PREHISTORIC ANGLESEY

PREHISTORIC ANGLESEY

THE ARCHAEOLOGY OF THE ISLAND
TO THE ROMAN CONQUEST

SECOND EDITION

by

FRANCES LYNCH
M.A., F.S.A.

THE ANGLESEY ANTIQUARIAN SOCIETY

© Anglesey Antiquarian Society 1991

1st edition 1970
This revised edition 1991

ISBN 0 9500199 7 6

The Committee of the Anglesey Antiquarian Society wish to record their appreciation and thanks to the Ynys Môn Borough Council for their financial assistance in publishing this series.

Published by The Anglesey Antiquarian Society, Llangefni, 1991,
Typeset by Stiwdio Mei, Pen-y-groes, and printed by W.O. Jones, Llangefni.

IN MEMORIAM

W. O. Stanley, Albert Way and E. Neil Baynes
without whom
so much of the prehistory of Anglesey
would have been lost.

FOREWORD

THIS book, the ninth in the series "Studies in Anglesey History", represents a revised version of Frances Lynch's original text published in 1970.

The highly acclaimed first volume has been out of print for a considerable time and the Publications Committee of the Anglesey Antiquarian Society is greatly indebted to the author for undertaking its revision.

The original text has been retained in full but has been prefaced by a discussion of currently held views and interpretations of prehistory in Britain and also supplemented by detailed descriptions of all the new excavations and discoveries in Anglesey during the past twenty years.

In promoting a series of specialist and definitive historical studies the Publications Committee has sought to achieve two major objectives: to publish a series of books which sheds light on an Island virtually unique in its historical, cultural and environmental character and to do so in a manner which would appeal to the academic community as well as to the general reader. The revised version of "Prehistoric Anglesey" clearly accords with this intention and the Publications Committee has every confidence that it represents another substantial step towards achieving both objectives.

Once again the Publications Committee wishes to record its appreciation of the support received from Ynys Môn Borough Council. Over the years the Council has shown considerable interest in the affairs of the Antiquarian Society and has supported its publication activities in a variety of ways. The Committee greatly values the links which have developed with the Council and expresses the hope that these can be maintained within a context of changing local government structures.

GWILYM T. JONES
General Editor, July 1991

CONTENTS

LIST OF ILLUSTRATIONS

LIST OF ILLUSTRATIONS 1991

FOREWORD

THIS book is the third in the History of Anglesey series, and I am certain that it will be particularly welcome to the Anglesey County Council — for whose continued interest and support my Committee is very grateful — as by the publication of this work we have carried out the first part of the original plan put forward by the Council in 1957. This was to produce a comprehensive and consecutive history of the island from prehistoric times to our own; but at that time it was rightly felt that more research was needed before such work could be undertaken and the Council later decided to give its support to this present series of specialist studies on different aspects of the island's history.

It is fortunate for us that Miss Frances Lynch joined the Archaeology Sub-Department at the University College of North Wales in 1965 and we are grateful to her for agreeing to our request to publish the results of her research and recent excavations. The illustrations alone will make this book a source of valuable information for scholars interested in the wider field of British archaeology, and the text is an important contribution to the study of the early history of Anglesey.

HELEN RAMAGE,

General Editor.
1970

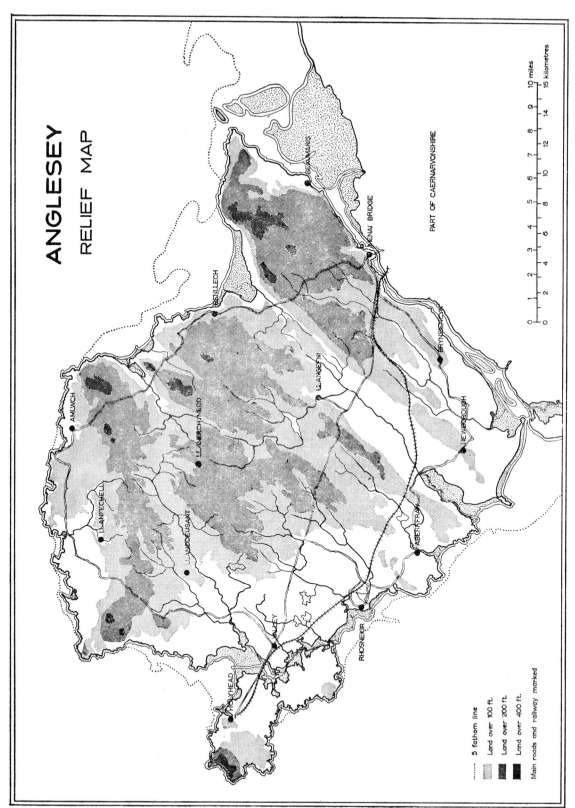

MAP 1 — Relief map showing main towns and roads.

PREFACE

In writing this book I have tried to keep technical discussion to a minimum and to bear in mind the needs of the general reader who has no previous knowledge of archaeology but who is interested in the objects and monuments which have survived from the remote past in his or her local area. Although the book is designed to treat the island as a whole, an index arranged by parishes has been added at the end so that it can be used quite easily as a guidebook. For such a purpose it may appear overloaded with footnotes, but these may be safely ignored. They simply refer to the original publications or indicate the source of further information for those who might like to follow up a particular problem.

I have made the illustrations as comprehensive as possible, not only because I hope they may help to make the past more tangible, but also because it is in them that the real value of the book will lie. For archaeology is such a fast-moving subject that, whereas the objective record stands, the historical framework and interpretation have to be continually altered and adapted to suit new information. One aspect in which recent research is making sweeping changes is chronology and the interpretation of radio carbon dating. At the time of writing this problem is still unresolved and I have preferred to retain the conventional carbon 14 dates calculated on the 5,568 half-life and have not attempted a calibration with the dendro-chronological calendar by which the actual dates for the Neolithic and Bronze Ages may be two or three hundred years earlier than formerly supposed.

My first debt of gratitude is to the Anglesey Antiquarian Society for inviting me to write this book and so stimulating me to deepen my knowledge of the island and its monuments and providing me with endless opportunities for enjoyable fieldwork and other pleasant activities connected with the collecton of material.

To individuals my debt is equally great. Among my professional colleagues I should mention in particular Mr. T. G. E. Powell and Mr. Colin Burgess who have helped me with a great deal of advice, information and criticism. Any errors which remain must be put down to culpable ignorance on my part. For helpful discussions on particular points I am grateful to Mr. C. H. Houlder, Dr. G. J. Wainwright, Dr. Ian Longworth, Miss L. F. Chitty and Dr. Anne Ross and for the provision of information and records I must thank Mr. A. H. A. Hogg of the Royal Commission on Ancient Monuments and Mr. Frank Bush, Mr. Martin Buckley and Mr. David Bark of the Archaeology Branch of the Ordnance Survey.

I should also like to thank Dr. H. N. Savory for permission to illustrate objects in the National Museum of Wales and for many kindnesses during the time I was there. I am also grateful to Mr. J. W. Brailsford and to Dr. Ian Longworth for similar facilities in the British Museum, to the Director of the Tolson Memorial Museum, Huddersfield, for permission to illustrate the Bodwrdin mould, and to Prof. A. H. Dodd, Hon. Curator of the Museum of Welsh Antiquities, Bangor, and to Mr. Dewi Jones, Hon. Secretary of the Anglesey Antiquarian Society, for allowing me access to the material under their care. I am also deeply grateful to the owners of material still in private hands for permission to draw and publish their finds and to the many farmers and landowners who have allowed me onto their land to examine monuments. In particular I should like to mention Messrs. O. R. and T. C. Pierce of Glan Alaw, Mr. H. T. Radcliffe of Presaddfed and Messrs. Jones of Fferam Rhosydd who so willingly gave permission for excavation on their land.

For help with the production of the book I must thank, first of all, Mr. Emrys Hughes who has taken such care to improve my spelling and punctuation and who very kindly took over so much of the work on the final preparation of the typescript. For useful criticism, comment and encouragement I must thank my parents, my colleagues at the University College of North Wales, amongst whom I should name Mr. P. A. B. Llewellyn and Mr. Bedwyr Lewis Jones; and, in particular, Mrs. Helen Ramage, the General Editor of this Series. For assistance with some of the illustrations I am grateful to Miss Enid Mummery and Mr. John Henderson who prepared the final drawings of the hill-forts for me. For the photograph of the Hendy head I am indebted to Mr. Brian Maidment. I must also thank Prof. Melville Richards for his help with Welsh spellings and place-names. Finally I must thank Gwilym Pritchard for agreeing to design the dust jacket for me and for expending so much time and effort on its production.

Finally I must record my indebtedness to former workers in Anglesey archaeology. Foremost amongst these are the late Mr. W. J. Hemp and the former staff of the Royal Commission whose Anglesey Inventory published just before the war marked a new era of accurate and comprehensive recording. It is a book on which I have relied heavily throughout and without which my task would have been immeasurably harder. My debt to the numerous assiduous recorders of the last century is scarcely less; men such as the Hon. W. O. Stanley, the Rev. Hugh Prichard, the Rev. W. Wynn Williams, the Rev. John Skinner, who spent a profitable ten days here at the beginning of the century, and the earliest Anglesey antiquary, the Rev. Henry Rowlands, though his records are sometimes more confusing than informative. So much would have been lost without their accounts of monuments and finds, for they lived at a time when antiquities were being destroyed on a large scale in Anglesey. At the beginning of this century the outstanding names are those of Harold Hughes and E. Neil Baynes, the guiding light of the Anglesey Antiquarian Society for many years. Without all these workers it would have been impossible to write this book.

FRANCES LYNCH.

Beaumaris.
May, 1970.

PREFACE

WHEN the Publications Committee of the Anglesey Antiquarian Society asked me to prepare a second edition of *Prehistoric Anglesey* which they had published in 1970 I was both flattered and dismayed, especially when they said that they planned to reproduce the original book as it stood with new material as a separate section. Whereas this arrangement cuts out a lot of tedious, detailed alteration it also means that views expressed twenty years ago, interpretations offered and predictions made will have to remain visible, to be measured against advances in knowledge and understanding of British prehistory in general and of Anglesey in particular.

This new edition, therefore, wraps itself around the original book with a series of preliminary sections which echo the original chapters and contain commentary on altered interpretations of prehistory on a broad front, pointing up those aspects of the original work which are most in need of the modification predicted in the original Preface. At the back are six supplementary chapters containing new finds and excavation results from Anglesey itself. These are essentially factual and have been written and illustrated in the same style as the original book. Finally, four new appendices have been compiled. One, which should have been in the 1970 book, lists all the Neolithic stone axes from the island; others contain information not available in 1970; new analyses of bronze implements and radiocarbon dates and the fourth simply lists palaeo-environmental information available from Anglesey. Cross-references to the original text are indicated as 'PA with appropriate page reference'; naturally it has not been possible to indicate in the original text where supplementary information is available or where views have been modified.

In 1970 no radiocarbon dates were available for Anglesey material but the general chronology used was derived from a growing series of dates from Britain as a whole. At that time the accuracy of those dates had been recently queried and it was becoming increasingly obvious that they were a good deal too young when measured against the natural clock contained in the annual growth rings of trees. In 1970 the problem had been identified, but not explained or remedied. In 1990 the problem remains largely unexplained (though some suggest that fluctuation in sun-spot activity may have something to do with it) but it can be remedied to a certain extent. In the intervening twenty years a great deal of work has been done on the dendrochronological record and master sequences for Britain and Western Europe have been built up, largely through the analysis of oak logs from the peats of Ireland studied in the Palaeoecology Laboratory of Queen's University, Belfast[1]. Such waterlogged wood can be dated both by measuring its growth rings and identifying their place on the master chart and by radiocarbon assay and thus the two clocks can be calibrated one against the other.

---

[1] A convenient summary of these problems and their solutions can be found in *Antiquity* 61, 1987, 'Special Radiocarbon Section', 97-138 with further comment in vol. 64, 1990, 203-4 and 315-8.

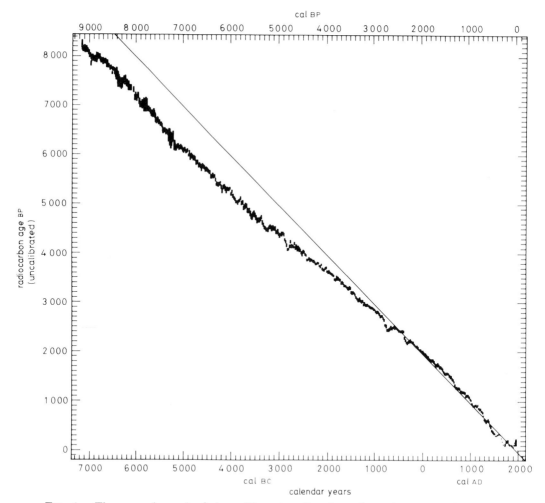

FIG. 1a. The general trend of the calibrated radiocarbon timescale compared to a 1:1 radiocarbon/calendar-age scale denoted by the straight line. Reproduced from *Antiquity* 1987 by kind permission of the Editor. BP means Before Present (ie 1950 AD).

Figure 1 reproduces the general calibration chart for Britain which shows that radiocarbon dates are too young by an amount which increases at a fairly steady rate the further back one goes. However it should be pointed out that the smooth curve conceals some awkward fluctuations, such as those around 2000 bc (4000 bp)[2] and during the Iron Age (2500 bp) which make the calibration of dates at those periods exceedingly difficult. While the use of calibrated dates is essential for the accurate assessment of broad chronologies, their use has removed yet further the goal of *precise* dating. Because of the nature of the counting process and the statistics which necessarily accompany its result, radiocarbon assay can only provide a band of time (normally now about 140 years) within which the true date is likely to die. Consequently events separated by less than 200 years cannot be confidently distinguished by radiocarbon dates alone. When the raw radiocarbon dates are calibrated the band is usually widened further, especially

---

[2] Bp means Before Present (ie 1950 when the technique was first developed). To obtain a bc/BC date simply subtract 1950 from the figure.

16

as it is recommended that results are quoted at two standard deviations, rather than one.

Partly because of these difficulties, but principally in order to maintain a consistent chronology throughout both parts of the new book I have decided to quote *uncalibrated* radiocarbon dates in the main text. These are indicated by the use of bc rather than BC, though it should be remembered that in the 1970 text BC stands for an uncalibrated chronology because this convention had not been standardised at that time (PA 13). In the Radiocarbon date list (Appendix) 3) the calibrated values are given, derived from the University of Washington Quaternary Isotope Laboratory computer, kindly operated for me by the Gwynedd Archaeological Trust.

As predicted in the Preface to the original text, archaeological understanding has seen many changes in the last twenty years. Not only have new finds, excavations and chronologies altered the historical framework of prehistory, but new theoretical approaches have changed the questions that are being asked of the material evidence, in some cases to an extent that leaves that evidence limping far behind[3]! Thus questions of status and social organisation now take precedence over artefactual identification and strict chronology in many archaeological reports and most may be the better for it, since the new questions often engage more directly with the readers' interest in the social and quasi-political life of the past[4]. Unfortunately the influence of the social sciences on archaeological writing has often had its normal baleful effect, producing a very abstruse vocabulary for some fairly simple thoughts. A development which must be acknowledged to be entirely beneficial is the integration of palaeo-environmental studies with archaeological excavation. As a result the essential environmental background to man's life on the island, a background which must have circumscribed all his activities, is much better known, both from information from archaeological sites themselves and from more strictly botanical studies.

In 1975 arrangements for rescue excavation in Gwynedd were put on a more permanent footing with the establishment of Gwynedd Archaeological Trust. As a consequence of this the University College became less directly involved in excavations in Anglesey, but I am grateful to members of the staff of the Trust, especially Mr David Longley, for their willingness to discuss their work with me and to provide me with information, often before full publication. I am also grateful for access to their Sites and Monuments Record. As before, I am grateful to the National Museum of Wales for granting facilities for the study of material in their care. I should particularly like to thank Dr Peter Northover for very generously providing me with the results of his metal analyses and with his considered views on their significance before their final publication. I am also grateful to Simon Timberlake for permission to publish his dates for the early mining at Parys Mountain, Ruth Watkin for information about her palaeobotanical studies at Llyn Hendref and Dr John Llywelyn Williams for help with the list of stone axes.

[3] A convenient compendium of theoretical approaches to archaeology: Ian Hodder *Reading the Past: Current Approaches to Interpretation in Archaeology*, Cambridge, 1986.
[4] A good example of the change towards social synoptic prehistory is R. Bradley *The Social Foundations of Prehistoric Britain*, London, 1984; also compare D. Clarke *et al*, *Symbols of Power in the Age of Stonehenge*, HMSO, 1985, with earlier exhibition catalogues.

LIST OF ABBREVIATIONS

A.A.S.	Anglesey Antiquarian Society.
B.M.	British Museum, London.
Camb. Arch. Assoc.	Cambrian Archaeological Association.
M.P.B.W.	Ministry of Public Buildings and Works.
N.M.I.	National Museum of Ireland, Dublin.
N.M.W.	National Museum of Wales, Cardiff.
R.C.A.M.	Royal Commission on Ancient Monuments in Wales and Monmouthshire.
U.C.N.W.	University College of North Wales, Bangor.

Journals:

Ant.	Antiquity.
Ant. J.	Antiquaries Journal.
Arch.	Archaeologia.
Arch. Camb.	Archaeologia Cambrensis.
Arch. J.	Archaeological Journal.
B.B.C.S.	Bulletin of the Board of Celtic Studies.
Cardiff Nat. Soc. Trans.	Cardiff Naturalists Society Report and Transactions
Dorset Arch. and Nat. Hist.	Proceedings of the Dorset Archaeological and Natural History Society.
Flintshire Hist. Soc. Public.	Flintshire Historical Society Publications.
Inventaria Archaeologica	Inventaria Archaeologica: An Illustrated Card Inventory of Important Associated Finds in Archaeology.
J. Co. Kildare Archaeol. Soc.	Journal of the Co. Kildare Archaeological Society.
J. Cork Arch. and Hist. Soc.	Journal of the Cork Archaeological and Historical Society.
J. Ecology.	Journal of Ecology.

J. Galway Arch. and Hist. Soc.	Journal of the Galway Archaeological and Historical Society.
J.R.S.A.I.	Journal of the Royal Society of Antiquaries of Ireland.
P.D.A.E.S.	Proceedings of the Devon Archaeological Exploration Society.
P.P.S.	Proceedings of the Prehistoric Society.
P.R.I.A.	Proceedings of the Royal Irish Academy.
Proc. Belfast Nat. Hist and Phil. Soc.	Proceedings of the Belfast Natural History and Philosophical Society.
Proc. Bristol Univ. Spelaeological Soc.	Proceedings of the University of Bristol Spelaeological Society.
Proc. Royal Society	Proceedings of the Royal Society.
Proc. Soc. Antiq. London	Proceedings of the Society of Antiquaries of London (forerunner of *Ant. J.*).
P.S.A.S.	Proceedings of the Society of Antiquaries of Scotland.
T.A.A.S.	Transactions of the Anglesey Antiquarian Society and Field Club.
Trans. Birmingham Archaeol. Soc.	Transactions of the Birmingham Archaeological Society.
Trans. Hon. Soc. Cymmrod.	Transactions of the Honourable Society of Cymmrodorion.
Trans. Lancs. and Cheshire Arch. Soc.	Transactions of the Lancashire and Cheshire Archaeological Society.
Trans. Woolhope Soc.	Transactions of the Woolhope Society.
U.J.A.	Ulster Journal of Archaeology.
Univ. London Inst. Archaeol. Ann. Report	University of London Institute of Archaeology Annual Report (or Bulletin).

HUNTERS AND
STRAND-LOOPERS

THE twenty years since the publication of the first edition have not produced any Palaeolithic finds from Anglesey. The earliest evidence of man still belongs to the earlier Mesolithic phase, around 7,000 bc as confirmed by radiocarbon dates from the new, more extensive, excavations at Aberffraw.

However, during these twenty years the antiquity of man in Wales has been greatly extended by the discoveries in the cave at Bontnewydd, in the Elwy valley, Clwyd[1]. Here the debris of a campsite, possibly at the entrance, had been swept by the river into the back of the cave. In that debris were numerous handaxes, and teeth and bones from more than one individual, demonstrating occupation by man almost a quarter of a million years ago, as early as any site in the south of England. This hunting band must have been close to the limits of exploitable land at that time and their descendants would have been driven south again when virtually the whole of Wales was overwhelmed by the ice of the later glaciations.

The survival of evidence such as that at Bontnewydd is very much dependent upon the accident of burial within caves, hence the concentration of our knowledge of all phases of the Palaeolithic within the limestone regions of Clwyd and the Gower Peninsula[2]. The remains of camps on the open tundra, such as might have existed in Anglesey at this time, will have been entirely swept away by the advance of the later ice.

In 1970 it was true to say that nearly all the evidence of post-glacial, Mesolithic occupation in Wales came from coastal locations, suggesting an economy very closely tied to maritime and wildfowl resources. Since then quite a number of upland sites have been discovered, on the Denbigh Moors and in the Brecon Beacons, which show a more balanced distribution of hunters across the country and a greater variety of prey. By and large these upland sites tend to belong to the later half of the period, after 5,000 bc[3].

The question of the transition from a hunting to a farming economy was discussed briefly in 1970 (PA 51-2). Opinions about the extent to which the native Mesolithic population was transforming its own lifestyle without the intervention of new colonists have been developing in the last twenty years. Despite the presence of foreign crops and animals, some have claimed that the transition was effected

---

[1] H.S. Green, *Pontnewydd Cave, a Lower Palaeolithic Hominid Site in Wales*, NMW, Cardiff, 1984.
[2] A convenient summary of the Welsh Palaeolithic can be found in Jacobi, 'The Upper Palaeolithic in Britain with special reference to Wales' in Taylor (ed) *Culture and Environment in Prehistoric Wales*, BAR 76 Oxford, 1980, 15-99.
[3] R. Jacobi, 'The Early Holocene Settlement of Wales' in Taylor *op. cit.*, 131-206.

without colonisation[4]; others have been more conservative but have pointed out that the adoption of the new economy must have been a matter of complex cultural choices, not of overwhelming numbers or of simple environmental determinism[5]. Since truly transitional sites must be rare and probably unrecognisable the discussion has been carried on at a largely theoretical level, each new proposition containing certain attractive insights but remaining, inevitably, beyond the range of objective proof.

[4] J.G.D. Clark, *Mesolithic Prelude*, Edinburgh, 1980 and R.W. Dennell, *European Economic Prehistory*, London, 1983.
[5] J. Thomas, 'Neolithic Explanations Revisited...', *Proc. Prehist. Soc.*, 54, 1988, 59-66.

THE NEOLITHIC PERIOD:
THE FIRST FARMERS

As mentioned in the previous section, recent work on the earliest development of agriculture has emphasised the crucial role of specialised and manipulative hunting strategies, both in Europe and in the Near East (which still remains a seminal area in the history of these changes). As more detailed studies are made, the complexity of the process and the variety of stimuli are becoming clearer and it is obvious that single all-embracing explanations must be judged inadequate at the level of the individual hunting band or farming family. However the statements on broad trends made in 1970 still have validity at a general level of discussion, though dates, even without calibration, must be pushed back at least a thousand years[1].

Farming communities are being recognised in Europe at earlier dates than those mentioned in 1970, but rather surprisingly the British and Irish evidence, where the uncertain definition of the earliest Neolithic settlements still remains a problem, has not been pushed back correspondingly far. Whereas there are now many more farming sites occupied at around 3,300 bc, none has yet produced a date of 4,000 bc[2].

The large wooden and stone tombs of western Europe have continued to be a subject of study and controversy. Interest has moved away from typological definitions and Continent-wide comparisons since most archaeologists have become content to view these monuments in smaller regional perspective and to concentrate theoretical discussion instead upon matters of use and their role within society[3]. Here emphasis has been placed upon the relatively short period of funerary use in contrast to the long history of significance to the local community as evidenced by alterations and additions to the structure, and upon the distribution of these impressive buildings within the landscape. In such themes stress is laid upon the role of the monuments, not primarily as ancestral tombs but as symbols of tribal continuity and land ownership.

The excavation of Din Dryfol and particularly of Trefignath with their clear demonstration of multi-period building have contributed to this debate, though the lack of a dominant tomb style in Anglesey has made it less attractive to theoreticians than some smaller islands.

[1] B. Bender, *Farming in Prehistory*, London, 1975.
[2] I. Kinnes, *Proc. Soc. Antiq. Scotland*, 115, 1985, 19-21.
[3] A general, Europe-wide summary can be found in Evans, Cunliffe and Renfrew (edd) *Antiquity and Man*, London, 1981; a good example of a regional study in D. Fraser, *Land and Society in Neolithic Orkney* BAR 117, Oxford, 1983 and a short summary of the theories by C. Renfrew in *Scientific American*, Nov. 1983, 128-36.

Since 1970 regional variations within Neolithic Britain, hinted at in *Prehistoric Anglesey* (58), have been more sharply defined. Although Causewayed Camps have been found in the English Midlands[4] their absence from the west and the north has been confirmed. However in the south-west defensive enclosures have now been recognised at this date, introducing a new element of warfare into this period previously envisaged as essentially peaceful. The frontier of these two societies, the agressive south west with its relatively straightforward but defensive villages and the traditional 'Windmill Hill Culture' area with its multi-layered political structures, seems to have lain in Dorset and along the Cotswolds[5]. The social framework of the large population concentrated in Yorkshire has yet to be characterised, for settlement sites remain elusive, but some distinctive society may be expected since burial monuments show regional peculiarities and the later history of the region suggests a frontier of some kind on the Humber.

The situation in Wales is much as it was in 1970 in that the chief expressions of Neolithic life remain the tombs and a scatter of settlement debris. The number of such settlements has increased but they still indicate isolated farmsteads rather than enclosed villages which might imply more elaborate political organisation. The large tripartite wooden house at Llandegai (PA 60) has now been dated to around 3,000 bc[6] and another has been found beneath the tomb at Gwernvale in the Usk valley[7]. In fact it is becoming apparent that this style of house, so similar to those on the Continent, was the norm for most parts of Britain and Ireland though they are still difficult to pick up on chalk subsoils.

In Anglesey the number of occupation sites has been increased but none has produced good structural evidence. Beneath the tomb at Trefignath a scatter of broken pottery suggests occupation at a date around 3,000 bc and two hearths not far away at Tŷ Mawr belong to the same horizon. The hilltop site, Capel Eithin near Gaerwen, has produced radiocarbon dates and some enigmatic 'foundation trenches' which indicate activity of some kind at a date close to 3,000 bc but there is no archaeological material to give precision to this. The pottery from Din Dryfol suggests that tomb was built at about this time and the early context for Graig Lwyd axes at the Llandegai house means that the settlement areas identified by the clusters of these finds could also belong to the early Neolithic. Thus the apparent but improbable absence of Early Neolithic material noted in 1970 (PA 118) has been remedied.

Set alongside the tombs, and with the environmental and agricultural evidence coming from modern excavations such as that of Trefignath, these sites are beginning to fill out our understanding of the use of the island at the turn of the third millennium[8]. The activity at Gaerwen, and the axes at Rhostrehwfa, well away from the more densely occupied coastal lands, are an indication that the centre may not have been so empty at this time as is traditionally supposed,

[4] R. Palmer 'Interrupted Ditch Enclosures in Britain...', *Proc. Prehist. Soc.*, 42, 1976, 161-86.
[5] R.J. Mercer, *Hambledon Hill: A Neolithic Landscape*, Edinburgh, 1980; P.W. Dixon on Crickley Hill in *Scientific American*, May 1979, 142-50 and C. Renfrew 'Monuments, mobilisation and social organisation in Neolithic Wessex' in Renfrew (ed) *The Explanation of Culture'*, London, 1973, 539-58.
[6] Date in Lynch in Boon and Lewis (edd) *Welsh Antiquity*, Cardiff, 1976, 65 and plan in Lynch 'Wales and Ireland: a fluctuating relationship,' *Arch. Camb.*, CXXXVIII, 1989, 1-19. Fig 1.
[7] W.J. Brintell and H.N. Savory, *Gwernvale and Penywyrlod...*, Camb. Arch. Mon. 2, Cardiff, 1984, 51-4.
[8] R. Holgate, 'Neolithic Anglesey: A Landscape Study' BBCS, 30, 1982, 153-64, makes an attempt to identify preferred settlement locations for early and late sites but the thesis is perhaps a little too heavy for the evidence to bear, certainly as to chronological distinctions.

but it remains true that the distribution of Neolithic activity lay predominantly on the better soils.[9]

Excavation since 1970 has not only provided confirmation of Early Neolithic activity, but greatly increased the Late Neolithic evidence from Anglesey. Pottery from the closure of the final chamber at Trefignath and from Capel Eithin joins that already known from Bryn yr Hen Bobl and Castell Bryn Gwyn (PA Fig. 63-4) as indications of the presence of eastern fashions, possibly even people, on the island in the last centuries of the third millenium bc. This eastern connection is reinforced by the discovery of Grooved Ware at Capel Eithin, and less certainly at Trefignath, a style which in 1970 had not been certainly identified anywhere in Wales. It is now being found much more widely, both in South Wales and in the Marches, and is indicative of a considerable shift of interest and connection. In the earlier Neolithic the cultural links lay westward, in Ireland; by the end of the period Anglesey, and Wales as a whole, seems to have turned eastward and to have been 'captured' by fashions and connections which lay in the lowland zone[10].

[9] W.F. Grimes, *Antiquity*, XIX, 1945, 169-74.
[10] F.M. Lynch, 'Wales and Ireland: a Fluctuating Relationship', *Arch. Camb.*, CXXXVIII, 1989, 1-19.

MAKERS OF BEAKERS
IN ANGLESEY

THE appearance of Beaker pottery in Europe and in Britain epitomises the difficulty and uncertainty of writing history through inanimate objects. In 1970 the discovery in Britain of a new style of pottery, almost identical to that used on the Continent, was confidently interpreted as evidence for the arrival of new people in numbers sufficient to change many fundamental aspects of life (PA 120).

Ever since 1912 when Lord Abercromby first made a detailed study of the material, this historical reconstruction had been one of the more secure points in British prehistory and in 1970 it was reinforced by a new *corpus* which claimed to identify seven waves of invaders from the Rhineland area[1]. But, very soon after this major publication appeared, doubts began to be expressed about the truth of this interpretation[2].

In *Prehistoric Anglesey* emphasis was laid on the changes in technology, house types, burial practice and general social ethos which seemed to accompany the appearance of this new pottery. But it was also pointed out that many things associated with Beakers in Britain were of entirely native origin and that, in the earliest stages at least, their makers and those of Fengate ware were difficult to tell apart (PA 121). The new view stresses the similarities rather than the changes and suggests a new mechanism and a new timetable for the introduction of those changes. The new mechanism is seen as a process of essentially internal social development linked to the adoption of European symbols for the expression of the new power structures within native society. The new timetable, which has shown that the period of transition is longer than originally thought and that the changes are staggered and not all appear to be contemporary with the adoption of new pottery styles, has added to the difficulty of maintaining the original simple 'invasion' explanation.

The new explanation builds upon insights into the structure of society in more densely populated areas of Britain in the Middle and Later Neolithic, a structure in which the individual 'chieftain' was becoming more visible through the accumulation of personal wealth. Thus it is believed that the two social trends — individuality and personal wealth — which distinguish the Bronze Age most clearly from the Neolithic were emerging within Britain without outside intervention, but in parallel with similar developments in several areas of Europe.

[1] Lord Abercromby *Bronze Age Pottery*, London 1912; D.L. Clarke *Beaker Pottery in Great Britain and Ireland*, Cambridge 1970.
[2] C.B. Burgess and S.J. Shennan, 'The Beaker Phenomenom: some suggestions' in Burgess and Miket (edd) *Settlement and Economy in the 3rd and 2nd Millenium BC*, BAR 33, Oxford 1976, 309-27 and various articles in *Glockenbechersymposion Oberreid 1974*.

What gives the 'Beaker Period' its apparent uniformity is the adoption of a particular type of pot by all these emerging 'elites'. The attraction of the pots may have their use in particular ceremonies which reinforced the social position of the participants — hence their appearance in graves where their presence could ensure the continuance of that status in the after-life. The occurrence of the earliest metal goods in these same graves would be simply an indication of the wealth and power of the occupants, not their ethnic background.

This theory aims to reconcile the obvious signs of social change with the continuance — indeed, expansion — of purely native institutions such as the Henge monuments. However it deals in realms of interpretation which can never be susceptible to final proof and since the theory is a product of an 'intellectual fashion' for the negation of large-scale 'invasions' in prehistory, one may suspect that the pendulum has swung too far. The question of skull shape and a different physical stock, which was such a major plank in earlier arguments, has been largely neglected in the present discussion because its genetic relevance is not clear[3]. It may re-emerge again, especially in the south where all the changes seem sharper, for it should be remembered that the Norman Conquest involved very few 'invaders' and substituted one broadly similar ruling class for another. The debate over the meaning of Beaker pottery has broadened our understanding of the complexity of social development but has not solved the problem of recognising and identifying the particular political event.

As far as Anglesey is concerned, the down-playing of any foreign element in the 'Beaker phenomenon' undoubtedly fits the picture well. The early Beaker pottery (PA 123) is found in native contexts, in tombs where it suggests that it has been acquired by the native elite. Where it occurs on settlements, as at the new site, Capel Eithin, it is usually mixed with British styles of pottery. The distinctive single graves belong to a later phase and a secondary spread from England (PA 125). The fact that their occupants all belong to the earlier, diolchocephalic group (PA 127) emphasises that fact that the movement by this stage is certainly one of ideas and social rites.

---

[3] F.M. Lynch in P.S. Harper and E. Sunderland (edd) *Genetic and Population Studies in Wales*, Cardiff, 1986, 19-20.

DEATH IN THE
BRONZE AGE

A GOOD deal of new material relevant to this chapter has been found since 1970 but, in contrast to the Beaker pottery discussed above, its historical interpretation has changed little. It is still appropriate to point out that most of the Bronze Age burial monuments in the island cover multiple cremations which suggest that a family or group orientated society, with few militaristic overtones and without conspicuous variation in wealth, held sway in Anglesey. Tentative remarks about the link between barrows and ceremonial circles (PA 162) have been confirmed and may be expanded in the light of more recent excavations in other parts of North Wales[1].

In 1970 there was little specific comment that one could make about the Standing Stones of Anglesey despite their number. Since then a radiocarbon date for the stone at the centre of Bedd Branwen (PA 152) suggests an Early Neolithic date for its erection, which is not sustained by other evidence. The excavation of the Cremlyn South Stone did not provide evidence of date but did suggest a long history of interest in that spot, although there were no ancilliary structures such as have been found frequently during recent excavations in South Wales[2].

The rediscovery of a cup and ring stone from the Llwydiarth Esgob area has provided the only example of this kind of antiquity from Anglesey, but since we know nothing of its original context it has not added to our understanding of these enigmatic carvings.

The one major Bronze Age excavation has been at Capel Eithin where an unmarked cemetery of seventeen cremation burials was found. The range of pottery and grave goods is very similar indeed to the nineteenth century discoveries at Cae Mickney (PA 196-9). The one important new element on this site is the length of time during which the cemetery was used. The radiocarbon dates suggest that this was a period of at least 700 years during which styles of pottery and burial customs changed very little[3]. One date, in fact, suggests a revival of interest in the site, despite its lack of monumentality, during the Iron Age.

This extension of the period of use is at variance with the preferred interpretation of the much shorter spread of dates from the barrow, Bedd Branwen (see radiocarbon date list Appendix 3). For reasons which were largely stratigraphic

---

[1] F.M. Lynch, 'Ring Cairns in Britain and Ireland: their Design and Purpose', *Ulster J. Archaeol*, 42, 1979, 1-19
[2] G. Williams, *The Standing Stones of Wales and South West England, BAR, 197, 1988.*
[3] A similar longevity and tenacity is demonstrated by dates from an 'urnfield' at Bromfield in Herefordshire, Stanford, *Proc. Prehist. Soc.*, 48, 1982, 279-320.

and stylistic it was thought that this monument was used by only two or three generations (PA 163 and 207-8). However the combination of late dates and absence of stylistic change in the pottery at Capel Eithin, may prompt some caution in accepting this interpretation at Bedd Branwen.

Another facet of the continued use of the one site through from Early to Later Bronze Age is the stability of community that it implies. Such stability may not be entirely surprising in a lowland, relatively fertile island such as Anglesey, but much of Britain and especially its higher, more marginal regions, seem to have suffered a considerable climatic and hence economic and social crisis in the centuries around 1000 bc.

During the earlier Bronze Age good weather had permitted an expansion of settlement onto upland areas like Dartmoor and the Cheviots where a prosperous but perhaps in the long-run damaging agricultural economy took root[4]. With the onset of bad weather around 1000 bc this economy collapsed. The fate of the population is not directly legible in the archaeological record but many upland farms were abandoned and most ceremonial and religious traditions seem to have come to an end, at least in the regions most seriously hit[5]. Such an economic crisis must undoubtedly have put a great deal of stress on the social and political fabric of both directly and indirectly affected areas and it is at this period that many defended settlements were founded.

Because the uplands have seldom been worked with such intensity again, the evidence for Bronze Age farming often survives with remarkable clarity. Unfortunately the huts and fields which can be recognised on the Welsh hills have yet to be convincingly dated to the Bronze Age, but in general form they are closely comparable to the dated examples from Northumberland and the Pennines[6]. Because Anglesey has always been relatively intensively farmed the preservation of whole landscapes of Bronze Age date cannot be expected, but even isolated patches of settlement evidence have been elusive (PA 150), and remain so.

The coarse, straight-sided pots from Capel Eithin indicate the type of pottery that might be expected from Middle and Later Bronze Age contexts; it is not unlike that from Deverel-Rimbury sites in the south (PA 149) but by no means identical. Certainly the compact farmsteads of that region cannot yet be recognised in Anglesey, but the fact that mounds of burnt stone are now convincingly dated to the Bronze Age (PA 282) and on the Orkneys have been shown to relate closely to house sites[7], may give a pointer to where these settlements might have stood. However those that have recently been investigated on Anglesey seem to have had a more industrial purpose (see metalworking section).

[4] A. Fleming, *The Dartmoor Reaves,* London, 1989 and Spratt and Burgess (edd) *Upland Settlement in Britain,* BAR 143, 1985.
[5] C.B. Burgess 'Population, Climate and Upland Settlement' in Spratt and Burgess, *op. cit.,* 195-250.
[6] F.M. Lynch 'The Bronze Age' in T.C. Darvill, *The Archaeology of the Uplands,* London, 1986, 27-30.
[7] J. Hedges *Proc. Soc. Antiq. Scotland,* 106, 1975, 39-98.

INDUSTRY AND TRADE
IN THE BRONZE AGE

THE most important development in the study of the early metal industry in Wales within the last few years has been the recognition that direct evidence of prehistoric mining has survived at a number of sites in both North and Mid Wales[1]. It was naturally suspected that the abundant copper ores of the region would have been exploited by early man (PA 212, 218) but it was assumed that later workings would have removed all the evidence for small-scale Bronze Age activity. This has proved to be an over-pessimistic view. The campaigns of Duncan James, Simon Timberlake and others, following in the footsteps of Oliver Davies who, in the absence of radiocarbon dating could only venture a Roman date for the spoilheaps he sampled, have shown that Bronze Age mining was not only widespread but was undertaken on an impressively large scale.

On Anglesey the largest reserve of copper is at Parys Mountain and we now know that this was being mined by 1600 bc. This is the earliest date so far obtained for a mine in Britain, but it is unlikely to remain so if investigation continues, for copper was being used long before this. Nor is Parys mountain likely to have been the only ore body mined in Anglesey during the Bronze Age. W.O. Stanley commented upon the vein of copper in the cliffs near the Tŷ Mawr huts, Holyhead, which he felt might have been used by bronzesmiths in that settlement (PA 246) and the numerous small ore deposits in the north east of the island might well repay archaeological investigation.

The background to this industry lies, of course, outside the island. The ultimate origins of metallurgy are to be found in Anatolia, probably as early as the 7th millenium bc, and were based on the hammering of 'native copper'. The earliest evidence for high temperature processes involving copper, melting and smelting, is ambiguous and it is not yet clear which is the earlier. Nonetheless it seems that these processes were being developed during the 5th millenium bc and were in regular use in the 4th. At the same time metallurgy is first recognised in Europe, in the Balkans, and was concerned with gold as well as copper. Whether or not these European developments were completely independent of those further east is not yet apparent[2].

It took many centuries for metalworking to develop from these first industries producing tools and trinkets in the 4th millenium bc to a stage where metal was the regular choice for everyday products. After the first flowering of the European

[1] P. & S. Crew, *Early Mining in the British Isles*, Plas Tan y Bwlch Occ. Paper 1, 1990, Snowdonia Nat. Park.
[2] *Pace* C. Renfrew, 'The autonomy of the south east European Copper Age,' *Proc. Prehist. Soc.*, 35, 1969, 12-47.

industry there was a marked reduction in the quantity of metal in circulation. Some link this to the working out of the oxide/carbonate ore deposits first exploited and the need to look further afield for new metal sources and to develop techniques for smelting sulphide ores. In this way metallurgy is seen as spreading to the Carpathians and the Alps by the 3rd millenium bc[3].

By the late 2nd millenium bc, when metal first reached Britain, Central Europe was undoubtedly a major producer and is the likely source of the daggers found in rich graves in southern England. But in Ireland the preponderance of copper axes and the moulds for making them suggest an independent industry, perhaps with a background in the far south west of Atlantic Europe where an early flowering of metallurgy is known at certain restricted sites[4]. Unfortunately the lack of finds from graves in Ireland makes it very difficult to correlate the date of the English and Irish material, but it is assumed that the Irish is slightly earlier, certainly as far as production is concerned since southern England, where the earliest products are found, did not have resources for manufacture until enough metal was in circulation for re-cycling[5].

In the last twenty years a great deal of work has been done on the analysis of metal tools. Allied to typological studies this has greatly refined our knowledge of the development of alloys[6] and has helped to define workshop traditions. Identification of the source of ores has always been more difficult because of chemical changes during processing but with larger samples and new methods of analysis this area, too, can be approached with more confidence.

In Wales this analytical work has been especially thorough and wide-ranging due to a comprehensive programme initiated and supported by the Board of Celtic Studies and the National Museum of Wales[7]. This work has suggested that the earliest stages of Welsh metalworking owed a great deal to Ireland. The earliest products were made from Irish metal and even when Welsh ores were used the designs were of Irish derivation (PA 215). But at the end of the Early Bronze Age more contact was made with the southern English industries which, under German stimulus, were becoming increasingly important and innovative (PA 218). It is at this time that we have definite evidence for the mining of local ores but they did not hold a monopoly, for metal seems to have been traded in many forms: as raw material, as finished products and as scrap for re-cycling[8].

One of the most important results of the Welsh analysis programme has been the confirmation of the particularity and importance of the Acton Park Complex (PA 228-9). This group of metalwork was first defined in typological terms and was recognised as being of special importance because of the early appearance

[3] Useful summary in A. Sheridan, 'A reconsideration of the origins of Irish metallurgy,' *J. Irish Archaeol.*, 1, 1983, 11-19.

[4] See articles by Harbison (pp.97-105) and Burgess (pp.207-14 especially p.213) but see also Craddock (p.376) in M. Ryan (ed) *Origins of Metalworking in Atlantic Europe*, Dublin 1979.

[5] S. Needham in Ryan *op. cit.*, 265-93.

[6] S. Needham *et al.* 'Developments in the Early Age metallurgy of southern Britain,' *World Archaeology*, 20, 1989, 383-402.

[7] Carried out by Dr Peter Northover, first at UCNW, Bangor and subsequently in Oxford. The final report is to be published by the Board of Celtic Studies; but a summary was published as an Appendix in H.N. Savory, *Guide Catalogue of the Bronze Age Collections*, NMW, Cardiff, 1980, 228-43.

[8] P. Northover, 'The Exploration of the Long-distance Movement of Bronze in Bronze and Early Iron Age Europe,' *Bull. Univ. London Inst. Archaeol.*, 19, 1982, 45-72.

of the fully developed palstave, the pre-eminent tool of the Middle Bronze Age[9]. Analysis of the metal used reveals that much of it could have come from Snowdonia with a possible second source in north east Wales/Marches. Many of the axes have a significant lead content probably deriving from the co-smelting of galena with the chalcopyrite copper ore. The quantities of lead are sufficient to have an observable effect on the properties of the finished bronze so that the choice should be regarded as deliberate[10]. Taken with the strange and seemingly experimental palstaves from the Moelfre Uchaf hoard, Betws yn Rhos, and the ultimate high standard of finish of the Acton Park palstaves, it all suggests a locally based industry with a flair both for metallurgy and for innovative design. The wide distribution of their distinctive metal mix, found as far afield as Holland and Brittany[11], is an indication of the success and influence of these workshops. This success was achieved at a time when imports of bronze from the Continent into south east England were at a low level and the Welsh industry was able to fill the gap, despite other metalworking areas, notably south west England with both copper and tin, being supposedly better placed to serve the markets of the south east.

In the following centuries this dominating position was lost and the organisation of the metal trade becomes more complicated. The production of weapons and of tools seems to diverge and a great number of the former are imported from France; so much so that at the beginning of the Late Bronze Age the south of England and north western France are virtually indistinguishable. Whether this link was purely commercial, or had political overtones one cannot be sure, but it should be remembered that the 'Penard Phase' covers the period of climatic and agricultural crisis which must have led to unrest in most parts of Europe.

The French industries were less dominant in the north and west and in the second half of the Late Bronze Age many local workshops can be recognised producing tools for relatively restricted regional markets. It is to this phase that the new Bodwrog hoard belongs. This group contains a mixture of weapons of distant origin and tools with much more local characteristics — a combination which is quite typical of hoards of the period. It is not surprising that the only find of prehistoric metalwork in the last twenty years should belong to the Late Bronze Age since the quantity of metal circulating at that time was high; but it is interesting that, in an island with metal resources and with relatively fertile land, this should be only the third such hoard found. In East Anglia, and in the south east of England generally, the quantity of metal in use and disuse is immeasurably greater, suggesting that it was at this time that underlying economic differences across the country became firmly and permanently established.

The way in which the new iron technology came to usurp the power of bronze is still very obscure[12]. Identification of small pieces of the new metal in hoards

[9] The group was first defined by Colin Burgess. His chapter (pp.243-86) in J.A. Taylor (ed) *Culture and Environment in Prehistoric Wales*, (BAR 76, 1970) provides a most valuable summary of the development of Welsh bronze industries.
[10] P. Northover, *NMW Catalogue*, 233-4. I am grateful to Dr Northover for aditional comments on this industry.
[11] P. Northover, *op.cit.*, 1982, Fig. 5.
[12] C.B. Burgess 'A Find from Boyton, Suffolk and the end of the Bronze Age in Britain and Ireland' in Burgess and Coombs (edd) *Bronze Age Hoards*, BAR 67, Oxford, 1979, 269-83.

of bronzes is becoming more frequent, especially in France, which suggests that the period of familiarisation may have been longer than originally imagined, but the mechanism of the change remains unknown and the iron sword in Llyn Fawr, Glamorgan, with a date of about 600 bc, is still regarded as the formal precursor of the new age (PA 251).

THE CELTIC IRON AGE

As with all periods of change, our understanding of the processes by which the Bronze Age became the Iron Age has undergone some serious rethinking over the past twenty years. In line with the interpretation favoured for earlier periods, the role of invaders has been played down in face of the back-dating of hillfort beginnings and our better understanding of the internal pressures of the Late Bronze Age (PA 255).

However, on the Continent more recent excavations, finds and theoretical work have demonstrated a most complex situation. Work on earlier chiefdoms has shown that the social structures of the Iron Age are hardly new (PA 253), though one may expect centralised control to wax and wane as political entities are battered by circumstances both natural and man-made. Increased precision of dating and of distributions has, in some areas which maintained close commercial links with the Mediterranean, revealed the rise and fall of power bases in a way which may encourage archaeologists to speak in terms which come close to the type of political history written by Thucydides and Livy[1].

In the light of the rise, the eclipse, and movement of tribes and alliances recognisable in southern Europe it would be naive to imagine that no groups could cross the English Channel; but certainly a large-scale replacement of population is no longer contemplated and the terminology of invasion is eschewed[2]. Despite their convenience the terms 'Iron Age A, Iron Age B and Iron Age C' are seldom used now and the period is divided into simple chronological sections 'Early' (c.500 to 350 bc), 'Middle' (350-100 bc) and 'Late' or 'Pre-Roman Iron Age' (100 bc to 43 AD). The Belgae must still be recognised as an intrusive group but the date of their arrival is the centre of some controversy[3]. In these last years of prehistory in which individuals appear as minters of coins or as minor actors on a broader, literate European stage, the difficulties of reconciling archaeological, stylistic chronologies with brief and often vague historical records are acute. Confusion in the radiocarbon calibration curve (p. 16) during this period only adds to the problems, though such a crude scale could not have helped to distinguish between the generations of Belgic chieftains.

One of the major supports for ideas of massive invasion in the Iron Age used to be the number of hillforts in the country, all apparently built at this time.

[1] T. Champion *et al. Prehistoric Europe*, London 1984, Chapters 9 and 10 provide a convenient summary of these developments.
[2] B. Cunliffe *Iron Age Communities in Britain*, 2nd ed. London, 1978.
[3] A. Birchall, *Proc. Prehist. Soc.*, 31, 1965, 241-367, Cunliffe *op. cit.* Chapters 5 and 6.

Already in 1970 (PA 255) it was becoming clear that many of them were much older, and since then many more Late Bronze Age palisaded hilltop settlements have been recognised (either through stratified artefacts or by radiocarbon dating) and we know much more about the ecological disaster which led to the atmosphere of fear and possessiveness that they represent. However it should not be forgotten that the sixth century bc, the traditional beginning of the Iron Age, does seem to be a period of renewed anxiety, for several sites were refortified with more substantial ramparts at that time and new foreign weapons make an appearance in some parts of the country[4].

North Wales is a region which has been shown to contain several Late Bronze Age palisaded sites without foreign, Hallstatt weaponry[5]. The social stresses which led to this development, therefore, must be reckoned to be local — a view which is in line with the current interpretation of the Castell Odo pottery (PA 256) and which might be expected in an upland area taking the brunt of the worsening climate.

Apart from the excavation of the Roman structure within Caer y Tŵr, Holyhead[6], there has been no work on the hillforts of Anglesey since 1970 so new datings cannot be confirmed for these sites (PA 258-78), though it may be expected that some of them will turn out to have as long a history as those on the mainland.

Whereas the date of the Anglesey hillforts must remain imprecise, more can now be said with confidence about the Iron Age dating of some of the stone hut circles (PA 279). Excavations at Tŷ Mawr, Holyhead, and Bryn Eryr, Llansadwrn, have shown that both these agricultural settlements were established in the Iron Age and continued in occupation through the Roman centuries and beyond. It had been thought (PA 149) that some of these round huts might prove to belong to the later Bronze Age but that prediction has not yet been fulfilled. Rather it seems that these very numerous and visible settlements may mark a horizon of agricultural expansion associated with a period of improved climate in the second century bc[7]. One cannot claim that all the stone huts on the island will share these early beginnings and long period of prosperity, but the results of these two excavations and the confirmed Iron Age date for VCP (Very Coarse Pottery PA 277)[8], do open up possibilities for such sites as Din Lligwy where the discovery of many prehistoric flints has always hinted of earlier occupation.

Apart from some sherds of this coarse pottery — VCP — which are not so much vessels as travelling containers for salt loaves from the Midlands, very few artefacts of Iron Age date have been found in the island, apart from the famous

[4] Burgess in J.A. Taylor (ed) *Culture and Environment in Prehistoric Wales*, BAR 76, Oxford, 1980, 276.
[5] D.W. Harding (ed) *Hillforts: Later Prehistoric Earthworks*, London 1976 contains summaries of relevant excavations: Breiddin (293-302), Moel y Gaer, Rhosesmor (303-17) together with a useful summary of broader Welsh Iron Age issues by H.N. Savory (237-91). For Dinorben see *Current Archaeology*, 1980, 336-8.
[6] P. Crew, *Arch. in Wales*, 21, 1981, no. 49, 35-6.
[7] J. Turner 'The Iron Age' in Simmons and Tooley (edd) *The Environment in British Prehistory*, London, 1981, 250-80.
[8] Elaine Morris, 'Prehistoric Salt Distributions...', BBCS, 32, 1985, 326-35.

votive deposit in Llyn Cerrig Bach (PA 285-313). This material is frequently illustrated and discussed but the only concentrated re-assessment of Sir Cyril Fox's conclusions has been that of Dr Savory in an anniversary address to the Anglesey Antiquarian Society in 1972[9].

Here he points out that the 'poverty' of the Welsh Iron Age is more apparent than real because it stems from an absence of pottery for which fine wooden vessels might be a more than acceptable substitute. Furthermore he argues that subsequent discoveries suggest that a flourishing school of decorative bronzework was established at an early date in the Irish Sea region which could be the source of the fine shield boss and crescentic plaque at Llyn Cerrig Bach. He also draws attention to the possibility that the dagger 139 (PA Fig.82) was made in Ireland rather than south west England[10], further reducing, but not entirely removing, the regional imbalance among the offerings which has presented difficulties of interpretation (PA 312-3). Discovery of quite extensive ironworking in North Wales has also raised the possibility that much of the ironwork might be relatively local and a proposed new study of the iron bars, always confidently interpreted as currency from south west England, may lead to some reassessment of their role and origin[11]. However, very recent analysis of some of the bronzework from the deposit (Appendix 2) has tended to confirm the south western link and also the wide range of date covered by the material, thus supporting the broad sweep of the original interpretation.

Our understanding of the situation in Anglesey immediately before the Roman conquest of 60 AD has been reinforced by two important finds in the last few years. Tacitus' comments about the presence on the island of political refugees from the south east (PA 319) have been neatly confirmed by the discovery of two La Tène III brooches fashionable among the Belgae on the eve of the conquest. These join the final deposits at Llyn Cerrig Bach and the sword from Gelliniog Wen (PA 284) as tangible evidence for the presence here of fighters from already conquered Belgic areas to boost the native resistance to the Romans.

[9] H.N. Savory 'Llyn Cerrig Bach Thirty Years On', TAAS, 1973, 24-38.
[10] Etienne Rynne's opinion quoted in Savory op.cit., 36.
[11] Peter Crew in B. Burnham and J. Davies (edd) Conquest, Co-existence and Change, Lampeter, 1991, 150-60. I am grateful to Mr Crew for discussion of this material and for permission to refer to his current work before publication.

I

HUNTERS AND STRAND-LOOPERS
IN ANGLESEY

ANGLESEY is an island and this simple fact gives it, like all other islands, a distinctive personality of its own. This distinctiveness is increased by its geographical position, being the only extensive area of low-lying, fertile and easily accessible land in a region of high and barren mountains. This has made it attractive to settlers in all periods of history and its reputation for agricultural productivity in the early Middle Ages underlines the fertility and significance of the island in the economy of North Wales, especially Gwynedd, at all times from the Neolithic onwards.

Anglesey was relatively well populated in prehistoric times, not only because of its fertility and openness in contrast to Snowdonia, but because of its central position in the Irish Sea. At a time when all inland areas were still densely wooded and the forests housed several dangerous species of animals, sea travel was both faster and safer. Consequently, throughout prehistory, since the time of the first farmers who were certainly competent boat-builders and sailors, the Irish Sea was the main highway of communication in western Britain and Ireland. Anglesey, then as now, was an ideal staging post on journeys north and south, and especially east and west, and, as a result, partook to some extent in most of the technological and social developments of the cultural provinces which lay on either side of it.

Anglesey essentially belongs to the western province; it is well within the Highland Zone as defined by Sir Cyril Fox,[1] and its links with Ireland, Scotland and the north of England, as well as with the rest of Wales, are strong throughout the prehistoric period. However, because of their central position on one of the main lines of communication and trade between the north west and southern England, itself in close touch with Europe, the inhabitants of Anglesey were exposed to new ideas from the south-east, which did not reach other parts of Wales. In fact, it is the alternate waxing and waning of these western and eastern traditions which forms one of the unifying themes of the island's prehistory, together with the consequent mixture of ideas which often results in structures or artifacts which are peculiar to Anglesey.

Although Anglesey is an island it has never been very difficult to reach. It is well known that the Romans invaded it by simply swimming across

---

[1] C. F. Fox, *The Personality of Britain,* National Museum of Wales, 1932. (1st. ed.).

37

the Straits, and it is probable that the first men who set foot here had walked over dry land in the same way as men had entered eastern England, crossing only a narrow river in the Middle Reach of what is now the Menai Straits. Holy Island would likewise have been joined to the mainland, and Malltraeth marsh would have been a broad dry valley.

I do not propose to discuss the geology of Anglesey which has been covered already in a previous volume in this series,[2] since, complex and fascinating as it is, it is not especially relevant to prehistoric settlement patterns on the island. The later cover of glacial drift and the resulting light or heavy soils are more significant since a light, well-drained soil was always more attractive to primitive agriculturalists without heavy tools.[3] This preference for light soils can be seen in the distribution of archaeological monuments and finds, and in the emphasis, more marked in the Romano-British period than others, on settlement on the limestone areas around Benllech, Penmon and Brynsiencyn, for limestone will always provide a well-drained soil. However, this preference for light soils and for coastal areas which would be less densely wooded is not absolute, for there are stone axes from the swampy central region and, by the Bronze Age, it is clear that a good many people actually lived in the Alaw valley and around Llyn Frogwy, areas which were considered rather unhealthy in the Mediaeval period.

Although the complicated geological history of Anglesey is not strictly relevant to this study, there is one aspect which is important for our understanding of the environment of the earliest inhabitants, and that is the alterations in sea level which resulted from the gradual melting of the ice cap which had covered the whole of Britain as far south as the Thames valley. Water had been locked up in these glaciers and consequently there was a rise in sea level when this water was released as the ice melted. In the north this rise in sea level was partly counteracted by the gradual rising of the land after the weight of the glaciers had been removed. The interaction of these two factors makes the history of the coasts around the north Irish Sea extremely complex, a complexity increased by the fact that these relative movements occurred more than once, for the temperature fluctuated and the ice advanced and retreated several times so that there are many levels of raised beaches and layers of submerged peat around our shores.[4]

However it is fairly certain that at the time man first appeared in Anglesey, perhaps around 6,000 B.C., the sea level, though rising, was still relatively low, with the island linked to the mainland, and land supporting a growth of trees in what are now Holyhead, Trearddur, Cymyran, Red

[2] W. E. Jones, (ed.), *The Natural History of Anglesey*, 1968, 11-30.
[3] W. F. Grimes. *Ant.* XIX, 1945, 169-74.
[4] Summarised in various works e.g., J. A. Steers. *The Coastline of England and Wales,* 1948. 475-501; H. Godwin. *Proc. Royal Society,* Series B. CLIII, 1961, 227-320 and J. C. Schofield. *New Zealand J. of Geology and Geophysics,* VII. 1964, 359-70. I am grateful to Mr. Richard Clark, Marine Science Lab., UCNW, for help with this problem.

Wharf and Lligwy Bays and southward from Newborough into Caernarvon Bay. Under exceptional conditions it is still possible to see the roots of the trees which grew on these shores, embedded in a layer of submerged peat.[5]

The major transgression of the sea which flooded this land and completely submerged the easternmost valley, now the Menai Straits; the series of pools and valleys between Holy Island and Anglesey; and almost breached the isthmus between Red Wharf Bay and Malltraeth, seems to have reached its maximum between 5,000 and 3,500 B.C. This culmination established the coast much as it is now. In the south of England another major period of flooding occurred in about 500 A.D., the climate having grown increasingly wet since about 500 B.C.[6] This later flooding was extensive in such areas as the Somerset Levels and the East Anglian Fens, but its effect further north has not been measured. It may have affected sensitive areas such as Malltraeth and Valley, but the continuing uplift of the ground in the north may well have kept pace with this rise in sea level.

Changes in climate were less dramatic but were more significant for early man for by them his entire environment was gradually altered, changing in time from open tundra, to steppe, to dense woodland with an accompanying change in the animals available for him to hunt and eat.

There is evidence of man's presence in Britain from about 200,000 B.C., well before the end of the Last Glaciation. He would have been roaming widely over an open landscape hunting the large animals such as mammoth, woolly rhinoceros and reindeer which thrived on the tundra. The mammoth (elephas primigenius) whose bones were dredged from the mud of Holyhead Harbour,[7] however, almost certainly lived free from the danger of attack by man, although a few men were active in North Wales between 30,000 B.C. and 20,000 B.C. for flint tools of Aurignacian type have been found in the limestone caves of the Clwyd Valley, at Ffynnon Beuno and Cae Gwyn.[8] Such a population would have been very small and it is doubtful if it would have been permanent. It is possible that these men may have belonged to a single tribe whose immense hunting grounds might have stretched from Wales to North Germany. The tools found in the Denbighshire caves show close similarities with those from Ilsen Höhle, near Leipzig.[9]

It is thought by some that Britain may have been completely depopulated as the climate worsened and the ice advanced for the last time

[5] E. Greenly. *Proc. Liverpool Geological Soc.*, XV, 1928, 55-62, H. Godwin. *J. of Ecology*, XXXI, 1943, 199-247.

[6] Godwin. 1961. *loc cit.*

[7] Discovered in the 1880s and presented to the Nat. History Mus., Kensington, by W. O. Stanley. I am grateful to Capt. G. Butterworth of Holyhead for drawing my attention to this find.

[8] C. B. M. McBurney, *in* Foster and Daniel (edd.), *Prehistoric and Early Wales*, 1965, 23, 27-9.

[9] V. Toepfer, *Ausgrabungen und Funde.* Berlin. (D.D.R.) III, 1958, 153.

Fig. 1 — Magle-
mosian arrow 34"
long) with micro-
liths set in resin:
Loshult, South
Sweden (after J. G.
D. Clarke).

(c. 19,000 - 13,000 B.C.).[10] The hunters only returned as the temperature gradually rose and their prey turned northwards in search of open tundra in front of the slow advance of temperate woodland in Central Europe.

The advance of woodland over open grassland meant a change in the animals available for man to hunt.[11] Large prey such as mammoth and the huge reindeer herds on which man had previously concentrated his attention gradually died as their natural habitat was eroded, and man had to turn to the smaller woodland species such as ox *(bos primigenius)*, bison, bears, horse and red and fallow deer. In hunting these he would have the lion, hyena and wolf as his rivals, not to mention wild cats and other small carnivores. Palaeolithic man had adapted his whole way of life to the hunting of particular species of animals, and when these became scarce a considerable re-orientation was necessary. Not only were the tools and weapons altered, but whereas, before, one successful hunting expedition might provide food for many days, the smaller size of the game now available must have meant that a larger proportion of men's time and energy must have been spent in hunting. On the other hand the increase in vegetation must have greatly extended the range of vegetable foods, roots, seeds, fruits, nuts and leaves, that could be conveniently gathered.[12]

The main characteristic of the tools of this period, known conventionally as the Mesolithic (Middle Stone Age), is a decrease in size and the concentration on small flint points. These points, in many cases really tiny, are known as microliths and may have been mounted in a variety of ways. Some may have been used alone as arrowtips (very effectively as the aurochs from Vig, Denmark, indicates, for it had been killed by just such a tiny point).[13] Others may have been arranged to form composite tools, barbed arrows, knives and such like. Microliths were not the only flint implements made, but they tended to be the most distinctive; heavy flint axes were developed to cut trees and branches, and tools such as awls and scrapers were used in the preparation of skins for making containers and

[10] McBurney. *op cit.,* 30.
[11] *See* I. W. Cornwall. *Prehistoric Animals and their Hunters,* 1968.
[12] *See* G. W. Dimbleby. *Plants and Archaeology,* 1967.
[13] N. Hartz and H. Winge. *Aarboger* XXI, 1906.

probably clothing. Nor was flint the only raw material, a vast number of weapons and tools were made from bone and antler as they had been in the earlier period, but unfortunately these do not survive so well. Barbed points seem to have been chiefly used as fish spears. Fishing, in rivers and on the coasts, had now become an important source of food and in fact some coastal communities may have lived almost entirely off fish and shell-fish.[14]

At the time when man may have returned to Wales, Anglesey would still have been cold and dry, with birch and pine as the only trees. In South Wales and in Derbyshire there are inhabited caves dating from this period (c. 10,000 - 8,000 B.C.) which contain flint implements showing strong links with the old Palaeolithic traditions, but alongside them are a number of smaller points, the forerunners of the true Mesolithic industries of this country.[15] None of these have yet been found in North Wales or Anglesey, but as the climate gradually improved the human population may be expected to have increased and spread.

By the time the Mesolithic hunters are likely to have reached Anglesey (c. 6,000 B.C.) the summers had become warmer, with hazel, pine and alder replacing birch as the dominant trees, and mixed oak woodland making its first appearance.[16] The animals living in these woodlands may have included deer, bison, bears, forest horse, pig, elk, hyaena, lion, wolf and certainly ox for the bones of one have been found in the peat of the submerged forest at Trearddur Bay.[17]

It is in this setting that we first have direct evidence of man's activity in Anglesey, and at this period the setting is particularly important because man, as a hunter and food gatherer, was still entirely dependent upon his environment and did not yet take any organised steps to alter it to his own advantage. The evidence for Mesolithic people in Anglesey, as in most of Wales, is inadequate because it consists only of chance finds of characteristic flint implements, but it is possible to supplement this rather meagre source with fuller information gained elsewhere where living sites have been found *in situ*.

Most of these well-documented sites lie beneath the low-level peat of Denmark and north Germany where, because of the water-logged conditions, netting, basketry, tools of wood, bone and antler have all survived alongside the flint work.[18] And since the peat also preserves the record of the contemporary vegetation in the form of fossil pollen it is possible to gain a very full picture of the forests which surrounded the camp sites and the animal and vegetable food which could be gathered from them.

[14] *See* J. G. D. Clark. *Prehistoric Europe: the Economic Basis*, 1952, 22-90, for a comprehensive survey of early hunting and gathering.
[15] C. B. M. McBurney, *in* Foster and Daniel (edd.), *Prehistoric and Early Wales*, 1965, 31-4.
[16] *See* H. Godwin, *The New Phytologist*, XXXIX, 1940, 370-400 for a short survey of vegetational history and pollen zonation.
[17] TAAS. 1931, 142.
[18] *See* J. G. D. Clark, *The Mesolithic Settlement of Northern Europe*, 1936.

A study of the plants collected and the age of the animals killed can reveal the time of year during which camps were occupied, for, like all hunters and gatherers, the Mesolithic people of Europe had a seasonal cycle of movement. In the course of the year they might visit several camping sites in order to take advantage of varying environments and the different food sources and raw materials they offered. For instance, they might camp beside inland lakes in the winter and spring for wild-fowling and the collection of shed antlers, an important source of raw material for harpoons and such like; while in the summer they may have lived on the coasts, fishing and strand-looping. The evidence of superimposed deposits suggests that they came back to the same camps time and again.

The variety of small animals, birds and fish that were available in the forests of Europe at this time meant that man had to diversify his hunting techniques and it is during this period that many of the ingenious traps and snares still used by poachers and others were first invented. The design of these fish traps, bird snares and tread traps reveals an intimate knowledge of the habits of the animals sought and in the thousands of years of their use they have not been bettered, for recent examples are almost identical to the Mesolithic types. Striking examples of this are the salmon weels still used in Sweden and those found in a Stone Age level at Holbaek, Jutland, and the blunt wooden arrows used to stun birds and small animals prized for their fur. These have been found on Danish Mesolithic sites and are still made by the Eskimos.[19]

In Britain, for the most part, our information is far more limited. Sites are normally recognisable only as a scatter of flint tools and the debris of their manufacture with perhaps a spread of charcoal where fires had been lit, and a few scattered stake holes which may be the remains of tents and windbreaks.[20] There is only one site, Star Carr, near Scarborough, from which anything like a full picture can be gained.[21] The Mesolithic camp site had been set up in a reed swamp on the shore of a lake. The lake had dried up and filled with peat which covered and preserved most of the organic remains which would have completely decayed under drier conditions.

The camp was set on a specially prepared platform of birch branches and brushwood laid down to consolidate the swampy margins of the lake. Two felled trees projected from it into the lake and might perhaps have been used as some sort of landing stage. A paddle was found, but no remains of the boats which may have been of skin. There was no indication of huts on the platform, but from its size (200 - 240 square yards) the group who used it may be judged to have consisted of four or five families, perhaps about 20 men, women and children.[22] Judging by the animal

[19] J. G. D. Clark, 1952, op cit. Pl. II and p. 37, fig. 14.
[20] e.g. Deepcar, Yorks. (PPS. XXX, 1964, 1-24), and Farnham, Surrey (PPS V, 1939, 98-107).
[21] J. G. D. Clark. Excavations at Star Carr, 1954.
[22] This size is very typical of contemporary sites in Europe (see comparative table: op cit., 8).

remains and the quantity of food they represent, the site was occupied during the winter and again in April, over a period of perhaps six or seven years.

The occupation of the inhabitants during these visits was mainly hunting and the preparation of tools for immediate and for future use. For instance the absence of fish bones suggests that they did not fish much in the lake, but a great number of antler fish spears were found on the site which shows that, having gathered shed antlers in the surrounding forests, they were busily preparing tools for use at a fishing camp, perhaps on the coast. They were also making flint tools from nodules that could be gathered from the local boulder clay. The debris of this flint knapping was scattered all over the platform, but tended to be concentrated in certain spots where individuals must have sat working close to the fires. The implements produced included axes for tree-felling, microlithic points for arrows, burins or chisels for cutting antler, and awls and scrapers for use in leather-working as well as flakes and blades for general cutting purposes. The antlers of the stags they hunted, and the shed ones that they picked up, were a valuable source of raw material which they used in preference to bone for the long barbed points which they made up into fish spears. The heavier elk antlers were cut from the skull and perforated to make mattocks, probably used for grubbing up roots and such like.

The antler points and microliths might be lashed to their shafts with sinews or stuck on with resin. A number of rolls of birch bark were found on the platform, the material having been collected and stored in this convenient way, presumably for future use. This use may have been the making of containers and boxes of various kinds, as is done in Finland to this day, or possibly boiling to extract the resin.[23]

The animal bones, the residue of numerous meals, provide direct evidence for the hunting activities of the group. The gathering of edible roots and rhizomes must also have been important but the evidence has not survived, while in April young nettles and such like could have provided a lot of nourishment. The animal chiefly hunted was the red deer (the bones of at least 80 specimens were found) followed by roe deer (33), elk (11), ox (9) and pig (5); there was naturally some wild-fowling on the lake, grebe being the principal bird caught. The main hunting weapon was the bow and arrow and certain stag frontlets may have been worn as stalking masks. These frontlets consist of a spread of antlers on the top part of the skull. This bone has its edges ground down so that it could be worn as a cap, and has either two or four holes through which thongs could be passed for tying it on. The weight of the antlers was reduced by splitting and hollowing the beams and tines. It is not certain whether these head-dresses were worn in magical ceremonies to increase the hunter's luck or whether they were used as a practical aid in the hunt itself to

[23] Finnish containers illustrated in *Clark*, 1952. op cit., Pl. XIIa.

disguise the hunters. Either use can be paralleled among recent hunting communities.

Mesolithic people were helped in their hunting by dogs, or perhaps it would be truer to say that the dogs were helped in their hunting by people, for the advantages to be gained by co-operation would be mutual. It is possible that the " domestication " of the wolf/dog was effected without any conscious effort on the part of the hunters whose camps, with their plentiful remains of bone and offal, would be naturally attractive to scavenging dogs, which, with an inborn propensity to accept pack leader-ship, could be trained relatively easily. It is difficult to tell the difference between a domesticated dog and a wolf from the skeletal material, but certain modifications in the jaw (probably due to a poor diet) distinguished certain animals found on Mesolithic sites from either wolves or jackals. The skull from Star Carr is possibly the earliest evidence for the domesti-cated dog in Europe.[24]

Burials, which loom so large in the record of later prehistoric periods, are seldom found.[25] None belonging to the Mesolithic period have been found in Britain and only a few have come to light on the Continent. These are usually simple individual burials, often within the settlement area. Occasionally the bodies are accompanied by a few tools or arrow heads and, at one celebrated site in Brittany, stag antlers had been arranged around the head. One very remarkable German find dating from this period consists of " a nest of skulls " (buried successively as severed heads) and hints at the existence of gruesome and elaborate rituals which may have been akin to head-hunting.

The people living at Star Carr belonged to a widespread woodland culture which flourished in Denmark, eastern England and the area now covered by the North Sea. These tribes, which shared a common tradition of tool-making particularly adapted to their forest environment, are known as Maglemosians, after a very typical site in Denmark. A distinctive feature of their equipment is the possession of axes for tree-felling. The radio carbon date obtained for the site of Star Carr itself, 7,530 ± 300 B.C., indicates an early stage in the emergence of this group as a recognisable entity.[26]

It would be wrong to suggest that all the details of life as lived at Star Carr can be applied to Anglesey during the Mesolithic period. Firstly, the information from Star Carr relates to a time at least 1,500 years before there is any evidence for man in Anglesey; to the Pre-boreal climatic phase, cold and dry, with forests of birch and pine, rather than the warmer Boreal phase in which thicker deciduous woodland becomes dominant. Secondly, the Maglemosians as such did not reach the west of these islands

[24] PPS XXVII. 1961, 35-55 on the Star Carr dog in particular and J. Clutton-Brock *in* Brothwell and Higgs (edd.), *Science in Archaeology*, 1963, 269-74 on the subject in general.
[25] Summarised in J. G. D. Clark. *Cambridge Ancient History*, 1965, Vol. I, Chap. III, 34-6, 43-5, 49.
[26] Clark. 1954. *op cit.*, 12.

though it is possible that some of the coastal groups living around the Irish Sea in the later part of the Mesolithic may be in some way related to or descended from this eastern group. There are axes, for instance, of Late Maglemosian (Horsham) type in Pembrokeshire.[27]

However, certain basic factors would have remained constant: the emphasis on hunting; the seasonal nature of camping sites; the small size of the communities; the use of all available organic materials and the production of microlithic flint points of various kinds. The use of barbed antler points may have been more exclusive; certainly none have survived from the southern coasts of the Irish Sea.

In Anglesey and in Wales as a whole most of the Mesolithic sites are to be found on the present-day coast, and the post-Mesolithic rise in sea level may have flooded others which were even nearer the sea.[28] However, the occasional discovery of microliths in Montgomery and Radnorshire, and in the make-up of the barrow at Bedd Branwen in the Alaw valley, indicates that Mesolithic man did penetrate inland and that his economy could exploit both a forested and a coastal environment.

The coastal economy, however, is clearly the dominant one. Although sand dune areas such as Newborough Warren may well have been less extensive than now because of thicker tree cover, such sites were obviously popular, as were low hills overlooking the shore. The shore could have provided much of Mesolithic man's food and many of his raw materials. From small boats he could have caught salt-water fish, while river mouths would have held fresh-water species and estuaries and cliffs would have yielded a harvest of birds, birds' eggs and shell-fish. This last source of nourishment was relied on heavily. In many parts of Europe there are vast mounds of discarded shells, mostly oyster and mussel (happily mixed with a number of dateable tools and weapons), which are the residue of innumerable Mesolithic meals.

Several of these shell middens exist in Anglesey, principally on Newborough Warren. None of them have been dated, though a bone needle of unspecific type was found in one in 1926.[29] It is not certainly Mesolithic, and in fact it cannot be said that all shell middens must date from this period because this kind of strand-looping existence could provide a living for people at any period. A family living at Penmon during the Roman period relied on shell-fish to a very large extent and accumulated quite a considerable mound of refuse.[30]

Apart from these middens of uncertain age the only finds of Mesolithic date from Anglesey are five groups of flint implements, all but one from the shore. The shore would, of course, have been the source of the flint, in the form of pebbles cast up on the beach. These would have originated

[27] G. J. Wainwright. PPS XXXIX, 1963, 108-14, 126.
[28] The most recent summary of the Mesolithic period in Wales is G. J. Wainwright, op cit., 99-132.
[29] E. N. Baynes. TAAS. 1927, 34-7.
[30] C. W. Phillips. Arch Camb., 1932, 247-59.

in the Antrim chalk or in the submerged flint seams in the bed of the Irish Sea. A sixth Mesolithic site may have been revealed by erosion of the submerged forest surface in Holyhead Bay. Flint flakes, sharpened bone tools and two skulls with other human bones were reported from this drowned land-surface which must be pre-Neolithic, but unfortunately the scraps of flint are all unworked, the bone 'tool' is not convincing, and the human bones do not appear to be ancient.[31]

It is impossible to date the Mesolithic finds exactly, or even approximately. The microlithic element has certain affinities with "Sauveterrean" flint-working traditions which in the east of England were flourishing by about 6,000 B.C. but continued well after that date.[32] Analysis of pollen in coastal peat covering comparable flint implements in Pembrokeshire suggested a date in Pollen Zone VIIa, that is, after 5,000 B.C.;[33] while the chip from a polished stone axe found amongst the Mesolithic flints at Aberffraw may indicate a very late date indeed, after 3,500 B.C. and contemporary with the earliest farmers.[34] Thus the range of possible date is enormous. The latter end of it seems more feasible for the few finds which survive.

The find which has the closest affinities with distinctive traditions of microlith making is the scalene triangle fortuitously included in the make-up of the Bronze Age barrow, Bedd Branwen (NGR SH/362849).[35] This is quite closely comparable to some of the microliths from the "Sauveterrean" sites at Prestatyn, Flintshire, and Port St. Mary, Isle of Man.[36] People making flints of this type were widely distributed in Britain and seem to have a preference for areas which would be only thinly wooded, such as the Pennines.[37] However, on the basis of a single find it would be unwise to state that this is definitely a "Sauveterrean" point for the ascription of any group of finds to a particular flint-working tradition is based on the relative quantity of certain types of point, rather than the simple presence or absence of any particular implement.

For this reason it is impossible to make any constructive comments about the group of three flint flakes found at Moryn Bay (now Porth Forllwyd) near Lligwy (NGR SH/504872).[38] Two of them are waste flakes and are not illustrated. The other is also a waste piece, but more distinctive, being what is termed a "microburin". These pieces are the result of making microliths in a particular way: the thick butt of the flake is

[31] L. Williams. TAAS. 1950, 94-5. The finds are in the custody of the AAS.
[32] PPS. XXI. 1955, 3-20. Peacock's Farm, Cambridgeshire, dated to Pollen Zone VIc. *See* H. Godwin. *Proc. Royal Society*, Series B. CLIII, 1961, 227-320 for the date.
[33] PPS. XXIX. 1963, 128-9.
[34] A similarly late date can be suggested for the microlithic flints at Newborough, also mixed with later Neolithic types.
[35] Fig. 2 no. 11. There is another piece of flint from this mound which might be broken microlith.
[36] Prestatyn: PPS. IV. 1938, 330-2. Nos. 29-38. Port St. Mary: PPS. I, 1935, 73, fig 3. Nos. 24-5.
[37] PPS. XXI. 1955, 3-20.
[38] Fig 2. No. 12. In NMW. W. F. Grimes. *The Prehistory of Wales*, 1951, 163, No. 276.

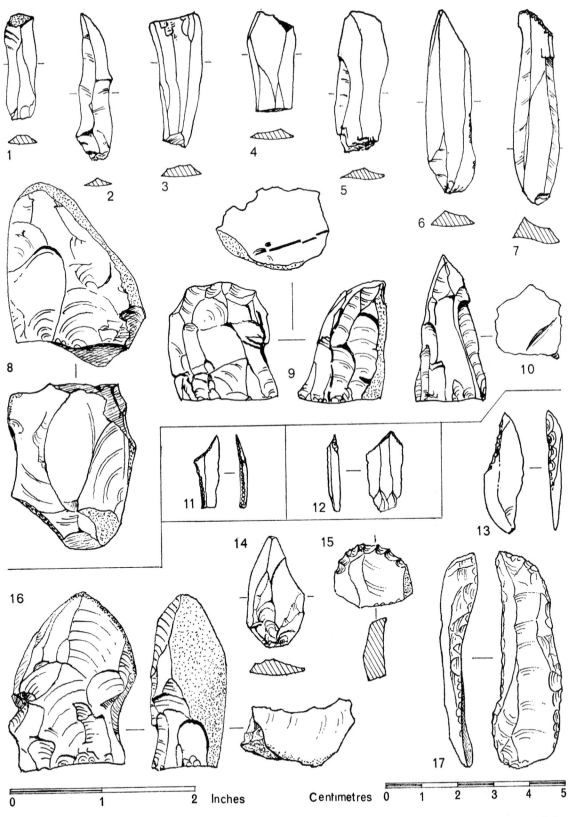

FIG. 2 — Mesolithic flints from Anglesey. Aberffraw : 1-7, selection of blades; 8-10 cores; 11, microlith from Bedd Branwen, Llanbabo; 12, microburin from Moryn Bay, Lligwy; 13-17, flints from Penmon.

removed and the curved point of the microlith is formed at the same time by working a notch in the side of the flake, then snapping it across at the waist (Fig. 3, No. 1 shows the other half of this process well). This method of working is found within the " Sauveterrean " tradition, but is not exclusive to it.

The group of eighteen flints from Penmon might well have stood a better chance of attribution but, in fact, all but five are waste flakes.[39] Two of these are the butts of broad, multi-ridged blades and two are small leaf-shaped flakes suitable for microlith production. Amongst the five worked pieces is a large core, the remains of a beach pebble from which a number of small flakes have been struck. Some of these must have been very short and the core was probably thrown away as no longer capable of producing usable blanks. The small, steeply worked scraper is a type common on most Mesolithic sites, as is the one microlith present, an obliquely blunted point. This type was popular with nearly every microlith-making group. The large worked flake is rather unusual but could be compared to some from the south Wales coast, from Nanna's Cave, Caldey and Nab Head, Pembrokeshire.[40] In fact, the Penmon site clearly belongs to the series of Welsh coastal sites which are distinguished by their very lack of distinction.[41] They have produced cores, flakes and microliths, mostly obliquely blunted points, but none of sufficient quality or quantity to make it possible to define their cultural background at all closely, beyond suggesting that the industries are all the products of groups responding to a similar coastal environment, perhaps descendants of the original Palaeolithic population. The large flakes from Caldey and Penmon might hint at this.

The fifth implement, a small leaf-shaped flake with a thinned butt, can be classified as a " Bann Flake ", a type of point particularly common on the coastal sites of the north of Ireland and in the Bann valley.[42] These occur quite frequently on the Welsh coastal sites as well, but the unity of culture on either side of the Irish Sea was not complete, for even unspecialised microliths like the one from Penmon are virtually unknown in Ireland. The Bann Flake may be indicative of a relatively late date. In Ireland they occur on beaches of the maximum sea level (c. 4,000 B.C.) and certainly continued to be used in the Neolithic. In Anglesey there is one from the megalithic tomb at Lligwy.

The largest group of Mesolithic flints from the island has not yet been definitively published.[43] I include drawings of them here by permission of the excavator, Mr. C. H. Houlder. They were found scattered on the old ground surface beneath an Early Bronze Age barrow at Trwyn Du,

[39] Fig. 2. Nos. 13-17. In NMW. W. F. Grimes, op cit., 161, No. 249.
[40] Caldey: Arch. Camb., 1955, 107, fig. 14. nos. 8 & 12. Nab Head: PPS. XXIX, 1963, 109, fig. 6, no. 32.
[41] PPS. XXIX. 1963, 115-26.
[42] H. Movius. The Irish Stone Age. 1942. passim.
[43] They are briefly mentioned in PPS. XXIX, 1963, 123.

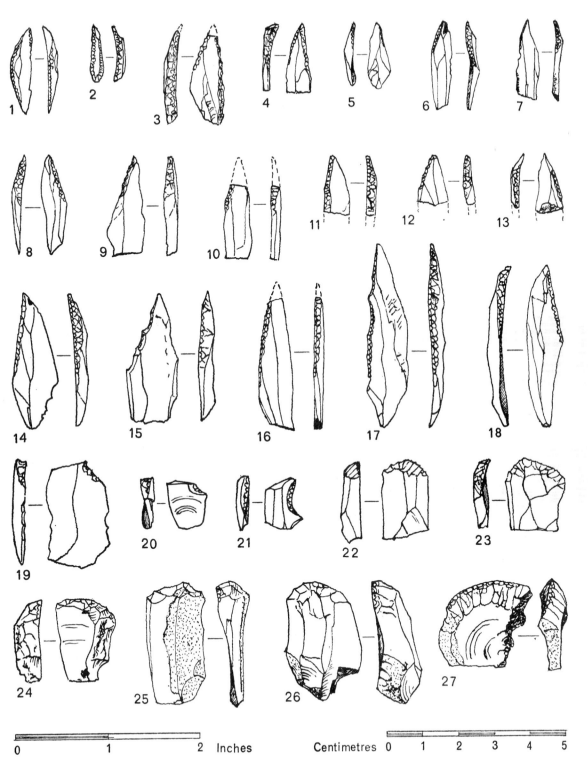

FIG. 3 — Mesolithic flints from Aberffraw. 1-18 microliths; 22-27, scrapers.

Aberffraw (NGR SH/352679). Others can still be picked up from eroded surfaces nearby (Fig. 4).

The area was clearly quite a large-scale working site. The collection includes 25 cores of which 10 would have produced very useful narrow flakes; 11 transverse flakes struck from the edge of cores to rejuvenate the striking platform; 6 microburins and a good deal of less distinctive waste from microlith working, snapped butts, etc., as well as quantities of large flakes and rough lumps.

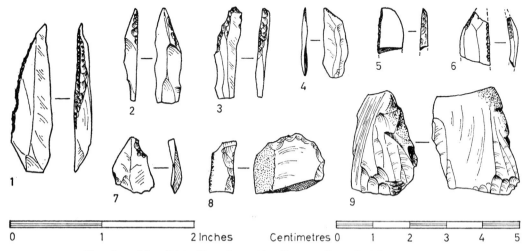

FIG. 4 — Mesolithic flints from Aberffraw, collected February 1970.
1-6, microliths; 7, microburin; 8, scraper; 9, core.

The finished implements include a lot of well struck flakes and blades which vary in width from ¼″ - ⁷⁄₁₀″, and are normally about 1½″ - 2″ long. Most of them are multifacetted. A selection is shown in Fig. 2, Nos. 1-7. There are 14 small scrapers, 8 of them end scrapers made on flakes of variable quality. Fig. 3, No. 22 is a very neatly made example entirely typical of Mesolithic flint-working. There are 5 flakes which may have an intentionally cut burin or chisel-edge, but they are all rather doubtful. Two are on core trimming flakes and may be simply the result of unsuccessful attempts to remove flakes.

There are 25 microlithic points of which 15 are the undistinctive obliquely blunted points that are to be found on so many Welsh coastal sites.[44] (12 illustrated: Fig. 3, Nos. 6-10; 12-16, 18). Two (Nos. 11 and 17) have steep working straight down one side. This roughening of the surface may have given a better purchase to the resin with which it was stuck to the shaft. Two others (Nos. 3 & 4) have worked points and No. 2 is a minute rod, or needle-shaped point, steeply worked all round. No. 1 is a crescent

---

[44] Others not mentioned are broken.

or elongated trapeze, a relatively distinctive type with a " Sauveterrean " background. However, the group as whole cannot be ascribed to the " Sauveterrean " tradition because of the lack of scalene triangles and the predominance of the obliquely blunted point. So, in spite of the quantity and quality of the material, the flint-workers at Aberffraw can be no more closely classified than those at Penmon. It can be said, however, that the Irish connection is not so strong, for there are no " Bann Flakes " among the numerous flakes and blades, which all tend to be parallel-sided.

The date at which this community flourished may be relatively late, for the debris included several flakes of stone, one of which had come from a polished stone axe, quarried at the commercial site on Mynydd Rhiw, Lleyn, and typical of the subsequent Neolithic period.[45] Although this was an open, surface site before it was covered by the barrow and so contamination with later objects is not impossible, the association does suggest that these Mesolithic hunters and fishers may have preserved their native traditions, living, unaffected and unmolested, alongside the intrusive farmers for some considerable time.

A similar situation may have existed on Newborough Warren, not far away.[46] Unfortunately the microliths from this site have been lost, but two obliquely blunted points (Fig. 32, Nos. 6 & 7) and three points worked down one edge (Fig. 32, Nos. 8-10) can be recognised in the published drawings. The collection is a surface one and the site, close to Bryn Llwyd (NGR SH/396645), was occupied over a long period and a mixture is inevitable. However, the predominance of later types, Neolithic arrowheads and scrapers, and the close juxtaposition of finds. of all periods, does suggest that the settlement may have been continuous, representative of the final assimilation of the Mesolithic natives and the Neolithic newcomers.

Like all fundamental changes in history, and more especially in prehistory, the borderline between the hunting and gathering cultures of the Mesolithic and the new farming communities of the Neolithic, is a blurred one even though the first farmers must be recognised as foreign colonists. One of the factors contributing to this haziness is the relationship of the hunters to their prey. As with the present day Lapps it is possible for men to " farm " animals without actually enforcing any kind of physical control, and there is some evidence from the south of England to suggest that the later Mesolithic people may have kept cattle confined close to their settlements.[47] The difference between this and true domestication as practised by the contemporary farmers on the Continent is hard to recognise.

The period from 4,000 - 3,000 B.C. must have been a time of considerable crisis for the coastal Mesolithic groups, for large tracts of their hunting territory were fast disappearing beneath the sea and new communities,

---

[45] See below pp. 72-5.
[46] T. Pape. TAAS. 1927, 23-33 and 1928, 21-7.
[47] Oakhanger, Selbourne, Hants. PPS. XXVI, 1960, 246-62.

which lived very differently from themselves, were settling in their areas. However, the land was still thinly populated and there is no evidence of direct antagonism between the two groups, although in the long run the farm clearings must have slowly encroached upon the native forest and reduced the habitat of the wild animals on which the Mesolithic hunters depended. But, while hunting and fishing were successful, there would be little incentive to change their way of life, even if the advantages of farming did gradually become apparent, so there is no reason to suppose that Mesolithic groups did not survive for many centuries alongside, but distinct from, the Neolithic farmers. Before returning to consider the impact of these first farmers on Anglesey it will be necessary to consider the beginnings of agriculture in its wider setting.

II

THE NEOLITHIC PERIOD: THE FIRST FARMERS IN ANGLESEY

THE beginning of a Neolithic period has been recognised by differing criteria over the years. The early antiquarians defined it as a change in stoneworking techniques: the introduction of polished stone tools. Later the significant factor was considered to be pottery. Now, with more extensive excavation and knowledge of settlement sites, the important change is seen to be one of economy; from a rather parasitic and insecure system of hunting and gathering, to a more settled life of food production through the planting of crops and the domestication of animals.

This was a revolutionary change, certainly one of the greatest in the history of mankind, since a settled life in which one man could produce more food than he, himself, needed is the necessary basis for the development of city life and all that it implies for the growth of technology and sophistication. Although this change was revolutionary it was certainly not sudden, nor was it universal. It was only in naturally favoured areas, places with a varied and temperate environment, that the potential advantages of manipulating, rather than simply using, his resources would occur to man.[1]

As far as Europe and Western Asia are concerned, the critical area was just north of the Euphrates valley where the foothills lie between the desert and the equally arid mountains. It is here that the wild ancestors of wheat, oats, barley, and of sheep and goats are to be found.[2] The cereal plants have the advantage of growing well in dense stands and being easily harvested, giving a high return for relatively little effort. Apart from the dog, the first animals to be domesticated, sheep, goats and cattle, are all gregarious, used to living in herds and accepting the leadership of an individual animal and so readily amenable to management by man once he had established his dominance.[3] This control might possibly be made easier by a decline in the health and strength of the animals under conditions of primitive farming. It is in fact this reduction in size which is used to differentiate the bones of domesticated from wild animals on these early settlement sites.[4]

---

[1] For a general discussion of this subject *see* R. J. Braidwood and G. G. Willey (edd.), *Courses Toward Urban Life*, 1962, especially pp. 330-59.
[2] S. Piggott, *Ancient Europe*, 1965, 35-9.
[3] For information on animal domestication *see* F. E. Zeuner, *A History of Domesticated Animals*, 1963.
[4] But *see* E. S. Higgs and M. R. Jarman, *Ant.* XLIII, 1969, 31-41, for doubts about this.

Inevitably the early stages of this process in which certain patches of cereals and certain groups of animals were simply guarded and fenced rather than sown or bred in captivity will be difficult, if not impossible, to recognise. At the present time caves in northern Iran are producing sheep bones which show signs of domestication at a date of c. 8,000 B.C.[5] Whether agriculture was carried on at the same time is not known: the two need not go together although their advantages are complementary.

It is certain that by at least 7,000 B.C. agriculture was well established in many places in the Near East, in Palestine and in southern Anatolia.[6] The settlements were by that time populous villages, or even towns, in which artisans and priests as well as farmers can be seen to have lived. Amongst the domestic animals, selective breeding had so advanced that several distinct breeds can be recognised, and careful cultivation of cereals had greatly increased the grain size and decreased the loss at harvesting by developing strains in which the grain was retained longer within the husk.

In the main river valleys, where annual floods renewed the fertility of the land, permanent settlements prospered and developed into the historic cities of Mesopotamia and Palestine. Elsewhere there was an inevitable deterioration as the soil became more and more exhausted by constant cropping unbalanced by additional manuring. This meant that primitive farmers were continually having to take in new land and even having to move their settlements every few years.[7]

It is possible that agriculture was developed independently in the east Mediterranean, probably in Greece which possesses many of the necessary conditions, but contact between the two areas must have been close and in general terms the history of western Europe is not altered by this possibility.[8] It still remains true that the earliest farming communities on the Continent have their immediate origins in the east Mediterranean, whether they were indigenous or had crossed from Anatolia. The knowledge of the techniques of farming and of pottery (which happen to go together in Europe) appears to have come to western Europe by two routes: around the northern shores of the Mediterranean and up the Danube valley. This latter route provides a wide corridor of particularly fertile loess soils on which the tree cover may have been relatively less dense and it was the scene of a definite movement of colonisation. Communities of people recognisable by their distinctive pottery styles and their large wooden houses of a peculiar wedge-shaped plan, can be seen moving slowly north-westwards, reaching the Rhine round about 5,000 B.C.[9]

In peripheral areas the story is less clear. Certain elements in all

[5] Iran Caves: Braidwood and Howe, *in* Braidwood and Willey, *op. cit.,* 136.
[6] J. Mellaart, *Catal Huyuk,* 1967, 18 and 52, and Perrot *in* Braidwood and Willey, *op. cit.,* 153-60.
[7] C. Clark and M. R. Haswell, *The Economics of Subsistence Agriculture,* 1967, 34-52.
[8] R. Pittioni *in* Braidwood and Willey, *op. cit.,* 221-3.
[9] S. Piggott, *op. cit.,* 50-60, for a convenient recent summary.

European Neolithic cultures must have come originally from the East, namely the cereal crops themselves and domesticated sheep and goats since their wild ancestors did not occur in Europe. But other plants and vegetables and wild cattle and pigs were widespread on the Continent, and it is possible that many of the new ideas were learnt and applied by the original Mesolithic inhabitants living in the forests which surrounded the Danubians' clearings. The evidence for animal husbandry with very little arable farming among the Ellerbek and Ertebolle peoples in north Germany and Denmark suggests that this process of 'acculturation' may explain the quick spread of farming beyond the areas actually inhabited by new-comers.[10]

The Danubians did not penetrate to western France or Spain. Here the first farming communities belonged to the Mediterranean groups, recognisable by their pottery decorated with cardium shell impressions. Their settlements are on the whole less elaborate than those of the Danubians and there is a good deal of evidence for their having lived in caves.[11] Indeed, their main building activity seems to have been concerned with large and complex tombs for the communal burial of the dead. This interest in the rites of burial, which may reflect fertility cults particularly linked with ancestor worship, can be found in many parts of western and northern Europe although, naturally, the tombs take varied forms. One of the major distinctions would seem to be between grouped individual burials eventually covered by a single mound, like those in Poland, Denmark and Brittany;[12] and the single communal chamber in which the bodies are mixed together, as found in Almeria, southern Spain and in the later series of megalithic or large-stone tombs which become the dominant form in most parts of Europe.[13]

Controversy continues to surround the origins and significance of the varying styles of architecture in these monuments and it will continue to do so because they are the most durable and complete (and in many areas the only) structure of this period left for us to study. It has been considered that the different tomb styles represent communities of differing origins, but new work in Brittany seems to suggest that these differences may be simply religious and that the different traditions were adopted by pre-existing farming communities who all had their ultimate origins in eastern France where burial practice had been much more simple.[14] Therefore, though the superficial differences between the various types of Neolithic

[10] H. Schwabedissen *in* Braidwood and Willey, *op. cit.*, 260-3.
[11] E.g. Escalon de Fenton. L'abri de Chateau-neuf-les-Martigues' *Gallia Préhistorie*, XII, 1956, 1-106, and J. Arnal. 'La Madeleine,' Zephyrus, VII, 1956, 30-79.
[12] K. Jazdzewski, *Poland* (Ancient Peoples and Places), 1965, 90-2; O. Klindt Jensen, *Denmark* (Ancient Peoples and Places), 1957, 39-42; P-R. Giot. *Brittany* (Ancient Peoples and Places), 1960, 109-14, but the dating has been revised since this book was published. *See* Giot, *Annales de Bretagne*, LXIX, 1962, 31-3.
[13] Recently summarised *in* H. N. Savory, *Spain and Portugal* (Ancient Peoples and Places), 1968, 85-115.
[14] J. L'Helgouach, *Les Sépultures Mégalithiques en Armorique*, 1965, 90-6, 100-6.

tombs are large and were, no doubt, important in the eyes of the builders, it is unlikely that they represent any great differences in way of life, economy, ultimate origins or basic attitudes.

The earliest Neolithic groups in the British Isles, as elsewhere, are difficult to recognise.[15] The introduction of wheat, barley, sheep and goats must indicate the arrival of actual colonists, but, since the size of their boats, probably made of skin and wickerwork, must have been limited, these groups would inevitably be small and probably isolated. They brought with them not only a knowledge of farming but also of pottery making, a highly traditional craft in which styles change only slowly. It should be possible, therefore, to discover the particular area of northern France or Germany from which these colonists came by a comparison of pottery types in use on both sides of the Channel. Unfortunately this approach has not proved particularly rewarding except in south-western England, Devon and Cornwall, where pottery from the earlier sites does have several points of comparison with that in Brittany.[16] One of the difficulties may be that we have not yet discovered the earliest sites, since most of our evidence comes from inland areas and from monuments whose very size suggests that they must be the products of a well-established society. By 3,000 B.C., therefore, we may be looking at traditions which have already gone through almost a thousand years of separate development and internal mixture.

It is certain that the main characteristics of southern English society in the Neolithic are the result of a great deal of local amalgamation for, though certain strands can be linked to Continental origins, these origins are diverse, stretching from north-eastern Europe to Brittany. The total complex cannot be paralleled in any one place.[17] Settlement sites in southern England are strangely uninformative, because the only tangible remains are small pits, filled with rubbish, which were probably originally dug for the storage of grain.[18] There are no postholes or other evidence of houses so it must be assumed that the people lived in light shelters, possibly tents. However, wood must have been available since, before they could cultivate the land, they would have to clear it of trees; they were certainly capable of large-scale carpentry for their burial mounds cover elaborate wooden structures.

These Long Barrows are some of the most characteristic monuments of this " Windmill Hill " (the name given to the Neolithic groups in the south of England). They are long mounds of earth and chalk, higher and broader at the east end where the burials are concentrated. The bodies normally lie in a state of some confusion in a restricted area marked out by a wooden fence or by isolated posts. The procedure seems to have been to

[15] S. Piggott, *Neolithic Cultures of the British Isles*, 1954, is the most comprehensive guide to the Neolithic period in Britain, especially the main southern English group, the Windmill Hill Culture, but it is out of date now in some matters.
[16] A. Fox, *South West England* (Ancient Peoples and Places), 1964, 27-35.
[17] S. Piggott, PPS, XXI, 1955, 96-101, for an early statement of the problem and a review of the evidence.
[18] Field *et al.*, PPS, XXX, 1964, 352-381.

leave the bodies exposed for some time in these ' mortuary enclosures ' while a sufficient number accumulated; then a final funeral ceremony took place and the bodies and the enclosure were covered by a large mound built of material obtained by digging deep ditches at either side. Once this had taken place the bones could not be touched, but there is evidence to suggest that, in the interval between death and final burial, certain bones might have been removed for use in religious ceremonies.[19]

The exact origins of this particular burial custom is one of the great problems of British archaeology to which no satisfactory answers can be found at present. Communal burials under long mounds are fairly wide-spread in Europe, but the trapezoid plan of English Long Barrows is difficult to explain. It has been compared to the similar shape of the Danubian houses, but the only place where both houses and Long Barrows are found is southern Poland and here the barrows are of the grouped individual burial type. There is also a problem of chronology if these Middle Neolithic Polish barrows are to be considered ancestral to the English group since Long Barrows were already being built in Wiltshire by 3,200 B.C.[20]

A similar problem of origin applies to the other communal monument built by these people, the Causewayed Camps. These are non-defensive enclosures, usually sited towards the summit of low hills, consisting of a circular area delimited by from one to three concentric banks and ditches interrupted by a number of wide causeways. There is no evidence of structures inside them and, though there is a great deal of debris in the ditches, broken pottery, animal bones, tools and hearths, there is nothing to suggest that these sites were permanent settlements. They seem to have been places where people came for short periods to carry out some unknown social activity. From the frequent association of ox, sheep and pig bones in the ditches it has been suggested that these camps were the setting for large annual sacrifices which, possibly, also incorporated rituals involving human bones, perhaps from Long Barrows.[21] In addition, these gatherings must have provided an opportunity for trade in raw materials, tools and animals.

A study of the grits used to temper pottery found in the ditches of these camps has revealed that much of it must have been made many miles from where it was found.[22] There is a strong possibility, therefore, that people came from a distance and that these Causewayed Camps represent small tribal centres, their existence hinting at some sort of social or political organisation over and above the immediate family group. In any case the building of these camps and the Long Barrows must have been a communal effort requiring considerable administrative skill, not

[19] S. Piggott, *West Kennet Long Barrow Excavations 1955-6*, 1962, 67-8.
[20] P. Ashbee, *Arch. C.* 1966, 45-7.
[21] A. Keiller, *Windmill Hill and Avebury*, 1965, 17-21.
[22] A. Keiller, *op. cit.*, 19, 43-8.

least in ensuring an adequate food supply for the work force. This fact alone means that agriculture must have been flourishing, a conclusion borne out by the fact that about 90% of the animal bones at Windmill Hill (the most completely excavated of the Causeway Camps) were from domesticated animals.[23] Hunting had become an insignificant factor in the economy.

In western Britain and Ireland the situation was somewhat different. Long Barrows and Causewayed Camps do not exist, nor do the quantity of grain storage pits. In place of the Long Barrows are large stone tombs covered by stone cairns instead of earthen mounds. They are clearly an equivalent tradition, linked to western areas of the Continent rather than Northern Europe. Their precise relationship to the Long Barrows is not clear; they are broadly contemporary and there are bound to have been mutual influences. Possibly the trapezoid cairn which covers some types of megalithic tombs may be one such borrowing from the Long Barrow traditions. Grain was certainly grown in south-west England and in Ireland but the absence of storage pits in the area may hint at a greater emphasis on cattle rearing, perhaps because of the rather wetter climate in the west.[24] The few settlement sites which have been found have revealed traces of substantial wooden houses, another contrast with southern England. Causeway Camps are not found west of Dorset, and no equivalent non-funerary monuments are known. Since our knowledge of the uses of these camps is so speculative, it would be wrong to place too much weight on this absence, but it might possibly suggest a less tightly organised society.

The history of Wales and Anglesey is very closely linked to that of south-west England and of Ireland throughout the Neolithic period. A radio carbon date of 3,050 ± 95 B.C. for Neolithic pottery from a pit at Coygan, Carmarthenshire, compares very reasonably with the date of 3,230 ± 150 B.C. for the site at Hembury in Devon.[25] This latter site is considered among the earliest sites in the British Isles, not only because of this date but because of the variety of shapes amongst the pots found there and the number of lugs or handles that they possess. These lugs can be compared fairly closely to some from the Néolithique Primaire of Brittany and provide some of the best evidence there is for direct links across the Channel.[26] In turn, the pottery from Hembury and from contemporary sites at Hazard Hill, Devon, and Carn Brea, Cornwall, can be linked to that from the settlement at Clegyr Boia, Pembrokeshire, with similar cupped

[23] A. Keiller, op. cit., 142-5.

[24] Grain at Hembury. A. Fox, op. cit., 31. Pollen analysis in Ireland and grain impressions on sherds. Smith and Willis, UJA, XXIV-XXV, 1961-2, 16-24. There was a very high proportion of cattle bones at Lough Gur, Co. Limerick. O'Riodain, PRIA, 56, C. 1954, 366.

[25] G. Wainwright, Ant., XLI, 1967, 66. I would consider the Coygan site to be rather later than Clegyr Boia, Pembs., which has provided material comparable to Hembury. Hembury date: A. Fox, Ant., XXXVII, 1963, 228-9.

[26] Summarised in A. Fox, South West England, 1964, 29-32. Original publication: D. M. Liddell, PDAES, 1930-35.

lugs.[27] The pottery from Devon is predominantly bag-shaped whereas that from Pembrokeshire contains a number of shouldered forms (i.e., an open bowl with a concave neck and a sharp angle between neck and rounded base). These shouldered bowls are particularly common in Ireland and are symptomatic of the continual interaction between Ireland and Wales at this time.

In North Wales we have rather little pottery and no radio carbon dates to guide us in the definition of an Early Neolithic phase of settlement. However, the pottery from the West Chamber of the tomb at Dyffryn Ardudwy, Merioneth, is very similar to that from Clegyr Boia and may be confidently claimed as early, although there is really insufficient comparative material from that area to establish this beyond all doubt.[28] The West Chamber at Dyffryn Ardudwy is a Portal Dolmen, a type of megalithic (or large stone) tomb which is very widespread in the Irish Sea area. They occur in Carmarthenshire and Pembrokeshire, both known to have been settled in the Early Neolithic and the occurrence of early pottery in direct association with one in Merioneth establishes fairly clearly that the building of these tombs is to be linked with the culture of the earliest farmers in Wales.

These Portal Dolmens are easily recognisable by the distinctive arrangement of stones at the front of the single chamber. These stones are set in an H plan, two high stones flanking a closing slab which may reach almost to their tops. This portal is much taller than the square chamber behind it so the large capstone is normally set at a slope. In Wales, one can find chambers in which these features are no longer very marked, though still recognisable, a fact which suggests that this tomb-type has a long, uninterrupted history in the area.[29]

Inevitably the stone tombs have survived much better than the less substantial houses of the living and we have tantalisingly little information about the way of life of their builders. The excavations at Clegyr Boia, Pembrokeshire, revealed the remains of a number of huts, an outdoor hearth and a large midden.[30] The framework of the huts was of wood and the gabled roof was supported by a row of large posts down the centre. The walls may have been of wattle and daub or, more likely, of turf with a foundation of stones, some of which survived on the site. The only source of light and air would have been the doorway, which was large. In this case, the fire was outside, but similar wooden houses have been found in Ireland where the hearth was inside.[31] At Clegyr Boia the largest house, 22 ft. by 12 ft., was rectangular, but another hut on the site might have

[27] Hazard Hill: C. H. Houlder, PDAES, 1963, 2-31. Carn Brea: C. Thomas, *Cornish Archaeology* I, 1962, 104-6. Clegyr Boia: A. Williams, *Arch. Camb.*, 1953, 20-47.

[28] Preliminary report: T. G. E. Powell, *Ant.*, XXXVII, 1963, 19-24. Full report forthcoming in *Arch.*

[29] *See* F. M. Lynch *in* T. G. E. Powell *et al.*, *Megalithic Enquiries in the West of Britain*, 1969, 124-48.

[30] A. Williams, *loc. cit.*

[31] Lough Gur: O'Riordain, PRIA, 56, C., 1954, 297-459.

been round. However, the rectangular shape is more normal, having been found at Lough Gur, Co. Limerick; Haldon, Devon; Nottage, Glamorgan, and Llandegai, Caernarvonshire.[32] The last two sites probably date from the Middle-Late Neolithic so this style of building must have lasted a long time.

No true villages have been found in the west, but at both Lough Gur and Clegyr Boia there were a number of houses loosely grouped together without any defensive earthworks.[33] In fact, all aspects of life at this time give an impression of peacefulness. There may have been a need for protection against the animals of the forest such as wolves, but there are few signs of any antagonism against other men: no aggressive weapons and no camps or fortresses. The farmers' time would seem to have been spent in clearing woodland, sowing crops, tending animals and making tools, as well as performing religious rituals. Many of the tools must have been made from wood, but unfortunately these seldom survive and we only know about those made from bone, antler, flint or stone. Flint, which can be easily chipped into shape, is rare in Wales and much must have been imported from the chalk areas of Antrim or southern England. However, the igneous rocks of Wales are suitable for the production of larger tools, especially the ubiquitous stone axes which can be ground and polished to a sharp edge.

These heavy axes cut down trees very efficiently and, since farmers were frequently having to clear new land as their old plots became exhausted, they must have been highly prized. Certain stones were exploited on such a large scale that the production of some axes must have been a commercial enterprise.[34] The workers on these 'axe factories' must, therefore, have been specialists, though the work was probably only of a seasonal or part-time nature. In the south the evidence for a similar large-scale working of flint can be seen in the mines at Cissbury, Sussex, and Grimes Graves in Norfolk.[35]

In Anglesey, we have little direct evidence for the type of life lived by the Neolithic inhabitants, but it is unlikely to have differed greatly from that lived on the mainland of Wales. We have no evidence for houses, nor of the type of agriculture practised, but the people were certainly concerned in the trading of axes from the great factory sites of the Graig Lwyd group at Penmaenmawr and Llanfairfechan. Like other groups in Wales, they buried their dead in communal stone tombs, and these tombs provide the best evidence for the Neolithic settlement of the island.

Megalithic tombs differ considerably from area to area in the plan of the chamber, in the shape of the covering cairn and probably in burial

[32] Lough Gur: *op. cit.*, 443-7. Haldon: S. Piggott, *Neolithic Cultures of the British Isles*, 1954, 33-5. Nottage: H. N. Savory, *Cardiff Nat. Soc. Trans.*, LXXXI, 1950-2, 75-92. Llandegai: C. H. Houlder, publication forthcoming.
[33] Clegyr Boia has natural defences but Lough Gur has virtually none.
[34] Evens *et al.*, PPS, XXVIII, 1962, 209-66, especially 233-40.
[35] S. Piggott, *op. cit.*, 1954, 36-45.

rituals. But it is normal for one or two particular styles to predominate in any given area, reflecting the traditions of a presumably homogeneous population. On the mainland of North Wales the Portal Dolmens would seem to represent the mainstream of tradition on to which ideas from other regions are grafted.[36] In Anglesey, on the other hand, discussion of the tombs is rendered confusing by the lack of any clearly dominant tradition. Few of the tombs can be unequivocably linked to other groups elsewhere; the geographical distribution is mixed and some must represent entirely local developments.

Sixteen megalithic tombs survive on the island at present. Their distribution is mainly coastal and it is noteworthy that most of them lie on, or close to, areas of light, easily drained soil.[37] The main concentrations lie on the limestone areas around Brynsiencyn and close to Benllech and Moelfre. The surviving monuments must represent only a proportion of those that existed originally; even in the eighteenth century the Rev. Henry Rowlands was able to record a number of sites in the Llanidan area which have subsequently vanished without trace.[38] There are, in fact, a number of eighteenth and nineteenth century accounts of destroyed sites, but unfortunately all are so vague that no archaeological conclusions can now be drawn from them, except that the distribution of tombs must have been remarkably dense in the areas around Brynsiencyn and Moelfre, the parts of the island where surviving tombs are still most common.[39] The pattern of distribution, therefore, is not materially altered.

Since there is such a mixture of traditions in Anglesey it is difficult to reconstruct the historical sequence, that is, to decide which tombs were built by the first farmers and which represent traditions brought in by later groups. Types of tomb which are similar to those built elsewhere will be dealt with first, and a date may be hazarded for some on the basis of this foreign evidence.

Such a group, which may belong to an early phase in the history of Neolithic settlers in Anglesey, are the simple Passage Graves. They have a widespread distribution in the Irish Sea area but are never found in large numbers. In Anglesey there are three. The tombs in question are Bodowyr, Tŷ-mawr and Tŷ Newydd, all situated towards the south-western corner of the island.

Bodowyr, near Llangaffo (ANG 6. NGR SH/463682) is the best preserved.[40] It consists of a small polygonal chamber formed by five upright

[36] F. M. Lynch in T. G. E. Powell et al., Megalithic Enquiries in the West of Britain, 1969, 107-48.
[37] W. F. Grimes, Ant., XIX, 1945, 169-74.
[38] References to tombs in Mona Antiqua Restaurata written about 1723.
[39] The most convenient and comprehensive summary of these accounts is in E. Neil Baynes, Trans. Hon. Soc. Cymmrod., 1910-11, 3-91.
[40] The reference numbers refer to the illustrations and to the gazetteer of tombs in T. G. E. Powell et al., Megalithic Enquiries in the West of Britain, 1969, 296-300, where full references to the literature will be found. The National Grid references have been given to assist in location, though in fact nearly all the megalithic tombs are marked on the 1″ O.S. map.

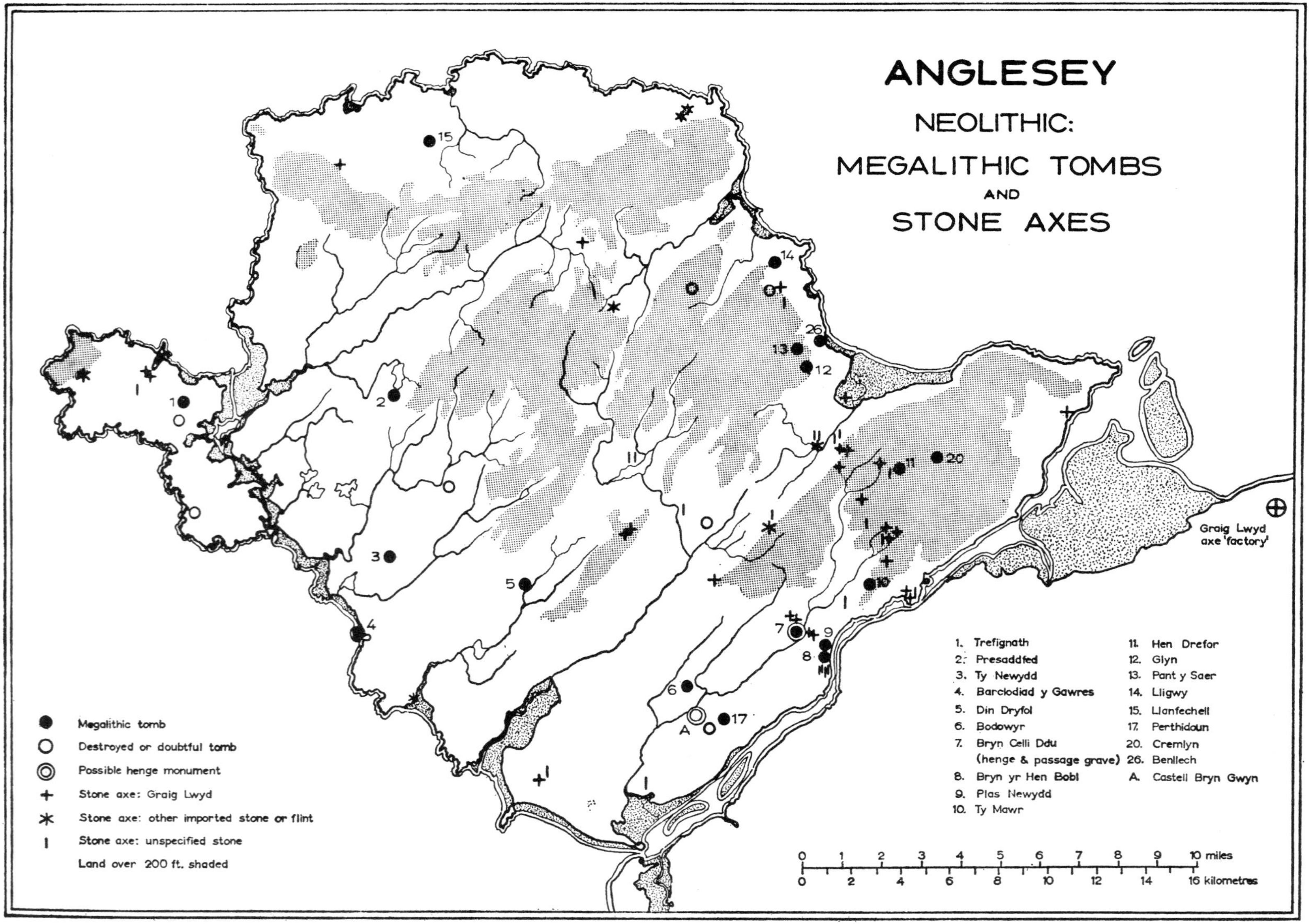
ANGLESEY
NEOLITHIC:
MEGALITHIC TOMBS
AND
STONE AXES
Graig Lwyd axe 'factory'
1. Trefignath
2. Presaddfed
3. Ty Newydd
4. Barclodiad y Gawres
5. Din Dryfol
6. Bodowyr
7. Bryn Celli Ddu (henge & passage grave)
8. Bryn yr Hen Bobl
9. Plas Newydd
10. Ty Mawr
11. Hen Drefor
12. Glyn
13. Pant y Saer
14. Lligwy
15. Llanfechell
17. Perthidoun
20. Cremlyn
26. Benllech
A. Castell Bryn Gwyn
Megalithic tomb
Destroyed or doubtful tomb
Possible henge monument
Stone axe: Graig Lwyd
Stone axe: other imported stone or flint
Stone axe: unspecified stone
Land over 200 ft. shaded
0 1 2 3 4 5 6 7 8 9 10 miles
0 2 4 6 8 10 12 14 16 kilometres

MAP 2 — Neolithic monuments and finds.

stones (one is now fallen), covered by a mushroom-shaped capstone. The size and shape of this chamber is similar to that of other small, simple Passage Graves in the Irish Sea area, for instance Hanging Stone, Burton,

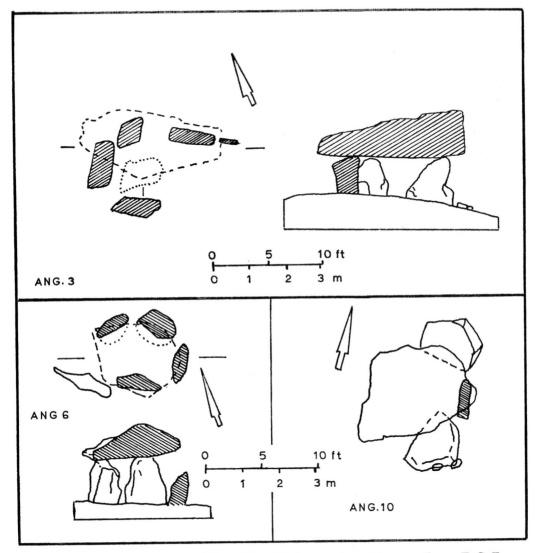

FIG. 5—Plans and sections: Tŷ Newydd and Bodowyr; plan: Tŷ-mawr. From: T. G. E. Powell *et al.*, *Megalithic Enquiries in the West of Britain* (Liverpool U.P. 1969).

Pembrokeshire, and Ballintoy, Co. Antrim.[41] The chamber would have been covered by a small round cairn of stones and access would have been gained by a short passage, formed of upright stones like the chamber itself. At

[41] Hanging Stone: W. F. Grimes, PPS, II, 1936, 131. Druid Stone, Ballintoy, C. Antrim: J. M. Mogey, UJA, IV, 1941, 49-56.

Bodowyr all sign of the passage has disappeared, but the entrance to the chamber is marked by a low stone on the eastern side. Whereas the supporters of the capstone are 5 ft. high, this stone is only 2 ft. 9 in. and does not appear to have been broken. It can reasonably be interpreted as a sill-stone across the entrance. This is not a common feature in tombs of this simple type, but does occur in more elaborate later Passage Graves.[42] It may be considered a peculiarity of this type of tomb in Anglesey, since it occurs at another site, Tŷ-mawr, near Llanfair Pwllgwyngyll (ANG 10. NGR SH/539722). This tomb is extremely badly ruined but enough survives to show that the capstone had originally stood on supporters some 4 ft. high, while the eastern sill-stone was only 2 ft. high.[43]

The third member of the group, Tŷ Newydd, close to Rhosneigr, (ANG 3, NGR SH/344738) is the only one to have been excavated, but unfortunately the contents are unhelpful for any close dating of the site.[44] The chamber here is oval in plan and covered by a very narrow capstone. This narrowness may be due to breakage in the recent past.[45] When the tomb was excavated in 1936, the area of the chamber was found to have been delimited by a spread of charcoal, with an area of burnt earth at the east end where it was considered the passage had opened into the chamber proper. Unfortunately neither the exact position nor the length of this passage are known with certainty, since the stone-holes in which lost supporters might have stood were not recognized, or possibly not recognizable since the tomb is built on a rock outcrop. However, despite the unsatisfactory nature of the passage itself, it is reasonable to include this tomb amongst passage graves, since there is a reliable tradition that it had been surrounded by a circular cairn.[46]

No human bones, either burnt or unburnt, were found in it and it is not known whether the objects found in the layer of charcoal covering the floor are primary to the tomb, that is, were put in by the original builders. It is possible that they belong to a later phase when the tomb may have been reused. The objects found were a very fine barbed and tanged arrowhead, 9 small pieces of pottery belonging to a Beaker and a small chip of flint said to come from a polished flint axe. The axe could belong to any phase of the Neolithic, but the Beaker pottery decorated with simple lines of cord ornament, and the arrowhead, must date from the very end of the period.

Objects of this Beaker phase have not infrequently been found in megalithic tombs, but they are normally accompanied by objects from an earlier date and can clearly be interpreted as a late use of the tomb. It cannot be proved that this is the correct explanation here, but the

[42] For instance in many of the Cruciform Passage Graves in Ireland.
[43] This was first pointed out by H. Prichard in *Arch. Camb.*, 1873, 22-7.
[44] Excavation report by C. W. Phillips, *Arch. Camb.*, 1936, 93-9.
[45] An appropriately-shaped stone in shown lying close to the chamber in Skinner's drawing, made in 1802. (Published: *Arch. Camb.* Suppl., 1908, 46).
[46] It used to be enclosed by a circular wall, diameter *c.* 100 ft., *Arch. Camb.*, 1936, 98.

dating of the simple Passage Graves elsewhere, principally in Brittany, Devon and South Wales, suggests that as a group they represent an early phase in megalithic building traditions in the Irish Sea area, and since they are rare, this phase was probably shortlived.[47] It is, therefore, likely that at Tŷ Newydd the barbed and tanged arrowhead and the Beaker are secondary.

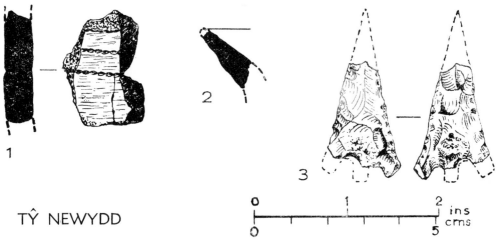

TŶ NEWYDD

FIG. 6 — Finds from Tŷ Newydd. 1-2, sherds of Beaker pottery; 3, barbed and tanged arrowhead. From T. G. E. Powell *et al.*, *Megalithic Enquiries in the West of Britain* (Liverpool U.P. 1969).

None of these three tombs retains any vestiges of its surrounding cairn. If it is right to suggest that they belong to the family of Passage Graves, one would expect these cairns to have been round, and in fact at Tŷ Newydd, as already mentioned, and at Bodowyr, there are nineteenth century accounts which hint at the former existence of circular cairns.[48] It is also normal for Passage Graves to be built in commanding positions and this is in fact true of all three sites, especially Tŷ Newydd, which is built on the summit of a low hill.

Another small but distinctive group of tombs may be discussed next, although their chronological position is unknown. Like the simple Passage Graves, they clearly belong to a larger family of tombs found in the Irish Sea area, the Court Cairns of northern Ireland and the segmented galleries of south-west Scotland.[49] The exact origin of this class of monument is obscure, but in both Scotland and Ireland they were certainly being built during the early phases of the Neolithic period. In both areas, however, they have a long history, during which changes and alterations can be seen

[47] Britanny: J. L'Helgouach, *Les Sépultures Mégalithiques en Armorique*, 1965, 21-120. Devon: Broadsands: C. A. R. Radford, PDAES, 1957-8, 147. Pembrokeshire: Carreg Samson: F. M. Lynch, forthcoming.
[48] *Lewis's Topographical Dictionary*, Vol. 2, 1833, 66.
[49] Court Cairns: de Valera, PRIA, 60, C., 1960, 9-140. South West Scotland: Scott *in* T. G. E. Powell *et al.*, *Megalithic Enquiries in the West of Britain*, 1969, 175-246.

taking place, these changes concentrating mainly on the entrance area and the arrangement of the chambers within the cairn. This particular type of tomb consists of a line of small square compartments, one behind the other, divided by low, transverse or septal slabs. Entrance to this continuous gallery was through two high stones at the eastern end, these portal stones being somewhat similar to those found in Portal Dolmens. In Ireland, the entrance area was further emphasised by the building of large semi-circular facades of upright stones on either side of the portal, thus providing a ceremonial forecourt in front of the tomb. All Irish court cairns have this facade in one form or another, but in Scotland this feature appears to be an addition, an idea imported from Ireland at some time in the Middle Neolithic when the basic tradition had already been established for some time in Scotland.[50]

The Anglesey tombs have many points of similarity with this group in the north Irish Sea area, but it is not clear how close this relationship was, nor at what time in the Neolithic this particular community came to the island. They differ in detail from tombs in all three areas of likely origin, north-east Ireland, south-west Scotland and the Isle of Man. In Anglesey, the group is unusually widely scattered, and it is probable that other tombs belong to it but are now too damaged to be recognisable.

The best preserved of these "Long Graves" is Trefignath on Holy Island (ANG 1. NGR SH/259805). The surviving structure is between 30 and 40 ft. long and is relatively complete. At the east end is a portal area and stretching behind it are the remains of three, or possibly four, rectangular chambers divided from each other by slabs reaching almost to the full height of the side stones. The first chamber is intact, the second completely destroyed, the third much ruined. The fourth chamber is conjectural for at present there are only four fallen slabs beyond the end of the third chamber. Whether or not these represent the remains of a fourth chamber is uncertain.

The north side of the portal has been disturbed and the surviving stone is out of place. However, the original arrangement can clearly be seen on the southern side. Here there is an entrance stone 6 or 7 ft. high, behind which is a slightly lower one. It is not uncommon to find double portal stones in Scottish sites, but the unusual feature of Trefignath is that these stones stand with their long axes parallel to that of the chamber, whereas the more normal arrangement is to find them at right angles to it.

The chamber behind the portals is rectangular, 8ft. by 4ft. The two side stones are from 3 ft. to 4 ft. high and directly support two overlapping capstones. The upper one has probably slipped back from an original position in which it would have covered the portal as well. A transverse slab across the back of this chamber reaches almost the height of the side stones and thus prevents actual access from one chamber to the other. This

---

[50] J. G. Scott, *loc. cit.*

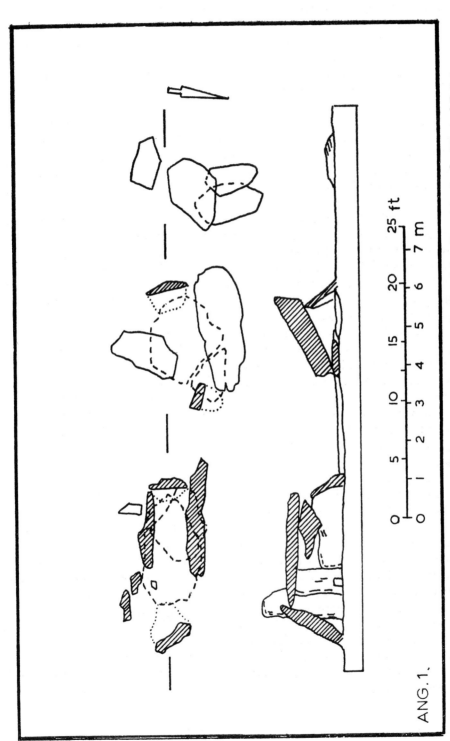

ANG. 1.

FIG. 7 — Plan and section: Trefignath. From: T. G. E. Powell *et al.*, *Megalithic Enquiries in the West of Britain* (Liverpool U.P. 1969).

is a very unusual feature and cannot be paralleled in any of the segmented galleries in either Scotland or Ireland. The second chamber has been entirely destroyed but did originally exist, since the Royal Commission found that the basal layer of the cairn ended in a line where the uprights had been removed.[51] Most of the stones of the third chamber survive, but all have been knocked from their original positions by the fall of the capstone. The transverse slab between the second and third chambers has not survived, but a small jambstone remains in position here. The northern sidestone which would have leant against this jambstone is also present. The western end of this chamber is marked by another high septal slab. Like the slab between the first and second chambers, this is sufficiently high to have blocked access further westward. It is possible, however, that this stone is not a septal but the final backstone of the gallery since the existence of the fourth chamber is doubtful. There are four large stones here, but all of them are lying on the surface and may well not be in their original positions.

As it stands at present, the Trefignath tomb differs from the Irish and Scottish galleries because of its closed chambers, without access from one to the other, and because of the position of its portal stones and the absence of a facade. It might be possible to argue that the facade here has been removed but, since early accounts of the site which describe the removal of the cairn make no reference to any facade stones, it is unlikely that they ever existed.[52] The site is built on a knoll of rock and the deposit of earth around it is extremely shallow; whether it would reveal stone holes is doubtful. A measure of doubt must remain on this point, but, by and large, the absence of facades at other similar sites in Anglesey does add weight to the belief that this feature never existed at Trefignath. The absence of a facade is characteristic of the earlier tombs in Scotland, but it is doubtful whether Trefignath should be equated with this phase, because all these Scottish tombs without facades are considerably smaller.[53]

Din Dryfol (ANG 5. NGR SH/396725), the second member of this group, is, at the time of writing, in the course of excavation.[54] The chambers had been virtually destroyed but it was hoped to reconstruct the plan by establishing the position of stoneholes. This has not been entirely successful because most of the stones had not been set into prepared holes. However, it is clear that the tomb consisted of three large rectangular chambers entered from the north-eastern end through a double portal, somewhat similar to that at Trefignath, but with the stones set at right angles to the line of the chambers. Unlike Trefignath, access from one chamber to the other seems to have been completely unimpeded.

The tomb is set on a narrow ledge on the side of a steep rocky hill. On

[51] R.C.A.M., *Anglesey*, 1937, 22.
[52] *Arch. Camb.*, 1867, 234 and *Arch. J.*, XXXI, 1874, 1-2.
[53] J. G. Scott, *loc. cit.*
[54] Excavations by the writer on behalf of M.P.B.W. A summary of the final results will be published in TAAS.

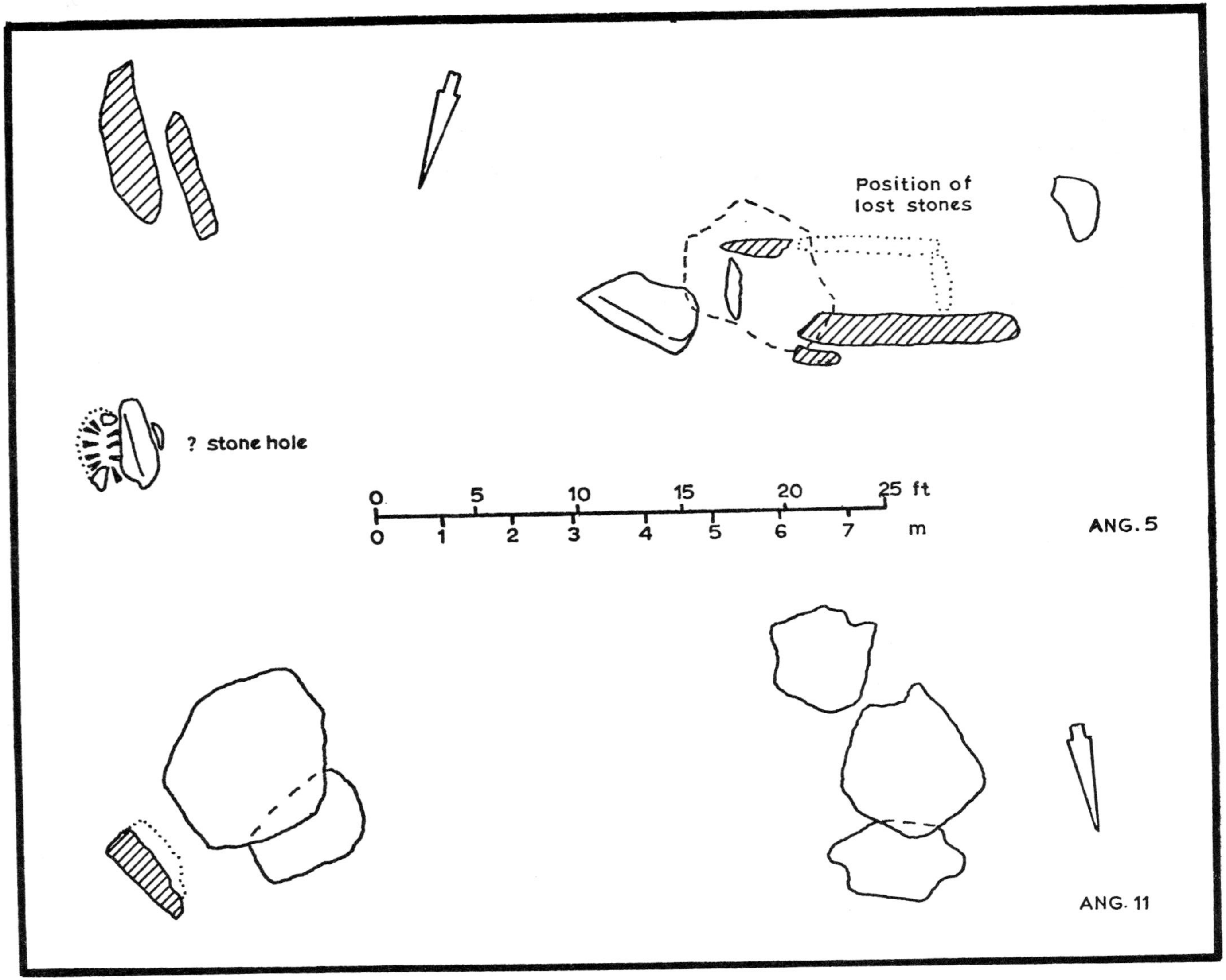

Fig. 8 — Plans: Din Dryfol and Hendrefor. From: T. G. E. Powell et al., Megalithic Enquiries in the West of Britain
(Liverpool U.P. 1969)

? stone hole

Position of
lost stones

ANG. 5

ANG. 11

0 1 2 3 4 5 6 7 m

0 5 10 15 20 25 ft

the eastern side, there is scarcely room for a facade next to the portal. The western side has not yet been investigated. There was no evidence for a stone blocking in front of the entrance. This contrasts with the practice in Scotland and in Ireland where stones were normally built up against the portals to prevent any later access. The ledge stretches for a distance of about 200ft. behind the chambers, and surface indications suggest that this whole area would originally have been covered by the long rectangular cairn.

The finds from the chamber area were not plentiful, but they included a number of small flint implements and some tiny sherds of plain ,undecorated pottery with simple rims. Unfortunately too little pottery has been found as yet and the flint implements are not sufficiently distinctive to give a close indication of date.

The third member of the group is an even more seriously ruined tomb on the other side of the island at Hendrefor, near Beaumaris (ANG 11. NGR SH/551773). Besides a high portal stone at the eastern end of the tomb, there is very little left except two groups of stones some 20ft. apart. When the western group was standing it consisted of a capstone on two supporters, perhaps sidestones of a rectangular chamber. It had already fallen when Thomas Pennant visited the monument in 1783.[55] In 1802 the eastern group was still standing, the capstone supported at a slope by the portal stone and another stone which appears, in Skinner's drawing, to be directly behind it.[56] This group was thrown down in 1825.[57]

Our knowledge of the monument in the nineteenth century, however, does not make classification very much easier since nothing is known about any structures connecting the two groups. A study of the ground between them offers no clues about this nor about the position of any second portal stone. However, the height of the existing stone and the overall length of the monument, which is 42ft., lead one to the conclusion that, on the present scanty evidence, its tentative classification as a "Long Grave", similar to Trefignath and Din Dryfol, is reasonable.

Barclodiad y Gawres (ANG 4. NGR SH/329707), magnificently sited on the top of a cliff on the south-west coast of the island, is one of the finest and most interesting of all the North Welsh tombs. It is a cruciform chamber with decorated walls, set in a round mound, altogether typical of a type of tomb found in Ireland, notably in the Boyne valley.[58]

The stone structure consists of a narrow passage some 23ft. long built of large upright stones leading into a large central chamber with three side chambers branching off it. The western chamber is more elaborate

[55] T. Pennant, *Tours in Wales,* 1783, iii, 41.

[56] J. Skinner, *Ten Days Tour through the Island of Anglesea* (published as a supplement to *Arch. Camb.,* 1908, 86-7).

[57] A. Llwyd quoting her father's MS. *See* E. Neil Baynes, *Trans. Hon. Soc. Cymmrod.,* 1910-11,30.

[58] It was excavated in 1952-3: *see* T. G. E. Powell and G. E. Daniel, *Barclodiad y Gawres: The Excavation of a Megalithic Chamber Tomb in Anglesey,* 1956.

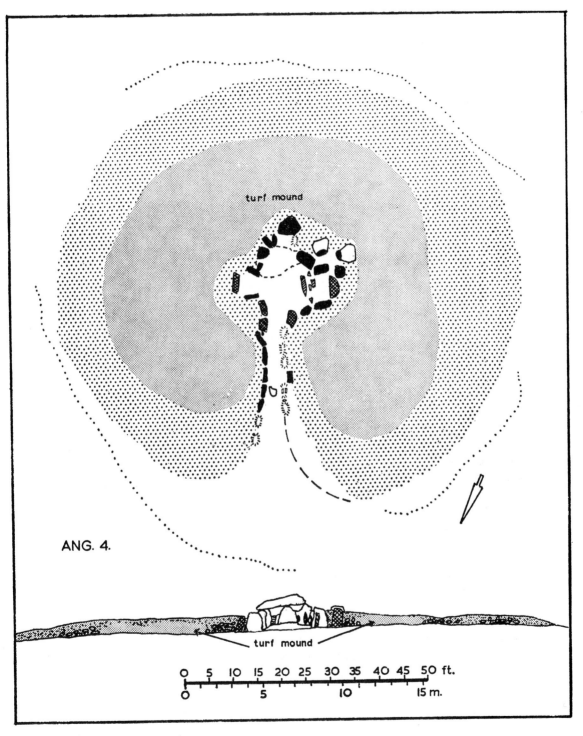

ANG. 4.

turf mound

turf mound

0 5 10 15 20 25 30 35 40 45 50 ft.

0   5   10   15 m.

FIG. 9 — Plan and section: Barclodiad y Gawres. From: T. G. E. Powell *et al., Megalithic Enquiries in the West of Britain* (Liverpool U.P. 1969).

than the others since it has an annexe to the south of it, and the front had been closed by complex stone blocking. This blocking, consisting of transverse slabs leaning against three uprights, had probably been put in position after the funeral had taken place, although it would, theoretically, have been possible to move the transverse slabs at any time. All but one of the roofing stones have been removed. The normal system of roofing these tombs is for the passage and side chambers to be covered by slabs resting directly on the uprights, or on one or two layers of intervening corbels. The central chamber, too wide to span in this way, is covered by a corbelled dome, each succeeding layer of corbels overlapping the lower one until the gap is sufficiently narrow to be filled with a single capstone. Some of these vaults are up to 20ft. high, but at Barclodiad y Gawres it is unlikely to have exceeded 8 or 9 feet.

All the uprights had been securely set in prepared stoneholes and most of them were backed by heaps of large boulders. However, the mound, 90ft. in total diameter, was chiefly composed of turves and only the outer edge was stone. A good deal of the mound had eroded away and it had been robbed for wall-building materials, so there is a possibility that it had been finished originally with a thin skin of stones to give the impression of a cairn entirely built of stone. Comparable mounds composed mainly of turves have been found at Fourknocks and other Cruciform Passage Graves in the Boyne valley.[59]

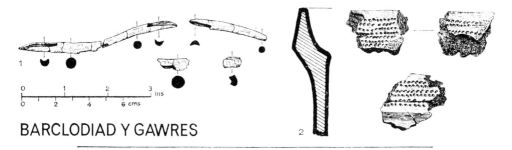

BARCLODIAD Y GAWRES

FIG. 10 — Finds from Barclodiad y Gawres: 1, burnt pin; 2, sherds of a Collared Urn (secondary burial). From: T. G. E. Powell *et al., Megalithic Enquiries in the West of Britain* (Liverpool U.P. 1969).

The burial rite was cremation, as in all tombs of this type. The undisturbed remains of two men were found in the west side-chamber, the burnt bones lying directly on the old ground surface and spreading over into the annexe. The east and back chambers had both been dug into in the past and nothing remained of the burial deposits except a few scraps of bone in the corners. With the bones in the west chamber were two broken and burnt pins of polished bone or antler. Such pins, which may have been used to hold together clothing, are commonly found amongst

[59] P. J. Hartnett, PRIA, 58, C., 1957, 200-4 and Site L, Newgrange (publication forthcoming).

the bones in Irish tombs together with stone beads and small stone balls which were not found at Barclodiad y Gawres.[60]

The central area had not been used for burial, but had been the scene of some ritual performances probably connected with the funeral. A fire had been lit on the floor in the centre and allowed to burn for some time. While it was still glowing, a quantity of stew was poured over it and the fire quenched by covering it with pebbles and limpet shells. The components of the stew, recognisable by tiny fragments of bone, were wrasse, eel, whiting, frog, toad, natterjack, grass snake, mouse, shrew and hare. Together they would have produced a scarcely edible mixture, but one which must surely have been connected with magical practices of some kind.

The entrance to the passage may have been another centre of ritual activity. Nothing exceptional was found beyond the end of the passage. In fact, the whole of that area had been badly disturbed and many of the passage stones had been removed, although the stoneholes remained visible. The remarkable lack of such stoneholes at the western end of the passage suggests that the last two or three stones did not support a roof, an arrangement which may have been more common in tombs of this type than was originally supposed.[61] The outer end of the passages have normally been found carefully and intentionally blocked, and the passage usually becomes more substantial at the inner point where this blocking ends. Therefore, one may suggest that the outer, unroofed end of the passage was a temporary formality to be filled in with blocking, which probably reached almost to the roof of the inner passage. However, the final lintel of the inner passage cannot have been covered since this is the point at which tombs have almost invariably been entered in the recent past. A peculiar structure above the entrance at Newgrange (the most famous of these tombs in Ireland), which covers a gap in the passage roof, hints at ceremonies designed to foster some intangible contact between the living and the dead.[62] If a gap was left between the top of the outer passage blocking and the lintel of the inner passage the same result could have been achieved at Barclodiad y Gawres and other sites less elaborate than Newgrange.

However, the most remarkable feature about this tomb is the series of decorated stones.[63] There are five of them, three at the end of the passage where it enters the central chamber and one in the east and west chambers. These designs have all been made by lightly pocking the smooth surface of the stone with a hard stone chisel. Only on Stone 22 has the pattern been deeply cut; the others are, admittedly, rather difficult to make out.

[60] Cf. Fourknocks: P. J. Hartnett, op. cit., 228-48.
[61] See F. M. Lynch, 3rd Atlantic Symposium, Arhus, publication forthcoming.
[62] C. O'Kelly, Illustrated Guide to Newgrange, 1967, 16, Pl. 11.
[63] For further discussion of these stones see F. M. Lynch, Arch. Camb., 1967, 1-22. The very poor spiral in the centre of Stone 19 is illustrated in that article, but not here.

FIG. 11 — Barclodiad y Gawres: decoration on Stone 22. (Reproduced from *Archaeologia Cambrensis*, by kind permission of the Editor.)

0   6   12   18   24   INCHES

0   10   20   30   40   50   CENTIMETRES

FIG. 12 — Barclodiad y Gawres: decoration on Stone 5. (Reproduced from *Archaeologia Cambrensis*, by kind permission of the Editor.)

They have never been emphasised by painting, but in torchlight the play of shadows would make them very effective.[64]

This type of entirely abstract art is found frequently on the cruciform tombs in Ireland but is not found in any other kind of megalithic tomb in the British Isles. Decorations are often found on the walls of tombs in Brittany but the repertoire of motifs and symbols is different.[65] There have been several attempts to interpret the designs but none have been convincing. It is generally agreed that the motifs chosen must have some religious potency and significance, and it is possible to cite parallels between the use of lozenges and zigzags in this art and on the carved bones in Spanish megalithic tombs, which are said to represent the Mother Goddess or Earth Goddess.[66]

The Barclodiad y Gawres stones are outstanding among examples of this art because of the way the motifs are manipulated in order to produce an integrated pattern on each stone. The execution of these designs has not been uniformly successful and the presence of earlier, partly erased, patterns obscures the situation on Stone 8 and at the top of Stone 22.

The patterns can be best appreciated from the drawings and I will not attempt to describe them here. The integration of the designs can be contrasted with the scattered motifs on the stones at Loughcrew, Co. Meath,[67] and compared to the large-scale composition on the two stones at Seefin, Co. Wicklow; the better stones at Newgrange; the magnificent series being revealed by the current excavations at Knowth; and two of the stones in the Southern Tomb at Dowth.[68] This latter comparison is very close indeed, but since the chronological sequence of these tombs in Ireland is not known in detail, these stylistic comparisons are not helpful in dating Barclodiad y Gawres, although on *a priori* grounds one would suppose it to be earlier than Loughcrew and, possibly, broadly contemporary with Newgrange.

A close comparison with Newgrange is helpful because a radio carbon date for the building of this tomb has recently been obtained.[69] This gives a range of 2,500 B.C. to 2,400 B.C. and, although one should not date a whole group of monuments from one example, it seems reasonable to suggest that Barclodiad y Gawres was built at some time within a century or two of those dates.

The tomb is the only surviving example of its type in the island, but there is a possibility that a destroyed site at Tregarnedd near Llangefni

[64] Several stones at Newgrange and elsewhere have been uncovered for the first time in recent excavations and none has shown any sign of pigment or even charcoal.

[65] F. M. Lynch, *op. cit.*, 13-7.

[66] H. N. Savory, *Spain and Portugal* (Ancient Peoples and Places), 1968, Pls. 19 and 33. *But see* A. Fleming, *World Archaeology*, I, 1969, 247-61.

[67] *E.g.* Pls. 56 and 57 *in* G. E. Daniel and S. P. O'Riordain, *Newgrange* (Ancient Peoples and Places), 1964.

[68] Seefin: E. Rynne, JRSAI, XCIII, 1963, 85-6. Newgrange: C. O'Kelly, *op. cit.*, *passim*. Knowth: G. Eogan, PRIA, 66, C., 1968, 336-42, figs. 23-7. Dowth: F. M. Lynch, *op. cit.*, figs. 9 and 10.

[69] *Ant.*, XLIII, 1969, 140.

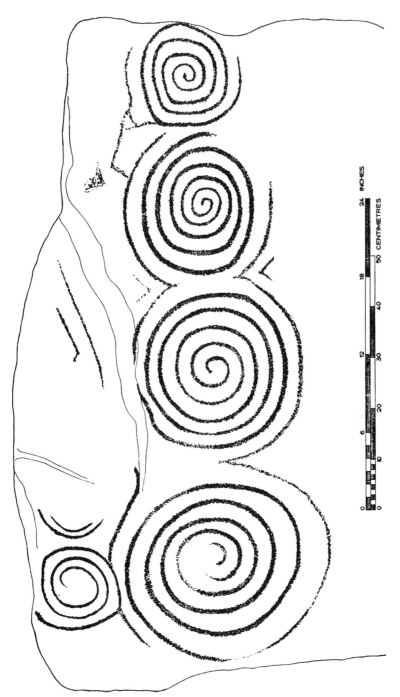

FIG. 13 — Barclodiad y Gawres: decoration on Stone 8. (Reproduced from *Archaeologia Cambrensis*, by kind permission of the Editor.)

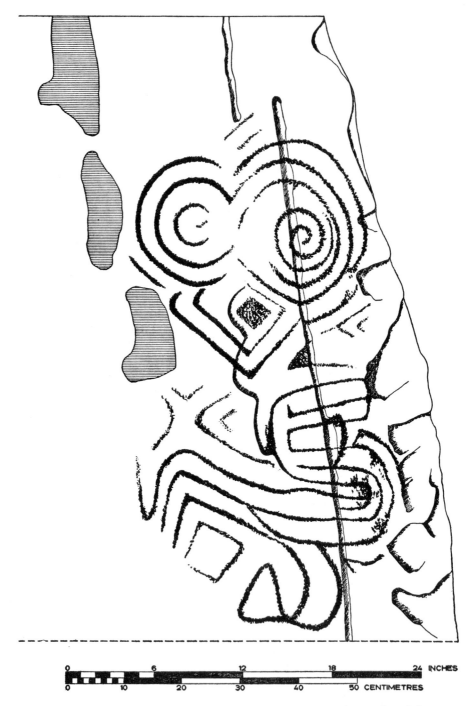

FIG. 14 — Barclodiad y Gawres: decoration on Stone 6. (Reproduced from *Archaeologia Cambrensis*, by kind permission of the Editor.)

(ANG 27. NGR SH/472748) had been similar. Pennant compared it to Bryn Celli Ddu, the only other Passage Grave known at the time, but goes on to speak of "numerous passages" which suggests that he might have been looking at a cruciform chamber.[70] In any case, these Anglesey tombs must represent only a small community, in close contact with more flourishing groups in Ireland, but apparently not making a great deal of headway in the island, which was certainly already occupied by groups with other traditions of tomb building. On the mainland of Wales there are none, but the remains of another isolated tomb of this group survive at the Calderstones, Liverpool.[71]

One of the major problems of the history of Anglesey during the Neolithic period is the absence of Portal Dolmens on the island. These tombs, as already mentioned, exist in fairly large numbers in the Lleyn Peninsula and in the Conway Valley, where their very characteristic architecture is easily recognisable. Their non-existence in Anglesey might be explained by suggesting that the island was already inhabited by other groups at the time when the builders of Portal Dolmens were spreading northwards from the Cardigan Bay area. But this is unlikely since, apart from the simple Passage Graves which are few in number, there do not seem to be any sufficiently early tombs in Anglesey; for in Merioneth the Portal Dolmens are almost certainly Early Neolithic, while the majority of Anglesey tombs would seem to belong to the Middle or even to the Late Neolithic period.

The absence of genuine Portal Dolmens is even more surprising in view of the possible influence of Portal Dolmen designs on certain of the peculiar local variant type of tombs on the island. These tombs, such as Pant y Saer and Bryn yr Hen Bobl, have small rectangular closed chambers which can be best explained as imitations of Portal Dolmens, although without the characteristic high portal. The peculiarity of the portal area at Trefignath may possibly also be due to a certain amount of influence from this same quarter. An early drawing of a tomb at Llanfechell (ANG 15. NGR SH/361920), which is now simply a heap of fallen stone, shows what appears to be a high closed front which is very suggestive of a Portal Dolmen, but unfortunately not much confidence can be placed in such drawings.[72]

Pant y Saer (ANG 13. NGR SH/510824) is a small tomb situated on a raised limestone plateau just outside Benllech. It has been dug into several times, notably in 1875 when an intrusive cist or grave, probably dating from the Beaker period, was removed; it was finally extensively excavated in 1932 by Sir Lindsay Scott.[73]

The chamber, which is only 8ft. square, was built over a large pit

[70] T. Pennant, *Tours in Wales*, 1783, iii, 51.
[71] J. Forde-Johnstone, PPS, XXIII, 1957, 20-39.
[72] Published *in* G. E. Daniel, *Prehistoric Chamber Tombs of England and Wales*, 1950, Pl. 3.
[73] 1875 excavations: W. Williams, *Arch. Camb.*, 1875, 341-8. 1932 excavations: W. L. Scott, *Arch. Camb.*, 1933, 185-228.

excavated into the rock. It is formed by three large uprights which support
a capstone which has tilted over to the east because of the crumbling of
the eastern stone. The west side is open at present and it is not certain how

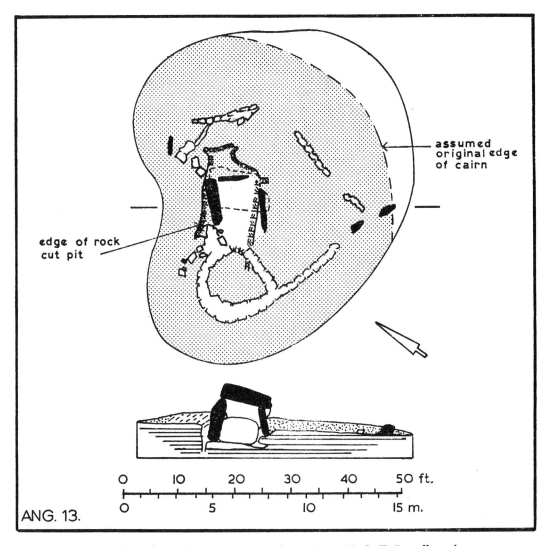

ANG. 13.

FIG. 15 — Plan and section: Pant y Saer. From: T. G. E. Powell *et al.*,
Megalithic Enquiries in the West of Britain (Liverpool U.P. 1969).

it was originally closed, for the stones lying there in 1932 were not deeply
set. It is possible that the closure here was removable, because it is the
only means of access to the chamber.

The chamber is surrounded by the remains of a small kidney-shaped
cairn with a marked indentation, or forecourt area, to the north. The
shape of this cairn was defined by a low wall of limestone and gritstone

blocks. There are other walls within the cairn and some small upright stones at the back which tend to confuse the picture, but there seems no reason for disagreeing with the excavator in this matter of cairn shape. At the north, the forecourt walls run up to the ends of the northern stone of the chamber, showing that this stone marks the front of the tomb, although it would be impossible to enter from this side. A stone at the north-east tip of the forecourt wall is reminiscent of the orthostatic facades of Irish Court Cairns, or, perhaps more pertinently, of the one added to

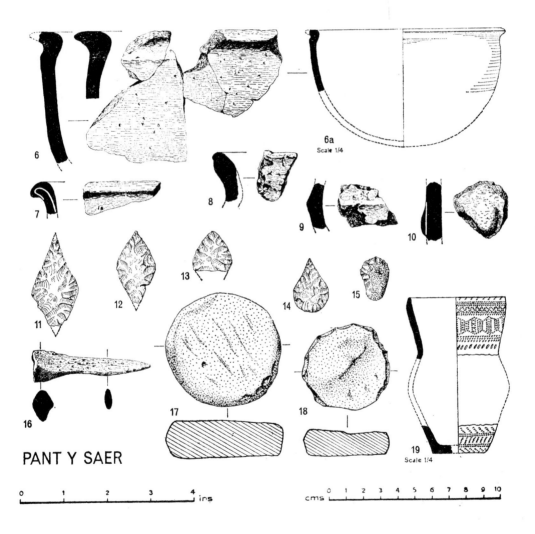

PANT Y SAER

FIG. 16 — Finds from Pant y Saer: 6-10, sherds of undecorated Neolithic pottery; 11-14, leaf-shaped arrowheads (see also Fig. 31, 1); 15, flint scraper; 16, polished antler point; 17-18, stone discs; 19, reconstruction of Beaker (later burial, see Chapter 3). From: T. G. E. Powell *et al., Megalithic Enquiries in the West of Britain* (Liverpool U.P. 1969).

the Portal Dolmen at Pentre Ifan, Pembrokeshire.[74] In any case, the existence of this forecourt is likely to be due to Irish influence whether direct or indirect, and by analogy with the date of the introduction of forecourts to Scotland this phase may be equated with the Middle Neolithic (roughly 2,800 to 2,400 B.C.).[75]

This date is consistent with the pottery found in the chamber and in the forecourt. The sherds from the forecourt were mainly from a large, undecorated, bag-shaped pot which had been placed at the foot of the northern stone of the chamber. Together with pieces of another pot, a scratched pebble, a portion of human skull and some animal bones, these seem to represent an offering laid at the formal entrance to the tomb. This deposit was subsequently covered by sloped stones when the forecourt was blocked. This blocking is a common feature of both Portal Dolmens and Court Cairns and seems to mark a final closure of the tomb, though in tombs such as this, with no actual entrance at the front, the blocking might have been built before burial had ceased.

Where the deposit inside the chamber was found undisturbed, the lowest levels were found to contain three arrowheads and sherds from several undecorated pots. One of the arrowheads is of chert, not flint, and two have a distinctive lozenge shape characteristic of the north of Ireland, where the raw material may have been obtained. The pottery is all very fragmentary but there are several rims, one shoulder sherd and one lug. The paste is well-fired, smooth and leathery, with limestone tempering. This compact paste contrasts with the corky fabric found at Dyffryn Ardudwy; at the settlement site at Llandegai, Caernarvonshire; and, to a lesser extent, even with the other Anglesey site at Bryn yr Hen Bobl. However, the limestone shows that it must have been made locally in spite of the similarity of the heavy, expanded rims to those on Abingdon Ware from southern England.[76] This style of pottery seems to have been in vogue at a period when southern English influence was being widely felt in the west and north, a period to be broadly equated with the Middle Neolithic.[77]

This tenuous link with southern England may also be seen in the burial rite at Pant y Saer. Although our present evidence suggests that cremation was the normal rite in the Irish Sea area, the bodies here were not burnt. The remains were those of fifty-four persons, men, women and children, among which were nine full-term foetuses suggestive of many deaths in childbirth. The number of people found in such a small chamber may be considered evidence for successive burial over a long period. The absence of most of the skulls and long bones might be due to the work of earlier excavators, but, taken together with the evidence from the undisturbed

[74] W. F. Grimes, *Arch. Camb.*, 1949, 2-23.
[75] J. G. Scott *in* T. G. E. Powell *et al.*, *Megalithic Enquiries in the West of Britain*, 217-22.
[76] E. T. Leeds, *Ant. J.*, VII, 1927, 438-64 and VIII, 1928, 461-77.
[77] *See* comments by J. G. Scott, PPS, XXX, 1964, 156-8.

tomb at West Kennet, Wiltshire, it is perhaps indicative of the deliberate removal of bones for ritual purposes.[78]

Other objects found in the course of the excavations include a piece of silicified shale, flaked rather like the rough-out of an axe; a piece of antler and a bone point, possibly used in leather-working; and two stone discs chipped to a round shape. The use of these is not known; they might possibly have been used in hunting small animals. Similar objects have been found in the megalithic tomb at Tŷ Isaf, Breconshire, and in tombs in Brittany where they have been interpreted as weights.[79] The neck and base of a Beaker were found in the upper levels of the chamber, together with a lump of iron pyrites used as a strike-a-light. These are likely to have come from a cist built into the tomb at a later date and will be discussed with the other Beaker graves.

Bryn yr Hen Bobl (ANG 8. NGR SH/519690) can be compared to Pant y Saer for several reasons, but principally because it is equally difficult to exactly parallel outside the island. They share the peculiar kidney-shaped cairn, the small closed chamber and the use of inhumation. It was excavated in 1929-35 by Mr. W. J. Hemp.[80]

The chamber at Bryn yr Hen Bobl is larger than at Pant y Saer, and it has three upright stones edging the forecourt and flanking the high entrance stone. This stone is now broken but originally must have reached almost to the roof. It has two small holes in it which are natural in origin, but they may have influenced the choice of this stone. The actual entrance to the chamber is difficult to determine. It may have been at the back where a stone has been cut back at floor level, but there has been so much recent disturbance at this point that certainty is impossible.

A great deal of the cairn survives at this site. It is a high, kidney-shaped mound of loose stone, the base surrounded by one, and possibly two, dry stone walls. At the back this walling is clearly designed to retain the cairn mass, but in the area of the forecourt the arrangement becomes more complicated. On the north side there are three walls, two of which apparently end abruptly, while on the south a considerable length of walling is missing. The excavator believed that this was not due to disturbance, but the sloped sealing stones in his photograph do have the appearance of collapsed material.[81] Dry stone walling had also been used to block the forecourt. At least one good wall was built directly in front of the entrance stone and a considerable area beyond that was filled in with sloped stones as at Pant y Saer. The amount of earth and charcoal amongst these blocking stones contrasted with the very clean stone of the cairn.

Before it was covered, four fires had been burning in the forecourt just

[78] S. Piggott, *West Kennett Long Barrow* . . . , 1962, 67-8.
[79] Ty Isaf: W. F. Grimes, PPS, V, 1939, 119-42. Champ-Grosset en Quessoy, Brittany: L'Helgouach, *Annales de Bretagne*, LXXII, 1965, 24, fig. 6, nos. 4-7.
[80] W. J. Hemp, *Arch.*, LXXXV, 1935, 253-92.
[81] W. J. Hemp, *op. cit.*, Pl. LXXVII, fig. 1.

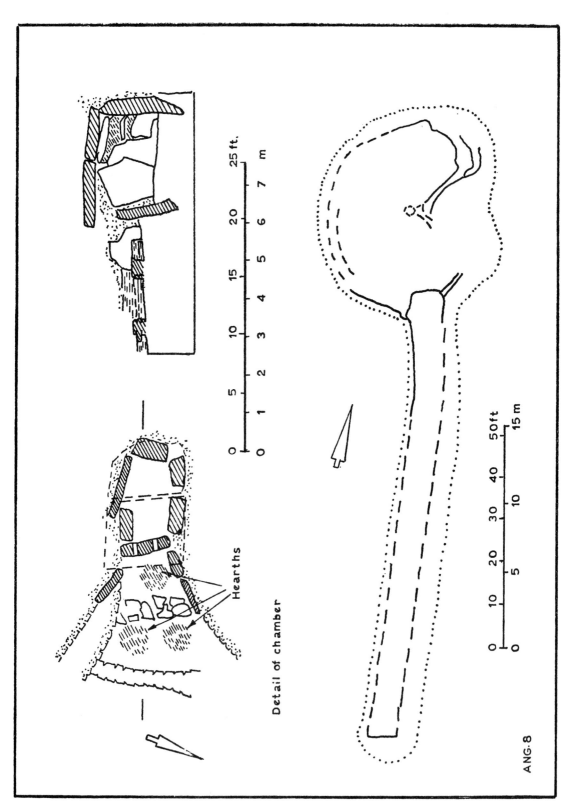

Detail of chamber

ANG·8

Fig. 17 — Plans and section: Bryn yr Hen Bobl. Dotted line indicates edge of cairn spread, line shows position of dry stone walling (See

in front of the entrance stone. These may represent four different ceremonial occasions. Some broken pieces of pottery (unspecified) were found on these stone hearths. Apart from a few scraps from the chamber and a plain bone pin, these were the only finds belonging to the tomb.

However, a great deal of pottery was found elsewhere on the site, all of it coming from the old ground surface beneath the "terrace" to the south of the cairn. This "terrace", 330ft. long and 40ft. wide, is an unique feature whose significance is quite unknown. It is a raised platform of stones surrounded by a wall 2ft. high. It had been built before the cairn, but possibly the interval was only a few days for the two were certainly bonded together by the tomb-builders. It contained nothing beyond what had been incorporated from the underlying settlement area, but it must have long retained a certain significance or sanctity because a Bronze Age urn burial was found close to the southern end.

All the bones in the chamber were unburnt, but they were in an extremely mixed and broken condition. This could have been an original feature, but it is more likely to be due to eighteenth century digging in the

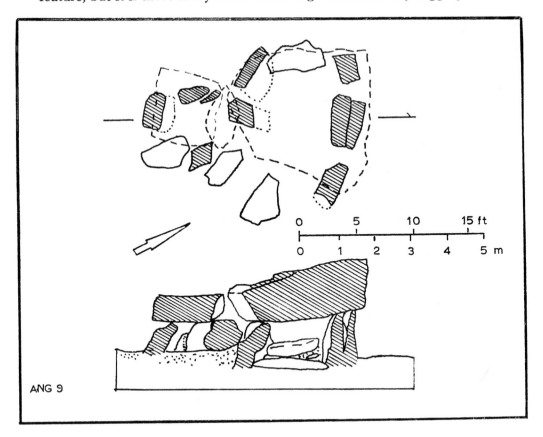

FIG. 18 — Plan and section: Plas Newydd. From: T. G. E. Powell *et al.*, *Megalithic Enquiries in the West of Britain* (Liverpool U.P. 1969).

chamber and in the cairn.[82] Burials, which might have been Iron Age or
Early Mediaeval in date, had been found in the top of the cairn and these
bones were eventually shovelled into the chamber as well. Therefore it is
impossible to say how many Neolithic bodies it had contained, but about
twenty individuals, men, women and children, were found in 1929-34, all
incomplete. Small quantities of burnt human bones were also found on the
old ground surface just outside the southern end of the "terrace". It is
possible that these are connected with the urn burial and belong to the
Bronze Age rather than the Neolithic.

Close to Bryn yr Hen Bobl is another tomb, Plas Newydd (ANG 9. NGR
SH/520697), which, impressive though it is, is impossible to classify.[83] It
consists of two elements, a large northern chamber with three high stones
in a row at the north end, and a small structure with its own capstone at
the south. This southern part has been variously interpreted as a passage

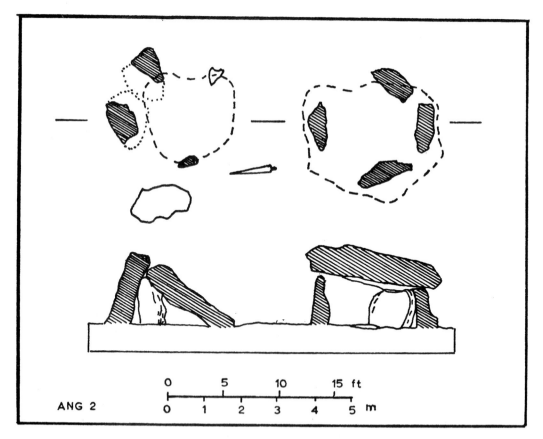

ANG 2

Fig. 19 — Plan and section: Presaddfed. From: T. G. E. Powell *et al.*,
Megalithic Enquiries in the West of Britain (Liverpool U.P. 1969).

[82] H. Rowlands, *Mona Antiqua Restaurata*, 2nd ed., 1766, 215.
[83] *See* comment by W. F. Grimes, PPS, II, 1936, 131.

or as a side chamber, but both views are complicated by the fact that access between the two parts is blocked by a vital supporter of the northern capstone.[84] It has doubtless suffered some interference from eighteenth century landscapers and, at present, no suggestions about its ancestry can be put forward with any confidence, especially as it is situated in an area of particularly mixed traditions.

Presaddfed (ANG 2. NGR SH/348809) is another tomb which, though well preserved, cannot be easily assigned to any group. It consists of two groups of stones some 6ft. apart. There is no evidence that they were ever linked, but they do lie roughly on the same axis. The northern group is ruined, only one large stone remaining upright, with a smaller one leaning against it. Behind them is a fallen capstone. The southern group is still standing. The remaining stones delimit a polygonal area, but if the northern group are to be part of a passage, access from it would be impossible because the north stone of the southern group would block the entrance. It has been suggested that the stones are the remains of two small Passage Graves, side by side, but the position of the monument on low land on the floor of a marshy valley makes it very unlikely that the site is that of a Passage Grave.[85] The siting would suit a Portal Dolmen, but it cannot be one of these. However, some connection with the Trefignath/Din Dryfol group might tentatively be suggested.

Unlike the last two, many tombs are obviously unclassifiable because they are so ruined. Many of the monuments drawn by early antiquaries seem to have been in this class, but at the present day only two certain examples survive in Anglesey, Perthiduon (ANG 17. NGR SH/480668), and Cremlyn (ANG 20. NGR SH/567776).[86] Only the capstone and one fallen supporter survive at Perthiduon. When Rowlands drew it there seem to have been three stones lying beneath the capstone.[87] There is an intriguing record of " brass chisels " being found beneath this stone, but a later report says " nearby " and this is more likely to be true.[88] Only one stone survives at Cremlyn at present. It is of interest in that this presumed chamber is associated with a natural mound as at Lletty'r Filiast, Llandudno.[89]

A group of three sites on the limestone area between Moelfre and Benllech are also, strictly speaking, unclassifiable, but for another reason. In all three the capstone is the most prominent feature and its shape

[84] W. J. Hemp, Arch., LXXXV, 1935, 253.
[85] G. E. Daniel and T. G. E. Powell, PPS, XV, 1949, 175.
[86] E. Neil Baynes, Trans. Hon. Soc. Cymmrod., 1910-11, 3-91 passim mentions several sites about which nothing very useful can be said now. Treban, Maen Chwyf, Bod-ddeiniol and Pentretraeth, are almost certainly natural boulders or erratics and not tombs at all. The same is true of the huge stones at Henblas although a later burial had been made close to them. Only one upright stone remains at Trearddur, Plas Meilw and Rhoscolyn on Holy Island but there are good records of a tomb on Bodafon Mountain (Arch. Camb., 1867, 344) at Llanallgo (Skinner, 1802, Arch. Camb. Suppl., 1908, 81-2) and at Carreg y Fran (Rowlands, op. cit., 93-4, Pl. VI, 2).
[87] H. Rowlands, op. cit., 93. Pl. VI, 3.
[88] Arch. Camb., 1846, 467 and 1869, 264.
[89] W. F. Grimes, PPS, II, 1936, 124-5.

governs the structure beneath it. In none of them has there been any effort
to make the chamber conform to any recognised style, and the governing
principle seems to have been to produce a suitable space for burial with
the minimum of effort.[90] This fact alone suggests that this kind of burial
chamber should be placed towards the end of the period when the strength
of the original traditions was waning.

In Anglesey this typological judgement is supported by the finds from
one of the excavated examples, Lligwy (ANG 14. NGR SH/501860).[91] The
structure here consists of an enormous capstone (18ft. by 16ft.) supported
on three of the eight variously shaped stones placed beneath its edges.
The entrance was probably at the east between the two largest stones.
Some flat stones were found in this area in 1909 when the tomb was fully
excavated, but it is unlikely that a chamber like this ever had a formal

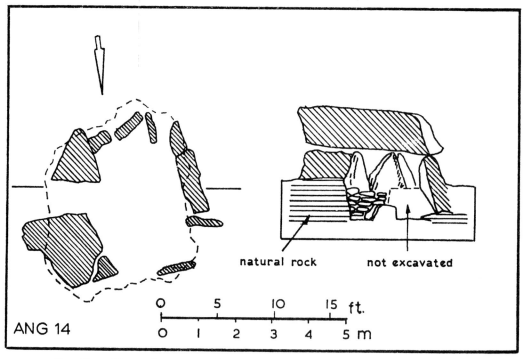

natural rock   not excavated

ANG 14

FIG. 20 — Plan and section: Lligwy. From: T. G. E. Powell *et al.*, *Megalithic
Enquiries in the West of Britain* (Liverpool U.P. 1969).

passage. Like Pant y Saer, which is only a few miles away, the chamber
had been built over a pit which gave a depth of 6ft. beneath the capstone.
The low supporters rested either on the rock at the edge of the pit or upon

[90] G. E. Daniel, *The Prehistoric Chamber Tombs of England and Wales*, 1950, 46-51 discusses this type which he describes as ' sub-megalithic '.
[91] E. Neil Baynes, *Arch. Camb.*, 1909, 217-31.

rough dry stone walling. No indisputable remains of cairn survived, but there had been a considerable build-up of earth and stones around the chamber.

In 1909 the chamber was found to have become filled with a good deal of sterile soil, but beneath that the burial deposit lay apparently

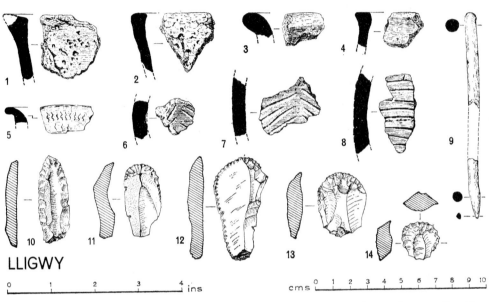

LLIGWY

FIG. 21 — Finds from Lligwy: 1-4, undecorated rimsherds; 5, rim decorated with cardium shell; 6-8, decorated sherds; 9, polished bone pin; 10, flint 'slug' knife; 11-14, flint scrapers. From: T. G. E. Powell *et al.*, *Megalithic Enquiries in the West of Britain* (Liverpool U.P. 1969).

undisturbed. It was divided into two layers by a kind of paving of flat stones. The upper layer contained black earth, broken bones, both human and animal, and a few flints and sherds of pottery. It was covered by a layer of limpet shells. The lower layer contained similar black earth with rather more bone and some more flints and pottery. This deposit rested on a mass of mussel shells. Human teeth, a flint scraper and a bone pin were found at a depth of 4ft. just outside the north side of the chamber, where they were likely to have been thrown by earlier diggers.[92]

The bones were unburnt, all very mixed and broken, as at Pant y Saer. Between fifteen and thirty people were represented, men, women and children, amongst whom at least three had a peculiar wide jaw, which hints at a not unexpected family relationship.[93] It is unfortunate that the exact stratigraphical position of most of the pottery is not known; the only certain fact is that a small everted rim sherd decorated with cardium shell

[92] E. Neil Baynes, *op. cit.*, 224-5.
[93] E. Neil Baynes, *op. cit.*, 226-9.

impressions, and thus comparable to Beakers from Newborough Warren, was found above the paving.[94] This suggests that the last burials in the tomb may be contemporary with Beakers, dating from between 2,000 and 1,800 B.C. The date of building is not fixed by this, but none of the other pottery looks early. The undecorated sherds are too featureless to be diagnostic, and the three grooved pieces could be equally compared to decorated pottery from some of the later Scottish tombs or to southern English Grooved Ware, which is certainly a feature of the late Neolithic.[95] The bone pin might be appropriate to either context. The flint " slug knife " is a type found quite often in Court Cairns in Ireland, but the only other datable example in Anglesey comes from Castell Bryn Gwyn, which is definitely a Late Neolithic site.[96]

Another flint knife very similar to the one from the tomb was found in the area of the later stone huts a few hundred yards away at Din Lligwy. The excavation of this Romano-British settlement produced quite a few flint implements of earlier date (Fig. 31, Nos. 10-16) which suggests that, as is so often the case, the huts may have covered a habitation site long

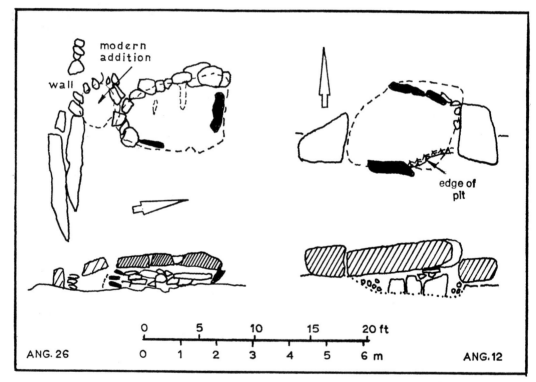

FIG. 22 — Plans and sections: Benllech and Glyn.

[94] S. Piggott, *Arch. Camb.*, 1933, 68-72.
[95] *Cf.* Unival: W. .L. Scott, PSAS, LXXXII, 1947-8, 20, fig. 6, no. 7. Grooved Ware: S. Piggott, *Neolithic Cultures of the British Isles*, 1954, 338-43.
[96] A. E. P. Collins, UJA, XVII, 1954, 28.

since abandoned.[97] Apart from the slug knife and a "petit tranchet derivative" arrowhead like the one from Bryn yr Hen Bobl, the implements are not particularly distinctive, being mostly scrapers, but both the arrowhead and the knife indicate a date towards the end of the Neolithic; no doubt the settlement was contemporary with the building of the tomb.

Two other sites which have affinities with the tomb at Lligwy are Glyn and Benllech. The site at Benllech (ANG 26. NGR SH/519826) was only recently discovered and was totally excavated in 1965.[98] As at Lligwy, the main feature was the capstone supported by rough dry walling and upright stones with an entrance at one corner. It was very low, but no pit had been cut into the rock under it. There were no finds to indicate a prehistoric date, but the size of the capstone suggests it.

On the other hand, bones and other relics (unspecified) were found in the nineteenth century at Glyn (ANG 12. NGR SH/514817).[99] Here, an outcropping slab of limestone had been levered up and shifted sideways a little to rest on the neighbouring slab, then the front and back had been propped and filled with small uprights. The existing hole was then deepened to give a height of 4ft. 6ins. beneath the capstone. It is doubtful whether such a grave would ever have been completed by a covering of cairn stones.

Bryn Celli Ddu (ANG 7. NGR SH/508702), probably the best-known monument in the island, has been left till last because it must have been one of the last megalithic tombs to be built in Anglesey. In spite of its similarity to Passage Graves in Brittany, which ought to indicate an early date, the tomb must have been built in the Late Neolithic period because it is superimposed on another religious monument, a Henge, of a type which first appears in southern England towards the end of the Middle Neolithic (at the earliest).

These Henges (a name borrowed from Stonehenge) seem to have been open-air sanctuaries, the scene of unknown ceremonies, which sometimes involved the erection of circles of upright stones and the burial of small quantities of burnt human bone.[100] They are invariably circular, the area demarcated by a bank and ditch, normally with the ditch inside the bank. It is possible that these religious centres were less closely linked to burial (and presumably ancestor worship) than the earlier Long Barrow/megalithic tomb group of monuments, but they might perhaps be a development of the Causewayed Camp, in that the rise of Henges in southern England seems to be paralleled by a gradual decline in the use of the former monuments.

Like the Causewayed Camps themselves, the Henges have no

---

[97] In the National Museum of Wales: 42.395/1/a-k.
[98] F. M. Lynch, Arch. Camb., 1966, 11-26.
[99] Arch. J., XXXIII, 1876, 192. E. Neil Baynes, Trans. Hon. Soc. Cymmrod., 1910-11, 44-7. Neil Baynes and Lord Boston made some small excavations at Glyn in 1909.
[100] The most recent general discussions of these monuments are in R. J. C. Atkinson et al., Excavations at Dorchester, Oxon., 1951, 81-96, and G. J. Wainwright, PPS, XXXV, 1969, 112-33.

Continental prototypes and are, as far as we know, an entirely English development. If the typology is correct, the earliest monuments, those at Dorchester, Oxfordshire, were very small circles of pits surrounded by a bank.[101] The pits appear never to have held posts but to have been simply dug and filled in. Cremations occur in the top of this filling, but they seem to represent a secondary use of the site, which had not been designed for burial. The first monument at Stonehenge (the bank, ditch and Aubrey Holes) was a Henge of this kind.[102] Another version of this open air monument is Avebury, an enormous enclosure containing several circles of widely spaced upright stones.[103] A third type is seen at Durrington Walls and Woodhenge (not far from Stonehenge).[104] The internal structures here were of wood, circular and very probably roofed. Thus there are many varieties of these sanctuaries in which the main unifying factor is the circular arrangement of features and the enclosing bank and ditch. All three seemed to be broadly contemporary and can be dated by the pottery (found most abundantly in the roofed variety) to the last phase of the Neolithic and the beginning of the Early Bronze Age. Another common feature of all three types is their tendency to be grouped, on flat land close to rivers, the complex of monuments consisting of two or more Henges, sometimes with an avenue of posts or stones, or a " cursus " (two parallel banks and ditches running for many yards or even miles across country).

The entrance to all three types of enclosure may be across one or two causeways. Since without excavation it is difficult to classify the internal structures unless they are of stone, a classification according to the number of entrances has been established. This has shown that the sites with a single entrance are Late Neolithic in date, while the ones with two opposed entrances belong to the Beaker period, the final phase of the Neolithic. Stone circles are more frequently found inside the double entrance type.[105]

Henges occur fairly widely in southern England and in the north, but are less frequent in Scotland and definitely rare in Wales and Ireland.[106] In Wales the two best examples are at Llandegai near Bangor, Caernarvonshire. These monuments were discovered only recently, by air photography, so it is not impossible that more sites may come to light in a similar way. The Llandegai complex included two large Henges, a Cursus and some small circular ditches, one probably a small Henge, the others perhaps the remnant of ploughed out round barrows.[107] One of the Henges had a single entrance with an internal bank and a miniature cremation circle just outside the causeway. This circle of pits containing several cremation deposits is

[101] R. J. C. Atkinson, op. cit.: excavation report on these sites.
[102] R. J. C. Atkinson, Stonehenge, 1956.
[103] A. Keiller, Windmill Hill and Avebury, 1965, 187-216.
[104] Woodhenge: M. E. Cunnington, Woodhenge, 1929 and S. Piggott, Arch. J., XCVI, 1940, 193-222. Durrington Walls: interim report, G. J. Wainwright, Ant., XLII, 1968, 20-6.
[105] R. J. C. Atkinson, Excavations at Dorchester, Oxon., 1951, 90-1.
[106] G. J. Wainwright, PPS, XXXV, 1969, 115 (fig. 1).
[107] Interim report, C. H. Houlder, Ant., XLII, 1968, 216-21.

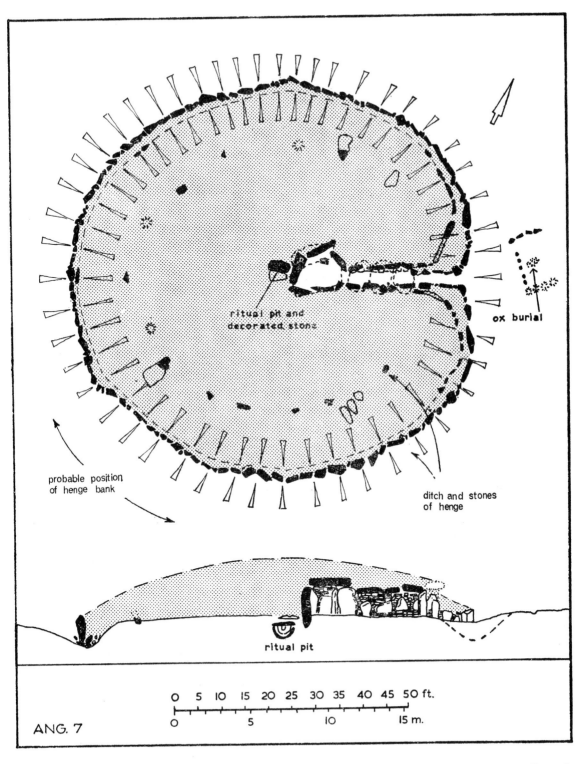

ox burial

ritual pit and
decorated stone

probable position
of henge bank

ditch and stones
of henge

ritual pit

ANG. 7

0 5 10 15 20 25 30 35 40 45 50 ft.

0   5   10   15 m.

FIG. 23 — Plan and section: Bryn Celli Ddu, Henge and Passage Grave. From: T. G. E. Powell *et al.*, *Megalithic Enquiries in the West of Britain* (Liverpool U.P. 1969).

very reminiscent of the Dorchester Henges. There were no internal features except a series of refilled holes towards the centre. A cremation burial had been made at the foot of the bank, the bones covered by a stone used for polishing stone axes. An unused axe had been carefully placed in another pit in the foot of the bank. This probably represents an offering and, together, the two finds suggest that the monument was built and used by people engaged in the axe trade. The pottery from an earlier house in the vicinity suggests that these people were not newcomers, but it is likely that they had adopted the new ideas represented by the Henge as the result of contact with southern England brought about by trade.[108]

The second Henge at Llandegai had two entrances, with a multiple cremation burial in a large pit outside the more important southern one. The centre was marked by another cremation, and three Beakers without any accompanying bones were found in small pits in the south-west quadrant. Apart from this there were no internal features, neither pits, posts nor stones.

The Henge at Bryn Celli Ddu is much smaller than the ones at Llandegai, but it is more elaborate in that it contained a free standing circle of stones and possibly even some central feature.[109] However, the great importance of the site lies in the fact that it preserves a rare instance of direct contact between two religious traditions. In the south the Henge may perhaps reflect a natural and gradual development of existing ideas, but in the west the old traditions must have lasted longer and were clearly not dead at the time when these new sanctuaries were introduced. For soon after it was erected, the Henge at Bryn Celli Ddu was deliberately destroyed by adherents of the older tomb-building religion (if one may use this term " religion ").

The Henge bank, which one would expect to have been outside the ditch, has completely disappeared at Bryn Celli Ddu, but this is not surprising, not only because it is on agricultural land but also because the material is likely to have been used by the Passage Grave builders for their mound. The ditch is well preserved. It is 69ft. in diameter, about 17ft. wide and over 6ft. deep. Like other Neolithic ditches, it would have been flat-bottomed, but the excavations in 1928 did not investigate the bottom adequately. It was partly silted by the time the Passage Grave was built over it, suggesting that the monument had been in use for some years before it was destroyed. The 1928 excavations did not locate the causeway (or causeways) and this has led some people to doubt that the site is a true Henge. However, it must be remembered that in 1928 the excavators were not looking for a causeway and cut only a few sections across the

[108] The ' house ' was in the area covered by the later Henge. The ditch of that earthwork had cut through one corner of it (C. H. Houlder, op. cit., 219).
[109] The site was excavated by Mr. W. J. Hemp in 1928. The excavation report (Arch., LXXX, 1930, 179-214 and Arch. Camb., 1931, 216-50, makes no reference to a Henge because all the features beneath the cairn were considered to be contemporary with the Passage Grave.

ditch. The most likely position for a causeway is on the east where the passage of the tomb is at present, and it is doubtful whether this area could have been adequately dug because of the danger of undermining the uprights. The gap in the free-standing circle of stones on this side is also suggestive.

A penannular circle of fourteen large upright stones had stood within the area enclosed by the ditch. Small deposits of burnt human bone and shattered quartz had been buried at the base of some of these stones: for instance, the complete cremation of a girl aged between eight and ten years close to stone n, and the almost complete cremation of a girl of fifteen at the foot of stone j.

All the stones (except possibly o, which had already fallen) had been deliberately damaged in some way by the Passage Grave builders before they were covered by the cairn. This in itself suggests that the sequence here represents a period of conflict. Sometimes one monument may be found simply covering another without unnecessary damage, or stones may be removed and reused, but here, not only had five stones been removed, six had been shattered and, of two knocked over, one had also been buried. Even more telling is the fact that three recumbent stones had each been broken in situ by dropping other heavy stones onto them.[110]

The stones of the Henge circle are not very regularly spaced, but it was found that lines drawn between stones diametrically opposite each other all crossed at the point now occupied by a central pit, which had been dug through the grass-grown surface of the Henge by the Passage Grave builders. This siting suggests that the present pit might have replaced an earlier central feature which had been dug out and destroyed.[111] However, this must remain hypothetical since, apart from the strange arrangement of the stones, no evidence survives.

The interval between the building of the two monuments is proved by the growth of grass over the interior and the partly silted ditch. This grass, as it decayed, had formed a recognisable layer of purplish-blue clay which covered the whole area under the cairn except where it had been cut through for the erection of the uprights of the Passage Graves. This " purple floor " was recognised as a significant layer by the excavators in 1928, but was misinterpreted because at that time little was known about the reactions of buried soils. The purple " floor " was considered to be an intentional deposit, proving that all the elements on the site were of the same date and that the ditch had been dug by the Passage Grave builders.[112] The intentional nature of such layers was only questioned later by work on non-religious sites where such preparation of the ground would not be

---

[110] W. J. Hemp, op. cit., Pl. LII, fig. 1.
[111] Central features, usually a group (or ' cove ') of large upright stones are occasionally found within Henges: e.g. Cairnpapple (S. Piggott, PSAS, LXXXII, 1947-8, 112-4 and Avebury (A. Keiller, op. cit., 198-202).
[112] W. J. Hemp, op. cit., 204-5.

expected.[113] These subsequent investigations have shown that the striking colour and clayey consistency are entirely due to natural changes which occur when organic material (e.g., grass) decays without oxygen (for instance when buried beneath a cairn or mound of earth).

Before the Passage Grave was erected, a curious ceremony seems to have taken place in the centre of the pre-existing Henge. The possibility that there may already have been some stone or post or pit there has been mentioned above. The edge of the present pit clearly cuts through the old turf (the " purple clay floor "), so it must belong to the later phase, but its presence may be explained by a need to rededicate the site. This pit is

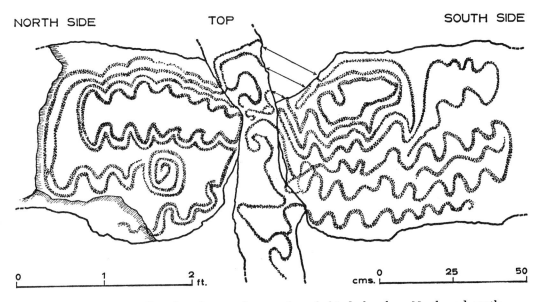

FIG. 24 — Bryn Celli Ddu: decorated stone from behind chamber. North and south relate to the position of the cast on the site. (After W. F. Grimes.)

oval, about 4ft. in diameter and 4ft. 6ins. deep. A fire had been lit in it and some wood and a burnt human ear bone had been placed in the bottom. The significance of the human ear bone, which is from an adult, is quite unknown, but it must have been an abiding one, for ear bones are conspicuous among the finds from Anglesey barrows in the Bronze Age.[114] The pit had been partly filled with what had been dug out of it, topped with turves and finally covered with a flat stone set some 2ft. below the original surface.

Lying beside the coverstone was another one, larger and partly decorated with a meandering pattern of spirals and wavy lines. This pattern runs over the top from one side to the other, which suggests that the stone

[113] M. J. O'Kelly, *J. Cork Arch. and Hist. Soc.*, LVI, 1951, 29-44.
[114] *See* Bedd Branwen and Treiorwerth *infra*.

was designed to stand upright. Such a free-standing pillar is unique in the British Isles. It might perhaps be compared to some of the decorated menhirs in Brittany, where the sinuous lines found on the Bryn Celli Ddu stone can be paralleled on the base of the stone at Manio.[115] In technique,

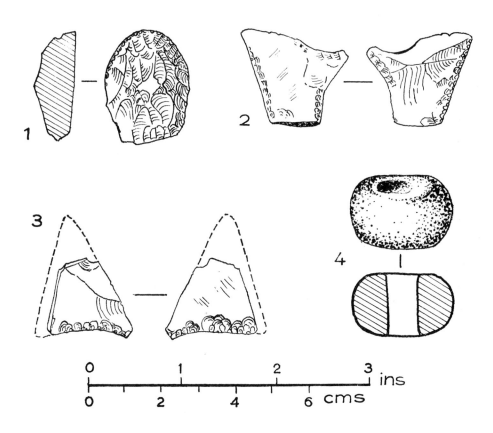

FIG. 25 — Finds from Bryn Celli Ddu: 1, flint scraper; 2-3, flint 'petit tranchet' arrowheads; 4, stone bead.

the pocked lines can be compared to those at Barclodiad y Gawres, but though in a very broad sense they both belong to same family of abstract art, the similarities between the two styles are not very close. This stone may have played a part in ceremonies to reconsecrate the site, and was then carefully buried.

The Passage Grave built over the Henge is a classic example of a type best seen in Brittany; it has a polygonal chamber (7 to 10ft. across) with

[115] P. R. Giot, *Brittany* (Ancient Peoples and Places), 1960, 39.

a long passage, the whole covered by a large circular cairn with a double kerb.[116]

Inside the chamber is a tall, free-standing pillar neatly dressed to an almost circular shape. It is not structural and so presumably must be, like the art, an abstract representation of some religious symbol. Such pillars are very rare; there are a few in Spain (but these may have been structural) and there are square ones at Carrowkeel, Co. Sligo, and at Clettraval in the Hebrides, both Passage Graves, though neither is very similar to Bryn Celli Ddu.[117] There is one small spiral carved on an upright on the south side of the chamber. It is very crudely cut and there may be a doubt about its authenticity.

Very few bones or other objects were found in 1928, but there are earlier records of both burnt and unburnt human bones having been found on the floor of the chamber and of the inner passage.[118] A broken arrowhead and some limpet and mussel shells were also found there in the nineteenth century. The finds from the cairn were equally meagre and, apart from another late type of arrowhead, are not very helpful for dating either monument.

The passage is 27ft. long and 3ft. wide. It is divided into two parts, the inner passage 16ft. long and 5ft. high, roofed by large capstones, and the low outer passage 10ft. long and never roofed. The junction between them is marked by a portal with two tall stones, which originally supported a large lintel. Two noteworthy features of the inner passage are the low wall or bench along the north side and the two upright stones set in niches just beyond the portal on the south. The significance of both is obscure. Benches occur occasionally in tombs in Spain and the Orkneys, and the small uprights have been compared to similar stone " Baetyls " in Spanish tombs.[119] There is a comparable stone in a niche in the passage at Barclodiad y Gawres, whence the idea may have come to Bryn Celli Ddu.

The inner passage was never blocked, but access to it was prevented after the final funerals had taken place by the systematic filling of the outer passage with stones and earth incorporating some cremated human bone. The inner edge of this blocking was marked by a row of quartz boulders, a material often used in important parts of Passage Graves. Although the earth and stone filling this low passage might be interpreted as a natural collapse of cairn material, the discovery of bone amongst them would seem to preclude this. Recent work on similar tombs in Ireland suggests that this blocking would have completely covered the outer passage, leaving only a fairly narrow gap open beneath the lintel of the portal. It has already been suggested that a similar arrangement may have existed at Barclodiad

[116] J. L'Helgouach, *Les Sépultures Mégalithiques en Armorique*, 1965, 55, fig. 23.1; 64. fig. 26.2.

[117] Spain: G. & V. Leisner, *Die Megalithgräber der Iberischen Halbinsel. I. Der Suden*, figs. 15, 18-21. Carrowkeel, Co. Sligo: R. A. S. Macalister *et al.*, PRIA, 29, C., 1912, 326-7. Clettraval, N. Uist: W. L. Scott, PSAS, LXIX, 1934-5, 488.

[118] Early accounts, chiefly by F. D. Lukis, quoted *in* W. J. Hemp, *op. cit.*, 179-82.

[119] G. & V. Leisner, *op. cit.*, Pl. 116.4.

y Gawres. The gap would not have allowed actual physical entry, but might have been designed as a means of communication or communion between those outside and the spirit of the dead inside.[120]

The importance of the portal as the ceremonial door of the tomb is further emphasised by the arrangement of the circles of kerbstones which mark the edge of the cairn. These kerbstones were set up in the bottom of the Henge ditch. They vary in size, being larger at the front. They were linked by dry stone walling which rose above them to form a neat surface and give stability to the cairn.[121] The kerb is double, but around the back the inner circle was invisible, serving only to reduce pressure on the outer stones. In the front, however, it emerges as a feature in its own right, rising above the outer passage and curving in to reach the portal where it provides a wall to hold back the cairn from this ceremonial area.

Although the outer passage was concealed once the funeral (or funerals) had taken place, the area just in front of it had been the scene of certain ceremonies. On the original surface, just to the right of the entrance, was a small platform of white quartz pebbles, and hearths had been built up against the kerb on either side. Nothing comparable has been found outside Breton Passage Graves, nor was anything found at Barclodiad y Gawres, but similar oval platforms of pebbles, often quartz, have been found outside several of the Irish Passage Graves, including Newgrange itself.[122] Hearths are more common, having been found outside the entrances to many different kinds of tombs. They may have been used in the preparation of ceremonial feasts. When the outer passage was blocked, this forecourt area was also covered by fan-shaped layers of carefully placed stones extending for 6 - 8ft. beyond the entrance. Amongst this blocking were the remains of fires and also a human cremation burial.

Beyond the blocking outside the ditch, there had been an arrangement of stone and wattle surrounding the skeleton of a small ox. The enclosure was three-sided, the north and south closed by small upright stones, and the west side formed by a 6ft. length of what may have been wattling; only the small post holes survived. There was no direct evidence for the date of this burial; the bones were so well preserved that they might even be modern, but their position in the centre of the enclosure makes this unlikely. The deposit is normally considered to be an extension of the forecourt features belonging to the Passage Grave. However, it has been laid out on a different axis and, if the causeway across the Henge ditch is in fact under the passage, the deposit might be compared with the pits outside the

---

[120] F. M. Lynch, *3rd Atlantic Symposium, Arhus,* forthcoming.
[121] These outer walls seldom survive but there is evidence to suggest that at several sites, e.g. Newgrange, Co. Meath and Barnenez, Brittany, the cairns were steep-sided and walls would have been necessary to preserve the shape. *See* J. L'Helgouach, *op. cit.,* 22-4 and fig. 6.
[122] Newgrange, main tomb. Publication forthcoming. Knowth, Site 8. Publication forthcoming.

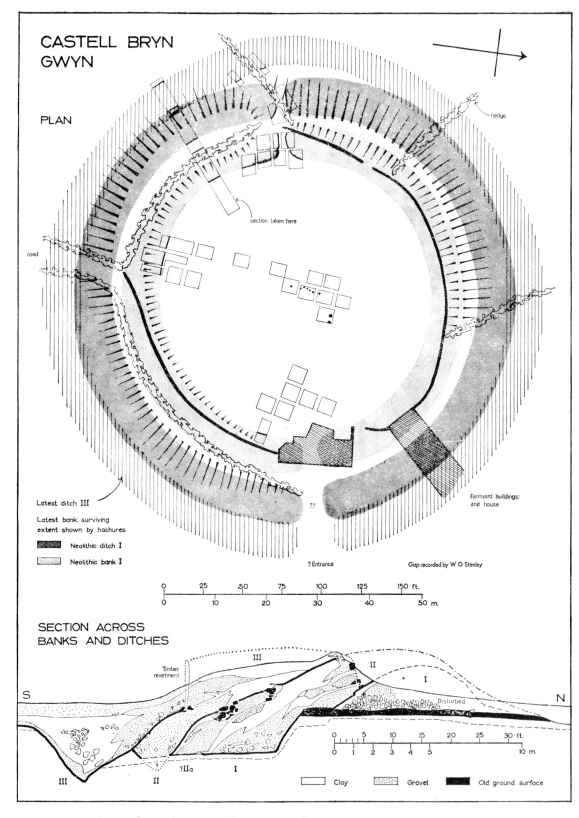

CASTELL BRYN GWYN

PLAN

section taken here

hedge

road

Latest ditch III

Latest bank: surviving
extent shown by hachures

Neolithic ditch I

Neolithic bank I

??

? Entrance

Gap recorded by W O Stanley

Farmyard buildings:
and house

0	25	50	75	100	125	150 ft.
0	10	20	30	40	50 m.	

SECTION ACROSS
BANKS AND DITCHES

III

II

I

Timber
revetment

S

Disturbed

N

III II ?IIa I

0	5	10	15	20	25	30 ft.
0	1	2	3	4	5	10 m.

Clay   Gravel   Old ground surface

FIG. 26 — Plan and section of banks: Castell Bryn Gwyn. (After G. J. Wainwright.)

entrances of the Henges at Llandegai.[123] Either way the use of an ox would not be surprising in view of the important part these animals played in the economy of the people.

The siting of Bryn Celli Ddu close to the river on fairly level land is appropriate to a Henge complex. There are no visible remains of other similar monuments in the vicinity, but it is not inconceivable that air photography might reveal others as at Llandegai.[124] However, the treatment meted out to the one at Bryn Celli Ddu would not lead one to expect to find many more in Anglesey not far away, but there is an anomalous site at which Late Neolithic pottery has been found, which has several of the features of a Henge.

Like Bryn Celli Ddu, this site at Castell Bryn Gwyn (NGR SH/466671) has been altered and adapted, but at a much later period.[125] Most of the bank visible today dates from the Roman period or later, though it may have been first adapted as a defensive site in the Iron Age.

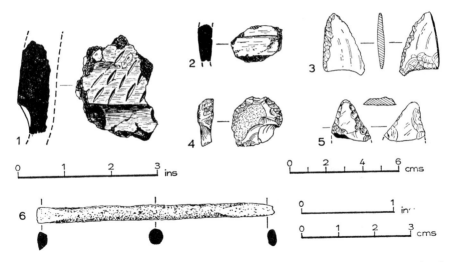

FIG. 27 — Finds from Castell Bryn Gwyn: 1, sherd of Fengate ware; 2, sherd of ?Beaker pottery; 3, 'petit tranchet derivative' arrowhead; 4, flint scraper; 5, flint 'slug' knife; 6, bronze awl. (1-5, half size; 6, full size.)

The original monument, dated to the Neolithic period by stratified finds, was a circular area about 130ft. in diameter surrounded by a bank 25ft. wide and perhaps 6ft. high. Outside this there was a flat-bottomed ditch, 7ft. deep and 20ft. or more wide. Both bank and ditch were interrupted by a very narrow causeway on the south-west side. In 1874 the tenant of the

[123] C. H. Houlder, *Ant.*, XLII, 1968, 218.
[124] The excavators found a section of another smaller ditch just to the south west of the large one and there is a Bronze Age barrow in the next field with a standing stone a few hundred yards away to the north. These may be suggestive, as is the number of stone axes found in the area.
[125] Excavated in 1959-60 by Dr. G. J. Wainwright. *Arch. Camb.*, 1962, 25-58.

farm remembered that there had been a gap in the surviving rampart (III), in the position now occupied by the farm house.[126] It is reasonable to assume that this would have corresponded to a similar gap in the early bank and ditch, but this is not, of course, proven.

There are no visible structures in the central area, and excavation in 1959-60 revealed only a few isolated postholes just north of the centre and a scatter of occupation debris on the east near the present farm house. This material included several flints, amongst which was an arrowhead similar to one of those from Bryn Celli Ddu, and part of a " slug knife " like the one from Lligwy. With them were some scraps of thick and heavily gritted pottery and some larger sherds of similar paste, which can be recognised as Fengate Ware because of the characteristic pit beneath the overhanging collar. This is a style of pottery current in southern England at the end of the Neolithic period.[127] The late date is further emphasised by the discovery of a small bronze awl with this pottery, indicating that the actual date of activity on the site must be near to 1,600 B.C., although the pottery would lead one to suggest a date closer to 2,000 B.C.[128]

The structure of the bank at this period is quite elaborate.[129] It has a core of boulders which must have been brought from a distance, since they cannot have been derived from the ditch. When the flat-bottomed ditch was dug the material from it must have been heaped on top of the boulders, the inner edge of this bank being revetted with a low stone wall. The shape of the ditch, with its wide flat bottom, is particularly character-istic of Neolithic ditches all over the country and can be seen at both Bryn Celli Ddu and Llandegai.

If the monument is to be considered a Henge, comparison with the northern circle at Llandegai is apt: in both cases the bank is sited abnormally, inside the ditch; the causeway is very narrow and it is placed on the same exis, 260° east of North. Against this may be set the evidence of occupation, the apparent absence of ritual activity either inside or outside the bank, and the elaborate nature of this bank which looks rather more like a rampart than the simple heaps of earth which normally make up Henge banks. However, it must be admitted that, if it is not a Henge, Castell Bryn Gwyn must have been a heavily defended settlement and, as such, would be out of place in the Neolithic period in Britain, even if it is argued that the inhabitants with their " English " background might have feared some antagonism from the natives.

The later history of the site is equally confusing. The single section (Fig. 26) cut through the bank and ditch reveals a very complicated situation; its interpretation is made yet more difficult by the very awkward nature of the gravels and clays of the subsoil and the banks. The first ditch

[126] W. O. Stanley, *Arch. J.*, XXXI, 1874, 319-26.
[127] A. Keiller, *Windmill Hill and Avebury*, 1965, 78, fig. 34 (I. F. Smith).
[128] It is a true 10% tin-bronze (*Arch. Camb.*, 1962, 55).
[129] *See* the section, Fig. 26. This is a simplified version. The original is in *Arch. Camb.*, 1962, 30, fig. 3.

and bank are dated to the Neolithic by the finds; the last one to the Iron Age, or later, by the shape of the ditch and the use of timber revetting on the bank.

Between these two periods the mass of the bank had been pushed forward over the original ditch and another, or possibly two further ditches, had cut away its outer edge. One may assume that the original bank would gradually silt into the ditch, but there may have been some destruction to help this process, for the top and back of the first bank have been removed.

The main obstacle to a four-phase interpretation is the origin of a thick layer of clay which runs from the top of the bank, forward of the original lip of ditch I, down to the bottom, where it appears to be cut into by a later ditch (IIa), and by a revetment wall presumably related to this ditch. This deposit must have been an addition to an already silted bank and ditch, so it is odd that it should reach the bottom of the ditch. A three-phase interpretation ignores the apparent corner of ditch IIa and explains all the spreads of clay and gravel as part of a single rampart provided with two revetment walls, one 6ft. inside the bank. There is no evidence to date this reorganisation, whether it was carried out in one or two stages.

The section shows the ditch, or ditches, in question to be flat-bottomed, which would be indicative of a Neolithic or Early Bronze Age date. The first three ditches were apparently cut to exactly the same depth, a coincidence which would be remarkable, particularly in this difficult gravel subsoil. One wonders, therefore, whether these ditches have been fully excavated. They show very little evidence for normal silting, which must have occurred even if they were open for only a few months, and the deliberate filling of the third ditch was noted at a very low level, suggesting that it did not long pre-date the final ditch. It is therefore suggested, but very tentatively, that ditch II, and possibly the putative ditch IIa as well, were V-shaped like the final one; that the sequence represents the fortification of a rather degraded Neolithic bank and ditch; and that these fortifications were altered twice in fairly rapid succession.[130] Such changes are quite frequently found in the ramparts of Iron Age hill forts.

It remains very doubtful whether the Neolithic bank and ditch should be considered a Henge, but it is certain that the inhabitants had some close connection with the south of England. This south-western corner of the island seems to have received a good deal of influence from the south during the Late Neolithic, for not only is there the Henge at Bryn Celli Ddu and the pottery from Castell Bryn Gwyn, but the bulk of the pottery from beneath the " terrace " at Bryn yr Hen Bobl is decorated in English styles. As at Llandegai, there is some evidence to show that the settlement at Bryn yr Hen Bobl was connected with the export of stone axes from Wales to England.

---

[130] Henge A at Llandegai, where the bank was inside the ditch and thus amenable to use as a defensive earthwork, was re-used during the Iron Age when at least one large wooden house was built inside it. C. H. Houlder, *Ant.*, XLII, 1968, 220.

The finds from beneath the "terrace" at Bryn yr Hen Bobl (NGR SH/519690) clearly relate to a settlement on the site abandoned before the tomb was built.[131] The lapse of time is unknown but may not have been long, since the scraps of pottery from the tomb were said to be similar to those beneath it.[132] The site may be identified as a settlement from the charcoal, dark earth, broken pottery, animal bones and stone-working waste, but unfortunately there was no evidence of structures in the limited area exposed in 1935.

Identification of the charcoal from the site showed that the neighbouring woodland was of the "damp" oakwood type, with oak predominant and hazel and hawthorn common.[133] Birch, maple and ash were also present, with a little alder and willow. The animal bones, most of which actually came from the blocking of the tomb, were recognisable as sheep, ox and pig, the normal farm animals of the period.

The artifacts are naturally of more interest since they give some indication of the cultural background of the inhabitants. The pottery is basically of two kinds: decorated and undecorated, the latter being better fired and less heavily tempered with grit.

It is possible to reconstruct one of the undecorated bowls; roughly hemispherical, with a simple lug, and an out-turned rim which had been made by adding an extra piece of clay to the top. This type of developed rim is quite common amongst the undecorated pottery and might be compared to those from Pant y Saer, and also to some from the house which pre-dates the Henges at Llandegai. There are several small sherds from shouldered bowls in the assemblage which, together with the characteristic corky texture which is seen on many Welsh sites, indicates that the group living here was not entirely foreign.

There are several pieces of rather thin pottery with a bright red surface, but this is probably simply an indication of better firing. Another peculiarity of the group is the shallow grooves found on some pieces. It is difficult to know whether this is intended as decoration or is simply the result of rather rough tooling. One sherd is possibly lightly decorated with cardium shell impressions, but since they are neither clear nor consistent this decoration should be regarded as doubtful.

Five or six pots may be represented among the undecorated sherds. They are all exceedingly fragmentary. The quantity of decorated pottery is larger, but it is unlikely that more than half a dozen pots are represented. The discovery of some of the undecorated pieces under the "terrace" is recorded in the excavation report, but the exact position of the decorated sherds is not given.[134] However, it is claimed that the majority of all the

---

[131] This was first recognised by Professor Piggott, *Neolithic Cultures of the British Isles*, 1954, 180.
[132] S. Piggott, *Arch. J.*, LXXXVIII, 1931, 155, though it is not mentioned in the excavation report.
[133] H. A. Hyde *in* W. J. Hemp, *Arch.*, LXXXV, 1935, 281-3.
[134] W. J. Hemp, *op. cit.*, 269, but the reference is to the wrong figure. For " fig. 3, no. 12 " read " fig. 2, no. 12 ". (Information from Mr. Colin Gresham).

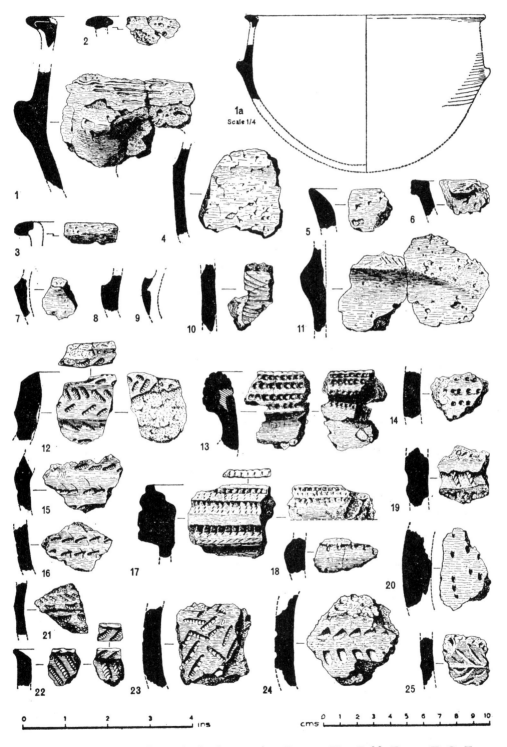

Fig. 28 — Pottery from beneath the 'terrace' at Bryn yr Hen Bobl. From: T. G. E. Powell *et al.*, *Megalithic Enquiries in the West of Britain* (Liverpool U.P. 1969).

finds came from a prolific area beneath the south-western corner of the " terrace ", therefore it may be assumed that the two types of pottery were genuinely associated on the site.

The decorated sherds are on the whole much thicker than the undecorated ones and a good deal of quartz grit, which gives them a rougher appearance, has been added to the clay. The decoration is carried out in a variety of techniques: whipped and twisted cord impressions, diagonal and vertical stab marks, and finger nail impressions. These techniques, and in particular the use of whipped cord " maggot impressions ", are commonly found on pottery of the Peterborough style in England. However, some of the rim forms are less typical. This situation whereby Peterborough decoration is added to pots of rather unusual shape is found quite often in areas away from the main centres of its use.[135] At Bryn yr Hen Bobl the presence of undecorated shouldered bowls serves to underline the fact that this is a mixed community.

Three large, elaborate rims are present and also a varied selection of body sherds, but it is difficult to reconstruct the full profile of any pot.[136] The majority of pieces may have belonged to one pot with a flat collar decorated with " maggot " impressions above a short hollow neck and rounded shoulder. The rest of the body, which may have been deep and elongated, was decorated with lines of stab marks crossing fingernail impressions.

There is a single sherd which may have come from a Beaker.[137] It is decorated with whipped cord and with a comb stamp, a technique much used on Beakers. The sherd is thin, made of hard, compact clay with very small grits, which again is more characteristic of Beakers than of Peterborough ware. On the evidence of this sherd both the settlement and the tomb should be dated after 2,000 B.C., but, since the exact findspot is not known, too much weight should not be given to it. The subdivision of the Peterborough style to which the main group of decorated pottery belongs, the Mortlake style, seems to have been current rather earlier, and perhaps a date of about 2,300 B.C. would be more appropriate, taking into account the undecorated pottery as well.

The making of small tools in flint and stone must have been part of the domestic activity of any Neolithic community, but the particular interest of the quantities of waste flakes found at Bryn yr Hen Bobl is that they seem to indicate some commercial activity over and above what would be needed in the settlement itself.

[135] *E.g.* Hedderwick. *See* comment *in* S. Piggott, *Neolithic Cultures of the British Isles,* 1954, 310. Cairnholy I, Wigtonshire, produced a pot rather similar to the one mentioned below. S. Piggott and T. G. E. Powell, PSAS, LXXXIII, 1948-9, 120, fig. 8.4.
[136] The very heavy overhanging rim is similar to the one from Gop Cave, Flintshire, which was found with two Late Neolithic " English " belt sliders (Boyd Dawkins, *Arch. Camb.,* 1902, 172, fig. 7). The neighbourhood of Gop also seems to have an area involved in the axe trade. (See below).
[137] Fig. 28, no. 21.

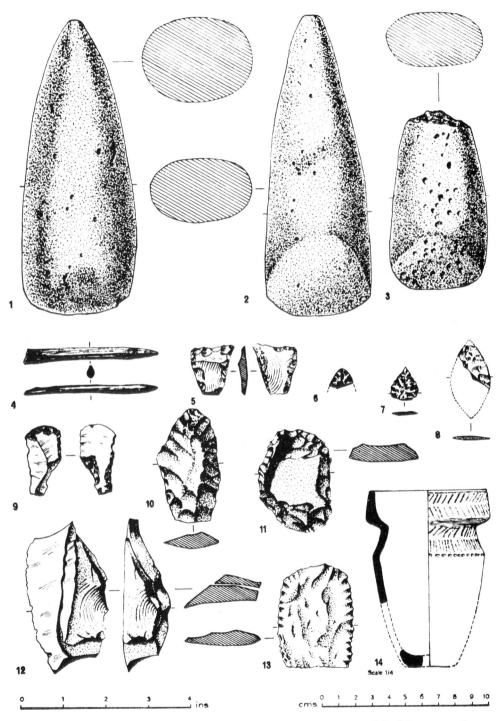

Fig. 29 — Finds from Bryn yr Hen Bobl: 1-3, stone axes; 4, polished bone pin (from chamber); 5, 'petit tranchet derivative' arrowhead; 6-8, leaf-shaped arrowheads; 9, flint scraper; 10-13, tools made from Graig Lwyd stone; 14, Collared urn from later burial at end of 'terrace' (see Chapter 4). From: T. G. E. Powell *et al.*, *Megalithic Enquiries in the West of Britain* (Liverpool U.P. 1969).

The flintwork is not especially interesting. The raw material is beach pebbles such as can be picked up around the coasts of Wales, and the common tool is the convex scraper, possibly used in cleaning skins and hides, which occurs on every site in the country and is not a distinctive type. It is noteworthy that two were made not from flint but from Graig Lwyd stone. The arrowheads are various: three leaf-shaped and one "petit tranchet derivative". This latter is very similar to the one from Bryn Celli Ddu and may be considered a Late Neolithic type.[138]

Four stone axes were found, two of them broken. Whereas the chips, flakes and other stone-working debris were all of Graig Lwyd stone from the factory site at Penmaenmawr, the completed axes were all made from local Anglesey dolerite. Polished axes of Graig Lwyd stone had certainly been present on the site at some stage, for several small tools had been made from broken pieces on which the polish is still visible. The evidence would therefore suggest that, except for re-used waste, the Graig Lwyd stone being worked was not for home consumption, and that the settlement may be interpreted as a workshop site at which Graig Lwyd axes were finished and prepared for export. Direct evidence of this work was found in the form of a hone, used for polishing axes, which came from amongst the cairn material near the northern end of the " terrace ".[139] The stone was not used as a quern for corn grinding since the areas of polish are narrow bands such as could be produced only by grinding the blade of an axe.

The production of stone axes on a commercial scale in certain parts of the country has already been mentioned briefly. The extent of this trade has only recently been realised as the result of an extensive programme of petrological thin sectioning.[140] Certain rocks, such as the Preselau "blue stone" used at Stonehenge and the spotted augite granophyre from Penmaenmawr are known to originate in a restricted locality and are easily recognised by eye. Macroscopic work on these distinctive rocks before the war first revealed the existence of a trade in stone and outlined the potentialities of the method of study, especially if refined by the use of the microscope on less easily identified rocks.[141]

As a result of this work it has been possible to recognise at least twenty-five axe groups of known origin and plot their patterns of dispersal. In five instances it is not only the general area of production that is known, but the actual factory-sites themselves. It is evident that most factories had a virtual monopoly of their home area and also a flourishing export trade. This distant trade usually focussed on the comparatively densely populated

[138] J. G. D. Clark, *Arch. J.*, XCI, 1934, 32-58.
[139] W. J. Hemp, *op. cit.*, Pl. LXXXI, fig. 1.
[140] ' Sub-committee of the South Western group of Museums and Art Galleries (England) on the Petrological Identification of Stone Axes'. 3rd Report, PPS, XVII, 1951, 99-158. 4th Report, PPS, XXVIII, 1962, 209-266. (This last is the latest and most comprehensive, giving descriptions of the rocks, information on factory sites, lists of products and discussion). The Graig Lwyd group of factory sites have recently been exhaustively studied by the RCAM., *Caernarvonshire I*, 1956, xli-lvii.
[141] T. A. Glenn, *Arch. Camb.*, 1935, 189-218.

downlands of Wiltshire, which possessed no suitable stone, although they were rich in flint.

The factory-sites are all on rather bleak scree slopes where the raw material was readily available in suitable blocks. Only at Mynydd Rhiw near Abersoch was the stone obtained by quarrying.[142] The quarries are not very deep, being simply a series of large pits following a dyke of metamorphosed rock, but the geological knowledge which their accurate placing implies is considerable. At Mynydd Rhiw there were hearths and working places in abandoned hollows, but there was no evidence of permanent living on the site. The fires and the few small tools found nearby were simply evidence of picnic sites where the workers ate and sheltered from the wind during the day. At other sites such as Graig Lwyd, Langdale in the Lakes, and Tievebulliagh in the north of Ireland, the only evidence of man's activity is the quantity of struck flakes and broken, roughed-out axes found among the scree.

It would seem, therefore, that men went up to the factory-site daily and spent the day collecting stone and chipping it to a rough shape to reduce the load to be carried back to the finishing site. No complete implement has ever been found on a factory-site. The lengthy process of grinding and polishing was done in greater comfort at settlements in the valleys, sometimes several miles from the source of the stone. The organisation of the Rathlin and Tievebulliagh sites in Co. Antrim is interesting in this respect. Only rough-outs are found at the factory-sites, while both finished and unfinished axes have been found in the surrounding valleys within a radius of fifteen miles.[143] No rough-out has been found outside this area, indicating that the export trade was in finished implements only. It is likely that the other factories were organised in the same way, though there is one instance of unworked stone exported from Graig Lwyd.[144]

The distances over which the finished axes were exported were very great: axes from the north of Ireland have been found in Kent, and Cornish axes at Flamborough Head. The mechanics of this trade are not known, but, judging by the quantities of chance finds of axes in certain areas, well-established trade routes must have existed. Not unexpectedly, since the goods must have been very heavy, rivers appear to have been used as much as possible, and a few sites on the coasts may even have been used as depots for the collection and further dispersal of products from a number of factories.[145] In England the products of Graig Lwyd, Tievebulliagh, and Langdale are often found in the same areas, a fact which suggests that the dispersal of products from these three factories around the north Irish Sea basin may have been concentrated in the hands of one group.

In Wales two sites which might have been depots are Prestatyn in

[142] This site has been excavated. C. H. Houlder, PPS, XXVII, 1961, 108-43.
[143] E. M. Jope, UJA, XV, 1952, 33-4.
[144] Nailsworth, Glos. *See* 4th Report, PPS, XXVIII, 1962, 217.
[145] Suggestion by Mr. C. H. Houlder, PPS, XXVII, 1961, 138.

Flintshire and Merthyr Mawr Warren in Glamorgan.[146] Both are on the coast with good sea and land communications and both have produced scraps of broken axes from more than one factory: at Prestatyn were found Graig Lwyd, Langdale and Mynydd Rhiw; at Merthyr Mawr, Graig Lwyd, Mynydd Rhiw and Group VIII (which probably comes from near St. David's in Pembrokeshire). There are likely to have been several finishing sites working on Graig Lwyd stone, but so far only two are known: Bryn yr Hen Bobl and Llandegai.

Both these sites show contact with, and influence from, England. This poses the questions: who were the people who organised this trade, and when did it begin? The question of date falls into two parts: the beginning of local exploitation, and the establishment of an export market. The people living at such early settlements as Hembury, Hazard Hill and Carn Brea in the south-west peninsula were already, before 3,000 B.C., using axes made from stone from recognised factory-sites.[147] Similarly the Tievebulliagh stone was already being used for axes at a date around 3,000 B.C.[148] Whether these sites were producing on a commercial scale at this date it is impossible to say, but it is obvious that suitable stone was recognised and exploited from a very early date, probably from the first arrival of farmers who would immediately need tools to clear the forest.

There is no direct evidence for the date of the beginning of axe production in North Wales. It is interesting to note that there is a Portal Dolmen on the slopes of Mynydd Rhiw, and that two stone pendants from the later Portal Dolmen at Dyffryn Ardudwy may be made from Mynydd Rhiw stone.[149] Beyond this, however, there is little to connect the axe factories with this group of early megalithic tombs and, in fact, there are no tombs of any kind in the coastal area around Penmaenmawr. However, we know very little about the first farmers in North Wales unless they were building tombs, and the evidence from elsewhere makes it likely that the Graig Lwyd stone would have been used locally from an early date.

The main period of exportation, on the other hand, does not begin until the Middle Neolithic.[150] Graig Lwyd and other northern and western axes have been found in the higher levels of the ditches at Windmill Hill and at Late Neolithic settlements at Avebury and Amesbury in Wiltshire. Radio carbon dates for Graig Lwyd axes found in the peat at Shapwick, Somerset, and Upware, Cambridgeshire, are 2,600 ± 120 B.C. and 2,980 - 2,740 B.C., the latter dated from the Fen Clay in which it was found. It would be wrong to suggest that all the axe factories were producing and exporting at the same time, but, by and large, the evidence does suggest that the export

[146] C. H. Houlder, loc. cit. Several sites are grouped under the name 'Prestatyn': Gwaen-ysgor, Dyserth Castle, Gop Cave and Field 56 & 56b, Prestatyn.
[147] 4th Report. PPS, XXVII, 1962, 233.
[148] Tievebulliagh axe from Newferry on the River Bann: C14, date 3330+170 B.C. (D. 36). W. A. Watts, Ant., XXXIV, 1960, 112.
[149] T. G. E. Powell, Ant., XXXVII, 1963, 23, fig. 4. Macroscopic identification only.
[150] 4th Report, PPS, XXVIII, 1962, 234-5 lists these instances of N. Welsh and other axes found in southern England.

trade for most of the groups reached its peak during the Late Neolithic period and in some cases continued into the Early Bronze Age.

It has been said that the country-wide dispersal of stone axes is not due to trade as we understand it, but rather to an exchange of gifts.[151] The argument is based on analogy with modern primitive societies which is perhaps more applicable to luxury articles, such as the beautiful polished jadeite axes found quite widely in Britain, than to the mundane tools which are under discussion here. It is impossible to judge such things with confidence at this distance in time, but some evidence from Llandegai may be brought forward in favour of the trading interpretation. Amongst the waste material from the settlement there was a good deal of very high quality, shiny black flint, far superior to anything obtainable from the Welsh coasts, and almost certainly derived from southern English chalk.[152] Flint was a valuable raw material for small tools and one which was difficult to obtain in Wales and, therefore, a highly suitable object for barter. Thus in the rubbish pits of Llandegai one may perhaps see both ends of the trading system.

Direct contact between North Wales and southern England, evidenced by the Henges at Llandegai and the pottery at Bryn yr Hen Bobl, may thus be explained as one of the results of this trade. However, it is still difficult to say whether people actually came up to North Wales from the south, whether it was the other way round, or whether the contact was normally through intermediaries. The English pottery at Bryn yr Hen Bobl suggests small-scale immigration from that area, whereas at Llandegai, where English religious ideas were adopted, the people retained their Irish Sea traditions of pottery and no southern English artifacts were found. Whether newcomers, like those at Bryn yr Hen Bobl, were the initiators of the trade it is impossible to say. Some of the evidence from Mynydd Rhiw and from Prestatyn hints at a Mesolithic background to some of the workers and, perhaps, to the men who travelled with the axes, and who may well have been semi-professional middlemen.[153] It would not be surprising to find the descendants of the Mesolithic hunters involved in this activity, since such men would have had a tradition of mobility.

It it clear that the Middle and Late Neolithic were periods of integration among the varied groups in these islands, when ideas on many aspects of life were being exchanged and adapted. The trade in stone axes is simply a very clear example of this process in action.

Chance discoveries of stone axes are frequently made, and up to fifty

[151] J. G. D. Clark, *Economic History Review*, XVIII, 1965, 1-28.
[152] Unlike the stone axes, the exact origin of any piece of flint cannot be identified, therefore one has to rely on the rather subjective criterion of quality, and chalky white cortex if it is present.
[153] Mynydd Rhiw: C. H. Houlder, PPS, XXVII, 1961, 135-9. Prestatyn: there are a large number of Mesolithic flints from Field 56b and elsewhere in that area. *See* G J. Wainwright, PPS, XXIX, 1963, 125.

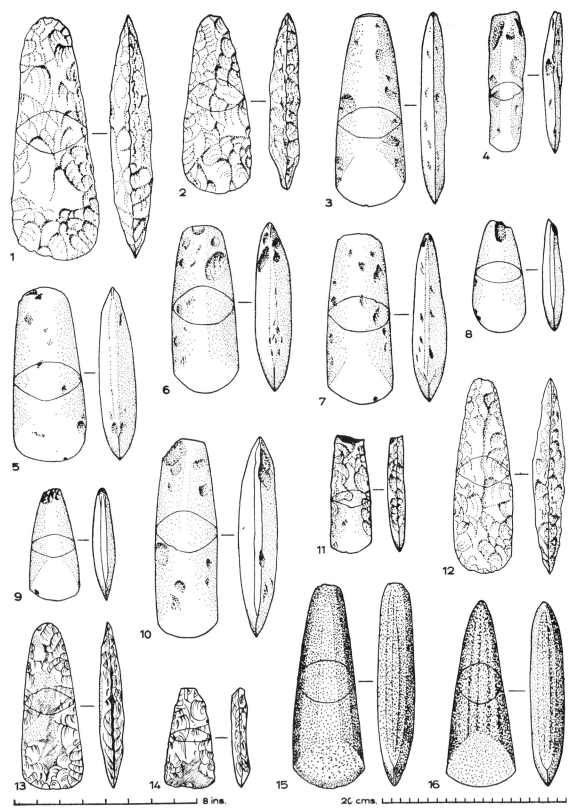

FIG. 30 — Stone axes from Anglesey: 1-2, rough-outs from Rhostrehwfa; 3, Rhos-y-bol; 4, Llansadwrn;
5, Ffynnon Dudur, Pentraeth; 6, Llanfihangel Esceifiog; 7-8, Cerrig Dewi; 9, Llaneilian; 10, 'Anglesey';
12, Llandyfrydog; 13, Llaneilian; 14, Cwm, Holyhead; 15 Penmynydd; 16, Pentraeth. 1-3, 5-6, Graig
Lwyd stone (Group VII); 9-10, Langdale (Group VI); 11-12, Mynydd Rhiw (Group XXI); 13-14, flint;
15, Cornwall (Group I); 16, ?French origin; 4, 7-8, unspecified stone. Cross-section shown on front view.

axes have been found at various times in Anglesey.[154] Fifty per cent of these are made from Graig Lwyd stone (Group VII in the Council for British Archaeology system of classification). Four are rough-outs or unfinished axes, straight from the factory.[155] The two found with other axes at Rhostrehwfa, near Llangefni, must represent the projected work of some individual who lived in the vicinity.[156] The proponderance of Graig Lwyd axes is to be expected in an area so close to their source, but the products of other factories did manage to penetrate the market to some extent.

The other North Welsh factory, Mynydd Rhiw (Group XXI), never as important as Graig Lwyd, is represented by two axes and a chip from an axe found at Trwyn Du, Aberffraw, beneath the Bronze Age barrow. One of the axes is a rough-out found at Llwydiarth Esgob, Llandyfrydog, and the other is a small partly-polished one without an exact provenance. The very productive factory at Langdale in the Lake District (Group VI), which exported a great many axes southwards, as well as into Scotland and Ireland, is represented by two axes, one from the north coast at Llaneilian and the other unprovenanced within the island. The factories on the coast of Cornwall concentrated chiefly on the southern English market, and their axes are found in large numbers in the west country and Wiltshire.[157] Axes of Group I, the largest of the Cornish groups, are, however, found further afield, so it is not surprising that the one Cornish axe in Anglesey, from Penmynydd, belongs to this group.

The stone axe is such a simple, functional tool that there is very little significant variation in shape from factory to factory, nor in the course of the long period of their use. However, it does seem that some small details are characteristic of certain factories and their finishing sites.[158] For instance, the Graig Lwyd axes always have a pointed oval section, while the axes from Langdale have normally been flattened by grinding down a narrow facet along the side (though this feature is not confined to this group). Because of the nature of the greenstone used, the Cornish axes always have a rounded section, a feature which can be well seen in the one from Penmynydd, and also on the ungrouped dolerite axe said to come from a barrow in Pentraeth which, because of its strange triangular shape, is thought to be French in origin.[159] However, a round section is not

---

[154] Lists in RCAM., *Anglesey*, 1937 and in the " Additions and Corrections " included with the 1960 reprint. Only the Rhostrehwfa axes and the flint axe from Llaneilian need be added to these lists at present, though a new list may be necessary when the Ordnance Survey have finished their current investigations.

[155] Not all these axes have been sectioned and examined petrologically, but the identifications are certain because this is a stone which can be recognised easily by eye if an unweathered area is visible. I am grateful to Mr. C. H. Houlder for generously lending me his records of all the Anglesey axes sectioned under the Council for British Archaeology scheme.

[156] These axes were found with a small polished chert axe and possibly with others not collected. I am grateful to Mr. Martin Buckley of the Ordnance Survey for this information and to Mr. E. Williams for allowing me to see the chert axe in his possession.

[157] The distribution pattern for most of the British factories can be found *in* PPS XXVIII, 1962, 209-266.

[158] This aspect has not been much studied, *but see* C. Fell, PPS, XXX, 1964, 39-55.

[159] H. N. Savory, *Arch. Camb.*, 1940, 245-6.

restricted to southern axes, for the local axes at Bryn yr Hen Bobl all share this feature, perhaps because they were made of rather intractable dolerite. In spite of the difficult nature of the raw material, it is clear that a certain standardisation in size was aimed at; for instance, three Graig Lwyd axes from Anglesey (Pentraeth, Llanfihangel Esgeifiog (Fig. 30, Nos. 5 and 6), and Penmon) are almost identical in size, as are the smaller rough-out from Rhostrehwfa and the finished axe from Rhos-y-bol.[160] This must be more than a coincidence and it indicates the skill and professionalism of the craftsmen who worked in this industry.

In spite of the number of axes from Graig Lwyd and other factories, many axes were not commercial products and were probably made from local rocks or suitable erratic boulders. So far, no evidence has come to light to suggest that any of the Anglesey rocks were exploited on a commercial scale, although there are a few examples of Anglesey axes in other parts of North Wales. The one found at Llandrillo-yn-rhos, Denbighshire, has a rounded section like the local ones from Bryn yr Hen Bobl.[161] It is made from a diorite found near the Anglesey Monument in Llanfair Pwllgwyngyll.

The distribution of these axes in Anglesey can be best appreciated from the map. It is notable that the distribution of axes and tombs does not coincide closely. Axes occur most frequently in the south-eastern corner where tombs are relatively rare, while there are virtually none in the south-western area where there are at least four tombs. The number of axes found close to Bryn Celli Ddu is perhaps worthy of comment, and may reflect the interest of the original Henge-builders in the axe trade here as at Llandegai. The quantity of finds strung out along the road from Menai Bridge to Pentraeth is remarkable and must be indicative of something more than simply the collecting activity of the Vicar of Llansadwrn in the last century, although such factors should not be forgotten.[162] The distribution of axes suggests that Neolithic settlement of the island was more extensive than the distribution of tombs would lead one to suppose, and that possibly other groups of farmers may have existed who, because they did not build elaborate tombs, are unknown to us.

Flint axes are rare in North Wales and are, without doubt, imports either from Antrim or from southern England.[163] One was found recently at Llaneilian.[164] It is only partly polished, but it may be a re-chipped implement rather than a rough-out, for a squared, polished facet is visible on

[160] The larger axe from Cerrig Dewi (unsectioned) is also exactly the same size.
[161] Ellis Davies, *Prehistoric and Roman Remains of Flintshire*, 1949, Appendix, 441-2, Thin section number DEN 7.
[162] The collections of the Rev. E. Evans form the bulk of the Anglesey Antiquarian Society collection today. *Arch. Camb.*, 1908, 292-4 and TAAS, 1915, 17-20.
[163] The Sturges Collection in the British Museum contains three narrow flint axes (nos. 101, 101a & b) marked " found in Anglesea but probably Irish ". This collection contains several more very fine flint implements similarly marked. They are all types common in Ireland and it seems reasonable to suppose that they were actually found there rather than in Anglesey.
[164] TAAS. 1959. 58.

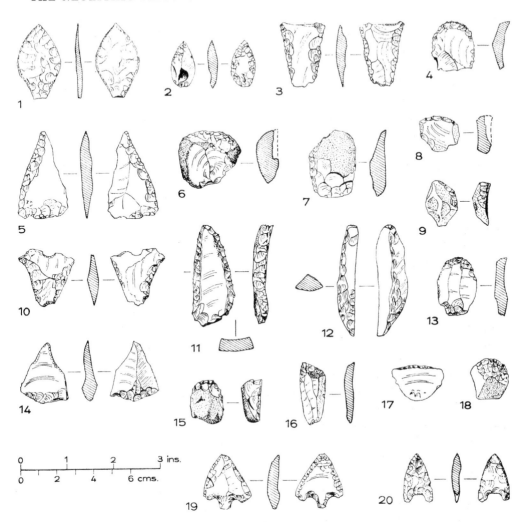

FIG. 31 — Flint implements from Anglesey: 1, Pant y Saer; 2, Llanidan; 3-4, Dwyran; 5, near Castellior, Llandysilio; 6, Llangaffo; 7-9, 'Ogo Arian', Pentre-eiriannell; 10-16, Din Lligwy; 17-18, Cors Bodwrog (After W. O. Stanley); 19, Gate Farm, Bodedern; 20, Gwynfa, Marianglas.

the side. A rather poorly shaped one with a polished blade survives in the British Museum; it is one of four said to have been found at Cwm, Holyhead, in the last century. The original account by W. O. Stanley states that the four axes were found at Cwm, near the Tŷ Mawr hut circles, together with several large flakes and a very big nodule of flint.[165] It is implied that all the axes were of flint, at least two being unfinished. Such a find would be highly significant in any discussion of a trade in flint, but

[165] *Arch. J.* XXXI. 1874. 296-7. 301.

unfortunately confidence cannot be placed in the details as the information was gathered some time after the event.

Another possible instance of a trader's hoard of flint, worked and unworked, is recorded by Stanley.[166] This was found in Cors Bodwrog, near Gwalchmai, and because of the thick white cortex it was suggested that this was flint mined from the chalk. Unfortunately, the information is again inadequate and the account rather confused. However, it is possible to recognise amongst the surviving material from several Anglesey sites certain implements and pieces of waste flint which are of very much higher quality than the usual Welsh flint.[167] They are black or very dark brown, glossy, semi-translucent, and without the flaws which often make pebbles so awkward to work. Although, unlike stone axes, their provenance cannot be proved, it is conceivable that these represent the return on the trading of axes to southern England. Such flints occur at Lligwy and on Newborough Warren. It would be interesting to see whether they occurred only on the later sites, but in Anglesey we have no certain Early Neolithic material against which this hypothesis could be checked.

Small flint implements are not especially common finds in Anglesey, nor in Wales as a whole, because of the scarcity of the material.[168] Amongst such chance finds scrapers (perhaps used for dressing hides) and unspecific worked flakes are the most frequent, but because such simple tools are used throughout the prehistoric period they cannot all be assigned to the Neolithic. Arrowheads are more distinctive and can be dated with greater accuracy.

Arrowheads found on the earlier Neolithic sites in the British Isles are normally leaf-shaped; thin flakes carefully worked on both surfaces and neatly chipped to a pointed oval or lozenge outline. There is a good series of such arrowheads from the tomb at Pant y Saer, but in the island as a whole they are rare.[169] There is a small one found at Llanidan and there is a single example among the quantity of flint implements from New-borough Warren.[170]

More common are the triangular arrowheads belonging to the class called "petit tranchet derivative", and dated to the latter half of the

---

[166] *Arch. J.* XXI. 1864. 168 and XXXI. 1874. 297. A similar hoard was found more recently at Penmachno, Caerns. (*Arch. Camb.* 1939. 106-7) and several have been found in the north of Ireland L. N. W. Flanagan. UJA. XXIX. 1966. 82-90 and P. Woodman UJA. XXX. 1967. 8-14).

[167] A large scraper, possibly Bronze Age in date, is recorded from Ponciau Moorings, Menai Bridge. It may have been made from mined flint (TAAS. 1954. 101).

[168] Collectors are also rare. There is at present one assiduous collector in Anglesey, Mr. H. Hooton of Benllech, to whom I am grateful for information about most of the chance finds recorded here and for permission to draw the best examples. His collection does not contain any implements of the standard of those in the Sturges Collection which makes the ascription of these flints in the British Museum to Anglesey even more unlikely. The Neolithic objects should perhaps be listed all the same. 138a — large lozenge shape javelin head, characteristic of the north of Ireland. 138c — very fine leaf shaped arrowhead. 149a — long and narrow *petit tranchet derivative* arrowhead.

[169] One of the arrowheads shown here in fact belongs to the Pant y Saer group. It was found on one of the spoil heaps after the excavation. It is in Bangor Museum.

[170] T. Pape. TAAS. 1928. 24. fig. 1, no. 5. (Reproduced here as Fig. 32).

Neolithic and to the very beginning of the Bronze Age.[171] Such arrowheads have been found at Bryn Celli Ddu (two examples), at Bryn yr Hen Bobl, and at Castell Bryn Gwyn, all sites which can be dated on other grounds to the Late Neolithic. One also occurred among the flints from Din Lligwy, and two have been found as strays: one at Llandysilio, not far from Castellior where a number of stone axes have been found, and one at Dwyran which was found with a small scraper of grey flint. This latter, with a narrow transverse blade, belongs to Class B. They are quite clearly not piercing arrowheads but are apparently very effective against small game and birds.

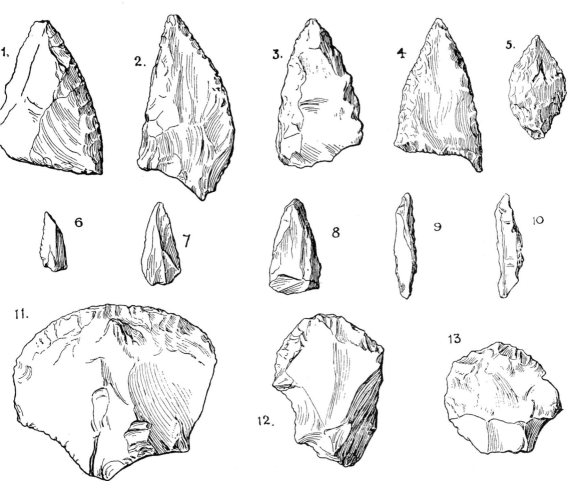

FIG. 32 — Flint implements from Newborough Warren. (Reproduced from TAAS by kind permission of the Editor.) (Full size.)

[171] J. G. D. Clark *Arch. J.* XCI. 1934. 32-58 for a comprehensive study and classification of this type. Recently several have been found at the Henge Monument at Durrington Walls, Wilts. and in the Beaker period settlement outside the tomb at Newgrange, Ireland.

The one from Llandysilio belongs to Class G, triangular in outline, with one naturally sharp edge. It is not clear how these were mounted, or even whether they were used as arrowheads at all, for they are sometimes very large and may have been knife blades. Four good examples of this type were found on Newborough Warren, close to the rocks at Bryn Llwyd.[172] This area produced a great many flints (mostly waste flakes but including a number of good scrapers and many undistinctive worked flakes), two polished stone axes, and several sherds of Beaker pottery which will be discussed in the next chapter. Since this type of arrowhead and the stone axes could belong either to the Late Neolithic or to the Early Bronze Age, it is difficult to be certain of the date at which this coastal settlement began. The presence of a few Mesolithic flints and of a leaf-shaped arrowhead do suggest, however, that a few people may have been living there spasmodically throughout the Neolithic period, and that the community was perhaps simply enlarged by the arrival of new people after 2,000 B.C.

Arrowheads are perhaps not very important, but such conclusions as may be drawn from them confirm the evidence of the more impressive relics of the period. The majority of Neolithic monuments and artifacts belong to the middle and later periods; there is no satisfactory evidence for farming and tomb-building on the island during the Early Neolithic, although it seems unbelievable that such a favourable and well-sited area should be uncolonised at this time. It is to be hoped that some of the megalithic tombs may eventually be shown to belong to an early phase of settlement.

However, by the Middle Neolithic it is clear that a number of communities with differing traditions of tomb-building had settled in the island and had to some extent merged, pooling their ideas to produce variants not found elsewhere. Local developments of this kind suggests a long period uninterrupted by foreign contacts, but it is doubtful whether such a period of isolation really existed, for Anglesey played a considerable part in the trade in stone axes, a trade which must have fostered a wide movement of people and ideas.

That this trade did forge links with distant areas is clear from the mixture of pottery styles at Bryn yr Hen Bobl and the introduction of new religious monuments at Llandegai and Bryn Celli Ddu. But despite these innovations the tomb-building traditions remained strong and, perhaps, survived longer in Anglesey than anywhere else, for the tombs were still

---

[172] Pape *loc. cit.* and TAAS. 1929. 95. Another one illustrated by him (no. 3) is very probably a fifth but the drawing is inadequate. Unfortunately all these arrowheads and the Mesolithic flints have disappeared. Bangor Museum received only the sherds, several boxes of waste flint and a box of scrapers. There is a small arrowhead of Class G in the Bangor Museum, together with a small flint knife probably of Beaker date. Their provenance is not certain but there is a possibility that they were found near Hologwyn, Llanddaniel Fab.

in use when the next group of newcomers arrived. These were the European people who made Beakers and brought with them influential new ideas, the knowledge of metal and the practice of single burial. But for all that, the traditions of collective activity and burial initiated by the first farmers never completely died out.

III

MAKERS OF BEAKERS IN ANGLESEY

THE next phase in the history of Anglesey is clearly marked archaeologically by the appearance of new types of pottery and the adoption of a new burial rite. It is during this phase, too, that metal objects gradually begin to appear in the record. These changes in material equipment are accompanied in certain instances by the arrival of a new physical type, broader and more heavily-built than the earlier Neolithic people. Thus it is possible to recognise groups of new people actually coming into the British Isles at this time which, on conventional dating, is from about 2,000 B.C.[1]

These people are recognisable all over Europe and the British Isles by their characteristic pottery of remarkably uniform paste and design, their habit of single burial, and their warlike equipment, either bows, arrows and wristguards, or daggers and battle-axes. They seem to have spread very rapidly over the entire Continent, probably from a centre in north-east or Central Europe.[2] It is extremely difficult to unravel the inter-relationships and chronological positions of these various groups because they seem to have covered such large distances so rapidly, and while, in some places, they remained distinct from the pre-existing Neolithic populations, in others they appear to have merged into them and are, at first, recognisable only by their distinctive pottery.

All the same, these groups who, in northern and eastern Europe at any rate, consistently buried their dead in single graves, do seem to herald the marked change in social climate which distinguishes the warrior/trader-orientated Bronze Age from the family-dominated farming communities of the Neolithic. This is not to say that the social structure was ever completely changed, but the appearance during the Bronze Age of individuals accompanied by personal possessions of great value suggests that a social stratification was growing up in which personal leadership might be more important than family position. It is possible, too, that economic factors encouraged this development. There is evidence that during this period the climate was becoming drier, a circumstance which, together with the amount of forest clearance carried out by Neolithic farmers, would produce

[1] Recent general surveys: S. Piggott *in* Foster and Alcock (edd.), *Culture and Environment*, 53-91, and D. L. Clarke, *Palaeohistoria*, XII, 1966, 179-98. (Preliminary note in advance of a major study).

[2] There is still considerable controversy on the exact place of origin of these people. The two main alternatives are Central Europe (Hungary) and Iberia. (*See* S. Piggott, *Ancient Europe*, 1965, 100-2).

ideal grazing conditions over large areas of Europe. As a result, there seems to have been a greater emphasis on cattle-herding which, in turn, would lead to greater mobility and probably an increase in raiding and local skirmishing. The rise of skilled bronzesmiths and the growth of long distance trade in raw materials and finished objects must also have tended to weaken earlier traditions, although widespread trade and a certain amount of specialisation had already existed during the Neolithic period.

However, none of these traits would seem to have been fully developed among the Beaker people who first came to the west. Although it seems likely that they were the first people to introduce a knowledge of metal and metal-working to Britain,[3] they are essentially a Neolithic group existing alongside native Late Neolithic peoples who, in southern England, made the Mortlake, Fengate and Grooved Ware styles of pottery. Several ideas of pottery decoration and design, especially the Beaker flat base which begins to be used for Fengate pots, were exchanged between them. It is also notable that the Beaker people used, and even built, many of the native sanctuaries of Henge type, and it is more than likely that they took a large part in the flourishing trade in stone axes which seems to have reached its peak during the Late Neolithic period.[4] Similarly some of the earliest Beaker settlers may have adopted the prevailing system of collective burial, for a very fine Bell Beaker was found in the filling of the West Kennet chambered tomb, and sherds of early Bell or Corded Beakers have often been found in the chambers of megalithic tombs, both in these islands and in Brittany and Spain.[5]

Most of our information about these people in Britain, however, comes from what may be a slightly later phase and is from graves. This means that we know very little about their houses, fields or social organisation. The few houses which have been found suggest that the settlements were smaller (possibly only a single isolated house), and perhaps less permanent than Neolithic ones like Clegyr Boia. The houses were definitely flimsy, stake rather than post structures, and tend to be oval and small, sufficient only for a single generation family.[6] Although specialised cattle kraals are known from the Netherlands and may be presumed to have existed in Britain, arable farming still continued, evidenced by grain impressions in sherds and a broken quern on a site in Cornwall.[7] Barley appears to have replaced wheat as the most popular crop.[8]

[3] H. J. Case, Palaeohistoria, XII. 1966, 141-77.
[4] Henge B at Llandegai, Caerns., provides a good example of such a link between Beaker people, Henges and the axe trade. C. H. Houlder, Ant., XLII, 1968, 216-21.
[5] West Kennet: S. Piggott, West Kennet Long Barrow: Excavations 1955-6, 1962, 43-5. Scotland: A. S. Henshall, Chambered Tombs of Scotland I, 1963, 109-10 and passim. Wales: F. M. Lynch in T. G. E. Powell et. al. Megalithic Enquiries in the West of Britain, 1969, 149-74 passim. Europe: J. L'Helgouach, Les Sépultures Mégalithiques en Armorique, 1965, 115-7; H. N. Savory, Spain and Portugal, 1968, 166.
[6] Unpublished lecture by D. D. A. Simpson, Bristol 1969.
[7] Anlo cattle Kraal: H. T. Waterbolk, Palaeohistoria, VIII, 1961, 59-60. Quern at Gwithian, unpublished.
[8] H. Helbaek, PPS. XVIII, 1952, 204-7

The first Beaker people in Britain may be represented by a small group of widely scattered pots of classic European Bell Beaker form. The use of this particular kind of pot suggests that they may have come over from the western coasts of France. However, the bulk of the early Beakers from Britain are of a type found mainly in the Netherlands, showing considerable similarity to the Corded Ware pots of Northern Europe. The first settlers who came in any numbers, therefore, would seem to have come from the lands round the mouth of the Rhine, and to have crossed to eastern England and to Scotland where the closest analogues to the Dutch pots are to be found. The earliest type seem to have been simply decorated by winding twisted cord around the pot while the clay was wet. It is these, known as " All-over-corded " Beakers which are most commonly found as sherds in the megalithic tombs. The first two types of Beakers that appear consistently in single graves are the Scottish Short-Necked Beakers, similar in shape and decoration to those found in Holland, and the Bell Beakers, found further south in eastern England, which have a decorative peculiarity (pendant triangles close to the base) linking them to contemporary pots in the Rhineland. Subsequent to this immigration phase, there is considerable change and development in the shape and decoration of the pottery and in the type of weapons placed in the grave. Some of these changes, particularly those concerned with weapons, were no doubt brought about through renewed contact with Europe, though at this stage it may not have involved any large-scale immigration.

In England the direction taken by the changes in pottery was towards a greater elaboration of pattern and an increase in the height of the vessel's neck, which resulted in the appearance of the native Long Necked Beaker, so common in southern England and Wales. Throughout the period the rite of single burial was practised with the body lying crouched in a grave or a stone box or cist, dug into the ground and frequently covered by a round mound or barrow.[9] In Scotland the early graves are not usually marked by a barrow, but south of the Tees such flat graves are rare and by the end of the period it is usual for the site of the burial to be marked by a mound of considerable size. This trend may have been influenced by the increased importance of barrow building on the Continent.

In contrast to the Neolithic practice by which no specific grave goods were placed with the dead, it was customary for the Beaker people to be buried with a standardised set of equipment.[10] In the earlier phases, this included a Beaker, usually standing behind the head and possibly containing liquid; some archers' equipment; a stone wrist guard and a number of barbed and tanged arrowheads; and, occasionally, a tanged copper knife. These are the first metal objects found regularly in Britain, but they are,

---

[9] In Yorkshire, and occasionally elsewhere, Beaker graves contain two or three bodies, probably buried successively.
[10] Fully discussed by S. Piggott in Foster and Alcock (edd.), *Culture and Environment*, 53-92. There appears to be little essential difference between his views and those of Clarke.

on the whole, rare. The later Long-Necked Beaker are usually found with a different " weapon group ": the archers' equipment has been replaced by stone battle-axes and rivetted daggers, which by now are made of bronze, a much harder and more effective metal than copper but one which requires a knowledge of alloying. Another distinctive object common in these later Beaker graves is the jet or shale button with converging drilled perforations (V-bored). These are sometimes accompanied by pulley rings with similar perforations; together they may have formed a belt fastening. These daggers, battle-axes and buttons quite often occur in inhumation graves without pottery of any kind, and it looks as if by this time the original Beaker traditions were being diluted both by a re-emergence of native customs (seen in the occasional use of cremation, and the appearance of Food Vessel and Collared Urn pottery) and the influence of Continental ideas (new weapon-types and an increased knowledge of metallurgy).

The number of Beakers and allied objects found in Anglesey is comparatively small and most of them date from the later phase character-ised by Long Necked Beakers. However, the early period, during which the newcomers were merging with the existing Neolithic population, is represented on the island. Two tiny sherds of Corded Beaker and a barbed and tanged arrowhead were found in the chamber of the Passage Grave at Tŷ Newydd (ANG 3), and a rim sherd, possibly from a Beaker decorated with cardium shell impressions, came from the upper layer of burials at Lligwy (ANG 14).[11] Beakers are typically made of a fine clay with little or no stone grit, and baked to a brick red colour. There are sherds of this paste amongst the pottery from Castell Bryn Gwyn found alongside the Late Neolithic Fengate ware, and there is a possible sherd of Beaker from the site beneath Bryn yr Hen Bobl (ANG 8).[12] The mixture of Fengate and Beaker pottery at Castell Bryn Gwyn is not surprising, especially if the site is really a double-entrance Henge, and the presence of a bronze awl, which implies a date of about 1,600 B.C., underlines the fact that the older native traditions persisted for a long time after the first arrival of Beaker people.

Sand dunes have always been attractive to early settlers, since they are accessible, relatively free of trees and have a good food supply in the form of fish and shellfish. Sherds and flints of all periods have been picked up from coastal areas in England, Wales, Scotland and Ireland, but unfortun-ately the remains of houses and such-like are very rarely found. The dunes on Newborough Warren have already been mentioned in connection with Mesolithic and Late Neolithic flints. Among the finds picked up from the surface close to the spine of rock called Bryn Llwyd were sherds from at least a dozen Beakers.[13]

None of these is represented by more than one or two sherds, and it is impossible to say a great deal about them or the settlement from which

---

[11] Fig. 6 and Fig. 21, no. 5.
[12] Castell Bryn Gwyn: Fig. 27, no. 2; Bryn yr Hen Bobl: Fig. 28, no. 21 and p. 70 above.
[13] T. Pape, TAAS, 1927, 23-33 and 1928, 21-7.

they must have come. Most of them are very simply decorated with rows of twisted cord or cardium shell impressions (Fig. 33, Nos. 1-4, 7-10). Others have faint, widely spaced finger-nail marks (Fig. 33, Nos. 5, 17), and some have more intricate patterns made by a square-toothed comb (Fig. 33, Nos. 12-15, 18). On Fig 33, No. 16, the most elaborate, the technique is not clear. There are a few undecorated sherds and some thick pieces with a good deal of stone grit. These may have come from domestic bowls and storage jars about which little is known, because they are never placed in the graves. Little can be said about the shape, beyond remarking on the preponderance of cordons beneath the rims. The one surviving shoulder suggests a classic Bell Beaker profile.

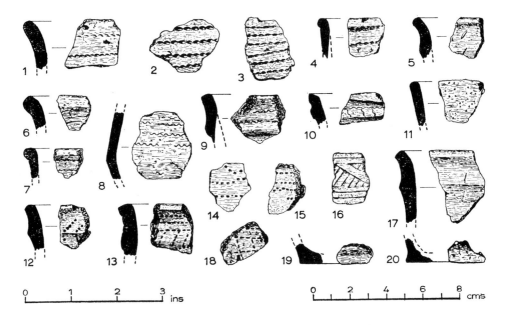

FIG. 33 — Sherds of Beaker pottery from Newborough Warren.

The assemblage would seem to be the debris of people most closely related to the early groups of Beaker settlers who made cord decorated pots, although the presence of hyphenated decoration made with a comb may imply some contact with slightly later groups from southern England. The faint finger-nail marks and the cordons beneath the rim are both features characteristic of the earlier Beakers in the British Isles, to which an approximate date of 2,000 - 1,800 B.C. may be given. It is not possible to define the antecedents of this particular group of people very closely, but similar coastal communities of Beaker people lived at Dalkey Island, Dublin; Glenluce Sands, Galloway; and Merthyr Mawr Warren,

Glamorgan.[14] This last site has produced evidence for a trade in stone axes. The people at Newborough may have been engaged in similar activities, for two axes (one from Graig Lwyd) have been found in the area, but the association with the Beaker pottery is not direct.[15]

The lop-sided triangular arrowheads ("petit-tranchet derivatives") found at Newborough have already been discussed in the previous chapter. Their context on the island is certainly Late Neolithic and they do not seem to be a type confined to the Beaker-making community, although very fine examples occurred with Beaker pottery at Newgrange, Ireland.[16] Elsewhere in Britain the typical Beaker and Early Bronze Age arrow is barbed and tanged, in the latter period very precisely shaped. These arrowheads are surprisingly rare in Anglesey, the only examples known to me being the one from Tŷ Newydd (ANG 3); a small, rather roughly made one, probably of Beaker date, picked up near the Treiorwerth barrow, Bodedern; and a variant form, having no central tang, from Gwynfa, Marianglas (Fig. 31, Nos. 19 and 20).[17] Although metal goods were gradually becoming available, small tools in flint were still much used throughout the Early Bronze Age, and flake knives such as those from Tŷ'n y Pwll and Porth Dafarch are frequently found in Beaker graves and as stray finds.

Whereas the sherds from Tŷ Newydd, Lligwy and Newborough suggest the presence of Beaker people in the island at an early date, perhaps around about 1,800 B.C., the Beakers found with single burials in Anglesey are all of a later type. They all have the long neck and elaborate decoration that are characteristic of the native Beakers made in southern England, but whether they are the work of people who came solely from that area is doubtful, because of the presence of jet at Merddyn Gwyn and the absence of a barrow over the cist at Rhosbeirio. These are both features which suggest contact with the north. The number of graves in question is too small for the distribution to be very significant, but, by and large, these later Beakers occur in areas away from the south-west corner, where the best evidence for earlier Beaker and Neolithic occupation is found.

Probably the most interesting of the Beaker burials in Anglesey is that at Merddyn Gwyn (NGR SH/521792), near Pentraeth. Unfortunately the entire barrow was destroyed in 1907 when a railway line was laid between Holland Arms and Red Wharf Bay; the information was gleaned very hurriedly in the course of this destruction.[18]

[14] Dalkey Island: G. D. Liversage, PRIA, 66, C., 1968, 53-233. Glenluce: I. McInnes, PSAS, XCVII, 1963-4, 40-81. Merthyr Mawr: J. Ward, *Arch. Camb.*, 1919, 323-52. Dalkey Island, just south of Dun Laoghaire, has produced sherds from pots very similiar indeed to those from Newborough (e.g. *op. cit.*, fig. 9, 53).

[15] TAAS, 1928, 22-3 and another axe found by Mr. T. C. Lethbridge, now in the Museum of Archaeology and Ethnology, Cambridge.

[16] M. J. O'Kelly, *3rd Atlantic Colloquium, Arhus*, 1969, unpublished.

[17] Ty Newydd: Fig. 6, no. 3. I am grateful to Mr. H. Davidson, Gate Farm, for showing me the arrowhead from Bodedern and to Mr. John Williams Hughes for allowing me to publish the one from Marianglas.

[18] The recording was initiated and several of the pots saved by the Rev. E. Evans of Llansadwrn. The final report is by Mr. Harold Hughes, *Arch. Camb.*, 1908, 211-20.

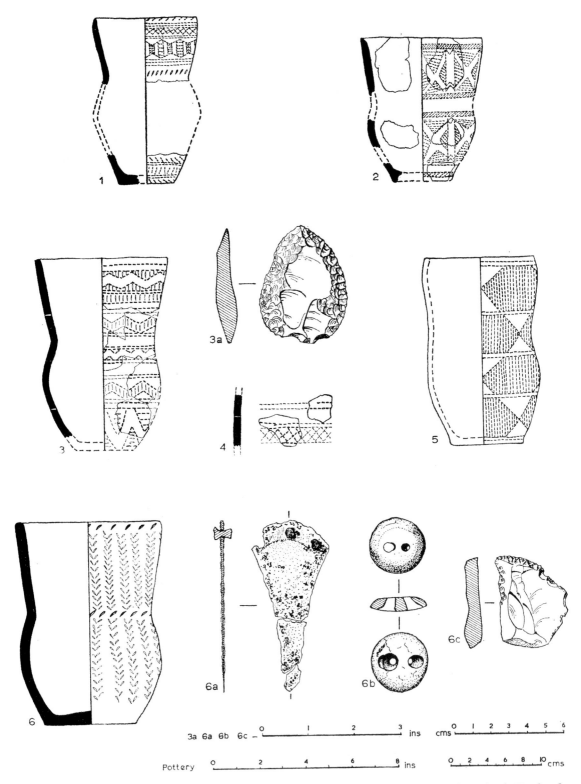

Fig. 34 — Beaker pottery from Anglesey: 1, Pant y Saer; 2, 'Llanbabo'; 3-4, Porth Dafarch II, sherds of two Beakers from the central grave and flint knife from the mound; 5, Rhosbeirio; 6, Merddyn Gwyn, Beaker, knife, jet button and ? flint flake from the central grave. (See Fig. 52 for plan of Merddyn Gwyn.)

The cairn was oval, about 45 × 50ft. in diameter, composed of large limestone blocks and surrounded by some sort of kerb or wall, also of limestone. The surviving height was something less than 6ft. (Fig. 52). Almost in the centre was the grave, dug 1ft. into the gravel subsoil. The exact dimensions are not given, but the depth beneath the capstone was 3ft. This cover was supported at the north end by a large upright stone which stood in the grave. Other supporters were removed before a record was made, but it was presumed that they had stood, not in the grave but on the old ground surface. There was apparently some burnt soil and charcoal on the floor of the grave.

In the grave was a crouched skeleton lying on its left side, with the head towards the north. A complete Beaker stood behind the head and the body was accompanied by a small bronze blade, a jet button and a roughly flaked flint or chert knife.[19] The body was that of a middle-aged man about 5ft. 9ins. in height with a long, narrow skull (dolichocephalic).[20] This last feature is surprising since elsewhere in Britain the Beaker people are distinguished from the earlier population, who were almost exclusively dolichocephalic, by having broad, round heads (brachicephalic). This peculiarity is shared by other Beaker burials in Anglesey, Porth Dafarch and Tŷn y Pwll, so it may be further confirmation of the late date of this group. By that time a considerable mingling of the populations may have taken place, although perhaps insufficient data precludes any certainty on this point at present.

The grave goods, Beaker, knife and button, are typical of contemporary graves in many parts of the country. Both the system of attaching the blade to the haft, of horn or wood, by rivets, and the use of V-bored buttons seem to have reached this country ultimately from the Rhineland at a date which may be centred on 1,600 B.C.[21]

Amongst Welsh Beaker burials, metal knives are rare and, on the whole, these communities do not give the impression of being very rich or successful.[22] There is no evidence of their having exploited the local copper ores and it is doubtful whether these Beaker groups would have had any practical knowledge or experience of metallurgy. The knife from Merddyn Gwyn is very small and the concave sides suggest heavy use and much whetting. The jet button, which was probably made in Yorkshire, is evidence of trade in non-essential objects, but it is not a particularly fine example of its type. It is made of good material and is well polished, but the normal buttons are conical with the perforations concealed, whereas this specimen looks somewhat sub-standard.

[19] The flint knife illustrated is assumed to be the one in question, but there is a slight uncertainty about it because the original flake was said by Greenly to be of grey chert and the original list of the Evans Collection does not state that this flint (no. 55) was found at Merddyn Gwyn (TAAS, 1914-15, 19).
[20] Report by Sir Arthur Keith, *Arch. Camb.*, 1909, 254-5.
[21] S. Piggott in Foster and Alcock (edd.), *Culture and Environment*, 78, 82-8.
[22] There are two major articles on Welsh Beakers: H. N. Savory, BBCS, XVI, 1955, 215-41 and W. E. Griffiths, PPS, XXIII, 1957, 57-90).

The Beaker is well-made, but not elaborately decorated. The pattern consists of vertical lines of paired diagonal marks made with a finger-nail. The rim and waist are encircled by a single row of deeper finger-nail marks, but none of these marks cause any rustication of the surface. This system of decoration is found on earlier Beakers, as at Newborough, and commonly on later ones, where the pairing is characteristic and often accompanied by a pinching up of the clay not seen here. Two Beakers similar to this in shape and decoration have been found in Wales: one with a burial at Plas Heaton, Henllan, Denbighshire, and the other in a small pit inside the double-entrance Henge at Llandegai, Caernarvonshire.[23]

At a later date, probably 1,500 - 1,400 B.C., the mound at Merddyn Gwyn was enlarged and several other burials added.[24] One frequently finds this continuity in the use of burial places throughout the Early Bronze Age. This may possibly be an expression of family tradition by which later generations aim to be buried in the dynastic barrow. In the Salisbury Plain area, where this seems to have been particularly common, the tradition clearly goes back to the Beaker period, but not beyond, since there are no Bronze Age insertions into Neolithic Long Barrows. The arrival of the Beaker people, who settled in large numbers there, must have meant a break with the past in this respect. In the west, where the Beaker people were fewer and more scattered, the change may not have been so abrupt. In Anglesey, for example, there are instances of Bronze Age burials inserted into Neolithic mounds (Barclodiad y Gawres and Bryn yr Hen Bobl),[25] though even here it is more often a Beaker barrow which is the focus of later cemetery groups.

The three barrows at Porth Dafarch, Holy Island (NGR SH/234801) exemplify such a cemetery in use over two or three hundred years, possibly by successive generations of the same small community who would have lived by farming and fishing in the area. The three barrows lay close together in a line running back from the shore. They had been heavily disturbed in the Roman period when a group of huts had been built over and around them. They were all entirely removed in the last century and the site is now covered by the road. The one closest to the sea (Porth Dafarch I) was dug into by a farmer in search of stone in 1848, and the others were excavated in 1875 by W. O. Stanley.[26] Stanley published details of the finds from all three sites, but some of the facts remain uncertain. This is not surprising for the complexity of the site might well baffle even the best modern excavator. Part of the site was in fact re-excavated just before the last war by the late Mr. B. St. John O'Neil when the structure of the

[23] Henllan: Wynne Ffoulkes, *Arch. Camb.*, 1851, 274-80. Llandegai: C. H. Houlder, *Ant.*, XLII, 1968, Pl. XXXI. b.
[24] Discussed in the next chapter.
[25] Fig. 10, no. 2 and Fig. 29, no. 14.
[26] W. O. Stanley, Porth Dafarch I, *Arch. J.*, VI, 1849, 226-39; and *Arch Camb.*, 1868, 222-31. Porth Dafarch II and III, *Arch. J.*, XXXIII, 1876, 129-43; and *Arch. Camb.*, 1878, 22-38.

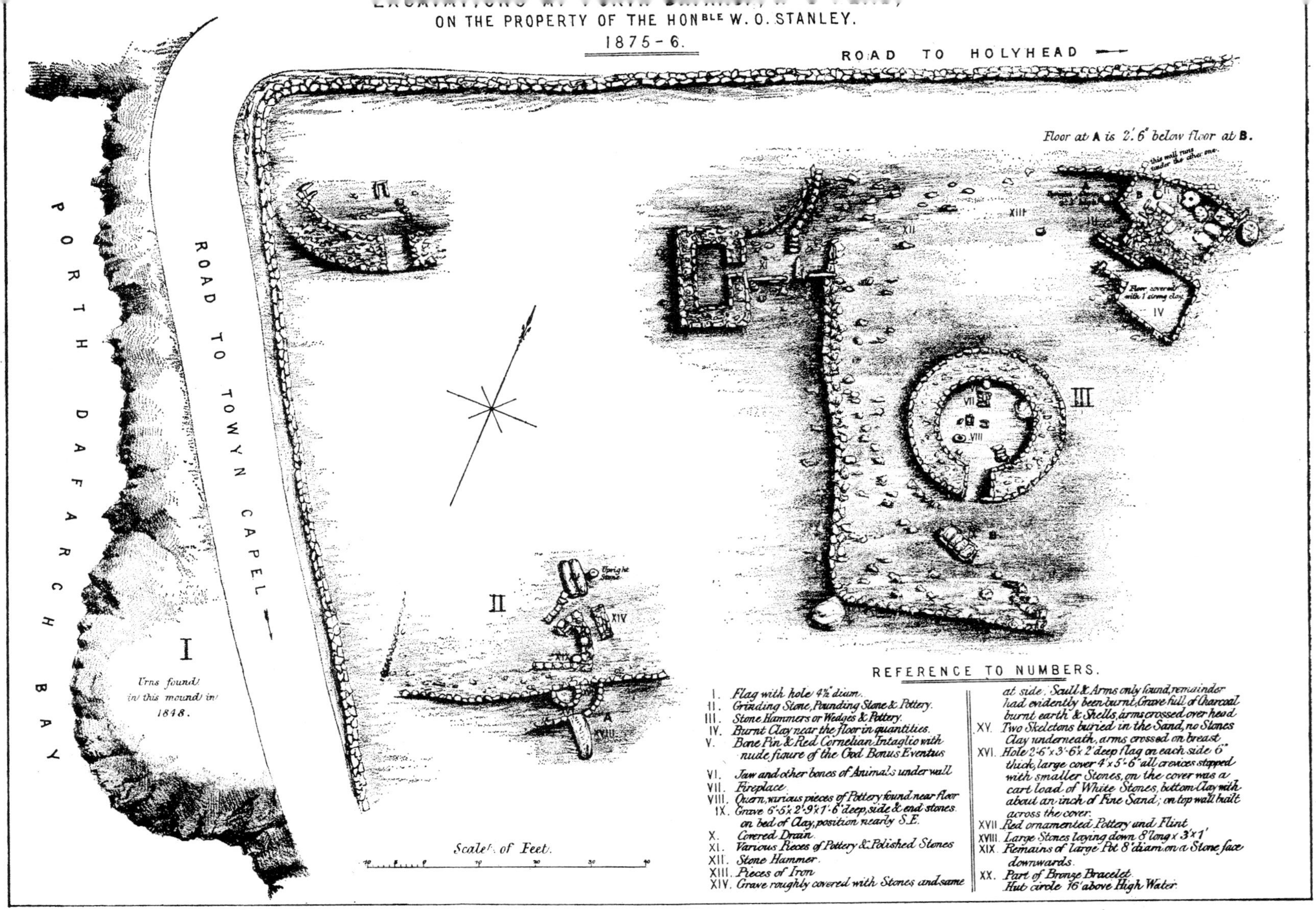

EXCAVATIONS AT ....
ON THE PROPERTY OF THE HON.ble W. O. STANLEY.
1875–6.

ROAD TO HOLYHEAD →

Floor at **A** is 2'.6 below floor at **B**.

ROAD TO TOWYN CAPEL →

PORTH DAFARCH BAY

Scale of Feet.

I
Was found in this mound in 1848.

REFERENCE TO NUMBERS.

I.— Flag with hole 9½" diam.
II.— Grinding Stone, Pounding Stone & Pottery.
III.— Stone Hammers or Wedges & Pottery.
IV.— Burnt Clay near the floor in quantities.
V.— Bone Pin & Red Cornelian, Intaglio with nude figure of the Ded Bonus Eventus.
VI.— Jaw and other bones of Animals under wall.
VII.— Fireplace.
VIII.— Quern, various pieces of Pottery found near.
IX.— Grave 6'.6 x 2'.9 7'.8 deep side & end stones on bed of clay position nearly S.E.
X.— Covered Drain.
XI.— Various Pieces of Pottery & Polished Stones
XII.— Stone Hammer.
XIII.— Pieces of Iron.
XIV.— Grave roughly covered with Stones and same.

XV.— Scull & Arms only found remainder had evidently been burnt. Grave full of Charcoal burnt earth & Shells arms crossed on breast.
XVI.— Two Skeletons buried in the Sand no Stones Clay underneath, arms crossed on breast. Hole 3'.6 x 3'.6 x 2' deep flag on each side 6" thick, large cover 4'.5'.6 all crevices stopped with smaller Stones, on the cover was a cart load of White Stones, bottom clay with about an inch of fine Sand, on top wall built across the cover.
XVII.— Bed ornamented Pottery and Flint
XVIII.— Large Stones laying down 8' long x 3' x 1'
XIX.— Remains of Large Pot 8" diam in a Stone face downwards.
XX.— Part of Bronze Bracelet. Hut circle 76 above high Water.

FIG. 35 — Porth Dafarch: Stanley's excavations. (Reproduced from *Archaeological Journal* by kind permission of the Editor.)

later huts was elucidated, but nothing more was learnt about the Bronze Age burials.[27]

There is a possibility that Porth Dafarch I may have covered a burial of Beaker date as well as later cremation urns. A stone cist, apparently of appropriate size, was found somewhere beneath the cairn and though nothing was found in it since it appeared to have been previously rifled, bones were found nearby.[28] Whether these were unburnt is problematical. Whatever the date of Porth Dafarch I, it is certain the Porth Dafarch II was built to cover a burial of the later Beaker period.

The details of this second mound are obscure because it had been disturbed at least twice: once when Romano-British huts and enclosure walls were built over it, and again when three extended inhumations, probably Early Mediaeval in date, were inserted in the top. The original burial, presumably central, seems to have been fairly complex. It was covered by a mound of sand, perhaps incorporating some settings of stones; the size is not given, but it must have been quite large.

The cist, 3ft. 6ins. × 2ft. 6ins. internally, was built of four large stones with smaller ones closing all gaps. It was covered by a large capstone (5ft. 4ins. × 4ft.) on which lay a heap of white quartz pebbles.[29] A large fallen stone (8ft. × 3ft.) was found just beyond the southern end of the cist. It is conceivable that originally this may have stood upright as a marker for the grave, like the one at the foot of the remarkable Beaker grave on Cairnpapple Hill, West Lothian.[30] Nearer home it could be compared to the large fallen stone found close to the cist at Tŷ'n y Pwll, Llanddyfnan.[31] The small-scale plan published by Stanley shows two arcs of stones surrounding the end of the cist.[32] It is not clear whether or not they belong to the Bronze Age level but, if they do, they hint at some sort of pattern of stones laid out beneath the mound like the settings of boulders found at Aberffraw encircling a D-shaped grave which probably belongs to the same period.[33]

The cist contained the crouched skeleton of a young woman, together with the broken remains of two Beakers.[34] One of these is reasonably complete and may have been intact when originally deposited, but the other is represented by only three sherds (Fig. 34, Nos. 3-4). The presence of two Beakers in one grave is unusual, but instances, such as the Cairn-

---

[27] *Arch. Camb.*, 1940, 65-74.
[28] W. O. Stanley, *loc. cit.*
[29] White quartz pebbles are frequently found in significant positions with prehistoric burials of most periods (for instance, they were much used in Neolithic Passage Graves). In some parts of Wales the association continues to the present day. *See* A. D. Rees, BBCS, VIII, 1935, 87-90.
[30] S. Piggott, PSAS, LXXXII, 1947-8, 88-92.
[31] *See* below, p. 99.
[32] *Arch. J.*, XXXIII, 1876, Pls. between pp. 128 and 129, and facing p. 139. (*See* Fig. 35).
[33] *See below*, p. 101.
[34] *Arch. J.*, XXXIII, 1876, 139 is ambiguous. It is implied that the body was in the cist but it is also stated that the cist was empty. A probable explanation is that the cist was not *filled* with sand or gravel.

papple grave mentioned above, could be brought forward, though it is normal for both pots to be complete.[35] Perhaps this point should not be over-stressed here in view of the rather haphazard nature of the excavation. There were no other grave goods, but two worked flints were found in the body of the mound.[36] One is a large flake knife (Fig. 34, No. 3a). As at Merddyn Gwyn, measurements of the skull show a closer similarity to the earlier Neolithic population than to the Beaker group.[37]

The reconstructed Beaker is elaborately decorated with a combination of coarse comb stamps and finger-nail impressions.[38] The scheme consists of a series of horizontal bands of filled and unfilled chevrons, with a panel of deeper chevrons at the base. The waist is emphasised by a double row of deeper finger-nail impressions as on the Pant y Saer and Merddyn Gwyn Beakers. The combination of comb stamp and finger-nail decoration can be found on another Long Necked Beaker from Bishops Canning, Wiltshire, which also has the horizontal bands of weak chevrons.[39] This Wiltshire comparison emphasises the southern English background to the later Welsh Beakers as a whole, and to this one in particular, on which the lowest panel of decoration is so reminiscent of the pendant triangles which are characteristic of Long Necked Beakers in the south. The use of reserved pattern and the very deep chevron at the bottom are, however, features popular in south Wales, which may be the immediate origin of the people burying their dead at Porth Dafarch.[40]

The second Beaker can be easily distinguished from the first by its different colour and paste, even though it has been decorated by much the same sort of comb impressions.

The discovery of a small undecorated Collared urn not far from the primary cist suggests that the barrow was reused at the time when Porth Dafarch III and possibly I were being built. A number of cremation burials associated with Collared urns and small accessory vessels were found in these two barrows. They will be described more fully in a later chapter.

Although in southern Britain Beaker burials are usually found beneath a mound, this is not essential; in Scotland it is, in fact, rare. In Anglesey there is one example of such an unmarked cist grave: that found in the 1860s at Rhosbeirio near Llanfechell (NGR SH/392914).[41] However, it must be remembered that the site was in a farmyard and the barrow might well have been removed previously. The cist was dug into the ground, 3ft. 6ins. square and covered by a large capstone. Four large slabs formed the walls,

---

[35] *Loc. cit.*, 89. Also Penarth, Caerns. (Griffiths, PPS, XXIII, 1957, 66), original report. *Arch. Camb.*, 1910, 399-402.
[36] *Arch. J.*, XXXIII, 1876, Pl. opp. p. 140.
[37] Subsequent report by Sir Arthur Keith, *Arch. Camb.*, 1909, 329.
[38] This is a new reconstruction made from surviving sherds in the British Museum.
[39] *Devizes Museum Catalogue*, 95, no. 122.
[40] W. F. Grimes, *Arch. Camb.*, 1961, 30-70 (especially 52-6).
[41] W. O. Stanley and Albert Way, *Arch. Camb.*, 1868, 271-2.

and there was a stone on the floor. On this lay a crouched skeleton with the Beaker near the head.

Unfortunately the pot has been lost, but a photograph from which Stanley's engraving was taken survives[42] (Fig. 34, No. 5). This shows the proportions well, but there is some doubt about its actual size. If it was 8ins. tall, as Stanley says, the diameter of the mouth must have been about 5ins., not 3⅝ins., which is the measurement that he gives. If he was right about the diameter it can only have been 6ins. high. Comparison with other pots suggests that the former measurements are the more likely, though both would be conceivable.

The decoration is carried out entirely by notched comb impressions, and the general scheme is very similar to that on a Beaker from Llanharry, Glamorgan, which has the same sinuous profile and slightly inturned rim.[43] The neck is rather shorter on this type than on the standard south Welsh Long Necked Beaker, and it is possible that their ancestry is closer to the early Short Necked Beakers, of which there are some good examples on the south Welsh coast.[44] In the absence of other grave goods one cannot confidently say that the Rhosbeirio burial is earlier than the others in Anglesey; this is a possibility.

Another Beaker which must be mentioned here is the one said to have been found in the barrow called Bedd Branwen at Llanbabo (NGR SH/362849). The original account of the opening of this mound in 1813 refers to the discovery of a virtually complete Collared urn containing burnt bone, but there is no mention of any other sherds nor of any unburnt bone.[45] In 1821 this urn was in the possession of a man living in Chester; in 1834 it was presented to the British Museum. When W. O. Stanley and Albert Way were preparing their important paper on Bronze Age burials in Anglesey, published in 1868, they had the urn examined and found the sherds of a Beaker and part of an unburnt skull inside; the sherds were wrapped in a piece of paper which said that they were part of Branwen's urn.[46]

It has been assumed since then that Bedd Branwen was a Beaker barrow, reused at a later period, and that both the primary and secondary burials had been disturbed in 1813. However, recent large-scale excavation of the site failed to produce any evidence for a Beaker burial and, moreover, it was clear that the entire barrow had been built at a date around 1,400 B.C., contemporary with the urn burial.[47] One must conclude, therefore, that the association of the Beaker and the urn was a mistake for which the chequered history of the urn between 1813 and 1834 gave ample opportunity.

[42] In the Penrhos Papers, UCNW Library, MS. 860.
[43] W. F. Grimes, *Prehistory of Wales*, NMW Catalogue, 1951, 261, fig. 73, no. 11.
[44] Map. W. E. Griffiths, PPS XXIII, 1957, 81.
[45] Richard Colt Hoare, *Cambro-Briton* II, 1820, 71.
[46] *Arch. Camb.*, 1868, 233-40.
[47] F. M. Lynch, TAAS, 1966, 1-31. Interim report.

Luckily the Beaker sherds have not been thoroughly cleaned and still retain a good deal of mud on the impressed surface. This mud is a peculiar yellow colour, similar to that found in the Alaw valley in the vicinity of Bedd Branwen. It is possible, therefore, that the Beaker did originally come from that neighbourhood and was automatically associated with the name Branwen, as were all antiquities found in the valley, especially in the early nineteenth century when the Celtic revival prompted renewed interest in the site.[48] It has been decided, therefore, to rename this Beaker " Llanbabo ", and to include it in this discussion of Anglesey Beakers, though in the absence of a true archaeological context it cannot add much to our knowledge.

It is an elaborately decorated Long Necked Beaker, probably rather smaller than average (Fig. 34, No. 2). It is decorated entirely with notched impressions made with a fine comb. The decoration is arranged in panels in which the saltire cross, left plain, is the main motif. This technique is reminiscent of the " Bar Chevron " Beakers of South Wales, but this pattern is more elaborate than is usual in that style.[49]

The presence of Beaker sherds in the chambers of megalithic tombs has already been mentioned. The situation at Pant y Saer (ANG 13), however, is not strictly comparable to that in other tombs, but, at the same time, it is not a typical Beaker single-grave burial. Unfortunately, we are dependent for most of the relevant information on an account of 1875 in which the significance of all that was found was not fully understood.[50]

The main outline, however, is not in doubt. Lying diagonally across the chamber, and dug into the earlier deposits, was a rectangular stone cist covered by a large capstone (6ft. × 2ft. 3ins.). The cist was long and narrow (4ft. 4ins. × 1ft. 2ins.), rounded at the north-west end. The walls appear to have been dry built, and on the floor was a thick bed of shingle. The rounded end and the use of dry walling are unusual, but they reappear in another Anglesey grave, Tŷ'n y Pwll, to be discussed below.

Inside the cist were the remains of two skeletons which, to judge by the plan given, were lying in some disorder. They had been crushed by the settlement and collapse of some of the walling, and may have been disturbed by burrowing animals; even so, it seems impossible to believe that two bodies had been laid out there in the normal Beaker way, especially considering the narrowness of the cist. To find two bodies in the same grave is itself unusual, and one is forced to admit that the burial rite used here must owe a good deal to the earlier Neolithic tradition of collective burial

[48] For instance, beads found somewhere on the bank of the Alaw have been uncomprom-isingly labelled " Princess Branwen's Beads " though there is nothing to connect them with the barrow.
[49] Part of a very similar one was found at Penarth, Caerns. (W. E. Griffiths, PPS, XXIII, 1957, 65, fig. 4.1) and another with the same general scheme comes from Dalkey Island (G. D. Liversage, PRIA, 66, C, 1968, 209, fig. 11.179).
[50] Williams and Prichard, *Arch. Camb.*, 1875, 341-8. *Résumé in* W. L. Scott, *Arch. Camb.*, 1933, 187-91.

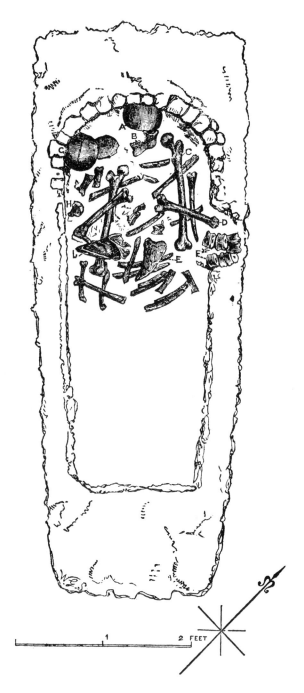

PANT Y SAER CROMLECH.

A. Flattened Skull.
B. Lower Jaw.
C. Femur.
D. Humerus.

E, F. Ribs, Vertebræ, etc.
G. Skull.
H. Fragment of Os Pubis.
L. Shoulder Blade.

FIG. 36 — Pant y Saer: Wynn Williams's plan of the cist (Reproduced from *Archaeologia Cambrensis* by kind permission of the Editor.)

and the possible use of ossuaries.[51] This link is, of course, strongly under-lined by the reuse of a megalithic chamber in the first place.

The dating of these burials to the Beaker period is not proved beyond all doubt. There was no mention of pottery or other grave goods in the 1875 report, but in 1933, when the chamber was re-excavated, a quantity of sherds from a Long Necked Beaker were found in the upper 6ins. of the deposit, in an area which had not been touched by the earlier excavators.[52] Whether the Beaker could have been removed from the cist at some time previous to 1875 is perhaps doubtful, but it is not inconceivable that this pot had been placed on the ledge where it was found by the people who inserted the cist. A small nodule of iron pyrites, probably used as a strike-a-light was found amongst the material thrown back after 1875. It is quite likely that this came from the cist as such nodules are often found with Early Bronze Age burials.[53]

The Beaker is not quite complete; the sherds represent most of the neck and some of the base of a LongNeckedBeaker of rather smaller than average size (Fig. 34, No. 1). Since the body does not survive it is possible that the neck is, proportionately, not very long and that, like the Rhosbeirio one, it may be more closely related to the earlier Short Necked Beakers than, for instance, the "Bar Chevron" ones. The decoration is made chiefly by comb impressions, but there is a row of deep finger-nail marks around the waist similar to those on the Merddyn Gwyn Beaker. The pattern is a complex one in which a band of filled hexagons forms the main motif. This design is unusual but can be compared to that of the handled Beaker from Cwm Du, Breconshire.[54] Both the hexagon motif and the handle are features of northern Beakers.[55]

Reference has already been made to the fact that objects, such as V-bored buttons and battle-axes, often associated with Long Necked Beakers, are sometimes found in graves without any pottery. It would seem that by the time these objects became fashionable the habit of placing pots in the grave was dying out, although the inhumation rite practised by the Beaker people still survived. In Anglesey there are two graves which almost certainly belong to this horizon, although there are, in fact, no distinctive grave goods. There are, however, structural peculiarities which, together with the crouched inhumation rite, link them with the other Beaker burials in the island.

The first to be described is that at Tŷn y Pwll, Llanddyfnan (SH/509784). The barrow is the easternmost one of a group of five running

---

[51] Several of the Yorkshire barrows excavated by Canon Greenwell (*British Barrows* 1877) contained more than one burial and more careful excavation suggests that bodies may have been added to existing burials (N. Thomas, *Trans. Birmingham Archaeol. Soc.*, LXXXII, 1967, 58-76. Such a practice might explain the situation at Pant y Saer.
[52] W. L. Scott, *op. cit.*, 205.
[53] W. L. Scott, *op. cit.*, 218-9, fig. 20.e. W. Greenwell, *British Barrows*, 1877, 41, fig. 31 illustrates one together with a flint rod.
[54] W. F. Grimes, *Prehistory of Wales*, NMW Catalogue, 1951, 261, fig. 73, no. 6.
[55] Outline scheme: D. L. Clarke, *Palaeohistoria*, XII, 1966, 179-98.

east-west across the summit of a rocky ridge.[56] It stands next to a large
barrow which contained a number of rich burials dating from about 1,500
B.C. Both these mounds were excavated in 1908 by Mr. E. Neil Baynes
when they were threatened with destruction by the farmer.[57]

The barrow was something over 60ft. in diameter and about 4ft. high.
Although it had been ploughed and stones had been removed from the east
and south sides, no secondary burials had ever been disturbed and none
were found in the excavation. The mound appears to have been built of a
mixture of soil, gravel and stones, presumably heaped up without any
design or elaboration. Just west of the centre a large pit had been dug
through the old ground surface to a depth of about 3ft. 9ins. Inside this,
a complex stone structure had been built containing a crouched inhumation
of an adult man. Behind his head was a small serrated flint flake. The sides
had been used as a knife and the bulbar end as a strike-a-light. Like the
other Bronze Age inhumation burials from Anglesey, this man has a
dolichocephalic skull suggesting that his ancestry lay amongst the earlier
Neolithic population.

The structure in which he was buried was built in two stages. An area
2ft. 3ins square was surrounded on three sides by a wall of small stones
set in clay about 12ins. wide and 8ins. high. The fourth side seems to
have been closed by small upright stones. The body had been placed inside,
lying on his left side, with his head resting against the south-eastern wall
and his wrists lying on top of the south-western one. The second stage of
building involved the addition of a mass of stone to the south-eastern side
of the cist, forming a solid triangular area 4ft. 3ins. by 2ft. 6ins. long.
The south-western and north-eastern walls of the cist were then raised
10ins. (covering the man's wrists) and continued around the apex of the
triangle to make a D-shaped structure which was then covered by a
rectangular capstone 5ft. 2ins. by 3ft. 5ins. by 8ins. Certain stains on the
bones and a stalagmitic deposit from the limestone capstone suggested
that the body might have been covered with leather or skins.[58] The grave-
pit had been back-filled with gravel above the capstone, which was some
14ins. below the old ground level.

The report makes brief mention of another large slab of limestone
(approximately 5ft. by 3ft. by 8ins.) standing on its longer side just to the
north of the cist. Although this is not stated, it presumably stood on the
old ground surface and may have been intended to act as a marker to the
grave (although one would have expected it to have stood at the end

[56] The three other barrows were recognised by Miss Sidney Lloyd and Mr. W. J. Hemp,
    Arch. Camb., 1941, 97-8.
[57] Excavation report on both barrows: Arch. Camb., 1909, 312-32 (Tŷ'n y Pwll, pp. 325-32).
    Both barrows have been variously referred to as Tŷ'n y Pwll I and II or as Llanddyfnan I
    and II. In order to avoid this confusion and because the earlier barrow always had to be
    called II, it has been decided to use the farm name (Tŷ'n y Pwll) for the Beaker Barrow
    and the parish name (Llanddyfnan) for the later one.
[58] Pieces of this deposit are in the National Museum of Wales (42. 395/8).

rather than the side of the cist). It can be compared to the fallen slab at the foot of the Beaker cist at Porth Dafarch, Holyhead.

The second D-shaped grave is at Trwyn Du, Aberffraw, under a small barrow excavated in 1956 by Mr. C. H. Houlder (NGR SH/352679).[59] Since it is set in an area of sandy soil it is not surprising that the body did not survive, for unburnt bone is quickly dissolved away in such acid conditions.

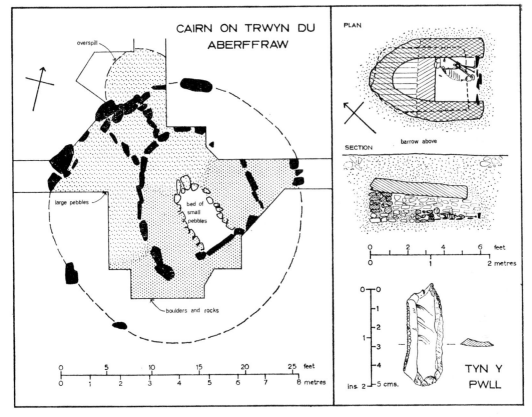

FIG. 37—Plan of cairn at Trwyn Du, Aberffraw (after C. H. Houlder). Tŷ'n y Pwll: plan and section of central grave (after E. N. Baynes), and worked flint flake from the grave.

The barrow was built of stone: boulders and rock in the south-eastern part, and large water-rolled pebbles in the north-western half. It was very small, only 25ft. in diameter, but covered an elaborate arrangement of stones carefully set into the underlying sand. These stones, which were about 2ft. long, formed a kerb to the cairn itself, and an inner D-shaped enclosure linked to the kerb by two, or possibly three, radial lines. The enclosure surrounded a grave 6ft. long and 3ft. wide which was partly filled with small pebbles. These pebbles may originally have covered the body.

[59] Interim report, PPS, XXIII, 1957, 228-9.

These barrows, characterised by D or boat-shaped graves and inhumations without pottery, form part of a small group of such burials found in various parts of England and Wales. The dating cannot be precise because of the frequent absence of pottery, but one of these burials, that at ʒutton 268, Llandow, Glamorgan, was associated with a Bell Beaker and tanged arrowheads.[60] This grave was set in a very large rock-cut pit, the contracted skeleton surrounded by low stones marking out a boat-shaped enclosure, narrower than, but otherwise generally similar to, that at Tŷn y Pwll.

Two elongated D-shaped pits comparable in size to the Aberffraw grave were found beneath a barrow, Bedd Emlyn, at Clocaenog, Denbighshire.[61] One of these is thought to have held the body in some sort of coffin, and the other perhaps a bier. Both of them had been roughly filled with stones thrown in around the wooden containers. The only direct evidence of date was a flint flake like that from Tŷn y Pwll, but it was clear that the pits were earlier than an Enlarged Food Vessel and cremation burials later inserted into the barrow.

A third example of this type of grave in Wales is the very complex monument at Twyn Bryn Glas, Cwm Cadlan, Breconshire.[62] The central feature is a boat-shaped structure with dry-built walls like the cist at Tŷn y Pwll, but without any capstone. Around this were other D-shaped walls and settings of stones reminiscent of those beneath the cairn at Aberffraw. The date of erection is obscure, since the excavator suggested that the structure had been altered on more than one occasion. The central area did, however, produce sherds from a handled Beaker, a Collared urn and an accessory cup, which suggests a date roughly comparable to that of the others.

The origin and significance of this particular type of burial cannot be clearly known. The shape of the grave may suggest a boat-symbolism in which the spirits of the dead are carried by water from this world to the next. This explanation may well lie behind the series of burials actually placed in dug-out canoes, but it cannot be brought forward so confidently to explain the D-shaped graves in which the connection with boats is very tenuous. Concentric stone settings rather like those at Aberffraw, Twyn Bryn Glas and, possibly, Porth Dafarch II can be found beneath the mounds of certain Passage Graves in Ireland, but since no direct link can be shown the similarity may not be significant.[63]

These graves are widely scattered in space and time, therefore they are unlikely to represent the burials of any particular cultural or family group. It is possible that they might belong to men of a special status in society, but this we can never know. All that can be said is that they seem to be

[60] C. F. Fox, *Arch.*, LXXXIX, 1943, 89-126. The Bell Beaker from this grave is very similar in shape and decoration to some sherds from Newborough Warren (Fig. 33, no. 12 in particular).
[61] H. N. Savory, *Trans. Denbighshire Historical Soc.*, X, 1961, 7-22.
[62] D. Webley, BBCS, XIX, 1960-2, 56-71.
[63] The best example is Townley Hall II, Co. Meath. G. Eogan, JRSAI, XCIII, 1963, 37-81.

the forerunners of the rather more numerous barrows of the later phase of the Bronze Age, which cover carefully built structures of stone or wood.

The small badly ruined cairn on the headland, Mynydd Bach, just north of Barclodiad y Gawres (NGR SH/328708), may also have covered a burial of the Beaker period, although the evidence is extremely tenuous.[64] The cairn had a diameter of 40ft. In the centre was a large grave, 5ft. by 3ft., formed of seven low uprights, open to the north-west. This grave had been rifled in the past, and when the site was excavated in 1953 nothing was found except a single sherd which, from its colour and paste, might have come from a Beaker. This identification is supported by the two facts that no scraps of burnt bone were found, and that the grave was large enough to have contained an inhumation.

The number of stray finds which can be ascribed specifically to the Beaker people is not large. The paucity of barbed and tanged arrowheads has already been mentioned; other pieces of archers' equipment, such as wrist guards, are completely absent. Apart from the dagger in the grave at Merddyn Gwyn and perhaps the awl at Castell Bryn Gwyn, the early metal objects from the island are not certainly connected with the Beaker people, although it was clearly at this time that metal objects were first known in the island.

In the south of England graves containing rivetted daggers, like the Merddyn Gwyn one, often contain a stone battle-axe as well. Although none of the Anglesey Beaker graves contains one, two have been found by chance in the north-western corner of the island, at Tŷ Mawr, Holyhead, and Treiorwerth, Bodedern.[65]

These weapons, possibly more prestigious than effective, are part of the influx of new ideas from Central Germany which entered Britain in the wake of the first Beaker immigrants at a date around 1,700 B.C. They seem to have been fashionable for about three hundred years, during which period certain variations in shape occur.[66] The type associated with the Long Necked Beakers is the simplest, with rounded butt, an unexpanded blade and the hole, drilled from both sides (hour-glass perforation), set in the widest part. Later battle-axes are more elaborate in shape, with expanded blades and wide, semi-circular butts. The average length is about six inches and it is characteristic of battle-axes that they are neatly made and have the surfaces ground or polished.

Like the Neolithic working axes, battle-axes and the rougher axe-hammers, which were probably tools, were made at commercial centres.[67] Most of the earlier factories were out of production by this time (for instance, no battle-axes made from Graig Lwyd stone have been found), but some of the Cornish ones, such as the very prolific Group I, may have

---

[64] T. G. E. Powell and G. E. Daniel, *Barclodiad y Gawres*, 1956, Appendix C, 71.
[65] In the AAS Collection and the National Museum of Wales respectively.
[66] For a recent study of these implements *see* F. E. S. Roe, PPS, XXXII, 1966, 199-245.
[67] These later factories are included in the discussion *in* PPS, XXVIII, 1962, 209-66.

continued on a small scale. While some died, others prospered; for example,
the Preselau factory in Pembrokeshire (Group XIII), which produced very
few Neolithic axes, greatly increased its output at this time, perhaps because
the prestige of this stone had been enhanced by its use at Stonehenge.
Other factories start up for the first time and seem to have specialised in
battle-axes and axe-hammers. The best known of these is Cwm Mawr on
the Shropshire/Montgomeryshire border (Group XII), and another is
probably sited on the Whin Sill in the Teesdale/Hadrians Wall area (Group
XVIII).[68] Both early and late types of battle-axes were produced at these
factories, which may consequently be dated from about 1,700 to 1,400 B.C.

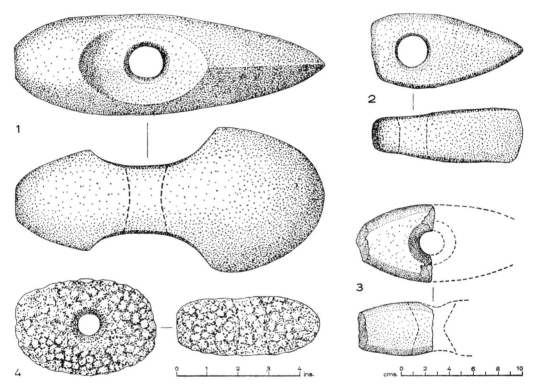

Fig. 38 — Battle-axes from Anglesey: 1, Maen Gwyn, Coedana; 2, Treiorwerth,
Bodedern; 3, Tŷ Mawr, Holyhead; 4, ?macehead, Porth Dafarch, Holyhead.

Both the early battle-axes from Anglesey are small. The one from
Treiorwerth, found recently in digging a water main near the house, is
odd in that the blade is thicker than the butt; otherwise the most interesting
thing about it is that it is almost certainly a product of the factory, or
factories, working the Whin Sill in the north of England. The one from
Tŷ Mawr, a chance find from Stanley's excavations, might well have been

[68] Cwm Mawr: Shotton, Chitty and Seaby, **PPS**, XVII, 1951, 159-67.

more interesting; it is neatly shaped and polished, but unfortunately it is broken and the blade does not survive. It is made from a quartzite grit, probably local. A chip of similar polished rock which had come from a battle-axe broken before 1,400 B.C. was found in the make-up of the mound at Bedd Branwen.

The oval stone found during W. O. Stanley's excavations at circular huts near Pen y Bonc, Holyhead,[69] is only very tentatively included amongst this group of Bronze Age stone implements. It is made from a dark-grey dolerite, now badly weathered. Its shape was unlike the other Romano-British hammers found by Stanley; it may possibly have been some sort of "macehead" or ceremonial stone belonging to an earlier settlement at the site. The area had certainly been inhabited at this period for there was a barrow close by.

In Anglesey the only example of a later battle-axe is that from Coedana, near Llannerch-y-medd.[70] This was found at Maen Gwyn with another smaller one, now lost.[71] It is very elegantly shaped and beautifully made, and must certainly be considered a prestige weapon rather than a tool, although it is very much larger than the normal battle-axe. The shape, with deep blade and conical butt, is typical of a group of weapons found most frequently in Scotland and the north of Ireland, although the proportions here are unusually elongated.[72] This group often has decoration in the form of concentric grooves outlining the central portion. They have occasionally been found with Cordoned urns which suggests a date around 1,500 - 1,400 B.C.[73] This type of pot, characteristic of Scotland and Ireland, has been found in Anglesey, at Llanddyfnan and Treiorwerth, so the discovery of this northern type of battle-axe is not surprising.

The axe-hammers are a much cruder type of implement, virtually changeless and never found in graves. Consequently it is impossible to date them closely beyond saying that they belong to the Bronze Age and must be broadly contemporary with the battle-axes, since they are much the same shape and are frequently made from the same stone. The blade is never very sharp; on the other hand, the butt is fairly well adapted for use as a hammer and especially heavy stones, such as picrite, are popular. Their precise use is not known. Some examples are worn along one side, suggesting that they might have been used as ploughshares, though the hypothesis has never been convincingly demonstrated.

Twelve or thirteen of these implements have been found in Anglesey, but none has any archaeological context. Three of them are unprovenanced within the island;[74] the records of two others, from Llannerch-y-medd and

[69] *Arch. J.*, XXVI, 1869, 321 and fig. 17. Part of another which was apparently similar was found at Ty Mawr.
[70] Now in the National Museum of Wales.
[71] TAAS, 1931, 143.
[72] PPS, XXXII, 1966, 212. Scotsburn and Crichie groups (Bann type in older terminology).
[73] *E.g.* Laheen, Co. Donegal, JRSAI, XCVII, 1967, 39-44.
[74] One was in the Geological Museum. London, in 1927; the other two were in Bangor Museum but one appears to have been lost.

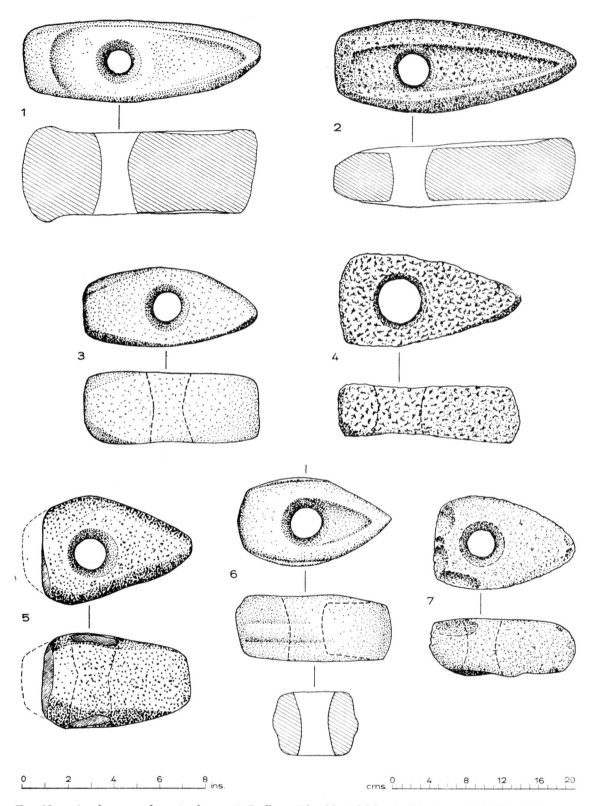

Fig. 39 — Axe-hammers from Anglesey: 1, Bodlew, Llanddaniel-fab; 2, 'Anglesey'; 3, Plas Cadnant, Llandysilio; 4, Llwydiarth Esgob, Llandyfrydog; 5, Llanfaethlu; 6, Bodowyr, Bodedern; 7, Plas Newydd, Rhos-y-bol.

from Cefn-mawr, Newborough, are rather doubtful;[75] the distribution of the others has been shown on Map 4, where it can be seen that they are scattered evenly across the island without any notable concentrations.

It is debatable whether the long, narrow axe-hammers, such as the one from Bodlew and the two unprovenanced ones,[76] should not be considered in the same class as battle-axes, for they are simply larger versions of the plain Beaker battle-axe, and it must be admitted that the size distinction is a purely arbitrary one. They are normally as carefully made and the occasional dishing, or hollowing, of the top and bottom surfaces on both types is an additional link. The Bodlew example is further distinguished by having a slightly expanded butt, which is characteristic of the rather more developed series of battle-axes. The Bodlew type is fairly rare; there is another plain axe-hammer from near Trefriw Caernarvonshire, made of the same rather pleasant greenish stone, but it has not got the expanded butt.[77] The two unprovenanced ones belong to a rather larger group represented by others almost identical from Lampeter, Cardiganshire, and the Corwen area of Merioneth.[78]

The remainder are clearly tools, although the small one from Bodedern is quite elaborately shaped. The ribs can scarcely have strengthened the stone and look very much as if they were copied from a model in some other material, perhaps metal, though such a metal prototype has never been found. Two of these axe-hammers are factory products: the one from Llwydiarth Esgob is from Cwm Mawr, Shropshire (Group XII); and the one found at Llanfaethlu is made from Preselau stone (Group XIII).[79] This latter has been damaged in the recent past and the butt flattened and polished, perhaps by use as a doorstop. The one from Rhos-y-bol, which is in private hands, has not been sectioned, but its triangular outline is rather suggestive of a factory product, for this shape would seem to be common among them.[80]

It is virtually impossible to suggest a date within the Bronze Age for these tools, but the fact that none of them has an expanded blade means that they may well belong to the earlier phase, closer to 1,700 than 1,400 B.C.

[75] I am grateful to Miss L. F. Chitty for these references: one was known from a rough sketch made by Mr. W. J. Hemp; the Llannerch-y-medd one was seen by her in the J. E. Griffiths Collection in Bangor Museum, but it is not there now and is not recorded in the accessions book. Two other axe hammers, the ones from Lledwigan and the Malltraeth area, have also been mislaid.

[76] the one in London is described in *Arch. Camb.*, 1928, 226. The exact provenance of the Bodlew axe hammer is rather doubtful. It appears in the RCAM list in 1937 as from Tre'r Dryw Bach, Llanidan, and in the 1960 list of corrections and additions it appears twice, as from Llanidan and as from Bodlew, Llanddaniel-fab. Mr. Awyne Jones of Bryn-siencyn, the present owner, claims that the second provenance is the correct one and I have followed him in this.

[77] RCAM. *Caernarvonshire I*, 1956, lxi, fig. 14.3.

[78] BBCS, XV, 1952-4, 158 and Pl. 1 and *Arch. Camb.*, 1932, 408.

[79] Llanfaethlu one previously published: *Arch. Camb.*, 1935, 277, fig. 5.

[80] I am grateful to Mr. Glyndwr Thomas of Llanddeusant for information about this axe-hammer and to Miss Jones, Rhos-y-bol, for allowing me to draw it.

The appearance in Anglesey of people who made Beakers and followed the practice of single burial marks not only a clear horizon in the archaeological record, but also a significant phase in the history of the island. It is possible that by the time they reached Anglesey the impact and strangeness of these European invaders may have been considerably reduced by years of settlement in Britain, but they may still have been the initiators of several changes. When they first arrived, megalithic tombs were still in use and Bryn Celli Ddu had only recently been built, yet their new burial traditions did in part prevail. Although their system of single burial was soon submerged by a variant of the older collective tradition, the round barrow and the practice of burying personal possessions with the dead survived.

The most far-reaching change for which, on present evidence, the Beaker people were responsible was the introduction of metal tools and weapons to the island. There is no evidence that they manufactured these here (though they might have been the first to recognise the potentialities of the local copper ores) and only a minority of the group were rich enough to possess such objects, but with their appearance the stage is set for the part Anglesey was to play as a vital link in the trade routes between Ireland and Britain throughout the ensuing Bronze Age.

However, before the subject of Bronze Age trade is discussed, other burials should be described to show how the older traditions and cultural groupings re-emerge in a new form after this brief period of change.

IV

DEATH IN THE BRONZE AGE

THE term " Bronze Age " reflects a technological division of history which could well not correspond to any truly relevant change in the life and attitudes of contemporary people, but in fact there does seem to be a genuinely different atmosphere about this period of history, at least in the first few centuries. In contrast to the Neolithic farming communities, closely knit and organised for co-operative effort, the Bronze Age people, buried alone with their display of personal wealth and military equipment, seem individualistic and aggressive. This contrast is first seen with the Beaker-making immigrants discussed in the last chapter, and perhaps reaches its peak in the latter part of the Early Bronze Age when a class of artistocratic and war-like chieftains has clearly emerged to partake in a flourishing international trade in luxury articles.

The peasant values of the third millenium, however, were never quite eclipsed, and the history of the later part of the Bronze Age sees the reappearance of small and apparently peaceful farming communities not greatly different from their Neolithic predecessors. Meanwhile, in the north and west of these lands the initial break with the family-orientated traditions of the Neolithic had been far less sharp than in the south.

Our knowledge of man's varied activities during this period is unfortunately uneven and disconnected. There are several strands involved : graves and burial ritual; everyday life on the settlements; local industries and the development of a bronze technology with its attendant growth in trade; but it is seldom possible to combine all these factors into a single historical narrative.

For the earlier part of the period, graves furnish a good deal of information about the personal possessions of richer members of society; these luxury articles illuminate a vast nexus of trade extending throughout Europe to the Mediterranean. This picture is supplemented by the finds of bronze hoards and of moulds which record the gradual development of native technology. Unfortunately, however, the basic economy on which this brilliant superstructure of ornaments and prestigious weapons rested is very inadequately known, for we have no settlement sites which can be dated to this period (c. 1,600 - 1,400 B.C.).

This phase, one of the most brilliant and fascinating in British prehistory, is known as the " Wessex Culture " because our knowledge of it is derived almost entirely from a group of rich graves centred on the Salisbury Plain area.[1] These graves normally contain the body of a single individual surrounded by his, or her, personal possessions, weapons and jewellery. Many of these objects are of gold and very beautifully made, revealing a standard of craftsmanship which is almost incredible at this date. Many of these fine daggers and ornaments can be shown to have close connections with the Continent, whence some may have been imported, along with the raw materials such as amber and gold.

The appearance of these individual graves with all the appurtenances of power and wealth suggest a highly stratified society with warrior chieftains at its head, constituting, since women, too, were wealthy, a dynastic aristocracy. This has given rise to the theory that these leaders were an intrusive group, a band of invaders from the Continent, either from Brittany or Central Europe, who, with their superior weapons, conquered the local population and imposed themselves as overlords.[2] The occasional rich grave in more distant parts of the country could be interpreted as evidence for colonial domination by adventurers from the centre in Wessex.

This "invasion hypothesis", which tends to explain every change in Britain by the advent of new peoples, is now becoming unfashionable and greater stress is being laid on evidence for continuity.[3] This evidence is quite considerable. It can be pointed out that the individual graves of warriors first appear, not in 1,600 B.C. (the traditional date for the beginning of the "Wessex Culture"), but with the advent of the makers of Beakers about three hundred years earlier, and that the wealth of Wessex was partly spent in improving the earlier Beaker monuments such as Stonehenge (though that in its turn represented a development of the native Henges), while the rich graves themselves appear under barrows which are part of cemetery groups in which the founder's grave normally dates from the Beaker period.[4]. Moreover, the bulk of the evidence for foreign contact lies in small, expensive objects which are more suggestive of commercial activity than folk movement. Pottery is unfortunately rare in the earliest Wessex graves (as in all late Beaker burials), but where it does occur it belongs to the native British Collared urn series, apart, that is, from the small Aldbourne and Grape cups which may represent an exotic fashion with its roots in Brittany, a phenomenon parallel to the accessory cups which are found in other parts of the country.

In this view the "Wessex Culture" represents not an invasion but the culmination of the new trends introduced by the makers of Beakers once these newcomers had successfully merged with the native Late Neolithic populations; but why this group in Wiltshire, Hampshire and Dorset should suddenly become so rich still remains obscure. This is the period of the

[1] The most comprehensive discussion of this material is in S. Piggott. PPS. IV. 1938. 52-106, but it features to some extent in all books and articles about the Bronze Age.
[2] This theory is argued in Piggott loc. cit.
[3] J. G. D. Clark. Ant. XL. 1966. 172-189.
[4] Or even as secondary burials in such barrows, e.g. Upton Lovell G2.

first widespread use of metal and it is one in which trade, in both raw materials and manufactured goods, would have become essential to many groups. The Wessex chieftains were only one of several such European communities who perhaps benefited from the quickening of economic life at the time;[5] but, unlike eastern Europe, Wessex had no natural resources with which to trade. It has been supposed, therefore, that they gained their wealth by acting as middlemen between Europe and Ireland, selling Irish raw materials and goods to the German industries. However, Europe is known to have had adequate supplies of its own and though Irish objects did reach northern Germany, there are so few of them in Wessex itself that it is scarcely feasible to see this through trade, if it existed, as the basis of the chieftains' wealth.[6] This leaves agriculture as a likely source of prosperity, but our ignorance of contemporary settlements leaves us without definite information about it, though it should not be forgotten that the Salisbury Plain area must have been one of the richest agricultural districts even in Neolithic times and already the centre of many trade routes pioneered by the sellers of stone axes.

It is possible that the pendulum has swung too far in attributing the whole Wessex phenomenon to native enterprise and commercial cunning, for the history of the British East India Company shows how complex and far-reaching the developments of merchant activity can be. But whatever the exact situation in Wessex itself, outside the main spheres of influence, and certainly in Anglesey, there is no need to suggest any invasion. The people who became rich enough to buy exotic objects were clearly members of the native population, however they may have come by their wealth.

This period of prosperity lasted for about two hundred years. After 1,400 B.C. a few imports continue to trickle in,[7] but by and large the population seems to have been thrown back on its own resources. Like its rise, the eclipse of the "Wessex Culture" is largely unexplained, but it would certainly have been difficult to keep open the trans-continental trade routes in the period of seemingly general unrest which follows the brilliant Early Bronze Age societies in Europe.[8]

In the course of these prosperous two hundred years there were several changes in British life, amongst which were the gradual re-emergence of cremation as the universal burial rite and the introduction of the two-valve mould. The former change emphasises the reassertion of native Late Neolithic traditions, while the industrial innovations are one of the results of foreign contacts. These two criteria, cremation burial and a new type of dagger made in the double mould, are important archaeologically

[5] S. Piggott. *Ancient Europe.* 1965. 113-160.
[6] Wessex metal analysis: D. Britton and E. E. Richards, *Archaeometry* IV, 1961. 39-52. Irish trade: J. J. Butler. *Palaeohistoria* IX. 1963. (monograph) *passim.*
[7] e.g. the Pelynt dagger and Topsham double axe, dated c. 1250-1200 in the Aegean. PPS. XVIII. 1952. 237-8.
[8] S. Piggott. *Ancient Europe.* 1965. 145, 157-60.

because they can be used to divide the material into two groups, Wessex I and II, which have a chronological significance.[9]

The inhumation graves of Wessex I, exemplified by the famous burial under the Bush Barrow, Wiltshire, are especially rich in gold and are characterised by a wide flat dagger attached to its haft by a large number of rivets (Bush Barrow daggers). These earlier graves are virtually restricted to the area of Wessex itself. In the second half of the period, after 1,500 B.C., the graves contain cremation burials with fewer gold objects but with rather finer and more effective daggers having a thick midrib and a sinuous, ogival outline (Camerton-Snowhill daggers). They also contain a number of pins and other ornaments imported from Central Europe, or alternatively native-made bone copies of these imports. A good deal of amber from the Baltic was imported in both phases, and Egyptian faience appears towards the end of the period. This artificial material, a type of blue glass, is the subject of some controveresy at the moment. It was originally believed that it must all have been imported from the Middle East,[10] but there is now a possibility that some of it may have been manufactured in this country.[11]

A general expansion of prosperity seems to have occurred during Wessex II, for it is to this period that most of the rich graves outside Wessex belong. The situation in Anglesey is fairly clear. All the graves contain cremation burials, and the majority of the grave goods, where they can be closely dated, are related to Wessex II. However, some of the things fashionable in Wessex I in the south obviously percolated northwards rather slowly, for in Anglesey they are found associated with objects belonging to Wessex II (1,500 - 1,400 B.C.).

After this date (1,400 B.C.), which marks the beginning of the Middle Bronze Age, the habit of burying personal possessions with the dead began to die out, and the only way in which later burials can be dated is by studying the development of pottery styles, an uncertain and rather subjective criterion, for, in the present state of research, it looks as if one community could be using several styles at the same time. Settlements dating from this period have been found recently in the south and west of England, and it is hoped that the stratified deposits which they yield may help to solve these problems.[12] At the moment, unfortunately, these results cannot be applied to Wales because the pottery found in Cornwall is a restricted local type and while the Deverel-Rimbury and related pottery

[9] First suggested in A. M. ApSimon. *Univ. London Inst. Archaeol. Ann. Report*. X. 1954. 37-61, and later expanded by R. J. C. Atkinson in an unpublished lecture to the C.B.A. Bronze Age Conference. 1960.
[10] J. F. S. Stone and L. C. Thomas. PPS. XXII. 1956. 37-84.
[11] R. G. Newton and C. Renfrew. *Ant*. XLIV, 1970, 199-206.
[12] Cornwall: Gwithian, A. C. Thomas. *Gwithian: Ten Years' Work 1949-58*. (1958). The situation in the south-west is summarised in A. Fox. *South West England*. (Ancient Peoples and Places) 1964. 86-96. Dorset Shearplace Hill. P. A. Rhatz and A. M. ApSimon. PPS. XXVIII. 1962. 289-328.

is found quite widely in southern England its makers did not spread into North Wales.

The appearance of these small farming settlements which can be linked with simple urn burials, often in pre-existing barrows, gives greater depth to our picture of Bronze Age life. The Deverel-Rimbury settlements, dating from about 1,200 B.C., seem to have been small, compact farmsteads with one or two houses facing onto a yard enclosed by a stockade and surrounded by a few square fields. Droveways through the groups of fields may have led to open grazing on higher ground. The houses excavated have proved to be built of wooden posts, roughly circular in plan, often with a porch over the entrance.[13] In Wales one or two oval huts, rather flimsily built, have come to light beneath barrows, but nowhere have compact settlements with fields been found.[14]

The majority of the Cornish Bronze Age settlements are groups of stone huts having a double wall of uprights with a rubble core, on which the rafters of the conical wooden roof would have rested. There has been a good deal of controversy in the past about the date of these huts, but the excavations at Gwithian, with its well-established pottery sequence, have confirmed the early date. It would seem to follow that this type of farm must have lasted with little change almost to the end of the Roman period, for more elaborate versions of the same huts have produced Romano-British material.[15] North Wales has a great number of stone hut circles which are structurally very similar to the ones in Devon and Cornwall, but so far none of the Welsh examples excavated has produced evidence for a date earlier than the Roman occupation.[16]

Anglesey still contains several groups of these huts and, up to the last century, used to contain a great many more. However, since they are normally clustered in what may almost be termed "villages", it is very unlikely that any of them are early. Moreover, the bulk of the material from them can be firmly dated to the later part of the Roman period.[17] The discovery of a Late Bronze Age hoard and some other early objects in the area of the Tŷ Mawr huts should not, of course, be forgotten, but there is nothing to associate them directly with the settlement, and nothing of similar date was found among the plentiful material from other sites in the island.

Analysis of the pollen in the soil used to build the burial mound, Bedd Branwen, near Llanddeusant, shows that the Bronze Age landscape, in that area at least, was not very different from our own.[18] The barrow had

---

[13] Shearplace Hill. *loc. cit.*

[14] Sant-y-nyll, St. Brides super Ely, Glam. H. N. Savory. *Cardiff Nat. Soc. Trans.* LXXXIX. 1959-60. 9-25.
Llandow, Glam. and others C. F. Fox. *Ant. J.* XXI. 1941. 97-127.

[15] A. Fox. *loc. cit.*

[16] RCAM. *Caernarvonshire.* III. 1964. lxxxvii-cvi summarises the situation in Wales.

[17] Anglesey sites discussed in RCAM *Anglesey.* 1937. lxvii-lxxxiii.

[18] I am grateful to Prof. G. W. Dimbleby of the Institute of Archaeology, London, for carrying out this pollen analysis and for his interpretation of the results.

been built in an open meadow especially rich in buttercups, and there were woods in the vicinity containing oak, hazel and alder. These wood-lands were rather more extensive than today; in isolated parts of the island they would still have been very dense. The amount of cereal pollen is slight but it is enough to show that crops were grown in the district, though, like today, open grazing may have been more important to the economy.

The absence of houses and fields, since we must exclude the stone hut circles, suggests that the houses were made of wood, like the earlier Neolithic ones, and were sited on the lower ground where modern agriculture has destroyed all trace of them. There is a possibility that the Beaker settlement on the coast at Newborough Warren may have continued into the later Bronze Age, but unfortunately there is no evidence for houses, or even hearths. All we have is some charcoal and sherds from a Collared urn found close to Bryn Llwyd.[19]

Throughout the Middle Bronze Age, the period of these farmsteads in the south of England, there is increasing evidence for the growth of a native bronze industry but even though it concentrated on tools rather than weapons, these implements have seldom been found in the settlements and are never placed in graves. It follows that our knowledge of this bronze technology tends to exist in a vacuum. This situation becomes even more apparent in the Late Bronze Age (c. 900 - 500 B.C.) when the number of bronze implements increases enormously whereas our knowledge of the contemporary settlements or graves is particularly sparse.

The archaeology of Anglesey reflects this situation very clearly: for the Early Bronze Age we have a good deal of information from graves, none of which can be given a definite date later than 1,400 B.C.; for the Middle Bronze Age we have a series of rather mundane tools; while in the Late Bronze Age we have some interesting hoards which obviously reflect a revival of trade, but we know nothing of the men who organised it. These later centuries will be dealt with in the next chapter, because all our knowledge of man's activities in the island at that time is connected with trade and industry.

Another strand which must have run alongside all this commercial activity is that of religion and ritual, but an overlap between the two can seldom be demonstrated. Both radio carbon dating and the sophistication of the structure show that the final rebuilding of Stonehenge took place during the "Wessex" period. Presumably other stone circles elsewhere in the country were being erected at the same time.[20] However, excavation of these monuments has always been so unproductive of finds that it is very difficult to give a date to any particular monument, and even more difficult to suggest what their purpose might have been. They are open-air

[19] T. Pape. TAAS. 1928. 21-2.
[20] 1620 B.C. ± 110. (I-2384) *Ant.* XLI. 1967. 63-4. A recent general discussion with parti-cular reference to Wales: W. F. Grimes *in* Foster and Alcock (edd) *Culture and Environment.* 1963. 93-111.

circular sanctuaries and, as such, must be related to the earlier Henge
monuments, several of which, such as the one under Bryn Celli Ddu,
contained settings of stones. It is possible that periodic visits there might
have been dictated by the calendar or the stars, but the significance of
what went on within the circle may never be known to us.

Anglesey contains no surviving stone circles, but two possible sites were
recorded in the Brynsiencyn area. One of these, at Tre'r Dryw Bach
(NGR SH/468673), had been an oval enclosure of smallish stones.[21] Nothing
survives there now and it is impossible to come to any worthwhile
conclusions about it. The other site, not far away at Bryn Gwyn
(NGR SH/463669), is probably genuine, but only two stones survive today.
Rowlands, at the beginning of the eighteenth century, records three large
stones and the stump of a fourth which he said formed the arc of a circle
about 40ft. in diameter.[22] Subsequent observers saw variously more, or
fewer, stones and only serve to complicate the record.[23] In 1939 the Royal
Commissioners claimed that part of a circular ditch and bank could be
seen surrounding the site (which would convert it into a monument
comparable to Avebury), but Prof. W. F. Grimes, who saw the site during
the same period, doubts its existence.[24] Certainly nothing is visible today.
The two surviving stones are extremely large, and if the others had been
comparable the circle would have been a very imposing monument. It is
interesting that it should be sited so close to the possible Henge at Castell
Bryn Gwyn, and if both are genuine it is a further argument for the
continuity of the type.

If the Bryn Gwyn stones were never part of a circle they may have
been simply a pair of Standing Stones or Meini Hirion. These monuments
occur widely in Anglesey, but it is virtually impossible to be certain that
all the examples are ancient.[25] Many of the smaller ones may be cattle
rubbing-stones, some may be mediaeval boundary markers, and some may
even be early mediaeval gravestones, for there are at least two from
Anglesey which have Christian inscriptions.[26] Even the ancient ones may
have been erected for various reasons. Excavation has shown that some
mark the position of cist burials (or, alternatively, that people were buried
at the foot of the stone), while others are related to trackways, especially
across open moorland.[27] Many have produced no evidence for either use or
date.

[21] W. Wynn Williams. *Arch. Camb.* 1871. 34-40.
[22] H. Rowlands. *Mona Antiqua Restaurata.* 2nd ed. 1766. 89-92. Pl. IV.
[23] These are listed and discussed in RCAM. *Anglesey.* 1937. xlvi-xlviii.
[24] RCAM. *loc. cit.* and W. F. Grimes *in* Foster and Alcock (edd.) *Culture and Environment.*
    112-3.
[25] See Map 3. The majority are listed in RCAM. Anglesey and there are useful lists and
    discussions by E. Neil Baynes. *Trans. Hon. Soc. Cymmrod.* 1910-11. 60-78 and by H.
    Senogles. TAAS. 1938. 24-9.
[26] Bodfeddan, Llanfaelog and Llanol, Llanbabo. See RCAM, *Anglesey* 1937. civ.
[27] This has been convincingly demonstrated by C. A. Gresham. *History of Merioneth.*
    Vol. I. 1967. 56-63.

None of the isolated stones in Anglesey has been excavated, but Stanley records a tradition that a cist containing bones, arrowheads and spearheads had been found in digging between the two stones at Plas Meilw, Holyhead (NGR SH/227809).[28] These two stones, identical in shape and size, stand only 11ft. apart. This pairing of stones is rare, but there is an even more remarkable group of three at Llanfechell (NGR SH/364917), and there are two instances of stones placed not more than a few hundred yards apart at Cremlyn, Llanddona (NGR SH/5777), and near Llanfairynghornwy (NGR SH/3390). This last site possibly had three stones originally.[29] It is doubtful if we could ever know the significance of such siting, which seems to be rather more common in Anglesey than elsewhere.[30]

✗ The excavation of the barrow, Bedd Branwen, which has a standing stone at the centre, revealed that this stone has stood for some time as a monument in its own right.[31] At its foot was a large shapeless pit containing nothing but charcoal and three abraded sherds of Beaker which may be considered to give a date for the stone's erection. This date would agree reasonably well with that obtained in Cornwall where pots of this kind have been found at the foot of several stones.[32] Their use and veneration, however, must have continued for several centuries, for a Food Vessel, a style of pottery which developed somewhat later, was found at the foot of a stone at Glynllifon, Caernarvonshire,[33] and the Bedd Branwen one was incorporated into a barrow built about 1,400 B.C. Thus, as a group, they are likely to be broadly contemporary with that other Bronze Age monument, the barrow. In Anglesey their distribution is very similar. The placing of a maen hir at the west end of the barrow cemetery at Llanddyfnan (NGR SH/502786) is perhaps significant, though not all the barrows are visible from it.

Whether the standing stones should be considered burial monuments in the strict sense is perhaps doubtful, for it is clear that the normal Bronze Age grave was marked by a mound or barrow. These mounds were always round in plan, though the size may vary considerably. This consistent use of a circular mound is in line with contemporary Continental practice and is one of the later Beaker innovations which survive the re-emergence of native ideas towards the end of the early Bronze Age.

These round barrows may be simple piles of earth or stones, or may be quite elaborately built structures, incorporating circles of wooden posts or upright stones.[34] A single monument may be built of varied materials, grass

---

[28] *Arch. J.* XXIV. 1867. 238. In *Arch. J.* XXVI. 1869, 310, he mentions the possibility of a stone circle around them as well.
[29] The site of the third (NGR SH/337904) is marked on the OS 1:25,000 map.
[30] There are some paired stones in Flintshire. (Ellis Davies. *Prehistoric and Roman Remains of Flintshire.* 1949. 250-2).
[31] F. M. Lynch. TAAS. 1966. 6-7.
[32] Summary in A. Fox. *South West England* (Ancient Peoples and Places) 1964. 67-8.
[33] *Arch. Camb.* 1875. 381-2 and 1932. 199-201.
[34] For a general discussion of barrows see P. Ashbee. *Bronze Age Round Barrow in Britain.* 1960. *passim.*

turves, specially dug clay, loose earth or stones. It is possible that some of the more elaborate monuments may have been built over quite an extended period of time, with the different parts representing successive stages in a complex ritual. Such a situation is, of course, difficult to prove;[35] but when a monument has simply been enlarged to accommodate later burials, this is normally fairly obvious.

At the beginning of the Bronze Age the burials covered by these barrows were by inhumation, the bodies usually lying crouched in a rectangular grave sunk a few feet below ground. The graves were usually individual, containing only one person accompanied by a few of his or her personal possessions, jewellery, tools or weapons, and a pot probably containing food or drink. This is the classic single-grave burial introduced from the Continent by the makers of Beakers. It was also practised by the people who made Food Vessels, a type of pottery contemporary with the later Beakers. The origin of these Food Vessel people is rather obscure. Their style of pottery has several points of similarity with European Single Grave cultures and with Beakers, but also has connections with the native, Late Neolithic, traditions.[36] These native traditions become even more apparent in the Collared urns, the large storage jars which are the standard burial urn in most parts of the British Isles by the end of the Early Bronze Age.[37] These urns contain the cremated bone and may be protected by a small stone box or cist; on the other hand, they may be put into a hole or simply incorporated into the body of the mound as it is built. They may be standing upright or be inverted, more frequently the latter. Several variations of these practices may be found in the same barrow.

The classic barrows of the "single-grave cultures" were intended for one individual, as the name implies, but in fact it is unusual to find a barrow which does not cover more than one burial. This is particularly true in the north and the west where the Neolithic traditions of collective burial may have been stronger. There are three ways in which such multiple burial mounds might occur. The first, perhaps, should not be considered a true multiple burial in that the bodies were put in individually at different times. Such mounds are common in the south of England, where the primary burial is often an inhumation accompanied by a Beaker, while the other burials are definitely secondary, placed in holes dug into the pre-existing mound.[38] Whether or not these later burials were all successive is seldom clear. The second situation involves a primary burial in the centre, obviously more important than the other, satellite, burials around the edge, which must, however, have been made at the same time, since they are covered by the undisturbed mound. Th third arrangement involves a number of burials of equal importance. There is either no primary burial and no secondaries,

[35] *But see* I. F. Smith and D. D. A. Simpson. PPS. XXXII. 1966. 132-3 and P. Christie. PPS. XXXIII. 1967. 336-66.
[36] A. M. ApSimon. *Univ. London Inst. Archaeol. Ann. Bull.* I. 1958. 24-36.
[37] I. H. Longworth. PPS. XXVII. 1961. 263-306.
[38] See P. Ashbee. *op. cit.* 43. Fig. 10 for explanation of terms.

or, in some cases, there may be two or more groups, several primaries and several secondaries, but each group was buried together at one time (this presumably involved storage of the burnt bone).

It is often difficult to distinguish the second and third situations archaeologically, and perhaps their social significance was not very different. It is possible to interpret the second situation as the grave of a leader and his ritually slaughtered followers, an extreme of social stratification; on the other hand it may simply represent a family grouped around its head, each dying naturally and stored until an appropriate number had accumulated. The third situation definitely lends itself to this family interpretation, and it is interesting that these true multiple burials without primaries are found most commonly in western parts of Wales, in Ireland, Scotland and the north of England — Sir Cyril Fox's " Highland Zone " — where one may expect new ideas to be diluted and transformed by the persistence of earlier traditions : in this case, the practice of collective burial as seen in the megalithic tombs which continued to be built in Anglesey right up to the beginning of the Bronze Age.

The distribution of barrows in Anglesey is shown on Map 3.[39] There are a number of reasons why this map cannot hope to be definitive. The principal one is the difficulty of recognising an artificial mound in a landscape abounding in hummocks and grass-grown knobs of rock. It is possible that several of the presumed barrows shown here are in fact natural features, and it is equally possible that some genuine Bronze Age mounds have been passed over because, by and large, the mounds which excavation has shown to be burial monuments are low and inconspicuous. A further complication occurs when a natural hillock has been enlarged and used for burial. This seems to have been the case with the barrow just south of Din Dryfol (NGR SH/395724).

It is unlikely, therefore, that the distribution shown on the map is complete, but it is probably representative. While the distribution of burial monuments alone is not a sure guide to the settlement of the living, the combined distributions of barrows and tools (Maps 3 and 4) should give us some indication of the settlement pattern. Both are scattered fairly evenly over the island and there are few notable concentrations. It is clear that the Bronze Age population seems to have kept to the lower ground and the river valleys, seldom venturing above the 200ft. contour. In contrast with the Neolithic period there is now evidence for activity in the northern part of the island and in the rather boggy and heavily wooded central area. This spread may be the result of both a drier climate and an increase in population.

When one looks at the distribution of monuments, the emphasis on the coastal area bordering the Straits appears to be less strong than in the Neolithic, but this may be simply the result of more intensive agriculture

---

[39] The monuments are listed in Appendix I.

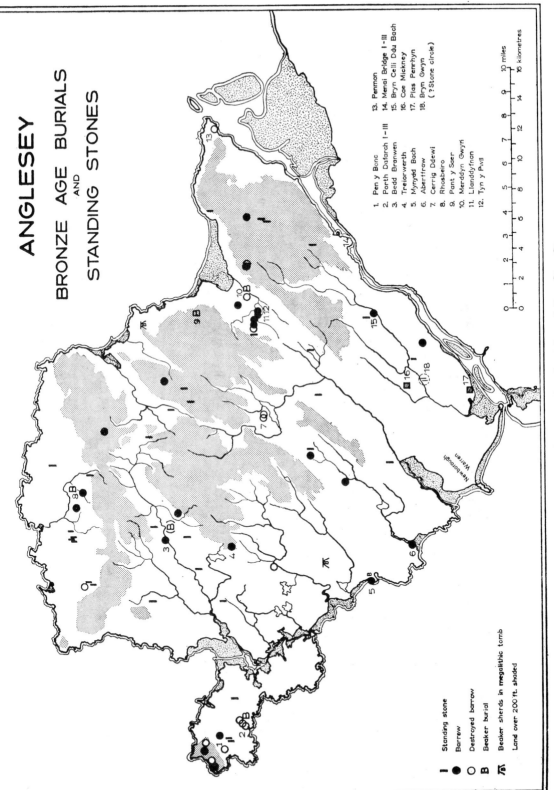

ANGLESEY

BRONZE AGE BURIALS
AND
STANDING STONES

1. Pen y Bonc
2. Porth Dafarch I–III
3. Bedd Branwen
4. Treior-werth
5. Mynydd Bach
6. Abertfraw
7. Cerrig Ddewi
8. Rhosbeirio
9. Pant y Saer
10. Merddyn Gwyn
11. Llanddyfnan
12. Tyn y Pwll
13. Penmon
14. Menai Bridge I–III
15. Bryn Celli Ddu Bach
16. Coe Mickney
17. Plas Penrhyn
18. Bryn Gwyn
    (? Stone circle)

Newborough
Warren

- Standing stone
- Barrow
- Destroyed barrow
- B Beaker burial
- Beaker sherds in megalithic tomb
- Land over 200 ft. shaded

0 1 2 3 4 5 6 7 8 9 10 miles
0 2 4 6 8 10 12 14 16 kilometres

MAP 3 — Distribution of Bronze Age burials and Standing Stones.

here or the use of unmarked cemeteries like Cae Mickney and Plas Penrhyn, for a good many bronze implements have been found in the area. Two other areas must have been fairly densely populated; the northern end of Holy Island and the higher land surrounding Red Wharf Bay. The distribution of barrows near Holyhead is supplemented by finds of several bronze implements, but remarkably little has been found in the Llanddyfnan area, except for stone axes. These tools are traditionally assigned to the Neolithic period, but their use certainly continued into the Bronze Age and, in fact, three of the axes from Pentraeth are said to have been found in a round barrow.[40]

The siting of individual barrows is quite varied. Some are in very conspicuous positions, such as the cairns on top of Holyhead Mountain, Mynydd Bodafon, and Mynydd Llwydiarth; and others, such as Treiorwerth and the one on top of Pen y Morwydd, Rhosbeirio, are equally prominent. On the other hand, several are set on the valley bottom, close to rivers. Amongst these are Bedd Branwen, Cors y Bol, the barrow near Din Dryfol, and the one near Rhosisaf, Llanddona. A few, like the very fine one at Garn, near Brynsiencyn, are on the hillslope.

Since most of the barrows excavated in Anglesey have proved to be cemetery-mounds rather than single graves, it is not surprising that there are very few cemetery groups. There are two certain examples of such grouping, at Porth Dafarch and at Llanddyfnan, both of which are centred upon a Beaker period single grave.[41] It is possible that the destroyed barrows at Cerrig Dewi, Llangwyllog, had also formed a small cemetery group.

In the south of England, especially the Wessex area, the external appearance of barrows is often quite elaborate, with surrounding ditches, berms and banks.[42] In Anglesey and in Wales generally none of these occur, and before excavation all the barrows appear to be simple cairns or mounds. Sometimes denudation reveals something of the internal structure, but this is rare. The cairn, Gorsedd Gwlwm, near Holyhead (NGR SH/227816), is one such.[43] It is a small cairn, about 40ft. across, surrounded by a low kerb. Off centre, on the west side, are three upright stones, about 3ft. high, roughly in line. If these are part of a cist it must have been extraordinarily large, and there is even a possibility that the site might be a small megalithic tomb.

Only excavation can answer such questions and provide information about the communities who built the barrows, about their ancestry, the source of their religious traditions and their contacts, through trade and other means, with neighbouring and distant groups. All such excavated burial monuments in Anglesey of which any record survives are described below.

[40] *Arch. Camb.* 1940. 246.
[41] See Chapter III.
[42] P. Ashbee. *op. cit.* 24-9.
[43] Plan in RCAM. *Anglesey.* 1937. 23.

The earliest round barrows in the island have already been mentioned in connection with the makers of Beakers. Apart from the rather doubtful case at Pant y Saer, these all covered single inhumation burials. The only other Bronze Age inhumation from Anglesey may well be contemporary with these later Beakers, though the grave goods which accompanied it suggest that the pottery, now lost, would have belonged to the Food Vessel class.

Unfortunately this grave at Pen y Bonc, near Tŷ Mawr, Holyhead (NGR SH/219815), was dug out by the farmer in 1828; information about it only reached W. O. Stanley during the 1860s.[44] Therefore one should not place too much reliance on the details, especially the reputed discovery of a coin in the grave, which is highly unlikely.

The size and material of the barrow are not mentioned, but the 3ft.

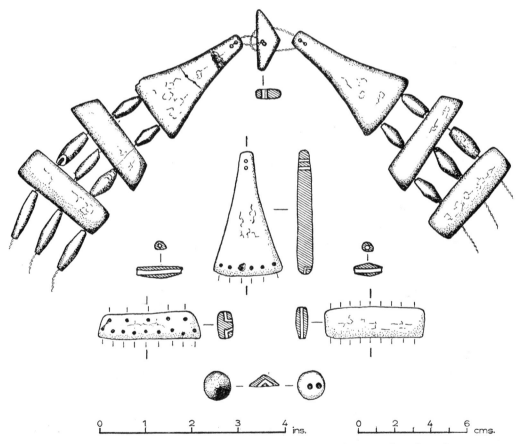

FIG. 40 — Pen y Bonc: Jet button and remains of jet necklace. Underside and sections of main components shown.

[44] Account published by Stanley's brother-in-law, Albert Way. *Arch. J.* XXIV. **1867.** 257-64 and *Arch. Camb.* 1868. 423-33.

square grave was cut into the rock and covered by a capstone. No bones appear to have been found, but this is not unusual when the body has not been burnt. Inside the grave were two broken "urns" about which nothing is known, and two bronze armlets which have also been lost. Lying in a corner, and, therefore, presumably not on the body, was an elaborate jet necklace from which several beads survive. There was also a V-bored jet button of the type found at Merddyn Gwyn.

This group of objects constituted one of the richest grave groups ever found in Anglesey: it is regrettable that so little of it remains today.[45] The necklace was a complex ornament with several strands of biconical (fusiform) beads in the front kept apart by flat spacer plates lying over the shoulders. These jet necklaces are part of a fashion for crescentic neck ornaments which is quite widespread in Europe. This particular type, with the fusiform beads and the spacer plates, is common in Scotland where the centre of manufacture may have been in Angus.[46] Spacer plate necklaces also occur in the north of England, presumably made of local jet, but they usually contain small disc beads as well as fusiform ones.[47] The Pen y Bonc necklace is rather unusual in having plain spacer plates. These plates normally carry punched decoration in simple geometric patterns, but there are two undecorated ones from Scotland, from Bogheadly, Kincardineshire, and Rothie-Norman, Aberdeenshire.[48]

Our knowledge of the bronze armlets is tantalisingly inadequate, but one may guess that they were bands of sheet metal about 1-2 inches deep, the edges slightly out-turned and the central area perhaps decorated with a simple raised pattern. Such armlets have also been found in Scotland, with a crescentic jet necklace at Melfort, Argyll,[49] and with a flat dagger and a jet necklace without spacer plates at Masterton, Fife.[50] It is probable that there armlets were hammered up from the continuous bronze rings or the bars sometimes found in metal-workers' hoards of the Migdale-Marnoch tradition.[51] Products of this school of metal-working, which flourished in the earlier part of the Early Bronze Age (around 1,500 B.C.), are found principally in the north and west of the British Isles, but, apart from the ubiquitous flat axe, distinctive objects from this group are relatively rare in Wales.

Although this grave was undoubtedly a rich one, there is no evidence here of contact with the "Wessex Culture" in the south. Both the armlets and the necklace, and probably the "urns" as well, relate to the north to northern England and especially to Scotland. Pottery from the later sites in Anglesey confirms these links and also reveals close ties with Ireland,

[45] The remains of the necklace and the button are now in the British Museum.
[46] G. Callander. PSAS. L. 1915-16. 201-240.
[47] J. H. Craw. PSAS. LXIII. 1928-9. 154-89.
[48] G. Callander, op. cit. 215.
[49] Inventaria Archaeolgica. G.B. 25.
[50] A. S. Henshall and J. C. Wallace. PSAS. XCVI. 1962-3. 145-54.
[51] D. Britton. PPS. XXIX. 1963. 263-83 and below p. 176-9.

suggesting that the enduring relationships were with the lands bordering the Irish Sea and with northern England, accessible along the north Welsh coast, while contacts with the south are likely to have been more superficial and perhaps almost entirely commercial.

Pen y Bonc is unusual among the Anglesey barrows, not only because it covers an inhumation but because it was built for one burial. The majority of barrows excavated in Anglesey have provided evidence of several burials, although the circumstances of recovery have not always been ideal and it is seldom possible to be certain whether they represent simultaneous or successive burials.

A site where the true multiple burial rite can be proved and well illustrated is Bedd Branwen, Llanbabo (NGR SH/362849). The barrow is low and rather inconspicuous, standing on the floor of the valley very close to the River Alaw in the centre of a slight natural rise in the bend of the river. Its most obvious feature is the large stone protruding from the centre. The doughnut-like profile is largely original, reflecting the design of the structure beneath. Another mound not far away, in Cors y Bol (NGR SH/376843), has the same hollow centre and may cover a similar cairn ring.[52]

The mound, which is the traditional burial place of Branwen, daughter of Llŷr, was first dug into in 1813 when a Collared urn in a small cist was found.[53] In 1868, when the urn was re-examined in the British Museum, some sherds of a Beaker and some unburnt bone were found in it.[54] This led to the assumption that the barrow was originally built to cover a Beaker burial and later enlarged to take cremation burials. However, large-scale excavation in 1967 showed that this was erroneous; the entire barrow dates from about 1,400 B.C.[55]

The mound, which is an elaborate one, is designed around the central stone which must have already existed as a monument in its own right for some time.[56] A hole dug through the old ground surface at the foot of the stone may have played some part in rededication ceremonies before the barrow was built, although its content of stone and charcoal gives no hint of what these ceremonies might have been.

The area to be covered by the cairn ring must first have been marked out, and three of the burial urns, L, H and C, placed in small holes carefully dug for them so that they stood just about flush with the old ground surface. L and H were accompanied by smaller accessory vessels placed nearby. All these pots were then covered by a cairn ring a triangular bank of stone, 8ft. wide and 2ft. 6ins. high at the apex, encircling the central stone

[52] I am grateful to Dr. J. M. Lewis of the National Museum of Wales for drawing my attention to this site.
[53] *Cambro-Briton*. II. 1820. 71. quoted in *Arch. J.* VI. 1849. 237-9 and in *Arch. Camb.* 1868. 233-40.
[54] *Arch. Camb.* 1868. *loc. cit.*
[55] F. M. Lynch. TAAS. 1966. 1-31.
[56] See above p. 116.

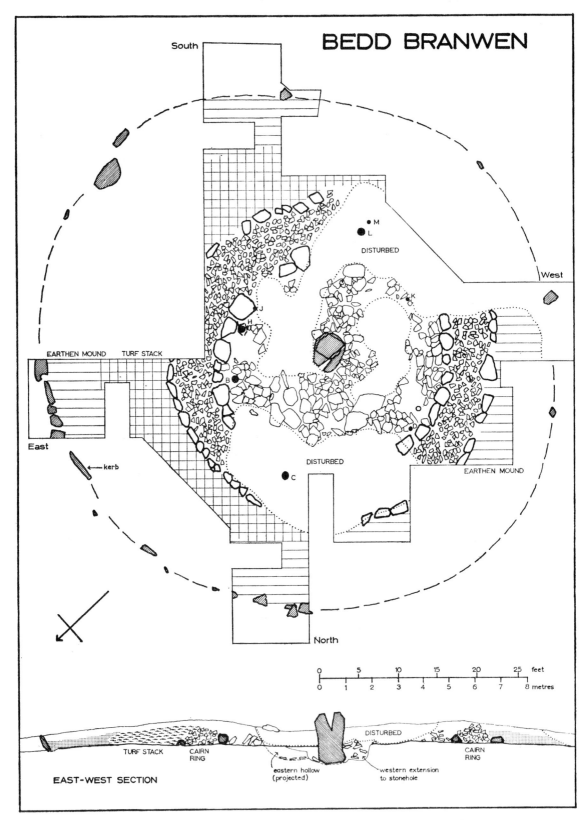

FIG. 41 — Bedd Branwen: Plan and section of the barrow as excavated, 1967.

at a distance of 12ft. The cairn ring was centred on the standing stone, but the kerb, which was erected next, was marked out from a point a little to the east of this stone. The hole for the stake used to mark out the circle was found during the excavations. The kerb, 65ft. in diameter, was a ring of stones standing end to end. Some of them can still be seen protruding through the modern surface. On the east, between the cairn ring and the kerb, was a crescentic stack of turves covering the outer slope of the cairn ring. These turves seem to have been designed to compensate for the lack of concentricity between the cairn ring and the kerb. The rest of the mound between the kerb and the cairn ring was built of earth, probably brought to the site in baskets. The central area was filled with large slabs sloping inward towards the central stone. Considerable disturbance here makes it uncertain whether or not such slabs filled the entire area. The bulk of the evidence suggests that the mound was never very high, with the central stone always visible.

Barrows built around a central stone, or having one on the top are rare in Britain, but not unknown. The tall stones at the head of the Beaker graves at Tŷ'n y Pwll and Porth Dafarch II have already been mentioned; the barrow at Kilpaison, Pembrokeshire,[57] completely covered a central standing stone; and at Llanfachreth, Merioneth, a large stone, standing on top of the cist, emerged through the centre of the barrow.[58] The last two instances are of graves roughly contemporary with Bedd Branwen.

Cairn rings are perhaps more common, though they are usually found surrounding a single primary burial. However, the association with multiple burials which have no standard form of barrow, is found in Wales at Mynydd Carn Goch, near Swansea; at Capel Cynon, Cardiganshire, and Cefn Golau, Flintshire. A similar association occurs in Ireland at Dun Ruadh, Co. Tyrone.[59]

The origin of the cairn ring is obscure. It occurs in a relatively early context at Overton Down in Wiltshire, where a flint ring covers burials dating from the earlier phase of the Wessex Culture (1,600 - 1,500 B.C.) and surrounds a Long Necked Beaker burial of the same date.[60] It is probable, however, that the majority are slightly later than this and contemporary with the practice of burying circles of stakes beneath the barrow. Like these stake circles, cairn rings occur spasmodically in various parts of the country and may well share the same (unknown) significance.[61] A direct link can be postulated at Tregulland, Cornwall, and Pant-y-Dulath, Flintshire, where the cairn ring had been built over and between

[57] *Arch. Camb.* 1926. 1-35.
[58] *Arch. Camb.* 1926. 406-9.
[59] Mynydd Carn Goch: *Arch. Camb.* 1856. 63-7 and 1868. 252-5.
     Capel Cynon: *Arch. Camb.* 1905. 62-9.
     Cefn Golau: *Flintshire Hist. Soc. Public.* XIII. 1952-3. 91-7 and XV. 1954-5. 112-37.
     Dun Ruadh: *Proc. Belfast Nat. Hist. and Phil. Soc.* 2nd Series I. 1935-6. 50-75.
[60] PPS. XXXII. 1966. 122-55.
[61] See discussion in P. Ashbee. *The Bronze Age Round Barrow in Britain.* 1960. 60-5.

two concentric stake circles.[62] In the linear cemetery at Letterston, Pembrokeshire, two barrows were surrounded by stake circles and the third contained a cairn ring.[63]

The Letterston barrow covered a cairn ring built to resemble a miniature stone circle of the embanked type.[64] It had a circle of upright stones set into its inner edge, and a narrow entrance passage; the central area was bare of features, but there was a burial in the passage. The fact that it is in a barrow cemetery, contains a burial and was almost immediately covered with turves and made to look like a normal barrow, all stress the link between the Embanked Stone Circles and the normal burial mounds. The embanked and free-standing stone circles were clearly not designed primarily as burial monuments, but rather, one supposes, as religious centres. However, they do contain certain burials, and monuments such as Circle 278 at Penmaenmawr, Caernarvonshire, may be something in between the two.[65] In design and size it is very similar to Bedd Branwen without its earthen covering. It produced a single urn containing earth and charcoal like Pot K from Bedd Branwen; the radio carbon date (1,405 ± 150 B.C.) obtained for this site is very similar to the archaeological dating of the Anglesey monument.[66]

There are a number of cairn circles and ring cairns on the western uplands of Wales which must also be part of this Bronze Age continuum from stone circle to burial mound, but unfortunately they have been largely neglected by field workers, and virtually none have been excavated.[67] One near Aberystwyth dug recently produced evidence of ritual activity and should perhaps not be considered a normal burial mound.[68] Like the stone circles, these monuments are most frequently found on the high moorland and are rare in Anglesey. The mound in Cors y Bol (and Bedd Branwen itself before excavation) might be classified as ring cairns, though they are not typical because of the presence of filling in the centre.

One can confidently postulate some connection between the stone circles, the ring cairns and the cairn rings incorporated into several barrows, but one cannot, at this distance in time, speculate upon the reasons for this link, principally because we know so little about the functions of stone circles or the significance of the circular setting which appears in various forms throughout the Bronze Age.

It is clear, however, that Bedd Branwen itself was built as a burial mound. The first group of these burials has already been mentioned. They

---

[62] Tregulland: *Ant. J.* XXXVIII. 1958. 174-96.
   Pant y Dulath: unpublished.
[63] Letterston I and II: *Arch. Camb.* 1948-9. 67-87.
   Letterston III: BBCS. XX. 1962-4. 309-25.
[64] W. F. Grimes *in* Foster and Alcock (edd) *Culture and Environment.* 1963. 95.
[65] PPS. XXVI. 1960. 318-22, 327.
[66] PPS. XXVIII. 1962. 387.
[67] The best information on these is in E. G. Bowen and C. A. Gresham *History of Merioneth.* Vol. I. 1967. 84-94.
[68] Information from Mr. A. H. A. Hogg prior to publication, for which I am very grateful.

must all have been made at the one time, before the cairn ring was built. At a later date another group of burials was inserted into the mound, whether at one time or successively it is impossible to say. These four or five burials were all placed around the inner circumference of the cairn ring between its large edging stones and the sloped stones of the central area, some of which must have been removed to make room for them. The interval between the primary group and the secondary burials cannot have been long, perhaps a generation, for the placing within the circle is so accurate that the concealed structure must have been well known. Furthermore, Pot J from the first group is almost identical to Pot F from the second, and the grave goods and burial ritual are the same in both series.

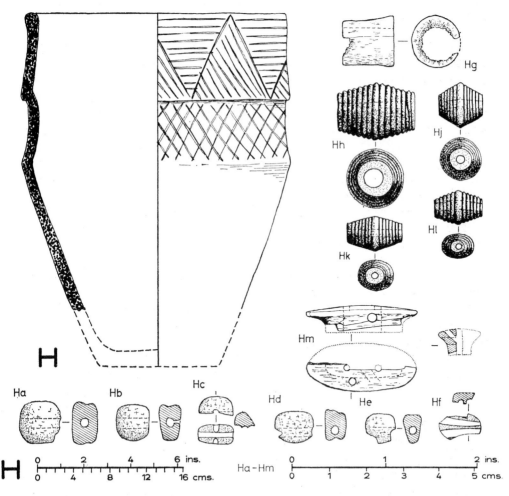

FIG. 42 — Bedd Branwen: Pot H with amber (Ha-Hf), jet (Hh-Hl) and bone (Hg) beads and bone pommel (Hm) from primary group.

Pot H, a large Collared urn rather clumsily decorated with rough incisions, contained the richest of the burials, although all the primary series must be considered of equal status. The pot was standing inverted in a five-sided cist which was rather too small for it. This pot and the one found in 1813 were the only ones to be protected by a stone box, although C had a few stones placed around it. The bones inside were those of an adult man who had suffered from osteoarthritis.[69] Amongst the bones were a simple polished bone bead and the bone pommel from the hilt of a small knife: both had been burnt, presumably on the body at the time of cremation.

The pommel could well have come from a bronze knife like the earlier one from Merddyn Gwyn, but there was no sign of any metal blade among the bones, so either the blade was retained by the relatives as too valuable to sacrifice or the knife was a special funerary model perhaps made from wood. The regularity with which such bone pommels are found without blades in cremations, and the existence of a dagger made from bone at Crug yr Afon, Glamorgan, add weight to the latter argument.[70]

After the bones had been placed in the pot, a small necklace of jet and amber beads had been dropped in on top of them. This necklace consisted of four jet beads and six or seven amber ones. Such composite necklaces are found fairly frequently in the south of England (the one from Upton Lovell, Wiltshire, is a well-known example),[71] and it is likely that the amber was obtained from that area, since a great deal of it was imported into Wessex from Denmark at this time. In the context of Wales, where amber is virtually unknown in the Early Bronze Age, even this small necklace is indicative of considerable wealth. The shape of the beads is unusual, and the multiple borings in two suggest that they may have been made from reused material, like those from the Knowes of Trotty, Orkney.[72]

Though the material is less exotic, the jet beads are perhaps more spectacular than the amber ones. All four, graduated in size, are biconical and very neatly grooved over the entire surface. Such beautiful workmanship must surely represent a *tour de force* considering the primitive tools which were available. Although biconical or fusiform jet beads are common in many parts of these islands at this time, occurring principally in crescentic necklaces like that from Pen y Bonc, carved ones are very unusual. There are a few grooved shale beads covered with sheet gold from some of the very rich graves in Wessex, and there are three rather

---

[69] I am very grateful to Dr. F. P. Lipowski and Dr. T. F. Spence of the University of Birmingham for the identification of the bones from Bedd Branwen and Treiorwerth.
[70] Bone pommels without blades at: Merddyn Gwyn: below p. —
Marian Bach, Cwm, Flints. NMW. 410. unpublished, and Rhiw, Caerns. RCAM. *Caernarvonshire* III. 1964. xxxviii. Fig. 10, nos. 8 & 9.
Crug yr Afon blade: BBCS. XX. 1962-4. 78-82.
[71] *Devizes Museum Catalogue.* 108. no. 342.
[72] *Inventaria Archaeologica.* GB 33. nos. 12-22.

roughly made ones in faience from Carnkreis, Boscregan, in Cornwall,[73] but in fact the best parallel for the Bedd Branwen beads comes from Anglesey, from Treiorwerth, a barrow less than three miles away. Other details to be discussed later confirm the link between these two monuments.

Close to Pot H, standing inverted in a shallow hole beneath one of the edging stones of the cairn ring, was a smaller pot, J, a Collared urn with a very narrow rim and a "necklace" around the shoulder (Fig. 45). It contained dark earth and charcoal and, at the bottom, the two petrous temporal bones of a new-born infant. These bones had been burnt and, since they are extremely hard, it could be argued that if the head of a new-born child were cremated nothing else would remain. However, the discovery at Treiorwerth of a pot containing dark earth and the ear bones of a six-year-old child, whose skull would certainly survive cremation, shows that their separate burial was not a matter of survival but of deliberate choice. There were two other instances of this custom at Bedd Branwen: Pots M and E each contained a pair of infant ear bones, and each pot accompanied a normal burial urn.[74]

There are three instances of this peculiar practice at Bedd Branwen and one at Treiorwerth; outside Anglesey it is unknown. It is very suggestive of some unpleasant ritual, probably sacrifice, accompanying the funerals of certain special individuals, but the significance of the ear bones themselves remains a mystery. They are set deep in the skull and could hardly be associated with hearing without an extraordinary knowledge of anatomy, nor are they an especially attractive shape. It is interesting to recall that the only bone in the dedicatory pit behind the Passage Grave at Bryn Celli Ddu was a burnt adult ear bone, but this ceremony must have taken place at least 400 years before the burial at Bedd Branwen.[75] However, it does hint at a long-standing tradition in the island and supports in a small way the theory that these multiple burial sites reflect the same family-orientated social system as the megalithic tombs.

The placing of ear bones in the accessory vessel is unknown elsewhere, but the presence of a smaller pot beside the burial urn is not uncommon. These pots may be completely empty, contain simply earth and charcoal, or may have a token quantity of bone in them. Some of the very small Collared urns found by Canon Greenwell in Yorkshire are in this third class, but he does not say whether any standard group of bones was involved.[76] It is possible, therefore, that the accessory vessels, whatever they contain, simply represent minor variations on the same ritual, people outside Anglesey leaving a less vivid memento of their activities. For even at Bedd Branwen the practice was not uniform: K, a small pot, probably

[73] Carnkreis: Illustrated in P. Ashbee. *The Bronze Age Round Barrow in Britain.* 1960. Pl. XVIII. 3.
[74] Pot E had been smashed and only one earbone was actually found.
[75] *Arch.* LXXX. 1930. 196 and above, p. 60.
[76] W. Greenwell. *British Barrows.* 1877. 287, Parish of Goodmanham. Barrows LXXXIII and LXXXIV.

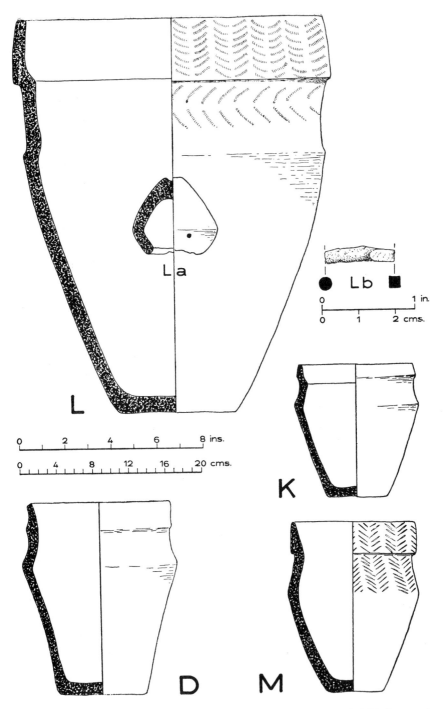

Fig. 43 — Bedd Branwen: Pots L, La, M and bronze awl (Lb) from primary group. Pots K and D from later group.

originally paired with a burial urn removed by disturbance, contained earth and only a tiny piece of bone which was not an ear bone; B, C and D were burial urns without any accompanying vessel at all; and at Treiorwerth Pot 3 contained no bone at all, only earth and charcoal.

Pot L, a large elegant Collared urn decorated with whipped cord impressions, was found beneath the cairn ring. Not only was it accompanied by an accessory vessel, M, which contained a pair of baby's ear bones, but it contained an accessory cup (La) which had been placed upside down on top of the bones inside the urn. The function of these little cups is not known: they are normally found inside larger urns but do not usually themselves contain bones. Their shape and decoration varies, but they frequently have one or more holes in the side. This latter fact has led to the use of the term "incense cup", and to the suggestion that they may have been used to hold glowing coals, perhaps those used to light the pyre.[77] This seems to be as good an explanation as any, but nothing has been found that directly proves or disproves it. Pot La contained a few pieces of charcoal.

It is a small, undecorated, biconical pot with a single hole at the shoulder. Its vase-like shape is somewhat unusual, the normal biconical form being much squatter, but it can be compared to the plain one from Porth Dafarch I, Holyhead (Fig. 53, No. 2). It is made from a rather soft, friable clay containing very well-crushed grit and has been baked to a brick-red colour. The colour and texture contrast strongly with that of the Collared urns which are made from a hard brown clay containing large, angular grits. This contrast is a normal feature, accessory cups always being softer and less heavily gritted than the large urns.

The use of the accessory cups seems to have been fashionable for a time during the later part of the Early Bronze Age. They occur most frequently in the later Wessex Culture graves and, outside that area, in association with contemporary objects such as faience beads. They occur very often with the urns in Welsh multiple burial sites, most of which seem to belong to the century 1,500 - 1,400 B.C.[78] Exactly when the fashion died out is not clear, since after 1,400 B.C. dateable objects no longer occur in the graves and changes in pottery styles are an unreliable guide for chronological purposes. The origin of these small pots is obscure. The ones from Wessex have certain decorative links with Late Neolithic pottery from Brittany, an area closely linked by trade to southern England. The biconial type common in the Irish Sea area has no obvious connection with Brittany, but may be derived from further south. The practice as a whole may, therefore, be associated with the Atlantic seaboard of Europe and may have been spread through the agency of trade.

[77] W. O. Stanley and Albert Way. *Arch. Camb.* 1868. 258-9. Greenwell (*op. cit.* 81-3) approved this opinion.
[78] General discussion of all Welsh examples by H. N. Savory. BBCS. XVIII. 1958-60. 89-118.

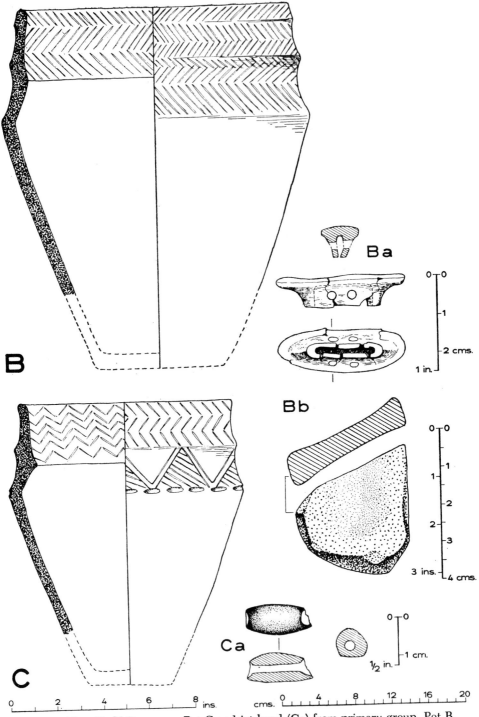

FIG. 44 — Bedd Branwen: Pot C and jet bead (Ca) from primary group. Pot B, bone pommel (Ba) and hone (Bb) from later group.

The only other object associated with Pot L is part of a bronze awl found in the earth filling the mouth of the pot. Awls, which may have been leather-working tools, are frequently found with Bronze Age cremations, most often with the remains of women.[79] In this instance, the bones were those of an adult of unknown sex. Other examples from the island are from Cae Mickney and Menai Bridge, both found with burials, and one from Castell Bryn Gwyn, associated with very Late Neolithic pottery.

Pot C was buried diametrically opposite L beneath the cairn ring. It is an urn of rather unusual type, having an upright collar, a profile which is common in Anglesey but rare elsewhere. It is decorated with sharp incisions and has a neatly cut "necklace" around the shoulder. It was a burial urn containing the bones of one individual, unaccompanied by any accessory vessels. The only grave-offering was a single bead, plain, highly polished and made of good quality jet. It is possible that originally it may have formed part of an elaborate necklace like that from Pen y Bonc, but there are plenty of instances of single beads being worn as ornaments in their own right. It had not been burnt, and had been placed at the bottom of the pot before the bones were put into it.

The other pots, B, D, E and F, K, and the pot found in 1813, contain a slightly later series of burials, though, as already mentioned, the interval is not likely to have been a long one. They are all placed around the inner edge of the cairn ring, and there are two instances of paired pots, one containing an ear bone, though, unfortunately, in both cases they had been disturbed.

Pot D (Fig. 43) contained a very simple burial of an adult of unknown sex. There were no grave goods, no accessory vessels, and the pot itself was small and undecorated.

The burial in Pot B was also unaccompanied by any accessory vessels, but amongst the bones there was a small bone pommel very like the one from Pot H. Again there was no sign of the rest of the knife, neither of the blade, nor of the hilt. The pommel itself had been burnt. However, after the bones had been placed in the pot and the mouth plugged with a clod of earth, a roughly shaped sandstone hone on which to sharpen the non-existent blade had been pressed into the top. More elegant whetstones are often found in contemporary graves in the south of England, where the bronze knives were normally included as well.[80]

The bones from Pot B, a large urn with an upright collar like that on Pot C, were those of an adult man. The majority of them were inside the pot which had been closed with earth before it had been buried, but other bones had been placed loose in the hole before the pot was put in. These bones come from the same body, an arrangement which shows that they must have been gathered from the pyre in two groups. The variable weight

[79] Greenwell. op. cit. 458-78. resumé of contents of Yorkshire graves.
[80] Devizes Museum Catalogue, passim and PPS, XXIX, 1963. 411-2.

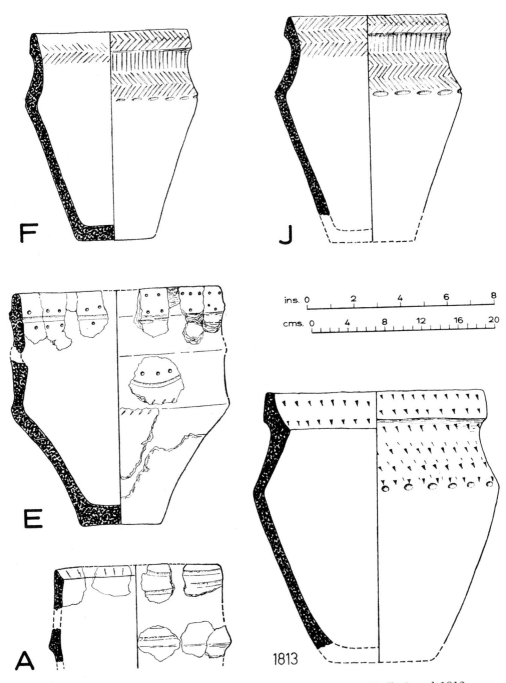

ins. 0   2   4   6   8

cms. 0 4 8 12 16 20

FIG. 45 — Bedd Branwen: Pot J from primary group and Pots F, E, A and 1813 urn from later group.

of bone in the urns certainly suggests that often only a representative sample of the bones might be buried.

Both Pot F and Pot E had been disturbed and badly broken. They must have been standing on the old ground surface, one upright and one inverted, just inside the circumference of the cairn ring. They therefore form a pair comparable to Pots L and M. There was some bone in the base of Pot F, but only a little earth in Pot E, with a single ear bone from an infant. In view of the destruction of the pot, it is reasonable to assume that it originally contained a pair like Pots J and M.

Pot F is remarkable for its similarity to Pot J, but Pot E is unlike any of the others. It had been badly broken and not much survives, so the reconstruction is necessarily tentative.[81] It is coarsely made with a rather haphazard decoration made with the end of a reed, the dots arranged around shallow channelling. The shoulder is marked by finger-nail impressions, probably in two lines. The suggested reconstruction shows it to have been a tall, ridged Food Vessel, a profile not found at other Anglesey sites. Such Food Vessels occur most frequently in Yorkshire, where they normally have a bevelled rim. Welsh versions of this type, which occur at Coity, Glamorgan, and Llanllechid, Caernarvonshire, are, like Pot E, roughly made and crudely decorated.[82]

It is probable that Pot K was originally one of a pair. It is a very small undecorated Collared urn which contained brown earth, a small quantity of charcoal, and one small piece of bone, not an ear bone. It was standing inverted on the old ground surface near the inner edge of the cairn ring, and very close to an area of considerable disturbance. A quantity of burnt bone was found in this area, no doubt part of the burial which Pot K had accompanied.

It is possible that the burial urn found in 1813 might have come from here. The account of its discovery says that it was found inverted in a covered cist, as was Pot H. However, since no hole was found from which such a cist might have been removed, it must presumably have been built above the old ground surface, placing the urn with the group of later burials. This pot, a Collared urn with a "necklace" feature like Pots J, F and C, contained the burnt bones of a woman, some of which had been stained green, perhaps from contact with bronze, but apparently no metal or other grave goods were found.

Broken sherds were found in various parts of the disturbed mound. The majority, which were from Pot A, came from the vicinity of C, where there was also a good deal of burnt bone. These remains must represent another of the later series of burials.

Bedd Branwen is perhaps the most interesting of the Bronze Age barrows in Anglesey because in it so many strands of Bronze Age life are

[81] I am grateful to Dr. Ian Longworth for this reconstruction.
[82] H. N. Savory. BBCS. XVII. 1956-8, 196-233. Fig. 10, nos. 1 & 3; Fig. 11, no. 1.

combined. It has a standing stone as its focal point; the structure of the mound is a complex one, incorporating ideas probably borrowed from the non-sepulchral religious monuments of the time; while the practice of multiple simultaneous burial emphasises the continuing strength of the family structure and the traditions which still united the western parts of these islands as they had in the Neolithic. The pottery illustrates the variety of shape and decoration current within the one community as effectively as it demonstrates the insularity of their inspiration, for some of the forms, especially the upright collar, are virtually restricted to Anglesey. On the other hand, some of their more exotic possessions indicate long-distance connections and trade in luxury articles, showing the Anglesey population participating in the widespread commercial activity exemplified in southern England by the term " Wessex Culture ". The ritual which involved the separate burial of ear bones must remain unexplained, but it is a reminder that many aspects of Bronze Age life and religion would appear savage and barbaric to us today, for life may have been very cheap in a society where raids and skirmishes must have been endemic.

The evidence from Bedd Branwen would not be so compelling if it were unique, but, in fact, the conclusions stated can be supported by information from other barrows less extensively excavated.

The group of five barrows near the village of Pentraeth has already been mentioned. They form a linear cemetery in which the earliest burial is an inhumation in a boat-shaped cist, which must date from the very beginning of the Bronze Age.[83] Some 200 yards west of the Tŷn y Pwll

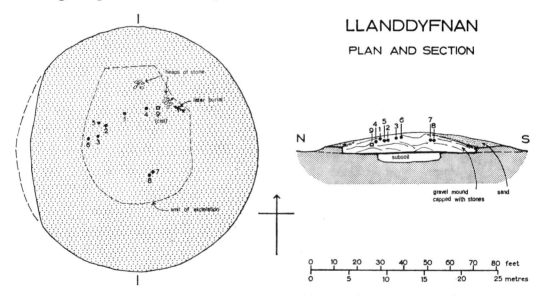

Fig. 46 — Llanddyfnan: Plan and section of barrow showing position of urns.
(After E. N. Baynes.)

[83] See above p. 99-101.

barrow is another, known as Llanddyfnan (NGR SH/508784), which was excavated at the same time.[84] There has been no excavation of the other three, which are now so ploughed down as to be scarcely visible.

The Llanddyfnan barrow was a large one, about 100ft. in diameter and surviving to a height of 7ft. It was set on the summit of the gravel ridge and was a composite mound built of stones, gravel and sand. There was no elaborate internal structure: in the centre there was a circular heap of gravel, 40 - 50ft. in diameter and 5ft. or 6ft. high, which was covered by a layer of stones perhaps about 2ft. thick. This was in turn covered by sand which merged with the present topsoil. There was no evidence that this layering was due to successive enlargements, for though there were no burials on the old ground surface all the pots were found within the central gravel mound.

The absence of any features on the old ground surface is unusual; it emphasises the absence of a primary burial, as does the scattered distribution of the urns which avoid the centre of the barrow. The burials must have been made while the mound was in process of construction. This system is relatively common with what have been termed " satellite " burials and was also used in the multiple burial site at Treiorwerth, near Bodedern, where there were actually some burials on the old ground surface as well, though none was in the centre.

All the pots were relatively close to the modern surface and three had been disturbed by ploughing before the excavation began. It is impossible to say now whether the higher ones might have been later additions, but, as at Bedd Branwen, it is likely that any interval was short for the grave goods all suggest a similar date, between 1,500 and 1,400 B.C. Excepting Urns 7 and 8, the burials were all placed in a rough arc in the northern half of the mound, about 15ft. from the centre. A similar concentration on one side of the barrow was found at Treiorwerth.

Urn 6 was closest to the modern surface, being found with its inverted base no more than 4 inches below the grass. However, it was closely surrounded with gravel without any protective cist, so it must have been buried as the mound was being built.

The urn itself was badly broken, but the impression left in the gravel showed it to have been 10ins. high and 8ins. in diameter. It was barrel-shaped, with two encircling ribs and decorated with twisted cord impressions. It belongs to a class of pot called Cordoned urns, more common in Ireland and Scotland than in Wales. The few that have been found here come, as might be expected, from western parts of the country.[85]

Urn 6 contained burnt bone and a flat piece of bronze badly damaged by heat. This object has since been lost, but it is recognisable from a photograph as the butt of a razor-knife. These small blades, with an

[84] E. Neil Baynes. *Arch. Camb.* 1909. 312-25.
[85] e.g. Kilpaison, Pembs.: *Arch. Camb.* 1926. 1-35 and Treiorwerth, Ang.

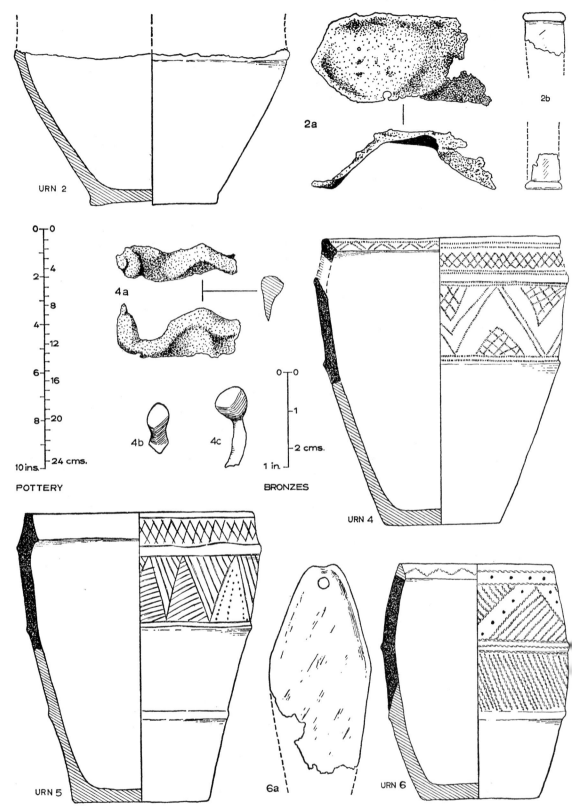

URN 2

2a

2b

0 ─ 0
2 ─ 4
  ─ 8
4 ─ 12
6 ─ 16
8 ─ 20
10 ins. ─ 24 cms.

POTTERY

4a

4b

4c

0 ─ 0
  ─ 1
  ─ 2 cms.
1 in.

BRONZES

URN 4

URN 5

6a

URN 6

Fig. 47 — Llanddyfnan: Urns 2, 4, 5 and 6 and contents. (2b, 4b, 4c and 6a after E. N. Baynes. Urn 2 and the hatched parts of the others are now lost and have been copied from E. N. Baynes's drawings.)

elongated triangular butt and a single rivet hole, are known from Ireland, where they seem to be a local development of the tanged and riveted Late Beaker knives.[86] They were probably used in the same way as the tanged razors current in western parts of these islands at the end of the Early Bronze Age. The Llanddyfnan one must have been very similar to those from Cremation 36 at Knockast, Co. Westmeath, and Carrowjames II, Co. Galway.[87] In both these instances the razors were in Cordoned urns and, in fact, all the Irish razors have been found in pots of this type.[88] It is interesting to see the connection holding good in Anglesey, although the reason for this constant link is unknown.

Urns 1, 2, 3 and 4 were all standing upright and must have been buried to about the same depth, with their tops about 9ins. below the modern surface. Urns 1 - 3 were broken by the farmer. The sherds and most of the contents have since been lost, but they were seen by Neil Baynes who wrote the excavation report.

Urn 1 was entirely destroyed and nothing is recorded about it except that it was small and contained bone. Only the lower half of Urn 2 survived. It had a low-set rib, as have most of the pots from this site, and must have been a large urn. It had contained burnt bone, amongst which were three fragments of bronze, all badly damaged by fire. The largest of these pieces survives. It is basically a flat piece of metal 2ins. long and almost an inch wide. It was possibly some sort of blade of a small knife or perhaps a razor like that from Urn 6, but it is too badly damaged for certainty. The other two pieces sound more interesting, but unfortunately they have been lost. They were both part of the same object, a narrow strip of bronze, about ⅜in. wide, decorated with a raised design and having both ends rolled over. The length is unknown, for only half an inch at either end survived, but there is a strong possibility that these scraps were the remains of a bracelet like the one from the Migdale hoard, Scotland.[89] Such bracelets are rare, but were part of the output of the same Migdale-Marnoch school of metal workers who may have made the lost armlets from Pen y Bonc. This tradition flourished around 1,550 B.C., so the bracelet may well have been old, possibly an heirloom, when worn by the person buried at Llanddyfnan.

Urn 3 was also found at a depth of 9ins., certainly covered by a stone and probably protected by a cist. The pot had been decorated with twisted

[86] S. Piggott *in* Foster and Alcock (edd) *Culture and Environment.* 1963. 73, fig. 16. The object was first recognised as a razor by W. F. Grimes. (*Prehistory of Wales.* 1951. 216), and was discussed by J. J. Butler and I. F. Smith. *Univ. London Inst. of Archaeol. Ann. Report* XII. 1956. 52.
[87] Knockast: PRIA. 41. C. 1934. 232-84, fig. 5. D.
   Carrowjames: *J. Galway Arch. and Hist. Soc.* XVIII. 1939. 157-67, fig. 7. e.
[88] E. Binchy-Laffan *in* E. Rynne (ed) *North Munster Studies.* 1967. 51.
[89] D. Britton. PPS. XXIX. 1963. 264, 279-81 and A. Henshall. PPS. XXX. 1964. 426-9. The Migdale one is the only one with a repoussé design.

cord impressions in a design of straight sloping lines and had contained bones.[90]

Urn 4 was a large pot, also 9ins. below the surface and described as standing upright on the gravel, so it might possibly be a later insertion. It was protected by a cist of horizontal stones covered by a flat capstone. A cist built of horizontal stones is unusual, but the cist (Burial 9) found at a greater depth in the mound was similarly constructed.

This urn contained burnt bones and three pieces of bronze, again badly distorted by fire. The surviving piece has been so much melted as to be unrecognisable, but one of the pieces subsequently lost seems to have been a knob on a thin stem, an object which might originally have been a pin like the one from Timsbury (Camerton), Somerset.[91] These dress ornaments are imports from Central Europe and are rather rare even in Wessex, but there is another from North Wales, from Cremation 5 at Cefn Golau on Moel Famau, Flintshire,[92] so the presence of one in Anglesey would not be so surprising.

Urns 4 and 5 are rather similar in general shape and design. Urn 4 is decorated with a very fine pointed comb and Urn 5 with deeply incised lines. They are both cordoned and barrel-shaped with slightly inturned rims and, though they are much larger, must be related to the more classic Cordoned urns such as Urn 6.

Urn 5 was found at a depth of 1ft. 3ins., rather deeper than the others close to it. It was standing inverted, enclosed in the gravel of the central mound without any protective cist. It contained the burnt bones of what might have been a woman or young man, unaccompanied by any grave goods.

Burial 9 was the last of those found in the northern half of the barrow. It consisted of burnt bone placed on the gravel without any pot but protected by a small covered cist built of horizontal stones. This cist was found at a depth of 1ft. 9ins. There were no grave goods.

In the southern half, which was less extensively excavated, only one burial was found. This burial, in Urn 7, is of particular interest and has sometimes been described as the primary burial; it is no more primary than any of the others and might even have been a later insertion. It was found at a depth of 10ins., inverted in a stone cist, with the mouth resting on a thin layer of gravel which overlay sand. The presence of sand suggests that this burial was in the outer layer — not in the central gravel mound — but the generalised section (Fig. 46) and the fact that Urn 6, very near the surface, was encased in gravel, show that the outer coating of sand did not

[90] Sherds in Bangor Museum answering this description are labelled " Merddyn Gwyn " but there is a possibility that this is a mistake since the original owner, the Rev. E. E. Evans, was associated with the excavation of both barrows. See below p. 152 and Fig. 52 no. 3.
[91] PPS. IV. 1938. 76, fig. 14.
[92] M. Bevan-Evans and P. Hayes. *Flints. Hist. Soc. Publics.* XV. 1954-5. 119.

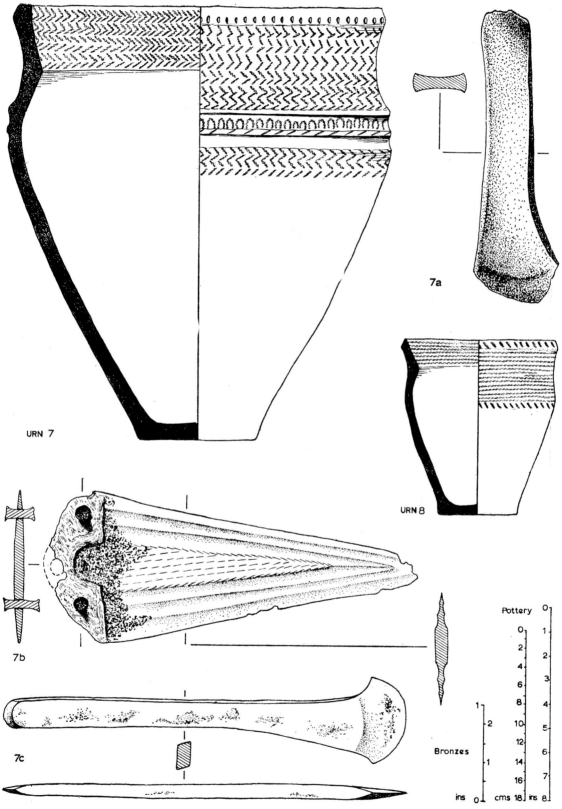

URN 7

7a

URN 8

7b

7c

Pottery

Bronzes

ins   cms 18 ins

Fig. 48 : Llanddyfnan : Urns 7 and 8 and contents.

survive at the centre. It is probable, therefore, that Pot 7 was placed within the gravel mound, but perhaps a large hole had been dug for its insertion and filled with sand.

Urn 7 was a burial urn accompanied by an accessory vessel like the ones from Bedd Branwen. The two pots are described as "touching", so presumably they were together in the one cist. Urn 7 was inverted and Urn 8 was found broken, on its side, with the mouth away from Urn 7. Originally it must have been standing upright, an arrangement recalling Pots E and F at Bedd Branwen. Unlike the Bedd Branwen pots, however, Urn 8 was empty; it contained neither earth nor ear bones.[93]

When this ritual involving the burial of accessory vessels is more fully studied and understood, it may well emerge that this practice of leaving an empty pot is quite a common variation. In Wales, there are examples of the practice at South Hill, Talbenny, Pembrokeshire, and at Llangwm, Denbighshire.[94] This last comparison is apt because not only is the burial rite similar, but the pottery used is comparable. In both cases the accessory vessels are small pots, best described as Vase Food Vessels. They have simple internally bevelled rims, with concave necks decorated with lines of twisted cord. The body of the Llangwm example is decorated down to the base, a feature typical of this kind of pot in Ireland, while the Llanddyfnan one, being plain below the shoulder like most British Bronze Age pottery, suggests a more distant relationship with Ireland.

The large urns in both cases have the upright collar seen on Pots B and C at Bedd Branwen. This is a rather unusual profile, but one relatively common in Anglesey, where it may be the result of stylistic influences from Ireland reacting on the local Collared urn tradition and producing a straightened version of more classic pots such as the 1813 urn from Bedd Branwen.

The Llanddyfnan and Llangwm burials must also be broadly contemporary. The Llangwm urn contained a segmented bead of faience traditionally dated to the end of the Early Bronze Age, and the Llanddyfnan pot contained three bronze implements characteristic of the "Wessex Culture."

One of these implements, the miniature axe, must have been on the body when it was cremated, since it has been badly twisted by the fire; the other two are unburnt and had been pushed down among the bones after they had been put into the urn. Finally, a piece of antler, 5ins. long and rubbed smooth at each end, had been placed on top of the bones. This piece has since been lost and it is impossible to know its original use.[95]

[93] There is a reference (*Arch. Camb.* 1909. 323) to one piece of bone in this pot. This was assumed to have come from the broken burial urn.
[94] Talbenny: C. F. Fox. *Life and Death in the Bronze Age.* 1959. 51-4.
    Llangwm: Ellis Davies. *Prehistoric and Roman Remains of Denbighshire.* 1929. 275-81.
[95] Several unexplained pieces of antler or bone occur in Wessex graves. (*Devises Museum Catalogue* nos. 212, 289, 290, 325, 385, 386).

The axe is just over 3ins. long, with a blade originally $^{13}/_{16}$ins. wide. It is impossible to say whether it was a functional tool or a ritual miniature version of such a tool. It has very weak cast flanges but no noticeable median ridge, though the butt has been thinned. Its parallel sides and elongated proportions suggest a link with the full-size cast-flanged axes of the Arreton Down tradition, the first native industry to use the Continental two-valve mould.[96]

A very similar miniature axe was found in the Breach Farm barrow, Glamorgan, another rich Welsh burial which shows contact with the influential Wessex area.[97] In that area itself there are comparable axes from Barrow 7, the Ridgeway, Dorset, and Wilsford G58, Wiltshire.[98] The latter accompanied an inhumation, while the former was with a cremation burial but in association with two daggers of the earlier Bush Barrow type. It seems, therefore, that these small axes must have been current about 1,500 B.C. and may occur in graves of either Wessex I or II.

The comparison with the Breach Farm barrow is particularly close, because at that site the axe was again accompanied by two other bronze implements. They were so badly corroded that they crumbled away to dust almost immediately, but in the ground they were just recognisable as a small dagger and a " chisel " with a splayed blade and a tang. This group of objects, therefore, may have been a standard set of equipment for some particular activity, perhaps connected with archery, for the Breach Farm grave also contained a pair of stone arrow-shaft smoothers, objects which have occurred with small axes and chisels at other sites.[99]

The " chisel " and the knife-dagger are more firmly placed in Wessex II, suggesting a date for the whole group closer to 1,400 B.C. than to 1,500 B.C. The knife-dagger has a grooved triangular blade reminiscent of those on Bush Barrow daggers, but the three rivets and the decoration in the central panel link it to a hybrid group, contemporary with the Camerton-Snowshill daggers of Wessex II. These have recently been studied in detail by Mrs. Proudfoot, who has shown that they occur with cremation burials in association with characteristic German imports such as crutch-headed pins, and have a distribution which is virtually restricted to the West Country, especially the Dorchester area, where the type may originate.[101] For while they are clearly related to Continental daggers with pointillé decoration, they are unlikely to be imports, because on all the French and German examples the dots form a pattern, rather than simply filling the area, as here. The Llanddyfnan dagger shows a further variation in that

[96] D. Britton. PPS. XXIX. 1963. 258-325.
[97] W. F. Grimes. PPS. IV. 1938. 107-121 (113, fig. 4).
[98] Ridgeway: *Dorset Arch. and Nat. Hist.* LVIII. 1936. 18-25.
    Wilsford: *Devizes Museum Catalogue.* 102, no. 213.
[99] Arrowsmoothers and axe and/or 'chisel': Breach Farm; Wilsford; Collingbourne Kingston (see below) and Froxfield, Hants. (Winchester Museum, *ex info.* C. B. Burgess).
[101] E. V. W. Proudfoot. PPS. XXIX. 1963. 395-425.

the punch marks are short lines rather than dots. The variation is a slight one, however, and it should not be necessary to adduce elaborate parallels to explain it. The lost dagger from Winterbourne Monkton seems to have been decorated by dashes in the same way, and this came from near Dorchester itself.[102]

The 'chisel' is basically such a simple object that it is difficult to classify and date precisely. It is completely flat with a sharp semi-circular blade which would not be ideal for use as a chisel. Its identification as a chisel is still more suspect because the butt has also been brought to a sharp edge. It looks as if it was a double-ended cutting implement of some kind with a handle in the centre. This might perhaps explain the unusual length of the tang. An implement found on the sandhills at Glenluce, Wigtownshire, is very similar in size and proportion, but it does not have

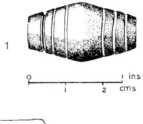

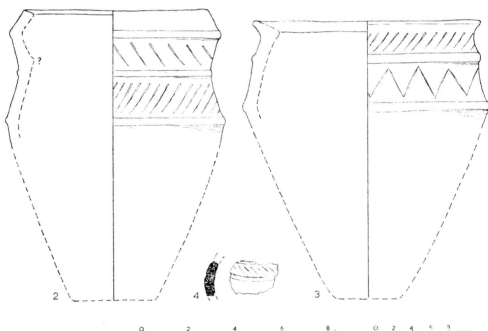

FIG. 49 — Treiorwerth: pottery and jet bead from disturbed areas.
(1-3 after W. O. Stanley; 4, found in 1968 excavations.)

[102] *ibid.* 408. and fig. 8, no. 11.

the sharpened butt.[103] More useful for dating are two small implements from barrows, one from a grave at Collingbourne Kingston, Wiltshire, which also contained an arrow-shaft straightener like the ones from Breach Farm, and another from a barrow on Arreton Down, Isle of Wight, in which a Camerton-Snowshill dagger was found.[104] However, neither of these 'chisels' is exactly the same as the Llanddyfnan example.

The community buried at Llanddyfnan show the same combination of local and exotic traits as the family at Bedd Branwen. The pottery, with its Cordoned urns and Food Vessel, possibly reveals rather closer links with the north, links which are confirmed by the Irish and Scottish metal work. However, here as at Bedd Branwen the really expensive items came from the south, from the territory of the Wessex chieftains who, we may presume, set the fashions for the rest of the country. But the southern burial customs were not followed, for the Llanddyfnan barrow is a typical western multiple burial site, sharing with Bedd Branwen the ritual which involved the burying of accessory vessels, but in this case without the ear bones.

The barrow at Treiorwerth, near Bodedern (NGR SH/354806), has several points of similarity with both Llanddyfnan and Bedd Branwen, but disturbance of the mound in the Early Mediaeval period and more recently has been so extensive that a great deal of important information has been lost.

The barrow is sited in a prominent position on the top of a rocky ridge overlooking Llyn Llywenan and the flat lands stretching west to Holy Island. The mound is still quite noticeable though it is surrounded by a forestry plantation. The barrow is 48ft. in diameter and about 6ft. high. It was a simple cairn of large stones capped with a thick layer of orange/yellow clay which also filled the interstices between the stones. The position of Pot 2, which stood on top of the clay layer, suggests that some of the dark earth which at present forms the topmost layer may be an original Bronze Age deposit; alternatively, the thickness of the yellow clay, now 1ft. 7ins. at most, may have been much reduced in the course of its long history of destruction.

This history began at an early date, when at least three inhumation cists, built of thin upright stones, were dug into the top of the mound. Two of these (6ft. long and 1ft. 4ins. wide) were for adults, and the third (2ft. 6ins. by 1ft. 6ins.) was for a child. No bones survived because of the acidity of the soil, and there were no grave goods of any kind. This last fact and the east-west orientation of the tombs suggests that they may be early Christian graves, though it is strange to find them in a pagan mound and so far from a church. There is a possibility that they might date from the Roman period, a suggestion supported by the reputed finding of Romano-

---

[103] Sir John Evans. *Ancient Bronze Implements.* 1881. 166. fig. 192.
[104] Collingbourne Kingston: *Devises Museum Catalogue.* 112, no. 387.
    Arreton Down: PPS. XXVI. 1960. 275, fig. 6, 4.

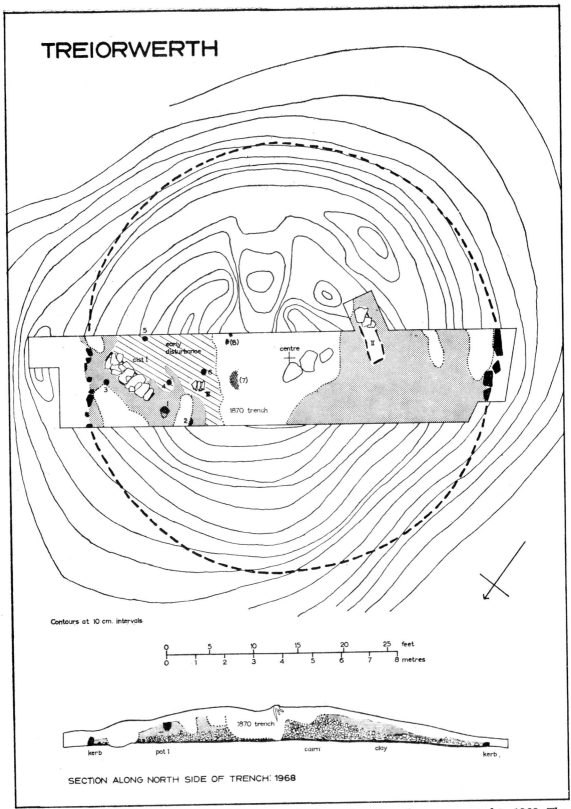

TREIORWERTH

Contours at 10 cm. intervals.

early disturbance

cist 1

centre

1870 trench

SECTION ALONG NORTH SIDE OF TRENCH: 1968

kerb   pot 1   cairn   clay   kerb.

FIG. 50 — Treiorwerth: contour plan of barrow with plan and section of area excavated in 1968. The position of Bronze Age pottery and the Early Mediaeval cists are shown.

British pottery in the top of the mound,[105] though the absence of grave goods makes this unlikely. Moreover the type of cist is almost identical to those found close to old churches[106] and, though it seems strange, it is not unknown for presumably Christian burials to be found in earlier barrows. There was a very similar cist with an extended inhumation in the Kilpaison barrow, Pembrokeshire,[107] and at four other Anglesey sites: Llanddyfnan, Merddyn Gwyn and Porth Dafarch II and III, there were extended inhumations which are likely to belong to this same period.

When the Cambrian Archaeological Association put a trench into the mound in 1870 they found that they were not the first to have dug there.[108] Near the centre they found one group of undisturbed cremated bones without any pottery, lying in a mass of charcoal. [109] All the other urns and deposits that they came across had already been mixed and broken. At least three pots must have been involved, one of which may have contained the large jet bead found in the course of this rather hurried digging.[110] This bead, with grooves apparently filled with a white material, is very similar to the ones from Pot H, Bedd Branwen, indicating contact with the same supplier of luxury goods.

In 1968 a further trench was cut right across the mound at right angles to that dug in 1870.[111] This revealed the simple structure of the barrow and produced six more urns and another cremation burial without pottery. This burial (7) and Pot 6 were in shallow holes dug into the old ground surface beneath the cairn, while pots 1 and 3 had been incorporated into the barrow as it was being built. This was the same system as that used at Llanddyfnan and, as at that site, the burials were confined to a restricted area of the monument.

Pots 4 and 5 were clearly secondaries, put in at a slightly later date, since one could see the outline of the pits dug for their insertion. Unfortunately, they had been badly broken and only the base survived in each case. There were some burnt bones close to Pot 4, which must have been a burial urn, but none was found in the vicinity of Pot 5, which contained only black earth. The status of Pot 2 is more doubtful, but the weight of the evidence suggests that it, too, was secondary. It was standing inverted on top of the yellow clay; there was no pit visible, but the whole area had been heavily disturbed and the pot itself badly broken. It had originally contained bone.

From the primary group there were two or three burials and two pots

[105] *Arch. Camb.* 1875. 126-8.
[106] Graves near Llanrhuddlad and Llechcynfarwy churches. TAAS. 1935. 189-91.
[107] *Arch. Camb.* 1926. 1-35.
[108] E. L. Barnwell. *Arch. Camb.* 1873. 195-7.
[109] Stanley, in republishing the pottery (*Arch. Camb.* 1875. *loc. cit.*) implies that unburnt bones were found but there is no mention of these in the original account.
[110] The two pots published by Stanley and a third, of which one sherd was found in the filling of the 1870 trench during 1968 excavations.
[111] Excavation report forthcoming in *Arch. Camb.*

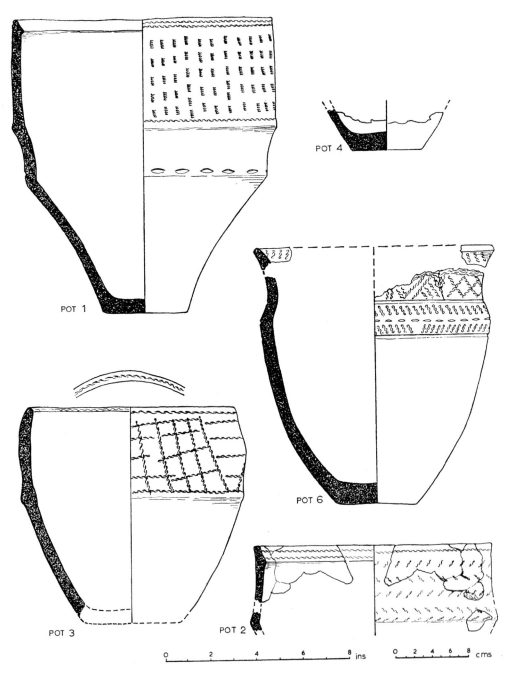

POT 4

POT 1

POT 6

POT 3

POT 2

0   2   4   6   8 ins

0   2   4   6   8 cms

FIG. 51 — Treiorwerth: pottery from the 1968 excavations. Pots 1, 6 and 3 are primary; pots 2 and 4 are secondary.

without the normal content of bone. Although these can be closely compared to the accessory vessels at Bedd Branwen, at Treiorwerth, there was no obvious pairing of the pots.

Pot 1, a large urn with a deep collar and a very narrow base, was in the clay layer above the cairn. It was tightly packed around with clean clay and must have been buried as this layer was being built up. It was covered with a flat stone which lay flush with the top of the clay. The pot is decorated with twisted and whipped cord impressions, and around the shoulder there is a line of oval notches cut out, with a thumb-nail making a 'necklace' feature like the ones on several pots from Bedd Branwen. The bones were those of an adult male and a woman of about twenty; they had no grave goods.

Burial 7 was also without grave goods and had been put into a bag rather than a pot, for the bones were lying in a compact mass in a shallow hole. They were the remains of a young adult of unknown sex. The cairn would originally have covered them, but it had been removed by the excavators of 1870. The bones may actually have been the remainder of the mass of bone found in 1870 and partly left *in situ*. Alternatively, another group of bones found somewhat scattered a few feet away may be what they were referring to. This burial of a young adult, who may have suffered from tuberculosis, had probably been in a similar hole before it was disturbed.

Pot 3 had been standing upright on a small nest of stones near the eastern edge of the barrow. One side was intact, surrounded by the stones of the cairn, but the other had been removed by a recent hole which had been dug down to the bedrock. The pot was a small Cordoned urn rather similar to Urn 6 from Llanddyfnan, but less barrel-shaped and without the lower cordon. It is rather roughly decorated with twisted cord mainly in a cross-hatched design with one triangular panel of horizontal lines. It contained only earth with a little charcoal.

Pot 6 was found inverted in a shallow hole beneath the cairn. It had been damaged before burial (most of the rim had been broken off) and the weight of the cairn had crushed it still further. It is an unusual pot, perhaps rather a Food Vessel than a Collared urn. The fabric is more compact than that of the average Collared urn; the shoulder is much more rounded, and emphasised by two shallow channels or grooves — a technique of decoration rare on Collared urns. However, it does share the 'necklace' feature with the contemporary Collared urns. A single sherd from what must have been a similar pot was found in the disturbed area in the centre of the barrow (Fig. 49, No. 4).

Pot 6 contained mostly earth and charcoal, but mixed with it were a few pieces of burnt bone. These included the petrous temporal bones (ear bones) of a child about six years old, the crowns from several teeth and some thin fragments of the vault of the skull, all probably from the same child. The impression given is that the ear bones were the intentional deposit and that the outer pieces were accidentally gathered up with them.

This practice links Treiorwerth very closely with Bedd Branwen; the two communities or families must have shared the same religious rituals and beliefs in some detail. This is not surprising since the two sites are only a few miles apart and their contemporaneity is confirmed by the presence of very similar jet beads at both. What is rather more surprising is the difference in pottery styles favoured by the two groups.

The barrow at Merddyn Gwyn, Pentraeth (NGR SH/521792), was built at the beginning of the Bronze Age to cover an inhumation burial accompanied by a Beaker.[112] The barrow at that time had been a small oval cairn surrounded by a kerb of large limestone blocks. Towards the end of the period, some time in the fifteenth century B.C., it was re-used and enlarged by the addition of a capping of earth which increased its size by about 28 feet. However, before it was covered, the original cairn had been disturbed and the kerb removed in the north-eastern quadrant.

The stones seem to have been replaced in part by gravel, but at least some of this gravel may have been introduced at a much later date, when a grave for an extended burial, without grave goods, was dug. This grave, orientated east-west, was sunk about 3ft. into the subsoil and was filled with limestone blocks from the original cairn. Above it, the mound was of gravel. The precise date of this burial is not clear, but it is probably Early Mediaeval, like the intrusive cists in the top of the barrow at Treiorwerth.

Although the barrow had been enlarged for later Bronze Age burials, at least one had been placed in the original cairn. This was one of the large urns (4 or 5) with a deep collar. It had been smashed by the railway's mechanical excavator, so no details of the burial are recorded. It may have been buried after the enlargement had been made and the position of the original cairn forgotten.

The only burial to be found *in situ* was that in 1 which had stood inverted, presumably on the old ground surface and certainly close against the kerb of the earlier cairn. The pot, which is technically an Enlarged Food Vessel, is typologically very interesting because it retains a well marked interrupted groove around the shoulder, the sort of feature which is thought to be ancestral to the residual 'necklace' seen on so many of the Collared urns in the island. The bones it contained were those of a woman, and amongst them was a small bone pommel almost identical to those from Bedd Branwen.[113] There was no sign of any metal blade: this is clearly another instance of the custom of burying part of the object as symbol of the whole, or, more probably, of using a special funerary version, perhaps made of wood.

Six feet away, but not found *in situ*, were the remains of a small pot

---

[112] Report by Harold Hughes compiled from his own and others' observations made during the destruction of the barrow to make way for the railway. *Arch. Camb.* 1908. 211-20 with additional notes, p. 297.

[113] This was subsequently lost. The damage suggests that it had been burnt, but this is not stated. There was also one bone from a dog in the urn.

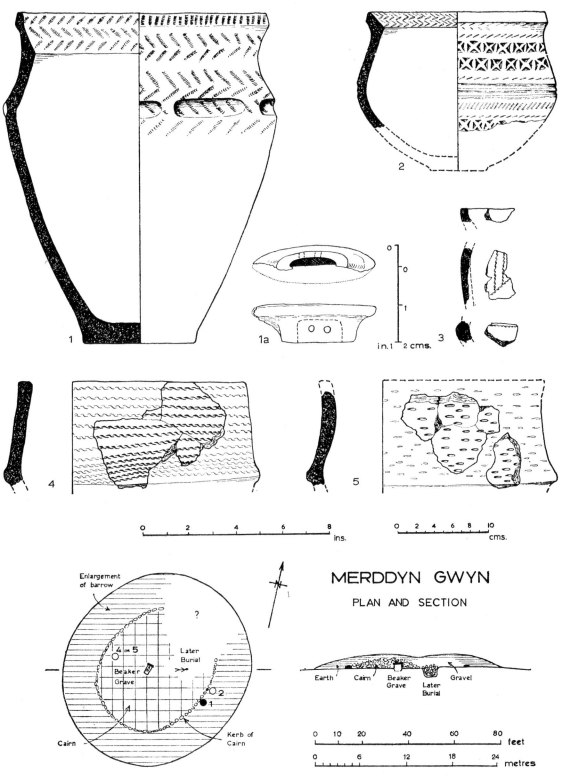

MERDDYN GWYN

PLAN AND SECTION

FIG. 52 — Merddyn Gwyn: plan and section of barrow; pottery and grave goods. (Plan, section and 1a after Harold Hughes; 3, broken sherds doubtfully ascribed to this barrow. See Fig 34 for Beaker, etc.)

at present unique in Anglesey.[114] It is a Bowl Food Vessel decorated with an elaborate pattern carried out in false-relief technique. This system of decoration, in which the motif is left in apparent relief by pressing down the surrounding area with a spatula, is very commonly found on these bowls in Ireland, where this bowl, and the taller Vase Food Vessels which are rather more common in Anglesey, found some of their inspiration. Although both types are broadly contemporary in Ireland, there is a possibility that the Bowls went out of fashion rather earlier than the Vases, a factor which may explain their scarcity in the Anglesey barrows which, by and large, belong to the latter half of the Early Bronze Age. Both kinds of Food Vessel differ from the urns in being more carefully made and decorated, the clay containing only well crushed grit. This may reflect a difference in domestic use, the urns probably acting as storage jars in the home.

Bowl Food Vessels often accompany inhumations; even where they are found with cremations, it is very unusual for them to actually contain the bones. It is not stated that the Food Vessel from Merddyn Gwyn contained bone, but since it was already broken when found, one cannot say that it definitely did not. It does remain a possibility, however, that, since they were found close together, Pots 1 and 2 formed a pair after the manner of Bedd Branwen and Llanddyfnan. In any case, their position close to the kerb of the Beaker barrow suggests that they were both buried at the same time, that is, when the enlargement was made to cover them.

The second of the large urns (5), which must have been at least twelve inches in diameter, has also been broken by the mechanical excavator, and its position within the barrow is not recorded. Harold Hughes says that no decoration was observable; this is strange, since the sherds now in Bangor Museum clearly show a pattern of oval impressions. These look as if they are an imitation of wicker work. One must remember that baskets and such-like would have been in constant use alongside the more durable pottery vessels.

In Bangor Museum there are also a few sherds from another urn, decorated with twisted cord (3), which is said to come from this barrow at Merddyn Gwyn. In the report there is no mention of any further urns, but it is perfectly possible that there had been other burials which had been destroyed without record by the railway excavators. Alternatively there is a possibility that these sherds come not from Merddyn Gwyn but from Llanddyfnan, for the surviving sherds answer perfectly the description of Urn 3 from that site.[115] The original owner, the Rev. E. Evans, was associated with the excavation from both barrows.

The surface beneath the barrow is said to have been burnt over a considerable area and pitted with large holes filled with earth; unfortunately the record of these holes in the old ground surface is incomplete.[116] They are

[114] The lost ' urns ' from Pen y Bonc may have been of this type. It was first identified by W. E. Griffiths. TAAS, 1956, 6-8.
[115] Arch. Camb. 1909. 316.
[116] Additional notes. Arch. Camb. 1908. 297.

said to have been 3ft. across and 3ft. deep, dimensions which make them far too large to have been stake or post holes : they must remain an enigma. It is not stated whether they lay under the original barrow or its enlargement. It is also said that three human skulls, several animal bones and two flint flakes were found in the make-up of the mound, but the exact position of these finds is not given. The discovery of human bones casually thrown in to the mound as it was being built up is not uncommon, and is another aspect of the rather macabre side of Bronze Age life.

The barrows at Porth Dafarch, Holyhead (NGR SH/234801), provide another instance of the use of burial places for many centuries (Fig. 35). Porth Dafarch II, the central barrow in the group of three, was built to cover the Beaker burial described in the previous chapter. It was subsequently reused, but apparently not enlarged, when the other barrows were being built. The only urn recorded was found not far from the Beaker grave, inverted on a stone and protected by a small stone cist.[117] It is described as 8ins. in diameter and undecorated. In the British Museum, with the Beakers from this barrow are two sherds which are probably from this urn. One of them has three wide grooves, suggesting that the pot might have been rather similar to the one from Porth Dafarch I. This pot contained no bones and must originally have accompanied a burial urn which Stanley did not find.

Porth Dafarch I, a small low cairn about 30ft. in diameter, stood about 60ft. nearer the sea than Porth Dafarch II. It was dug into in 1848 by a local farmer, from whom W. O. Stanley obtained details of the finds.[118] There is a possibility, already mentioned, that this barrow, too, might have been built during the Beaker period, for there was a large empty stone cist found somewhere beneath the cairn. However, Stanley's account of this is somewhat confused; he states that it was built of four stones, but then compares it to the Early Mediaeval cist at Towyn y Capel which contained at least twelve slabs. Since both Porth Dafarch II and III had been disturbed by Early Mediaeval graves, the question must remain open.

Two urn burials are recorded from this barrow. They both contained accessory cups and may, therefore, be roughly contemporary with the building of Bedd Branwen. The first one was found 2ft. from the surface of the cairn. The height of the barrow is not given, but there is a strong presumption that this burial was in the body of the cairn, not on the old ground surface. However, as the evidence from Llanddyfnan shows, this does not necessary mean that it was a later insertion.

The urn was inverted and had been protected by a flat stone placed over it and some pebbles set around the rim. It contained the bones of a woman of perhaps 24 years, some bones of a dog, a single bronze rivet, and

---

[117] W. O. Stanley, *Arch. J.* XXXIII. 1876. 138-41. Plan opp. p. 129 and *Arch. Camb.* 1878. 34.
[118] *Arch. J.* VI. 1849. 226-39 and *Arch. Camb.* 1868. 222-31.

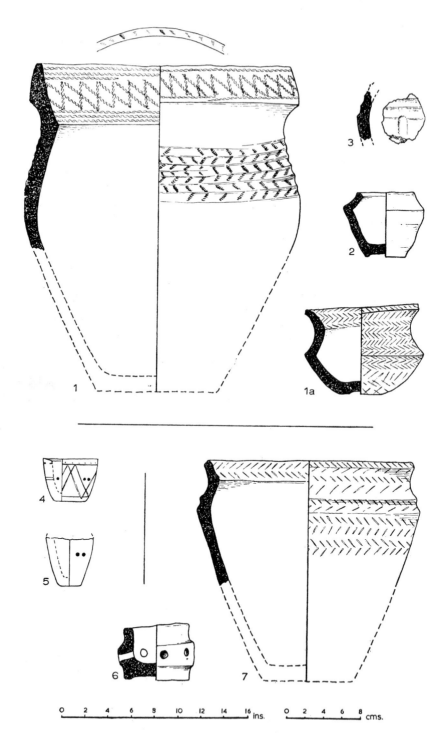

FIG. 53 — Pottery from various sites: 1, 1a and 2, Porth Dafarch I;
3, Porth Dafarch II; 4-5, Flagstaff Quarry, Penmon; 6-7, Cerrig Dewi,
Llangwyllog. (4-5 after the Rev. E. Owen.)

it had been inverted over an accessory cup which was standing upright on a small flat stone. This cup had been lined with braken and contained the incomplete skeleton of a very young child. Unfortunately the bones from the two pots had become rather mixed by the time they were sent for examination, and the surviving bones from the child burial are not listed. The death of a mother and child might very possibly be natural, but the incompleteness of the child's skeleton is strongly suggestive of ritual practices akin to those at Bedd Branwen.

The urn is a large Collared urn with the characteristic internal moulding of the rim. It is elaborately decorated with twisted cord on the collar, and whipped cord 'maggots' on the shoulder between the wide grooves or fluting. This corrugation of the surface is a rather unusual variant of the grooving which is fairly common on Food Vessels and related pottery. It seems to have been popular in this community for it occurs again on the sherd from Porth Dafarch II.

The accessory cup is rather larger than is usual in this group, and it should not perhaps be classified as such.[119] It has been considered as a miniature Food Vessel, but, though the fabric and decoration would be appropriate, the shape is not typical. Typologically, therefore, it is anomalous, but clearly it was being used in the same way as the normal accessory cups and vessels.

The second burial was found "adjacent" to the first. It was in an inverted urn without any protective cist. This urn, which had presumably held bone, also contained an accessory cup which is said to have contained "ashes". This word is rather ambiguous, but presumably there was some bone in this pot as well. The large urn had been smashed and none of it was preserved; the accessory cup survived intact.

This is a small bipartite pot of which the closest analogue is the one found inside Pot L at Bedd Branwen. They have similar proportions and share an absence of decoration and an omphaloid base, but the one from Porth Dyfarch has no perforation in the shoulder and is rather less carefully made, though the clay is more compact and better fired than that of the urns.

Very little is known about the Bronze Age levels of Porth Dyfarch III; it was completely overlain by Romano-British huts and enclosures and had been further disturbed by a long stone cist with an inhumation burial.[120] All the Bronze Age burials had been removed before W. O. Stanley arrived on the scene, and there is no record of them beyond the fact that there were several, some in urns and some in small 'beehive' cists without pottery. Some had certainly been interfered with at an early date, for a Roman gem and a decorated bone pin were found very close to one cist. A dry stone

[119] H. N. Savory. BBCS. XVII. 1956-8. 206. Dr. Savory considers it to be a Food Vessel. It is, however, similar to a small accessory vessel found with a Collared urn at Tyringham, Bucks. PPS. XXVII. 1961. 279. fig. 10.
[120] W. O. Stanley. *Arch. J.* XXXIII. 1876. 132-8.

wall, 2ft. 6ins. high, was found somewhere in this mound. It might possibly have been a kerb to the barrow, but it might equally have been part of an enclosure wall of later date.

Unfortunately even less is known about the barrows at Cerrig Dewi, Llangwyllog (NGR SH/440780).[121] Their exact position is not recorded, but they probably stood on the low promontory which overlooks what must then have been an area of bog drained by the Cefni. It is said that several barrows were levelled by the farmer in 1869 or thereabouts. The number is not given, but it is likely that they were a small cemetery group like that at Llanddyfnan.

Only two pots were rescued from this destruction (Fig. 53, Nos. 6 and 7). The one said to have contained bone is a small urn or Enlarged Food Vessel with a high grooved shoulder. The other is a peculiar accessory cup said to have been empty when found. It is not known whether they came from the same barrow.

The accessory cup is unusual and unlike any of the others found in Anglesey or North Wales.[122] It is basically a straight-sided pot with a thick central band pierced by seven large holes. These holes are much larger than the usual paired perforations, and it is possible that they represent a clumsy attempt to make an open-work cup. This type is admittedly rare in Wales, but there is one from Bryn Seiont, Caernarvon, not so very far away.[123] The Cerrig Dewi cup is made from a rather soft red clay similar to that used for the accessory cup at Bedd Branwen and it has an omphaloid base like the one from Porth Dafarch.

Accessory cups have normally been found associated with much larger pots which contained the burnt bones. However, they are sometimes found without any other pottery, lying on top of, or beside, a pile of cremated bone. In Anglesey there is only one instance of this practice: in a barrow at Penmon where, in fact, two accessory cups were found.

The site was on the top of a prominent headland now partly removed by the Flagstaff Quarry (NGR SH/634806). It was in the course of quarrying operations that the cairn was discovered in 1889.[124] It seems to have been extremely small, only 3ft. long and oblong in shape, built of blocks of local limestone. It is very probable that this was only the central core of a larger earthen barrow by then badly denuded; not surprisingly in this very exposed position. This small cairn covered a slightly smaller grave cut into the underlying rock and containing a good deal of cremated bone and charcoal, with the two very small cups lying on top of it at one end. They were resting on their sides, mouth to mouth. Amongst the bones there was a perforated bone object, which was unfortunately lost. There was also

[121] W. O. Stanley. *Arch. J.* XXVII. 1870. 154-7.
[122] H. N. Savory. BBCS. XVIII. 1958-60. 115. D6. Dr. Savory considers it a " debased bipartite type ".
[123] *ibid.* 108. fig. 5, 6.
[124] Rev. E. Owen. *Arch. Camb.* 1889. 59-62.

something described as leather which might possibly have been the remains of a bag which had held the bones.

The accessory cups were subsequently lost, but an engraving of them exists and their dimensions are known (Fig. 53, Nos. 4 and 5). They are both much smaller than the other cups from Anglesey. The decorated one is complete; in shape it is a simple truncated cone, a shape which is rare in Wales and is considered more characteristic of eastern England.[125] It is quite simply decorated with incised lines and two pairs of holes piercing the walls about halfway down. The rim is described as "perforated, the holes forming two distinct circles around the inside and outside edges".[126] These do not show on the engraving.

From the engraving the second cup appears to be of a similar shape but slightly taller, undecorated and with only two holes. The description, however, states that the mouth had "jagged, uneven edges".[127] This suggests that the actual rim may not have been present. The pot might originally have been bipartite like the one from Bedd Branwen.[128]

The bone object was described as "a skewer or bone pin, ornamented round with an indentation, and a hole through midway between its ends".[129] It was compared to the bar of a steel guard passed through the button-hole of a waistcoat. It is probable that it was some sort of toggle, like the ones found by Mortimer in two Food Vessel barrows in Yorkshire.[130] These toggles are an interesting type, perhaps dating back to the Beaker period when people seem to have worn quite elaborately tailored clothes. A definite association with accessory cups would establish their long currency, but the association here should not be pressed because the identification of the object is tentative.

Several objects dating from the Bronze Age, both tools and burials, have been found in the vicinity of Menai Bridge. The Straits are narrow here, with firm ground on either side, making it attractive as a crossing point, then as now. There have been at least three separate discoveries of cremation burials between Cadnant and Telford's bridge. All of them came to light during road works and are, consequently, badly recorded. W. O. Stanley and Albert Way gathered the information together in 1868, but it is sometimes difficult to identify the surviving pots.[131]

The first discovery (Menai Bridge I) was made in 1825 in the grounds of Plas Cadnant while building the road to Beaumaris. Presumably the site was somewhere close to the shore, just south of Cadnant Bridge

---

[125] H. N. Savory. *op. cit.* 104.
[126] *Arch. Camb.* 1889. 61.
[127] *ibid.*
[128] The use of damaged pots is not unusual. A good deal of the rim of Pot 1a from Bedd Branwen was missing and most of the rim of Pot 6, Treiorwerth, had been broken off before it was buried.
[129] *op. cit.* 60.
[130] D. D. A. Simpson *in* Simpson and Coles (edd) *Studies in Ancient Europe.* 1968. 200, illustrated 199, fig. 45, 4 and 201, fig. 46. 3.
[131] *Arch. Camb.* 1868. 243-5.

(NGR SH/560728). Stanley records only one urn from here, the one that was formerly in the Caernarvon Museum; but sherds from two others, now in the British Museum, are said to have been found in cutting the road between Menai Bridge and Beaumaris. They were bought in 1875 from the Rev. W. C. Lukis who may have taken them away to the Channel Islands before Stanley heard of the find. Lukis's son was in Anglesey in 1865.

No details are known about the burials, not even whether they were marked by a barrow. The urns, if they belong together, are quite varied.

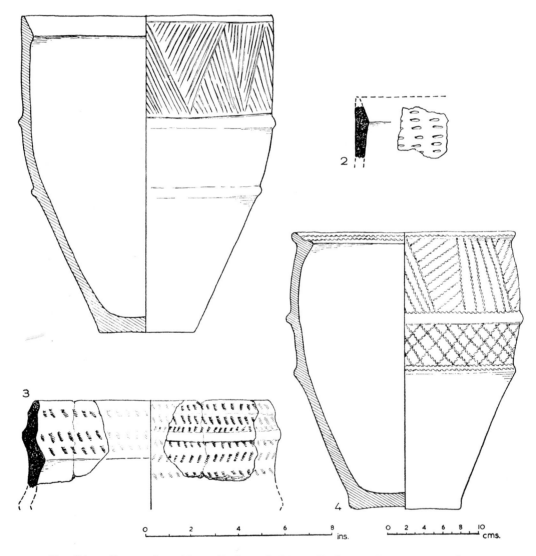

Fig. 54 — Pottery from Menai Bridge: 1, Menai Bridge II; 2-4, Menai Bridge I.
(1 and 4 after R.C.A.M.)

The most complete pot is an Overhanging Rim urn, a type traditionally considered to be slightly later in date than the Collared urns in which the collar, or rim, is less deep.[132] However, evidence from Bedd Branwen (Pot H) and Cae Mickney suggests that, in Anglesey at least, this distinction does not have much significance. Fig. 54, No. 3 has the peculiar upright neck characteristic of Anglesey and is very similar to Pot B from Bedd Branwen. Little can be said about No. 2 except that its decoration is almost identical to that on one of the urns from Merddyn Gwyn.

The second burial (Menai Bridge II) came to light in 1855 just opposite the Anglesey Arms Hotel (NGR SH/555717).[133] There were two pots involved; one certainly contained bone and had been protected by a cist. Nothing is known about the other which was sent to London. It is very unlikely that it is one of those at present in the British Museum since these were bought from Lukis. The other urn was in Liverpool Museum where it was destroyed during the war. It was a large pot with a deep collar, decorated simply with incised lines.

Nothing now survives from the third group (Menai Bridge III), found in 1864 close to the pier (NGR SH/558720).[134] This is particularly regrettable because these were the only burials here with grave goods. The finding of two urns is recorded; both contained burnt bones; in one of them there was a bronze awl, 3½ins. long, with one end pointed and the other flattened. It must have been closely comparable to the one from Cae Mickney (Fig. 55, No. 1a), which unfortunately is not so well preserved. One of the urns was undecorated and apparently of unusual shape.

Capt. Griffiths, who supplied Stanley with the information about this find, also sent a small bronze blade which he had found "amongst bones at the same spot".[135] This, presumably, was not from either of the pots mentioned above, but must have come from a third burial in the same group. The blade was 2½ins. long and ⅝in. wide; no rivet holes are mentioned. It is too narrow to have been a knife blade, but the measurements tally almost exactly with those of the small notched razor from Kilmore, Co. Westmeath, and the tanged razor from Cremation 14, Knockast, in the same county.[136]

No barrows are mentioned as covering the burials at Menai Bridge, but this is perhaps not surprising since they were within a built-up area. However, the lack of covering mound may have been original, for there are two known instances of unmarked burials in Anglesey, and at least one in Caernarvonshire.[137]

---

[132] W. F. Grimes. *The Prehistory of Wales*. 1951. 91-6.
[133] *Arch. Camb.* 1868. 243-4 and *Arch. Camb.* 1930. 405-7. Two years later a stone axe or battle axe of limestone containing fossil shells was found at the same spot.
[134] *Arch. Camb.* 1868. 245.
[135] *ibid.*
[136] Kilmore: E. Prendergast. JRSAI. XC. 1960. 5-9. fig. 2a.
     Knockast: H. Henken and H. Movius. PRIA. 41. C. 1934. 232-84. fig. 2. E.
[137] Llysdu, near Dolbenmaen, Caerns. *Arch. Camb.* 1861. 90; 1923. 311-2; and 1941. 190.

The largest and best known of these flat burial areas was at Cae Mickney, Llanidan (NGR SH/456683), where thirty-two burials were found in 1882.[138] The first urns were found by a labourer digging a ditch for a new hedge: the others were then excavated by Hugh Prichard of Dinam. He made a thorough search for the remains of a barrow, but could find none; all the burials were within 6 - 12 inches of the surface, and there was no increase in the stone content of the earth above them, nor was there any indication of a buried surface. Rowlands does not record any mound here in 1723, although he mentions a number of other possible earthworks in the area, most of which had disappeared by Prichard's time.[139] One may confidently state, therefore, that these burials had never been marked by a mound, though it remains possible that the area had been marked out in some way during its period of use, for the deposits were restricted to a circular area about 36ft. in diameter.[140] It is probable that this period of use was relatively short, perhaps one or two generations longer than Bedd Branwen, judging by the number of burials. However, the nature of the site, so close to the modern surface, means that no reliable information could ever have been gained on this point.

There were thirty-two burials in all. Seven of the cremations were simply set into a hole without an urn, the rest were contained in pots. They are not described in detail, but it is implied that most of the urns were inverted and protected by small stone cists, perhaps in some cases consisting of no more than top and bottom stones. However, some were unprotected and some were buried upright. Five of the urns had almost completely disintegrated; nine others were badly damaged, and thirteen were tolerably well preserved and are described in some detail by Prichard.[141]

There were no grave goods except an awl found in the urn illustrated in Fig. 55, No. 1. It is broken, and both ends are damaged, but it had not

[138] Hugh Prichard. *Arch. Camb.* 1882. 210-8. 'Cae Mickney' is a corruption of 'Cae Meini' but has been retained here because the site has become known in archaeological literature by this name. The name Cae Meini, which applies to the farm as a whole, should not be considered good evidence of a cairn.

[139] Henry Rowlands. *Mona Antiqua Restaurata.* 2nd. ed. 1766. 93. Pl. V. Discussed by Prichard. *op. cit.* 213-6.

[140] It is conceivable that the area might have been marked by a low bank, making something comparable to the southern English Pond Barrows. (See P. Ashbee. *The Bronze Age Round Barrow in Britain.* 1960. 25-7, 82).

[141] Twelve of these thirteen pots still survived in the 1930s when a selection of them were drawn at Dinam by the Royal Commission. Nine still survive in Bangor Museum to which they were transferred in 1942. These are shown in Figs 55 & 56. nos. 1-12. (1=Prichard 4; 2=P10; 3=P2; 4=P11; 5=P6; 6=P9; 7=P3; 8=P7; 9=P5; 10=P1; 11 = P13; 12 = P8). P12, a small undecorated urn was not drawn by the RCAM and has been lost. Fig. 56 no. 13 is in the Bangor reserve collection, unlabelled. It was drawn by the RCAM at Dinam so most likely belongs to this group, though it is not described by Prichard, which is strange since so much survives. Fig. 56 nos. 14-17 are also unlabelled in the Bangor reserve collection and can be ascribed to Cae Mickney with less certainty. However the accessions book lists " sherds of various Cinerary Urns " from the Dinam Collection and the great similarity between nos. 11 and 15 makes it more than likely that these are the sherds in question.

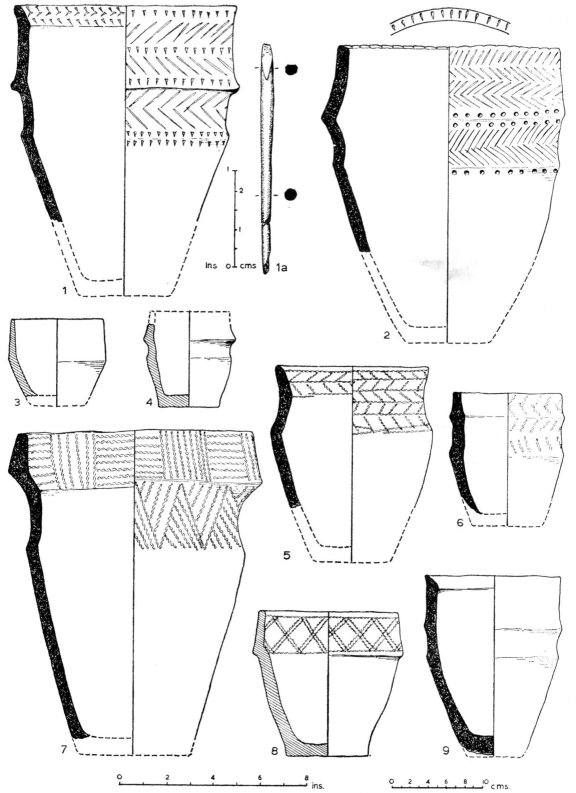

FIG. 55 — Pottery and metal awl from Cae Mickney, Llanidan. (3, 4 and 8 after R.C.A.M.)

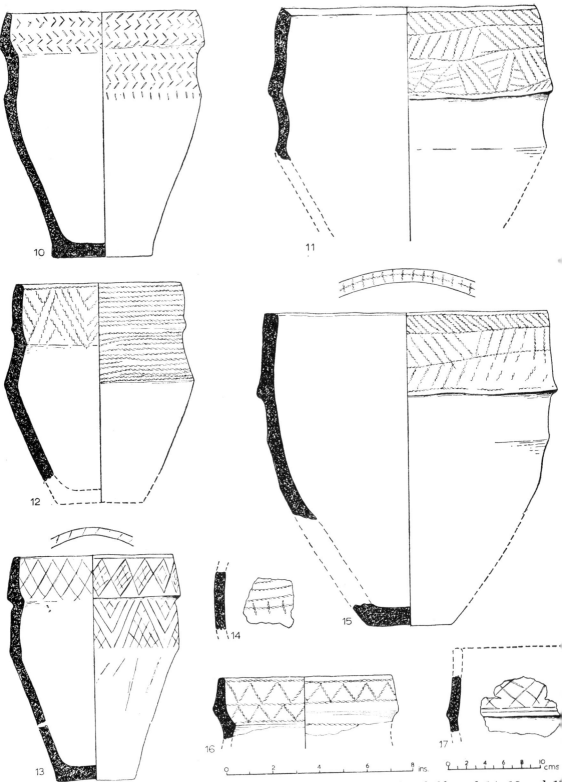

Fig. 56 — Pottery from Cae Mickney, Llanidan. (13 almost certainly, 15 probably and 14, 16 and 1 possibly from this site.)

been burnt. The metal used is not bronze but a mixture of copper and lead.[142]
The two form a mixture, not an alloy, and the resulting metal has an
attractive gold colour but would be far too soft for practical use as an
awl. Some of these pins, therefore, may have been used decoratively in
clothing or hair. The use of lead may imply experimentation on the part
of local smiths, who could probably obtain lead more easily than tin.

The seven unurned cremations and the twenty-seven pots make a total
of thirty-four, not thirty-two, so it might be presumed that the two accessory
cups were found inside two of the larger urns. If that had been the case,
however, it is strange that Prichard did not mention it, since he is careful
to record the awl. It is also strange that No. 3 should have lost its base if it
had been protected inside another pot. Consequently, it is more probable
that these cups had been separately buried but had not contained bone.
It follows from this that all the others must have contained bone, and
Prichard implies this, saying that their contents were "incinerated bones
with an unctuous black mould and ashes". However, some of the pots are
small, comparable in size to Pot M from Bedd Branwen, and one would
expect them to have been used in the same way, that is, as accessory vessels
containing mainly earth and charcoal. It is a pity, therefore, that Prichard
did not record the proportion of bone to mould in each pot, nor the relative
positions of the deposits so that one could check the occurrence of pairing.

I do not propose to discuss the pottery in detail at this point, but it is
perhaps worth making some general remarks. Like the other Anglesey
groups, Bedd Branwen, Treiorwerth and Llanddyfnan, the Cae Mickney
pottery is very varied, a number of different shapes and systems of
decoration being current in the one community; while, on the other hand,
there is a pair of pots, as at Bedd Branwen and Llanddyfnan, which are
so similar that they could well have been made by the same person (Fig. 56,
Nos. 11 and 15). These facts are relevant in discussing both the internal
and external chronology of such groups.

A very similar group of burials was found in 1928 not far from Cae
Mickney when levelling ground to make a tennis court at Plas Penrhyn
(NGR SH/455635).[143] The site was on gently sloping land very close to the
Straits and not far from a long-established ferry to Caernarvon. It is possible
that, like Menai Bridge, this area attracted Bronze Age settlers because of
the easy crossing to the mainland.[144]

Only seven pots were found, but since only a limited area was explored
others, no doubt, remain undisturbed. The extent of the burial area is not
exactly known, but two of the pots were 20ft. apart. Four pots were found
in situ, inverted, without any protective cists, and it is probable that of

---

[142] I am gateful to Dr. D. W. F. James, School of Electronic Engineering Science, UCNW,
for arranging this analysis and for discussing the results with me. This is the only example
of this metal known at present.

[143] E. Neil Baynes. *Arch. Camb.* 1929. 229-36.

[144] A good many Bronze Age burials and bronze implements have been found on the opposite
shore, close to the town of Caernarvon.

the others (broken by the workmen) only No. 7 was standing upright. It is not certain how many actually contained bone. No. 1 certainly did; they were the bones of a woman, mixed with charcoal. So did No. 4, which is exhibited in Bangor Museum with most of its content of earth and bone intact. The small pot, No. 6, contained a mass of dark material with a few tiny pieces of bone. No. 2 most probably contained no bone for its rim was found *in situ* filled with dark material including charcoal. The contents of No. 7 are not described, yet they must have survived since so much of the body of this pot is preserved. It is possible that the reference to a " dark substance, probably charcoal " without bone, which is said to have filled No. 4, applies instead to No. 7.[145] The report was written by Neil Baynes, who was not present when the pots were found, so such a mistake is understandable. The contents of Nos. 3 and 5, both badly broken, are not recorded.

It is clear, therefore, that among this group of seven pots only two contained a normal burial, while three contained no bone, or only a token amount. Even here, where the burials were simply placed in the ground without any permanent monument, it is obvious that the funerary ritual itself must have been quite elaborate, reflecting ideas which we cannot hope to interpret correctly today.

The most interesting pot in this group is the large Encrusted Urn (Fig. 57, No. 5), a type relatively rare in Wales but clearly related to the large series of such urns from Ireland and Scotland. This pot constitutes the strongest evidence for the influence of Irish fashions on the Bronze Age pottery in Anglesey, but it is not an isolated example and, in fact, in this group there are others, such as Nos. 2, 3 and 7, which show similar contact.

Nearly all the sites mentioned above have been those of multiple burials. It is presumed that in each case these burials were made on one or two occasions within a relatively short period, say twenty to fifty years. It has seldom been possible to demonstrate such a short period of use conclusively on the evidence available, but it is clear that this system of burial was prevalent throughout the island during the second half of the Early Bronze Age (about 1,500 - 1,400 B.C.). It may have continued into the later period, but reliable dating is not possible after 1,400 B.C.

There is, however, one barrow which may have contained a single central burial in the southern English manner. This is the small and much ruined cairn situated on the same ridge as Bryn Celli Ddu, some 40 yards south of the Neolithic tomb (NGR SH/507702). Skinner records that this cairn was dug into at the beginning of the last century, when an earthen ' pan ' and a wedge of gold were apparently found.[146] It is possible that this wedge might have been a bronze dagger, but this must remain speculative.

---

[145] *Op. cit.* 233.
[146] Rev. John Skinner. *Ten Days Tour through the Island of Anglesea.* 1802. 24. (Published as a supplement to *Arch. Camb.* 1908).

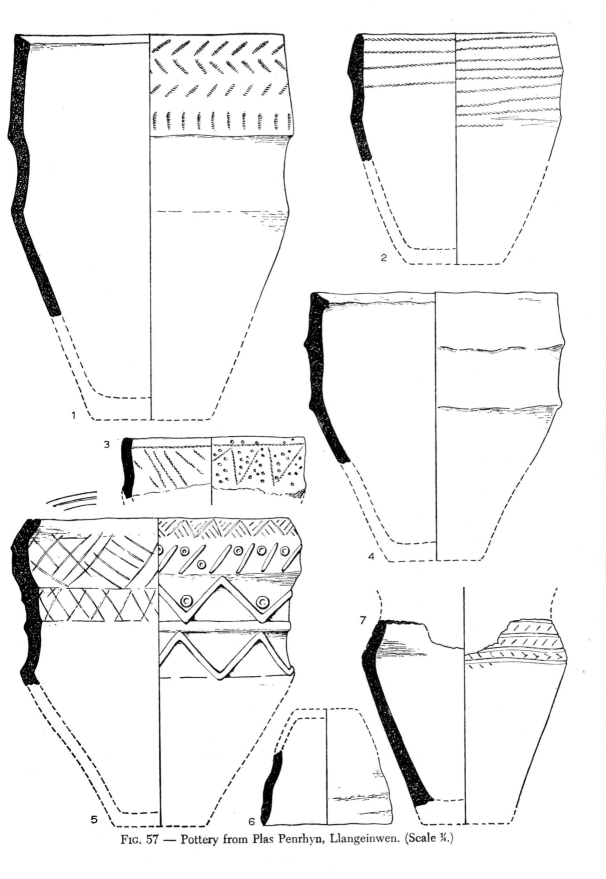

FIG. 57 — Pottery from Plas Penrhyn, Llangeinwen. (Scale ¼.)

This digging did a great deal of damage to the site, and there was very little left when it was excavated in 1929.[147] Enough survived to show that it had been built of small - medium stones mixed with some gravel and edged with a kerb of upright slabs about 68ft. in diameter. In the centre, buried in the ground with the capstone flush with the old surface was a small stone cist 9ins. by 24ins. by 14ins. deep, built of four upright slabs. This cist contained the cremated bones of one adult man, without any pottery or grave goods. Close to this cist were two patches of charcoal, amongst which were a few burnt bones. This whole area had been so thoroughly disturbed and dug over that it is not clear whether or not these represent other burials, such as one might have expected in Anglesey.

Because of the lack of finds, this site cannot be closely dated but it undoubtedly belongs to the Bronze Age. Its proximity to the Neolithic tomb is interesting in that it suggests that the sanctity of Neolithic burial areas did not end when burial in megalithic tombs ceased.[148] This is supported by evidence from other sites in the island where Bronze Age burials have actually been inserted into Neolithic cairns. Sherds from a Collared urn with plaited string decoration were found in the filling of the central chamber at Barclodiad y Gawres.[149] They had probably come from a burial dug into the top of the mound. At Bryn yr Hen Bobl, too, the sanctity of the site continued, for a small Collared urn, decorated with whipped cord and having a 'necklace' around the shoulder, was found inverted in a pit just at the end of the 'terrace'. It contained burnt bone.[150]

Many of the large Neolithic tombs known in the eighteenth century have since disappeared without trace, and it is probable that even more of the far less conspicuous Bronze Age monuments have been destroyed. There are incidental references to urns and burnt bones found in various parts of the island, for instance at Pen yr Orsedd, Rhos-y-bol (NGR SH/415884) and at an unspecified point close to the railway near Llangaffo, but no details are known.[151] A few slivers of talc, now in the National Museum of Wales, which were found amongst the bones in an urn from Cymynod, Bodedern (NGR SH/339777), are the only evidence for a destroyed barrow on that site.[152] The talc is likely to have come from

[147] R. S. Newall. *Arch. Camb.* 1931. 259-62.
[148] There is a small round barrow only about 100 yards away from the tomb at Din Dryfol. (NGR SH/395724).
[149] Fig 10 no. 2. T. G. E. Powell and G. E. Daniel. *Barclodiad y Gawres.* 1956. 59-61.
[150] Fig. 29 no. 14. W. J. Hemp. *Arch.* LXXXV. 1935. 269.
[151] Pen yr Orsedd: *Arch. Camb.* 1876. 105. where the urns are said to have been set in rows. Llangaffo: *Arch. Camb.* 1882. 210n. The mound, Crug Las, is not a barrow. The account of the excavation (H. Prichard. *Arch. Camb.* 1865. 196-200, 394) is confused and open to question on many points. The mound is in the centre of Malltraeth marsh which all the evidence suggests would have been inaccessible in the Bronze Age and the remains, recently re-excavated, are consistent with a mound of turves and clay resulting from eighteenth century drainage operations. I am grateful to Mr. Richard White of Llangristiolus, for information prior to the publication of his excavation report.
[152] W. F. Grimes. *The Prehistory of Wales.* 1951. 200. no. 593.

deposits near Holyhead. It is difficult to guess at its use or significance: it may simply have attracted the curiosity of its Bronze Age owner.

More is known about the burials close to the large stones at Henblas, Llangristiolus (NGR SH/426722), but a good deal of confusion remains.[153] The stones in question, which are huge glacial erratics, were long considered to be an artificial structure, some monstrous megalithic tomb, and have naturally attracted a good deal of legend and speculation. It seems clear that there were originally other stones, probably more erratics, in the vicinity, and that in removing these an urn containing burnt bones and a ring of blue glass were found. Even though the stones are a natural feature, this burial need not be doubted for they are a very remarkable phenomenon which must have attracted the attention and admiration of a people used to setting up meini hirion and other large stone monuments.

It is unfortunate that the ring of blue glass from this site has been lost, for there is a possibility that it might have been one of the faience beads which were very popular in the British Isles during the latter part of the Early Bronze Age. The description "a ring of blue glass" suggests that it might have been a quoit-shaped bead, a type of bead which is virtually restricted to these islands and is especially common in Scotland. It is around this specific type that the present controversy on the origins of British faience is centred. If this bead was genuine, it would add further evidence for the close contacts between Anglesey and south-west Scotland and the north Irish Sea area at this time.[154]

This contact with the north is confirmed by a study of the pottery from the various Bronze Age burials on the island. The vast majority of the pots belong to the class known collectively as Collared Urns, which are considered to have developed from the native Late Neolithic pottery, the Mortlake and Fengate styles of the Peterborough tradition.[155] This type of Neolithic pottery is very rare in Wales, and although it is found on two sites in Anglesey it is clear that the development of the standard urn had taken place elsewhere before it became current in North Wales. Both Beakers and Food Vessels must have been in use alongside the urns, and ideas of shape and decoration, especially from the latter group, must have influenced their development considerably. In fact, by the time most of the Anglesey barrows were built, there is evidence here on the island of a well integrated

---

[153] H. Prichard. *Arch. Camb.* 1866. 466-70.
[154] Beck and Stone (*Arch.* LXXXV. 1935. 249. S.63) mention a blue glass bead found near the River Alaw (*Proc. Soc. Antiq. London.* XIX. 1902. 50) and suggest that this might have been of faience. In 1935 it was mislaid, but has since been rediscovered. It is a large almost spherical bead of very pale blue glass and is not faience. It is probably mediaeval in date.
[155] I. H. Longworth. PPS. XXVII. 1961. 263-306. This is the most comprehensive modern work on the subject, but it only deals with the earlier urns. By using Longworth's analysis of traits it is possible to assign the majority of the Anglesey urns to his Primary Series, but in most groups there are one or two urns (such as H from Bedd Branwen) which have no Primary traits, yet are associated with pots having up to five. This may be due to new ideas overtaking a very conservative tradition in the island, but it suggests that a too rigorous adherence to such analyses may not be helpful in out-lying areas.

population; of a Bronze Age society that displayed a well-balanced mixture of native and foreign traditions in both pottery and burial customs.

Prehistoric pottery-making is believed to be basically a domestic activity, probably carried out by women, and one in which the power of tradition was so strong that any change would be resisted. However, individual women might have different cultural backgrounds, bringing with them ideas from varying traditions, so that one could expect a gradual evolution of shape and decoration, with the direction of these changes indicating the areas with which the local population maintained, or had maintained, connections. Further, the extent to which any given pot differs from the ancestral type should indicate its position in the evolutionary sequence, and hence its date. In practice, however, it is extremely difficult to apply these principles. Firstly, it is impossible to measure the power of a tradition which is emotive and, secondly, it is now clear that we are dealing not with a series of successive types but with a group of contemporary traditions which may be shared in various combinations by several groups, so that it is often difficult to isolate the basic types. As a result, one is thrown back on the system of dating by associated objects, daggers, beads, etc. This is a much more secure basis for argument, but, unfortunately, the practice of leaving grave goods is rather short-lived so that it becomes increasingly difficult to assign any pottery to the Middle and Late Bronze Age.

The pottery of Anglesey is especially difficult to classify because it results from such a mixture of traditions and types, a mixture in which the shape of one type of urn may be found with the decoration of another, and in which certain styles are virtually restricted to the island. This blurring of distinctions is not surprising considering its geographical position, easily accessible from all areas around the Irish Sea and, overland, across north-east Wales to England both north and south.

Typologically the complete pot from Merddyn Gwyn (Fig. 52, No. 1) may be the earliest. It certainly seems to have the closest link with the Food Vessel tradition, evident in the stopped groove around the shoulder, the herringbone decoration, and the very narrow rim, but the size and the internal moulding of the rim are features of the Collared urn. The emphasis on the Food Vessel aspects of this urn is strengthened by its probable association with the Bowl Food Vessel (Fig. 52, No. 2). This bowl is partly decorated in 'false relief' technique, a system very popular in Ireland, but it does not have the sagging profile of most Irish pots, and its design must owe a good deal to the northern English tradition of Food Vessel bowls. The stopped groove on the urn is also a feature very typical of Yorkshire.[156]

[156] H. N. Savory (BBCS. XVII. 1956-8. 196-233) has studied the Food Vessel element in the Anglesey pottery with special reference to Merddyn Gwyn, Cerrig Dewi and Llanddyfnan, Urns 7 and 8.

The two very large Collared urns from the site (4 and 5) have none of the features which are considered to distinguish the earlier pots of this class, and the stratification of the site suggests that they may have been buried at a later date.

Another urn which retains close links with the Food Vessel tradition is the one from Cerrig Dewi (Fig. 53, No. 7). It has the small bevelled rim and the close-set herring-bone decoration extending below the shoulder, which is characteristic of the type. The shoulder groove is set very high, producing a rather elegant profile which can be compared with several pots from the north of England.[157]

Similar grooves occur on the shoulder on Urn 7 from Llanddyfnan, as does the herring-bone decoration extending below the shoulder (Fig. 48). However, this pot has an internal rim moulding and an upright neck of the kind that is found on the Anglesey Collared urns. Urn 7 was associated with the Vase Food Vessel, Urn 8. This pot has the characteristic bevelled rim, but its slack profile is rather undistinctive. In Anglesey, however, it may be quite an important type, for there is another (Fig. 55, No. 5) from Cae Mickney (without a bevelled rim but with decoration in the appropriate place), while Pot 6 from Treiorwerth, with its concave neck and everted rim, may be simply an enlarged version of this type (Fig. 51). It is probable that No. 7 from Plas Penrhyn was very similar to the Treiorwerth pot: they share the use of channelled decoration, a rather rare technique.

Even though both Urns 7 and 8 from Llanddyfnan might be considered typologically early, they cannot have been made until after 1,500 B.C. because of the Wessex II knife-dagger inside 7. They must, therefore, be contemporary with a number of other styles current in the island. In fact, all these multiple burial sites reveal the same situation: there is considerable variation among the pots produced by a single community, but all these variants can be cross-referenced to other sites in the island and, whatever their theoretical typological position, these comparisons and the associated grave goods suggest that they are all roughly contemporary, dating from the latter part of the Early Bronze Age, when the earliest styles within the Collared urn series were gradually fading out.

The relative date of the pots from any multiple burial site is, of course, often doubtful, but reasons have already been given for believing that most of the Anglesey sites were used for only a short time. Llanddyfnan is a case in point (Figs. 47 and 48). Until recently Urns 4, 5 and 6 would have been considered secondary, regardless of the excavation evidence, because the style of pot was considered to be late, while Urns 7 and 8 were clearly early. However, a reassessment of the Cordoned urns has given due

---

[157] J. Abercromby. *Bronze Age Pottery*. 1912. Vol. II. nos. 484 (Durham) and 485 (Northumberland). One of the lost pots from Treiorwerth (Fig. 49. no. 3) was compared by Stanley (*Arch. Camb.* 1875. 126) to the Cerrig Dewi urn and, as far as one can tell from his drawing, the comparison was apt.

weight to the early date of the razors often associated with them and they are now recognised as a phenomenon of the Highland Zone — Scotland and Ireland — parallel to the Collared urns in the rest of Britain and, like them, stemming from native Late Neolithic traditions.[158] Like most of the Anglesey pots, these Cordoned urns are not entirely typical. Urn 6 is closest to the norm, but the second band of decoration is unusual. Urns 4 and 5 are an unusual type best paralleled in Scotland.[159] In fact, apart from the exotic objects in Urn 7, clearly status symbols, the whole bias of this community at Llanddyfnan, in both metalwork and pottery styles, is towards the north.

The people who were buried at Bedd Branwen had similar trading links with the south, but the jet beads and certain aspects of the pottery hint at links at some stage with the north of England. The pots here, like the surviving urn from Porth Dafarch, are all basically Collared urns of the normal English type (Figs. 42-5 and 53, No. 1), but a remarkable number (C, J, F and the 1813 urn) have the shoulder ' necklace ' which is so common on urns in Derbyshire and the Pennine region.[160] It occurs often in north-east Wales, indicating the overland route by which this idea came to Anglesey.[161] This feature is also found on the urn from Bryn yr Hen Bobl (Fig. 29, No. 14), and on Pots 1 and 6 from Treiorwerth (Fig. 51), a site closely linked to Bedd Branwen.

Although the 1813 urn and Pots L and K from Bedd Branwen are completely typical of the primary series of Collared urns, Pots B and C are not so typical because they have an unusually upright neck, a feature which has been mentioned already. Apart from the Llangwm urn from Denbighshire and two from the multiple burial site at Penmaenmawr, Caernarvonshire, it seems to be restricted to Anglesey.[162] The rims still retain some internal moulding, but the profile seen on the 1813 urn has been elongated and straightened. This fashion for straight-necked pots may very well have come to Anglesey from Ireland, where the contemporary Vase Food Vessel very frequently has this upright rim. The peculiarity of the Anglesey undulating neck is created by the reaction of this trend on the elaborately moulded collar of the Collared urn. This development is best demonstrated at Bedd Branwen, but can also be seen at Menai Bridge (Fig. 54, No. 3) and at Llanddyfnan (Urn 7). The extreme of the style is found at Plas Penrhyn (Fig. 57, Nos. 2 and 3) and at Cae Mickney (Fig. 56, No. 12). It is interesting that the best parallel for this last pot is one from

---

[158] J. J. Butler and I. F. Smith. *Univ. Lond. Inst. of Archaeol. Ann. Report* XII. 1956. 46-7.
[159] e.g. Abercromby. *op. cit.* vol. II. nos. 508 (Seamill, Ayrshire) and 509 (Pittodrie, Aberdeenshire).
[160] W. J. Varley. *Ant. J.* XVIII. 1938. 163-71.
[161] e.g. Bryn Bugeilen, Denbs. *Arch. Camb.* 1868. 247-9.
    Hillbury and Holt, Denbs. *Arch. Camb.* 1925. 177-84.
    Corwen, Merioneth. Grimes. *Prehistory of Wales.* 1951. 265. Fig. 77. 1. (a pot similar in many ways to Treiorwerth 6).
[162] Llangwm: W. F. Grimes. *op. cit.* 87. Fig. 28.
    Penmaenmawr: RCAM. *Caernarvonshire* I. 1956. lxiv. nos. 6 and 7.

Clonshannon, Co. Wicklow, showing that influences moved in more than one direction.[163]

A similar combination of Irish and British fashions, peculiar to Anglesey, occurs on the very odd Encrusted urn from Plas Penrhyn. The plastic decoration on pots of this class is extremely standardised, and the Plas Penrhyn example, with its large zigzags and pellets, made from added strips of clay, is very similar to several pots in Ireland and Scotland.[164] However, the curved rim and internal moulding are foreign to that tradition and must belong to the Collared urns. The result is a uniquely ugly pot, unless the lost pot from Treiorwerth (Fig. 49, No. 2), which seems to have applied cordons, can be considered similar.[165]

The pots from Treiorwerth vary considerably, but they are all linked by having very small bases (Fig. 51). This is an aspect of the ancestral Late Neolithic pottery to which this group obviously clung tenaciously. As a result Pot 3, which is a Cordoned urn and which should be barrel-shaped, has an unusual rounded body, and Pot 1, on which the 'necklace' rim, deep collar and system of decoration all suggest a late typological position, retains this feature so characteristic of the early urns.[166]

What remains of Pot 2 is also suggestive of a typologically later pot; its secondary position in the barrow makes this an acceptable possibility, as it does with the two larger urns from Merddyn Gwyn. However, Pot H from Bedd Branwen, which has all the characteristics of the theoretically later urns — the absence of internal moulding and decoration, the deep concave collar, and the complex, incised patterns including, in particular, the lattice on the neck — must be contemporary with the building of the barrow and contained beads which cannot be dated later than 1,400 B.C. So it should not be automatically assumed that similar pots, such as Nos. 1 and 4 from Plas Penrhyn or Nos. 1, 2, 11, 17 and 15 from Cae Mickney, are not strictly contemporary with the others from these sites, even though this cannot be convincingly demonstrated from the record of excavation.

This leaves remarkably few pots with any claim at all to date from the Middle Bronze Age. Apart from secondaries at Merddyn Gwyn and Treiorwerth, it leaves only Menai Bridge II and, possibly, I, where typologically the complete urn looks late but, if the one so similar to Bedd Branwen B is genuinely associated, even here caution must be adopted. If the blade from Menai Bridge III were really a razor, that burial, too, would belong to the same horizon as Llanddyfnan.

---

[163] A. Mahr and L. Price. JRSAI. LXII. 1932. 79. fig. 3. This is decorated to the base in the Irish manner. There are other pots with profiles reminiscent of Bedd Branwen Pot B at Irish multiple burial sites: e.g. Ballon Hill, Co. Carlow (Nat. Mus. Ireland. 1928. 446) and Greenhills, Co. Dublin (N.M.I. 1909. 24).

[164] C. F. Fox. Ant. J. VII. 1927. 115-33. A very close parallel is Abercromby, op. cit. vol. II. no. 532 from Ross.

[165] A pot from Yorkshire (Abercromby. op. cit. vol. II. no. 487) has the same peculiar profile, but without any hint of encrustation.

[166] I. H. Longworth. PPS. XXVII. 1961. 268.

In spite of the mass of material and information that has been gained over the years from Bronze Age burials in Anglesey, the period illuminated by this knowledge is a surprisingly short one: no more than about two hundred years, from 1,600 - 1,400 B.C. At the beginning of the period, the single inhumation at Pen y Bonc suggests the retention of the single grave tradition brought in by the makers of Beakers. But this did not last long, and by 1,500 B.C. it is obvious that the underlying Neolithic tradition of family or group burial had re-emerged in a new form to become the standard practice in Anglesey, as in Scotland, Ireland and other parts of northern and western Britain. This unity within the 'Irish Sea Province' is seen again in a predilection for similar types of pottery, and in more easily defined links such as trading in bronze tools and weapons.

This trade, however, reached eastwards as well as westwards and brought Anglesey into contact with the rich and brilliant 'Wessex Culture' of southern England, a group of chieftains whose taste for personal adornment and expensive weapons is to some extent reflected among the people buried at Bedd Branwen and Llanddyfnan. It is only for a short time around 1,400 B.C. that the goods and the customers can be linked in this way, but trade was not invented by the 'Wessex' merchants and it did not collapse with the contraction of the brilliant internationalism of the Early Bronze Age. It is, in fact, in the later centuries that the native bronze industries come into their own, and it is through this insular trade that we can follow the fortunes of Anglesey through the next few hundred years, although we have no graves or settlements to add depth to the picture.

V

INDUSTRY AND TRADE IN THE
BRONZE AGE

THIS chapter will deal with the evidence to be gained from a study of the metal implements found in the island. The vast majority of these tools and weapons have been found by chance, and so have no archaeological context by which they could be related to other aspects of contemporary life. However, since both tools and weapons are functional objects, it is possible to establish an independent chronology by plotting their growth in efficiency; by observing how early disadvantages are overcome, and the optimum use made of the minimum quantity of metal by the gradual alteration of old types and the adoption of new techniques. All these metal-working techniques require a great deal of knowledge, skill and experience, which presuppose the existence of specialists, and probably of industrial schools or traditions by which this knowledge could be passed on. So by examining details of technique and style employed in the production of groups of implements, it is possible to define local industrial traditions and to plot their distribution in space and time, following their fluctuating fortunes in the struggle for markets for their raw materials, and for their finished products.

It could be said that the germs of modern society are to be found in these developments. The use of complex manufacturing techniques must have led to the growth of a class of specialists who may have lived by the sale of their products rather than by their own farming. The discovery of merchants' and founders' hoards (new tools to be sold and old ones bought in as scrap metal) suggests that these craftsmen may have lived an itinerant life, moving quite considerable distances in search of raw material and customers. This reliance on raw materials, copper and especially tin, which are only available in limited areas of Europe, is another important factor in Bronze Age economy, and one which must have led to the gradual erosion of the independence and self-sufficiency of the small Neolithic farming communities. Neither widespread trade nor the existence of specialist workers is an entirely new phenomenon; the Neolithic trade in stone axes must have involved both, but as metal tools became more common the part played by commerce in everyday life must have increased and with it the dependence on the goodwill of distant communities. In the course of the period, trading relationships seem to have changed on more than one occasion and links were established for reasons which are not obviously geographical but which may well have been political. /

Like agriculture, knowledge of the processes by which metal could be extracted from certain stones and could be fashioned into implements is traditionally thought to have come to Europe from the Near East. Copper was being smelted and cast in Anatolia by 6,000 B.C., long before farming became established in these islands.[1] The methods by which this new knowledge spread to Europe are obscure, but it can be said that the date of the earliest metal objects in Bulgaria and Rumania may lie between 4,000 and 3,000 B.C.; by 2,000 B.C. complex metal working traditions were well established.[2]

As far as these islands are concerned, though copper is plentiful in the west, the knowledge of its use is clearly an introduced art. Some of the earliest metal objects in Britain are the daggers and knives found in graves with Beakers.[3] Like the pottery, these flat copper blades, held in the hilt by a tang, relate to similar objects found on the Continent. Certain technical details, such as the hollow ground edge, show links with the advanced metal working industry of south Germany. Germany continued to be a vital source of finished products and, perhaps, even of raw material; certainly of inspiration, throughout the Early Bronze Age while the native British industries were gradually developing and gaining competence.

In spite of the importance given by archaeologists to the earliest metal tools, it should be remembered that they are very rare, and several centuries must have elapsed before they were in general use. Throughout the Early Bronze Age, stone and flint continued to be used for knives, axes and hammers; for weapons such as battle-axes and daggers and, of course, for arrowheads and small tools such as scrapers. Apart from the large axe-hammers described in a previous chapter, Anglesey has not produced many stone tools of specifically Bronze Age type, though it must be remembered that a number of the polished stone axes appear to have come from Bronze Age contexts.[4] Barbed and tanged arrowheads are rare, and there are no reliable records of the discovery of any plano-convex flint knives, a tool frequently found with Food Vessels. There is, however, one of these very characteristic objects in the Sturges Collection in the British Museum which is said to have been found " in Anglesey ", but this provenance is doubtful.[5]

Not only were the earliest metal weapons rare, they were probably inefficient as well. The first implements were made from copper, a metal which is easily bent and does not keep a sharp edge well. It is rather

[1] J. Mellaart. Catal Huyuk. 1967. 217-8.
[2] C. Renfrew. PPS. XXXV. 1969. 12-47.
[3] S. Piggott in Foster and Alcock (edd). *Culture and Environment*. 1963. 53-91.
[4] See above. p. 120.
[5] Sturges Coll. 147. All the flints (very fine examples, made from good flint and therefore unlikely to have come from Anglesey) are marked ambiguously " found in Anglesea but probably Irish." No provenance within the island is given for any of them and they are all of common northern Irish types.

surprising that all the European industries should start by using copper alone, since the advantages of alloying were known in Central Europe at a relatively early date.[6] However, this may be partly explained by the fact that copper ores are widespread and can be smelted fairly easily, whereas the techniques of alloying need a great deal of experimentation and experience.

Since nearly all the Anglesey Beakers are late types, it is not surprising that no implements of pure copper have been found on the island. No tanged Beaker daggers or thick-butted flat axes exist, though the latter may have been made at an early date on the mainland of Wales, since a hoard of three was found on Moel Arthur, Flintshire, and another was found at Halkyn in the same area; analysis suggests that this might have been made from local ores.[7]

By about 1,700 - 1,600 B.C., contemporary with the later Beakers, rivetted knives like the one from Merddyn Gwyn had replaced the earlier tanged variety, and the knowledge of alloying techniques must have become widespread, for all the examples analysed have proved to be of bronze.[8] It is indicative of the late appearance of metal in Anglesey that the metal object with the earliest context is already made of bronze with a ten per cent tin content.[9] This is the awl from beneath the bank at Castell Bryn Gwyn which was associated with Late Neolithic pottery. This find emphasises the slowness of change, with many Neolithic techniques surviving virtually unaltered for a considerable time after the arrival of new peoples and ideas.

The principles of alloying were known by about 1,700 B.C., but the optimum proportions of tin and copper were scarcely standardised even in the later Bronze Age.[10] During the first few centuries there must have been a great deal of experiment both in the selection of ores and the use of alloys. It is in this period that copper containing a larger quantity of arsenic is used. The presence of arsenic produces a much harder metal and its properties were used with great subtlety. For instance, arsenical copper might be used for the blade of a halberd, while the rivets would be made of the softer pure copper.[11] Certain copper ores contain a good deal of arsenic naturally, but it is not yet clear whether the arsenic in the implements is simply due to the careful selection of arsenical ores or whether it represents a deliberate alloy, a specific mix in the crucible. The latter view is gaining ground at the moment.

The mixture of copper with tin to make bronze is certainly a deliberate

[6] S. Junghans, E. Sangmeister and M. Schroder. *Metallanalysen kupferzeitlicher und frühbronzezeitlicher Bodenfunde aus Europa.* 1960. 45-6, 54.
[7] Moel Arthur hoard: *Flints. Hist. Soc. Public.* XXI. 1964. 99-100. Halkyn axe: *Flints. Hist. Soc. Public.* XVIII. 1960. 169-71.
[8] I am grateful to Dr. D. W. F. James, School of Engineering Science UCNW, for the analysis of the Merddyn Gwyn knife. See Appendix II.
[9] *Arch. Camb.* 1962. 55-6.
[10] D. Britton. *Archaeometry.* IV. 1961. 39-52.
[11] Coghlan & Case. PPS. XXIII. 1957. 96.

alloy. Like all the early technological advances, this important knowledge came to Britain from the Continent, but it is possible that it was in this country that the optimum proportion of tin to copper was first widely used. The use of too small a quantity of tin will make no appreciable difference to the hardness of the metal, while the use of too much (over 12%) will make bronze rather brittle. The addition of 8 - 10% tin, however, will produce a hard metal which can be cast in a closed mould more easily than pure copper, and will withstand more subsequent work-hardening.

The first recognisable native metal working tradition is a fully bronze-using industry, based on the copper-rich highland areas of Britain. The bronze-smiths presumably got their tin supplies from Cornwall, but the best known centre of activity is Scotland and the school is called Migdale-Marnoch, after a hoard and a mould from that region, although other areas contained workshops making similar products.[12] The smiths had a characteristic repertoire, mainly thin-butted flat axes, but including a variety of personal ornaments and a few daggers. All these objects were made from flat castings produced in single-valve moulds; a great deal of hammering and annealing must have been necessary to achieve the final shape. All the moulds used were of stone, usually a block of sandstone with one flat face, into which was cut the shape of the desired object, or objects, for several moulds have matrices for more than one type. The molten metal would be simply poured into the matrix, sometimes previously greased with a carbon-based material, and allowed to cool, perhaps covered by a lid to prevent oxidization.

The date at which this tradition was flourishing is fairly clear; V-bored jet buttons, tubular beads and bronze ear-rings in the Migdale hoard[13] are types often found with late Beakers and the number of rivets in the Migdale-Marnoch daggers suggest a link with the early Wessex daggers of Bush Barrow type, so a span of a century on either side of 1,600 B.C. may be suggested. At this time there is little evidence for bronze manufacture in the south of England, where it seems likely that the daggers and axes were either imported or copied from the Continent rather than from the north or west of Britain.

Although there are plentiful deposits of copper ore in northern Anglesey which could well have been recognised and exploited by prehistoric man, there is no evidence that metal was actually worked in the island at this date, though the Bodwrdin mould indicates production at a slightly later period. Apart from flat axes, characteristic products of the Migdale-Marnoch tradition are relatively rare in Wales as a whole, but two graves in Anglesey contained ornaments which very probably belonged to this group: Pen y Bonc, Holyhead, which apparently contained armlets like those from Melfort, Argyll, and Llanddyfnan, at which there was a broken strip with repoussé decoration akin to that from the Migdale hoard itself.

[12] D. Britton. PPS. XXIX. 1963. 263-84.
[13] *Inventaria Archaeologica*. GB. 26.

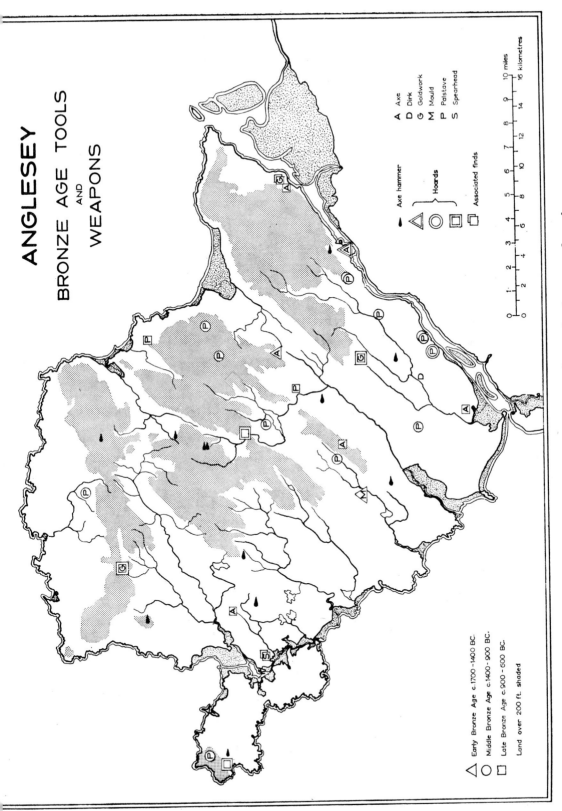

MAP 4 — Distribution of bronze implements and stone battle-axes and axe-hammers.

Ornaments form a surprisingly large part of the output of this group, but the flat axe-head must have been their chief standby. The typical Migdale axe has a thin, relatively narrow butt, concave sides, and slightly splayed blade. This simple type of axe is widespread in these islands, and it is probable that they were produced by more than one group of bronze-smiths working within the general Migdale-Marnoch tradition but producing local versions which differ in size and proportion. For instance, the relative widths of blade and butt would seem to distinguish the Scottish axes, and the moulds from which they were made, from another group of flat axes notable for their widely-splayed blades which, on present evidence, seem to be most common in Ireland and the west. For instance, the axes from the Migdale hoard have a blade/butt ratio of 100: 41 - 48, whereas the others, recently labelled " Killaha " after a famous hoard from Co. Kerry, have a ratio of 100: 26 - 32.[14]

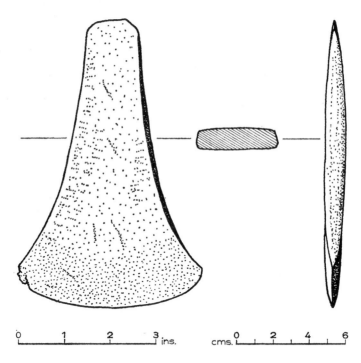

FIG. 58 — Flat axe of bronze from Ynys, Talwrn.

A small, unprovenanced axe from the Dinam Collection in Bangor Museum would belong to the former group. However, it is not certain that it was found in Anglesey, though the majority of the Dinam material was collected locally.[15]

[14] P. Harbison. PRIA. 67. C. 1968. 35.
[15] Comment by Sir Ivor Williams. TAAS. 1942. 44-6.

The one flat axe certainly from Anglesey, found at Ynys, Talwrn, belongs to the " Killaha " group, though this should not imply that it was made in Ireland, for the stone mould from Betws y Coed, Caerns., would have produced an axe of this type, as would the ones from Longden Common, Shropshire, and Altarnum, Cornwall.[16] The distribution of these moulds and axes suggests a close contact between bronze workers in Ireland and the west of Britain during this period, a contact which is evident in the similarity of many of their other products.

The date of these wide-bladed axes must fall within that of the Migdale-Marnoch tradition in general. Technologically they are the same as the Scottish ones, and the association of a " Killaha " type axe with a flat dagger at Parwich, Derbyshire, and with a dagger related to the Bush Barrow type at Aylesford, Kent, reveals a similar period of use.[17]

Other flat axes have almost certainly been found in Anglesey, but they have been lost and nothing useful can be said about them. A " bronze axehead of simple type in shape like the heater of a box-iron " is said to have been found in a " semi-circular fort " at Llanrhyddlad.[18] This was clearly a flat axe; the objects described as " gold tongues ", found on Mynydd Bodafon, can be identified as a hoard of flat axes with far less certainty;[19] the object found in the smaller cairn at Bryn Celli Ddu looks rather like an axe in Skinner's drawing, but may in fact have been a dagger of some kind.[20]

Although the Migdale-Marnoch and contemporary Irish industries used good metal and could produce a surprising variety of objects by elaborate hammering and annealing of their rough castings, their reliance on the single-valve mould meant that they were in what could be termed a technological cul de sac. Although midribs and low flanges could be produced by hammering, there is a limit to the amount of shaping which can be done after casting, so that avenues of development within these traditions were restricted.

The introduction of the two-valve mould is not precisely documented, partly because the standard of finish on Early Bronze Age objects is so high that the details of manufacture are usually obscured. However, the complex objects, such as metal-handled halberds, made in Europe during the currency of the Migdale-Marnoch tradition in this country, show that the use of closed moulds, and of cores to produce a hollow casting, was understood there at an early date.

The introduction of these new methods into these islands may be documented by the rise of two new industrial traditions during the fifteenth

[16] PPS. XXIX. 1963. 268, fig. 8; 267, fig. 6.
[17] Parwich: *Inventaria Archaeologica.* GB. 19.
    Aylesford: S. Piggott *in* Foster and Alcock (edd.) *Culture and Environment.* 1963. 87. fig. 20, 1-3.
[18] *Arch. Camb.* 1868. 272.
[19] J. Skinner. 1802. 75. (*Arch. Camb.* 1908. Supplement).
[20] *Op. cit.* 24-5.

century B.C., one in southern England and the other in Ireland. In southern England hoards containing finished products and metalworking tools appear for the first time, indicating a much larger production in this area than previously. Since the region lacks native ores, the workers must have been entirely dependent on distant suppliers for their raw materials. Ireland, on the other hand, had been a large producer of metalwork in the earlier phase, but both these new traditions drew their main inspiration from Central Europe, where prototypes of their daggers, axes, and spearheads are to be found.

These traditions, known as " Arreton Down " in England, and " Inch Island " in Ireland, share many common types and techniques and it is often difficult to distinguish the products of the two schools.[21] Both made weapons and tools, with the stronger emphasis on weapons, while small personal ornaments such as those made by the Migdale-Marnoch smiths are no longer found in the hoards. The hoard associations of the Continental prototypes, and the discovery of the native products in the later Wessex graves, Camerton-Snowshill daggers, for example, all confirm a date of 1,500 - 1,400 B.C. for this industrial phase.

Most of the products of these two industries show a technological advance over the Migdale-Marnoch types and over the Bush Barrow daggers. The ogival (Camerton-Snowshill) daggers are not only more elegant but also more effective, because of the wide thick midrib which made them completely rigid. The earlier flat daggers might be easily bent and one found at Grange, Co. Roscommon, had actually been rolled up.[22] The spearheads, which appear for the first time in bronze during this phase, are very similar indeed to the dagger blades. The typical Arreton Down product has a long tang and sometimes a separate collar to cover the end of the wooden shaft. Another type, with a socket and peg holes for attachment to the shaft, is rare, but there is one example in the Arreton Down hoard itself. In Ireland the socketed type was preferred, but loops rather than peg-holes were provided at the end of the socket to secure the shaft.

The Arreton Down axe also represents a notable advance in design and one which, like the design of the socketed spearheads, could not have been achieved without the use of a closed two-valve mould. The overall shape of these axes differs quite markedly from the earlier ones : they are narrower; the sides are straight and virtually parallel, while the expansion of the cutting edge is more abrupt, producing an almost semi-circular blade. The most important distinction, however, lies in the flanges. The Migdale-Marnoch axes are either completely flat or have only very low flanges

[21] D. Britton. PPS. XXIX. 1963. 284-97 for Arreton Down tradition. C. B. Burgess, forthcoming, for Inch Island. I am grateful to Mr. Burgess for allowing me to refer to his work prior to publication.
[22] P. Harbison. PRIA. 67. C. 1968. 51.

produced by hammering up the sides; the Arreton Down type have high flanges cast in the mould.

These flanges represent an improvement in design, since the axe-heads were hafted in a split cruck, with the butt pushed between the split ends of the shorter branch and then bound (see Fig. 59). Without a flange, therefore, there would be a tendency for the head to work loose by slipping from side to side. Axes with deep flanges would prevent this sideways movement and be much firmer in use. The earliest copper, thick-butted axes may well have been hafted through a hole at right angles to a straight handle, as were the Neolithic stone axes, but the introduction of the thin butt of Migdale-Marnoch type is indicative of the use of a split handle, and all subsequent developments in the shape of the axe-head confirms

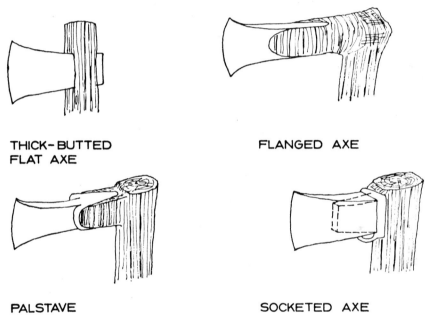

THICK-BUTTED
FLAT AXE

FLANGED AXE

PALSTAVE

SOCKETED AXE

FIG. 59 — Methods of hafting bronze axe-heads.

this: they are all improvements designed to eliminate the disadvantages of this system. One of these disadvantages must have been the tendency for the metal head to bite back into the handle as it was used. Although the central thickening on Arreton Down and contemporary Irish axes goes some way towards solving this problem, it cannot have been entirely eliminated at this stage.

The majority of the Arreton Down axes were very carefully finished, the flanges were hammered and ground into facets, all signs of casting seams and such like were removed and the surfaces polished. In addition, many were decorated, usually with parallel grooves or furrows on both faces and a cable effect on the sides of the flanges. This very high standard

of design and workmanship is characteristic of all the Early Bronze Age
metalwork, and it underlines the fact that any metal objects must still have
been rare and consequently highly valued and expensive. One decorated
axe-head found in a bog in Ireland was in a specially made leather case,
which not only shows how much they were treasured, but also suggests
that these especially fine axes may have been ceremonial rather than
utilitarian.[23] It is noteworthy that the metalworkers' own tools, chisels and
punches found occasionally in the Arreton Down hoards, are not so well
finished as the rest of their products.

The Arreton Down tradition was based upon the south of England, but
its influence was felt as far away as Anglesey. This expansion may be due
to a search for raw materials or, possibly, to the prestige of the fashionable
Wessex society with which there was some contact at this time (shown by
the amber beads from Bedd Branwen and the bronzes from Llanddyfnan).
These bronzes have already been discussed. The dagger is the most
characteristic object; in shape and decoration it is related to a sub-group
of the Camerton-Snowshill type, perhaps made in Dorset. The punch, or
tracer, decoration is quite typical of the Arreton Down school and can be
seen on one of the lost spearheads from the Arreton Down hoard itself.[24]
The small axe has very weak cast flanges and the proportions of an Arreton
axe, though clearly it is a special type of production, being so small. This
grave group is representative of the kind of prestigious bronzework
produced in the south of England, and there is little reason to consider
them anything other than imports into the island.

The remaining finds of Early Bronze Age metalwork, the Menai Bridge
hoard of axes (which emanates from the Arreton Down school) and the
Bodwrdin spearhead mould (which belongs to the Inch Island tradition),
both raise the question of local production. A hoard of finished axes like
that from Menai Bridge is, however, ambiguous. It might be the stock-in-
trade of a metalworker hidden while awaiting a boat for shipment to the
mainland for sale elsewhere, or it might be a merchant's cache of incoming
stock concealed for safety while he sold others elsewhere in the island.
(In either case the owner must have met with some disaster and been unable
to retrieve them.) The Bodwrdin mould, on the other hand, is clear evidence
for the presence of a smith on the island who could have been using local
copper.

The eight Menai Bridge axes were found in 1874 or 75 by workmen
quarrying for stone close to the Anglesey end of the bridge. They came
upon the axes at a depth of 7ft., six under one large stone and two under
another. W. Wynn Williams, who wrote the first account of the discovery,[25]
was told that near the spot there was a cave or shaft which was said to be

[23] Axe from Brockagh, Co. Kildare. *J. Co. Kildare. Archaeol. Soc.* XIII. 1961-3. 459-60, 462,
    Pl. 1.
[24] PPS. XXIX. 1963. 288. fig. 19.
[25] *Arch. Camb.* 1875. 294 and 1877. 206-11.

an old copper working, but he could not confirm this information and one should not place too much reliance upon it. The eight axes were quickly dispersed and even in 1877 only four could be traced.

Three of these survive today: Lord Clarence Paget's axe is in the British Museum; Capt. Griffith's came to the National Museum of Wales in the T. A. Glenn Collection; and the one formerly in the possession of Mr. Richard Davies is now in the Bangor Museum.[26] The one that had belonged to the landlord of the Anglesey Arms has been lost, but it was briefly described by Wynn Williams.

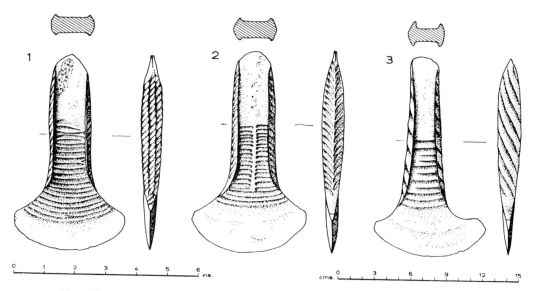

FIG. 60 — Menai Bridge hoard: three surviving axes from the original eight.

All eight axes are described as being very similar, varying only slightly in size, weight and details of decoration. Of those that survive, the ones in the Bangor and British Museums may well have come from the same mould; the dimensions and weight of the lost one (length 6ins., width of blade 3½ins., depth of flange ⅛in., width between flanges in centre 1in., weight 18½ozs.) suggest that it, too, must have been almost identical. The Cardiff axe is narrower and must have come from another mould. The fact that two or three seem to have been made in the same mould suggests that some form of permanent two-valve mould was used, rather than an investment mould which would have to be broken to remove each casting.

[26] 1. BM. 81. 12-24. 1.
2. NMW.44. 172. 1. Discussed in *Arch. Camb.* 1946-7. 117-9 where it is considered to be the one belonging to Mr. Richard Davies. But in view of the history of the Bangor one this is impossible and the differences, in weight and decoration, between it and the one illustrated in *Arch. Camb.* 1877 and said to belong to Capt. Griffiths, are so slight that they can be discounted.
3. Bangor Museum 2777. TAAS. 1923. 27.

All the axes are decorated but the ornament is slightly different on each. Fig. 60, Nos. 1 and 2, are decorated by the same hammered technique, and the patterns are variations of the same design: horizontal grooves on the face and herring-bone on the sides. All this decoration and the facetting of the flanges would, of course, be done after the rough casting had come from the mould, as would the final hammering and grinding of the blade, hence their slightly divergent outlines. The decoration on Fig. 60, No. 3, produces a rather different effect, a fluted rather than a grooved surface, and the flanges have been given a freer treatment.

Two of the surviving axes have been analysed (Fig. 60, Nos. 1 and 3).[27] Neither of them falls into any of the recognised metal groups, which might suggest that they were made from local Welsh metal, since the prehistoric use of Welsh ores has not yet been investigated. Fig. 60, No. 3, is remarkable for the quantity of tin (17%) which it contains.[28] Such a high proportion must have made it rather brittle, but it is possible that this was offset by some other advantage, perhaps of colour.[29] A whitish bronze may have been popular at this time, for the Arreton Down bronzes as a whole are noted for their high tin content, 13.8% on average.[30] Fig. 60, No. 1, contains a normal 12.6% of tin. Wynn Williams claimed that the lost axe contained a high percentage of copper, but this is doubtful in view of the other analyses.

All three axes are entirely typical of the Arreton Down tradition, even to the small groove which runs along the top of the arched butt and onto the upper part of each side. This is particularly clear on Fig. 60, Nos. 1 and 2, and on the undecorated Arreton Down axes in the hoard from Plymstock, Devon, which also contained one of the prototype European flanged axes.[31] Another feature which is indicative of the English origin of the Menai Bridge axes is the exclusive use of hammered and grooved decoration. The Irish smiths, who produced a basically similar axe, preferred a more elaborate decoration, usually made by incision or sharp blows with a tracer.[32]

The Menai Bridge hoard is very remarkable, for even single finds are rare so far beyond the central area of production. It is the only Arreton Down hoard in the Highland Zone of Britain; the nearest group of comparable material is in the Ebnal hoard from north Shropshire, an assemblage which contains products from both the Arreton Down and Inch Island schools.[33] Thus these two hoards provide rare and vital evidence

[27] *Archaeometry* IV. 1961. 50. Analysis nos. 93 and 94. See Appendix II.
[28] The Llanddyfnan dagger, another very ornamental piece, also has an extremely high proportion (16%) of tin. *op. cit.* 45. Analysis no. 16.
[29] The surface of this axe is far better preserved than the others, though this long term effect is unlikely to have impressed a Bronze Age buyer!
[30] *op. cit.*, 41-2.
[31] *Inventaria Archaeologica.* GB. 9. (the European axe is no. 14).
[32] For instance the one from Penrhyndeudraeth, Merioneth, is almost certainly Irish. (E. G. Bowen and C. A. Gresham. *History of Merioneth.* Vol. I. 1967. 47, fig. 22).
[33] L. F. Chitty. *Arch. Camb.* 1940. 27-30. To be discussed by C. B. Burgess and J. D. Cowen in a forthcoming paper.

of contact and interpenetration of the two traditions and their spheres of influence.

Little is recorded about the discovery of the Bodwrdin mould except that it was found close to the river Gwna, between the farms of Bodwrdin and Treddafydd in the parish of Trefdraeth.[34] It was first published and illustrated in 1846, after which the original was lost sight of, though happily not before a number of casts had been made from it. A few years ago the original came to light again in the Tolson Memorial Museum, Huddersfield, where it had been on exhibition without provenance.[35]

The object is a square-sectioned block of yellow sandstone, 9¾ins. long

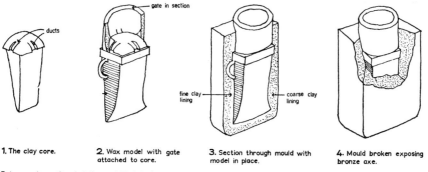

OPEN MOULDS

Used for flat axes, daggers, and similar simple forms.

BIVALVE MOULDS

peg to hold core in place

half of valve cut away to show interior

core

dowel hole

Without core, for solid moulded objects such as palstaves.

With core, for hollow and socketed objects such as spearheads.

WASTE WAX (CIRE PERDUE) CASTING

gate in section

ducts

fine clay lining

coarse clay lining

1. The clay core.

2. Wax model with gate attached to core.

3. Section through mould with model in place.

4. Mould broken exposing bronze axe.

Between stages 3 and 4 the mould is baked, the melted wax run off, and the resulting cavity filled with molten metal. The mould is broken to abstract the finished casting.

FIG. 61 — Types of moulds for casting bronze implements. (After W. F. Grimes.)

[34] *Arch. J.* III. 1846. 257.
[35] T. G. Manby. PPS. XXXII. 1966. 349 and Pl. XXXV.

and 2ins. square at the bottom, tapering slightly to 1½ins. by 1¾ins. at the top (Fig. 62). All four sides have been ground down to a perfectly flat surface in which a matrix has been cut. On faces 1 and 3 there is a finished matrix for casting a socketed spearhead; the matrix on 4 is unfinished, but was possibly intended for another spearhead; on 2 there is a tapered groove, which may either be the matrix for some kind of spike or awl, or may be another uncompleted carving. This block would have formed half of a two-valve mould. The other half would have been an identical block, and to make a casting the two would have been bound together and the molten metal poured into the resulting hole. In order to produce a good casting it is essential to align the two halves of the mould correctly. On the top of the Bodwrdin mould are cut three nicks which exactly correspond with the centre of the matrix on each face so that accurate alignment would be relatively simple.

In order to produce a socketed object, it is necessary to suspend a central core inside the mould. This must be held away from the walls so that metal will flow around it; it was usual to pin the lower end in place with small bronze strips or chaplets which were anchored into the core and fitted into small holes in the mould. As the molten metal flowed in the chaplets would fuse with it and the ends could be simply ground off when the casting came out of the mould. The other end of the core would probably have been fixed into a separate pouring head, which would have fitted into the flared end of the socket. Some sort of pouring head would be necessary to ensure that air and gases could escape from the cavity as the metal was being poured in.[36]

The Bodwrdin mould provides very good evidence for a practice which is seen on several moulds of this period, the prior dressing of the stone with some mixture containing carbon.[37] This may have been done to seal the stone or, like greasing a cake tin, to ease the removal of the casting, for it is noticeable that the dressing is thickest in the awkward spots, such as around the thin loops where there might be a danger of breakage. The mould may also have been preheated to prevent cracking, for the entire outer surface, not just the matrices, has been turned slightly pink.

Face 1 has the matrix for a socket-looped spearhead with a relatively thick socket and narrow blade. It would have had a lozenge-sectioned midrib, which may have been hollow for part of its length. At the base of the blade are two pairs of grooves for core supports. It is not clear why there should be two pairs, possibly the second set are vents to allow an escape of gas, but they seem too short and too neatly cut for this.[38] Perhaps the first pair was simply wrongly placed. The loops are set towards the base

---

[36] These techniques are discussed with special reference to the Bodwrdin mould in D. Britton. PPS. XXIX. 1963. 294-6.
[37] *Op. cit.* 276 and H. H. Coghlan, *Notes on the Prehistoric Metallurgy of Copper and Bronze in the Old World.* 1951. 112-5.
[38] See remarks in R. F. Tylecote, *Metallurgy in Archaeology.* 1962. 116.

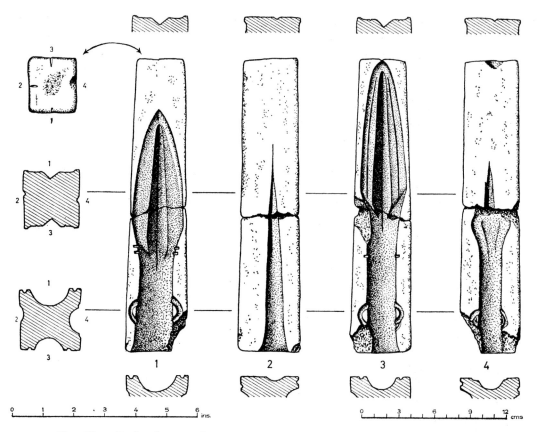

FIG. 62 — Bodwrdin: mould for casting spearheads. The four faces and the top are shown.

of the socket, a characteristic of Early Bronze Age spearheads by which they may be distinguished from Middle Bronze Age types with loops closer to the blade. The entire surface of this matrix is covered with the black waxy material which spreads onto the face of the stone for a few millimetres all round.

The matrix on face 2 may very well be unfinished. In its present state it would produce a sharp spike, perhaps socketed. This would be a useful tool, but nothing comparable to it has ever been found, so it seems more reasonable to suppose that it is not complete. However, in the top there is an alignment nick which exactly corresponds with the non-central position of the groove, and which presupposes the existence of its opposite number.[39] Moreover this matrix has been greased, especially in the upper half.

[39] It has been suggested that this is a mould for clay cores to fit spearheads on Faces 1 and 3 (PPS. XXIX. 1963. 295) but, if so, they would have been too narrow. It has been ingeniously suggested (Evans, *Ancient Bronze Implements of Great Britain*. 1881. 437-8) that this matrix was the pair of a more elaborate one in which the blade was fully cut, leaving only the midrib to be cut out of the second half. It is claimed that this system was used on a Middle Bronze Age mould from Campbeltown, Argyll (*op. cit.* fig. 525) but I doubt whether it would work with the Bodwrdin mould.

The matrix on face 3 is for a larger and more elaborate socket-looped spearhead. It is very long and narrow, with the loops well down on the socket. The blade is reinforced by a sharp rib on each side of the angular midrib. The midrib in this instance was almost certainly solid, with the end of the socket enclosing the blade like the hilt of a dagger. This is a certain indication of early date among spearheads. There is one pair of chaplet grooves, at the same height as the lower pair on face 1. There is a small runnel connecting the socket and the right-hand loop. This cannot be easily explained, but it seems to be intentional. The entire blade has been well coated with the black dressing, but on the socket it only occurs around the loops.

The matrix on face 4 was probably unfinished, even though there are traces of black dressing on the left-hand edge of the socket. The lower half of the matrix is complete, though the insides of the loops have been damaged; perhaps it could be used for another spearhead or, just possibly, a detachable collar or independent socket.[40] The base of the " blade " is almost flat, but a start has been made on cutting a triangular groove for the midrib above. If it had originally been designed as a collar, this groove must represent a subsequent adaptation. There is no alignment nick at the top, but a shallow scoop has been cut here, perhaps the beginning of a matrix inadvertently started upside down.

The background to the Bodwrdin mould lies in the Irish Inch Island tradition, though it is clearly the product of a local Welsh bronze-smith, and is the best evidence we have for the actual manufacture of bronze implements in Anglesey. There are no surviving moulds from the Arreton Down tradition, consequently, as in the later Bronze Age, the use of clay must be assumed. In the west, stone moulds were always more popular and continued in use right up to the Late Bronze Age in Ireland.[41] There are a number of four-sided tabular moulds belonging to the Inch Island tradition in Ireland, and the Bodwrdin one fits very neatly into the group, being very similar indeed to the well-known one from Lough Gur, Co. Limerick.

Although the one from Bodwrdin is the only Inch Island mould from Wales, a number of chance finds of finished implements reveal the impact of this tradition on the country and the extent of its sphere of influence. One of the most characteristic products is the spearhead with a looped socket, such as would be cast in the Bodwrdin mould. Although the blade form is very similar to that of the contemporary Arreton Down spearhead, the use of loops rather than peg holes on the socket distinguishes the two. Such end-looped socketed spearheads occur commonly in Ireland and are found occasionally in the west of Britain, as at Rodborough, Gloucestershire,

[40] Suggestion by D. Britton, quoted by Manby, PPS. XXXII. 1966. 349. Mr. Manby himself suggests that it might be a socketed chisel.
[41] For Irish Bronze Age moulds of all periods *see* H. H. Coghlan and J. Raftery, *Sibrium* VI. 1961. 223-44.

and in the Ebnal hoard mentioned above.[42] Although they are an Irish type, some were obviously manufactured in Wales. Not only do we have the Bodwrdin mould, but one of these spearheads found recently in Bala Lake, Merioneth, was clearly a local product, probably thrown into the water in disgust by its maker. It is a quite unsaleable object; the two sides of the mould had been inaccurately aligned, and the core was so badly off-centre that the metal had not been able to flow around it, leaving a hole in one side of the socket.[43]

The razor from Llanddyfnan and the lost blade from Menai Bridge III belong to a group of unpretentious personal equipment of a type which was becoming increasingly popular at the end of the Wessex period. The eclipse of the brilliant warrior societies is a phenomenon which can be traced all over Europe, and with them died the schools of high quality metal workers exemplified by the Arreton Down and Inch Island traditions, with their emphasis on impressive and elegantly decorated weapons. The Middle Bronze Age schools which emerge about 1,400 B.C. inevitably seem rather drab by comparison, but the period does see some interesting technological advances and a remarkable expansion in the use of metal for everyday tools.

It is not clear whether the tradition of placing personal possessions in the urn with the bones continued into the Middle Bronze Age in any real sense. It is certainly true that the rich weapons and ornaments found in the Early Bronze Age graves were not buried in the later period, for no Middle Bronze Age equivalents, neckrings or rapiers, have been found with burials. Razors and awls are occasionally found, as at Menai Bridge III and Cae Mickney, but there is no real evidence that these mark a later horizon than Llanddyfnan and Bedd Branwen, which contained similar objects together with rather richer accessories. It has even been suggested that, since all the datable graves belong to the Early Bronze Age, the custom of urn burial itself did not continue long into the Middle Bronze Age.[44] Unfortunately in the north and west there is no alternative form of burial which can be dated to the later Bronze Age, so this hypothesis must remain unconfirmed.

One consequence of the absence of grave finds is that the Middle Bronze Age objects, usually found by chance in ploughing or digging operations, can only be dated by typology and association; by their position on an assumed ladder of development; and by cross-referencing with contemporary objects found together in hoards. No hoards of this period survive in Anglesey and, as a result, all the information about the date and origin of the tools must be interpolated from elsewhere. The important metal working school which flourished in North Wales at the beginning of the period is, not surprisingly, the source of many of the tools from the island, but the

[42] *Arch.* LXXI. 1920-1. 140, Pl. 12, fig. 2.
[43] BBCS. XXI. 1966. 371-3.
[44] J. D. Bu'lock. *Trans. Lancs and Cheshire Arch. Soc.* LXXI. 1961. 37.

fashion for North European jewellery, which forms such a marked horizon later in south-west England, appears not to have reached Anglesey, nor the rest of North Wales for that matter. In fact, the over-all impression is that Anglesey was something of a backwater during the centuries after 1,400 B.C. and until about 700 B.C. when trade with Ireland, which seems to have been in abeyance in the Middle Bronze Age, picks up again during the Late Bronze Age and the island was once more the meeting point between the English and Irish spheres of influence.

The majority of Middle Bronze Age implements from Anglesey are palstaves, a developed form of axe, the standard tool of the period in the south of Britain. These implements go through a slow process of change, which spans the years from 1,400 B.C. to about 750 B.C. A few other bronze implements have been found which date from about 1,000 B.C., but these will be considered later in order to allow the palstaves to be discussed as a single group.

The Middle Bronze Age axes or palstaves were hafted in a split cruck, as were the earlier flanged axes, and the evolution of the palstave from the flanged axe is likewise moulded by the demands of this kind of hafting, coupled with the desire to economise on the amount of metal used. This new interest in economy; the appearance of specialist hoards containing only palstaves, with several made from the same mould; and the general deterioration in standards of finish (the casting seams have seldom been completely ground down on palstaves, which very rarely have the engraved or hammered decoration seen on earlier bronzes) must all indicate a change in the market. The craftsmen were no longer serving only the rich, who wanted weapons and tools designed to impress, and were presumably prepared to pay for them: they were now producing for a much wider, but perhaps more impoverished, market; for men who simply wanted efficient tools and who were not prepared, or not able, to pay for individual design and embellishment.

The advantages of the flanged axe over the flat axe have already been discussed; the main one is the prevention of sideways movement. However, since only half the axe head is held in the haft, flanges like the Arreton Down ones, extending the full length of the blade, are not strictly necessary Consequently one of the developments which occurs in the interests of economy and efficiency in use is a reduction in the length of the flanges until they are restricted to the upper half of the axe head. Axes at this stage of development, Haft-flanged Axes, are most common in Ireland, Scotland, and the north of England;[45] there are several in Wales, but none in Anglesey.

A disadvantage, unsolved by the Arreton Down smiths, is the tendency for axe heads hafted in a split cruck, to bite back into the shaft as they are used (see Fig 59). This problem was solved by placing a raised bar across

[45] M. A. Smith. PPS. XXV. 1959. 174-5. maps 4a and b.

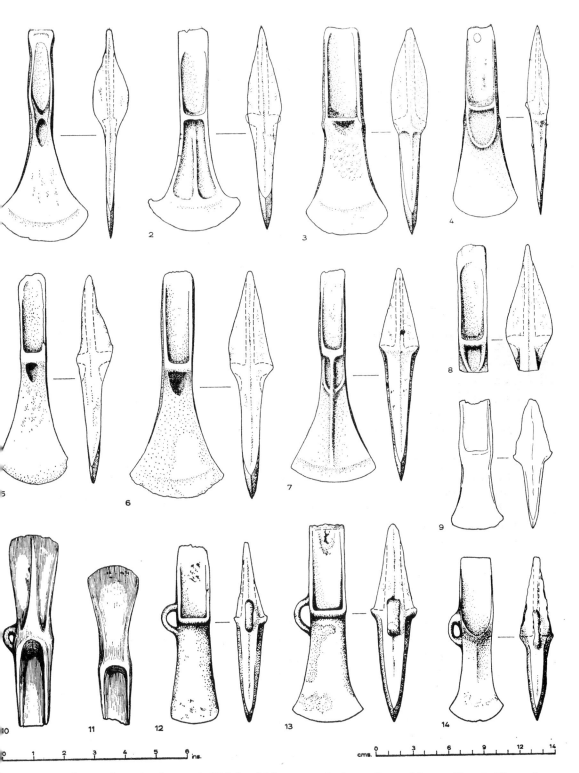

FIG. 63 — Palstaves from Anglesey: 1, Holyhead Mountain; 2, Cerrig Dewi, Llangwyllog; 3, Chwarelau, Llanfair Mathafarn Eithaf; 4, Plas Bodewryd, Bodewryd; 5, Bryn Celli Ddu, Llanddaniel-fab; 6, 'Anglesey'; 7, Bodrwyn, Cerrigceinwen; 8, 'Anglesey'; 9, Rhos-y-gad, Llanfair Pwllgwyngyll (after A. Way); 10-11, Near Porthamel, Llanidan (after W. Wynn Williams); 12, Lligwy; 13, Llangefni; 14, Poncyrefail, Llaneugrad (after C. B. Burgess).

the middle of the axe head as a stop against which the end of the shaft would abutt. Early axes of this type have a thin raised strip across the middle and are of uniform thickness on either side of it. The flanges on these " Bar-stop " axes may sometimes be restricted to the upper part: the two lines of development naturally go hand in hand.

An improvement on the bar-stop is the ledge-stop, which is character-istic of the true palstave. The thickness of the upper part between the flanges (the septum) is greatly reduced while that of the blade, where the strength and rigidity are really needed, remains the same or is increased. Below this stop the blade may be variously decorated with mouldings or ribs. Once the palstave type (with ledge-stop, thin septum, and flanges confined to the upper half) became established, perhaps by 1,400, certainly by 1,300 B.C., few significant changes are made and the chronological and regional groups can be best distinguished by small changes in proportions, blade shape and style of decoration.[46]

What appears to be the earliest implement of palstave type from Anglesey is the one from Holyhead Mountain (Fig. 63, No. 1).[47] The flanges are high and leaf-shaped, as viewed from the side, and the blade is widely expanded: features shared by the various forms of flanged axe and by early palstaves. The implement has certain anomalies which make it difficult to parallel exactly, notably the thinness of the blade, the curved stopridge, and the slightly expanded butt. Thin blades occur on two " Bar-stop " axes from North Wales, one from Dyserth, Flintshire, and the other from the Moelfre Uchaf hoard, Betws yn Rhos, Denbighshire; neither of them has an expanded butt, nor a curved stopridge.[48] The expanded butt can be seen on the peculiar object called a " chisel " from the Acton Park hoard, Wrexham, Denbighshire, which also has a remarkably thin and widely expanded blade, but no stopridge of any kind.[49] This " chisel " was found with fully developed palstaves, so it is probable that the hybrid implement from Holyhead was made by a craftsman of this Wrexham school.

The bronze-smiths of north-eastern Wales, whose main product was a particularly heavy version of the one of the standard early palstaves, were an extremely active group, in the forefront of developments in design.[50] The presence of some of their products in hoards in the Netherlands and north Germany is indicative of close contact with the Continental areas

[46] A convenient summary of early types of palstaves and their dates can be found in C. B. Burgess. *Monmouthshire Antiquary*. I. 1964. 117-24.
[47] In the National Museum of Wales. BBCS. XII. 1946. 59. Another palstave formerly said to have come from Holyhead Mountain is now known to belong to the Cemaes (Mont.) hoard. (*Arch. Camb.* 1958. 24).
[48] Dyserth: Ellis Davies. *Prehistoric and Roman Remains of Flintshire*. 1949. 119. (illustrated 107).
    Betws yn rhos: *Arch. Camb.* 1937. 335.
    An unprovenanced palstave in the Evans Collection (AAS. 2) also has a very thin blade but since the entire surface has been ground down to uncorroded metal in the recent past its size and shape cannot be considered significant.
[49] W. F. Grimes. *The Prehistory of Wales*. 1951. 253. fig. 65. 7.
[50] J. J. Butler. *Palaeohistoria*. IX. 1963. 51, 61, 62.
    C. B. Burgess. *Monmouthshire Antiquary*. I. 1964. 117-24.

from which the palstave idea was borrowed and several details of shape and decoration betray the influence of the later British flanged axes which must have been in use alongside the earliest native palstaves. The occurrence of palstaves, possibly made in Wales, in hoards of the Ilsmoor phase in Germany argues for a date close to 1,400 B.C. for their manufacture in Wales, a date which is supported by the typological similarities to the flanged axe.

The products of these metalworkers in North Wales have been grouped as the " Acton Park Complex ", after the hoard from Wrexham mentioned above.[51] The principal product was the " shield pattern " palstave of which several varieties were made, all of them distinguished by some form of shield-shaped decoration below the stopridge, either a raised moulding or a simple depression. One sub-group, which may possibly be the earliest, includes the Preeswood and Clochfaen types.[52] These are typologically closest to the flanged axe, having facetted flanges, a curved moulding on the blade like Irish decorated axes, and a strange, shouldered profile due to a slight increase in blade width at the bottom of the flanges. These characteristics are most marked on the Preeswood type, commonly found in the Marches. The Clochfaen type is closer to the variety found in the Acton Park hoard itself, but may be distinguished from it by its less clumsy proportions, especially the thinner blade and lower flanges.

The palstave found at Plas Bodewryd (Fig. 63, No. 4) is of this Clochfaen type, with low flanges and relatively thin blade. The shield is large and marked by a simple raised moulding. The shouldered profile is clear, though it scarcely increases the width of the blade. It is the only one of this type in Anglesey, but they are relatively common elsewhere in North Wales and the Marches, similar implements having been found at Llanfair Talhaearn and Colwyn Bay, Denbighshire, at Clochfaen, Montgomeryshire, and Weston-under-Penyard, Herefordshire.[53]

The broken palstave which was formerly in the T. A. Glenn Collection at Prestatyn (Fig. 63, No. 8), represents another variety of " shield pattern " palstave made in North Wales at this time.[54] The shield is very clearly marked by a heavy moulding which is, in fact, a continuation of the flanges. The shield is open, for the moulding is not quite continuous: a variation on the design seen again on a palstave from Llanidloes, Montgomeryshire.[55]

[51] Term first coined by C. B. Burgess. *Radnorshire Soc. Trans.* XXXII. 1962. 18.
[52] J. J. Butler. *op. cit.* 51 and L. F. Chitty. *Ant. J.* IX. 1929. 253-5. Clochfaen group unpublished.
[53] Llanfair Talhaiarn: Ellis Davies. *Prehistoric and Roman Remains of Denbighshire.* 1929. 226. (illustrated. 413).
Colwyn Bay: *ibid.* 197.
Clochfaen, Montgomeryshire: *Arch. Camb.* 1949. 275-6.
[54] TAAS. 1965. 2-6. It is said to have been found at Ty Mawr, Holyhead, but this is a provenance so commonly used for doubtful articles that it should be regarded with suspicion. The Prestatyn Collection has now been handed over to the Flintshire County Council.
[55] W. F. Grimes. *Prehistory of Wales.* 1951. 247. Fig. 59. 1.

The palstave is marked " Anglesey ", but it has no exact provenance within the island.

Fig. 63, Nos. 5 and 6, belong to yet another variety of " shield pattern " palstave in which the shield is marked not by a moulding but by a simple depression. No. 5, which is badly worn and corroded, was found in ploughing near Bryn Celli Ddu, Llanddaniel-fab.[56] The precise origin of the other is not known. It formerly belonged to Major Chadwick of Llangoed and is believed to have been found somewhere in Anglesey.[57] Both these palstaves are narrower than the typical Acton Park product, the Bryn Celli Ddu one notably so, a detail which, together with the loss of definition in the shield, might suggest a rather later date, closer to 1,300 than 1,400 B.C. The triangular outline of the flanges on No. 6 is another feature which may be considered typologically late.

In spite of the rough depression beneath the stopridge, the palstave from Chwarelau, Llanfair Mathafarn Eithaf (Fig. 63, No. 3) does not belong to the " shield pattern " group, though it should probably be included within the same Acton Park Complex.[58] It has the shouldered profile and the leaf-shaped flanges, which give it an early typological position and suggest a date comparable to that of the Clochfaen group. The septum is notably broader than on most palstaves and these rather heavy proportions invite comparison with others with a scattered distribution in Glamorgan, the Marches and north-east Wales.[59] It is also similar to the plain palstaves in the Voorhout hoard, Holland, a Continental hoard which contains " shield pattern " palstaves, and may even have been the stock-in-trade of a travelling Welsh smith.[60]

The very fine single-ribbed palstave from Llangwyllog (Fig. 63, No. 2) belongs to a well-defined group which has an eastern Welsh distribution rather similar to that of the type mentioned above.[61] These ribbed palstaves are typologically early, having a widely splayed blade, leaf-shaped flanges, occasionally a shouldered profile, but never a loop. An early date is confirmed by their association with " shield pattern " palstaves in the Acton Park hoard itself, by their export to the Continent and their inclusion in

[56] In the National Museum of Wales. BBCS. XVI. 1954-6. 209-10.
[57] It is now in the collection of Mr. Alwyne H. Jones, Brynsiencyn.
[58] In the National Museum of Wales; Grimes. *op. cit.* 176, no. 436. This Palstave, which was given to the Museum in 1939 by Col. Lawrence Williams, is in fact the one said to have been found at Maen Eryr, Tregaian (E. N. Baynes. TAAS. 1914. 18 and 1923. 27). The two reputed findspots are close to each other but unfortunately the Royal Commission (*Anglesey* 1937. lxiv-v) list it twice (nos. 53 and 66). The identity of the two is confirmed by Miss L. F. Chitty, *ex info.* E. N. Baynes. The provenance accepted by the National Museum of Wales is retained here to save further confusion.
[59] e.g. Llandaff, Glam.: Grimes. *op. cit.* 247. Fig. 59. 7.
   Llanrhumney, Glam.: BBCS. XXI. 1966. 373-4.
   Parc Farm, Llangadfan, Mont.: Private Collection.
[60] J. J. Butler. *Palaeohistoria.* IX. 1963. 52. Fig 11. f and g.
[61] Burgess Group II palstave: *Monmouthshire Antiquary.* I. 1964. 117-24. Original publication: *Arch. J.* XXVII. 1870. 157 & 163. It is now in the British Museum. The 'decoration' on the sides seen by Burgess is not really clear.

hoards there, dating from about 1,400 B.C.[62] Although there is one in the
Acton Park hoard, this type of palstave was made chiefly in south-east
Wales, and this example from Anglesey is, therefore, something of an outlier.

There is a record of an unlooped palstave from Cefn-mawr-isaf, Newborough, but the implement cannot now be traced. A very rough sketch
survives which shows it to have been 6ins. long:[63] the proportions are
similar to those of the Bryn Celli Ddu palstave, but it is undecorated.

The palstaves mentioned above have all belonged to the earliest phases
of production and to styles originating in Wales. At that time North Wales
seems to have been a major area of production and development, but in
later centuries this initiative appears to have been lost. The smiths seem
to have come under the influence of styles emanating from elsewhere, and
by the Late Bronze Age North Wales is remarkable for the conservatism
of its bronzework.

The unlooped palstave from Bodrwyn, Cerrigceinwen (Fig. 63, No. 7),
illustrates this point. It is not a specifically Welsh type, being one of a
widespread group of " trident pattern " palstaves found mainly in southern
England. They can be fairly closely dated, because they occur in hoards
with British versions of Continental neckrings, bracelets, etc., which, in the
south-west of England, form a well-marked " Ornament Horizon " at a date
between 1,200 and 1,000 B.C.[64] It was found near a tributary of the Gwna,
in an area containing hut circles, though any genuine association with the
huts is doubtful.[65]

This low-flanged, " trident pattern " type may be found either with or
without a loop, because they were current during the transitional time when
the loop was becoming a standard addition. Two bronze moulds, one for
an unlooped palstave, the other for an identical implement with a loop,
were found together at Deansfield, Bangor.[66]

There is a looped example of this kind of palstave in the Dinam
Collection, but it is unprovenanced and it is not even known whether it was
found in Anglesey.[67] It is possible that the hoard of " brass or copper
chisels " said to have been found close to the megalithic tomb at Perthiduon,
Llanidan,[68] contained palstaves which might very well have been of this
kind, for it is at this time, round about 1,200 B.C., that true mass-production
starts. Very large hoards of looped " trident pattern " palstaves have been
found at Cemmaes, Montgomeryshire, and Gloddaeth, near Llandudno; they

---

[62] Acton Park: Grimes op. cit. 253. fig. 65. 6.
  Rülow hoard, Mecklenburg: J. J. Butler. Palaeohistoria. IX. 1963. Pl. VIA. 8.
  Dating: Butler op. cit. 61-2.
[63] RCAM. Anglesey. 1937. lxv. no. 62. I am grateful to Mr. W. E. Griffiths for showing me
  the sketch in the Royal Commission's files.
[64] M. A. Smith. PPS. XXV. 1959. 144-87.
[65] Hugh Prichard. Arch. Camb. 1874. 10-7.
[66] RCAM. Caernarvonshire. II. 1960. lii. fig. 14.
[67] Bangor Museum 108. 41. 2.
[68] Arch. Camb. 1846. 467 and 1869. 264.

are very common as chance finds in north-eastern Wales, although the main weight of the distribution is in south-east England.[69]

The Irish connection, which was relatively strong in the Early Bronze Age (evidence from both implements and barrows), seems to have been weak during the Middle Bronze Age, perhaps because the various Irish experimental versions of the palstave/haft-flanged axe were less satisfactory than the standard Anglo-Welsh palstave. However, at about 1,100 - 1,000 B.C. some Irish metalwork begins to appear in Anglesey again and this trade becomes an important factor in the Late Bronze Age.

Anglesey has not produced any of the twisted gold neck rings that were made in Ireland at this time, examples of which have been found in other parts of Wales. There is, however, one Irish palstave (Fig. 63, No. 9) which was found in the middle of the last century at Rhos-y-gad, near the station at Llanfair Pwllgwyngyll.[70] It is said to have been found with another looped palstave which was larger. Both have subsequently been lost, but a good drawing survives of the Irish implement.[71] Albert Way, who first published the group, rightly described the smaller as Irish, but made no comment on the origin of the other, which may be assumed to have been a normal British type.

The implement is very small, as is so much Irish bronzework; it is unlooped and has a plain blade. The stopridge is very high, a trend seen in the later British palstaves as well, and it is likely that the ledge stop was undercut, although the drawing unfortunately does not show this feature which is an infallible guide to Irish manufacture. It is notoriously difficult to date Irish palstaves because so few have been found in hoards, but a probable date for this type is the Annesborough/Bishopsland Phase, the Irish equivalent of the British Ornament Horizon, giving a date of about 1,200 - 1,000 B.C., or a little later.[72]

A rather similar Irish palstave has been found in Llanrug, near Caernarvon, and a lost one from near Porthamel, Llanidan, may also have been comparable. This, too, was found with a larger looped implement. A drawing of both was published (Fig. 63, Nos. 10 and 11).[74] The smaller of the two, which was said to contain a lot of copper, is much the same size as the Rhos-y-gad one, and has a similar waisted profile. The height of the stop-ridge is not indicated. The larger one had a narrow blade with a thick, tapering midrib. This type of midrib can be found on looped Irish palstaves, though it is normally shorter. A better comparison may be with the

[69] Cemmaes: *Arch. Camb.* 1902. 240 and BBCS. VIII. 1935-7. 96-7.
   Gloddaeth: *Arch. Camb.* 1941. 205.
   General distributions: PPS. XXV. 1959. 169-70. maps 2 and 3.
[70] *Arch. J.* XIII. 1856. 85 and *Arch. Camb.* 1856. 124.
[71] In Way's papers in the library of the Soc. of Antiquaries, London. I am grateful to Miss L. F. Chitty for a copy of this drawing and to Mr. C. B. Burgess for drawing my attention to it. Mr. Neil Baynes was mistaken when he suggested that the actual implement was still in London. (TAAS. 1923. 27).
[72] C. B. Burgess. *Arch. J.* CXXV. 1969. 1-45.
[73] RCAM. *Caernarvonshire.* II. 1960. 1. Fig. 13. 12.
[74] W. Wynn Williams. *Arch. Camb.* 1867, 283.

"transitional" palstaves in several of the northern English hoards belonging to the Wallington tradition, dated to about 900 B.C.[75]

Another "transitional" palstave, with a markedly curved stopridge but no midrib, only a slightly ridged blade, was found at Poncyrefail, Marianglas, Llaneugrad (Fig. 63, No. 14).[76] This must belong to the same period as the one discussed above, and probably has a northern English background, though exact parallels are difficult to find. It is notable that all these later palstaves are much smaller than the early ones.

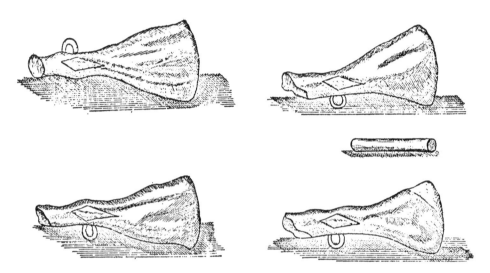

FIG. 64—Hoard from Y Rhiedd, Llanidan. (Reproduced from *Mona Antiqua Restaurata*, by the Rev. Henry Rowlands.)

Henry Rowlands records a hoard of bronze implements found at Y Rhiedd, Maes Mawr Gad, Llanidan.[77] They have subsequently been lost and it is difficult to interpret Rowlands's bad drawing with any certainty. This drawing shows a length of what appears to be hollow tube, and four implements with loops, wide blades, and some suggestion of decoration in the shape of a lozenge in the centre. The ends appear to be slightly broken, but they are shown in the same convention as the tube, suggesting that these blades, which are clearly related to palstaves, may have been socketed.[78] This impression is reinforced by his description which speaks of "their loop holes and sockets" and in which they are contrasted, by implication, with a non-socketed palstave owned by Rowlands. If these were indeed socketed palstaves, they are an extremely rare and interesting

[75] C. B. Burgess. *Bronze Age Metalwork in Northern England.* 1968. Shelf and Roundhay hoards. fig. 6. 7 and fig. 7. 1a.
[76] *Arch. Camb.* 1938. 135-6. It is in Manchester Museum.
[77] H. Rowlands. *Mona Antiqua Restaurata* 2nd. ed. 1766. Pl. II. Fig. 2. and p. 86.
[78] This suggestion was first put forward by C. B. Burgess. *Arch. J.* CXXV. 1969. 3. footnote 11.

type, only one other example being known, that from St. George, near Abergele, Denbighshire.[79]

This type is clearly experimental and must date from the time when socketed axes were first coming into use, perhaps to be equated with the Penard Phase, about 1,000 - 900 B.C.[80] The conservative palstave-making industries were clearly affected by the introduction from the Continent of this new type, although at first it did not make much headway. In spite of the fact that socketed axes were first made in this country in about 1,200 B.C., they were not widely used until some four hundred years later. The hollow blade, which was more economical to produce, would not have had the weight of the palstave, which must have remained in use for heavy woodwork, perhaps until the very end of the Bronze Age.

The design of late palstaves, like the ones from Lligwy and Llangefni (Fig. 63, Nos. 12 and 13),[81] shows strong influence from the socketed axe, especially in the narrowness and thickness of the blade and the overhanging stop-ridge, which is reminiscent of the collar on socketed axes. In fact, when the upper part was hidden by the binding the two implements must have looked very much alike. There is an unprovenanced palstave in the Evans Collection (Anglesey Antiquarian Society, No. 3), which has three vertical ribs beneath the stop ridge, showing strong influence from the common varieties of ribbed socketed axes.

Both the Lligwy and Llangefni palstaves with their squared stop-ridges and plain blades can be compared to the palstaves from the Guilsfield hoard, Montgomeryshire, which seems to have been deposited about 750 B.C.[82] This hoard is particularly important for dating the Welsh material because it contains rare examples of implements which, though current in England, never seem to have reached the far more conservative smiths (or consumers) further west. Another interesting association is the hoard from the Great Orme, Llandudno, which contained a palstave very similar to the Lligwy one, and two gold "lock rings" or hair ornaments like those found at Gaerwen.[83] This gives a similar eighth century date for this luxury trade with Ireland in which Anglesey played a large part and which may well have made several of her inhabitants quite rich.

In most areas of the country, throughout the Middle Bronze Age, the rather mundane palstave is the commonest implement; finds of weapons, dirks, rapiers and spearheads are comparatively rare. From Anglesey, one small dirk and two spearheads survive. There are, however, records of other spearheads which may have belonged to this period; " several bronze spear-

[79] BBCS. XII. 1948. 125-6.
[80] This experimental phase discussed in C. B. Burgess. op. cit. 3-9.
[81] Lligwy: TAAS. 1923. 26. In Bangor Museum on loan from the National Museum of Wales. Llangefni: BM. WG. 1839. Published in the Reliquary VI. 118 and RCAM. Anglesey. 1937. liii. fig. 4.
[82] G. Davies. Ant. J. XLVII. 1967. 95-108.
[83] H. N. Savory. BBCS. XVI. 1954-6. 51. Pl. 1. 2. and Arch. Camb. 1958. 14-6, 56-7 and Pl. V.B.

heads" are said to have been found at Rhuddgaer, Llangeinwen, close to the shore of the Menai Straits;[84] a "head of a hunting-spear of bronze" is recorded from the north-west coast, apparently found at Tyn-y-nant, Llanfwrog;[85] Neil Baynes mentions another from Cae-maes-mawr, Llanrhwydrys;[86] and there is a further reference to spearheads from Rhos-y-gad, Llanbedrgoch.[87] Unfortunately, all these weapons have vanished without trace and their authenticity cannot be vouched for.

The dirk was found at Tre'r Dryw, Llanidan (Fig. 65, No. 1). Nothing is known about the circumstances of discovery; it was part of the collection of E. Neil Baynes and is now in the National Museum of Wales, Cardiff.[88]

The blade is 6¾ins. long and ⅛in. thick in the centre. It has been slightly bent and the edges are ragged, the combined result of use and corrosion. For the most part the surface is good, covered with a glossy brown patination. The trapeze-shaped butt has been damaged and the two rivet holes torn. The edges are bevelled on either side of a wide, very slightly domed midrib, and the butt has also been thinned a little where it would be covered by the hilt.

A trapeze-shaped butt with two rivet holes is normal to the Anglo-Irish series of these weapons and may occur on both the long, elegant rapiers, like the ones found at Maentwrog, Merioneth,[89] or on these rather less impressive dirks which must have acted as all-purpose hunting and fighting knives, like the Highland dirk of more recent times. The shape of the butt is not a very close indicator of date; the blade section may be more significant.[90] However, though the Llanidan dirk has a wide, flat midrib which would place it in Burgess's Group IV, its general shape and proportion make it unlike other members of that group; in many ways it is closer to the earlier weapons of Group II. The majority of weapons of Group IV (such as those from Maentwrog) may be dated to the end of the Middle Bronze Age, about 1,100 - 800 B.C., whereas the Group II rapiers would have been current about 200 years earlier. Rare hybrid types, such as the Llanidan example, are consequently difficult to date or categorise, but local manufacture at about 1,200 B.C. may be tentatively suggested.

Rapiers and dirks were a popular form of weapon in the western half of Europe, and it is clear that they were made by most of the schools of metalworkers operating in western France, Ireland and Britain. Wales does not contain very many examples, but the hoard of fifty rapiers found in the

[84] E. Neil Baynes. TAAS. 1923. 27.
[85] 3rd Rep. *Soc. Nat. Hist. and Antiq. of Anglesey, Caernarvon and Merioneth.* 25th Oct. 1835.
[86] E. Neil Baynes. *loc. cit.*
[87] *Arch. Camb.* 1904. 84.
[88] RCAM. *Anglesey.* 1937. liii. fig. 6 and TAAS. 1923, 26.
[89] *Inventaria Archaeologica.* GB 10.
[90] C. B. Burgess. *Trans. Architectural and Archaeol. Soc. of Durham and Northumberland.* New Series. I. 1968. 3-26.

seventeenth century at Beddgelert, Caerns., is the largest ever found in these islands.[91]

The spearheads are in the possession of Mr. M. Plews, of Valley, who found them while digging on the marshy land between Valley and Four Mile Bridge.[92] They both came from the same spot, about 9ft. apart, but were not found on the same day. It is not possible to state definitely that these two are truly associated, that is, were lost or hidden at the same time, although this is quite probable.

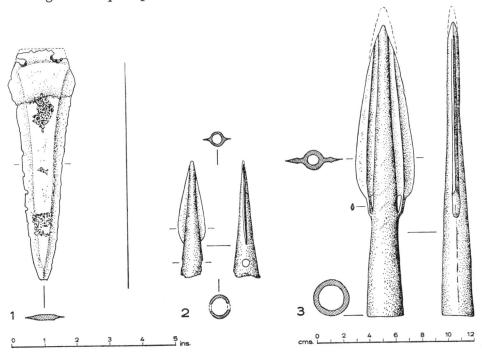

FIG. 65 — 1, knife-dagger, Tre'r Dryw, Llanidan; 2-3, spearheads from near Four Mile Bridge, Valley.

The larger of the two is a basal-looped spearhead with a ridged blade and a circular midrib. Its present length is 8½ins., but it may originally have been a little longer for the top seems to have been worn down by frequent sharpening. As a result, the blade may now have a more leaf-shaped outline than it did when new. This point is relevant because straight-sided blades such as this one came into production at a rather later date than the leaf-shaped ones, although these latter continued alongside them.[93]

Theoretically, these basal-looped spearheads, in which the loops merge with the base of the blade, are a development of the end-looped type such

[91] RCAM. *Caernarvonshire*. II. 1960. fig. 13. 3-8 and liv. no. 97.
[92] I am grateful to Capt. Butterworth of Holyhead for bringing this find to my notice and to Mr. Plews for kindly allowing me to publish the spearheads.
[93] C. B. Burgess. *Bronze Age Metalwork in Northern England*. 1968. 19-22.

as the Bodwrdin mould would have produced. It is difficult, however, to give precise dates to the various stages in this ideal sequence. Export to the Continent suggests that the basal-looped type may have been made as early as 1,300 B.C., but in this country such an early date cannot be actually proved because of the paucity of hoards. They appear in hoards such as Taunton and Maentwrog, of the 12th - 11th century B.C.; in Scotland, Ireland and the north of England they may be found as late as 800 B.C.[94]

The small spearhead would have been fixed to its shaft by a rivet or peg passed through the two holes in the side. This system of securing the head had first been used by the Arreton Down smiths in the south, but had been superseded by loops until it was reintroduced from the Continent about 1,000 B.C.[95] The type is so simple and basic that it is impossible to date with any precision; it could have been made anytime from about 1,000 B.C. (Penard Phase) onwards. There is a small spearhead, very similar to this one, in the Pant y Maen hoard, Carmarthenshire, which dates from about 800 - 750 B.C.,[96] but if the two Valley spears are genuinely associated, a rather earlier date would be preferable.

Apart from the palstave from Rhos-y-gad, evidence for contact with Ireland during the Middle Bronze Age is negligible, but from the eighth century B.C. onwards trade between Anglesey and Ireland seems to have revived. The most dramatic evidence of this is the quantity of Irish goldwork from the island, but, before this is discussed, two less exciting finds should be mentioned. These are the small socketed axe with cable moulding from Beaumaris and the plain, bag-shaped axe found at Rhuddgaer, Llangeinwen, and now unfortunately lost.

The Beaumaris axe is very small and has a remarkably thin strap-like loop. Although the surface is badly corroded, the cable moulding around the collar, which is a characteristic feature of many Irish axes of this period, is clearly visible on one side. The chronology of the various types of Irish axes has yet to be worked out in detail, but a lost axe from the Guilsfield hoard, Montgomeryshire, had cabling round the mouth, suggesting that the type may have been reaching Wales by about 750 B.C.[97]

The lost axe from Rhuddgaer is known only from a description and a rough sketch from memory.[98] It clearly had the splayed blade and flaring neck of the Irish bag-shaped axes, and had a simple collar moulding. In north-east Wales there are several Irish socketed axes, and one from Cerrigydrudion, Denbighshire, may have been very similar indeed to the one from Rhuddgaer.[99]

[94] Continental evidence: J. J. Butler. *Palaeohistoria* IX. 1963. 98-102, 239.
   Taunton and Maentwrog hoards: *Inventaria Archaeologica.* GB 43 and 10.
[95] Burgess *op. cit.* 5, 42, note 35 and *Arch. J.* CXXV. 1969. 34 and note 6.
[96] W. E. Griffiths. BBCS. XVII. 1956-8. 118-24.
[97] E. L. Barnwell. *Arch. Camb.* 1864. 212-21. (the original publication).
[98] I am most grateful to Miss L. F. Chitty for sending me a copy of this sketch made for her by the brother of the original owner.
[99] Ellis Davies. *Prehistoric and Roman Remains of Denbighshire.* 1929. 82. It is now in St. Asaph Cathedral.

Stray finds of socketed axes are not very common in Anglesey, perhaps because the palstave seems to have survived for so long in the island, as in the rest of North Wales. Only two other finds are known, one a large ribbed axe from Parc, Llangristiolus,[100] and the other a small square-sectioned axe from Tŷ Croes, Llanynghenedl.

Around 750 - 700 B.C. a number of regional schools specialising in socketed axes came into being. The best known are those centred on Yorkshire and South Wales; both produced axes decorated with three vertical ribs on either face.[101] The two can be distinguished by certain details of design, notably size (the south Welsh axes are large and rather clumsy); the position of the loop (which is set rather low in the Yorkshire type); and the moulding of the collar (the ribs spring directly from the collar in South Wales, while in Yorkshire there is always a second moulding interposed). Unfortunately, the Parc axe cannot be assigned to either of these two schools: the well-finished sloping collar is foreign to the South Wales group, and the loop is too broad; the ribs do not spring directly from the collar, but the moulding is too slight for the Yorkshire type and the loop is set too high.

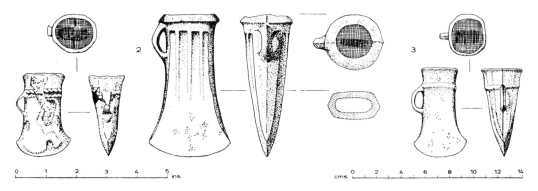

FIG. 66 — Socketed axes from Anglesey: 1, Beaumaris; 2, Parc, Llangristiolus; 3, Tŷ Croes, Llanynghenedl.

Although the Yorkshire and South Welsh centres have been the most closely studied, it is clear that ribbed axes were produced elsewhere: in Ireland, for instance, where the smiths were making an axe very similar to the Yorkshire one. It would not be surprising, therefore, to find local centres of production outside south-east Wales using the South Welsh axe as a model. The Parc axe would seem to be a product of one of these, for its size, hexagonal section and high loop are all very close to the standard type seen in such hoards as St. Fagans and Llantwit Major, Glamorgan.[102]

[100] TAAS. 1945, 23-4.
[101] See map in H. W. M. Hodges, UJA. XIX. 1956. 40. fig. 6.
[102] W. F. Grimes. *The Prehistory of Wales*. 1951. 254. Fig. 66. 12-6. 257. Fig. 69. 1-12.

The axe from Tŷ Croes is much less distinctive.[103] It is basically square sectioned, but there is a slight facetting on the sides. There is a very low moulding just above the loop. The type is simple and quite widespread. A number of similar axes occur in large hoards from eastern England, such as Reach Fen and Meldreth, Cambridgeshire,[104] which also contain objects similar to those in the Llangwyllog and Tŷ Mawr hoards from Anglesey. This stray axe may, therefore, belong to the same horizon, c. 750 - 600 B.C.

The growth of trade with Ireland during the eighth and seventh centuries has already been mentioned. The most spectacular evidence for this trade and for its importance is the number of gold ornaments made in Ireland which have been found in the island. Unfortunately, most of these precious and attractive objects have since disappeared, and that is not altogether surprising. One hoard, three gold bracelets and a " bulla ", has been lost in its entirety. It was found some time before the middle of the last century " near the earthworks of Castell Crwn in Llanfflewyn parish ".[105] The accuracy of this is a little doubtful because Castell Crwn is not in Llanfflewyn. The Royal Commission give the find-spot as Ynys Gwyddel, Llanfflewyn, which is just under two miles away from Castell Crwn.[106] The bracelets may be presumed to have been like those from Gaerwen, and it has been suggested that the " bulla " may have been a hair ornament, or " lock ring ", like the Gaerwen ones.[107] The Irish goldsmiths did, however, produce genuine " bullae ", or hollow pendants, so there is no real reason for supposing that the Llanfflewyn one was not like the famous one from the Bog of Allen or the one from the Kinnegoe hoard, Co. Armagh.[108]

The hoard found in 1856 at Gaerwen consisted originally of eleven gold bracelets and eleven gold hair ornaments or " lock rings " — the largest hoard of these objects ever found.[109] Only two of each now survive. They were bought by an itinerant trader soon after their discovery and sold by him to a silversmith in Newcastle-upon-Tyne. At some stage Canon Greenwell acquired the four objects now in the British Museum.

The exact use of the " lock rings " is not known. It is thought that they may have been used to catch a bunch of hair at the temples, or perhaps

---

[103] TAAS. 1965. 2-6. It was in the Collection of the Prestatyn UDC, now handed over to the Flintshire County Council.

[104] *Inventaria Archaeologica.* GB. 17 and 13. There is a very similar axe from Dinas Bran, Llangollen (Ellis Davies. *Prehistoric and Roman Remains of Denbighshire.* 1929. 254) an area always open to English influence. Its presence suggests the route by which the Tŷ Croes axe reached Anglesey.

[105] Albert Way. *Arch. J.* XIII. 1856. 295.

[106] RCAM. *Anglesey.* 1937. lxv. They do not give any authority for the change. They also state (1960 *Corrections and Additions.* 4.) that, according to the British Museum, two of the bracelets may have been in existence in 1946 in private possession. It has not been possible to discover anything more about this.

[107] Albert Way. *loc. cit.* and others.

[108] PPS. XXX. 1964. 303. fig. 15. 8 and 333.

[109] Albert Way. *Arch. J.* XIII. 1856. 295. It has always been assumed that the Gaerwen in question was the village of that name in the parish of Llanfihangel Ysceifiog but Neil Baynes (TAAS. 1923. 27) lists it as Gaerwen, Llanfair yn Cwmmwd. He does not comment on this and it may be simply a mistake on his part.

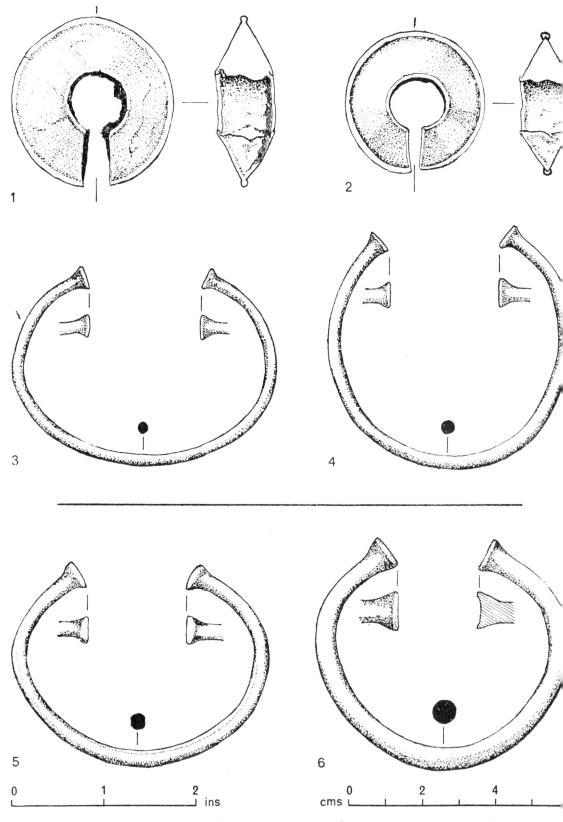

FIG. 67 — Gold ornaments from Anglesey; 1-4 surviving 'lock rings' and bracelets from Gaerwe
5-6, bracelets from Beaumaris.

incorporated into plaits. Others have suggested that they might have been worn as ear-rings, but they are not sprung and would probably have slipped off rather too easily. They are penannular objects with a hollow triangular cross-section. Basically they are two opposed cones supported in the centre by a tube. The manufacture of these objects must have been exceedingly delicate and time-consuming, for they can be made from as many as six separate parts; moreover, in Ireland, the face plates were normally made not from sheet metal but from minute gold wires soldered together.[110]

The two surviving "lock rings" from Gaerwen are of different sizes and each has been made in a slightly different way. The larger one is made from very thin gold sheet (now rather crushed). It consists of a central tube ⅗in. long and two undecorated face plates attached to each other by being very neatly overlapped around the outer circumference and folded in over the ends of the tube in the centre. The circle is split at one point and the open ends have been closed by folding the ends of the central tube outwards and attaching them neatly to the ends of the face plates. The other one, 1½ins. in diameter, is made of slightly thicker gold sheet and is consequently in better condition. The principle of manufacture is the same, but in the centre the tube has been folded out over the face plates and around the outer circumference, the plates are held together not by overlapping but by a separate C-sectioned gold tube. The open ends have been closed in the same way by folding back part of the central tube.

The bracelets are round-sectioned bars of solid gold with slightly expanded ends. These simple bracelets are found fairly commonly in Ireland itself, notably in the Great Clare Find (Mooghaun North, Co. Clare), where no less than one hundred and thirty-eight bracelets similar to the Gaerwen ones were found, together with gold collars and two "lock rings".[111] These gold bracelets must have been a convenient way of carrying personal wealth then, as in succeeding centuries, and consequently would have been very popular as a trading item. The Gaerwen hoard was no doubt the property of one such trader, perhaps on his way to the north of England where the "lock rings" are found in quite large numbers. Two other examples, from the Great Orme and from Portfield, near Whalley, Lancashire, indicate the route taken by the Irish traders of this time.[112] The ultimate goal may have been Scandinavia for, though the "lock rings" themselves are not found there, the popularity of Scandinavian fashions and Baltic amber in Ireland are indicative of close contact between the two areas.

The quantity of objects in the Gaerwen hoard suggests that it was the stock-in-trade of a merchant, but the Beaumaris find, only two gold brace-

[110] For a comprehensive discussion of these objects see G. Eogan. PRIA. 67. C. 1969. 93-148.
[111] PPS. XXX. 1964. 335.
[112] Great Orme: BBCS. XVI. 1954-6. 51, Pl. 1, 2.
   Portfield: *British Museum Quarterly.* XXXII. 1967. 8-14.
   G. Eogan. PRIA. 67. C. 1969. 107-11 for comment on the distribution and trade routes.

lets, may have been personal property, presumably belonging to a native of Anglesey who had hidden his wealth in a time of danger.[113] The bracelets are very similar to the Gaerwen ones and were no doubt made in Ireland, but they are very much more substantial and look less like a standard trade object. One terminal is very slightly cupped, but the others are flat and all are evenly expanded.

The bracelets are too simple to be closely datable, but the "lock rings" were probably being made in Ireland between 850 and 600 B.C., and the associations with a late palstave in the Great Orme find, and with a Yorkshire socketed axe at Portfield, give a date of 750 to perhaps as late as 500 B.C. for the period when this trade was passing through Anglesey and North Wales.

Wealth passing through an area does not necessarily indicate a high level of prosperity among the local inhabitants; unfortunately, we have no other strands of evidence which we could use to gauge the means of livelihood and standard of living of the local population at this time. We have no houses or farms which can be certainly dated to this latter end of the Bronze Age, and we have not even got such evidence as can be deduced from burials.

However, the Beaumaris find suggests that some of the valuable metal work stayed in the island and this impression is confirmed by the hoard found in 1854 near Llangwyllog church. This hoard contained a bronze razor, tweezers, a bracelet, a necklace of amber and jet beads, and some bronze studs and rings, which seem to have been embellishments to horse harness. All of them were in good condition, and the collection seems to have been the personal possessions of a relatively wealthy individual who had to hide his belongings hurriedly in a moment of crisis. Judging by the number of similar finds from all over the country, the Late Bronze Age must have been a time during which such moments of crisis were uncomfortably frequent. This was, of course, a period of considerable unrest on the Continent, where Hallstatt/Celtic warriors were ranging widely over Germany, France, Belgium, Switzerland, and even Spain.[114] Evidence for invasions, and such like, in Britain is far less clear, but it seems that the political tensions built up by the advance of these new peoples may well have spilled over into this country.

The objects in the Llangwyllog hoard were all found together in the bank of a small stream, a tributary of the river Cefni, which had just been widened (NGR SH/430797). Presumably, they were originally hidden in a hole, or perhaps a burrow, but it was not noted whether this hiding place had been marked by a stone, as was often the case. The hoard was first published in 1865 by Albert Way, who listed the objects and illustrated

[113] The bracelets are now in the British Museum. Nothing is known about the circumstances of the find. The reasons for burying valuables cannot, of course, be known. Fear is a reasonable inference but large and spectacular finds from bogs may have been deposited as offerings, perhaps to water gods. (See Llyn Cerrig Bach, Chapter VI, below).
[114] European situation summarised in S. Piggott. *Ancient Europe*. 1965. 168-207.

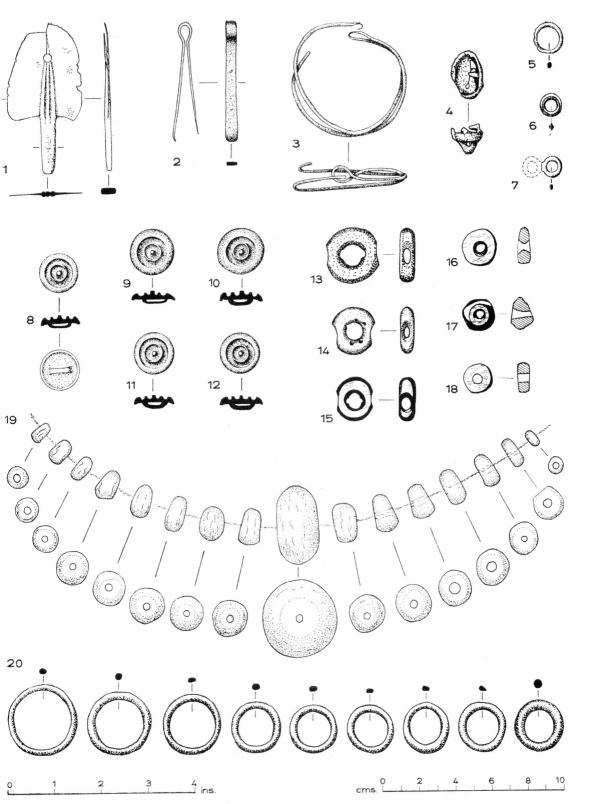

FIG. 68 — Hoard from Llangwyllog: 1, razor; 2, tweezers; 3, bracelet; 4, ?mount; 5-7, small bronze rings; 8-12, harness studs; 13, hollow bronze ring; 14, stone ring; 15, jet ring; 16-18, jet beads; 19, necklace of 16 amber beads; 20, 9 bronze rings.

most of them.[115] His list is very slightly inaccurate in that he mentions only four bronze studs and thirteen bronze rings, not mentioning the perforated jet ring. It does not seem likely, however, that the objects at present in the British Museum are anything other than the entire hoard as it was found.

The razor and the tweezers are toilet articles. Razors of this kind, double-edged, with a notch or a hole at the top, are relatively common throughout Britain during this period: an almost identical one was found in the Thames at Wallingford, Berkshire, for instance, with a group of objects very similar to those in the Tŷ Mawr hoard from Anglesey.[116] They are a native type developed from the simple leaf-shaped blades which were contemporary with the rivetted razor from Llanddyfnan. The tweezers are a rare type, and may appear in this country as the result of the contacts with western France, which are quite marked throughout this period. It is interesting that the huge hoard from Vénat, Charente, contained double-edged razors, tweezers and hooked bracelets like the Llangwyllog one, together with bronze versions of the Irish " lock rings ".[117] The not unexpected combination of razor and tweezers can be found again at Feltwell Fen, Norfolk, in a hoard which also contained part of a gold " lock ring " and an amber bead, both suggestive of contact with the west.[118] Another instance can be cited, this time from an inhabited cave, Merlin's Cave, Symond's Yat, Herefordshire, where there were also various pieces of horse harness, as at Llangwyllog.[119]

The bracelet is very simply made from a long piece of thin bronze wire, doubled over and lightly twisted, with the ends flattened and bent over to make a small hook. One of these ends has been broken, the only sign of damage among these objects. French versions of this type of bracelet in the Vénat hoard have already been mentioned. Another well known example was found in the Heathery Burn cave, Co. Durham, among a large number of other things: bronze vessels, horse harness, Irish goldwork, and more mundane bronze and bone tools. It is thought that the cave was a workshop for a group of bronzesmiths working there around 700 - 600 B.C.[120]

The amber necklace is a very fine one, and all the beads survive in good condition. Some of the amber used is translucent, but the majority of beads are of an opaque, bright yellow amber which seems to have been especially popular at this time; nearly all the Irish Late Bronze Age amber is of this kind, and it is more than likely that the Llangwyllog necklace was bought

[115] Albert Way. *Arch. J.* XXII. 1865. 74 and *Arch. Camb.* 1866. 97-111.
[116] Evans, *Ancient Bronze Implements of Great Britain.* 1881. 167 and 218, fig. 269. The reason for the notch and the hole may haves been a practical one. The cut would enable the bronze smith to sharpen and thin the blade by hammering, for it would absorb the spread of the metal and allow it to overlap. This is clearly seen on the Llangwyllog example.
[117] *Inventaria Archaeologica.* France. Fasicule. 1. F6.
[118] *Inventaria Archaeologica.* GB.. 35.
[119] C. W. Phillips. *Univ. Bristol Spelaeological Soc. Proc.* IV:I. 1931. 22.
[120] *Inventaria Archaeologica.* GB. 55. Bracelet: p. 1, no. 6.

from an Irish trader rather than directly from Denmark.[121] Apart from the sixteen amber ones, there are also three jet beads which probably were strung as part of the same necklace, though their place of origin is likely to have been northern England. The harness studs show that their owner had contacts not only with Ireland, but also with areas to the east.

Apart from the rough casting (Fig. 68, No. 4), which cannot be adequately identified (it appears to have a shank, and may have been a mounting for some kind of stud), all the other objects are harness rings or embellishments. This fashion for loading horses with expensive trappings becomes quite widespread during the seventh century B.C. In this, Britain was no doubt influenced by Continental trends where the horse-riding Hallstatt/Celtic warriors were rapidly converting the horse and chariot or wagon into the status symbol *par excellence*. The spread of the fashion may also have been helped by a desire, common in disturbed times, to convert wealth into easily moveable objects — not only gold bracelets for your wife, but expensive harness for your horse.

The range of horse trappings at Llangwyllog is not especially impressive if compared, for instance, with the large hoard from Parc y Meirch, near Abergele, Denbighshire,[122] but the five ridged studs are beautifully made and must have represented a considerable investment. They each have a wide loop at the back and were probably threaded on the bridle. Rather similar studs in the Parc y Meirch hoard have four loops at the back and were specifically designed to hold crossed straps. Studs very similar indeed to the Llangwyllog ones were found in the hoards from Reach Fen, Cambridgeshire, and Kensington, London, but they are a rare type and it is possible that they were actually imported from Germany.[123]

The other objects are mostly simple rings. There are nine rather crudely made ones probably used to link straps. One of the smaller rings has a lozenge section and had been well polished, while the smallest one has been broken from a double link. These double link chains are fairly common in Ireland; they often occur in the rather dull Irish harness hoards where the only horse trappings are bronze rings of various sorts and sizes.[124] The hollow ring with lateral perforations (Fig. 68, No. 13) is another type which is probably Irish in origin: their exact use is unknown. Apart from the bronze version, there are two other laterally perforated rings at Llangwyllog, one made from stone (Fig. 68, No. 14) and the other from jet. Both are, to my knowledge, unique. The jet ring would scarcely seem to be a practical

[121] There is a great deal of Baltic amber in Ireland at this time when other Scandinavian fashions in jewellery and ornaments were also popular, e.g. gorgets and large dress pins. See G. Eogan. PPS. XXX. 1964. 302-7).
[122] Arch. Camb. 1941. 1-10.
[123] Inventaria Archaeologica. GB. 17 and 52 and C. F. C. Hawkes Ant. J. XXXVII. 1957. 153-6.
[124] PPS. XXX. 1964. 307-9.

piece of harness; on the other hand, it might possibly have been part of an armlet like the one in the Ballytegan hoard, Co. Laois.[125]

With all personal hoards it is difficult to guess how old the various objects may have been when they were hidden, but all the objects here, including the ridged studs which are the rarest and, therefore, theoretically the most closely datable, could have been available during the century 700 - 600 B.C. Perhaps the same crisis which caused them to be hidden away led to the concealment of the gold bracelets in Beaumaris.

A similar mixture of Irish and English objects occurs in the other Anglesey hoard dating from this period, that found in 1832 under a stone near the hut circles at Tŷ Mawr, Holyhead (NGR SH/216823).[126] Its discovery so close to the huts has often raised the question of whether some of the huts may not date from the Bronze Age. The surviving structures, however, when they were excavated in the eighteen-seventies, produced convincing evidence of their construction and use in the Romano-British period, with maximum occupation in the third and fourth centuries A.D.[127] But these excavations also produced a few objects: the broken battle-axe; what appears to be a stone macehead; and a faulty casting of a socketed bronze axe; items which suggest an earlier occupation of the site.[128] The faulty casting and the fact that the Tŷ Mawr hoard (nearly all broken objects, probably scrap to be melted down) most probably belonged to a bronze-smith, suggest that metal working may have been carried out there in the earlier period, as it certainly was in the later. The attraction may have been the copper lodes which outcrop in the cliffs not far away.[129]

Few of the objects in the Tŷ Mawr hoard are rare or distinctive types, and it is probable that most of them were made locally. However, the source

[125] A recent discovery, publication forthcoming. The armlet consists of three twisted bronze wires let into the sides of a hollow bronze ring.
[126] *Arch.* XXVI. 1835. 483 contains the first mention of the finding of the hoard, part of which was sent to the British Museum by W. O. Stanley in 1853. These objects are accessioned as 53. 10-31. 1-5 and are illustrated in this book as Fig. 69, nos. 6, 7, 8, 9, 14 respectively. The rest of the hoard was more adequately published by W. O. Stanley and Albert Way (*Arch. J.* VI. 1849. 236 and XXIV. 1867. 253-7 and *Arch. Camb.* 1868. 401-22). They do not mention the other group of objects although they do refer to the *Archaeologia* article. The later group were sent to the Museum in 1870 by W. O. Stanley's brother and are accessioned as 70. 11-26. 2-15. They are illustrated as Fig. 69, nos. 3, 4, 2, 1, 10, 5, 11, 12, 13, 19, 16, 18, 15, 17 respectively. The bracelet (53. 10-31. 1) the pin head (53. 10-31. 3) and the spearhead (70. 11-26. 2) have been mislaid. There is an unconfirmed report of the other amber beads having been found at Cwm in the Tŷ Mawr area (*Arch. J.* XXXI. 1874. 297). There is a socketed knife and a small socketed axe in the Bangor Museum (1/49 and 2/49) which the labels suggest may have come from the Tŷ Mawr hoard. The accessions book gives no warrant for this assumption and their excellent state of preservation makes it certain that they were never part of this hoard in which all the objects are badly corroded. The socketed knife is much larger, but in other ways almost identical to the one from Tŷ Mawr and the axe is similar to the one from Tŷ Croes. They may well have been found together but their provenance is quite unknown. They were given to the museum in 1949 by Mr. W. McMillan of Holyhead.
[127] W. O. Stanley. *Arch. J.* XXIV. 1867. 229-53; XXVI. 1869. 301-22 and XXVII. 1870. 147-54. 160-2.
[128] Albert Way. *Arch. J.* XXVIII. 1871. 149-50. fig. 4.
[129] *Arch.* XXVI. 1835. 483. *Arch. J.* XXVI. 1869. 310-11.

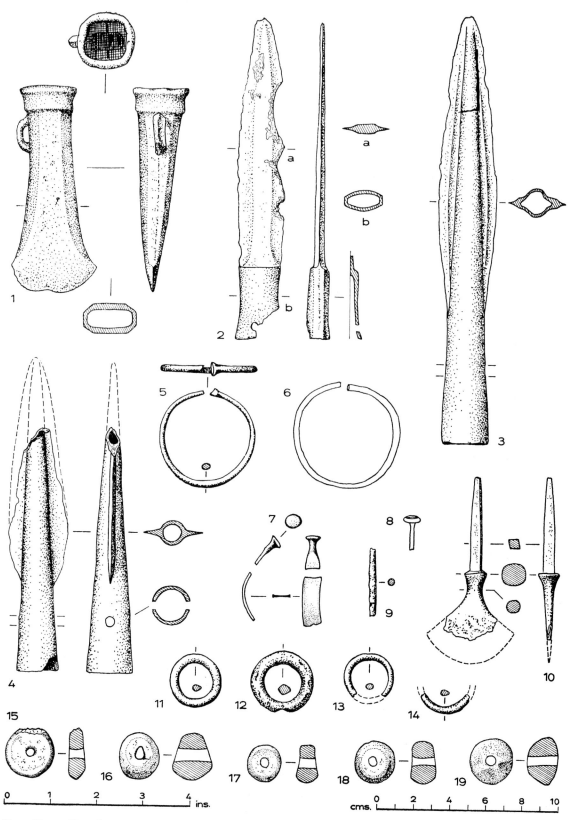

FIG. 69 — Hoard from Tŷ Mawr: 1, socketed axe; 2, socketed knife; 3-4, spearheads; 5-7 bronze bracelets; 8, head of a pin; 9, bronze rod; 10, chisel; 11-14, bronze rings; 15-19, amber beads. (6 and 8, after B.M. catalogue, 3 after C. B. Burgess.)

of the bronzesmith's inspiration was varied and his products can be roughly divided into two groups: those with an English or south-eastern background and those stemming from Irish traditions.

The former group includes the long, slender, facetted axe, the socketed knife, the smaller spearhead and the flat bracelet with buffet terminals. The five amber beads and the larger spearhead are clearly derived from Ireland; the bronze rings and the two plain bracelets are probably also Irish in origin, while the tanged "chisel", although a common type everywhere, has the strongly waisted outline which is considered typical of Ireland.[130]

The hoard contains a mixture of tools, weapons and personal ornaments. The beads and the two plain bracelets might have been worn by the owner, but all the other objects are damaged and are obviously scrap metal, while it is clear that the flat bracelet has been intentionally broken preparatory to re-melting in a small crucible. Such hoards of scrap metal are commonly found during the Late Bronze Age.

The tools and weapons do not warrant an elaborate discussion as they are all well-known types. A similar combination of socketed knife of Thorndon type, plain spearhead, and tanged "chisel" occurs in the hoard from Reach Fen, Cambridgeshire;[131] the octagonal-sectioned axe and the "Thorndon" knife are found again in the Feltwell Fen hoard from Norfolk.[132] This latter hoard also contains amber beads and part of a gold "lock ring", evidence that the Irish connection seen at Llangwyllog and Tŷ Mawr was not confined to Anglesey and the west. The larger spearhead (Fig. 69, No. 3), with its long, narrow, "willow leaf" blade, is a type characteristic of Ireland at this time.[133]

All three bracelets are made of bronze, though in styles frequently found in gold elsewhere. One of the two round-sectioned bracelets has been lost, but the drawing in the British Museum accessions book suggests that the ends were unexpanded. The survivor (Fig. 69, No. 5) is badly corroded and may be broken; one of the ends is evenly, but only slightly, expanded. Both are of very simple design and can be compared to bronze bracelets from the Beacon Hill hoard, Leicester (found with facetted axe and two plain spearheads, as at Tŷ Mawr), and the Heathery Burn Cave, Co. Durham, where a doubled bracelet, like the one from Llangwyllog, was also found.[134] The lost pin head and the short length of bronze rod, which may have been the shaft of a pin, can also find parallels among the varied material from this cave, which seems to have been the site of a workshop, probably frequented during the seventh century (700 - 600 B.C.).[135]

[130] As with earlier 'chisels' it is unlikely that these were actually used as a modern chisel. It has been suggested to me by Mr. Mansel Spratling that the wide, semi-circular blade would be well adapted to cutting leather. Irish chisels: UJA. V. 1942. 128-31.

[131] *Inventaria Archaeologica*. GB. 17, nos. 1, 44-5, 4 and 35.

[132] *Inventaria Archaeologica*. GB. 35, nos. 1 and 8.

[133] UJA. XIX. 1956. 35 and *Arch. J.* CXXV. 1969. 42.

[134] Beacon Hill: Jewry Wall Museum, Leicester. 3. IL. 1946.
Heathery Burn: *Inventaria Archaeologica*. GB. 55. p. 1. nos. 3 and 4.

[135] *ibid.* p. 8, nos. 95-103.

The broken bracelet with buffer terminal is a much rarer type and is unlikely to be local (Fig. 69, No. 7). The metal from which it is made has withstood corrosion much better than that of any of the other implements; that in itself suggests a different composition. The bracelet had been carefully made from a circular rod 4mm. in diameter; the end had been hammered down to create a flat round buffer terminal and the body had been hammered out into a strip 10mm. wide, with the edges slightly raised by further hammering. Such bracelets are extremely rare in bronze, but there are a few comparable examples in gold, for instance, in the Morvah hoard from Cornwall and the hoard from Tisbury, Wiltshire.[136] In all three cases, however, the body is curved, or otherwise more complex; it is the terminals which are similar, as are those on a gold bracelet from this same cave at Heathery Burn, mentioned in connection with the simpler bracelets.[137] Such flat bracelets, even when made of gold, are more frequently found in the south and east, and may be contrasted with the contemporary Irish styles, which almost exclusively favour a solid round body.

Both these hoards, from Llangwyllog and Tŷ Mawr, belong to the same period, the seventh century B.C., and though they differ in composition, they both suggest a similar economic situation. At this time, Anglesey is clearly on one of the main trading routes and so is open to industrial contacts and influences emanating from both Ireland and southern England, and even beyond. The Llangwyllog hoard is evidence of the varied possessions that a rich inhabitant of Anglesey might own, and the Tŷ Mawr hoard reveals the repertoire of a local smith, adopting tools and weapons from both east and west.

One aspect of Late Bronze Age metalwork in Britain which has not been mentioned is the composition of the metal used. Throughout the Middle Bronze Age, the standard alloy had been a mixture of 90% copper with 10% tin, but about 1,000 - 900 B.C. in southern England it became customary to add lead at the expense of tin, which had always been a rare metal and may have been difficult to obtain.[138] This added lead, which varies from 4 - 7%, improves the casting; the metal runs more easily, but the alloy is less strong than true tin-bronze and is less resistant to corrosion. However, these disadvantages are felt by the customer not the smith and, since there is no visible difference in the metals, he would have no redress! This reduction in quality may, however, have been off-set by an increase in quantity and perhaps a fall in price, for it is after this date that the very large specialist, mass-production hoards begin to appear.

Analysis for lead can, therefore, draw a line between the old-fashioned Middle Bronze Age industries, producing palstaves, rapiers and looped

---

[136] C. F. C. Hawkes and R. R. Clarke *in* Foster and Alcock (edd) *Culture and Environment* 1963. 230-5. Fig. 53 and Pl. XI.
[137] *Inventaria Archaeologica.* GB. 55. p. 1, no. 2.
[138] M. A. Brown and A. E. Blin-Stoyle. PPS. XXV. 1959. 188-208.

spearheads, and the Late Bronze Age smiths, who made the new types of socketed axe, peghole spearheads and swords, using the new type of alloy. This clear distinction, however, only applies to the south of England at this early stage. In the north the bronzesmiths were more conservative; they introduced a few new types but continued to rely mainly on their traditional products, the palstave and the basal-looped spearhead. Moreover, they did not adopt the new practice of adding lead to the alloy.[139] This development did not reach the north until about 800 - 700 B.C., when the new " Heathery Burn " school of metalworking finally superseded the older traditions. The Welsh bronzes have not been analysed, so it is not possible to give a date for the first production of lead-bronze in Wales. However, the number of " transitional " palstaves, and the clear links between North Wales and northern England at this time, make it more than likely that the Welsh smiths were equally late in adopting this new technique from southern England. Thus one may guess that the " transitional " palstaves, such as that from Poncyrefail, are made of tin-bronze, while the Parc and Tŷ Croes axes and the objects in the Llangwyllog and Tŷ Mawr hoards may be of leaded bronze. In fact, the first publication of the Tŷ Mawr hoard in 1835 states that the weapons are made from " a composition of tin, copper and lead ".[140]

Because of the technological bias of archaeological classification, the introduction of iron has assumed an importance which may not be entirely warranted. In this country, the introduction of this new metal is credited to the European people known loosely as " Celts " (and archaeologically as the Hallstatt and La Tène cultures), but their impact had already been felt in Britain and elsewhere before their military strength was reinforced by the use of this new and cheap metal. Their power lay rather in their new style of fighting with horses, chariots and slashing swords than in a coincidental change in raw materials.

Iron never superseded bronze for decorative metalwork, nor for sheet work, because it could not be cast; the manipulation of wrought iron involves some extremely complicated techniques of which the results could not always be guaranteed. In fact, the use of iron was at first restricted to objects such as swords, spearheads, knives, sickles, etc., in which strength and sharpness were more important than elaborate design. Although ironworking techniques were so different from those used for casting bronze, it is clear that the bronzesmiths made a valiant attempt to master the new material. Early examples of ironwork in this country — and Wales has produced some of the earliest examples known — suggest an effort to manipulate the wrought iron into unsuitable socketed shapes evolved through centuries of working cast bronze. Naturally, the tools were not very successful and few of them survive, but there are two interesting examples

[139] C. B. Burgess. *Bronze Age Metalwork in Northern Britain.* 1968. Appendix by R. F. Tylecote. 48-56.
[140] *Arch.* XXVI. 1835. 483.

from Wales: the socketed axe from the Berwyns, and the socketed sickle from the Llyn Fawr hoard, Glamorgan.[141] The earliest iron sword in these islands, an imported object, comes from this Llyn Fawr hoard, where it was found in conjunction with two beautiful bronze cauldrons of Anglo-Irish manufacture, a circumstance that would suggest a date of about 600 B.C. for the introduction of iron.[142]

No such finds have been made in Anglesey, so it is impossible to say at what date the new technology reached the island. It is likely that, as in Ireland, the Late Bronze Age traditions lingered on for some time and that the change, when it came, was very gradual. However, in view of the lack of evidence, this can be no more than a guess, and since we have no knowledge of either settlements or burials from the earliest Iron Age, it is extremely difficult to judge the impact of new people, or to suggest the size of any group of settlers. However, we may be fairly certain that, though new overlords might impose themselves on the island, the population was not radically altered. It must have continued to consist, basically, of the descendants of the first farmers and of the Mesolithic hunters, with an element from the later Beaker-making immigrants and perhaps small groups from Ireland, Scotland and the north of England, whose presence is reflected in the diverse traditions of pottery and metal-working that may be seen in Anglesey during the Bronze Age.

[141] Berwyn axe: *Arch. Camb.* 1855. 250-2.
Llyn Fawr hoard: *Arch.* LXXI. 1920-1. 133-140 and *Ant. J.* XIX. 1939. 369-404.
[142] C. F. C. Hawkes and M. A. Smith, *Ant. J.* XXXVII. 1957. 187-90.

VI

THE CELTIC IRON AGE

THE last six or seven centuries before the birth of Christ are notable in European history for the appearance of a group of boastful, aggressive, artistic and emotional tribes who were known to the Greeks by the generic term "Keltoi". It is during this period that the barbaric tribes from the wooded valleys of Central Europe, Germany and Switzerland first begin to impinge upon the consciousness of the literate Mediterranean societies, and it is in the writings of Greek historians and geographers that we get the first glimpse of the flesh and blood which clothed the cold realities of the archaeological record.

The Celts in life were so excessively warm-blooded that archaeology alone can do them scant justice (though their art gives some hint of their flamboyance), so the long quotations from Greek writers which follow need no excuse.[1]

"The whole race, which is now called Gallic or Galatic, is madly fond of war, high-spirited and quick to battle, but otherwise straightforward and not of evil character. And so when they are stirred up they assemble in their bands for battle, quite openly and without forethought, so that they are easily handled by those who desire to outwit them; for at any time or place and on whatever pretext you stir them up, you will have them ready to face danger, even if they have nothing on their side but their own strength and courage. On the other hand, if won over by gentle persuasion, they willingly devote their energies to useful pursuits and even take to a literary education. Their strength depends both on their mighty bodies, and on their numbers. And because of this frank and straightforward element in their character they assemble in large numbers on slight provocation, being ever ready to sympathize with the anger of a neighbour who thinks he has been wronged . . ."

". . . To the frankness and high-spiritedness of their temperament must be added the traits of childish boastfulness and love of decoration. They wear ornaments of gold, torques on their necks and bracelets on their arms and wrists, while people of high rank wear dyed garments besprinkled with gold. It is this vanity which makes them unbearable in victory and so downcast in defeat. In addition to their witlessness they possess a trait of barbarous savagery which is especially peculiar to the northern peoples, for when they are leaving the battlefield they fasten to the necks of their horses the heads of their enemies, and on arriving home they nail up this spectacle at the entrances to their houses . . ."

[1] Translations by J. J. Tierney. PRIA. 60 C. 1960. 189-275. The extracts are from Strabo (IV. iv. 2, 5.) ; Diodorus (V. 28, 30 and 31) and Athenaeus (IV. 36) who all based their accounts on Posidonius.

" . . . The Gauls are tall in stature and their flesh is very moist and white, while their hair is not only naturally blond, but they also use artificial means to increase this natural quality of colour. For they continually wash their hair with lime-wash and draw it back from the forehead to the crown and to the nape of the neck, with the result that their appearance resembles that of Satyrs and of Pans, for the hair is so thickened by this treatment that it differs in no way from a horse's mane. Some shave off the beard, while others cultivate a short beard; the nobles shave the cheeks but let the moustache grow freely so that it covers the mouth. And so when they are eating the moustache becomes entangled in the food, and when they are drinking the drink passes, as it were, through a sort of strainer. When dining they all sit not on chairs, but on the earth, strewing beneath them the skins of wolves or dogs. At their meals they are served by their youngest grown-up children, both boys and girls. Beside them are hearths blazing with fire, with cauldrons and spits containing large pieces of meat. Brave warriors they honour with the finest portions of the meat . . . They also invite strangers to their banquets, and only after the meal do they ask who they are and of what they stand in need . . ."

" . . . The drink of the wealthy classes (in Gaul) is wine imported from Italy or from the territory of Marseilles. This is unadulterated, but sometimes a little water is added. The lower classes drink wheaten beer prepared with honey, but most people drink it plain. It is called *corma*. They use a common cup, drinking a little at a time, not more than a mouthful, but they do it rather frequently . . ."

" . . . They wear a striking kind of clothing — tunics dyed and stained in various colours, and trousers, which they call by the name of *bracae;* and they wear striped cloaks, fastened with buckles, thick in winter and light in summer, picked out with a variegated small check pattern . . ."

" . . . Physically the Gauls are terrifying in appearance, with deep-sounding and very harsh voices. In conversation they use few words and speak in riddles, for the most part hinting at things and leaving a great deal to be understood. They frequently exaggerate with the aim of extolling themselves and diminishing the status of others. They are boasters and threateners and given to bombastic self-dramatisation, and yet they are quick of mind and with good natural ability for learning . . ."

These people who were described so graphically by the Greeks were not, however, a new phenomenon in Europe. What is new is our knowledge of their personality. Archaeologically they can be recognised as the descendants of the people represented in Central Europe by the Late Bronze Age Urnfields.[2] The immediate background of these Urnfield people was in the Middle Danube area from where they spread into Austria and Germany. They practised a simple cremation rite, and in the early stage they do not seem to have evolved a sharply stratified society; the chieftainship, which was such a marked characteristic of the later Celtic peoples, does not appear to be strongly developed as far as the evidence of tombs is concerned. Eastern horsemen, whose impact can be felt in the eighth century B.C., may have contributed in large measure to the development of chieftainship and of warfare in Central Europe, for by the time the Hallstatt Culture had emerged it is clear that both had been brought to a high pitch

[2] *See* T. G. E. Powell. *The Celts.* (Ancient Peoples and Places) 1958. Chapter 1 for the best account of the archaeological background to these people.

The Hallstatt Culture, recognisable during the seventh and sixth centuries B.C. in Bohemia, Upper Austria and Bavaria, was the first iron-using culture in Europe. It had links southward through Bosnia and the head of the Adriatic, whence the new technology was derived, but the preponderant element remained the old Urnfield population. The chieftains were buried, unburnt, on funerary cars (which in the early stages were four-wheeled waggons) together with their weapons, ornaments and all the equipment for a busy and successful life after death.

It is through these distinctive chieftain burials that the fortunes of the Hallstatt warriors can be traced. They were an aggressive and successful group who appear to have united other tribes under their rule, welding the rather diverse remnants of the older European populations into an amalgam which seems to have been prepared to acknowledge a single name: Celt. This name under which the Greeks included the majority of northern barbarians may originally have been the name of the dominant Hallstatt group. This group can be traced as they moved westwards across Europe: in the sixth century B.C. the rich graves are to be found in Switzerland and the Upper Rhine; in the fifth century they are in the middle Rhine area and in the Moselle valley, whence the chieftains move on to Champagne, and finally a small group, who may be related, appear in East Yorkshire in the second century B.C.

During the fifth century these rich aristocratic warriors imported a great many luxury items from the Etruscans and from Greece via the Greek colony at Marseilles. These fine objects, normally flagons and drinking services for wine, provided the native craftsmen with models from which they quickly evolved their own decorative style. This style, known as La Tène, was based in the last analysis on the rather formal acanthus and palmette patterns of Greek art, but it has none of the classicism and symmetry of the Mediterranean mind. In fact, the Celtic artists seem to revel in asymmetry, producing flamboyant flowing lines full of life and movement. Several stages can be recognised in the process by which La Tène art freed itself from reliance on southern models, but these need not concern us here beyond the fact that it is during the currency of the Continental Waldalgesheim style that this art reaches Britain. Once here, it develops in a way that is unique, and the products of British La Tène art are amongst the most beautiful in Europe.

The historical process by which Britain came within the orbit of the Hallstatt and La Tène cultures is less clear than the record of their progress on the Continent. The occasional appearance of Continental Urnfield swords in the tenth century B.C. and of horsegear (such as the hoard from Parc y Meirch, Denbighshire, and the studs from Llangwyllog) in the eighth and seventh centuries is difficult to interpret. It may be simply the result of trade, but it might also indicate the arrival of bands of adventurers, possibly heralding a later invasion.

Such an invasion of the south-east of England was believed to have taken place on a large scale in the fifth century B.C., bringing groups of settlers of mixed Urnfield and Hallstatt background over from the Low Countries to overrun the native Late Bronze Age farmers, as they themselves had been overrun by the La Tène chieftains in their own country. This view which postulates a massive influx of new people is now tending to lose ground as the archaeological evidence for these invaders, a very undistinctive, coarse pottery and the building of hill fortifications, is reassessed.[3] This new assessment is beginning to suggest that both the pottery and the hill-forts have more to do with the native British Late Bronze Age than with the European Iron Age. The pottery is admittedly so lacking in distinctive features that it could support either case, but the number of occasions on which well-dated Late Bronze Age metal implements have been found on hill-forts is now so large that they should no longer be interpreted automatically as accidental survival.[4]

However, a simple continuation of Late Bronze Age traditions does not fully explain why so many fortifications should be built at this period. Inter-tribal warfare might have increased, but it is also reasonable to suggest that there may have been an additional external threat, for it remains true that England did receive many European traits, including the use of iron, at about this time.

Whatever may be the outcome of these studies with regard to the status of these early groups, known archaeologically in Britain as Iron Age A,[5] it is clear that at some time during the Iron Age there was a migration to these islands of tribes who called themselves Celts, and that at the end of the third century B.C. there is a recognisable intrusion of people from northern France and the middle Rhine carrying with them the La Tène culture and art style.[6] These groups can be most easily identified on the south coast, but they are also found in the Irish Sea area where they may have been attracted by the availability of tin in Cornwall.

In the alphabetical scheme which has been adopted for distinguishing the various cultural groups of the British Iron Age, the people who introduced La Tène traditions are known as Iron Age B, or sometimes as Marnians, from the region of France whence many of them may have come. The final groups of invaders, known archaeologically as Iron Age C and historically as the Belgae, can be more clearly distinguished. Their emigration from northern France to southern England at the beginning of the first century B.C. is recorded by Caesar and, once here, their material culture and political organisation are sharply defined.[7] They used a distinctive wheel-turned pottery, practised cremation, and set up strong

[3] See J. G. D. Clark. Ant. XL. 1966. 185-7 and F. R. Hodson PPS. XXX. 1964. 99-110.
[4] e.g. Breiddin, Montgomery; South Cadbury, Somerset and Ivinghoe, Buckinghamshire.
[5] This scheme is outlined in C. F. C. Hawkes. 'The ABC of the British Iron Age' Ant. XXXIII. 1959. 170-82.
[6] E. M. Jope. 'The beginning of the La Tène Ornamental Style in the British Isles' in S. S. Frere (ed) Problems of the Iron Age in Southern Britain. 1961. 69-83.
[7] A. Birchall. PPS. XXXI. 1965. 241-367 and C. F. C. Hawkes. Ant. XLII. 1968. 6-16.

tribal kingdoms centred on large defended settlements or " oppida ", so
thickly populated and diversified that they warrant the name of " town ".
It was this latest group of overlords who proved to be the backbone of
native resistance to Rome in 43 A.D.

The history of the Iron Age is even more obscure in Wales than in
England because there has been less excavation, and amongst the excavated
sites very few have produced material in any quantity. Wales has its fair
share of Hallstatt metalwork, notably in the famous Llyn Fawr hoard
dated to 600 B.C., but it is difficult to associate this with any clear picture
of invasion or settlement.[8]

In North Wales the presence of Iron Age invaders, people with a
Hallstatt background, is perhaps indicated by the shouldered and finger-
printed pottery from Castell Odo, near Aberdaron.[9] The people who made
this pottery were living in circular timber houses within an unfinished
palisade. This settlement, being soon burnt down, may be easily interpreted
as the home of a small immigrant group who aroused the antagonism of the
natives. On the other hand, a recent study of the small quantity of Iron
Age A pottery from Wales as a whole has laid less emphasis on its exotic
nature and more on the continuity with already established types.[10] Thus
the early Iron Age invaders of Wales seem to be fading away like their
English counterparts.

The evidence for Iron Age B people in South Wales and the Bristol
Channel area is stronger, and recent work on their commercially-made
pottery and the excavations carried out in the last few years on the hill-forts
of the southern Marches presage a much fuller knowledge of their history
and activities. However, these results have yet to be finally synthesised.[11]
In North Wales our knowledge of the settlements and pottery of this period
is less certain, but we do have a remarkable quantity of early metalwork
of the highest quality in the British La Tène style.[12] Unfortunately, all these
pieces have been found in isolation and, like all luxury articles, are difficult
to interpret in terms of every-day life. They do seem to indicate, however,
the presence of skilled craftsmen working for chieftains whose taste had
been formed on the Continent towards the end of the third century B.C.
These rich objects pose particularly intractable problems when the apparent
poverty of the settlement material from even large sites like Dinorben is

[8] C. Fox. *Ant. J.* XIX. 1939. 369-404 and Hawkes and Smith. *Ant. J.* XXXVII. 1957. 187-90.
[9] L. Alcock. *Arch. Camb.* 1960. 78-135.
[10] G. J. Wainwright. *Coygan Camp.* Cambrian Arch. Assoc. 1967. 23-6.
[11] D. P. S. Peacock. PPS. XXXIV. 1968. 414-27 and excavation by Mr. S. C. Stanford
     published in *Trans. Woolhope Soc.* in the last few years.
[12] A booklet which conveniently brings together the best of this metalwork has been
     published recently by the National Museum of Wales. H. N. Savory, *Early Iron Age Art
     in Wales.* 1968. See also, H. N. Savory, BBCS, XX. 1964. 472-3 and F. Schwappach *in*
     Frey (ed) *Marburger Beitrage zur Archäeologie der Kelten. Festschrift für Wolfgang
     Dehn.* 1969. 213-87.

considered,[13] problems which are especially relevant to Anglesey in view of the remarkable finds from Llyn Cerrig Bach, to be described later.

As the Romans invaded the south-east of England there was a considerable movement of people, particularly the ruling classes, towards the west. Thus the arrival of the Belgae in Wales is very much a feature of the last few decades of independence. There is some evidence of their settlement in South Wales.[14] In North Wales, as so often, the evidence is less clear, but we have the testimony of Tacitus who says that North Wales, and Anglesey in particular, harboured many refugees.[15] In fact, they were present in such numbers and were so active politically that they constituted a serious threat to Roman authority and their existence was one of the main causes of the military campaigns against Wales.

Throughout Wales the main evidence of Iron Age activity lies in the hundreds of fortifications, large and small, which surround the tops of hills and promontories.[16] Only a small proportion of these have been excavated, so that attention has to be directed to questions of structure and size. But any attempt to interpret the visible remains in terms of the spread of particular groups with special structural traditions, is complicated by the fact that the defences of many sites were remodelled on a number of occasions, and by the length of time over which these sites might be used.[17] The possibility that some might have been built as early as the Late Bronze Age has already been mentioned. Moreover, in Wales excavation and chance finds have shown that many of the earlier defensive positions were resettled in the later Roman period and even in the Dark Ages, while some of the smaller sites may actually have been built in this latter period.[18]

Another problem is that we are not sure to what extent these often bleak and uncomfortable hilltop sites were permanent settlements. Recent excavations in the Malvern area suggest that the numerous hill-forts in the southern Marches were genuine villages, the area inside the ramparts filled with small, closely-set houses, of which the inhabitants worked the fields below the defences.[19] Others have suggested that very large enclosures, such as some of those on the Clwydian hills, should be regarded as cattle kraals for protection against rustling (endemic in Celtic society and the main-spring of a chieftain's life), rather than as normal villages.[20]

[13] Willoughy Gardner and H. N. Savory. *Dinorben, a Hillfort occupied in Early Iron Age and Roman Times*. NMW. 1964.
[14] Mynydd Bychan (*Arch. Camb.* 1954. 85-108 and 1955. 14-51); Llanmelin (*Arch. Camb.* 1933. 237-346); Sudbrook (*Arch. Camb.* 1939. 42-79) and Lesser Garth Cave (*Arch. Camb.* 1966. 27-44 with general discussion of Belgae in South Wales).
[15] Tacitus. *Agricola* XIV and *Annals*. XIV, xxix.
[16] A. H. A. Hogg *in* Foster and Daniel (edd) *Prehistoric and Early Wales*. 1965. 109-50 and many other writings by the same author which deal with the Welsh hill-forts in general and in detail.
[17] e.g. Dinorben (Willoughby Gardner and H. N. Savory *Dinorben*. 1964. *passim*).
[18] G. Simpson *in* Gardner and Savory *op. cit.* 209-220. and L. Alcock, *Dinas Powis, an Iron Age, Dark Age and Early Mediaeval Settlement in Glamorgan*. 1963.
[19] S. C. Stanford. forthcoming.
[20] L. Alcock. *Ant.* XXXIX. 1965. 184-95 where this whole problem is discussed in some detail.

Certain rocky hilltops, such as Holyhead Mountain, would not seem suitable for either purpose and should perhaps be considered occasional refuges for a scattered population in times of danger. The people sheltering inside such forts could not have held out against a prolonged siege, for most sites are without water, nor could they have prevented their enemies from burning their unprotected crops, but they might well be saved from the short but savage frontal assault which was the normal technique in Celtic warfare. That such defences were considered effective even against the Roman army is shown by Caractacus's hurried construction of stone ramparts around his camp before the final battle against Ostorius Scapula.[21]

There are eight or nine hilltop or promontory sites in Anglesey which may be considered hill-forts likely to have been built during the Iron Age. None of them has been scientifically excavated, but several have been dug into and most have produced some evidence for occupation in the Roman period. On analogy with other sites elsewhere, this may be considered a re-occupation, though only in one Anglesey site has anything been found which could be dated to the Iron Age. Structurally the larger forts are simple, with a single stone wall encircling the top of the hill. This type of site is common in Caernarvonshire where they are believed to represent the earliest tradition of fort building.[22] No clear evidence of date is available in Anglesey. Twyn y Parc and some of the smaller forts have multiple ramparts which may be earthen banks rather than walls. These might be products of a slightly later tradition, but little comment can be made in the absence of excavation.

Bwrdd Arthur or Din Silwy (NGR SH/585815) is perhaps the best known and certainly one of the more accessible hill-forts in Anglesey. It is sited on the top of a prominent flat-topped limestone hill behind Llanddona and is an easily recognised landmark from all directions.

The hill is naturally steep-sided and the only artificial defence is a single line of walling encircling the entire hilltop and set back a little from the crest of the slope. This wall has been destroyed in part by quarrying on the south and east sides, but elsewhere, especially on the north-west side, the foundations can be clearly traced in spite of a luxuriant growth of black-thorn. The wall is on average 8ft. thick, the inner and outer faces built of large upright slabs of limestone with an inner core of rubble, most of which has gone. The upright slabs are of variable size and shape, often triangular, and probably the interstices would have been filled, and the upper courses built, with heavy dry stone walling. This system of wall building is common in most limestone areas and can be seen again at the Romano-British village, or homestead, at Din Lligwy and, occasionally, in much later field walls in the district.

There are two original entrances through this wall, in the centre of the south side and on the west. The southern entrance is clearly the more

[21] Tacitus. *Annals*. XII. xxxiii-xxxv.
[22] RCAM. *Caernarvonshire* III. 1964. lxx-lxxxi.

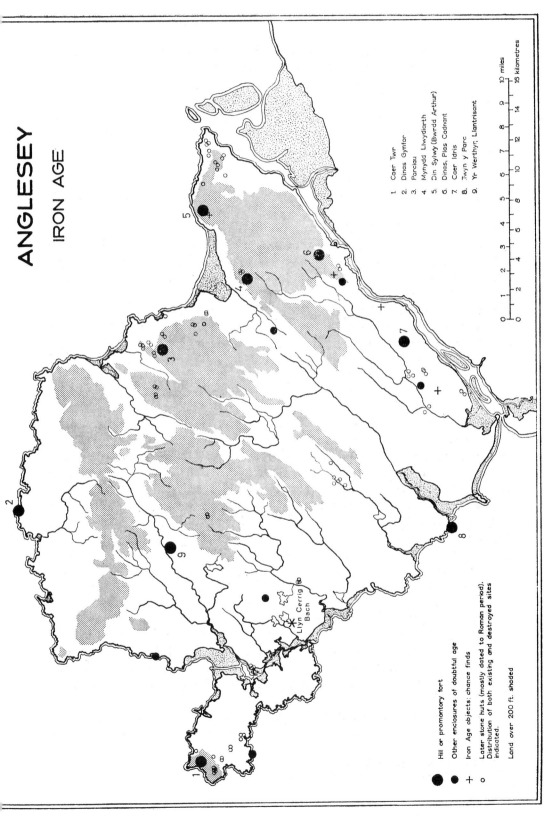

ANGLESEY
IRON AGE

1. Caer Twr
2. Dinas Gynfor
3. Parciau
4. Mynydd Llwydiarth
5. Din Sylwy (Bwrdd Arthur)
6. Dinas, Plas Cadnant
7. Caer Idris
8. Twyn y Parc
9. Yr Werthyr, Llantrisant

Llyn Cerrig Bach

Hill or promontory fort

Other enclosures of doubtful age

Iron Age objects: chance finds

Later stone huts (mostly dated to Roman period). Distribution of both existing and destroyed sites indicated.

Land over 200 ft. shaded

| 0 | 1 | 2 | 3 | 4 | 5 | 6 | 7 | 8 | 9 | 10 miles |

| 0 | 2 | 4 | 6 | 8 | 10 | 12 | 14 | 16 kilometres |

MAP 5 — Anglesey in the Iron Age.

important and is approached by a well-marked terraced trackway. This path may have been enlarged in recent times to take quarry traffic, but it must always have been one of the easier points of access to the interior. The entrance itself is some 15ft. wide and is defended by an overlap of the western end of the wall which turns inwards above the path. Plans by the Rev. W. Wynn Williams and the Royal Commission show a clear arrangement of upright stones here, but the area is at present covered with bushes and the end of the wall is completely obscured.[23]

The western entrance is no more than a simple gap in the wall which is slightly increased in width on its south side. It is approached by a very narrow track up the side of the rock, which is very steep at this point. It would be scarcely possible for more than one person at a time to come up this path. There may have been another small entrance at a point midway along the north-western side where another narrow track (certainly modern in its present form) approaches the wall. Here there are two groups of stones set at right angles to the wall which, between them, is slightly reduced in width as if this was a subsequent blocking.[24]

The area enclosed is about seventeen acres, all of it flat with a gentle slope to the north. The entire area would have been suitable for habitation, but there is no evidence for any surviving huts except close to the wall. Just to the east of the southern entrance is a semi-circular enclosure marked by a wall of upright stones. It was originally attached to the main defensive wall which has been quarried away at this point. Just north of the west entrance there is a large, roughly circular, depression and the remains of a wall which may mark the position of a similar structure built against the main wall. On the south-west side, close to the wall, is a sunken rectangular area which might be the foundation of another such building. The Rev. W. Wynn Williams mentions other possible structures against the wall, but it is impossible to recognise these today. In the eastern half, where the wall has been destroyed, there are some low rectangular mounds which may be modern " pillow mounds " for rabbits.

There has been no excavation inside the fort, but a good deal of material has been picked up there over the years. The main bulk of this has dated from the Roman period, and has included pottery of third and fourth century A.D. types and a quantity of coins.[25] A hoard of copper and silver coins, together with " rings, keys, buckles and clasps of copper " was found within the area in 1831.[26] The coins included issues of Nero, Vespasian, Constantius and Constantine.

Although the number of Roman finds suggests that there must have been a period of occupation here, as elsewhere, during the third and fourth

[23] *Arch. Camb.* 1869. 56-61. and RCAM. *Anglesey.* 1937. lxxi. (entrance).
[24] RCAM. *op. cit.* 82. point F.
[25] Angharad Llwyd. *History of Mona.* 1833. 265.
      Lewis' Topographical Dictionary. 1833. under ' Llanfihangel Din Silwy '. *Arch. Camb.* 1877. 339 and *Arch. Camb.* 1908. 296-7.
[26] *Arch. Camb.* 1869. 61. (quoting Angharad Llwyd).

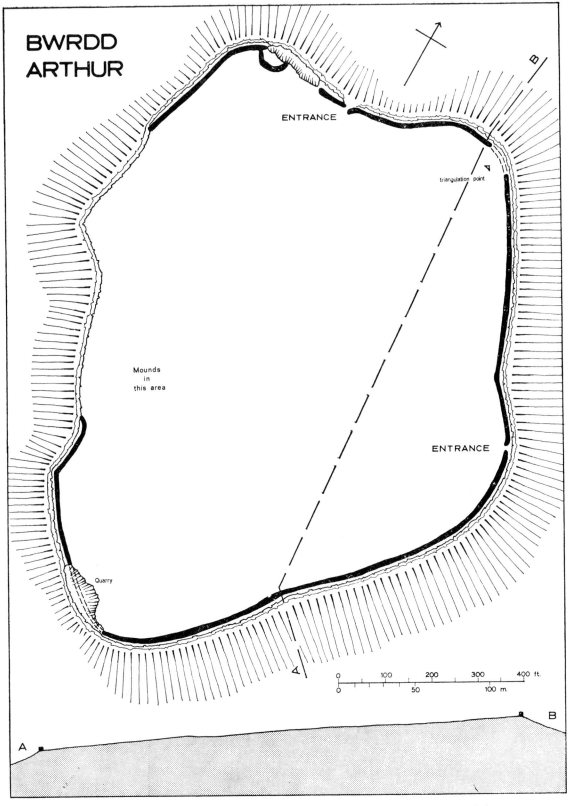

BWRDD
ARTHUR

ENTRANCE

triangulation point

Mounds
in
this area

ENTRANCE

Quarry

0   100   200   300   400 ft.
0   50   100 m.

A   B

Fig. 70 — Bwrdd Arthur, Llanfihangel Dinsylwy: Plan (after R.C.A.M.).

centuries A.D., there are two finds which are indicative of an earlier date, perhaps the period when the fortress was first constructed. These were both picked up in molehills but were not found together. The more important of the two has unfortunately been lost and only a description of it survives.[27] It was an iron ring-headed pin of Iron Age type. The shank had been bent back round the head, destroying the typical arching of the neck. These pins, which may be made of either bronze or iron, are characteristic of an early phase of the Iron Age in southern England, dating from about 300 - 200 B.C. They are not common in Wales, where Iron Age material of any kind is rare, but iron examples have been found at the coastal settlement at Merthyr Mawr Warren, Glamorgan, and at the large hill-fort, Dinorben, in Denbighshire, while a bronze one was found in the promontory fort at Stackpole, Pembrokeshire.[28] Their precise date in this area is not clear, but the presence of this pin at Bwrdd Arthur is definite evidence of a pre-Roman phase at the site, a phase during which the fortress was presumably built, to be re-occupied later as were so many Welsh hill-forts.

Another ring-headed pin, made in bronze, is said to have been found in Anglesey.[29] It belongs to a group of " projecting-head " pins which are otherwise almost entirely restricted to Scotland where they were fashionable during the first three centuries A.D. Even though an example has been found recently at Dinorben, Denbighshire,[30] it remains very unlikely that the bronze one really was found in Anglesey. It was thought to have come from W. O. Stanley's excavations at Tŷ Mawr, but if this were really so it is strange that he made no reference to it since it was in a very good state of preservation. After his death a number of varied objects were said to have been found at that site, without any apparent justification beyond the fact that the excavations were known to have been more productive than most.

The other find from Bwrdd Arthur which might be of Iron Age date is a short length of iron chain. The chain is quite small and might have been used for hanging pots over the fire. The oval links have been pinched together in the centre to prevent the chain twisting. This particular technique of chain-making is seen on the Iron Age gang chains from Llyn Cerrig Bach (Fig. 90), dating to just before the Roman conquest. Chains of this type, however, are rather more common in the succeeding Roman period, so it must be admitted that an Iron Age date for this piece is far from certain.

Another implement of doubtful date which might possibly belong to this period is the socketed antler tool found in the bed of a stream near

[27] W. F. Grimes. BBCS. V. 1929-31. 392.
[28] Merthyr Mawr: W. F. Grimes. *Prehistory of Wales*. 1951. 131, fig. 43, no. 12.
       Dinorben: Willoughby Gardner and H. N. Savory. *Dinorben*. 1964. 131-2; fig. 19, no. 2.
       Stackpole: W. F. Grimes. BBCS. V. 1929-31. 392.
[29] *Proc. Soc. Antiq. London*. n.s. XX. 1903-4. 347, mentioned in Willoughby Gardner and
       H. N. Savory. *Dinorben*. 1964. 132.
[30] *Loc. cit.*

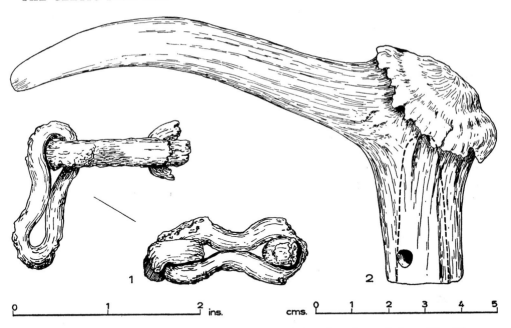

Fig. 71 — 1, iron chain from Bwrdd Arthur; 2, socketed antler pick from Llanddona. (2 after W. F. Grimes.)

Llanddona church.[31] In general shape it is very similar to the Neolithic picks found so frequently in the chalk ditches of sites such as Windmill Hill and Durrington Walls. It may seem unlikely that an antler pick would be much use against limestone, but such implements have been found in the bottom of the ditches at Dinorben and were presumably used in their construction. Some of these picks from Dinorben were large socketed tines which must have been fitted with wooden handles like the Llanddona example.[32] Such improvement on the natural tool is extremely rare.

The rampart wall at Caer y Twr (SH/219829) encloses an area of 17 acres, equal to that of Bwrdd Arthur, but the available living space is a great deal less because it is sited on the rocky summit of Holyhead Mountain. The western half of the site is dominated by steep bare crags interrupted by narrow gullies, but in the north-eastern quarter the ground is more level and less encumbered by rocks and scree, as well as being sheltered to some extent from the south-westerly winds. It is in this area, therefore, that any signs of permanent habitation might be expected, but in fact no hut circles are to be seen. This is not altogether surprising for even here the ground is barren and uneven with a great deal of bare rock which today supports an attractive but unproductive cover of gorse and heather. Caer y Twr is thus a good example of the " refuge " type of hill-fort, a strong point to which people living on the lower ground might retreat in

[31] *Arch. Camb.* 1937. 172-4.
[32] Willoughby Gardner and H. N. Savory. *Dinorben.* 1964. 173 and fig. 26. nos. 5 & 8.

time of danger, but which would not be occupied on any permanent basis. Such an explanation has not, of course, been proved by excavation, which has sometimes produced surprising results on equally isolated and wind-swept heights.[33]

As at Bwrdd Arthur, the defences at Caer y Twr take advantage of the natural lie of the land. The south-western side needs no artificial protection since it ends on a sheer precipice. The ascent from the south-east is also extremely difficult and no wall has been built along the top of the crags there. Elsewhere the area is enclosed by a strong rampart wall which has been carefully contoured to run along the top of the steepest slope, taking in several bastion-like crags in its course.[34] This wall has been destroyed along part of the west side, but elsewhere it is in good repair and still stands to a height of 10ft. in places.

The wall has an average width of about 11ft. and is dry built, with an outer and inner face of massive masonry and a rubble core. A number of the stones are very long and set at right angles to the face to bond the wall firmly. At certain points on the northern and eastern stretches of the wall Dr. Willoughby Gardner and the Royal Commission noticed the remains of a rampart walk about 4ft. wide and 3 - 4ft. above the ground.[35] This feature is now less recognisable. The breastwork in front of this rampart walk is about 7ft. in width, and Dr. Gardner suggested that this might have supported a further rampart walk at a higher level from which a better view of any activity outside the wall might be gained. Such a double walk is found at Caer Drewyn, near Corwen, and a single one exists at Tre'r Ceiri on Yr Eifl.[36] Some such arrangement must have been essential at these sites defended by such thick high walls if the defenders were to have any knowledge of what was going on outside. In this respect the natural bastions at Caer y Twr were also useful since they covered a considerable stretch of wall on either side.

There is only one entrance; at the north-east corner where a narrow gully leads into the interior. Advantage has been taken of this natural feature to provide an inturned entrance about 10ft. wide. The funnel-shaped passageway is overlooked and protected by the curved ends of the ramparts and by natural rock bastions. Any massive assault on the gate would be further reduced by the nature of the path itself, which is extremely rough and difficult, and twists in and out among a confusing series of ridges and gullies which tend to conceal the entrance until one is directly beneath it.

The weakest point in the defences is on the north side where a wide gully provides a gently sloping approach. This gully is closed by an

[33] e.g. Tre'r Ceiri on Yr Eifl. A. H. A. Hogg. *Arch. J.* CXVII. 1960. 10-24.
[34] See comment in RCAM. *Caernarvonshire.* III. 1964. cxvi, though there is no reason to suppose a Dark Age date for the building of Caer y Twr.
[35] *A   Camb.* 1934. 156-73, especially 160-3 and fig. 14. RCAM. *Anglesey.* 1937. 24.
[36] *Ar   Camb.* 1922. 118, figs. 5 and 7, and 1926. 257, fig. 20. *Arch. J.* CXVII. 1962. 11, fig. 1b.

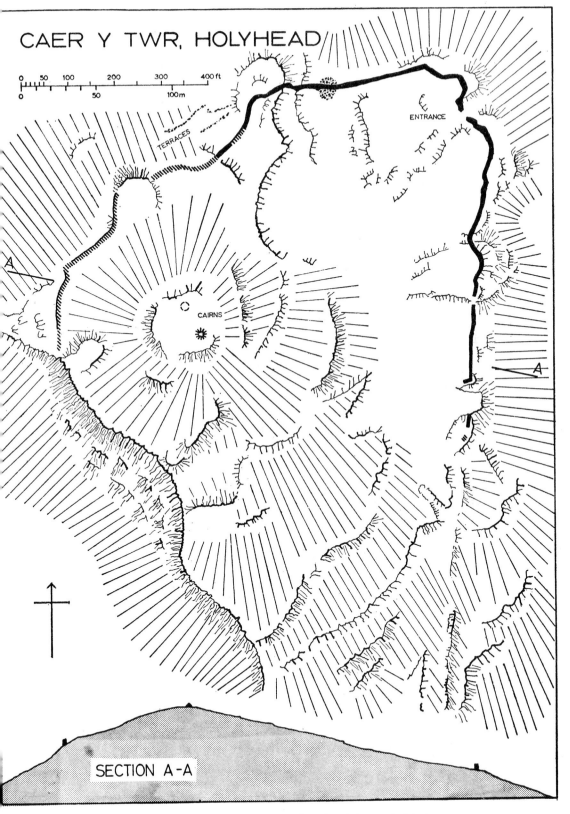

FIG. **72** — Caer y Twr, Holyhead: plan (after R.C.A.M.).

especially thick length of walling, but there is no additional defence. It is here that the rampart appears to have been partially destroyed, with the stone from the wall pushed down into the interior of the fort. Since most of the stone is on the uphill side, it has been suggested that this is not simply the result of natural collapse but rather of deliberate destruction by an enemy at some time during the occupation of the site.[37] Such destruction might be the work of the Romans or perhaps of later Irish raiders. There have been no finds from the interior of the fort to give a precise date of its building or occupation.

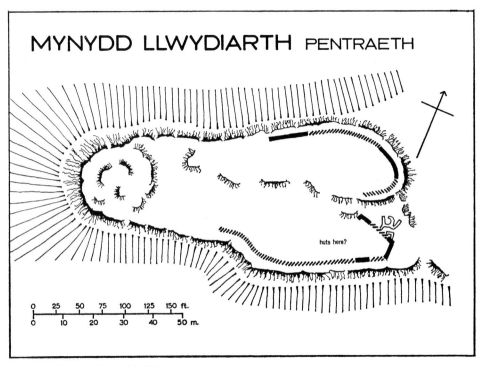

FIG. 73 — Plan of hill-fort on Mynydd Llwydiarth, Pentraeth (after R.C.A.M., at twice scale of Fig. 70).

The history of other hill-forts in Wales designed and built in the same way as Caer y Twr shows that such fortresses were constructed in the pre-Roman Iron Age but were quite often re-occupied temporarily during the Roman period. Such a history can be demonstrated at Bwrdd Arthur and may be suggested at Caer y Twr for, although there are no Roman finds from the fort itself, a hoard of late Roman coins was found on the eastern side of the hill, and there is even a possibility of some sort of Roman lighthouse having been built on the summit, while the surrounding hut groups have produced abundant evidence for a large native population

[37] Arch. Camb. 1934. 167.

in the third and fourth centuries A.D. who might have used it as a refuge
at time of danger or unrest.[38]

The remains of a similar fort on a much smaller scale are to be found
on a spur at the southern end of Mynydd Llwydiarth (NGR SH/538784).
The walls were already much ruined when the Royal Commission recorded
it, and the site has subsequently been planted over by the Forestry Commission and is now scarcely recognisable.

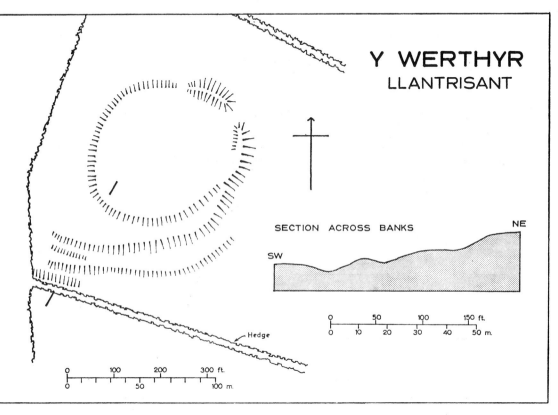

FIG. 74 — Y Werthyr, Llantrisant: plan (based on the O.S. map with the sanction of
the Controller of H.M. Stationery Office; Crown copyright reserved; at twice scale of
Fig. 70).

Like Caer y Twr, it takes full advantage of a naturally precipitous site,
and walls were built only at the eastern end where the slope is less steep.
The entrance here was arranged in a way that is reminiscent of Caer y Twr
with the walls turning in along a natural scarp to form a funnel-shaped
passage. The area enclosed is about one acre, a size comparable to many
enclosures in Wales, and, although the ground is rocky and broken, there

[38] W. O. Stanley. *Arch. Camb.* 1868. 396 (coin hoard) and T. Pennant. *Tours in Wales.* iii.
73-4, with discussion in *Arch. Camb.* 1934. 172. (lighthouse).

were remains of stone huts visible near the entrance and just outside it. Since these latter huts partly block the entrance, it could be suggested that they represent a later, and more peaceful, phase of occupation. A similar situation can be seen at Dinas, Plas Cadnant (Fig. 79), but the date of occupation in either case is unknown.

Another site which has been almost totally destroyed by agricultural activity over the years is Y Werthyr in Llantrisant parish (NGR SH/363843).[39] This enclosure is unusual for Anglesey in that it is set on the top of a low, rounded hill, not a naturally strong position, and the defences seem to have consisted entirely of earthen banks. These banks have been very much reduced and are now little more than scarps. The ditches outside the second and third banks can still be seen on the south side.

The inner enclosure is oval, about 100 yards long, with a simple entrance at the north-east end. It is doubtful whether there is a ditch outside this bank. The circuit of the outer banks and ditches is not clear, but they do not seem to be concentric with the inner enclosure. No finds have been recorded from the area. Such sites are notoriously difficult to date, but the presence of more than one bank and ditch is suggestive of a pre-Roman date and a comparison with the Early Iron Age site at Castell Odo, Aberdaron, might be put forward. However, a post-Roman or even an early Mediaeval date cannot be ruled out.

Recent excavation at a superficially similar site, Y Werthyr, Llanbeulan (NGR SH/374782), revealed that the bank which appeared to encircle this low hill was an entirely natural feature.[40] During the excavation, a bronze terret, or harness ring, of a type current in the second and third centuries A.D. or even later, was found in the topsoil, but this association is entirely fortuitous.[41]

The rocky and indented coastline of Anglesey is admirably suited to the construction of the type of coastal fort in which a promontory, or narrow tongue of land, is isolated by building a rampart across the neck at its narrowest point. Such promontory situations can provide the maximum of protection for the minimum of effort, a consideration which was obviously of some importance to Anglesey fortress builders, as their careful choice of naturally defended inland sites has shown. It is also probable that the freedom and convenience of sea communications were of importance to those who chose to live in promontory forts.

The best example of such a coastal fort in Anglesey is Twyn y Parc, Llangadwaladr (NGR SH/370650), a very rocky, narrow headland at the entrance to Malltraeth Bay.[42] This headland is cut off by quite elaborate and well-preserved defences. The main line is represented by a huge

[39] RCAM. *Anglesey.* 1937. 114.
[40] RCAM. *Anglesey.* 1937. 41. I am grateful to Mr. R. G. Livens for permission to mention the result of his excavation prior to his own publication.
[41] It is similar to those from Dinas Emrys, illustrated in W. F. Grimes. *Prehistory of Wales.* 1951. 133, fig. 44.
[42] Hugh Prichard. *Arch. Camb.* 1875. 349-58. and RCAM. *Anglesey.* 1937. 87-8.

rampart of earth and stone still standing to a height of 18ft. The entrance was at its western end, where it stops a few feet short of the present cliff edge. Erosion must have removed the outer side of the gateway and, perhaps, a continuation of the rampart protecting the narrow ledge of level ground which at present overlooks the western creek. The eastern end of this rampart and of the outer bank also seem to have suffered from erosion.

The outer defences are much slighter. On the west there is a low curved bank with a ditch and small counterscarp bank outside it. It runs from the end of the creek up to a narrow ridge of rock which seems to form a natural roadway into the fort, skirting the main rampart and terminating at the entrance. On the east the outer bank starts at this ridge and runs straight down to the edge of the cliff. It is strangely situated beneath a high outcrop which must have made it virtually useless from the point of view of defence. Although the builders may have intended to make a strong overlapped entrance through these outer defences the gap is in fact very wide and, all in all, these outer banks do not seem to have been very well designed. Presumably the inhabitants depended chiefly on the enormous strength of the inner rampart.

The total area of the headland is about eight acres, but only a small proportion of this is suitable for habitation. The eastern side ends in precipitous cliffs and is dangerously broken by outcrops and narrow gullies. The western side slopes more gently and is grass grown, and the southern tip is relatively flat, but both these areas are brutally exposed to the south-west winds and would not make ideal house sites. The most likely area for huts, though none are visible, is on the flat ground immediately behind the main rampart and especially at the south-eastern end where it is sheltered from the wind by overhanging cliffs. It is probable that quite a large number of huts could have clustered here and animals could have been allowed to graze over the rest of the interior. A supply of water would be available from a spring in the rocks above this flat ground. The inhabitants might have kept boats in the western creek, but it is doubtful whether it would be a very safe harbour, being boulder-strewn, narrow, and exposed.

"Sundry, random excavations" were made by Sir George Meyrick inside the area of the fort in 1938 and 1939.[43] From the level area inside the rampart he obtained two pieces of the rim of a Roman mortarium (grinding basin) of third-fourth century type comparable to those from Bwrdd Arthur and suggestive of a similar occupation at that period. Later he found an iron spearhead 10½ins. long and 3ins. broad, a crucible with traces of copper, and a stone pot boiler. The location of these finds is not given and they cannot be found now in Bangor Museum.

Dinas Gynfor, Llanbadrig (NGR SH/390950), is similar in many ways to Twyn y Parc, although very much larger, covering an area of about

[43] *Arch. Camb.* 1939. 98-9 and TAAS. 1945. 22-3.

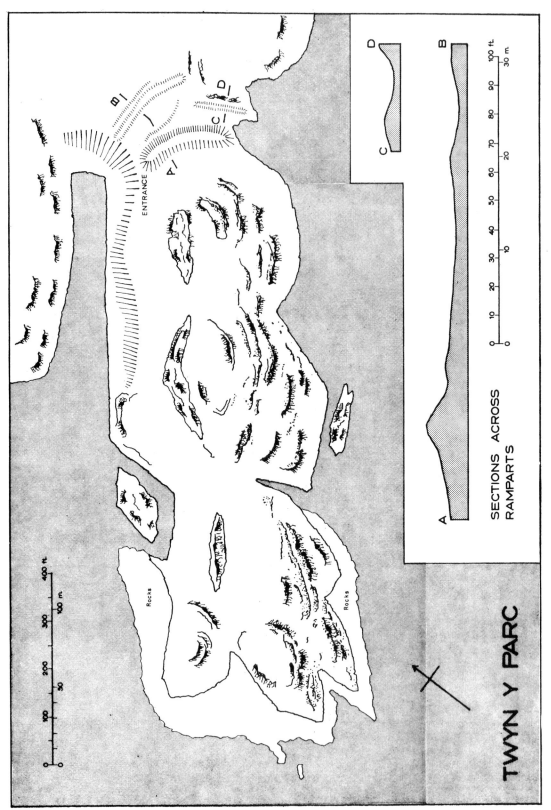

Fig. 75.— Twyn y Parc, Llangadwaladr: plan (after R.C.A.M.).

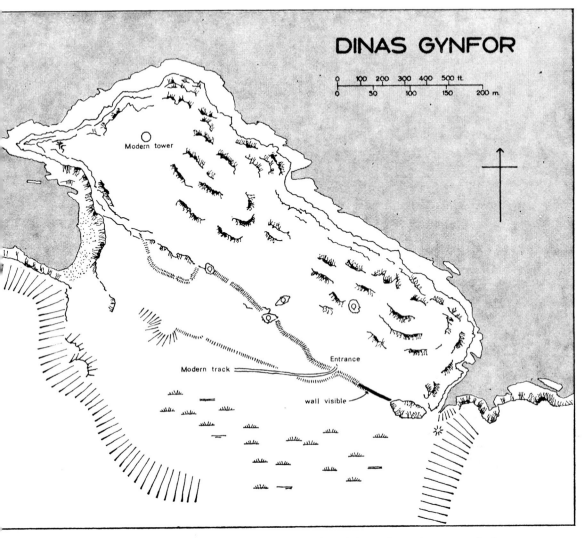

FIG. 76 — Dinas Gynfor, Llanbadrig: plan (reproduced from the O.S. map with the sanction of the Controller of H.M. Stationery Office; Crown copyright reserved; at about half the scale of Fig. 75).

twenty-four acres.[44] They are both long rocky promontories with steep cliffs to the sea and at both a considerable amount of the internal area is unsuitable for houses. However, Dinas Gynfor is joined to the mainland by a broad isthmus which has necessitated the building of longer and more elaborate ramparts than at Twyn y Parc.

This isthmus is occupied by a steep-sided marshy valley which must have formed a formidable barrier in itself. Above it, the side of Dinas Gynfor rises steeply to a height of 200ft. Along the crest of the slope is a

[44] W. Wynn Williams. *Arch. Camb.* 1876. 103-9 and RCAM. *Anglesey.* 1937. 37.

wide rampart, now grass grown and looking rather like an earthen bank. However, its true nature can be seen at the south-eastern end where a length of the wall face has been clearly exposd. This is dry-built from large blocks probably obtained from the irregular quarry ditch inside the line of the wall. Such a ditch is rare on Welsh sites where digging for stone is not normally necessary. However, though this ditch is not obvious today, its existence should not be doubted, for it is recorded as a " deep ditch " in 1866 when it was stated that large beach pebbles had been found in it.[45] Such pebbles might have been used as ammunition for slings. This inner rampart runs from a high " citadel " of rock at the south-east end to another boss about 400 yards to the west where it turns to incorporate a naturally terraced area, and continues along the top of the slope until the cliffs become precipitous, and artificial defence unnecessary.

Lower down the slope there is a further rampart, perhaps an earthen bank for most of its length, seemingly designed to protect a pathway which ran diagonally up the hill to a slightly inturned entrance through the inner rampart. There is much more stone in this outer bank where it approaches the entrance, and it is possible that there was a third rampart running for a short distance outside it here. However, the presence of a modern trackway has confused the issue somewhat. The Royal Commission mark a short length of rampart at the bottom of the steep eastern slope at the end of Porth Cynfor, but this is almost certainly a modern field bank. The rampart that they mark at the top of the eastern slope is also rather doubtful, although the natural gully here does make this corner a potentially weak point in the defences.

The northern half of the interior is very steep and rocky, but the southern side behind the rampart is relatively level and there is a flattish shoulder across the centre of the site, all of which would be suitable for habitation. Unfortunately, this area has been badly mutilated by nineteenth century quarrying for " china stone ", an altered felspar used in the manufacture of porcelain. The remains of a square enclosure may be seen in the south-eastern corner. It now appears as a grassy bank, but in 1866 it could be recognised as a wall. In view of the modern activity on the site it may not be ancient. Porth Llanlleiana is a good harbour (later used for shipping the " china stone "), and one which seems to have been well used by the fort builders, if the diagonal path can be considered to lead to it.

Nothing has been found at Dinas Gynfor to indicate the date of its construction or occupation. An Iron Age date may be suggested by analogy with other promontory forts.

Dinas, Holyhead (NGR SH/223794), a small promontory now virtually inaccessible from the mainland, may be a defensive site of the same period.[46] The high cliffs on the landward side are topped with a low bank, and the

[45] Hugh Hughes. *Hanes Amlwch a'i Gymydogaethau.* Eisteddfod Essay. 1866. Quoted in *Arch. Camb.* 1876. 104.
[46] RCAM. *Anglesey.* 1937. 24.

Royal Commission suggest that irregularities in the surface may cover the foundations of huts. The bank can certainly not be explained as part of any agricultural activity, so a defensive intention is possible. Another promontory cut off by a bank, Castell, near Trefadog (NGR SH/291859), is unlikely to be prehistoric.[47]

The idea of the defenced promontory is not confined to the coast; where suitable hill spurs are found inland they have often been isolated in the same way.

Caer Idris, Llanidan (NGR SH/494679), is one such site which takes advantage of a natural limestone scarp.[48] The defences here seem to have been quite complex although only a very small area may have been enclosed. Three or four closely set ramparts were constructed and an elaborate zig-zag entrance was contrived through them. The width of the entrance gaps, however, almost twenty feet across, seems to nullify these precautions. The site is now covered with trees and impenetrable undergrowth, a particularly unfortunate state of affairs since multivallate forts are rare in Anglesey. The only find from the site is a small sandstone rubber, circular, 1¾ins. in diameter, and marked with a cross like a hot-cross-bun; it was at one time the property of the Rev. W. Wynn Williams.[49]

A similar inland promontory fort may have existed in Llanfair Pwllgwyngyll village (NGR SH/534716), where the denuded remains of a bank and ditch can be seen cutting off the neck of the promontory on which the Anglesey Column stands.[50] Another site, at Tan-y-graig, in Llanffinan parish (NGR SH/505769), which has a comparable situation, is mentioned by the Royal Commission as a possible hill-fort, but it is now even more overgrown than when they saw it, and neither walls nor huts can be recognised.[51]

The best surviving example of the inland promontory fort is the one at Parciau, Llaneugrad, sometimes known as Bryn Ddiol (NGR SH/495847).[52] It is situated on the end of a low promontory of limestone, defended on the north and north-west by sheer cliffs about 50ft. high and on the east by a steep grassy slope. On the south-west the fort is isolated from the rest of the promontory by a series of three banks and ditches, the innermost one continuing along the crest of the slope on the east, and perhaps along the top of the cliff on the north-east, though here the evidence is not clear.

The south-western defences consist of three parallel walls of increasing height and thickness. There are rock-cut ditches outside them from which the stone would have been obtained. The outermost rampart is low, now little more than a ledge, and no stone is visible. The second one is higher

[47] RCAM. *Anglesey.* 1937. 69.
[48] RCAM. *Anglesey.* 1937. 103, 105. The size of the enclosure may have been reduced by quarrying on the north side of the road.
[49] In NMW. Wynn Williams Collection 19. 298A. 26.
[50] RCAM. *Anglesey.* 1937. 74.
[51] RCAM. *Anglesey.* 1937. 79.
[52] RCAM. *Anglesey.* 1937. 63.

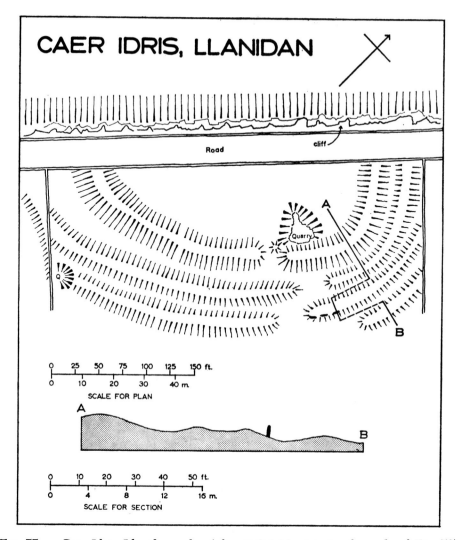

FIG. 77 — Caer Idris, Llanidan: plan (after R.C.A.M. at twice the scale of Fig. 70).

and built of very large limestock blocks. This rampart is carried round the south-eastern corner of the hill where it encloses quite a large flat area which might be considered an annexe to the fort. The innermost rampart is much higher and thicker than the others, and at the north-west end a length of the wall face has been exposed. In this part the wall is built of large blocks laid flat, but on the eastern side some upright stones can be seen, suggesting a wall built in the same way as that of Bwrdd Arthur. The rock-cut ditch continues around beneath this eastern wall as a ledge rather than a ditch and ends abruptly against a boss of rock about half-way along.

The entrance is on the south side. A causeway passes through the second

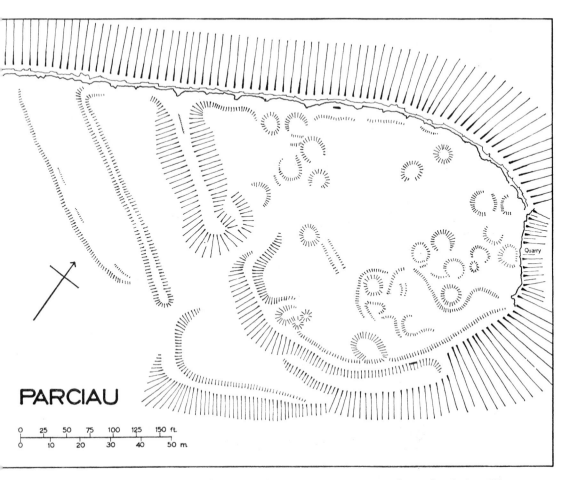

PARCIAU

Fig. 78 — Parciau, Llaneugrad: plan (after R.C.A.M., at twice the scale of Fig. 70).

rampart and crosses the inner ditch to pass through a gap in the inner rampart. The eastern end of the wall seems to be turned inwards at this point; the other side of the gateway is marked simply by an increase in height and width. The outermost rampart cannot be traced to the east of the entrance; on the west it curves inwards and probably made contact with the end of the second rampart.

The remarkable thing about Parciau is the quantity of hut foundations which can be traced inside the defended area. Over the entire area of one and a half acres, circular depressions can be seen, indicating the presence of stone huts each about 25ft. in diameter. If all these belong to the same period there can have been no room for animal grazing nor for any form of food production within the area of the actual village. This is in contrast to many of the large hill-forts where, it is suggested, animals could be kept and horticulture, if not agriculture, could be carried on within the defences themselves.

There have been three small excavations inside the area of the fort; one hut was dug into in 1867 by the Rev. Hugh Prichard and in 1923 E. Neil Baynes dug trenches across two others.[53] Both these excavations produced similar results: the rock floor of the huts was reached at about 1ft. 6ins. to 2ft. below the present ground level; these floors were covered with a dark occupation layer containing shells, animal bones, charcoal and iron slag, together with sherds of Romano-British pottery, glass beads, five fragments of box flue tiles and eight Roman coins dating from about 280 - 325 A.D. The pottery suggests a similar late third - early fourth century date.

Because the system of defence is so similar to that of pre-Roman hill-forts this site has traditionally been included in that group, but it must be admitted that excavation has so far produced no evidence of an early date. It would certainly seem that the visible remains of habitation date from a later period, but this may, of course, be simply another instance of the re-occupation of native sites seen elsewhere on the island. Excavation beneath the ramparts of these small sites is needed before the date of their construction can be known with any certainty and before these defended hilltop settlements can be meaningfully distinguished from the walled hut villages such as Din Lligwy which belong to the later Roman period.

A site which must have been very similar to that at Parciau formerly existed at Porthamel (NGR SH/508679).[54] It, too, was about one and a half acres in extent and was enclosed by two low ramparts on the south and east which ran up to a steep slope on the other two sides. Inside, the remains of at least fifteen huts were visible.

The settlement known as Dinas, near Plas Cadnant (NGR SH/552734), is another of these hilltop sites of very uncertain date.[55] It is situated, like so many early sites, on a rocky outcrop in a naturally defended position, but it contains not only the common round stone huts but also a series of small rectangular enclosures which elsewhere in North Wales are suggestive of Roman influence and date.

The flat-topped mass of rock on which it is sited is divided into three areas to which easy access is gained by two natural gullies. The western-most area is roughly triangular and contains the remains of at least five huts clustered close together, as well as two rectangular enclosures which abut against the outer wall, here quite well preserved. The central area is the highest and consists of a bare rock plateau on which there is no evidence of habitation. The third area is the most extensive and slopes gently to the east where the natural defences are weakest.

In this eastern area the remains of huts are scanty, but there is a row of well preserved rectangular enclosures in the centre and a wide rampart

[53] Hugh Prichard. *Arch. Camb.* 1867. 108-15, and Neil Baynes. *Arch. Camb.* 1930. 409-10.
[54] W. Wynn Williams. *Arch. Camb.* 1867. 281 (with plan).
[55] RCAM. *Anglesey.* 1937. 52-4. Other sites, now destroyed, may have been similar: e.g. Cadmarth, Trefdraeth. (*Arch. Camb.* 1871. 309-10).

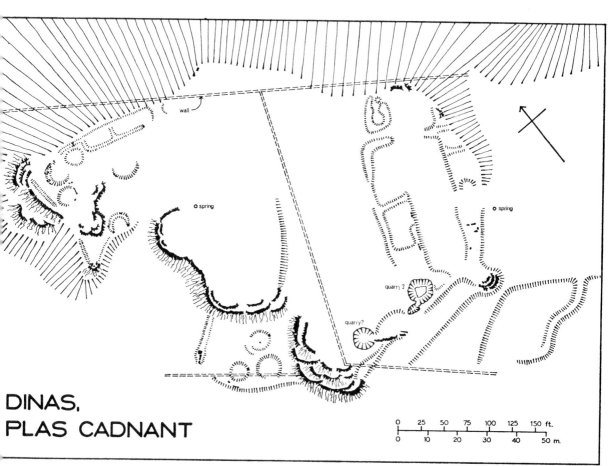

DINAS,
PLAS CADNANT

FIG. 79 — Dinas, Plas Cadnant, Llandysilio: plan (after R.C.A.M., at twice the scale of Fig. 70).

across the vulnerable slope at the east. This rampart appears to have been breached at a point where a rectangular hut has been built in the thickness of the bank. This modern destruction has caused some confusion because it has produced an entrance which appears to be flanked by rectangular guard chambers.[56] The presence of such guard chambers is a characteristic feature of a particular style of military architecture which can be seen in the major North Welsh hill-forts during the period immediately prior to the Roman invasion.

The reassessment of this entrance has consequently removed the best evidence for an early date of construction for the defences here. However, one other fact demands consideration in this context and that is the discovery of two pieces of extremely crude pottery on the site.[57] These are

[56] Willoughby Gardner and H. N. Savory. *Dinorben.* 1964. 86-90.
[57] RCAM. *Anglesey.* 1937. 54. (NMW. 38. 643/1).

beige/pink in colour with a soft, rather friable texture with no stone grit, and might be compared to the very coarse pottery found in Iron Age contexts in some of the Marcher hill-forts and at Dinorben, Denbighshire.[58] However, the absence of stone grit makes it unlikely that it really belongs to this class of pottery which has recently been the subject of much discussion.[59] The point at issue has been the Iron Age or Dark Age date of allegedly similar pottery from the Pant y Saer hut group.

Consideration of sites such as Parciau and Dinas, Plas Cadnant, which contain a number of hut foundations, raises the problem of the dating of the numerous round stone huts which are found both inside and outside enclosures in many parts of Anglesey and elsewhere in north-west Wales.[60] These hut circles are the remains of single-roomed round houses usually 20 - 30ft. in diameter. The thick stone walls, which can seldom have been higher than 2 - 3ft., would have supported the rafters of a high conical roof, probably covered with thatch or turves. The central support for the roof is variable; sometimes a single post, sometimes several, sometimes none at all. The doorway is normally wide, being the only source of light unless there was some central opening in the roof to allow the escape of smoke from the fire. The internal fittings were probably minimal and seldom survive, but in one case a raised sleeping area was found against the back wall, and in another what was perhaps a bed, in the shape of a rectangular stone box which could have been filled with heather or straw. Occasionally stone mortars have been found embedded in the floor, showing that daytime domestic duties were carried on inside the house, although one would imagine that such things would be done outside if possible. A few of the larger huts contained internal subdivisions, probably of wattling; some seem designed to form separate rooms, others simply to prevent draughts. It is noticeable that in Anglesey nearly all the doorways are sensibly facing away from the prevailing wind.

Houses such as these are a very basic type and seem to have remained the traditional form of dwelling for many centuries during which no variation in design or technique can be discerned. The walls may be built with either upright or laid stones, but since both techniques may be used in the same house this difference can have no chronological significance; nor can the system of roofing, where this is known; nor the size of the building. The only approach to the dating of unexcavated examples, therefore, is through a study of the grouping of huts, since many of them are found in enclosures of one kind or another.

One of the most conspicuous enclosures in which such huts are found are hill-forts of Iron Age type, among them sites, such as Conway Mountain,

[58] op. cit. 193-4 P. S. Gelling and S. C. Stanford. *Trans. Proc. Birmingham Archaeol. Soc.* LXXXII. 1967. 77-91.
[59] C. W. Phillips. *Arch. Camb.* 1934. 1-36. Pottery also illustrated in RCAM. *Anglesey.* 1937. lxxxi.
[60] A general survey of the facts, the theories and the literature can be found in RCAM. *Caernarvonshire.* III. 1964. lxxxvii-cvii. The Anglesey ones discussed in RCAM. *Anglesey.* 1937. lxxiii-lxxix.

which have not produced any Roman material.[61] Since the huts inside these forts, some of which can be clearly associated with the period of construction, are indistinguishable from those outside them, it is reasonable to assume that the tradition of building such huts must go back to the Iron Age, if not earlier. But, unfortunately, no huts outside the hill-forts have produced any evidence for Iron Age occupation and the problem is further complicated by the discovery at lower altitudes of Iron Age huts which, though admittedly round, are built of wood and not stone. In fact, all the stone huts which have produced dateable material are proved to have been occupied during the Roman period, and some, such as Pant y Saer, have even produced objects dating from the fifth and sixth centuries A.D.[62]

Apart from the remote possibility (already discussed, p. 210) of a Late Bronze Age date for some of the huts at Tŷ Mawr, Holyhead, and the alleged Iron Age date of coarse sherds from Pant y Saer,[63] the excavated Anglesey huts do not present a major problem. They have all produced Romano-British material, some in large quantities, which, together with their frequent grouping into what could almost be termed villages, leaves no doubt of their period of occupation, a period which places them outside the scope of this present volume. Since even those inside the area of presumptively Iron Age defences have produced an abundance of late Roman material, which must represent a secondary occupation of these sites, it is clear that the solution to the problem of the initial date of this tradition is unlikely to be found in Anglesey.

Another type of field monument constructed and used during a very long period is the farmstead defended by a circular bank and ditch. This type, known by a number of names, the commonest of which is "rath", is widespread in Ireland, where excavation has shown that the majority belong to the Early Christian period.[64] Despite this, it is thought that some of these homesteads may also date back to the Iron Age and perhaps earlier. Although this type of earthwork is so common in Ireland, it is not frequently found elsewhere except in Pembrokeshire, an area which shows many cultural links with Ireland. Recent excavation of such a site in that county, Walesland Rath, near Haverfordwest, has produced evidence of occupation during the Iron Age, so that in Wales, at least, several of these sites may be genuinely pre-Roman.[65]

The only visible earthwork in Anglesey which has analogies with this group is Castell Bryn Gwyn, Llanidan (NGR SH/466671).[66] This site has already been discussed in connection with the underlying Neolithic structures (pp. 65-7 and Fig. 26). The final reconstruction of the defences is

[61] W. E. Griffiths and A. H. A. Hogg. *Arch. Camb.* 1956. 49-80.
[62] *Arch. Camb.* 1934. 1-36.
[63] Gelling and Stanford. *op. cit.* 84-6.
[64] S. P. O'Riordain. *Antiquities of the Irish Countryside.* Third ed. 1953. 1-13 for a convenient summary.
[65] G. J. Wainwright. *Current Archaeology.* XII. January 1969.
[66] G. J. Wainwright. *Arch. Camb.* 1962. 25-58.

dated to after the arrival of the Romans by the discovery of a few sherds of Flavian pottery. But before that there had been one, or possibly two, earlier phases of rampart building which may be reasonably attributed to the Iron Age, on analogy with Walesland and with the situation at Llandegai where, as here, a surviving Neolithic enclosure was re-used.[67]

The interpretation and dating of Castell Bryn Gwyn are not altogether satisfactory since so little was found. Moreover, the analogy with the Irish or Pembrokeshire raths should not be over-stressed, since other convincing examples of such earthworks cannot be found in Anglesey. However, a number of crop-mark sites in the northern half of the island should, perhaps, be mentioned in this context. Air photographs have revealed several small circular enclosures with simple entrances which might be interpreted as raths.[68] Since nothing is visible on the ground and none have been excavated it is impossible at this stage to do more than simply draw attention to their existence.

Another type of antiquity which provides similar problems of dating are the mounds of burnt stone which occur widely in marshy areas or on moorland in many parts of Ireland and western Britain. Before excavation, these sites are recognisable as horseshoe-shaped mounds composed entirely of burnt stone mixed with charcoal and black earth. They normally open towards a small stream. Excavation will invariably reveal a large hearth in the central depression, often associated with a wooden or clay-lined trough.

All the evidence points to these sites being open-air cooking places, and recent experiments have shown that they can function very effectively. Excavation of a well-preserved example at Ballyvourney, Co. Cork, revealed a series of structures.[69] The central feature was a rectangular wooden trough (filled by seepage of bog water, though most troughs were filled manually) with a large paved hearth at either end. Close to one of the hearths was a smaller stone-lined pit, and on the other side was a small wooden hut which seems to have held a meat-rack and a butcher's block.

Inside the hut, carcasses could be stored and prepared: outside, the meat could be cooked by either boiling or roasting. Experiment showed that the water in the trough (100 gallons) could be brought to the boil in little over half an hour by shovelling in hot stones, and that the addition of only a few stones every quarter of an hour could keep it simmering gently for the 3 hours 40 minutes needed to boil a large joint of mutton (wrapped in straw to keep it clean). A similar joint could be roasted in the smaller stone-lined pit (previously heated by having a fire burning in it) by covering it with hot stones. It was found that these would need to be changed seven times in the course of 3 hours 40 minutes, but that, altogether, fewer stones were required for roasting than for boiling.

[67] C. H. Houlder. *Ant.* XLII. 1968. 220.
[68] I am grateful to the Archaeology section of the Ordnance Survey for allowing me access to their air photographs.
[69] M. J. O'Kelly. JRSAI. LXXXIV. 1954. 105-55.

The hot stones for both these methods, and for smaller cooking operations in pots or skins (if such took place),[70] would be obtained from the large hearth or hearths. The size of the hearth is governed by the need to keep a continuous supply of accessible hot stones. This is done by spreading the fire from one group of stones to the next. When the cooking is finished, the stone is shovelled out of the trough or roasting pit and gradually, over the years, builds up into the characteristic horseshoe-shaped mounds which survive today.

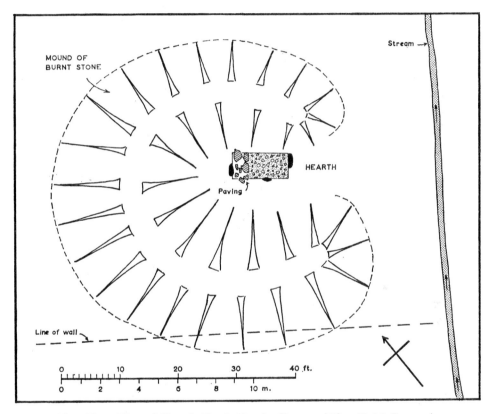

Fig. 80 — Plan of Hearth No. 1, Penrhosllugwy. (After E. N. Baynes.)

A group of three such cooking sites at Penrhosllugwy were excavated by Mr. E. Neil Baynes at the beginning of the century.[71] The three are close together (NGR SH/488857; 490859; 490859) on either side of a small brook; such grouping seems to be characteristic of the type.[72] None of them produced evidence for a wooden boiling trough, although water was readily available, but the two that were fully excavated each had a very large

[70] See Ant. XL. 1966. 225-7 and XLIII. 1969. 217-20 for experiments with this method.
[71] Arch. Camb. 1913. 201-14 (printed as a supplement to TAAS. 1913).
[72] Another has recently been found by the Ordnance Survey in the same area. NGR SH/487850).

clay-lined hearth at the centre. One had a paved area (4ft. × 2ft. 6ins.) at the upper end of the hearth which could be interpreted as a roasting pit. No evidence of a hut was found in either case, but the sites must have been used for a considerable period as the debris of burnt stone had built up into mounds 30 - 50ft. in diameter and up to 4ft. high.

Mounds of burnt stone have been recorded elsewhere in the island, at Llechcynfarwy and on Mynydd Llwydiarth, but no systematic search has been made and it is more than likely that others await discovery.[73]

The date of these outdoor cooking sites is very problematical; they are always found in isolated areas away from settlements, and dateable objects have never been found in direct association with them. On the other hand, the situation revealed at Ballyvourney corresponds exactly to the descriptions in early Irish literature to the hunting camps of the *Fianna*, young men who, while on military service, lived on the game they could catch in the wild.[74] The Irish laws imply that such camps could be used by anyone, but it is probable that individual groups would set up a number of camps in their own area and aim to use them in turn in the course of a season's hunting. The literary evidence, therefore, suggests that these sites belong to the first few centuries A.D., but pollen analysis, radio carbon dating, and the incidence of flint flakes suggest that this tradition, like so many that are preserved in early Irish society, has roots that may go back well into the Bronze Age.

The monuments and finds so far described can only be dated to the Iron Age in a very general sense, and it may be suggested that perhaps the greater part of their history lay in the Roman and post-Roman periods. There is one find, however, which unquestionably relates to the Celtic Iron Age warriors who must have formed the upper stratum of society in Anglesey in the centuries before the arrival of the Romans. This is the burial found in 1909 on the farm of Gelliniog Wen, Llangeinwen (NGR SH/459657).[75]

The burial was found accidentally and few details were recorded, but the body was apparently lying at full length with the feet towards the east. It was protected by a stone cist, one side of which was formed by a natural ledge of rock, the others by upright stones. The cist was covered by three large capstones. With the body was a long sword in its scabbard, perhaps attached to the belt with a ring, part of which survives. All three are made of iron and are badly corroded so that the details are difficult to make out.

The total length of the sword was originally about 2ft. 7¾ins., but 2ins. from the tip has since been lost. The tang is 5ins. long and the angular shoulder of the blade can just be seen emerging from the corrosion of the scabbard. The present width of the blade is 1⅝ins., but the Royal Commission drew it as 1¾ins., with an edge groove which cannot now be made

[73] Llechcynfarwy: TAAS. 1926. 23. Mynydd Llwydiarth: RCAM. *Anglesey.* 1937. 141.
[74] The literary background and the problems of dating are fully discussed by O'Kelly in JRSAI. LXXXIV. 1954. 147-50, 142-4.
[75] Harold Hughes. *Arch Camb.* 1909. 256-7, 367. RCAM. *Anglesey.* 1937. lxix. no. 1.

Fig. 81 — Iron sword in scabbard from the burial at Gelliniog Wen, Llangeinwen.

out.[76] The flat blade, long tang, angular shoulder and blade width (if the present measurements are correct) are all comparable to the La Tène swords from Llyn Cerrig Bach (Nos. 2 and 93 (Fig. 82) especially) which are considered to belong to Piggott's Group II.[77]

However, the scabbard presents some problems for, although its width (2ins.) and the indication of a simple, high-set strap loop invite comparison with the iron scabbards from Llyn Cerrig Bach (92 and 8, Fig. 82), the scabbard mouth appears to have been flat, a feature of later, south-east English swords of Group V. The indications of this straight end are now less obvious on the back than the earlier drawings suggest (perhaps the result of cleaning), while on the front there is a slight ogee mark which might possibly indicate a normal arched top to the scabbard.

Although it is not possible to place this sward definitely in either Group II or Group V, certain conclusions would be the same in either case. Both these types of iron sword are found chiefly in the south-east of England, Group V more especially in the Belgic areas, so the Gelliniog Wen sword may be considered an import from that region. Group II swords, though generally earlier, continue in production up to the first century A.D.; some could, therefore, be contemporary with swords of Group V which belong to the last phase of the pre-Roman Iron Age.

The presence of both Group II and Group V swords at Llyn Cerrig Bach might be explained as religious tribute, but the discovery of such a sword in a burial, with its owner, requires some other explanation. It is perhaps tangible evidence for the presence in the island of the southern refugees mentioned by Tacitus, in which case a date within the first century A.D. should be preferred.[78] The use of inhumation, however, suggests a non-Belgic background to the warrior buried at Gelliniog Wen for the Belgae always used cremation, whereas the rest of the Iron Age population, whose graves are rarely found, seem to have preferred inhumation, occasionally in stone cists, as here.[79]

The south-eastern origin of the Gelliniog Wen sword need not imply, of course, that its owner was equally foreign, but unfortunately we have no native Welsh burials of this date with which to compare it.[80] Until the Roman period and the establishment (or growth) of the hut villages, the life of the native population remains extremely shadowy. A great many exotic objects eventually found their way into the island, but these may have been largely irrelevant of the daily life of the normal inhabitant. It is here that Anglesey's apparent prestige as a religious centre — as a place

[76] It is now on exhibition in the NMW, Cardiff.
[77] S. Piggott. PPS. XVI. 1950. 1-28.
[78] Tacitus. Agricola. XIV.
[79] Early Iron Age Guide: British Museum. 1925. 121.
[80] The inhumation burials found in the early nineteenth century in the top of Bryn yr Hen Bobl might have dated from this period since a small glass bead, perhaps of La Tène date, was found with those thrown back into the chamber. Few details of these burials survive. (Arch. LXXXV. 1935. 254-5, 259 and 292).

where powerful sanctuaries and their guardians might attract the wealth of devotees — complicates the picture. Another factor which is difficult to assess archaeologically is the final influx of refugees from the richer south which is recorded by Tacitus. Certainly the limited evidence of Iron Age activity from the island as a whole would not lead one to expect to see a wealth of exotic military equipment in daily use amongst the inhabitants.

Yet the spectacular discoveries at Llyn Cerrig Bach include some of the most splendid works of prehistoric art from the whole of Wales, and as a group, illuminating as they do the military equipment, the artistic development, the manufacturing economy and the religious practices of the period just before the native cultures were eclipsed by Rome, they constitute one of the most fascinating and important Iron Age finds ever to come to light in these islands. It is all the more unfortunate, therefore, that they were found under such difficult circumstances.

The discoveries were made in 1943 when ground was being prepared for the construction of the Royal Air Force Station at Valley.[81] This preparation involved spreading peat over the sand, the peat being obtained for this purpose from a number of small bogs in the locality. The method employed was to drag the peaty mass to the margin of the bog with a large wire scoop like a trawler net. The peat was left for a few days to drain, then taken by lorry to the Station, dumped in heaps and then spread evenly over the sand by means of a harrow. It was during this final process that a number of metal objects and a quantity of bones were found in peat which had come from a small bog just to the west of Llyn Cerrig Bach (NGR SH/306765). The first object to be found was one of the iron gang chains which got caught in the teeth of the harrow. The story of how this nineteen hundred-year-old chain was successfully used to pull lorries out of the mud is well-known.

After this initial discovery, other objects were noticed and collected by the workmen on the site, Messrs. W. O. and R. Roberts, W. Jones and W. Rees, and by the Resident Engineer, Mr. J. A. Jones, who sent drawings of them to the National Museum in Cardiff. Once the importance of the finds was realised a thorough search of all the peat was made, but only in the peat which came from Llyn Cerrig Bach was anything found. The original source of the finds was conclusively demonstrated by the discovery of another gang chain, an iron tyre and one of the small embossed plaques at the bog itself. It is possible that a good deal more Iron Age metalwork remains in the lower levels of the bog and other pieces may be lying in the peat sealed beneath the runways of the aerodrome. Unfortunately, both areas are now inaccessible because of road works and developments carried out during the war.

[81] The circumstances of discovery and the content of this vitally important deposit have been fully described by Sir Cyril Fox in two publications for the NMW: *A Find of the Early Iron Age from Llyn Cerrig Bach, Anglesey. Interim Report.* 1945, and *A Find of the Early Iron Age from Llyn Cerrig Bach, Anglesey.* 1946/7 (hereinafter, Fox 1946/7). These are the authoritative accounts and I have relied very heavily upon them in the discussion which follows.

The area around Llyn Cerrig Bach is broken and rocky, with abrupt, bare outcrops of contorted rock and small lakes and marshy ground filling the hollows between them. In many ways it is a romantic and dramatic landscape and could even have been awe-inspiring before the railway and other modern developments broke in upon it. The precise position of the finds within the bog close to Llyn Cerrig Bach can be located with some accuracy; they all seem to have come from the edge of the bog at the foot of a sheer rock cliff. This cliff would have risen about 11ft. above the level of the lake at the time of the deposit, and its flat top would have provided an ideal platform from which the objects might be thrown into the water. The uncorroded state of those iron objects which had not been exposed for long on the Station, proves that they had sunk immediately into water, or beneath the surface of a very wet bog, indicating that during the Iron Age the lake had been larger, extending to beneath the rock platform.

People may throw things into pools and hollows for a number of reasons. The simplest would be to get rid of rubbish, but, though the finds from Llyn Cerrig Bach included a great number of animal bones and a good deal of the metalwork had been broken in antiquity, the restricted range of objects and the splendour of many of them make this explanation the least likely. Another reason which it would be easy for us to understand is a fear of attack and theft, the hiding of wealth in the hope of returning to collect it, or simply to forestall an enemy. Such an explanation may lie behind many hoards, such as the Late Bronze Age one from Llangwyllog, but the varying date of many of the objects found at Valley makes it unlikely that they could all have been thrown in the lake at the same time.

When the exclusively military nature of the objects, their splendour, the wealth they represent, and the amount of deliberate damage that has been done to many of them (damage which could not have occurred in normal use) are considered, it may be seen that the group answers very closely the descriptions of classical writers who record that the Celts: " after a victory, sacrifice such living things as they have captured and all the other booty they gather together in one place. In many tribal areas heaps of such objects can be seen piled up in sacred precincts ".[82] This quotation implies that masses of captured war gear might be found, offered to the gods, in consecrated areas on dry land; such finds have been made in Switzerland, but Strabo's description of the famous Gaulish treasure at Toulouse, known to consist of votive offerings: " some placed in sacred precincts and some in sacred pools ", shows that lakes and other watery spots might be equally hallowed.[83]

Archaeology bears this out, for it is remarkable how many fine prehistoric objects have been found in bogs or dredged from rivers. Although some of these objects may have been accidentally lost, it is unlikely that

[82] Caesar. de Bello Gallico. VI. xvii. (Loeb translation).
[83] Strabo. IV. i, xiii. Both passages are quoted by Fox (1946/7. 69-70) and the practice is discussed in more detail by Piggott (PSAS. LXXXVII. 1952-3. 4-8).

anyone would be so careless as to drop the many beautiful gold lunulae, and the incomparable shields recovered from the Thames at Battersea and the Witham at Lincoln, without making an attempt to retrieve them. The peculiarly deliberate arrangement of certain objects within a bog, such as the circle of bronze shields set upright in the bog at Beith, Ayrshire,[84] also suggests that their placing was deliberate, valuable offerings made to the " indwelling spirit of the pool ", and accepted by the god as the water, or the peat, closed over them.

Finds of this nature from all periods of prehistory indicate that this practice is of great antiquity and was not something invented by the Celts. However, the practice is most clearly attested amongst these people because it is specifically mentioned by classical writers, and because the number of finds of Celtic metalwork which can be interpreted in this way is impressive. Often the offering seems to have been made at one time, the loot from a single successful battle or raid, but, occasionally, as at Llyn Cerrig Bach and at Thorsbjerg, Denmark,[85] the objects range over several centuries: people coming back time and again to make their offerings at a particularly sacred spot.

Although the majority of finds are of military equipment, parade gear or arms captured in battle as Caesar implies, some offerings were not exclusively martial or aristocratic. Gregory of Tours describes a gathering at a lake in the Cevennes at which the peasants threw into the water offerings of bread, cheese, beeswax, rags, clothing, and other objects according to their standing; finds from southern Scotland may reflect a similar social situation.[86] These ceremonies described by Gregory were accompanied by three days of feasting. A similar custom might explain the quantities of bones of ox, sheep and pig from Llyn Cerrig Bach, though horse and dog bones must surely represent the sacrifice of captured animals. No human bones were found; presumably human sacrifices did not take place at this spot. Such sacrifices, graphically illustrated on the Gundestrup cauldron from Denmark,[87] played a not inconsiderable part in Celtic religious ceremonies and are known to have taken place in Anglesey, for Tacitus, speaking specifically of the Druids, or priests, on the island, says: " their religion enjoined them to drench their altars with the blood of prisoners, and to find out the will of the gods by consulting the entrails of human beings ".[88]

The vast majority of the one hundred and forty-four objects found at Llyn Cerrig Bach reflect an aristocratic society with masculine and military preoccupations; just such a society, fond of war, bravado and personal display, as is shown in the classical writings about the European Celts, and

[84] J. Coles. PPS. XXVIII. 1962. 189.
[85] Jankuhn. Forschungen und Forschritte. XII. 1936. 202, and Ant. XXVI. 1952. 22.
[86] Gregory of Tours. In Gloria Confessorum. Cap. 2. quoted by Piggott (PSAS. LXXXVII. 1952-3. 6.) in discussing three Scottish hoards.
[87] Illustrated in S. Piggott. The Druids. (Anc. Peoples and Places) 1968. Pl. 1.
[88] Tacitus. Annals. XIV. xxx. (trans. Dudley and Webster).

in the literature of their later counterparts, the epic tales of tribal fighting and cattle raiding in Ireland.[89]

Weapons, chariot fittings, and harness form the bulk of the collection. The weapons consist of swords, spears and parts of one or two shields which, like some of the spears, may have been ceremonial, parade gear.

Altogether, eleven swords are represented, two of them complete and two of them still in their iron scabbards. The complete swords (92 and 93) are 2ft. 3ins. and 2ft. 6ins. long respectively, an average size for swords of this date, but No. 7 may have been over 3ft. long originally.[90] The width of the blade is variable, but they divide broadly into two classes: those about 1½ins. wide and those 2ins. or more across. These may be later in date, although the absence of diagnostic features such as scabbards and hilt guards make it difficult to place them exactly. The simple iron scabbards (92 and 8) belong to the narrower series, and their arched mouths and plain loops place them in Piggott's Group II, a type which may have either the short loop as on 92 or the elongated one seen on 8.[91] The date of this group, to which most of the swords at Llyn Cerrig Bach belong, is difficult to establish precisely, it may range from before 125 B.C. to well into the first century A.D. It is possible that the individual swords at Llyn Cerrig Bach may vary a good deal in age, some of them probably being amongst the earliest objects in the lake.

Late swords must have been represented in the deposit since 10 and 11 are bronze mountings from wide scabbards, and 10 is a distinctive type which occurs frequently on the scabbards of swords of Piggott's Group V.[92] These swords, which are a Continental type, appear in the south-east of England at the beginning of the first century A.D. and may be characteristic of the Belgae. It is interesting that all the swords from Llyn Cerrig Bach, of whatever date, are southern in ultimate origin. The mechanics by which they reached Anglesey are obscure, for in both cases Llyn Cerrig Bach is very much an outlier from the normal distribution, although it must be admitted that remarkably little is known of Iron Age weapons in Wales, where even such prolific sites as Dinorben have produced virtually none. It is also noteworthy that there are no northern swords (Piggott's Groups III and IV) at Llyn Cerrig Bach, unless 12 may be considered the pommel of such a sword.[93] The resemblance is not very strong, and the fact that 12 is so flat would seem to militate against the comparison.

Recent cleaning has revealed that one of the swords from Llyn Cerrig Bach (2) has a maker's mark stamped on the blade.[94] Such stamps have been

[89] See K. Jackson. The Oldest Irish Tradition: A Window on the Iron Age. 1964.
[90] The numbers are those of the inventory of finds in Fox 1946/7. They are also used on the illustrations here which show all the decorative pieces but only a representative sample of the less ornamental objects.
[91] S. Piggott. PPS. XVI. 1950. 1-28.
[92] op. cit. 28.
[93] It is somewhat similar to the pommel on the sword from Hod Hill, Dorset. (PPS. XVI. 1950. Pl. II).
[94] H. N. Savory. BBCS. XXI. 1966. 374-6.

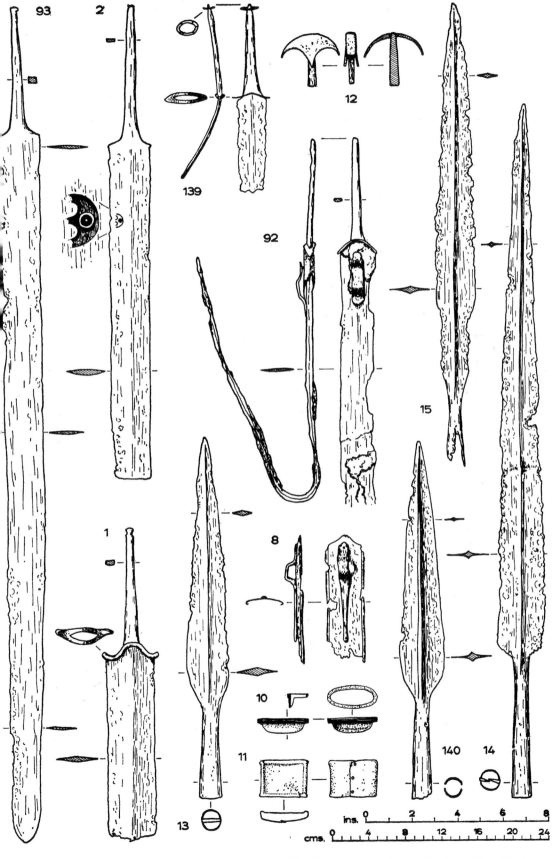

FIG. 82 — Llyn Cerrig Bach: iron swords, scabbards, dagger and spearheads. (After Fox.)

found occasionally on Continental swords, but none had previously been known from Britain. These marks must have been stamped onto the red-hot blade as it was forged and are presumed to be a guarantee of quality. However, recent analysis of the metal used for the Llyn Cerrig Bach swords has shown that they are all made from high quality steel, and that the blade of No. 2 is not notably better than the others.[95] Perhaps these stamps may have been magic marks protecting the user. No other instances of this particular semi-circular mark are known.[96]

By and large, daggers seem to have been rarely used in the British Iron Age, but there is a small group from habitation sites in Somerset which may be compared to the one from Llyn Cerrig Bach (139).[97] They are very similar to the Group II swords with which they must be contemporary and a date in the first century B.C. may be suggested. 139, with its arched bronze hilt guard, may be compared to one from Kingsdown Camp, Mells, Somerset.[98] 139 has, in addition, a small bronze ring which must have been part of the pommel.

The seven spearheads are all of iron, and though some of them are badly corroded, they seem to have suffered less deliberate damage than the swords, which have nearly all been broken or, like 92, bent. The ridged blades of the spears would have made them stronger, and 14 has clearly survived an attempt to bend it. These sharply ridged blades are typical of La Tène spearheads in this country and on the Continent, but the type does not alter much and it is impossible to date them closely. The great length of 14, 2ft. 5ins., and the even greater size of 16, which is broken, suggest that they were ceremonial rather than practical weapons. They all have small sockets indicating that they were throwing spears with light shafts of ash. A piece of the shaft survives inside the socket of 96.[99]

The normal Celtic shield, oval or rectangular in shape and often over 3ft. long, was made of wood, or wood and leather, with a wooden boss covering the central handgrip. On the Continent this boss, which was usually oval and sometimes incorporated vertical ribs to strengthen the board, was protected by a simple strip of iron.[100] In Britain, shields were more elaborately decorated: the bosses covered with polished bronze sheet often beautifully embossed or engraved; the ribs encased in bronze and decorative studs and plaques nailed onto the boards.

It is difficult to establish a detailed typology of these British shields since few have been found in dateable contexts.[101] Many of the finest have, in fact, been found in rivers and must be considered votive offerings. Since the body of the shield was wood, it is usually only the metal fittings which

---

[95] J. N. McGarth. BBCS. XXII. 1967. 418-25.
[96] Two recently found on swords from Hungary are similar but have a pointed oval rather than a circle in the centre. E. F. Petres. *Albia Regia*. VIII-IX. 1967-8. 35-42.
[97] E. M. Jope. PPS. XXVII. 1961. 340-1.
[98] *op. cit.* Fig. 14. no. 38.
[99] Fox 1946/7. 98. Appendix II by H. A. Hyde.
[100] *See* S. Piggott. *Ancient Europe*. 1965. Pl. XLIII. a & b. (compare British one, c, below).
[101] A recent attempt is by I. M. Stead. PPS. XXXIV. 1968. 173-8.

survive, the boss, the rib casing and the decorative plaques. The bosses
may be round or oval, the latter often extended to cover the ribs. The
magnificent shield boss from Llyn Cerrig Bach (98) belongs to this class
of elongated boss and, in particular, to a small sub-group which seems to
be characteristic of North Wales.[102] This sub-group is distinguished by
having arched sides, a design which may be considered an evolved version
of the Continental strip boss, infinitely more elegant and with the rib casing
attached. The hoard from Tal y Llyn, Merioneth, contains two shield
bosses which show their strip origin very clearly.[103] On the well-known one
from Moel Hiraddug, Flintshire, the boss and ribs are more closely
integrated, but the design echoes the earlier strip system.[104] At Llyn Cerrig
Bach the line of boss and rib is quite unbroken, and the engraved design
is independent of any functional ancestry.[105]

It is possible, therefore, to suggest a typological sequence in which
the boss from Llyn Cerrig Bach is the latest of the North Welsh examples.
This structural typology is supported by a study of the technique of
decoration. The makers of the Tal y Llyn shields outlined their embossed
patterns with a rocked tracer. This particular technique, which produces
a tiny zigzag line, is used on Middle La Tène ornaments on the Continent
and on a number of pieces of fine metalwork in Britain, most of which
may be considered early in the insular tradition.[106] A number of workshops
around the Irish Sea seem to have favoured this system, and there is
increasing evidence to suggest that much of the fine metalwork found in
Wales during this period may be locally made. Similarities over wide areas,
however, may imply that the individual craftsmen were highly mobile,
moving from household to household among the warrior chiefs who were
their patrons. Because, in Wales, we have not yet found the sites of any
of these households with attendant workshops, it is difficult to give a
precise date to this artistic activity. Stylistic analogies are notoriously
difficult to interpret, but certain elements in the Tal y Llyn hoard suggest
that the pieces were made about 200 B.C., though they may have been
finally hidden during the Roman period.[107] Consequently a date in the
second century — perhaps between 150 and 100 B.C. — might be suggested
for the Llyn Cerrig Bach shield boss, for on this the rocked tracer patterns
are in a slightly later style, paralleled on a sword scabbard of La Tène II
from La Tène itself.[108]

It is not proposed to embark on any elaborate analysis of the patterns
engraved on the boss; their beauty and liveliness can speak for themselves.

[102] H. N. Savory. BBCS. XX. 1964. 449-75.
[103] loc. cit.
[104] W. J. Hemp. Arch. Camb. 1928. 253-84.
[105] Part of what may have been another of this sub-group with a vertically arranged
    embossed pattern was found last summer at South Cadbury hillfort in the remains of
    a workshop. (Ant. XLIV. 1970. 46-9, fig. 2).
[106] E. M. Jope. PPS. XXVII. 1961. 312 and H. N. Savory. BBCS. XX. 1964. 455.
[107] H. N. Savory. BBCS. XXII. 1966. 88-103.
[108] H. N. Savory. BBCS. XX. 1964. 455, 470.

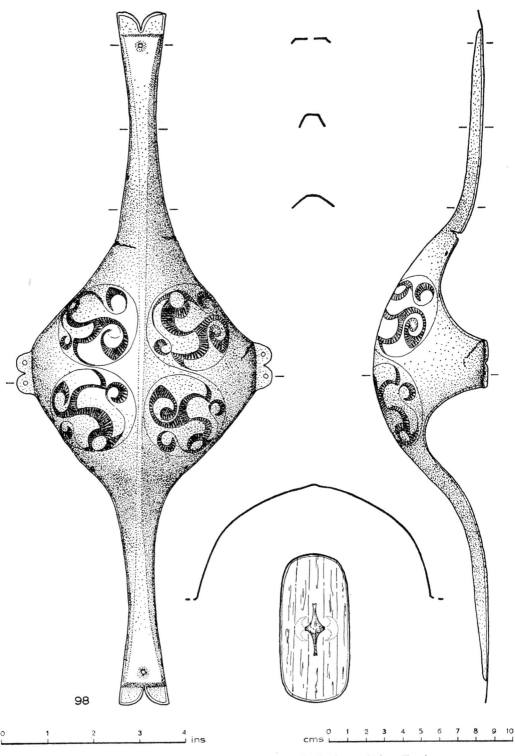

98

FIG. 83 — Llyn Cerrig Bach: bronze shield boss. (After Fox.)

Sir Cyril Fox has said of this design that its keynote is "unstable equilibrium; balance temporary and precarious, exciting, like that achieved by a man on a tight-rope", an analogy which exactly captures the feeling of these skilfully sketched roundels.[109] The basic three-armed figure, the "triskele" appears again and again in a variety of forms, simple or elaborate. Its popularity in all aspects of Celtic art may have been due to some magical significance. The variation here, the pointed "trumpet" terminal which looks a little like a puffin's head, is a distinctively British feature and may be found frequently on the remarkable series of decorated mirrors which are one of the high points in the development of native art in this country.[110] The design on the Llyn Cerrig Bach boss, with its use of "matting" to define the main elements of the pattern, is in many ways similar to those on the mirrors from Billericay, Essex, and Desborough, Northants,[111] but their use of more formalised, incised basketry "matting" suggests a rather later date of manufacture. Another comparison can be drawn between the shield boss and the decorated scabbard from Bugthorpe, Yorkshire: this underlines links with the northern group of craftsmen who preferred to use "matting" to define the pattern, rather than to reserve the pattern while roughening the background, as they did in the south. The Bugthorpe scabbard contained a sword of Piggott's Group III which could date from the end of the second century B.C., the date already suggested for the Llyn Cerrig Bach shield boss.[112]

In addition to their very fine bosses, the shields from Tal y Llyn and Moel Hiraddug were decorated with large pelta-shaped bronze plaques which were nailed to the shield on either side of the boss. The Llyn Cerrig Bach shield may have had similar additions, but they do not survive. Two small, bean-shaped plaques (17 and 18, Fig. 84) might have been some such shield fitting, but it is unlikely that they came from the same one as 98.[113]

It has been recently suggested that the crescentic plaque (75) might also have been intended as decoration for a shield.[114] Others have thought that it may have embellished a chariot.[115] Its true purpose cannot be determined beyond the fact that it was clearly designed to be nailed onto some flat surface, perhaps surrounding a circular protrusion.

This thin bronze sheet has been decorated in a repoussé technique with certain parts emphasised by engraved lines. On the Tal y Llyn boss the lines around the raised pattern were made with a rocked tracer, and the absence of this technique on the crescentic plaque might suggest a later

[109] Fox. 1946/7. 7.
[110] The development of these motifs is fully discussed in Fox 1946/7. 48-58 and in his later work, *Pattern and Purpose*. NMW. 1958. *passim*.
[111] Fox. 1946/7. 56. Fig. 31, A and B.
[112] S. Piggott. PPS. XVI. 1950. 12-14.
[113] Similar kidney-shaped plaques on a shield from Nimes, France, have been dated to the first century A.D.
[114] I. M. Stead. PPS. XXXIV. 1968. 178.
[115] Fox. 1946/7. 46-7.

date for this piece, perhaps around 100 B.C., a date which would seem reasonable on other stylistic grounds.

The design is another version of the " triskele " enclosed in a circle and framed by three fleshy leaves on either side. These elements which help to relate the circular pattern to the shape of the plaque are otherwise rather unfortunate for they add too much weight and detract from the clarity and liveliness of the central design. Originally the plaque would have been further embellished with four, or possibly five, ornamental studs. The asymmetrical " triskele " design, worked in two planes of relief, is lively, satisfying and attractive in its own right, but has gained an especial importance in any discussion of British La Tène art because it exemplifies a significant moment in the development of the native " triskele " designs : a moment when their origin in the Continental plant tendril patterns, ultimately of Greek derivation, is still recognisable, while foreshadowing the final resolution into complete abstraction exemplified in the British Mirror Style.[116]

Amongst the objects thrown into the lake were the remains of a number of chariots. Light chariots such as those from Llyn Cerrig Bach played an important part in Celtic warfare as the writings of Greek and Roman adversaries reveal.[117] They were designed to carry two people, the warrior armed with a sword, a shield and a spear, and his charioteer, who was probably a non-combatant. The chariots were not used in the melée of battle itself; the warrior would descend from it to fight hand to hand, while the chariot was held in readiness behind the lines for flight or pursuit, depending on the fortunes of war. Their tactical advantage was to move the warrior quickly to and from the place of combat and enhance his height, speed and fearsomeness in the preliminary phase of mutual abuse and verbal intimidation which was such a remarkable feature of Celtic battles. Since the chariots were simply means of transport, it is not surprising to find them in non-military contexts as well; a carving from Padua seems to show a man and his wife travelling in a chariot,[118] and in Europe and in Yorkshire during the early La Tène period it was traditional to use the chariot as a funeral car and to bury the warrior lying in it.

The use of these sophisticated vehicles, which are known to have been designed for speed, implies an open, grassy landscape and at least some rudimentary roads, neither of which is likely to have existed in Iron Age Anglesey where, even today, the terrain is broken and rocky in many areas.[119] It is surprising, therefore, that parts of so many different chariots found their way to Llyn Cerrig Bach. It would be interesting to know whether they were complete or dismantled when they arrived.

Most of the chariots are represented only by the broken iron tyres from

[116] This is discussed in great detail in Fox 1946/7. 48-53.
[117] e.g. Diodorus V. xxix.
[118] O-H Frey. *Germania.* XLVI. 1968. 317-20. Pl. 39.
[119] T. G. E. Powell *in* Foster and Alcock (edd) *Culture and Environment.* 1963. 165-7.

their wheels.[120] The various styles of tyre, differentiated by their width and shape in section (shown in Fig. 85), suggest that at least ten and perhaps twenty-two chariots might have been involved. The variations in tyre-form suggest further that these chariots had probably been built in different areas and at different dates, but insufficient comparative material has been found elsewhere to verify this hypothesis.

All the tyres, made from double shear steel, had been shrunk onto the wheel and had not been fixed with nails.[121] The absence of nails is a characteristic of nearly all the pre-Roman tyres in Britain and contrasts with Roman and, to a lesser extent, Continental Celtic practice where, although the tyre was shrunk on to give strength and elasticity to the wheel, nails were added to keep the tyres in place. Celtic wheelwrights were famous throughout the ancient world for the lightness and strength of their products, made with a single-piece felloe and a variable number of spokes, anything from six to twelve. Three foot was the most common wheel diameter at Llyn Cerrig Bach, but one wheel four foot across was included and there were five with a diameter of 2ft. 6ins.

The naves or hubs of such wheels are seldom found, but from Llyn Cerrig Bach there are eight or nine metal rings, about 5ins. in diameter, which would have fitted round the wooden naves to prevent their splitting. There are three complete nave-hoops of iron and four ornamental ones of bronze (35 - 38), which would have covered functional iron ones. One of these narrow iron bands (39) was in fact found, though it is rather too small to have fitted under any of the surviving bronze ones. The shape and decoration of the bronze bands can be very closely paralleled by some from Read's Cavern, Mendip, dated to the first century B.C.[122]

The wheel was kept in position by a metal pin passed through a hole in the axle and secured with a wire wound round each end. Two of these linchpins (42 and 43) were found at Llyn Cerrig Bach; as with so many of the chariot fittings, a full set was not recovered. 42 is an elegant piece, perhaps belonging to one of the chariots with bronze nave hoops, for the date of both could lie within the first century B.C. It has a bronze head and foot and an iron shank. This design was popular for a long time, occurring in the Arras grave in the second century B.C., and in the Stanwick hoard dated to around 50 A.D.[123] 43, made entirely of iron, is much simpler with a large ring head and an upturned foot. It belongs to a type found in the south of England during the first century B.C. and the beginning of the first century A.D.[124]

---

[120] The wheel is an attribute of certain Celtic gods. It is conceivable that wheels alone might have been offered at the sacred pool.
[121] Fox. 1946/7. 75-6, and S. Piggott. PSAS. LXXXVII. 1952-3. 12.
[122] *Proc. Bristol Univ. Spelaeological Soc.* I. 1920. 13-4. Two D-sectioned iron rings were found by Mr. W. O. Roberts of Rhosneigr between Llyn Cerrig Bach and the sea. It is impossible to say whether or not these simple objects are ancient.
[123] Arras: I. M. Stead. *The Le Tène Cultures of Eastern Yorkshire.* 1965. 33. fig. 15, no. 1. Stanwick: M. MacGregor. PPS. XXVIII. 1962. 46, nos. 75-7 and fig. 11.
[124] List in Fox 1946/7. 79.

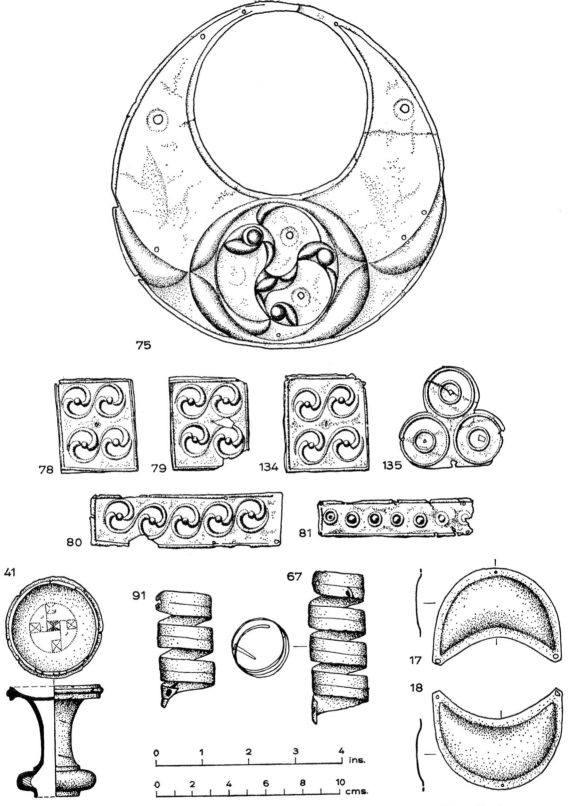

FIG. 84 — Llyn Cerrig Bach: pieces of decorative bronzework. (After Fox.)

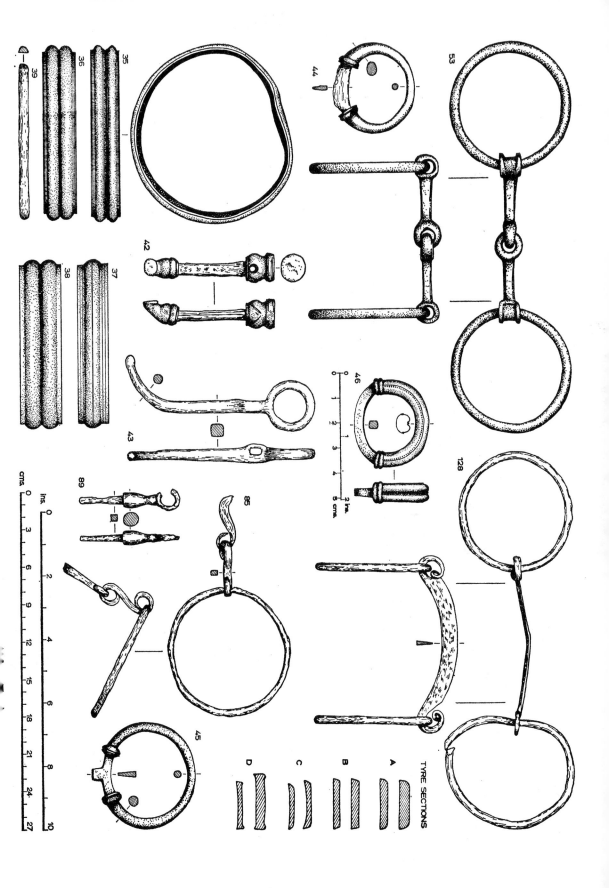

The body of the chariot would have been made entirely of wood or other perishable materials, so direct evidence for its size and shape have seldom, if ever, survived.[125] The only evidence available, therefore, is the representation of chariots, often schematic, on coins and gravestones, and the references, usually obscure, in early Irish literature. The distance between the tyres in chariot burials suggests a width of a little over 3ft.; the bodywork was probably square. The frame must have been of wood, but the floor may have been of stretched hide which would reduce some of the inevitable bumping and jolting. All the representations show low side panels, often with a double arcade, wooden framed, and probably filled with wickerwork. The chariot was obviously open at the back, but our information about the front is less satisfactory. Some Italian carvings suggest a curved and relatively high front panel,[126] as does the peculiar shaped hand-rail from Mont Eribus I, Belgium.[127] On the other hand, the position of the extended body in chariot burials and Caesar's references to charioteers who can run up the pole must surely indicate that in many types of chariot the front was open.[128]

It seems probable that the charioteer sat or crouched in the chariot, but the warrior is usually shown standing where it must have been very difficult to keep one's balance. Sir Cyril Fox suggested that there must have been hand-holds at the back, but these are not shown on any known representation. These side panels may have been embellished with metal plaques and such-like decoration, and it is more than likely that the small embossed strips and squares from Llyn Cerrig Bach (78 - 81, 134, 135, Fig. 84) had been nailed onto some part of a chariot frame. The very slight curve of the motifs on the strips suggests that they might have been placed on the arcaded side panels.

These thin bronze plates have been mechanically embossed with a die stamp. The regularity and formality of these designs contrast strongly with the lively asymmetrical patterns of the earlier art style exemplified by the crescentic plaque and the shield boss. Such rather dull decoration first appeared in this country with the Belgae, whose art had been strongly influenced by Rome, and in the succeeding centuries the style extended its influence over the native craftsmen in most parts of Britain. Embossed strips very similar to the ones from Llyn Cerrig Bach have been found in Belgic contexts in the south of England and in later, Romano-British, contexts at sites such as Lydney in Gloucestershire.[129] The chariot from

---

[125] Several studies of this problem have been made: Fox. 1946/7. 23-7; Piggott. *Ant.* XXVI. 1952. 87; Marien. *La Periode de La Tène en Belgique*: *le groupe de la Haine.* 1961, 173-8; Powell *in* Foster and Alcock (edd) *Culture and Environment.* 1963, 153-69; Stead. *Ant.* XXXIX. 1965. 259-65; Greene, lecture delivered to CBA conference on the problems of the Iron Age in the Irish Sea area, Cardiff. 1969. (Publication forthcoming).

[126] Stead. *op. cit.*

[127] Marien. *op. cit.* A peculiar shaped iron bar from Llyn Cerrig Bach (137) might be part of such a hand rail.

[128] Caesar. *de Bello Gallico.* IV. xxxiii.

[129] List and references in Fox 1946/7. 89.

which these decorations came must therefore be amongst the latest offerings at the lake.

The Celtic chariots were pulled by two small horses or ponies. The horse bones from the chariot burial at Arras, Yorkshire, indicated an animal of 13 hands, while the bones from Llyn Cerrig Bach itself suggest a pony of less than 12 hands.[130] The ponies were harnessed to the chariot by a central pole and a yoke, a system which was clearly adapted from ox carts and which had a very long ancestry in Egypt, Mesopotamia and Europe. Oxen pull from the top of the shoulder and the power is transmitted directly to the yoke. Horses, on the other hand, pull from the chest, so the neckband with which they were attached to the yoke would tend to strangle them and must certainly have reduced their performance. It is surprising, therefore, that it is not until the Middle Ages that the horse collar came into general use. Because this yoke harness is so inefficient, Sir Cyril Fox suggested that it might have been supplemented by traces from the lower part of the collar to a swingletree, or to the front of the chariot. These traces would transmit some of the pull and reduce the strain on the neck. Certain small hooks and rings from some chariot burials are suggestive of such traces, but the fact that this harness is never shown on any chariot representations in which reins and such like are clearly drawn, casts some doubt on this interpretation.[131]

The tip of the central pole from one of the chariots at Llyn Cerrig Bach has survived. The pole had been made from hawthorn or cherry wood, and the curved end had been sheathed with iron plates, strengthening it at the point where an iron bar had been passed through.[132] The yoke, attached to this bar by lashings, would have been of wood, probably padded and covered with leather. The metal fittings which survive suggest that two kinds of yoke were present: one with a smooth curve and upturned ends, a type which does not seem to have required the use of terrets or rein guides, and a peaked variety surmounted by four terrets through which the reins were passed.

The evidence for the first type of yoke is incomplete; only one of the decorative end caps survives (41, Fig. 84). This piece was interpreted by Sir Cyril Fox as a hand-hold, on analogy with a similar cap attached to a curved bronze horn from the chariot burial at Waldalgesheim, Germany.[133] However, the position of the Waldalgesheim horn on the chariot was not known, and a more recent study has suggested that these horns can best be compared to the upturned wooden knobs on the complete yoke from

[130] Arras: *Arch.* LX. 1906. 280.
       Llyn Cerrig Bach: Fox 1946/7. 97. Appendix I by L. F. Cowley.
[131] The clearest representation of harness is on the Padua gravestone. (*Germania* XLVI. 1968. Pl. 39). *See* Littauer. *Ant.* XLII. 1968. 27-31 for a discussion of some of the problems of horse harness.
[132] Detailed drawings in Fox 1946/7. 23, Fig. 12 and Pl. VI.
[133] Fox. 1946/7. 15-17. They were previously thought to be axle-caps. See also: S. Piggott. *Ant. J.* XLIX. 1969. 378-81.

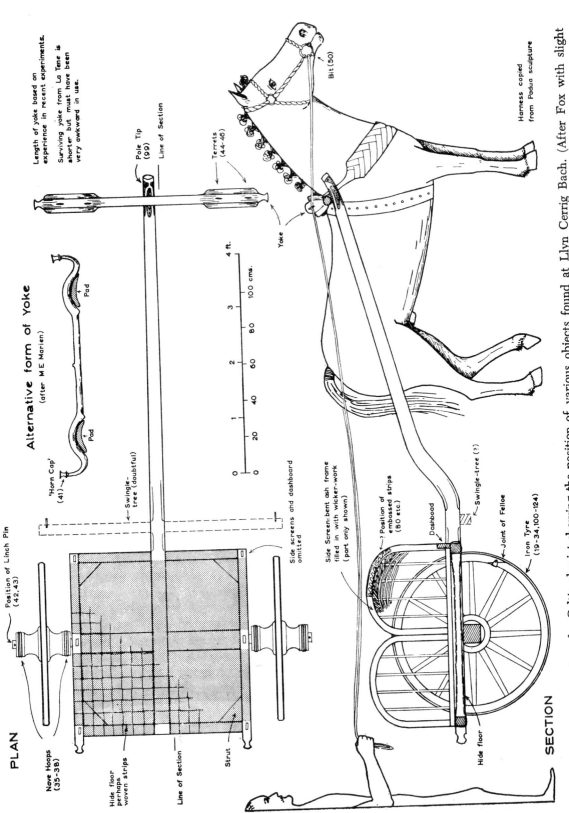

Length of yoke based on experience in recent experiments.

Surviving yoke from La Tene is shorter but must have been very awkward in use.

Pole Tip (99)

Line of Section

Terrets (44-45)

Yoke

Bit (50)

Harness copied from Padua sculpture

Alternative form of Yoke
(after M E Marien)

'Horn Cap' (41)

Pad

Pad

Swingle-tree (doubtful)

4 ft.

3

100 cms.

2

80

60

1

40

20

0

0

Side screens and dashboard omitted

Side Screen: bent ash frame filled in with wicker-work (part only shown)

? Position of embossed strips (80 etc.)

Dashboard

Swingle-tree (?)

Joint of Felloe

Iron Tyre (19-34, 100-124)

Hide floor

SECTION

PLAN

Position of Linch Pin (42, 43)

Nave Hoops (35-38)

Hide floor perhaps woven strips

Line of Section

Strut

Fig. 86 — Reconstruction of a Celtic chariot showing the position of various objects found at Llyn Cerrig Bach. (After Fox with slight modifications based on more recent discoveries.)

La Tène.[134] The upswept ends would prevent the reins from slipping down.

In shape and decoration 41 is a distinctively British version of the cap. Its elegant profile and concave top can be paralleled on a cap from Brentford, Essex, where the top is decorated with a raised pattern in the early Waldalgesheim style, which would suggest a date in the third or second centuries B.C.[135] The swastika decoration on the one from Llyn Cerrig Bach is a motif that appears on the famous Battersea shield, which may have been made in the first century B.C.[136] However, yokes of this kind continued in use up to the Roman conquest, for a cap of this type has been found at Maiden Castle, Dorset, in levels dating from 25 - 45 A.D. The main area of distribution is in southern England, in the south-east and in the Somerset area.[137]

The number of terrets from Llyn Cerrig Bach is surprisingly small, considering that each chariot should have had a set of four or five. Only three were found and they all must have come from different vehicles (Fig. 85). They are all of basically the same type; a ring with a flattened bar (in the case of 44, made of iron), which would have been embedded in the leather yoke cover. These rings stood upright on the top of the yoke and the reins passing through them would cause considerable wear on one side. Such rubbing is visible on 44 and on 46, suggesting that the latter is, in fact, a terret in spite of its small size.[138]

Of the three, 44 is the earliest and can be paralleled in the chariot burial from Hunmanby, Yorkshire, dating from the second century B.C. 45, with its projecting tongue, is a type found chiefly in the south-west of Britain at the beginning of the first century A.D. A more elaborate version of it appears in the Stanwick hoard from Yorkshire, which was hidden in about 50 A.D. 46 is probably another import from the south-west where the frilled decoration was particularly popular.[139] This same technique of joining bronze sheet is seen again in the bronze-covered iron bit, number 49 (Fig. 87), and was employed by the craftsmen at the Meare Lake Village, near Glastonbury. The manufacture of 46 is, in fact, peculiarly complicated. It must have been made on a foundation of three iron bars then covered with three separate sheets of bronze, all the joins embellished by tiny, regular punch marks, and the whole thing finally cast onto the bar.[140]

The only surviving parts of the horse harness are the metal bits, most of them beautifully made and obviously pieces of great value. 51 has a setting for a stud on one side only, a clear indication of its use on a two-horse vehicle. Although the others are symmetrical, it is almost certain that they, too, belonged to chariot ponies, for the Celts in Britain seldom rode horses.

[134] M. E. Marien. *La Periode de La Tène en Belgique*: *le groupe de la Haine*. 1961. 173, Fig. 66 where the yoke from La Tène is also illustrated.
[135] Illustrated in T. G. E. Powell. *Prehistoric Art*. 1966. 204. Pl. 198.
[136] Illustrated. *op. cit.* 239. Pl. 246.
[137] List and references in Fox. 1946/7. 77-8.
[138] Some of the Continental terrets are even smaller. Marien *op. cit.* 50, Fig. 21 and 176.
[139] List and references in Fox 1946/7. 79-80.
[140] Fox 1946/7. 37 and a letter from Dr. Plenderleith in the NMW.

There are several types of bits present, and the group may represent a considerable time range although in the present state of knowledge it is difficult to ascribe any single example to a particular date.[141] The ten or eleven three-link bits fall into three classes. One, number 55, made of solid bronze throughout, is an Irish type, distinguished from the British versions by having both holes in the side links in the same plane. It is a good example of Raftery's Type I which seems to have originated in north-east Ireland.[142] Since the exact chronology of the Irish Iron Age remains obscure, it is not possible to suggest a closer dating than 150 B.C. - 50 A.D.

The other two classes are both of British manufacture for they all have studs to prevent the rings turning in the loops and to restrict the area of wear.[143] This is a feature which does not appear on the Continent, even on the three-link bits from the Marne area which seem to be ancestral to the British series. Those in the first class, which includes 47, 48 and 49, are made of iron plated with bronze. In the case of 49 the side loops are plated, while the rings are covered with bronze sheet which has been joined by a decorative frilling technique similar to that used on terret 46. It is likely that both pieces were made in south-west England.

The second class are made entirely of bronze; the mouthpieces are cast solid, the rings are tubular and hollow like old-fashioned curtain rings. This type is represented by 50 and 51 and by four or five unattached rings which must have belonged to similar bits. One, 86, was considered to be a bracelet by Sir Cyril Fox because it is unusually small, but a bracelet would seem to be out of place in such a masculine and military assemblage as that from Llyn Cerrig Bach.[144]

Sir Cyril Fox suggested that there was a chronological difference between the iron bits and the bronze ones. He believed the iron ones to be earlier, since both the material and the simple design of the side loops associate them more closely with the Arras-type bits found in second century B.C. chariot graves in Yorkshire, whence the type is believed to have developed in Britain. The bronze ones, he suggested, were manufactured in south-west England, an area with local supplies of copper and tin, at a later date, evidenced by the more elaborate moulding of the side-loops.

More recent work on Iron Age bits has not adequately replaced the scheme outlined by Fox in 1946, but it has cast some doubt on the unitary nature of the line of development which he postulated. He himself recognised this when he pointed out that 49 is stylistically closer to 50 and 51 than to the other iron ones, in spite of its material, while the

[141] J. B. Ward Perkins. PPS. V. 1939. 173-92; Fox 1946/7. 27-34; J. Barber and J. V. S. Megaw. PPS. XXIX. 1963. 206-13; I. M. Stead. *The La Tène Cultures of Eastern Yorkshire.* 1965. 37-42.
[142] Not fully published. List in PPS. III. 1937. 427.
[143] No. 49 may not have had studs, but it is too badly damaged for certainty.
[144] Fox. 1946/7. 90.

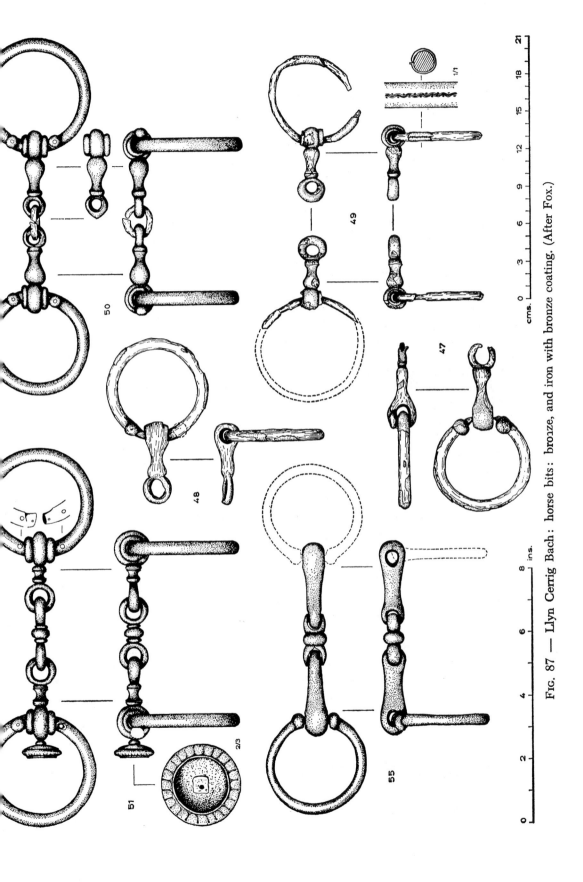

FIG. 87 — Llyn Cerrig Bach: horse bits: bronze, and iron with bronze coating. (After Fox.)

distinction in date has been further eroded by Dr. I. M. Stead in his recent study of the Yorkshire chariot burials.[145] It would seem, therefore, that all the more decorative of the Llyn Cerrig Bach bits may be of roughly the same date: manufactured during the first century B.C., perhaps not long after 100 B.C., in the south-west of England, where Bredon Hill, Gloucestershire, and Glastonbury, Somerset, can produce generally similar types.[146]

There is only one two-link bit (53) in the collection (Fig. 85).[147] It is very plain, made of solid bronze and may be a local product. Two-link bits are common in Iron Age contexts on the Continent, but are surprisingly rare in Britain. They are found in quantity only in the south-west of England, where they seem to date mainly from the first century B.C. and later.[148] They have a striking design an "eared" side-loop which may be recognised in its simplest form at Llyn Cerrig Bach. Another bit of this kind, rather more elaborate, was found at Carneddau Hengwm, Merioneth, which hints at a Welsh manufacture for some of this class.[149]

There is at least one plain iron bit (128, Fig. 85) in the deposit. The mouthpiece is a single curved bar with scroll terminals, which must have made it rather unpleasant for the horse. Similar bars were found at Ham Hill, a defended settlement in Somerset, and in the Lesser Garth Cave, Glamorgan, together with a group of Belgic bronzes.[150] Another ring with two S-curved links (85) has been identified as part of a bit;[151] with a third link it would be a suitable size, but the position of the wear on the ring precludes this identification, though it does not make it any easier to suggest what it might have been. The illustration shows the angle at which the link sits best in this worn notch (Fig. 85).

The rough bit and the iron strap junctions (56 and 57 — only one illustrated, Fig. 88), which are also paralleled at Ham Hill, do not look as if they had come from chariot harness, but rather from some sort of working cart. The tongs (131 and 132), sickle blades (65 and 144), and the object that may be a sort of palette knife (141), also imply that offerings might be made by people in the lower ranks of society, for it was not only the spoils of war which were acceptable to the spirits of the pool. Such tools must have been as valuable to the farmers and blacksmiths who had owned them as the swords were to the warriors. Their presence at Llyn Cerrig Bach foreshadows the peaceful nature of the later votive hoards such as those found in the south of Scotland.[152] These date from the end of the first century A.D. when the Roman invasion had put an end to the

[145] Stead. *op. cit.*
[146] List and references in Fox 1946/7. 83.
[147] There is a slight doubt about the provenance of this bit which was picked up from a part of the airfield outside, but close to, the area where the Llyn Cerrig peat had been dumped. Fox 1946/7. 83.
[148] Ward Perkins. PPS. V. 1939. 174-5, but see comment in Fox 1946/7. 33. note 2.
[149] Ward Perkins. *op. cit.* 175, Fig. 2.
[150] Ham Hill: Fox 1946/7. 34-5; Lesser Garth: Savory. *Arch. Camb.* 1966. 33-4. fig. 2, no. 2.
[151] Fox 1946/7. 34, 90.
[152] S. Piggott. PSAS. LXXXVII. 1952-3. 1-50.

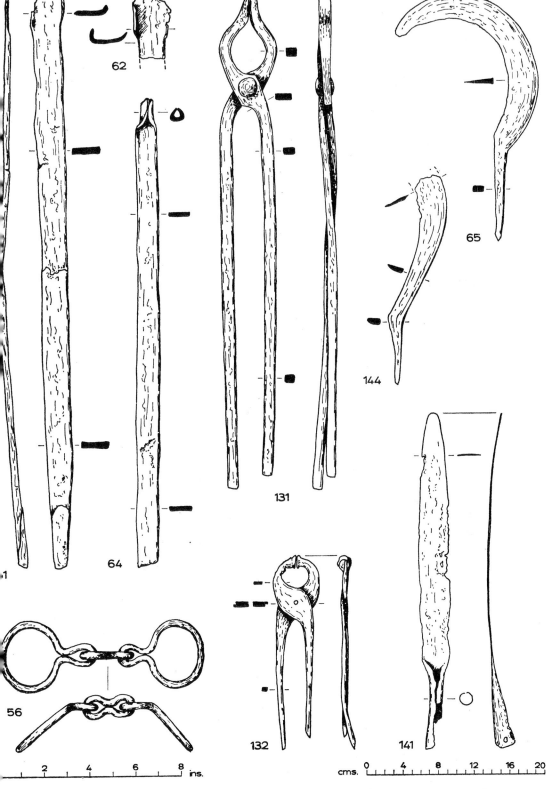

62

65

144

131

56

132

141

2   4   6   8   ins.

cms.   0   4   8   12   16   20

ɪɢ. 88 — Llyn Cerrig Bach: iron currency bars, tongs, sickles, strap junction and ? palette knife.
(After Fox.)

aristocratic life of cattle raiding and tribal warfare, reflected in the chariots and weapons at Llyn Cerrig Bach, but had not killed the old traditions, nor altered the religious practices.

Both the large tongs (131) and the smaller " gripping " tongs (132) must have been in use in a local smithy. Their design is so functional that it has scarcely changed during the last two thousand years, even down to the detail of having one shorter handle to enable an oval ring to be pushed over the end to hold the tongs closed. Such tongs first appear in this country during the Iron Age, when the art of smithing was introduced. It is probable that each chieftain's household would include at least one smith to make and repair equipment and weapons.

The balanced sickle is another Iron Age introduction to this country. The native Late Bronze Age versions were rather clumsier, with a profile similar to that of 144. This blade (144) has been interpreted as part of a scythe, an implement generally held to have been introduced by the Romans.[153] Since so little of the blade survives, it would seem unwise to claim that it proves a pre-Roman currency for the type. The widespread adoption of well-balanced sickles like 65 may be connected with an intensification of cereal-growing, which is reflected by the number of huge corn-storage pits on Iron Age settlement sites in southern England. The discovery of such sickles at places like Dinorben and Llyn Cerrig Bach shows that arable farming was not neglected even in highland areas, although it may not have been undertaken on such a large scale.[154]

The remains of two sheet bronze cauldrons were found (Fig. 89). Both had been much patched before they had been thrown into the lake, which suggests that they had been in actual use in some chieftain's household. The Celtic chieftains were renowned for their hospitality. It was a matter of both pride and duty for them to provide great feasts for their followers and guests, feasts at which vast quantities of food and drink were consumed while the bards or poets eulogised the great achievements of their leader and his ancestors.[155] The hearth and all its accoutrements, the firedogs, grid irons, and cauldrons with elaborate chains and supports, became the focus and symbol of the power of the chieftain and his ability to reward his followers, so it is not surprising to find these things in situations where their significance is obviously ritual. The ritual use of the cauldron is far older than the Iron Age in these islands, for most of the beautiful Late Bronze Age examples from Ireland have been found in bogs, and this aura of magic continues beyond the Roman period, to be incorporated in the myth and legend of the Mabinogion.[156]

The cauldrons are of different designs; 77 must have been hemispherical and belongs to a small group of globular cauldrons exemplified

---

[153] Piggott. *op. cit.* 9.
[154] Willoughby Gardner and H. N. Savory. *Dinorben.* 1964. 156, Fig. 24, no. 5 and 158-9. It is from the Romano-British levels of this site, which also produced a plough-share.
[155] e.g. Diodorus V. xxviii.
[156] e.g. in the story of Branwen.

by one from Battersea; 76 is shouldered and belongs to a group known as the " Spettisbury type ", although, unlike the others, it is made from a single sheet of metal.[157] Both of them have lost their iron or bronze rims and handles, although on 76 the position of the escutcheons which would have held the ring handles is clear. They have left a patch of lighter patination on the bronze. One of these escutcheons had been torn away in antiquity and the break had been repaired with a strangely shaped strip of bronze. It seems to have been a peculiarity of Celtic craftsmanship that they would always emphasise a repair, often profusely decorating the added metal, even if it wrecked the original design.[158] Thus the specially cut repair strip on the cauldron confirms its pre-Roman date, although such a single-piece shouldered cauldron would normally belong to the fourth century A.D. The simple Battersea type cannot be dated closely, having been made both before and after the Roman invasion. Here one may simply say that these cauldrons must belong to the later group of finds from Llyn Cerrig Bach.

There are surprisingly few things in the Llyn Cerrig Bach deposit which were manufactured in Ireland. The three-link bit has already been mentioned; the only other object brought from Ireland is the broken trumpet (74). The surviving piece is part of the lower half of a large semi-circular trumpet of a well-known Irish type of which the one from Navan, Co. Armagh, is the best known.[159] The disc at the mouth of the trumpet from Navan has embossed decoration which is similar to that on the Torrs champfrein (or pony cap) and is related to the early style of La Tène art in these islands, showing that this type of trumpet had evolved by the early part of the second century B.C. This same dating may be applied to the Llyn Cerrig Bach trumpet because of the use of a rocked tracer technique on the decorated repair-strip.[160] The small length of decoration on the trumpet itself is so worn that the technique used cannot be distinguished.

The trumpet is made from a tube of thin bronze riveted along its length to an inner strip of thin metal. The edge-to-edge seam is in the closest possible contact and at the broken end is brazed to form a smooth surface for decoration. This change of technique may have caused a slight leak which was covered by the repair strip, no doubt put on by the original craftsman. The cast bronze knob covered the junction between the two halves of the trumpet which, when complete, could have been over 4ft. long.

These trumpets have seldom been found in any informative context,

[157] List and references in Fox 1946/7. 42-4, 88 and in Piggott. PSAS. LXXXVII. 1952-3. 12-6, map. p. 18 and list, pp. 40-1.
[158] e.g. on the Torrs Champfrein, on the Thames helmet (Fox. *Pattern and Purpose*. 1958. 23, Fig. 16 and 50, Fig. 36b.) and on the trumpet from Llyn Cerrig Bach itself.
[159] T. G. E. Powell. *The Celts* (Ancient Peoples and Places). 1958. Pl. 44. The type is shown in the famous Roman sculpture of the ' Dying Gaul '. (illustrated *op. cit.* Pl. 3).
[160] First noticed by H. N. Savory. BBCS. XXII. 1966. 94.

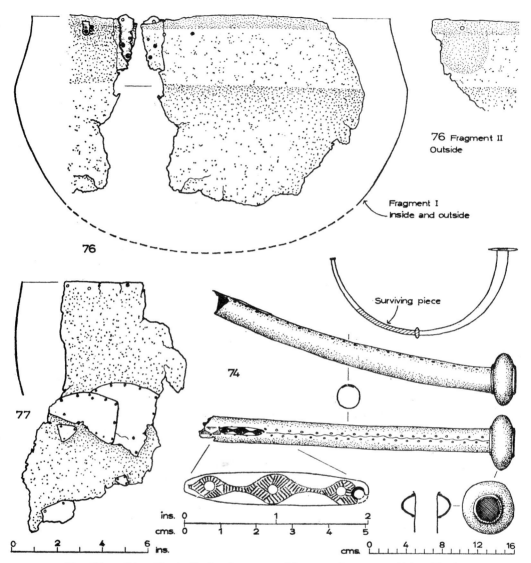

Fig. 89 — Llyn Cerrig Bach: bronze cauldrons and trumpet. (After Fox.)

but it is likely that they would have been used on ceremonial occasions (the Gundestrup cauldron shows a carnyx, an animal-headed trumpet, being blown during a sacrifice),[161] or before a battle as part of the general tumult and noise which heralded all military engagements amongst the Celts. Like so many things, they are not in themselves an innovation; many fine Late Bronze Age trumpets have been found in Ireland.[162]

The spirals of bronze ribbon (67 - 72, 91 and 133, Fig. 84) may also have

[161] Illustrated: Piggott. *The Druids*. (Ancient Peoples and Places). 1968. Pl. 1.
[162] J. M. Coles. PPS. XXIX. 1963. 326-56.

been part of ceremonial equipment, perhaps staves or wands of office. They had clearly been nailed onto some circular wooden object about 1in. in diameter, and a piece of wood still attached to 67 showed this to have been ash.[163] Since this wood has properties which would make it very suitable for chariot building, it is possible that these strips may have been wrapped round part of the frame. This interpretation is to some extent supported by the presence of a similar spiral of iron in a chariot burial from Armentières, northern France,[164] but the original comparison with the decorated bronze binding of a staff from the Romano-British temple at Fairley Heath, Surrey, may be closer to the truth.[165] The four staves for which we have evidence at Llyn Cerrig Bach, therefore, may be presumed to have played some part in the religious ceremonies on the site.

The long plain bars of iron, such as Nos. 61 - 64 and 130 (Fig. 88), have been interpreted as currency bars.[166] Although coins were already in use amongst the tribes of south-east England at the time of Caesar's arrival, he speaks of iron bars in use as a form of money among tribes further west.[167] Archaeology bears him out in general terms, but it is sometimes difficult to be sure which of the various types of iron bars are to be considered currency. Two classes may be distinguished: the sword-shaped bars found in Wessex (Durotrigan tribal area) and the spit-shaped bars, which predominate in the Malvern area and parts of Somerset. Both these types can be fairly confidently interpreted as currency because they are frequently found in hoards and are more or less consistent in weight, especially the sword-shaped ones which weigh from 20 to 22 ounces. A third class, "plough-share bars", can be regarded as currency with much less certainty. They are wider and more robust than either of the other classes and they have raised flanges or wings at the blunt end like those on the contemporary plough-shares.[168] Moreover, there is a considerable variation in length and weight amongst bars of this class, which are usually found singly or in possibly votive situations such as rivers. However, even the widest examples are a good deal narrower and much longer than functional plough-shares, suggesting that these should be regarded as symbolic shares, specially made for religious occasions, perhaps in connection with fertility.

There were five of these bars at Llyn Cerrig Bach. One (64) belongs to the spit-shaped group which may be looked upon as genuine currency. It is very similar to those found in the great hoard from the Malverns which contained about 300 bars tied up in two bundles.[169] 61 and 62 are good

---

[163] Fox. 1946/7. 98. Appendix II by H. A. Hyde.
[164] M. E. Marien. *La Periode de La Tène en Belgique; le groupe de la Haine.* 1961. 177, fig. 68, no. 10.
[165] R. G. Goodchild. *Ant. J.* XVIII. 1938. 391-6. Pl. LXXVII, LXXVIII.
[166] For a recent discussion of these bars, their classification and use, *see* D. Allen. PPS. XXXIII. 1967. 307-35.
[167] Caesar. *de Bello Gallico.* V. xii. iv. (Discussed: Allen. *op. cit.* 319).
[168] For plough-shares *see* F. G. Payne *Agricultural History Rev.* V. 1957. 74-84 and F. A. Aberg. *Gwerin.* I. 1956-7. 171-81.
[169] Allen. *op. cit.* 332.

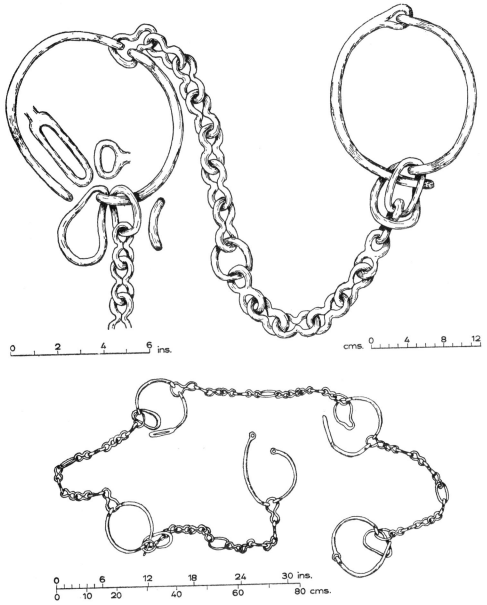

FIG. 90 — Llyn Cerrig Bach: iron gang-chain. Detail of neck-rings and locking device above. (After Fox.)

examples of the third class of bar, and the two fragmentary ones were probably similar to them. They may be compared to the one found in the Thames at Datchet, Bucks.[170] Whether these objects are currency or are specially made votive pieces, their presence at Llyn Cerrig Bach implies a

---

[170] Allen. *op. cit.* 333.

considerable journey beyond their areas of normal distribution which, for both classes, lay in the south of England. The same may be said of a great many of the fine things from Llyn Cerrig Bach. Although this may be partly due to an absence of excavation in Wales, it cannot be the whole answer and we must accept that, for reason which we cannot fully understand, a small lake in Anglesey received rich offerings from distant people for a period of over one hundred and fifty years.

Amongst the objects thrown into the lake at what may have been the final ceremony were two iron gang-chains (59 and 60). One is broken but seems to have been almost identical to the complete chain which was designed to hold five captives. The chains were made with five hinged neck-rings linked by a length of chain which allowed a distance of approximately 2ft. between each man. The neck-rings were closed by passing a pear-shaped loop through the elongated hole in one end and then running the entire chain through this loop (see Fig. 90). The last man presumably would have been tied to the man in charge of the party. The chain is made up from pinched loops which could prevent it twisting and getting entangled in use.[171] Both the design and manufacture of these chains is of extremely high quality, a quality which has stood the test of time, as their use in the twentieth century has shown.

FIG. 91 — Captives in a gang-chain. (Reproduced from Sir Cyril Fox, *Pattern and Purpose*, 1958, by permission of the National Museum of Wales.)

These chains are of Belgic origin, and date from the first half of the first century A.D. The Belgae, who came to Britain partly as the result of Roman activity in their homelands in northern France, are known to have played a large part in the slave trade, selling captives from the British tribes they conquered as slaves to the Romans. Very similar chains have come from Belgic contexts in south-east England, and they are occasionally seen on captives depicted on Roman and Romano-Celtic sculpture in Europe.[172] It is more than likely that other tribes in Britain took part in this lucrative trade in slaves, but they do not seem to have used these distinctive gang-chains. Thus the presence of the chains at Llyn Cerrig

[171] *See* technical report in Fox 1946-7. 38, 84.
[172] List and references in Fox 1946/7. 84-5.

Bach is strong evidence for direct contact with the kingdoms of south-eastern England in the period just before the Roman conquest. This affinity, whatever it may have meant in human and political terms, is strengthened by the presence of other Belgic objects such as the decorated bronze strips (78 and others), with their formal, almost Romanised, patterns, the scabbard mount (10), and the bronze cauldrons (76 and 77).

In searching for an explanation of how this great collection of military equipment found its way to Anglesey, it would be tempting to emphasise this last group, belonging to the final decades of native independence, and suggest that the weapons and chariots were thrown into the lake as a last despairing gesture by groups of southern refugees who had fled from the Roman advance and had hoped, perhaps, to establish a new centre of resistance in Anglesey. While it may be true that some of the latest objects had been brought northwards by such refugees, the power of the sanctuary at Llyn Cerrig Bach must have been established for a long time before their arrival. The earliest finds, the swords, shields and harness of second century B.C. date, were offered in this pool long before there was any Roman threat to artificially inflate the political importance of distant western areas.

The trophies which were traditionally dedicated to the gods were presumably won in relatively local inter-tribal fighting; the victorious side returning home with their booty to be offered to their own tribal god. In spite of the apparent poverty of the settlements in Anglesey and in North Wales as a whole, some very fine pieces of aristocratic equipment have been found in the area, including the Cerrigydrudion hanging bowl, the Moel Hiraddug shield, and the shields from Tal y Llyn.[173] It is not inconceivable, therefore, that many of the splendid weapons found at Llyn Cerrig Bach may have been captured in battles between local chieftains.

If this were so, the fact that so much of the material seems to have been manufactured in Somerset and beyond must imply either that Welsh chieftains imported a high proportion of their equipment or that their raiding expeditions took them a long way from the borders of their own territories. Both these implications may be doubted. The individuality of the North Welsh shield bosses and the high quality of their design suggest that skilled craftsmen were available within Wales itself to supply local needs. As regards long-distance raids, archaeology is inevitably ambiguous, but, in view of the spontaneous and disorganised nature of Celtic warfare and the liquidity of their political alliances, it is unlikely that large-scale campaigns could have been undertaken.[174] The number of chariots is another factor which suggests that the offerings at Llyn Cerrig Bach are something over and above the spoils of local wars. Although Tacitus mentions the use of chariots in the battle of Mons Graupius in Scotland,[175] they do not feature

[173] *See* H. N. Savory *Early Iron Age Art in Wales.* NMW. 1968.
[174] Strabo. IV. iv. 2.
[175] Tacitus. *Agricola.* xxxv.

in the records of any Welsh campaigns, and this is not surprising in view
of the unsuitable nature of the terrain.

One has to admit, therefore, that the small lake among the rocks and
dunes of Traeth Cymyran had rather more than local sanctity, and that
offerings might be made there by, or on behalf of, people whose homes
were two hundred miles or more away. How this spot came to have such a
supra-tribal significance is, of course, quite unknown. Its powers must have
been established during the second century B.C., if not earlier, long before
we have any classical writing relevant to the area which might help to
illuminate this kind of problem, which can scarcely be solved by archaeology
alone. By the end of the period covered by the offerings in the lake there
are, however, a few classical references which imply that Anglesey was a
religious centre of some importance, and was a seat, perhaps even the main
seat, of the Celtic priesthood in Britain, the notorious Druids.[176]

Any connection between the sacred pool of Llyn Cerrig Bach and the
Druids is speculative, but the link is attractive since the Druids of Anglesey,
who may have wielded power and influence far beyond the borders of
Wales, might well be responsible for gathering together such a varied and
impressive collection as that found in the lake. These Celtic priests have
been surrounded by a great deal of myth and legend, not least in the more
recent past, which has hindered the true understanding of their position
and activities.[177] Most of the classical writers base their comments upon
the early ethnographical writing of Posidonius, a Greek historian and
geographer of the second century B.C., who appears to have had considerable first-hand knowledge of his subject.[178] It would seem that the Celtic
priesthood, who held a very high social position, was divided into three
groups: Druids; *vates*, or diviners and seers; and bards, who composed
eulogies and satires to accompany feasting and ceremonial. There is some
confusion between the spheres of activity of the first two groups; perhaps
that of the *vates* was restricted more to religious ceremonial and attendance
at sacrifices. Caesar implies that the Druids, in particular, wielded political
as well as religious power, and were a rallying point for national resistance

[176] The specific references occur in Tacitus. *Annals*. XIV. xxix-xxx and *Agricola* xiv
and xviii. He nowhere actually states that Anglesey was a noted centre of Druidic
power, though the political refugees that he mentions more than once may have included
many Druids. The description of Anglesey as the main seat of the British Druidic Order
is that of commentators influenced by the large part played by the Druids in the battle
to defend the island (actual involvement in warfare was exceptional among Druids) and
the unusually determined effort made by the Romans to wipe out the Order and prevent
their sacrifices after their victory. Recent commentators have pointed to the finds at
Llyn Cerrig Bach in support of their view. They may also have been more strongly
influenced than they would care to admit by the theories of the Rev. Henry Rowlands
(*Mona Antiqua Restauranta* 1723) and his school of thought. Although it is worth
pointing out that Tacitus does not actually say that Anglesey was a renowned religious
centre, the implications and conclusions drawn by most commentators are probably
true: the island may well have contained an exceptionally large and influential community
of Druids.

[177] The most recent general survey of the literary and archaeological evidence and of the
romantic legend is S. Piggott. *The Druids*. (Ancient Peoples and Places) 1868.

[178] J. J. Tierney. 'The Celtic Ethnography of Posidonius'. PRIA. 60. C. 1960. 189-275.

against Rome, though he may be suspected of over-emphasising this point to suit his own propaganda.[179]

The ranks of the Druids were recruited from among the sons of the nobility who underwent a long training in special " schools " sited deep in the forests. This learning was entirely oral, transmitted through long verse narratives. The content of these traditions is difficult to establish, but the philosophy is not likely to have been very sophisticated. The Celts clearly believed in a very literal form of life after death, evidenced by the elaborate equipment in their graves; in the efficacy of sacrifice; and in prophecy from entrails, human and animal. In all of this ritual and ceremonial the Druids would have been proficient. Classical writers also credit them with considerable knowledge of natural science and astronomy. The Coligny Calendar with its lunar months and complex system of lucky and unlucky days is no doubt the product of Druidic learning in this sphere.[180] It is thought by some that the Druids were the guardians of customary tribal law, but this is less certain, for it was usual for the chieftain to be the arbiter of quarrels and law-suits. Druids may well have acted as political advisers to the chiefs for their prestige was clearly very high. Another factor in their exercise of power was their mobility. Whereas the lower ranks of society were tied to the land, and even the chiefs and their warriors were more or less confined to their own territories, the three ranks of the priesthood seem to have moved from place to place at will.

This mobility and the knowledge of the wider scene which it implies may in part explain their political importance.[181] The Druids may well have been the only group with any national consciousness and, as such, would be a natural target for Roman attack, quite apart from the abhorrence which their participation in human sacrifice engendered amongst the Romans, who had abandoned this practice about a hundred years previously. Their political influence and mobility could be reflected in the far-flung connections implied by the material in deposits such as that found at Llyn Cerrig Bach.

In view of the existence of such an important sanctuary on the island it is strange that direct evidence for native cults, in the form of stone heads or statues, is rare in Anglesey, and, up till 1969, could be said to be totally absent. This absence could be due either to the thoroughness of the programme of destruction and extermination undertaken by the Romans who, though they might tolerate innocuous local cults, were determined to wipe out the Druidic Order, or to the comparatively impoverished condition of Wales during the Romano-British period. For it is to this later period,

[179] Caesar. *de Bello Gallico*. VI. xiii, xiv.
[180] T. G. E. Powell. *The Celts*. 1958. 274-5, and Pl. 76. E. MacNeill. *Erin*. X. 1923. 1-67.
[181] Compare the position of the Sanuiya Order in the recent history of North Africa. E. Evans-Pritchard. *The Sanusi of Cyrenaica*. 1949.

rather than to the pre-Roman Iron Age, that most of this religious sculpture in Britain belongs.[182]

Another factor in the paucity of archaeological evidence is the very nature of the Celtic holy places themselves.[183] Classical writers relate how the Celts used to gather for worship in woods and groves, by pools and at the sources of rivers. Although excavation has shown that such groves might occasionally be artificial, in the form of wooden enclosures with settings of large posts, it is clear that many were in natural woods. Furthermore, although the long history of votive offerings at Llyn Cerrig Bach indicates a long-standing tradition, it was not necessary for such sacred pools or springs to be marked by any special structure.

The Celtic interest in wells, springs, and rivers is manifest all over Europe and it appears that certain particularly vital rivers may have been worshipped as gods, or it may have been believed that their power epitomised that of the god. In either case, the number of beautiful and valuable objects which have been found in rivers, and the names given to these rivers, must be significant. One of the longest rivers in Anglesey waters the fertile south-eastern corner of the island and is called the Braint. This name is thought to be related to that of the goddess Brigantia, the patron of the powerful tribe of the Brigantes, who ruled most of the north of England at the time of the Roman conquest.[184] There is no other evidence for the worship of Brigantia in Anglesey, but since the survival of such evidence is extremely haphazard, especially in only marginally Romanised areas where inscriptions are not to be expected, such ancient place-names (and river names are often the most ancient) should not be neglected. The large number of holy wells on Anglesey may be mentioned in this context, although there has been no excavation to indicate a pre-Christian history for any of them.[185]

Another feature of Celtic religion which is widespread both on the Continent and in Britain is an almost obsessive interest in heads, either actual or representational. This interest and the attendant belief that the head symbolises the whole man (or god) can be found all over the world and, in Europe, dates back at least as far as the Mesolithic period; it is during the Celtic Iron Age, however, that it reaches its highest point. Classical writers record how Celtic warriors would decapitate their fallen enemies and return home with the heads to be displayed as trophies on the walls of their houses, and how the heads of certain especially redoubtable foes would be embalmed and preserved amongst the most valuable possessions of a chieftain. In addition to actual skulls which are frequently found at sanctuaries or thrown into sacred wells, it was customary to depict severed heads in stone or wood.

[182] See Anne Ross. Pagan Celtic Britain. 1967, for a comprehensive survey of this sculpture and the cults it served.
[183] op. cit. Chapter 1 and S. Piggott. The Druids. 1968. 54-89.
[184] E. Ekwall. English River Names. 1928. 51, quoted in Ross, op. cit. 21, 361.
[185] Most of them are listed in RCAM, Anglesey. 1937.

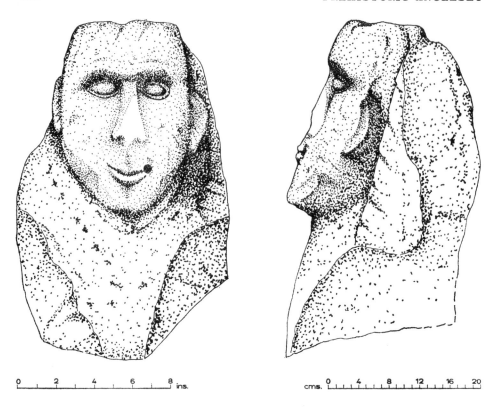

FIG. 92 — Stone head from Hendy, Llanfair Pwllgwyngyll.

A number of stone heads have been found which can be clearly recognised by certain attributes as those of divine beings. Some of these may be Janus heads, with two faces back to back, or may be three-faced, like the famous one from Corleck, Co. Cavan, while others may have a leaf crown or horns.[186] The identification of the individual gods represented is extremely difficult and, in most cases, impossible, but certain major groups can be recognised: gods and goddesses linked with the basic human concerns: love, war, fertility, health, and such like. Sometimes, however, the same god may be associated with several different aspects, and it seems that the chief tribal god should be seen as an all-powerful divinity caring in turn for all aspects of his tribe's welfare. The tribal god no doubt moved with the tribe when they conquered new areas; the Celtic goddesses, on the other hand, seem to have been more territorial, representing rather the fertility and power of a particular locality.

The only example of such a stone head from Anglesey has no obvious attributes of divinity, but on stylistic grounds it can be classed with other heads, considered to represent some local god, the focus of a small shrine, perhaps domestic, perhaps of wider significance.

[186] All these heads are discussed and illustrated in A. Ross. *Pagan Celtic Britain*. 1967.

The head, which is at present cemented onto the garden wall at Hendy, Llanfair Pwllgwyngyll (NGR SH/541725), unfortunately has no exact provenance.[187] It has been on the wall at Hendy for at least the last fifty years, and it is probable that it was originally found somewhere on the farm. The head has only recently been brought to the attention of archaeologists because, until a year or so ago, it was hidden in a hedge which grew behind the wall. When this hedge was cut down, the head was seen and photographed by Mrs. Holden, a cousin of the owners, Mr. and Mrs. T. Ollosson, who sent her photograph to the British Museum.

The head is carved from a triangular block of red sandstone which was very likely obtained near Lligwy.[188] The block is about 1ft. 6ins. high and the face carved on it is roughly life-sized. The shoulders and the back of the head have been left rough and the neck is barely indicated. The face, on the other hand, has been carefully and skilfully carved, and may have been painted or covered with a red clay.[189] The only damage is to the nose from which a large piece has been broken.

The most remarkable thing about the head is its strange twisted smile, unusual in Celtic sculpture in which the faces are often rather expressionless.[190] However, other details of the carving; the protruding eyes with their double outline, the beetling brow, the rather flat profile, the crescentic ears, and the narrow chin can all be paralleled in heads found in reputable Celtic settings. Amongst these the closest parallel is one from Laugharne, Carmarthenshire.[191] Although this has no true archaeological context, it may be assigned to an Iron Age rather than a Romano-British date, since it is carved on the top of a tall stone and may be compared to Continental pillar stones.

Another conspicuous feature of the Hendy head is the small hole, ⅜in. in diameter and ½in. - ¾in. deep, drilled in one side of the mouth. At first sight this might be taken for a modern addition, but exactly similar holes can be seen on a number of stone heads from Ireland and on a few from elsewhere. Since three of those concerned, Corleck, Co. Cavan, and the two from Greetland, Yorkshire, are three-faced heads, the genuine antiquity of this feature is not in doubt.[192] It is more difficult to suggest what it might signify; perhaps some pipe or branch might have been put in it for special ritual occasions. It is thought that the flattened top on many heads, including

[187] I am grateful to Dr. Anne Ross for drawing my attention to this previously unpublished head and to Mr. and Mrs. Ollosson for permission to draw and photograph it.
[188] I am grateful to Dr. David Jenkins, Dept. of Bio-Chemistry and Soil Science U.C.N.W. for giving me his opinion on this stone.
[189] Traces of paint have been found on a stone head from Gloucestershire, the paint used being a mixture of blood and charcoal. (ex info Dr. Anne Ross).
[190] But see the heads from Roquepertuse and Salzburg. (T. G. E. Powell. Prehistoric Art. 1966. 231, Pls. 232-3).
[191] A. Ross. Pagan Celtic Britain. 1967. Pl. 16a. and J. V. S. Megaw. Arch. Camb. 1967. 192-4. Pl. V.
[192] Corleck: J. Raftery. Prehistoric Ireland. 1951. Fig. 263, right, shows the face with the hole. Greetland: S. Jackson. Ant. XLII. 1968. 314-5. illustrated, Backpiece.

the one from Hendy, may have been for placing offerings. Some heads have been found which actually have a bowl-like hollow in the top.[193]

Although the bulk of the evidence suggests that the Hendy head represents some local Celtic diety and that it was probably carved during the pre-Roman Iron Age, it should not be forgotten that this dating is entirely based on stylistic comparisons. In an area where the Mediaeval sculpture is very simple and often rather crudely carved, such comparisons might be misleading. However, the angle of the head and the roughness of the neck and shoulders militate against its being a mediaeval church corbel, although a number of churches in Anglesey contain heads which are stylistically even less sophisticated.[194] In fact, the number of early pagan carvings which have found their way into Irish churches suggest that, far from the Hendy head being Mediaeval, some of the heads now in Anglesey churches may be pre-Christian in origin, though it must be admitted that none of them has any of the specific attributes of a Celtic head.

The later history of Iron Age Britain was to a large degree governed by the activities of the Romans in Europe. Caesar's Gallic wars, not surprisingly, caused a great upheaval amongst the Celtic tribes of France, many of whom sought help and often refuge among their cousins already established across the Channel. Thus the existence of Britain as a potential base for further hostilities was an ever-present threat to the projected Roman order in Gaul; its subjection became an inevitable target of Roman policy.

However, Caesar's campaign of 55 - 54 B.C., although a portent of what was to come, was not a major turning point in British history. Events in Rome itself necessitated his withdrawal from Britain before his initial conquests could be consolidated, and the flood of refugees continued unabated. In fact, recent work on the latest groups of Belgae in Kent suggests that they did not arrive in large numbers until about 50 B.C. and that their kingdoms in south-east England flourished chiefly in the period between the two Roman invasions.[195]

In 43 A.D., however, the Emperor Claudius initiated a serious attack on Britain with a large and well-supported army under the first governor, Aulus Plautius, who, before the end of his tenure of office in 47 A.D., had brought most of southern England under Roman control. It is possible that at first the Romans did not contemplate a military conquest of the whole of Britain but simply intended to protect their small but potentially rich south-eastern province by a system of alliances and buffer states among the tribes to the north and west of it. Such a buffer kingdom was established in the north of England, under Cartimandua, Queen of the Brigantes, but the policy was not achieved in Wales. Despite good relations built up from an early date with the Cornovii in the Shropshire area and the pro-Roman

[193] Ross. *op. cit.* Pl. 17.
[194] For a useful photgraphic survey of the stone heads on Anglesey churches *see* Hulbert Powell. TAAS. 1944. 19-48.
[195] A. Birchall. PPS. XXXI. 1965. 241-367.

attitude of the Demetae in south-west Wales, there was continuous trouble from the Silures in the south-east and the Deceangli and Ordovices in the north.

In 48 A.D., the second governor, P. Ostorius (Scapula), was campaigning in north-east Wales where his main adversaries were the Deceangli, who lived in Flintshire.[196] Since Tacitus says that he almost reached the Irish Sea,[197] it has been suggested that he was also fighting against the Ordovices of north-west Wales and that possibly his final objective may have been Anglesey, perhaps the stronghold of Druidism, certainly a *receptaculum perfugarum*. However, Scapula never reached Anglesey because a revolt among the Brigantes caused him to abandon the campaign and turn his attention to the north. It has even been suggested that this revolt in the north which saved Anglesey might have been engineered by the Druids. Some contacts with Brigantia are shown by pieces of northern metalwork in the ritual deposit at Llyn Cerrig Bach, but apart from this, evidence for such sophisticated diplomatic action is entirely lacking.[198]

It is difficult to know how much this campaign of 48 A.D. finally achieved in North Wales. Since the Romans were operating lead mines in Flintshire by 74 A.D., that area at least may have been genuinely pacified by Scapula. From 49 - 52/3 A.D. the Silures of South Wales occupied the attention of the Roman armies. Not only were the Silures themselves a particularly ferocious and war-like tribe, but their resistance was stiffened by the presence among them of Caractacus, who had been a chieftain of the Catuvellauni in the area north of London. After 47 A.D. he had been driven into exile rather than submit to the Romans, and since then had been a rallying point for resistance and rebellion. In 51 A.D. he and the Silures were defeated in a pitched battle somewhere in Montgomeryshire and he fled north to Brigantia, where Queen Cartimandua promptly handed him over to the Romans.

After Claudius's death in 54 A.D., and the accession of Nero, there seems to have been a period of uncertainty on the part of the Roman authorities, during which the whole future of the British province was in doubt and the activities of the governors were restricted to consolidating the southern part of the country. The decision to hold on to Britain seems to have been taken in 57 A.D., and campaigning began again with another attack on the Silures by Q. Veranius. Veranius died in the following year and was succeeded by Suetonius Paulinus who continued the campaigning in Wales.

By 60 A.D. Paulinus was in North Wales and, after successful fighting against the tribes on the mainland, he finally attacked Anglesey. His infantry were transported across the Straits in flat-bottomed boats, while the cavalry waded or swam. Tacitus vividly describes this scene, the final

[196] For this section I have leaned heavily on the work of Dr. Michael Jarrett, especially 'Early Roman Campaigns in Wales' *Arch. J.* CXXI. 1964. 23-39.
[197] Tacitus. *Annals.* XII. xxxii.
[198] Jarrett. *op. cit.* 25.

confrontation between the Roman army and the hard-core of the Celtic resistance defending their last stronghold.

" The shore was lined by a motley battle array. Women were seen rushing through the ranks of soldiers in wild disorder, dressed in black, with their hair dishevelled and brandishing flaming torches. Their whole appearance resembled the frantic rage of the Furies. The Druids were ranged in order, calling down terrible curses. The soldiers, paralysed by this strange spectacle, stood still and offered themselves as a target for wounds. But at last the promptings of the general — and their own rallying of each other — urged them not to be frightened of a mob of women and fanatics. They advanced the standards, cut down all who met them and swallowed them up in their own fires. After this a garrison was placed over the conquered islanders, and the groves sacred to savage rites were cut down ".[199]

It would be tempting to end the story here with the dramatic entry of Anglesey onto the pages of history, but, in fact, this disastrous battle did not mark the final triumph of Roman power in the island, for the control exercised by Paulinus was short-lived. While he had been in Wales, a widespread revolt had broken out in the south-east led by Boudicca, Queen of the Iceni, and Paulinus had to abandon his new conquests in order to suppress this rising which was threatening the future of his entire province.[200]

For the next ten years the governors of Britain were fully occupied with the unrest in the south and the difficulties and final downfall of their ally, Cartimandua, in the north; not to mention the political troubles of Rome itself in the year 69 A.D., when there were three rival claimants to the Imperial throne. Vespasian, who finally emerged as Emperor, clearly saw the need for a rapid conquest of the whole of Britain. Petillius Cerealis (Governor 71 - 74 A.D.) was occupied in the north, but his successor, Sextus Iulius Frontinus, was able to turn his attention to Wales and finally completed the conquest of the Silures in the south. He may also have campaigned in the north, for it was an attack by the Ordovices on a cavalry regiment stationed in their territory which was the immediate cause of the offensive launched by his successor, Iulius Agricola, as soon as he arrived in Britain in 78 A.D.

It was in this year, almost a generation after the first attack, that Anglesey was finally brought within the orbit of close Roman control. The changes which had taken place on the island in the course of this generation seem to have been fundamental, resulting in something not far short of the total demoralisation of the population. The initial victory of Paulinus was no doubt a traumatic experience, but it need not have been fatal. The nature

[199] Tacitus. *Annals*. XIV. xxx. (trans. Dudley and Webster).
[200] It has been suggested that the Boudiccan rising might have been engineered by the Druids to prevent the invasion of Anglesey (D. R. Dudley and G. Webster. *The Rebellion of Boudicca*. 1962. 52-60). Though the idea may seem attractive, there is no evidence to support it.

of the island is such that, having suffered defeat on the Straits,[201] a well organised opposition could fall back on Llangefni and hold the pass across the marsh. Since the Roman troops were soon recalled, it seems unlikely that they could have penetrated the western half of the island at all. Yet by 78 A.D. the spirit and temper of the inhabitants seems to have been completely changed.

By this one may perhaps measure the power and inspiration of the leaders of 60 A.D. These leaders may have been the Druids, who are known to have been present in large numbers at the battle, and against whom the Romans launched an especially determined attack. Tacitus records that the Druids, and the sanctuaries and rites over which they presided, were the particular target of the Romans after their initial victory, and it may be that this short campaign of extermination was entirely successful.[202] Those of the leaders who survived, either Druids or secular refugees from the south, may have abandoned the island and sailed for Ireland where at least one burial has been found, significantly, on the shore of Dublin Bay. From this burial at Lambay Island there is a bronze scabbard mount very similar to No. 10 from Llyn Cerrig Bach.[203] Both finds suggest the presence in the west of rich Celts from south-eastern England in the middle of the first century A.D., and it is tempting to interpret the Irish find as a further step in the flight of Celtic resisters before the encroaching Romans.

Support for the theory that the religious and political significance of Anglesey came to an end in 60 not 78 A.D. is to be found in the deposit at Llyn Cerrig Bach itself. In the middle of the first century A.D. there were a number of important changes in the style of native metalwork. These involved a much greater use of enamel and certain easily recognised new shapes in bits, terrets, and other equipment. The great hoard from Stanwick, Yorkshire, buried in about 50 A.D., is perhaps the best-known group of such metalwork.[204] The style reached South Wales, and is represented in the Seven Sisters hoard from Neath which probably dates from the period of relative peace amongst the Silures, from 58 to 74 A.D.[205] None of this distinctive metalwork was found amongst the mass of objects from Llyn Cerrig Bach, from which one may conclude that no offerings were made there after 60 A.D. at the latest.

The differing attitudes of the Roman generals, Paulinus and Agricola, towards Anglesey are also instructive. In 60 A.D. Anglesey was obviously a serious threat, and its invasion was a matter of predetermined policy. Paulinus had boats ready prepared and these may have been specially designed for the peculiar conditions of the Straits. In 78 A.D. Agricola's

[201] The shallows between Caernarvon and the Anglesey shore near Llanidan mark the traditional site of both Roman crossings.
[202] Tacitus. *Annals.* XIV. xxx.
[203] J. Raftery. *Prehistoric Ireland.* 1951. figs. 236-46. Mount (fig. 239).
[204] M. MacGregor. PPS. XXVIII. 1962. 17-57.
[205] W. F. Grimes. *The Prehistory of Wales.* 1951. 124, fig. 40. Date discussed in Jarrett. *Arch. J.* CXXI. 1964. 37.

expedition was undertaken on the spur of the moment, the conquest of Anglesey was something of an afterthought, which suggests that it was no longer a base for serious resistance to the Roman military advance on the mainland.

The gulf that lies between 60 and 78 A.D. may be measured by a comparison of Tacitus's tame account of Agricola's successful invasion with his description of the dramatic defence of the island against Paulinus.

" It was a sudden decision, and Agricola found himself without boats, but his resourcefulness and determination took him across. When all the soldiers had put down their packs, he selected from amongst his auxiliary troops those who were familiar with the channels and had such a life-long knowledge of swimming that they could control themselves, their weapons and their horses in the water. These he sent across so quickly and so suddenly that the enemy, who had been expecting a fleet or some naval expedition, were stupefied and demoralised to the extent that they believed that nothing could stand in the way of men with such an approach to war. Accordingly they petitioned for peace and surrendered the island ".[206]

Thus the story of prehistoric Anglesey comes to an end with the absorption of the island into the vast empire of the Romans. Its history as part of the Roman province of Britain is no less dependent than its prehistoric past on the evidence of archaeology for, after the initial drama of its conquest, Anglesey does not appear again in the world's literature for many centuries. The expansion of the stone hut villages implies a state of quiet prosperity for the inhabitants, and a life of agriculture and crafts-manship which was not far different from their earlier life, but a discussion of these succeeding centuries is well outside the scope of this book.

[206] Tacitus. *Agricola.* xviii.

LIST OF BARROWS SURVIVING IN ANGLESEY, SEE MAP 3

Holyhead Rural
Summit of Holyhead Mountain	NGR SH/219829	Virtually invisible
Garn	NGR SH/211825	Virtually invisible
Gorsedd Gwlwm, near Trewilmot	NGR SH/227816	Clearly visible

Bodedern
Treiorwerth	NGR SH/354806	Clearly visible

Llanbabo
Bedd Branwen	NGR SH/362849	Clearly visible

Llantrisant
Cors y Bol	NGR SH/376843	Not obvious

Rhosbeirio
Pen y Morwydd	NGR SH/385913	Clearly visible
Yr Efail	NGR SH/395910	Not obvious

Rhos-y-bol
Barrow near Pen y Fynwent	NGR SH/434889	Virtually invisible

Llanfihangel Tre'r Beirdd
Mynydd Bodafon	NGR SH/467848	Not obvious

Llanbedr Goch
Rhos-y-gad	NGR SH/515796	Visible

Llanddyfnan
Tyn-y-Pwll	NGR SH/509784	Visible
'Llanddyfnan'	NGR SH/508784	Visible
Two others	NGR SH/505785	Virtually invisible
	NGR SH/506786	Virtually invisible

Pentraeth
Mynydd Llwydiarth	NGR SH/541787	Virtually invisible

Llaniestyn Rural
Rhosisaf	NGR SH/574786	Not obvious

Llanddaniel Fab
Cairn near Bryn Celli Ddu	NGR SH/507702	Virtually invisible

Llanidan
Garn, Brynsiencyn	NGR SH/488670	Clearly visible

Cerrigceinwen		
Craig Las, near Mona	NGR SH/415748	Clearly visible
Aberffraw		
°Barrow near Din Dryfol	NGR SH/395724	Clearly visible
Trwyn Du	NGR SH/352679	Kerb visible
Llangwyfan		
Mynydd Bach	NGR SH/328708	Visible

LIST OF STANDING STONES IN ANGLESEY, SEE MAP 3

Holyhead Rural
Plas Meilw (Two stones)   NGR SH/227809
Near Trefignath   NGR SH/254809

Llanynghenedl
Tŷ Croes   NGR SH/317812

Llantrisant
Tregwelyth   NGR SH/340832
New Church   NGR SH/363837

Llanbabo
Bod Deiniol   NGR SH/368857

Llanfaethlu
Stone near the Black Lion   NGR SH/319863

Llanrhwydrys
South Stone   NGR SH/333904
North Stone   NGR SH/334906

Llanfechell
Triangular setting   NGR SH/364917
East Stone   NGR SH/370916

Bodewryd
Stone near Plas Bodewryd   NGR SH/406902

Amlwch
Stone near Werthyr   NGR SH/415928

Llandyfrydog
Stone near Dwyran   NGR SH/430858
Carreg Leidr   NGR SH/446843
Stone near Plas Llanfihangel   NGR SH/452831

* The drought in May and June 1970 revealed that this mound is composed of natural rock. The references to it on pp. 118 and 166, note 148, should be ignored.

Llanfihangel Tre'r Beirdd
    Maenaddwyn   NGR SH/461833

Llanddyfnan
    Stone near Tyn-llan   NGR SH/502786

Llanddona
    Stone near Cyndal   NGR SH/567799

Llansadwrn
    Stones near Cremlyn   NGR SH/571773
                                           NGR SH/571776

Llandysilio
    Plas Cadnant stone   NGR SH/554739

Llanddaniel Fab
    Stone near Bryn Celli Ddu   NGR SH/503703

Llanidan
    Trefwri   NGR SH/476678

Llanffinan
    Stone near Hirdre-faig   NGR SH/484745

Llangefni
    Lledwigan stone   NGR SH/456740

Trefdraeth
    Stone near railway, Malltraeth Yard   NGR SH/409693

Cerrigceinwen
    Craig Las, near Mona   NGR SH/416749

HUNTERS AND STRAND-LOOPERS

SINCE 1970 the major work in this period has been the excavation of the occupation and working site at Trwyn Du, Aberffraw (PA 48-51). The original excavations remain unpublished in detail but the erosion of the deposit signalled by the discovery of quite large quantities of worked flint at the top of the beach[1] caused a further excavation to be carried out in 1974[2]. The aim of this excavation was to rescue the archaeological material from the vulnerable zone at the edge of the sea and to consolidate that edge so that no more information would be lost within the foreseeable future.

The excavation of the coastal strip revealed two pits and a hollow which seemed to have been a focus for tool-making since artefacts were concentrated around it. Unfortunately no structures or hearths were found within the 52sq m (c.60 sq.yds.) excavated, nor was a great deal learnt about the economic life of the hunters since the bone of their prey could not survive in the acid, sandy soil. The only evidence of their food was burnt hazelnut shells thrown into a pit, but in reality a great variety of animals, birds and fish must have been caught and eaten. However it should be noted that, at the time when the site was first occupied — a good deal earlier than was originally thought — it must have been some two or three miles from the sea and marine food resources would not have dominated the diet.

More than 5000 pieces of flint and chert were found but only 309 (or 6%) were formally designed implements. The range of tools, mainly blunted points and scrapers, echoed that of the earlier excavations but the greater quantity of tools now available for study emphasises the dominance of earlier Mesolithic types in the assemblage[3]. Two new finds of some importance are flaked 'tranchet' axes, one made from a black chert and the other from a crystal tuff (Fig. 2a, 1 & 2 respectively). These small axes, designed to tackle the woodland environment of the time, are rare finds but very characteristic of the period. Up till now they have mainly been found in the south of England and south Wales; their discovery in Anglesey supports the early date for the settlement suggested by the preference for larger microliths, a date confirmed by two radiocarbon dates of 6700-6600 bc for charcoal from the working hollow[4]. This new chronological evidence means that Trwyn Du, together with one of the several camps on the crossing

[1] TAAS 1973, 170-5.
[2] R.B. White 'Excavations to Trwyn Du, Anglesey, 1974' *Arch. Camb.* CXXVII, 1978, 16-39.
[3] R. Jacobi, 'The Early Holocene Settlement of Wales' in J.A. Taylor (ed) *Culture and Environment in Prehistoric Wales*, BAR 76, Oxford, 1980, 131-206 (especially 139-49).
[4] See Appendix 3.

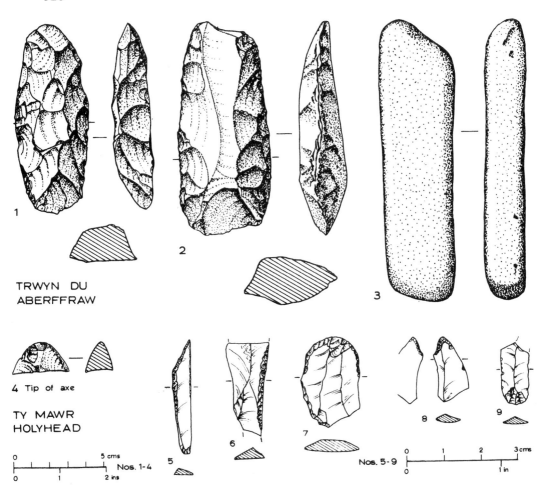

FIG. 2a.Mesolithic *tranchet* axes (1, chert and 2, crystal tuff) and 'limpet scoop' (3) from Trwyn du, Aberffraw. Chert axe tip (4), flint microliths (5, 6, 8); flint scraper (7) and flint microburin (9) from Tŷ Mawr, Holyhead. After White and Smith.

of the Clwyd at Rhuddlan[5] is one of the earliest Mesolithic sites in North Wales, having links with Maglemosian groups established in the north of England.

However the discovery of a chip from a polished axe of Mynydd Rhiw stone during the earlier excavations and the recognition of two unpolished flakes of Pembrokeshire stone (Group VIII) amongst the surface collections[6] suggests that the site was at least re-visited at a later period. The possibility that Mesolithic people were the first to recognise the special qualities of certain stones, which they may have transported over quite long distances, should not however be forgotten.

Excavations in the village of Aberffraw (NGR SH 355 690) later in 1974 revealed more flint scatters of Mesolithic date indicating temporary camps along

[5] H. Miles, *Flints. Hist. Soc. Publics.*, 25, 1971, 1-8 and Jacobi, *op.cit.*, 146.
[6] See Appendix 1.

the west side of the river. The artefacts were not susceptible to precise dating within the period[7].

Occupation of Holy Island during the Mesolithic is now well documented by a group of over a hundred flint and chert cores and flakes from among the huts at Tŷ Mawr (NGR SH 214 821)[8], by two cores found in eroding peat at Porth Ruffydd (NGR SH 216 800) and by 38 flakes and one microlith found during ploughing at Rhoscolyn (NGR SH 281 753)[9]. The Tŷ Mawr material comes from the excavation of later huts and, though no structures of Mesolithic date were found, the concentration of the finds and the evidence for flint knapping on the spot suggest a settlement of some permanence. As well as the debris of flint-working using a Late Mesolithic technique there were 7 microliths, 2 scrapers and 5 knives suggesting activity in the fourth millenium bc, but the presence of part of a tranchet axe (Fig. 2a, 4) like those from Trwyn Du hints at earlier occupation as well.

Re-examination of the flints from beneath the cairn, Bryn yr Hen Bobl, near Plas Newydd on the Straits (NGR SH 519 690) suggests that there, too, there may have been Mesolithic occupation before the early farmers built their tomb. No indisputable Mesolithic tools are present but the general impression of the collection is Mesolithic rather than Neolithic, nearly all the flakes being small and heavily patinated[10].

[7] R.B. White, *Arch. in Wales*, 1975, 25.
[8] C.A. Smith, *Arch. Camb.*, CXXXV, 1986, 12-23. and CXXXVI, 1987, 26.
[9] Both collections are in Bangor Museum (1984/153 and 1986/3).
[10] NMW 35, 377/35, 399.

THE NEOLITHIC PERIOD: THE FIRST FARMERS

THE most significant work relating to this period since 1970 has been the excavation of Trefignath chambered tomb (NGR SH 259 805) and the completion of the investigations at Din Dryfol (NGR SH 396 725) which throw much new light on the small group of 'Long Graves' on the island (PA 65-70) and provide incontrovertible evidence of multi-period construction of both sites. The other important developments have been the discovery of some domestic sites, confirmation of Early Neolithic phases and increased evidence for Late Neolithic activity in Anglesey.

The work at Trefignath, which involved the total excavation of the chambers and cairn, was occasioned by the collapse of the central chamber in 1971 and the decay of props in the eastern chamber by 1977. The excavation was carried out by Dr C.A. Smith, then Inspector of Ancient Monuments for the area. It has been fully published in a monograph together with the writer's excavations at Din Dryfol, for the two tombs have much in common[1].

The excavations revealed that, far from being a continuous gallery of three chambers with a pile of disturbed slabs at the western end (PA 66), it had consisted of three separate chambers built in succession from west to east and covered by an elaborately designed cairn which had been enlarged as each new chamber was built. This cairn overlay evidence for domestic occupation at a date around 3000 bc which will be described later.

The western chamber was the earliest structure; it stood on the highest point of the knoll and had opened to the north. It had originally consisted of five orthostats and perhaps two capstones. The capstones had been lost and the sidestones had collapsed like a pack of cards (PA Fig. 7), but four of the five survived and their stoneholes could be recognised. No burial deposit remained on the bare rock floor of the chamber. A thin scatter of stones surrounded it, their dark colour and rounded shape contrasting with the quarried blocks of the later cairns.

This first tomb may be reconstructed as a squarish chamber with a short low passage formed by a continuation of the eastern sidestone and by a stone on the west which narrows the access somewhat. The rather ragged cairn may be judged to be circular. It is not a classic design but may be justifiably equated with the group of small Passage Graves which run up both sides of the Irish Sea and have an arguably early date amongst the megalithic tombs of these

[1] C.A. Smith and F.M. Lynch *Trefignath and Din Dryfol: the Excavation of Two Megalithic Tombs in Anglesey*, Camb. Arch. Monographs 3, 1987.

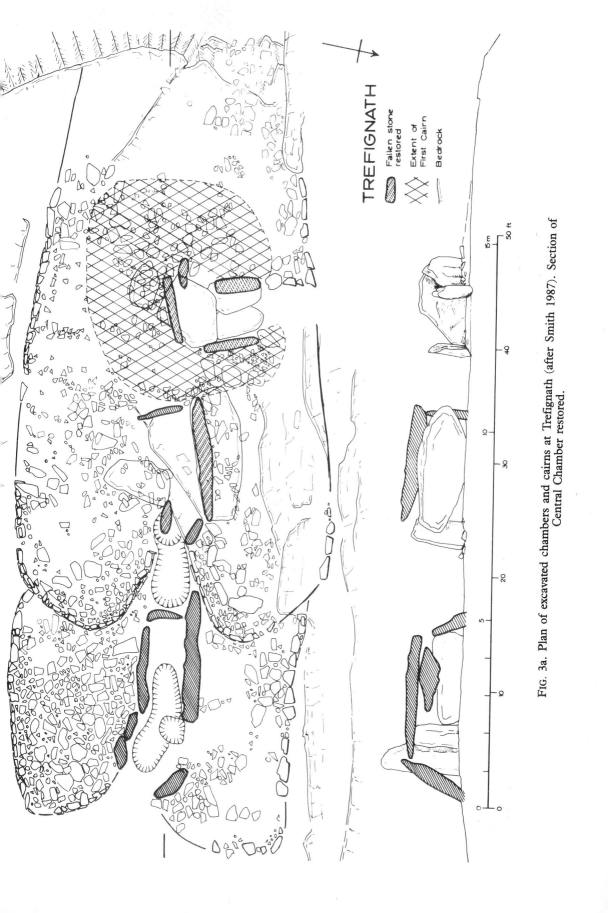

TREFIGNATH

Fallen stone
restored

Extent of
First Cairn

Bedrock

Fig. 3a. Plan of excavated chambers and cairns at Trefignath (after Smith 1987). Section of
Central Chamber restored.

islands.[2]. The stratigraphy suggested that the building of this chamber followed close upon the abandonment of the settlement which produced a radiocarbon date of 3100 ± 70 bc, confirming this dating horizon and providing a useful context for the other members of this group in Anglesey (PA 61-5).

The central chamber was built just on the eastern edge of the first cairn. It had consisted of a simple rectangular box with two portal stones at the east end. These portals do not give extra height to the chamber but they may have been covered by a separate, thicker lintel since the existing capstone is not long enough to cover the entire space. This chamber was built over awkwardly stepped bedrock and only two stoneholes were dug; the other stones were wedged against breaks in the rock. The forecourt had been badly disturbed and no burial deposit survived on the rock floor but it is possible that "urns and bones" mentioned in 19th century accounts of the site[3] came from this chamber. However one interesting sherd (K, Fig. 4a) was found in a crevice of the floor. It is a piece made from an unusual, non-local, clay decorated with a sharp groove, probably to be identified with southern English Grooved Ware (PA 90) and indicating that this chamber remained accessible into the later half of the Neolithic.

The date of its building is unclear. It must be later than the west chamber, but its builders seem to have maintained access to that chamber since the outer end of its passage is bonded into the wall of the second cairn. That wall was built from quarried blocks which very probably were obtained from the western end of the knoll on which the tomb stands where fresh breaks and ledges were found under the tail of the cairn. On one of these ledges were sherds from a carinated bowl (E, Fig. 4a) very similar to those in use in the earlier settlement, suggesting that the sequence settlement/western chamber/central chamber was a relatively rapid one.

The design of this simple box-like chamber would be appropriate to a relatively early date since it might be compared to putatively early versions of the Clyde Tombs of south west Scotland[4]. However the elaborate design of the wedge-shaped cairn and its cuspate forecourt have led people to look in another direction for the inspiration for the building of this monument[5]. Carefully walled cairns with an inner wall to take the pressure of the loose stone are characteristic of the Cotswold Severn group of tombs, a group whose influence can be recognised in North Wales[6]. This group could perhaps provide an equally convincing context for the abandonment of the Passage Grave design in preference for the long cairn and immediately accessible box-like chamber which was already popular in many parts of the Irish Sea Province.[7]

The final chamber to be built repeats many of the features of the central chamber. It is a rectangular box-like structure but this time with high portal stones; the forecourt was again cuspate and the extension to the cairn neatly walled, though

[2] F.M. Lynch, *Arch. Camb.* CXXIV, 1975, 15-35.
[3] Longueville Jones, *Arch. Camb.* 1855, 18-27.
[4] A.S. Henshall, *Chambered Tombs of Scotland*, vol. 2, 59-73.
[5] Smith and Lynch *op.cit.*, 23.
[6] F.M. Lynch in *Welsh Antiquity* (Boon & Lewis edd) Cardiff, 1976, 64-5.
[7] L. Masters in *Antiquity and Man* (Evans *et al.* edd) London, 1981, 161-76.

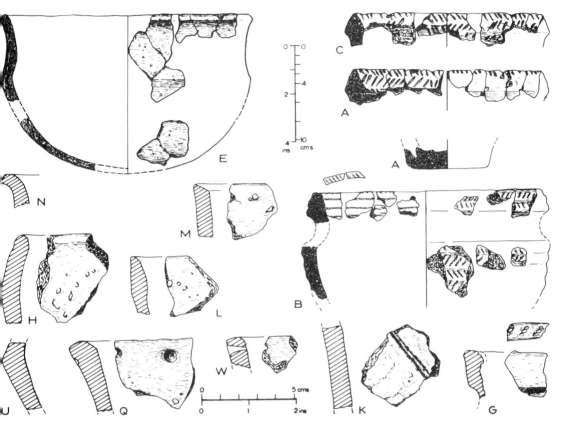

FIG. 4a. Pottery from Trefignath. N, M, H, L, U from pre-cairn settlement; E from shelf in 'quarry' (phase 2); K from Central Chamber (phase 2); A, B, C & G associated with final closured of tomb; Q unstratified. After Smith 1987. Pottery drawings with hatched sections are half size, those with dark sections are quarter size.

without duplication. This chamber was built into the forecourt of the central chamber and must have rendered it inaccessible; the cairn wall abuts directly against the wall of the second cairn providing incontrovertible evidence for the sequence of building and demonstrating that there was no 'extra-revetment' or masking material in front of that wall at the time. The portal consists of four stones; the surviving inner one (and presumably its missing partner) are the same height as the chamber sidestones, but the outer ones are an imposing 2m (6ft) high. This extra height gives this chamber an undoubtedly Scottish look. Some have suggested[5] that this high front gives Trefignath a place amongst the Welsh Portal Dolmens, strangely absent from Anglesey (PA 79), but though there is a general family resemblance amongst all these 'gailery graves', I would agree with Dr Smith that this version is more reminiscent of the Clyde type and is suggestive of a not surprising maritime connection with that region[9].

However the final ceremonies of blocking this chamber involved the use of decorated pottery of a generally southern English type. Pots A, B, C and G belong to the Peterborough family of wares (Fig. 4a) but analysis of the clay[10] revealed

[8] Masters op.cit., 171-2.
[9] Smith and Lynch op.cit., 26-9.
[10] Jenkins in Smith and Lynch op.cit., 60-73.

that they were locally made. Indeed their closest parallels are to be found in Anglesey, at the settlement beside Bryn yr Hen Bobl (PA 104-108), demonstrating the extent of south eastern influences in the island in the Late Neolithic. It had been hoped that a radiocarbon date for charcoal associated with some of these scattered sherds would have given a more precise date for this phase, but the results showed that the charcoal came from what must have been a period of disturbance and destruction during the Iron Age[11].

Din Dryfol (PA 68-70) was in course of excavation in 1970, but the work was not completed until 1980. With its tall portal stone and rectangular chamber the monument had always been known to have similarities to Trefignath which were, in general terms, confirmed by the excavation; hence their publication in the same volume[12]. However, though Din Dryfol was of multi-period construction, the chambers were not separate, but were combined into a single gallery of three or four chambers' length and, though comparisons with the pre-tomb pottery at Trefignath, suggest an early construction date for Din Dryfol, it does not seem to have had a long period of use.

The tomb stands on a rocky ledge on the northern slope of Dinas (NGR SH 396 725) with a very large portal stone at the east end and the remains of a rectangular chamber 9m (30ft) to the west. Excavation revealed that the area between had been very badly damaged by Romano-British agricultural and industrial activity and by a later road which had removed all evidence for the first two chambers. Very unusually most of the stones in this monument had been set on the surface, without stoneholes, which made the retrieval of the complete plan impossible. However the third and fourth chambers could be reconstructed with greater confidence, as could the massively built long cairn which was reasonably intact from this point westwards.

Because the fourth chamber is the most complete it is easiest to start the description of the tomb from the west. This fourth chamber had been very similar to the central chamber at Trefignath, a simple box with two unemphatic portal stones. A few scraps of cremated bone from two individuals (an adult and an immature person) were found in the badly disturbed chamber area and amongst the nearby cairn stones. The chamber was surrounded by a cairn built of exceptionally large blocks which extended for at least 35m (116ft) behind it running between raised ridges of rock on either side. On the south side this cairn was retained by a wall of large slabs laid horizontally, against which lent a fringe of smaller stones. It was not clear whether this 'Outer Cairn' was part of the original design or a later addition.

Immediately to the east of this chamber was an area of jumbled stones which resolved itself into two lines of carefully placed slabs which must have formed part of the walls of Chamber Three. This third chamber was very unusual in that the entrance was marked by two circular holes which appeared to have been designed to hold wooden portal posts rather than stones. These posts must have been removed before they had rotted since the holes were found to have been

[11] Smith and Lynch op.cit, 33.
[12] Smith and Lynch op.cit. note 1.

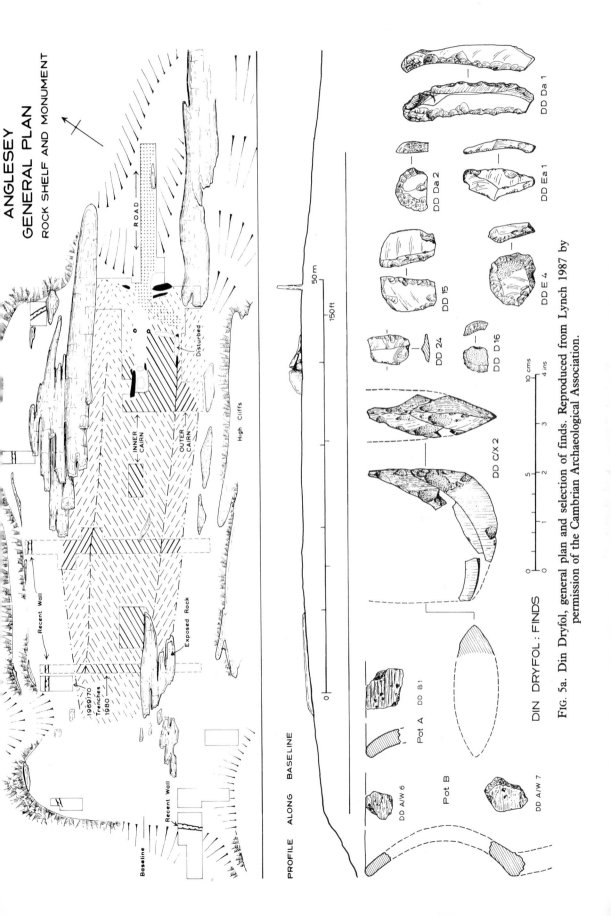

ANGLESEY
GENERAL PLAN

ROCK SHELF AND MONUMENT

ROAD

INNER CAIRN

OUTER CAIRN

High Cliffs

Disturbed

Exposed Rock

Recent Wall

Trenches 1969/70 1980

Recent Wall

Baseline

PROFILE ALONG BASELINE

0   150 ft   50 m

DIN DRYFOL : FINDS

DD Da 1

DD Da 2

DD Ea 1

DD 15

DD E 4

DD 24

DD D 16

DD C/X 2

Pot A   DD B 1

Pot B

DD A/W 6

DD A/W 7

0   5   10 cms
0   1   2   3   4 ins

Fig. 5a. Din Dryfol, general plan and selection of finds. Reproduced from Lynch 1987 by permission of the Cambrian Archaeological Association.

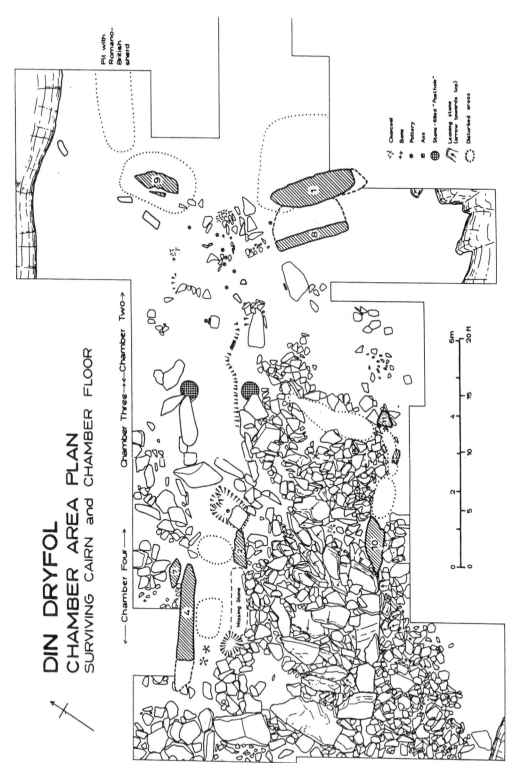

DIN DRYFOL
CHAMBER AREA PLAN
SURVIVING CAIRN and CHAMBER FLOOR

← Chamber Four → Chamber Three →←← Chamber Two →

Pit with Romano-British sherd

Missing Stone

✓ Charcoal
✝ Bone
• Pottery
▣ Axe
◉ Stone-filled "Posthole"
◿ Leaning stone (arrow towards top)
◌ Disturbed areas

0   5   10   15   20 ft
0   2   4   6m

Fig. 6a. Din Dryfol, plan of cairn and chamber floors. Reproduced from Lynch 1987 by permission of the Cambrian Archaeological Association.

completely filled by stones which cannot be interpreted as packing. Abutting the southern posthole was a narrow band of disturbance cutting through the cairn which was locally well-preserved. This disturbance ran up to a smashed orthostat where it turned at right angles towards a surviving upright stone which abutted the retaining wall of the inner cairn, this change in the nature of the cairn edge occurring opposite the front of Chamber Four. The specific nature of this disturbance suggested that a line of upright slabs, a straight facade and cairn edge, had been removed.

All structural details to the east of the postholes had been destroyed except the immediate portal area. One very large slab on the south remained intact with a lower stone of uncertain status behind it; on the north side the evidence was unsatisfactory but the shattered base of what must have been a much smaller stone survived in an area of disturbance. The distance between them suggested a rather wide chamber whose reality was confirmed by the distribution of sherds within its putative confines. The length of the gap between the portal and the posts at the front of Chamber Three (5m/17ft) suggested that the space would have been divided between two chambers but there was no specific evidence on this point.

It is fairly obvious that the wooden portal of Chamber Three and its straight facade must have formed the front of the tomb at some stage and that, when the front chambers were added, the posts must have been removed while they were still accessible and before they had rotted. This suggests that the sequence of events, producing a three-chambered gallery without any septal or division between the chambers, must have been relatively rapid.

Difficulties of interpretation relate to the details of the structure of Chamber Three with its unusual combination of wood and stone, to the possibility that its side walls were of laid slabs even though one fallen orthostat survived on the north side, and to its relationship to Chamber Four. The change in the nature of the cairn edge and the jumble of stones overlying a shallow pit just in front of Chamber Four make it possible to argue that this was the primary structure, a single chamber comparable to the central chamber at Trefignath and to others in south west Scotland. The pit and jumbled stones could then be interpreted as forecourt and blocking features, with Chamber Three built in front later as an independent chamber without access between them. The evidence is not conclusive either way, but the present writer has a slight preference for the three-period over the two-period interpretation (Fig. 7a).

The use of structural timbers in a megalithic tomb is very rare but not unknown. Only excavation can identify the practice so it may be more widespread than we know. Only some five instances are known at present[13]; they are not a coherent group, either in time or place, stretching as they do from the Channel Islands to the north of Ireland and occurring in a variety of different types of tomb. This technical device should not be confused with the presence of an entirely wooden monument beneath a later stone structure, as at Lochhill, Slewcairn and

[13] Smith and Lynch op.cit., 126.

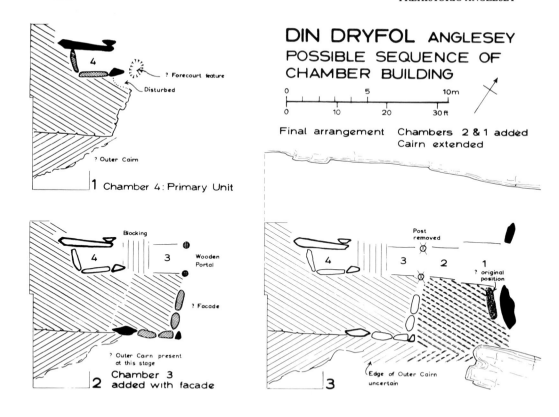

FIG. 7a. Din Dryfol, suggested sequence of construction. Reproduced from Lynch 1987 by permission of the Cambrian Archaeological Association.

Doey's Cairn which do form a coherent, early group in the north Irish Sea area[14].

Both the structural necessities of the use of wood and the close similarity of the pottery in the pit outside Chamber Four (Pot A, Fig. 5a) and on the floor of Chamber One (Pot B) combine to suggest that, despite its complex history, Din Dryfol was not in active use for a very long period. That period of use was in the Early Neolithic, around 3000 bc if one may judge by the similarity of the high quality pottery (albeit a very small amount) to that from Dyffryn Ardudwy, Llandegai and now the settlement beneath Trefignath. The last two sites both have dates of about 3000 bc[15]. This comparison also suggests that a box-like structure was being built at Din Dryfol at approximately the same time as the Passage Grave (West Chamber) at Trefignath, demonstrating that the variety of tomb-building styles which is such a feature of Neolithic Anglesey, was present in the island from a very early date.

The results of the excavations of Trefignath and Din Dryfol have implications

---

[14] Masters *op.cit.*, 167-8.
[15] Lynch in *Welsh Antiquity*, (Boon & Lewis edd), 1976, 63-5.

for the interpretation of Hendrefor (NGR SH 551 773, PA 70), the third member of the Long Grave family. It is possible that it, too, is an accretion of independent chambers rather than a badly damaged segmented gallery. Presaddfed (NGR SH 348 809, PA 87) is another tomb which might be looked at afresh in the light of these new excavations.

Since 1970 fieldwork has revealed at least one undoubted goosehouse in the Benllech area roofed by a megalithic slab[16]. This casts a great deal of doubt over the antiquity of the structure excavated in 1965 (NGR SH 519 826, PA 91) for which there was no evidence of prehistoric date, except the size of the capstone. It should no longer be included in a list of megalithic tombs.

Bryn Celli Ddu (NGR SH 508 702, PA 91-101) has been the subject of new articles listed in the footnotes[17]. Mrs O'Kelly's analysis is based, as mine was, on the insights provided by her husband's re-interpretation of the purple clay floor and her conclusions are broadly similar to mine. Prof. Eogan's suggestion that the ditch is not part of a Henge but simply an enlargement of the Passage Grave I find unconvincing. The widely spaced stones around the centre could never have been part of a kerb and the absence of the bank can be more satisfactorily explained (PA 94).

Ideas relating to evidence for occupation prior to the building of Bryn yr Hen Bobl (NGR SH 519 690, PA 83-6; 104-8), on the other hand, have been seriously changed. Re-examination of the flints suggest some earlier, Mesolithic, occupation (see p.329) and new information about the distribution of pottery has modified arguments about the date of the tomb. It was believed, in the absence of any firm statement in the excavation report, that decorated and undecorated pottery was found mixed together and that both came from *under* the terrace and the cairn (PA 106). This would mean that the tomb must be late, post-dating the appearance of Peterborough pottery in the island. Dr Colin Gresham, who took part in the excavation, has now put on record[18] his clear recollection that only undecorated pottery was found beneath the terrace and his belief that the decorated pottery may have come exclusively from the trenches at the back of the cairn. This means that, if the decorated pottery came from a settlement, it post-dated the cairn, which is therefore dated by the undecorated pottery alone and consequently could belong to the earlier Neolithic, but not necessarily so, since such pottery has a long currency.

In 1970 the absence of evidence for domestic settlement on Anglesey during the Neolithic could only be lamented (PA 60), but now it is possible to list four sites occupied at this time and to point more confidently to other places where such evidence might be found in the future.

The discovery of occupation debris under the cairn at Trefignath was an unexpected bonus of the tomb excavation[19]. This debris consisted of a scatter of sherds, all very small and abraded, and of flint and chert implements and flakes, together with a certain amount of charcoal trodden into the surface. Much

---

[16] At Cromlech Farm, NGR SH 588 824.
[17] C. O'Kelly, *Arch. Camb.*, CXVIII, 1969, 17-48 and G. Eogan. *Antiquity* LVII. 1983, 135-6.
[18] Colin Gresham, *Arch. Camb.* CXXXV, 1985, 225-7.
[19] Smith and Lynch *op.cit.*, 10-14.

of this material was securely stratified beneath the earliest cairn, demonstrating that the occupation had taken place before any of the tombs were built, but it spread more widely into areas where the cairn had been lost, so a certain amount must be considered technically unstratified. Unfortunately the only structural evidence was a group of four pits dug into this old ground surface; there were no postholes and no house, such as the one at Llandegai near Bangor[20], could be recognised.

The date of this occupation, which may have been connected with preparations for the building of the first burial chamber, is indicated by a radiocarbon date of 3100 ± 70 bc for charcoal from the surface and by the style of pottery. The remains of eight pots could be recognised amongst the twenty-four groups of sherds stratified beneath the first cairn (Fig. 4a); all are extremely fragmentary and none can be fully reconstructed even on paper but the shapes are consistent with the style known as Irish Sea ware[21], predominantly open shouldered bowls with some plain hemispherical cups, all undecorated and often having a corky but carefully smoothed surface. This pottery has been found at putatively early sites such as Clegyr Boia in Pembrokeshire and Dyffryn Ardudwy in Merioneth and associated with the house at Llandegai where there is a radiocarbon date comparable to that at Trefignath. It is also similar to the pieces put in the tomb at Din Dryfol, though of rather poorer quality as befits its domestic context here. Analysis of the clay[22] demonstrated that the pottery had been made locally on Holy Island.

The flint and black chert used for small tools had also been obtained locally and had been worked on the spot[23]. It was a homogeneous industry making mainly scrapers and knives with an *écaille* technique particularly characteristic of Neolithic flint working. This technique is normally thought to be characteristic of later rather than earlier Neolithic work, but its association here with an early date must cast doubt on that conclusion[24].

Analysis of the pollen surviving beneath the cairn and in a nearby bog[25] shows that before the tomb was built the area — now so open and windswept — had been thickly wooded but that the tomb-builders quickly made inroads into this oak woodland. The settlement was surrounded by open grassland with meadow flowers and there were traces of cereal crops and of celtic bean[26]. As time went on more and more land was cleared, for pollen from beneath the latest cairn shows a marked decline in tree species and a greater dominance of grassland. Pollen was not analysed in the soil beneath Din Dryfol but the charcoal used there in the Neolithic was mainly from oak and hazel[27], woodland appropriate to the Gwna valley.

A palaeoecological study of Tre'r Gof peat basin on the north coast (NGR

[20] F.M. Lynch. *Arch. Camb CXXXVIII, 1989*, 2-4, *Fig. 1*.
[21] Lynch in *Welsh Antiquity*, 63-5, Fig. 1.
[22] Jenkins in Smith and Lynch *op.cit.*, 60-73.
[23] Healey in Smith and Lynch *op.cit.*, 47-59.
[24] Smith in Smith and Lynch *op.cit.*, 12.
[25] Greig in Smith and Lynch *op.cit.*, 39-44.
[26] A rare find (Smith and Lynch *op.cit.*, 43)
[27] Denne in Smith and Lynch *op.cit.*, 130.

SH 360 935) where archaeological evidence, especially for the earlier periods, is extremely scarce, has provided a radiocarbon-dated sequence of vegetation changes[28]. This shows some very small-scale and short-lived clearances between about 4000 bc and 1800 bc. They are indicated by fluctuations in the quantity of birch and elm pollen and the presence of secondary woodland species such as holly, hawthorn and honeysuckle. After 1800 bc, during the Early Bronze age, human interference begins to increase, cereal pollen is occasionally found and all trees show some decline. However a pastureland vegetation with slight but regular cereal representation does not become fully established there until perhaps the Iron Age. Earlier work at Gors Goch (NGR SH 50 81) suggests a similar picture — some very short-lived clearances, perhaps during the Mesolithic or Neolithic, followed by gradual but relentless inroads into the natural woodland[29].

Other sites with evidence of apparently domestic activity belong to a horizon later than Trefignath, lying towards the end of the third millenium bc. The most important of these is at Capel Eithin, Gaerwen (NGR SH 490 727) where some evidence of wooden structures, albeit enigmatic, was obtained, associated with sherds of Grooved Ware, a Late Neolithic style found mainly in the south of England and until recently, thought to be absent from Wales. Its discovery in some quantity at Capel Eithin makes the attribution of the Lligwy pottery (PA 90; Fig.21.6-9) and Pot K from Trefignath to this style the more likely.

The site was on the top of a low but prominent hill which was to be the focus for burials in the Bronze Age and in the Early Christian period (hence the name, Capel Eithin). The nature of the Neolithic activity is less certain; indeed there remain many problems associated with the interpretation of this as yet unpublished excavation carried out by the Gwynedd Archaeological Trust in 1980/1[30]. These problems mainly concern the conflicting dates obtained from radiocarbon assay and traditional archaeological typology, and the difficulty of reconstructing any plausible structures from the multiplicity of pits, scoops and putative 'foundation trenches'.

The earliest dates[31] centre around 4000 bc and come from charcoal in postholes within a large, approximately trapezoid foundation trench (F69) for which there is no other dating evidence. Another pair of dates belong to the mid third millenium bc, comparable to some of the earliest dates for Neolithic activity in the Irish Sea region and earlier than anything yet found in Anglesey. These dates come from charcoal in postholes(?) in a curving foundation trench (F78), perhaps part of a round house, but the difficulty is that some pottery was found in this trench, one sherd at least belonging to the Peterborough style, current only in the Late Neolithic[32]. Similar Late Neolithic pottery, together with some sherds of Grooved ware, was found in a pit (F83) which produced a date of 2790 ± 80 bc which is also judged too early for the appearance of this style, especially in Wales.

[28] E.M. Botterill, *A Palaeoecological Study of Cors Gyfelog and Tre'r Gof: Lowland Mires in North Wales*, unpublished PhD thesis, Univ. Keele 1988.
[29] Seddon (unpublished) quoted in Botterill, 224.
[30] S.I. White, TAAS, 1981, 15-27 interim report.
[31] See Appendix 3.
[32] A more substantial version of a curving, possibly penannular, trench with postholes within it was found on the line of the Shell Oil Pipeline near Llanbedrgoch (NGR SH 505 808). There were no finds to date or explain it (White, BBCS, XXVII, 1977, 480-1).

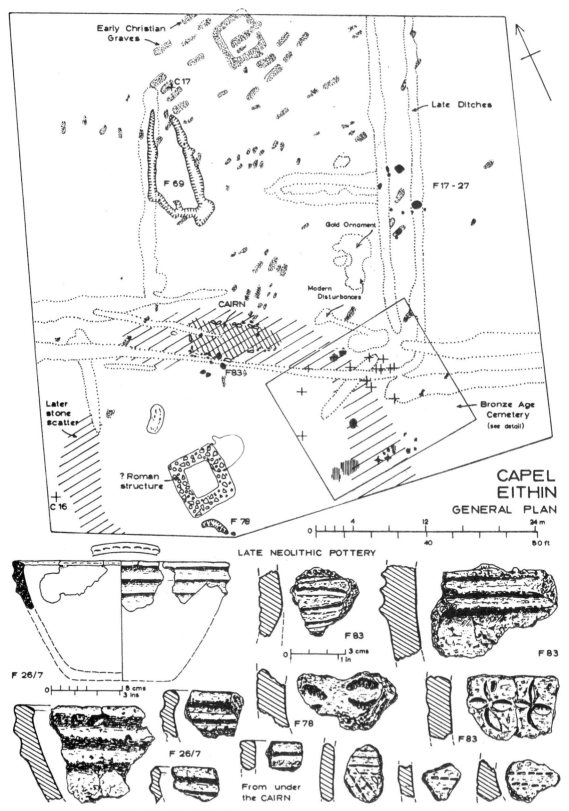

Early Christian Graves

C 17

F 69

Late Ditches

F 17 - 27

Gold Ornament

Modern Disturbances

CAIRN

F 83

Later stone scatter

?Roman structure

C 16

F 78

Bronze Age Cemetery (see detail)

CAPEL EITHIN

GENERAL PLAN

0   4   12   24 m
    40   80 ft

LATE NEOLITHIC POTTERY

F 26/7

0   8 cms
    3 ins

F 83

F 83

0   3 cms
    1 in

F 78

F 83

F 26/7

From under the CAIRN

FIG. 8a. Capel Eithin, general plan and Late Neolithic pottery.

Only in the north east quadrant of the site did the pottery and the radiocarbon dates accord. In that part of the site there had been four large pits or postholes (F17, 18, 23, 27) forming a trapezoid 4.5m-5m × 3m-3.5m (15-17′ × 10-11′9″). The structure is difficult to reconstruct since there were other contemporary postholes weaving through the area. In spite of considerable damage from later ditches, charcoal and potsherds were found in all four large pits and in three of the seven smaller postholes. This pottery consisted of several sherds of Grooved Ware, all belonging to the Woodlands sub-style[33] and representing six or eight different pots (Fig. 8a). In one instance joining sherds were found in separate pits. The burnt material in F17 included charred grains of emmer wheat and naked barley, confirming the agricultural basis of life at this settlement around 2000 bc (CAR 446) — a date which is much more acceptable for the appearance of this 'English' style of pottery in Anglesey than the other Neolithic dates from the site.

Interpretation of the activity on this site can only be attempted in the broadest terms. The presence of very old charcoal suggests burning, presumably by man, in the fourth millenium[34]. There was no Mesolithic material recognised amongst the 200 or more flint flakes from the site; nor is there anything, especially amongst the pottery, which could be considered to belong to the earliest Neolithic. For instance, there are only two or three undecorated corky sherds which might be compared to those from Trefignath, but the shape of the pot is unknown and they are associated with later pottery. No useful comments can be made about the putative structures at F69 and F78 except that the latter is rather more coherent, if incomplete. The nature of the stratigraphy does not permit a firm decision about how Late Neolithic pottery might have found its way into the filling of this foundation trench, but the general scatter of such material under the 'cairn' some 14m (44ft) to the north indicates activity on this part of the site at this time. The radiocarbon date for the hearth near the Bronze Age burials suggests that this, too, belongs to the Late Neolithic horizon. Presumably activity then was domestic, agricultural and perhaps industrial (a pit with fire-cracked stones (F78.II) is said to have contained a piece of Peterborough pottery) and involved the breakage of a range of pots in several current styles, including Beaker, all of them with an eastern background. Twenty-six metres (almost 100 yards) north east of this domestic area there may have been some tall wooden structure evidenced by the large pits F17-26.

The problems caused by the disparity of radiocarbon dates and archaeological material are demonstrated at another Anglesey site. The stone huts at Tŷ Mawr, Holyhead (NGR SH 212 821) were first excavated by W.O. Stanley who found, amongst a great deal of undatable material, some Romano-British pottery and

---

[33] Wainwright and Longworth, *Durrington Walls, Excavations 1966-8*, London, 1971, 238. Dr Longworth studied the pottery from Capel Eithin when it was first excavated. Both he and I remember a sherd with an applied 'knot' at the intersection of converging cordons. This is very characteristic of the Woodlands Style and it is particularly unfortunate that this sherd appears to have been lost before it could be drawn.

[34] The discovery of coal in one charcoal sample from the site might suggest contamination from fossil fuel which could cause misleadingly early dates. However no coal was observed in the samples dated (*pers. comm.* Quentin Dresser, CAR lab.).

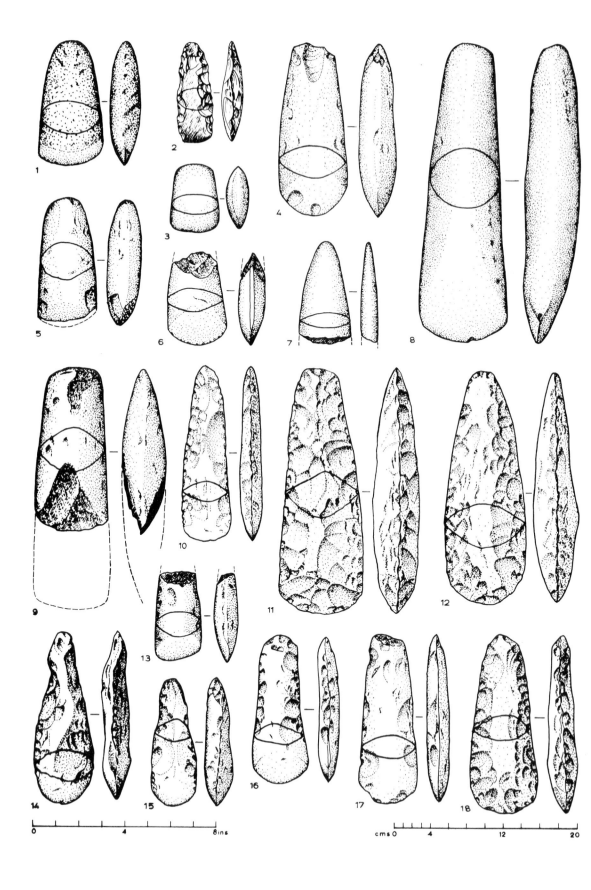

1   2   3   4   8

5   6   7

9   10   11   12

         13

14   15   16   17   18

0   4   8ins

cms 0   4   12   20

coins[35]; recent excavation has shown that the stone structures are earlier than that and that the site had been occupied at several periods[36]. The earliest material found belonged to the Late Mesolithic but two hearths, within an enclosure but judged to be below its occupation level[37], produced dates of around 2100 bc for which there was no supporting archaeological material. The excavator was tempted to suggest that Mesolithic traditions might have lingered here for an exceptionally long time as they did in the Hebrides[38], but this is surely special pleading and we must admit that many human activities may not leave datable cultural debris behind. The increasing use of radiocarbon dating will inevitably produce many more of these anomalies. We should therefore simply note two presumably domestic hearths of Late Neolithic date at Tŷ Mawr, perhaps contemporary with the final closure of the tomb at Trefignath, not so very far away.

A site which has been partially excavated at Tyn Lôn, Dothan (NGR SH 373 744) has considerable potential since it encompasses permanently wet areas where organic remains may be expected and has produced a variety of flint implements[39] and the butt of a polished stone axe. Spreads of stone, areas of burning and a length of shallow ditch suggest that evidence should be obtainable. So far the finds indicate some Mesolithic and Neolithic activity but the exact period cannot be pinpointed.

In 1970 it was said that the distribution of polished stone axes should be a good indicator of settlement and attention was drawn to areas where several axes had been found, although it was pointed out that some of these concentrations might be the result of collecting activity (PA 114). Discoveries since 1970[40], however, tend to confirm the importance of some of these areas, notably Llwydiarth Esgob (NGR SH 435 844) and the Wern/Castellior ridge behind Llandegfan (NGR SH 54 74) where a great number of querns have also been found. Nineteenth century records[41] speak of many stone huts and of a 'large cist with cremated bones' at this site which may well have seen prolonged occupation.

Mr Harry Hooton's flint collection which he kindly made available in 1970 (PA Fig. 31) has not only grown since that date, but has been the subject of more systematic study which has demonstrated several notable concentrations

[35] W.O. Stanley, Archaeol. J. XXIV, 1867, 229-42 and XXVI, 1869, 301-22.
[36] C.A. Smith, Arch. Camb., CXXXVI, 1987, 20-38 (Part IV: Chronology).
[37] C.A. Smith, Arch. Camb., CXXXIII, 1985, 20-1 and CXXXVI, 1987 24.
[38] C.A. Smith, Arch. Camb., CXXXVI, 1987, 26-7.
[39] Archaeol. in Wales 27, 1987, 32. I am grateful to Helen Jones the finder and excavator for information about this site.
[40] See Appendix 1.
[41] RCAM Anglesey 1937, 113.

FIG. 9a. 1. Hen Penclip, Menai Bridge; 2. Rhostrehwfa (found near PA Fig.30.1 & 2); 3. Ynys Uchaf, Brynteg; 4. Red Wharf Bay; 5. Trefarthen, Llangeinwen; 6. Wern, Llandegfan; 7. Newborough Warren; 8. County Hospital, Llangefni; 9. Pwll Fanogl, Llanfairpwll; 10. Penrhyn Gwyn, Llanddaniel Fab; 11. Clegyrdy Mawr, Talwrn; 12. Llwydiarth Esgob, Llandyfrydog; 13. Rectory, Penmynydd; 14. Pwll Fanogl, Llanfairpwll; 15. Ysgubor Fawr, Llaneugrad; 16. Wern, Llandegfan; 17. Plas Penmynydd; 18. Caer Elen, Bodedern.
1. Gabbro; 2. chert or flint; 8. quartz dolerite; 6. Langdale (Group VI); 10. close to Group VIII (S. Wales); 4, 7, 9, 11-18. Graig Lwyd (Group VII); 3, 5 not sectioned.

of finds[42]. Four of these concentrations occur along the Brynsiencyn ridge and on the coast to the east of it. The coastal finds, which include at least three polished axes, late Neolithic arrowheads, a scraper and flint knife and more than a dozen waste flakes, have come from the area between Trefarthen and Barras (SH 48 66)[43]. They suggest settlement in a very similar situation to that beneath Bryn yr Hen Bobl. The other concentrations, around Cae Mawr, Dwyran (SH 46 63) and Tanpencefn, Brynsiencyn (SH 47 66) lie on the crest of a ridge, in the latter case at a point where round huts were noted in the last century[44]. As at Castellior and at Din Lligwy, where many Neolithic flints have been collected[45], one may suspect repeated, if not continuous, occupation of fertile land. The Llanidan ridge near Pont Dic (SH 49 68) has produced many flints, but in less significant concentration. The emphasis on the south western corner of the island echoes that of recorded and surviving monuments and must reflect the relative fertility of the land in that area, but it should not be forgotten that these flints have been found on ploughed fields so that the record will be inevitably biased towards areas of present-day arable farming. In regions such as Anglesey, however, which are neither environmentally specialised nor particularly marginal, one may expect the farming population to have sought out and to have continued to occupy the better land from earliest times to the present day[46].

[42] I am grateful to Dr Robin Holgate who studied this collection as part of his work for an undergraduate dissertation at the Institute of Archaeology, for the loan of his notes.

[43] Hooton Collection and information from Mr J. Roberts, Trefarthen.

[44] RCAM *Anglesey*, 1937, 105

[45] The Hooton Collection contains 93 waste flints, 21 scrapers, 8 knives, 9 worked flakes and 2 arrowheads from the Plas Lligwy fields (SH 50 86).

[46] The Department of Archaeology at St. David's University College, Lampeter is currently (1990) testing the reality of this bias by a sampling programme in the productive south west and the apparently empty north east of the island. The results will not be available for several seasons.

MAKERS OF BEAKERS

No major finds of this period have been made in Anglesey since 1970. Sherds of Beaker pottery were found with other Late Neolithic pottery at Capel Eithin (NGR SH 490 727), a site discussed in the previous chapter. A broken axe-hammer of gabbro (CBA no.59) has been found at Llwydiarth Esgob (NGR SH 435 845), the second one from this farm which has also produced two Neolithic axes. Outcrops of dolerite nearby make it possible to suggest that this may heve been a production centre for stone tools and perhaps pottery[1].

The re-excavation of the Mesolithic site at Trwyn Du, Aberffraw[2], exposed a length of the kerb of the overlying cairn (PA 137) revealing that it had been built of alternate tall and short stones producing a crenellated effect which must have been intentional. Such architectural sophistication is being increasingly recognised amongst Bronze Age monuments previously considered tediously simple in construction.

Corrections: The findspot of the small axe-hammer from Bodedern (PA Fig. 39.6) was not Bodowyr, but Cae'r Meirch (NGR SH 330 796) about half a mile to the east. The drawing of the Beaker from Merddyn Gwyn (PA Fig. 34.6) is incorrect, showing only one of the two lines of fingernail marks around the waist.

---

[1] J.Ll. Williams and D.A. Jenkins in D.A. Davidson and M.L. Shackley (edd), *Geoarchaeology*, London, 1976, 115-35.
[2] R.B. White, *Arch. Camb.* CXXVII, 1978, 26.

DEATH IN THE BRONZE AGE

ALTHOUGH Standing Stones are only indirectly connected with burials, in Anglesey it is convenient to start the discussion of Bronze Age burial monuments with these conspicuous and often very imposing memorials. Since 1970 excavation information has become available for two stones in the island. The first is the squat stone which stands at the centre of the barrow of Bedd Branwen, Llanbabo (NGR SH 362 849). The excavation had demonstrated that the stone had stood as a monument in its own right before the barrow was built around it and it was thought in 1970 that its erection was dated by abraded sherds of Beaker pottery in the top of a large pit at its foot (PA 152). Such a date would be comparable to several other stones in Wales and elsewhere[1] but the radiocarbon date which became available later suggested that the stone was a great deal older (2973 ± 75 bc (BM – 452). A date in the Early rather than the Late Neolithic is very surprising and cannot be satisfactory explained[2]. It must remain anomalous, but cannot be totally ignored until a clearer pattern emerges from more dated excavations.

The second excavated stone is the southern stone at Cremlyn near Llansadwrn (NGR SH 571 773) which fell over in the spring of 1977. The stonehole and setting were examined before it was re-erected in a secure concrete base. This excavation[3] provided no evidence of stone settings, cists or prehistoric pits like those found regularly in recent years, close to Standing Stones in South Wales[4], and there was no direct evidence for the date or purpose of the stone's erection. However the investigation of its stonehole did reveal that it had probably replaced a wooden post, suggesting that the spot had previously been marked by a less permanent memorial whose exact position it had been deemed important to perpetuate. A similar situation had been recorded in Cornwall where the Long Stone at St Stephen-in-Brannel could be shown to have been the fourth stone set up on the site[5]. We can be certain, therefore, that the stones commemorated something of continuing importance to the community, but neither excavation revealed what that might have been.

The Standing Stones of Anglesey have been the subject of a more recent study[6] which lists evidence for the former existence of 69 stones, of which 45 are extant. This total includes two rows of small stones whose prehistoric dates

---

[1] G. Williams *The Standing Stones of Wales and South West England*, BAR, 197, 1988.
[2] F.M. Lynch, *Arch. Camb.*, CXX, 1971, 82.
[3] F.M. Lynch, 'The Investigation of a Standing Stone at Cremlyn, Anglesey', TAAS, 1980, 117-24.
[4] Williams, *op. cit.*, 48-53.
[5] H. & T. Miles, *Cornish Archaeology*, 10, 1971, 5-12.
[6] J. Wilson, BBCS, XXX, 1983, 363-89.

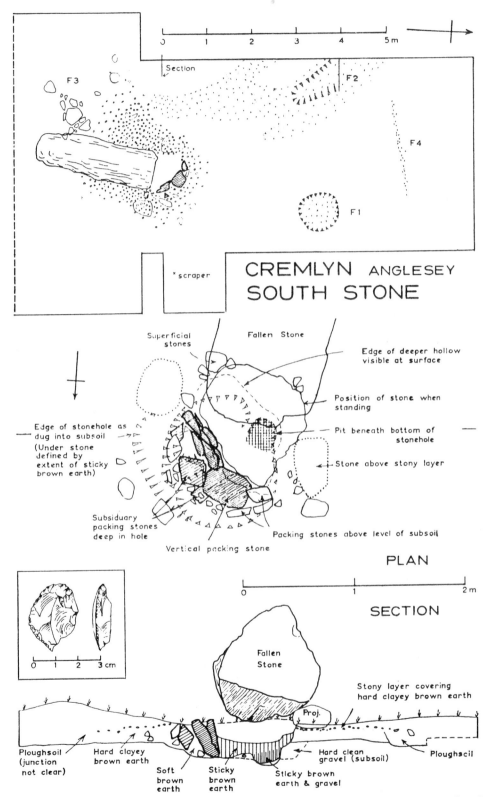

CREMLYN ANGLESEY
SOUTH STONE

Labels on plan/section:
F3, F2, F4, F1, Section, × scraper

Superficial stones
Fallen Stone
Edge of deeper hollow visible at surface
Position of stone when standing
Pit beneath bottom of stonehole
Stone above stony layer
Edge of stonehole as dug into subsoil (Under stone defined by extent of sticky brown earth)
Subsiduary packing stones deep in hole
Vertical packing stone
Packing stones above level of subsoil

PLAN

0   1   2 m

SECTION

0 1 2 3 cm

Fallen Stone
Stony layer covering hard clayey brown earth
Proj.
Ploughsoil (junction not clear)
Hard clayey brown earth
Soft brown earth
Sticky brown earth
Sticky brown earth & gravel
Hard clean gravel (subsoil)
Ploughsoil

FIG. 10a. Plan and Section of Cremlyn South Stone and its setting, with a flint scraper found in the topsoil. Reproduced from Lynch 1980.

are doubtful (one at Pentraeth and the other of Hafoty[7]). It also includes the Cunogusi stone at Llanfaelog[8] (NGR SH 356 746). This stone has a sixth century AD inscription on it, but it is unusually large for an Early Christian gravestone and a cup mark has recently been noticed on its western side[9] which may be an indication that this was a prehistoric stone reused for Christian purposes. Recent excavation by Gwynedd Archaeological Trust close to Maen Addwyn (NGR SH 461 833) revealed no ancient features of any kind but documentary research in connection with the work showed that the original Maen Addwyn had stood close to the road junction (NGR SH 460 840); when it was removed the name must have been transferred to the stone half a mile to the south[10]. This district, like Pen-yr-orsedd near Llanfairynghornwy (PA 152), must have had a notable concentration of these monuments, for there are two others within a mile of these.

Cup-marked stones and Cup and Ring Stones are enigmatic products of prehistoric activity. These markings normally appear on living rock, distant from datable monuments and without a clear association with any particular aspect of religion or ritual. It is normally believed that they belong to the Bronze Age and have some magic or religious connotations[11]. In 1970 none was known in

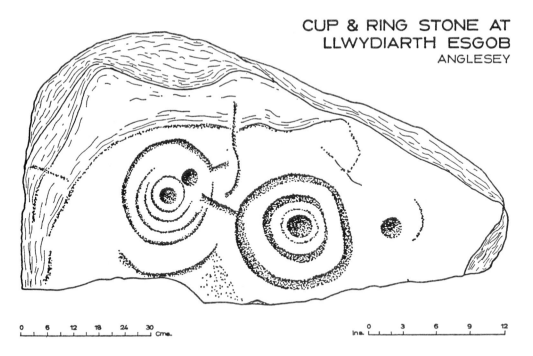

CUP & RING STONE AT LLWYDIARTH ESGOB
ANGLESEY

0   6   12   18   24   30   Cms.

0   3   6   9   12   Ins.

FIG. 11a. Llwydiarth Esgob Stone. Reproduced from Lynch and Jenkins 1974.

---

[7] One of the Hafoty stones was excavated in 1973 (White, BBCS, XXVII, 1977, 483-6) but evidence of date was ephemeral to say the least.

[8] RCAM *Anglesey*, 1937, 65.

[9] *Archaeol. in Wales*, 21, 1981, 20.

[10] I am grateful to David Longley (GAT) for this information.

[11] R.W.B. Morris, 'The Prehistoric Rock Art of Great Britain...' *Proc. Prehist. Soc.*, 55, 1989, 45-88.

Anglesey and they were very rare in Wales as a whole. In 1974, however, attention was drawn to a boulder with cup and ring markings standing in the garden of Llwydiarth Esgob near Llannerch-y-medd (NGR SH 436 844)[12]. Llwydiarth Esgob had been the home of Thomas Pritchard, a notable collector of antiquities and it was obvious that the stone had been brought to the house from elsewhere. But the size of the boulder and the fact that it is composed of a very rare horneblende picrite to be found in Anglesey only near Llannerch-y-medd, suggest that it did not come far. Unfortunately the outcrop from which it had been cut cannot be identified and so nothing can be said about the context of the find except that the carving with four cups and two sets of rings (Fig. 11a) is typical of such stones, which may be found most often in the Pennines, Northumberland and south west Scotland.

No new barrows have been identified or excavated in Anglesey since 1970, but the final report on the excavation of Bedd Branwen and the Treiorwerth barrow has been published[13]. The main results of the excavations which had taken place in 1966 and 1967 were incorporated in *Prehistoric Anglesey* (PA 159-72, 181-6) but the full publication includes details for which there was not room and the results of radiocarbon dating which were not available at the time of writing in 1970. Since that date more instances of the separate burial of infant earbones and the use of small bone pommels have come to light outside Anglesey[14].

Although no new barrow has been found, an 'urnfield' of some size was discovered on the hilltop of Capel Eithin (NGR SH 490 727) where there had been activity of some kind during the Neolithic[15]. Because this was a heavily ploughed field one cannot be certain that there had never been a cairn or mound over the burials; a similar question hangs over the 'urnfield' found in the last century at Cae Mickney (PA 196-9), a site which has many parallels to Capel Eithin.

Eleven Bronze Age burials were scattered over an area 13 × 7m (45 × 23ft) with a line of shallow pits and scoops containing mainly charcoal lying approximately parallel to the burials and some 3m (10ft) to the south (Fig. 12a). Two other cremations were found well away from the main group, one (C16) 30m (100ft) to the west and the other without an urn (C17) 30m to the north (Fig. 8a). The main group had been disturbed by two ditches which had cut through several of the burials and all of them had been damaged to a greater or lesser extent by ploughing. However it was possible to see that all the main group of cremations had been placed in pots and buried, either inverted or upright, in pits which were often a very tight fit. On two occasions (C9 and C12) the inverted urn had been protected by a flat slab over its base and in one (C13)

[12] F.M. Lynch and D.A. Jenkins, TAAS, 1974, 118-21.
[13] F.M. Lynch, 'Report on the Re-excavation of two Bronze Age Cairns in Anglesey; Bedd Branwen and Treiorwerth', *Arch. Camb.*, CXX, 1971, 11-83.
[14] F.M. Lynch, *Excavations in the Brenig Valley*, Cambrian Arch. Monographs,, *forthcoming* and G. Burenhult, *The Archaeological Excavations at Carrowmore, Co. Sligo. 1977-9*, Theses and Papers in Northern Archaeol., 9, 1980, 127.
[15] Interim Report: S.I. White, TAAS, 1981, 15-27. Bromfield in Herefordshire is a very similar site published since 1970 (Stanford, *Proc. Prehist. Soc.*, 48, 1982, 279-320) which has many parallels to Capel Eithin.

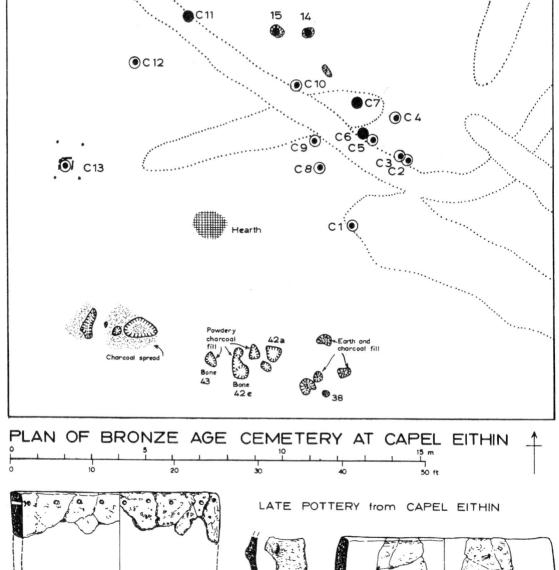

PLAN OF BRONZE AGE CEMETERY AT CAPEL EITHIN

Hearth

Charcoal spread

Powdery charcoal fill

Bone 43

Bone 42e

42a

Earth and charcoal fill

38

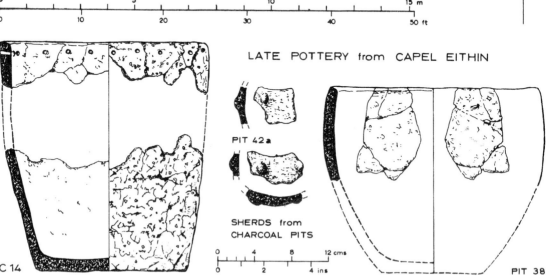

LATE POTTERY from CAPEL EITHIN

PIT 42a

SHERDS from CHARCOAL PITS

C 14

PIT 38

FIG. 12a. Plan of Bronze Age cremations and pits at Capel Eithin. Inverted urns: encircled dots; upright urns: solid dots. Later pottery from Pits 14, 42a and 38. Dotted outlines: later ditches (see Fig. 8a).

the urn had been inside a small stone cist which itself had been surrounded by some rectangular cover represented by four stakeholes. In two instances (C2 and 3 and C5 and 6) urns were paired, one containing the bone and the other being an Accessory Vessel. However in both instances the Accessory Vessels (C2 and 6) were badly damaged and the original absence of bone is a bit uncertain. C5 and C6 seem to have been placed in a single pit, but C2 and 3 were separate and a lignite bead (Fig. 13a), presumably a grave offering, is recorded with the Accessory Vessel, where it would be a bit unusual.

Most of the urns had been packed around with a great deal of charcoal and the group of pits to the south contained yet more. Charcoal obviously played a very significant role in Bronze Age funeral ceremonies; some of it probably came from the cremation pyre but other deposits were unusually fresh and pure and may have been made specially for ceremonial use. Two types of filling may be recognised among the pits to the south; five, which seem to form a close-set group, contained a 'powdery charcoal' while eight contained a stickier mixture of earth and charcoal, more likely the remains of the pyre. There were also two pits (42E and 43) which contained a more elaborate filling incorporating a few scraps of burnt human bone. In these pits the charcoal was concentrated at the bottom and sides and it is tempting to suggest that they may once have held a wooden box.

On the northern edge of the group of burials were two pits (14 and 15) which were very similar to Pits 42E and 43 in that they contained charcoal and a very few scraps of burnt human bone. They also contained pottery, in the case of 14 a coarse, straight-sided jar with holes under the rim (Fig. 12a). The sherds in 15 suggested a similar pot, but it was badly damaged. Such utilitarian pots are difficult to date on their own but radiocarbon dating of the charcoal in 15 revealed that these two pits were very much later than the others which they so much resembled. In fact the date (580 ±70 bc) suggests that they were dug during the Late Bronze Age or Early Iron Age, a date which is generally appropriate to the style of pottery used. Thus Chapel Eithin joins a growing list of burial sites which seem to have maintained a tradition of sanctity long beyond their main period of use, to see a revival of activity in the Iron Age[16]. It is all the more remarkable in this case where there seems to have been no visible marker or monument.

A high proportion of the burials have been radiocarbon dated and the results suggest that the site was used for 700 years during which the system of burial and style of pottery did not change very much[17]. Radiocarbon dates have to be used with great circumspection but one conclusion is inescapable — the site was in use for many generations. Within the long span three main periods may be recognised. The first period (centring on the 17th century bc) saw the burial of the main group of cremations (C6, C2, C11 and C12). They were already quite a widely scattered group since C11 and 12 are some distance from the others. A charcoal pit cut by Grave 35, up near the Late Neolithic 'structure' (F17-27) also belongs to this period but its association with the burials is uncertain (Fig.

[16] Stackpole in Williams *op. cit.*, 96-100; Plas Gogerddan in *Arch. in Wales*, 26, 1986, 29-31.
[17] Appendix 3.

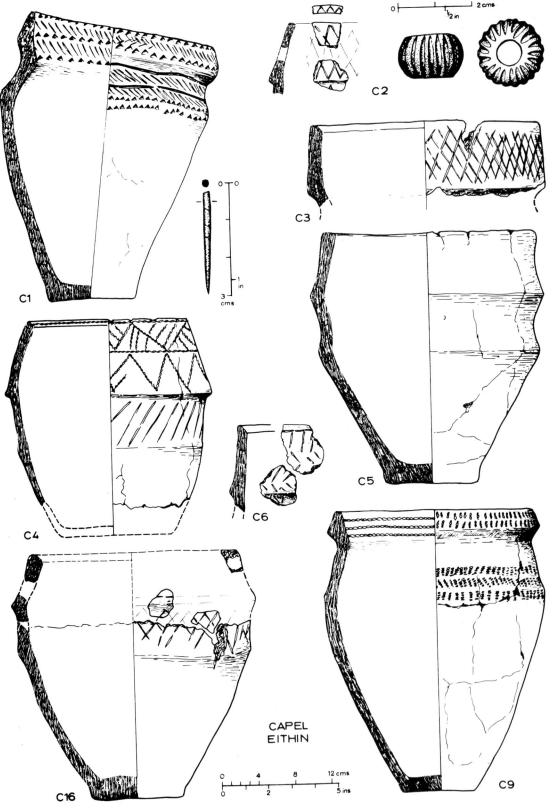

FIG. 13a. Burial urns from Capel Eithin. Jet bead from C2 and bronze pin from C1, full size.
Urn C7 is unillustrated because only the base remains.

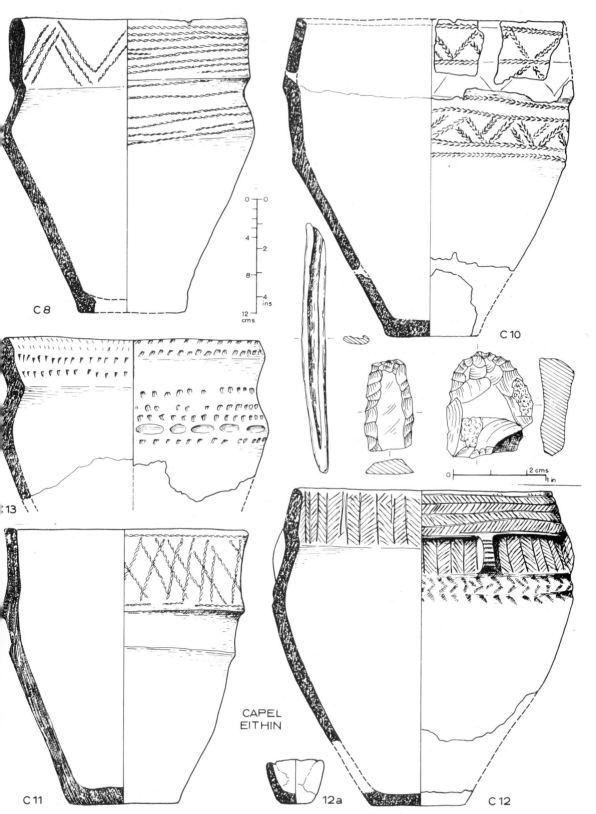

Fig. 14a. Burial urns and Pigmy Cup from Capel Eithin.
Bone point and flints from C10, full size.

8a). The second period centres on the 14th century bc and must have been broadly contemporary with the much shorter lived but more monumental burial sites at Bedd Branwen and Treiorwerth. This period is represented by two burials, C10 and 16, in every way similar to the earlier ones; C10 is placed close to them, but C16 is an outlier, some 30m (100ft) away (Fig. 8a). The third period, centring on the 11th century bc, saw one burial urn (C8) placed on the edge of the original group and the digging of two of the 'charcoal pits' (38 and 42a) to the west. Whether all these pits should be assigned to this late period is uncertain, but these two contained coarse sherds which would not be out of place in a Middle Bronze Age context (Fig. 12a). The burial urn, C8, however, is much earlier in style (Fig. 14a).

Another radiocarbon date which falls within this period is that obtained from the protected surface beneath a spread of stones designated 'Cairn'. The date and status of these is very uncertain. They do not seem to be the remnant of a stone monument over the Bronze Age burials; they appeared to be contained within an approximately rectangular kerb of larger boulders (10m × 3.5m (33′ × 11′6″) and were covered by an annular scatter of smaller stones which was thought to relate to a Roman structure lying 12m (40ft) to the south (Fig. 8a). Whatever the nature of these stones, they had protected a scatter of pottery of Late Neolithic and Bronze Age type lying on a surface which had been exposed during and perhaps beyond this third period of burial activity.

Over this long period only twelve adults and five children were buried in the cemetery; in four instances the children were buried with an adult, presumably the parent. One elderly female had suffered from osteoarthritis and two other elderly people had had trouble with their backs. The burial rituals seem to have been quite straightforward. In two instances (C3 and C5) the burial urn was accompanied by an Accessory Vessel but these did not contain anything like the intriguing earbones found at Bedd Branwen (PA 165).

The bones of a young child in C12 were accompanied by a small 'pigmy' or 'incense' cup but the grave goods, or personal possessions of the individuals buried, were few. The most interesting is a grooved jet or lignite bead from C2 which must be an import from Yorkshire like those from Bedd Branwen and Treiorwerth (PA 164, 183). All the other objects are more prosaic; a small sharp pin, probably bronze in C1, a split bone point in C10; some fragments of antler in C16 and some burnt flint implements and unworked flakes. Another bronze pin found in topsoil near the main group of pots may have come from a damaged urn. Although they were generous with their provision of urns to contain the bones (only C17 was without one) it is likely that both C10 and C13 were already damaged at the time of burial. The grave goods and pottery, therefore, do not give the impression that this community was wealthy at any time in its history but it was obviously tenacious of its traditions.

These traditions echo very closely those seen at Cae Mickney, Llanidan (PA 196-9) where a rather larger 'urnfield' was found in 1882. The pottery from Capel Eithin contains a similar range of shapes and decoration and the similarities between C8 and pot 12 from Cae Mickney (PA Fig. 56) are so close that one

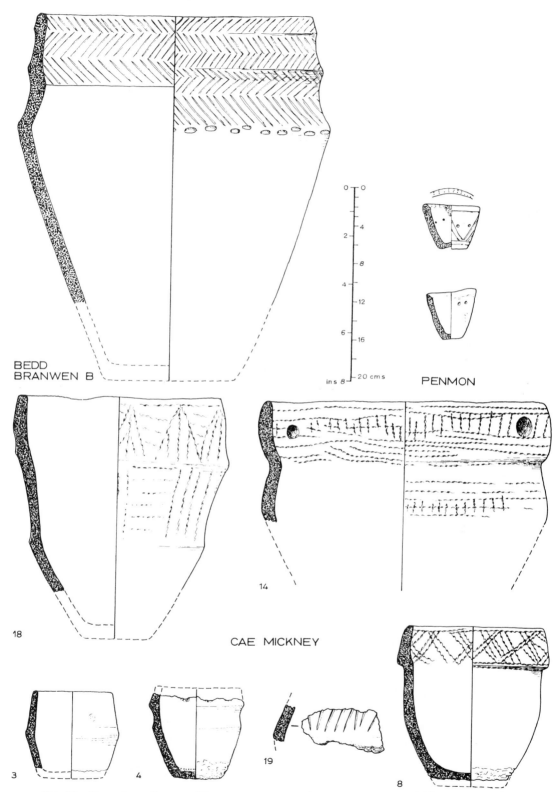

BEDD
BRANWEN B

PENMON

CAE MICKNEY

18

14

3

4

19

8

FIG. 15a. Recently re-discovered Bronze Age pottery. Bedd Branwen B: revised drawing (cf. PA
Fig. 44).

could believe that they were both made by the same potter. Other pots recall different Anglesey sites; for instance C13 has a Food Vessel-like profile reminiscent of Pot 2 from the early diggings at Treiorwerth (PA Fig. 49) and the unusual triangular spatula used on C1 is like that used to decorate the Bowl Food Vessel at Merddyn Gwyn (PA Fig. 52.2). The smaller urn, C4, is difficult to classify; in many ways it is similar to the Cordoned urns from Llandyfnan (PA Fig. 47.6) and Treiorwerth (PA Fig. 51.3) but it has a collar rather than a cordon and should perhaps be considered a true Collared Urn. This kind of ambiguity and the closeness of C1, 9 and 13 to Food Vessel profiles underlines the fact that in Anglesey and much of North Wales the two main styles of Bronze Age pottery were closely related and probably produced by the same potters[18]. It is certainly impossible to disentangle the stylistic traits shown by the large urn, C12, whose prominent vertical lugs and grooved shoulder are Food Vessel features, while the vertical neck and internal moulding belong to the Collared urn tradition, but especially that seen in Anglesey, which itself may have been influenced by Food Vessel styles in Ireland (PA 206). The pottery from Capel Eithin, therefore, fits well amongst the Early Bronze Age material already known from the island; what is more surprising is the longevity of these styles suggested by the spread of radiocarbon dates from this cemetery.

Since 1970 the Cae Mickney urns recorded by the Royal Commission but subsequently mislaid (PA 196 n.141) have been rediscovered in Bangor Museum. New drawings of nos. 3, 4 and 8 have been prepared together with drawings of sherds or previously unillustrated pots (14, 18 and 19). The two pigmy cups from Penmon (PA 193) have also turned up and are now in the National Museum of Wales[19]; new drawings have been prepared. A correction should be made to the illustration of Pot B from Bedd Branwen (PA Fig. 44); like Pots C, J, F and 1813, it has a faint 'necklace' around the shoulder.

The quantity of Bronze Age pottery excavated in Anglesey and the complexity and variety of the island's geology make it an ideal subject for compositional studies. One such study is in progress and preliminary results have been published[20]. Fifty-one sherds from Bedd Branwen, Treiorwerth, Cae Mickney, Plas Penrhyn, Llanddyfnan, Merddyn Gwyn and Bryn yr Hen Bobl were examined petrographically and eight were sampled further for heavy minerals and trace elements. This study (in which the petrographic analysis was the most illuminating) showed that the crushed rock used to temper the clay was predominantly of five types, mainly dolerites. This contrasted with the great variety of rock types which might be found in any sample of silts in the island and suggested that rocks were being specially selected for this role. The freshness of the fragments also suggested that the rock had been crushed and had not been collected from river gravels. The appearance of hornblende picrite from the Llwydiarth Esgob area in the pottery from Bedd Branwen and Treiorwerth

[18] F.M. Lynch, *Arch. Camb.*, CXXXIII, 1984, 30-2 and D.A. Jenkins in same, 45-7.
[19] NMW.84.89H.
[20] J.Ll. Williams and D.A. Jenkins in *Geoarchaeology*, (D.A. Davidson and M.L. Shackley edd), London, 1976, 115-35.

indicated a production centre not far from those sites, just as the presence of glaucophane schist at Plas Penrhyn showed that those pots had been made in the south east of the Island. The choice of such a limited range of available rock and the obvious preference for dolerite, a preference shared with other potters in the west of Britain[21], suggests a very specific knowledge of the qualities of the clay and filler which is indicative of professional production. This conclusion is at variance with the traditional view of a home-based pottery industry at this time[22]. When the study is complete it is hoped that the areas of production may be more closely pinpointed.

The problem of identifying Bronze Age settlements has still not been solved in Anglesey. Round wooden houses may be expected and these are notoriously difficult to find. Part of a shallow gully encircling a damaged hearth was found during the construction of the Shell pipeline near Pentraeth (NGR SH 506 793) but there was no dating evidence and to describe it as 'Bronze Age' would be optimistic[23]. Evidence from the Orkneys has shown that mounds of burnt stone (PA 280-2) may accumulate on Bronze Age settlement sites[24], but they may also be the products of industrial activity and those found recently in Anglesey will be described in the next section. However such indicators should not be ignored in the continuing search for this essential element in our understanding of man's life in the past.

[21] Stanford, *Proc. Prehist. Soc.*, 48, 1982, 279-320.
[22] Wardle, *Arch. in Wales*, 27, 1987, 16-7.
[23] R.B. White, BBCS, XXVII, 1977, 481-3.
[24] J. Hedges, *Proc. Soc. Antiq. Scotland*, 106, 1975, 39-98.

INDUSTRY AND TRADE
IN THE BRONZE AGE

SINCE 1970 there have been two major developments in the study of bronzeworking on Anglesey and one important new hoard of bronze tools has been found.

Parys Mountain near Amlwch has long been famous as a major source of copper ore. In the 18th and 19th centuries it was one of the world's most important copper mines[1] and the notable concentration in the island of large 'copper cake' ingots, some with official Roman stamps, has always hinted at a long history to mining in the area[2]. Because of the evidence for fire-setting in the old workings and the finds of primitive hammerstones on the hill[3], this was one of the sites selected for investigation by Oliver Davies during a survey of possibly early mining sites undertaken in 1937. He cut a section through what appeared to be an old waste tip and found a number of broken hammerstones and a good deal of charcoal but no diagnostic finds which would enable him (in the absence at that time of radiometric measurement) to assign a specific date to the workings. In accordance with the general opinion of the time he tentatively suggested a Roman date[4].

The search for early mining sites has been reopened during the last decade and, despite the fact that subsequent mining activity has inevitably destroyed a lot of the evidence, the results have been very rewarding[5]. The early sites have been recognised through the discovery of simple stone mauls and by the evidence of fire-setting against the mine walls. These mines normally seem to have been simple trench mines or short adits, but on the Great Orme at least, galleries descending over 30m (100ft) can be recognised amongst the maze of later workings[6]. The stone mauls, which are the simplest kind of tools, often just a beach pebble of hard rock, usually slightly modified by pecking a groove to secure a withy handle more firmly, were used to break out and crush the ore-bearing rock which had been weakened by the heat of burning a mass of timber piled against the face. They were frequently broken in the process and the spoil heaps

1 John Rowlands, *Copper Mountain*, AAS, Llangefni, 1966, reprinted 1981.
2 W.O. Stanley, *Archaeol. J.*, 30, 1973, 59-62.
3 C.S. Briggs in *Historical Metallurgy*, 10, 1, 1976, 43 referring to notes by Christopher Sykes of Sledmere (1796).
4 O. Davies TAAS, 1939, 40-2.
5 J. Ellis-Jones *Aspects of Ancient Mining and Metallurgy : Acta of a British School at Athens Centenary Conference*, Bangor 1988 and S. Timberlake *et al.* in *Arch. in Wales*, 1987 and 1988 for Welsh results, also P and S Crew (edd) *Early mining in the British Isles*, Plas Tan y Bwlch Occ. Paper 1, 1990, Snowdonia National Park, Maentwrog.
6 D. James in J. Ellis-Jones *op.cit.*, 115-21.

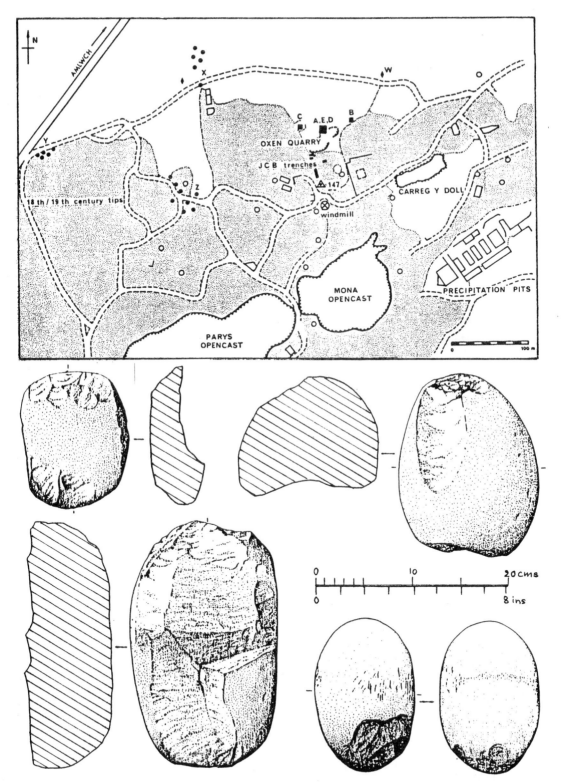

FIG. 16a. Parys Mountain, excavation sites (squares); surface finds of hammer stones (circles) and finds of slag, not *in situ*, (diamonds) with a selection of mauls. Reproduced from Timberlake 1988 by kind permission of the author and the editor.

contain large quantities of them interspersed amongst the waste rock and charcoal from the brushwood fires. The presence of this charcoal has revolutionised the study because, from it, it is possible to obtain reliable dates for the spoil heaps and for the fill of abandoned galleries. Radiocarbon dating has now demonstrated unequivocally that mines at Cwm Copa near Aberystwyth, on the Great Orme and on Mount Gabriel in Co. Kerry were being exploited during the Middle Bronze Age[7].

As a result of the success of his investigations in Cardiganshire Simon Timberlake decided to reopen Oliver Davies' excavations on Parys Mountain in 1988 in order to obtain charcoal for radiocarbon dating[8]. His trench through the same spoil heap revealed almost 2m (6ft) of mining waste. The top layers were clearly modern and they covered a thick layer of peaty soil which had built up between the period of the early workings and the resumption of mining in the 18th century. Beneath this were various lenses of waste rock and burnt material, a tip which included hammerstones and charred twigs throughout and incorporated at least one thick lens of charcoal which provided very secure samples for dating. These dates prove that ores were worked here in the 18th century bc[9]. This is at present the earliest date for copper mining in these islands.

The dated spoil heap is on the north side of the hill just below Oxen Quarry (NGR SH 443 906) which unfortunately must have removed the trench mine or adit from which the spoil was derived. Significant numbers of hammerstones have been found at three other sites on this north western flank of the hill where, because of glacial action, the ores are closer to the surface and would have been easier to locate and excavate in antiquity. All the hammerstones are very simple; so far none of the carefully made 'Grooved Mauls' have been found in a Bronze Age context. These mauls are especially common in Anglesey and the Bangor area[10], but have not been found in the mines, so their context and date remain uncertain.

⌐ Other new evidence for metalworking in the island is more enigmatic and difficult to interpret. Low, amorphous spreads of burnt stone and dark earth and charcoal have been recorded at a number of locations, always close to streams or marshy ground. Three are known in the Llantrisant area[11] and another may be easily seen near Bryn Eryr when the field is ploughed[12]. Another three examples were discovered in this Pentraeth area when the Shell Oil Pipeline was stripped[13]. Partial excavation revealed a very similar situation at each site; an amorphous spread of dark earth and burnt stones (predominantly dolerites) up to 30m (100ft) across but seldom more than 0.30m (1ft) thick might cover from

[7] *Arch. in Wales*. 28, 1988, 19.

[8] S. Timberlake, *Arch. in Wales*, 28, 1988, 11-14. Preliminary account.

[9] I am grateful to Mr Timberlake for permission to refer to this date before his full publication of the work.

[10] F.M. Lynch, *Bangor Museum Catalogue of Archaeological Material*, 1986, 64 and J. Pickin *Arch. in Wales*, 28, 1988, 18-9.

[11] A. Davidson in *Arch. in Wales*, 1984, 25 (where the NGR is wrong. Chwaen Hen is at SH 359 833) and TAAS, 1926, 23.

[12] NGR SH 541 759 (*Arch. in Wales* 1984, 25).

[13] R.B. White, BBCS, XXVII, 1977, 468-76.

one to six pits of variable size and about 0.3-0.5m (1-2ft) deep. These pits were filled with more cracked and burnt stones in a matrix of dark earth and charcoal. Occasionally the sides of the pit might be scorched red, but this was not always so. Sometimes the pits were cut into each other and there was one clear case of re-use suggesting a recurrent purpose.

Only one of the Anglesey sites provided any evidence of what this purpose might be. Site No. 6 near Tre-wyn, Llandyfrydog (NGR SH 454 852) was the only one that had been visible before topsoil stripping began. Excavation of a sample area revealed a single large pit, three possible postholes and some

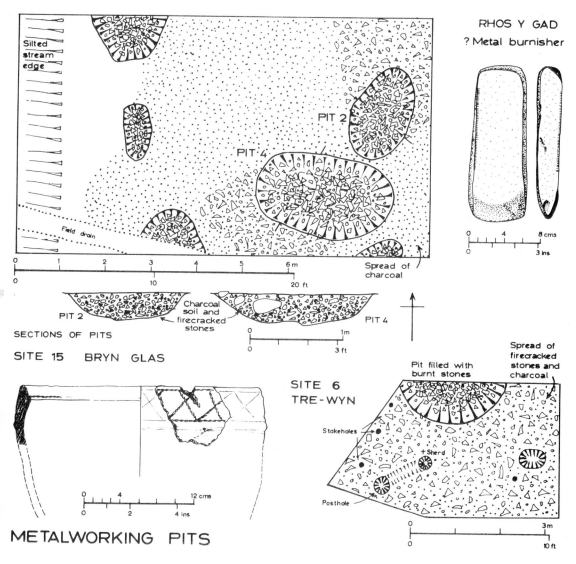

FIG. 17a. Plans of stone-filled pits at Bryn Glas and Tre-wyn with Bronze Age sherd from Tre-wyn. After White 1977. Probable metal burnisher from Rhos y Gad.

stakeholes. A sherd of Bronze Age pottery was found close to one of the postholes and a single piece of slag came from the stone-filled pit (Fig. 17a). It is notoriously difficult to identify metals from slag, but it is more than likely that this piece was the residue of copper smelting. Experiments have shown that it is possible to smelt copper in a pit such as this, though modern archaeologists have not built up sufficient experience to make their efforts very successful[14]. The presence of the pottery would suggest a date of about 1400 bc for the activity here but a radiocarbon date for charcoal from a similar pit at Site 3 near Dwigyr (NGR SH 418 916) came out at 2180 ± 100 bc which is surprisingly early if all these seemingly industrial pits are to be connected with metal working.

Very similar sites have been excavated at Rhuddlan in Clwyd and Graeanog south of Llanllyfni, but unfortunately neither site has been fully published so details are not yet available. At Rhuddlan one of a group of pits filled with charcoal and fire-cracked stones also contained Bronze Age pottery[15]; at Graeanog a group of similar pits produced evidence of intense burning but no slag; a very large mound of burnt stone had accumulated suggesting considerable industrial activity, but its exact nature is uncertain[16]. A similar uncertainty attaches to the activity evidenced by the large mounds of burnt stone at Carne in Dyfed which have a radiocarbon date as early as that from Dwigyr[17].

The presence of burnt stone and the invariable stream-side location suggest the need for heat and for hot water and there are many activities besides metalworking which might need such facilities. The traditional interpretation of burnt stone mounds is that they indicate cooking sites where large joints of meat were boiled in wooden troughs (PA 280-2). This explanation is still the most likely one for those high mounds which exhibit the characteristic crescentic shape. The mounds excavated by Neil Baynes at Penrhosllugwy (PA 281-2) and those on Mynydd Llwydiarth[18] are of this type and their height and relatively precise shape contrast strongly with the low amorphous spreads of stone which have been found to cover the 'industrial' pits. However, radiocarbon dating has shown that these cooking sites are also mainly of Bronze Age date and evidence from the Orkneys suggests that they are more closely associated with living sites than was previously believed[19].

The confirmation of early mining on Parys Mountain and the number of possible metalworking sites revealed by the random transect of the Shell Pipeline all indicate copper and bronze production on the island. It has often been forgotten that W.O. Stanley's excavations within the Tŷ Mawr huts near Holyhead in 1862 and 1868 revealed large quantities of fire-cracked stones associated with hearths and crushing mortars[20]. He was convinced that the occupants of the huts were

[14] J. Coles *Archaeology by Experiment*, London, 1973, 135.
[15] H. Miles, *Flints. Hist. Soc. Publics.*, 25, 1971, 1-8.
[16] I am grateful to Richard Kelly of Gwynedd Arch. Trust for information about this site before his final publication.
[17] H. James, BBCS, 33, 1986, 245-65.
[18] RCAM, *Anglesey*, 1937, 141.
[19] J. Hedges, *Proc. Soc. Antiq. Scotland*, 106, 1975, 39-98.
[20] W.O. Stanley, *Archaeol. J.*, 26, 1869, 301-18.

heavily involved with the metal industry, both copper and iron. It is regrettable that his finds are no longer available for study alongside similar evidence now coming from huts in Caernarfonshire, for early processing sites are proving even more elusive than the contemporary mines[21]. The number of moulds and other tools connected with this production is not especially high, but the very fine four-sided mould from Bodwrdin (broadly contemporary with the mining at Parys Mountain) should not be forgotten (PA 221-4). What was very likely a metal-burnishing tool was found in the last century at Rhos y Gad, Llanfairpwll (NGR SH 525 715) (Fig. 17a). It had belonged to the Rev. E. Evans and had been listed as a 'celt' or axe[22] but it can never have had a sharp blade and the degree of polish on it suggests that it had been a burnisher, imitating in shape the object on which it was to be used. Simpler rectangular burnishers are known from very early metalworkers' graves in the Netherlands[23]; there is an almost identical axe-shaped example from Penicuik in Midlothian[24] and another on view in the museum at Lough Gur, Co. Limerick which has the same, unexplained, nicks down one edge as on the Rhos y Gad piece.

Since 1974 a programme of analysis has been carried out on all Welsh bronze implements with the aim of identifying ore sources and metallurgical practices. This study has not yet been fully published[25] so the implications of the work in the wider field of British and Irish trade relations in prehistory cannot yet be assessed. The demonstration of early mining in Anglesey and Caernarfonshire must stimulate further consideration of the ore sources available. The broad results of this work are discussed more fully in the introductory chapter; here it suffices · to draw attention to Appendix 2 with the list of analytical results and a discussion of their implications kindly provided by Dr Peter Northover in advance of the full publication.

During the excavations at Capel Eithin near Gaerwen (NGR SH 490 727) a badly crushed gold ''lock ring'' was found in topsoil near a large roughly dug pit which cut through the centre of the site (Fig. 8a). The gold ornament was obviously in a derived position and the other contents of the pit suggested that it has been dug in the mid 19th century. It was at that time, 1856, that a large group of such ornaments was found at 'Gaerwen' (PA 239-42) and it is a reasonable assumption that this example had been dropped and crushed under foot in the excitement of that discovery[26]. The original record[27] is vague about the findspot and says that eleven ''lock rings'' were found with eleven bracelets. Since ''lock rings'' are more usually found in pairs it is easy to believe that the original deposit was twelve rather than eleven. Unfortunately the 19th century finders had dug

[21] I am grateful to Peter Crew, Plas Tan-y-Bwlch, for drawing my attention to this evidence.
[22] AAS Report 1914-15, 17. Evans Coll. no.16.
[23] D. Clarke *et al.*, *Symbols of Power in the Age of Stonehenge*, London, 1985, Fig. 4.3, Lunteren grave.
[24] Clarke *op.cit.* Fig. 4.6 (also mistaken for an axe!)
[25] Interim statement by J.P. Northover in H.N. Savory, *Guide Catalogue to the Bronze Age Collections*, NMW, Cardiff, 1980, 229-43.
[26] S.I. White TAAS, 1981, 24 and Plate 3. The ornament is 38mm across, the same size as the smaller one from the original group.
[27] See footnote 109, PA p.239.

such a large pit that no details survived about the original circumstances under which the treasure had been buried. This great hoard of gold must have been hidden here after the hill had ceased to be used for burials and before the revival of interest in the site in the Iron Age.

The only major group of Bronze Age tools found since 1970 was discovered in 1974 on the edge of Cors Bodwrog (NGR SH 406 775). In the last century a number of mined flints, presumably a trading hoard (PA 116 and Fig. 31.17-18), were found in the same bog but the exact position is not known. The bog drains into Llyn Hendref where palaeobotanical work has been undertaken. Unfortunately the pollen record is badly disturbed and interpretation is difficult, but the situation at about 1000 bc indicates that the lake level was high and the appearance of new herbaceous plants suggests that surrounding woodland was being opened up perhaps by burning, since charcoal occurs frequently. (Ruth Watkins, *pers. comm.*). The implication that extensive interference with vegetation did not begin until the Bronze Age accords with the distribution of monuments and finds (PA maps 3 and 4) which shows an increase in activity in this central part of the island at that date.

The bronzes were found on two separate occasions. The first group, two palstaves, two pieces of sword and an axe (Fig. 18a nos 1-4, 6) were found while the farmer was digging a hole to bury an animal, the others a few days later when relatives came to examine the hole more closely. The site is on the present edge of the bog and the tools were found under about 0.30m (1 ft) of peat on what may have been a slightly denser and more compact surface. The pieces were scattered over an area about 2m × 1m (6' × 3') but may be legitimately considered a single group[28].

The hoard consists of nine pieces; the tools, socketed axes, palstaves and a gouge with part of the handle lodged in the socket, are complete, though the axe and gouge are rather damaged and may have been thrown away as no longer really usable. The pieces of sword blade (3 & 4), the chape (7, the metal cover from the tip of a scabbard) and the razor (8), by contrast, are all very fragmentary and are presumably scrap for melting down and reuse. The palstaves look as if they may have been new and are perhaps products of the metalworkers themselves, for the group as a whole may well have come from a nearby workshop. There is no surface indication of occupation on the site which is right at the edge of the marsh, but such damp spots were not infrequently chosen for houses in the Late Bronze Age. The lakeside settlement at Ballinderry in County Offaly is a case in point[29]. It is not impossible that the Llangwyllog hoard (PA 242) came from another such site, for the setting is very similar. However, it should not

[28] I am most grateful to Mr and Mrs Lester of Caergeiliog for information about the circumstances of discovery and allowing me to study the hoard in its entirety. It remains in their possession and that of their cousin, Mr Len Williams, Bodwrog Farm. The gouge has been given to Dr Dafydd Alun Jones who has also very kindly allowed it to be studied and has generously given a fragment of the wooden handle in it to be dated by the British Museum. The first implements found were brought to Bangor Museum for identification and were published by Dr H.N. Savory in 'Some Welsh Late Bronze Age Hoards: Old and New', *Archaeologia Atlantica*, 1, 1975, 111-25 (Bodwrog 112-7).

[29] H.O'N. Henken, PRIA, 47C, 1942, 1-76.

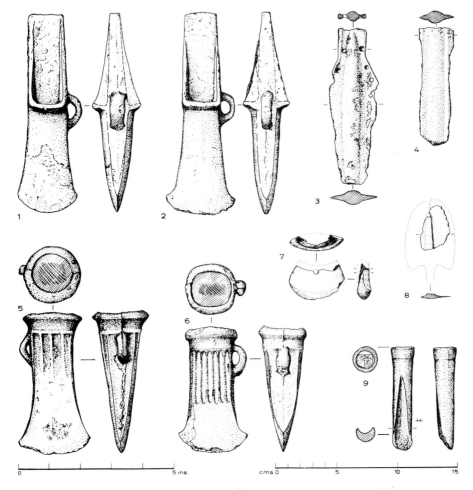

FIG. 18a. Late Bronze Age hoard from Cors Bodwrog.

be forgotten that the custom of making valuable offerings to water gods in lakes and bogs is well attested at this period[30], so finds like these may not necessarily imply settlement nearby.

Whether or not bronzesmiths were working at the edge of the bog it is very likely that the two large palstaves are the products of a local Anglesey tradition. Although they are very similar in size and appearance they are not actually from the same mould for the stop-ridge of 2 is much squarer than 1 and the metal-mix (Appendix 2) is different, but both are quite exceptionally massive, the blade being both broad and thick. This massiveness is unusual at this date but seems to be a feature of North Wales where customers were rather old-fashioned, preferring the palstave to the newer socketed axe forms. The closest parallels to The Bodwrog palstaves are one from Llangefni (PA 234, Fig. 63.13) and another from south Caernarvonshire in Bangor Museum[31] which share their massive proportions. The broken palstave found in Pigeon's Cave, Great Orme, with a

[30] R. Bradley, 'The interpretation of later Bronze Age metalwork from British rivers', *Internat, J. Nautical Archaeol.*, 8, 1979, 3-6 and 'Stages in the development of Hoards and votive Deposits' *Proc. Prehist. Soc.*, 53, 1987, 351-62.
[31] F.M. Lynch, *Bangor Museum Catalogue*, no. 119, Fig. 13.5.

gold "lock ring" like the ones from Gaerwen, has the same broad thick blade and is only slightly shorter. The massiveness and weight of these pieces distinguishes them from smaller palstaves of very similar design such as that from Lligwy (PA 234, Fig. 63.12) and those in the large workshop hoard from Guilsfield, Montgomeryshire, which date from the eighth century bc[32]. Both context and design suggest that the Bodwrog type is slightly later, probably seventh century bc.

The two socketed axes are rather more unusual; such tools are relatively rare in North Wales and neither belong to any of the standard groups. The larger axe (15) with three ribs on the face is similar in size and proportion to one from Chwilog in Lleyn[33] and another from Llanegryn in Merioneth found with a large palstave, not unlike those from Bodwrog, but with ribs below the stop-ridge[34], but both these axes have four ribs on the face. The smaller axe (6) with a ridged face is very unusual indeed; two unpublished axes from north east Wales are said to be broadly similar, but there are no close parallels known[35]. This, too, may turn out to be of local manufacture, but on this evidence it is not possible to prove it.

The gouge is a wood-working tool which was popular throughout the Late Bronze Age and, with very little variation, they are found from Ireland to northern France and beyond. This one has a flat collar which those in the Guilsfield hoard do not, although it is probably closer to them in date than to the collared one found with a Hallstatt sword at Brogynton, Salop[36]. The handle had broken off and its tip remained in the socket; it had been made from ash[37].

The pieces of scrap, being weapons and personal goods more susceptible to 'fashion', are rather more sensitive indicators of date; they also suggest more far-flung connections to the south east. The chape is the most exotic piece. It is the first one to be found in Wales, all the others have come from the south east, mainly East Anglia where they have been found at Gray's Thurrock, Felixstowe and Reach Fen in workshop hoards containing gouges and axes and broken spears and swords very much in the manner of this collection from Bodwrog[38]. At Reach Fen there were also some bronze studs very like those from Llangwyllog and a tanged chisel like that in the Tŷ Mawr hoard from Holyhead (PA Figs. 68 & 69). The razor from Bodwrog recalls that from Llangwyllog and the type is also found at another fenland site, Feltwell[39], where the hoard included a gold "lock ring" and amber beads as well as a pair of tweezers like those from Llangwyllog. These inter-connections demonstrate that the three Late Bronze Age hoards from Anglesey are all broadly contemporary, showing that, during the seventh century bc, people in the island (especially professional metalworkers

[32] NMW *Bronze Age Catalogue*, Fig. 40, 307 and Fig. 32, 268.
[33] Lynch *op. cit.*, Fig. 44, 285.
[34] NMW *op. cit.*, Fig. 44, 285.
[35] H.N. Savory, *Archaeol. Atlantica*, 1, 1975, 114.
[36] NMW *op. cit.*, Fig. 44, 288.
[37] I am grateful to Dr Pat Denne for this identification.
[38] Gray's Thurrock, *Antiq. J.*, 2, 1922, 105-8. Felixstowe, *Inventaria Archaeologia*, GB.16. Reach Fen, *Inv. Arch.* GB.17.
[39] Feltwell Fen, *Inv. Arch.* GB.35.

like those at Tŷ Mawr and Bodwrog) were in touch with both Ireland and the east of England, while producing locally designed pieces for a local market.

Many workshop or founders' hoards like that from Bodwrog contain pieces of broken swords and they are often a good indicator of date and commercial contacts. Unfortunately the two pieces from Bodwrog, which are not from the same blade, are not easy to place in context. They have unusually well-defined midribs which means that they do not belong to the standard British Ewart Park type, nor the common Continental Carp's Tongue variety which was popular in the south of England in the seventh century bc. However Dr Savory in his study of part of the hoard published in 1975[40] thought that they might prove to be a rare precursor of the Carp's Tongue variety and, as such, are of great potential interest.

In an island with a wealth of metal resources it is perhaps surprising that relatively so few prehistoric bronzes have been found, this small but interesting hoard being the only discovery in twenty years.

[40] H.N. Savory, *op. cit.*, 115-6.

THE CELTIC IRON AGE

IN 1970 it was recognised that the traditional Romano-British date for the groups of round stone huts which were common among the surviving field monuments of the island might need serious revision (PA 279). It was believed, however, that the evidence for a new chronology was unlikely to be found at any of the Anglesey sites. While the proof of a Bronze Age origin for these settlements in Wales is still elusive (despite plentiful evidence from other upland areas such as Dartmoor[1]), in fact recent work in Anglesey has been able to demonstrate that at least two of the hut groups on the Island were being occupied during the Iron Age. It is probable that many more were.

Because pottery was very rare or undistinctive during the Iron Age and in post-Roman times, occupation during these periods was almost impossible to recognise in the archaeological record, whereas the use of well-known and widely traded pottery in the second, third and fourth centuries AD made activity in the Romano-British period very easy to demonstrate. The distortions that this situation produced have now been remedied by the evidence obtained from radiocarbon and other chronometric dating systems. Despite the inherent imprecision of the method it has enabled new excavations to demonstrate much longer periods of occupation, often beginning in the pre-Roman Iron Age and continuing through into the Dark Ages. The centuries of prosperity and trade under Roman rule can now be seen as but an episode in an unbroken tradition of social and economic life in these farmsteads or small hamlets. The history of settlement on undefended sites now parallels more closely and more convincingly the history of occupation of hillforts which may be seen as simply occupying a different social niche.

The hut groups spread along the lower slopes of Holyhead Mountain have for many years been central to any discussion of the problem of later prehistoric settlement in Anglesey. The prospect of a Bronze Age origin has always been recognised since the Tŷ Mawr hoard (PA 246) was found nearby; Stanley's excavations laid bare the extent of the villages and provided evidence of their economic foundation, though his dating evidence proved misleading (at least for Tŷ Mawr) largely because of subsequent misunderstanding; and now excavations in the north eastern part of the Tŷ Mawr group (NGR SH 213 822) in 1978-82 have provided proof of occupation both before and after the Roman period[2].

In the mid 19th century the remains at Tŷ Mawr alone consisted of up to

---

[1] A. Fleming *The Dartmoor Reaves*, London 1989.
[2] W.O. Stanley, *Archaeol. J.*, 24, 1867, 229-42; 26, 1869, 301-22; 27, 1870, 147-64; A. Way, *Archaeol. J.* 28, 1871, 144-54; C.A. Smith, *Arch. Camb.*, CXXXIII, 1984 — CXXXVI, 1987 (see below).

fifty huts but many were lost to agricultural improvement before any excavation began. Stanley cleared at least ten huts in two campaigns in 1862 and again in 1868. He worked in the large circular huts and in the small semi-subterranean rectangular structures which he concluded were workshops. His finds were largely stone: mortars, grinding stones, hammers and pounders. At least one of the hammers[3] was grooved around the middle like those from the early mine sites and on one occasion a mortar was found filled with crushed quartz[4]; a good deal of slag which analysis suggested was from iron[5] was found around some of the hearths, together with what Stanley identified as 'moulding sand' and a great number of fire-cracked stones or 'pot boilers'. All in all it was a convincing picture of a community for whom metal processing was a major economic activity[6]. The presence of iron suggests that the main occupation was post-Bronze Age but Stanley was unable to date it very precisely. He found a good deal of 'coarse gritty pottery' which he felt was probably prehistoric but the only closely datable finds were 12 badly corroded Roman coins of the late second century AD from Hut C. These coins and the undoubted Roman pottery from the huts at Pen y bonc and Twr[7] have dominated thinking about the date of the settlement as a whole. Unfortunately the coarse pottery which might now be recognisable as Late Bronze Age or Iron Age never reached the British Museum where Stanley regularly sent his better finds[8].

In 1978, as part of a project to extend the public display of the site, it was decided to re-excavate Hut S and attendant structures[9]. This work by Dr C.A. Smith exposed a homestead, two huts and an enclosed yard, which had undergone quite a complex sequence of development. Fronting the homestead was a narrow field into which two structures, presumably huts broadly similar to the earlier ones, had been built some centuries later, by which time the original farm was ruined, but usable for storage and some crop processing. The discovery of several flint implements of Mesolithic type and Late Neolithic dates obtained from two hearths beneath soil built up within the yard reveal that the spot had been occupied on previous occasions, but the stone structures are likely to belong to the first millenium bc.

The first phase of the homestead cannot be dated but the second hut (S) had been built before 200 bc, the date obtained from a heap of limpet shells (164, Fig. 19a) thrown out at the back and lying against a wall which abuts the hut. It is likely that the modifications to that hut took place within a few generations for there was no Roman material found in the homestead either by Stanley or by Smith. In the third century AD there was some activity in a small hut (T4) at the foot of a steep bank or lynchet built up by soil creep in the ploughed

[3] *Archaeol. J.*, 26, 1869, Fig. 11 between 322 and 323.
[4] *loc. cit.* 306.
[5] Analysis: *Archaeol. J.*, 27, 1870, 152, ftnt.
[6] *Archaeol. J.*, 26, 1869, 310-18.
[7] *Archaeol. J.*, 27, 1870, 151-4.
[8] There are a few sherds (NMW 33.560.40-44) of what might be Late Bronze Age pottery from O'Neill's excavation of the huts at Porth Dafarch — a site of undoubted long occupation (PA 92).
[9] C.A. Smith, *Arch. Camb.*, CXXXIII, 1984, 64-82 (earlier work); CXXXIV, 1985, 11-52 (structural sequence); CXXXV, 1986, 12-80 (finds); CXXXVI, 1987, 20-38 (chronology and discussion).

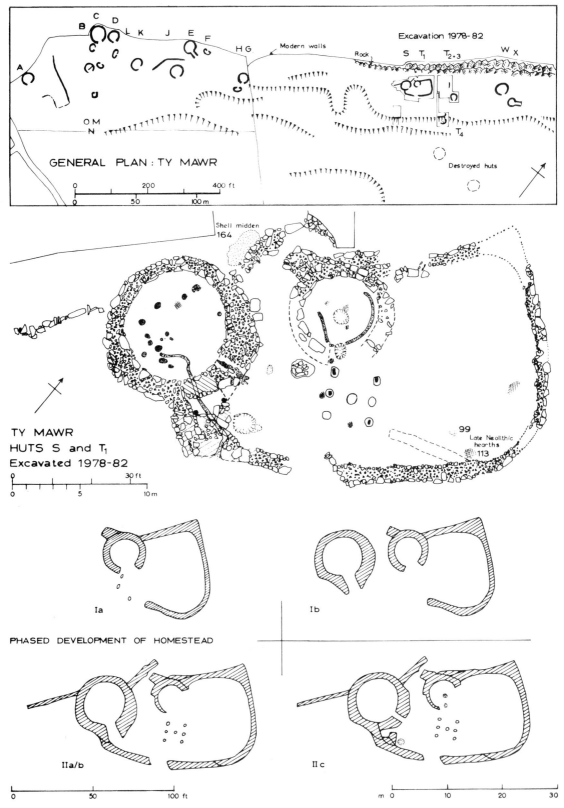

FIG. 19a. Tŷ Mawr huts. General plan after RCAM *Anglesey* and details and interpretation of S and T after Smith 1985 and 1987.

field above and this agricultural activity was renewed in the sixth century AD when straw was being burnt in the ruins of hut T1 and pits were dug into its floor. It was finally used as a dump for burnt stone, suggesting that some industrial activity continued throughout the life of the settlement, although the main living area, by this time, may have moved further along the slope.

Stanley had excavated the large hut (S) in 1868 and had found at least two hearths with evidence of metalworking. Unfortunately his work had removed the floor levels and nothing remained of the metalworking evidence. The bottoms of postholes survived to suggest a ring of roof supports, necessary in such a large building (7m/22ft). Examination of the walls revealed that the original doorway, with its long drainage gully, had been blocked and a new one provided when a re-alignment of the yard wall made access difficult (IIc). The awkward relationship between the original entrance and the extended yard wall is the basis for postulating a stage (Ib) when Hut S was free standing.

The chronological relationship between Huts S and T1 is not stratigraphically proven. Hut T1 had not been previously excavated but it had been very badly disturbed in antiquity so the floor levels and finds were disappointing. A drain was recognised, but there was no evidence for the original use of the hut which must have been rendered inaccessible by the building of the 'seven-post structure' in front of it. It was probably at this time (IIa/b) that the front half was actually demolished while the back wall became part of the enclosing yard. The structure in front of it is interpreted as a granary, a wooden sleeper beam building (3.40m (11′) square) raised on stone supports some 0.40m (1′4″) above the ground. This is a very unusual version of a common Iron Age storage structure — the 'Four-poster'; Stanley's plans, however, suggest that there may have been others amongst huts at Plas Meilw and Pen y Bonc[10].

The new excavations at Tŷ Mawr have demonstrated the long duration and complexity of settlement on the slopes of Holyhead Mountain. It is obviously simplistic to see all the huts as contemporary even when they are close together and it may be better to think of the straggle of buildings along the contour as a series of discrete clusters or homesteads[11] occupied at different periods, these periods including both pre- and post-Roman phases. These excavations have extended our understanding of the agricultural activities of the community — plough marks were found within the narrow field fronting the homestead[12], wheat, barley and oats were being grown in the sixth century AD and horses, cattle and sheep were being reared[13], but unfortunately little more was learnt about the industrial side of their life, so much stressed by Stanley in his analysis of the results of his own work.

Continuity of settlement from the later Iron Age through the Roman period and beyond has been demonstrated by recent excavations at another Anglesey

[10] *Archaeol. J.*, 26, 1869, 308-10. For a discussion of such granaries see H. Gent, 'Centralised storage...', *Proc. Prehist. Soc.*, 49. 1983, 243-67.
[11] *Arch. Camb.* CXXXVI, 1987, 29. Stanley's original survey emphasised the clustering within the group (*Archaeol. J.*, 24, 1867, 232).
[12] *Arch. Camb.*, CXXXIV, 1985, 44.
[13] *Arch. Camb.*, CXXXV, 1986, 64-69.

site, Bryn Eryr near Llansadwrn (NGR SH 540 757)[14]. Superficially this was a very different site from Tŷ Mawr in that the field evidence consisted of a square ditched enclosure in which no huts were visible. But buildings were revealed by excavation; they had been made from wood, turf and clay, but in size and plan they were very similar to those in Holyhead and the social group who used them must have had much in common with the occupants of Tŷ Mawr.

Like the Tŷ Mawr homestead the establishment at Bryn Eryr had grown over the years. The first phase, which has not been precisely dated[15], consisted of a single large hut (9m/30ft in diameter) within an incomplete enclosure formed by a narrow trench which must have held a simple wooden fence, a farm which had been created by clearing away alder and hazel woodland. The hut is best defined by the shallow 'eaves drip' gulley which would have collected the water off the conical roof. The wall had been of turf or clay for it was recognisable only as a spread a hard clay echoing the line of the eaves. The inside of the wall may have been lined with wattle and the roof was supported by a number of posts. A multiplicity of stone-covered drains ran across the floor, but they may belong to later periods for this house continued in occupation for a long time.

In the second phase the farm was remodelled on a much more impressive scale. A massive ditch (4m/13ft wide and 2m/6ft deep) was dug and the clay heaped up into a correspondingly large bank which covered part of the earlier fence. The original house continued to be occupied but another, slightly smaller, was built close beside it, the new wall covering a section of the original eaves gulley. The combined drainage was carried away by a ditch cutting through the western side of the bank while a hard standing was laid down in the eastern entrance. Substantial postholes in the farmyard can be grouped into three or more square structures which may be interpreted as granaries and, together with the imposing enclosure, they speak of a prosperous establishment.

Charcoal deposits from the bottom of the ditch have provided a date of about 150bc for this phase, perhaps a generation or so later than the enlargement of Tŷ Mawr. This is certainly the apogee of the Bryn Eryr farm and it may also be the period when a number of other impressive farms, Caer Leb near Brynsiencyn and Hendrefor for instance[16], were established. It has always been assumed that these big sites belonged to a period of prosperity under Roman rule, but a noticeable improvement of climate during the later Iron Age[17] may have encouraged an earlier period of agricultural expansion, for several previously undatable sites are now being shown by radiocarbon and archaeomagnetic assay to belong to this horizon[18].

Despite the impressive size of the farmyard, finds were not plentiful. There

[14] I am grateful to David Longley for information in advance of his full publication of the excavations of 1985-7. Interim reports in *Arch. in Wales*, 26, 1986, 42; 28, 1988, 57.

[15] The date CAR 1058 (290 ± 80 bc) comes from a length of palisade trench which cannot be related to the first house, but it is clearly earlier than the main ditch.

[16] RCAM, *Anglesey*, 1937 112 (Hendrefor) and 104 (Caer Leb).

[17] J.A. Taylor, *Culture and Environment in Prehistoric Wales*, Oxford, 1980, 125 and J. Turner in Simmons and Tooley (edd) *The Environment in British Prehistory*, London 1981, 261.

[18] Erw Wen, R.S. Kelly, *Proc. Prehist. Soc.*, 54, 1988, 119-30, 137-40; Crawcwellt West, Mer. dates not yet published, but see *Arch. in Wales*, 27, 1987, 41 and 28, 1988, 54-5.

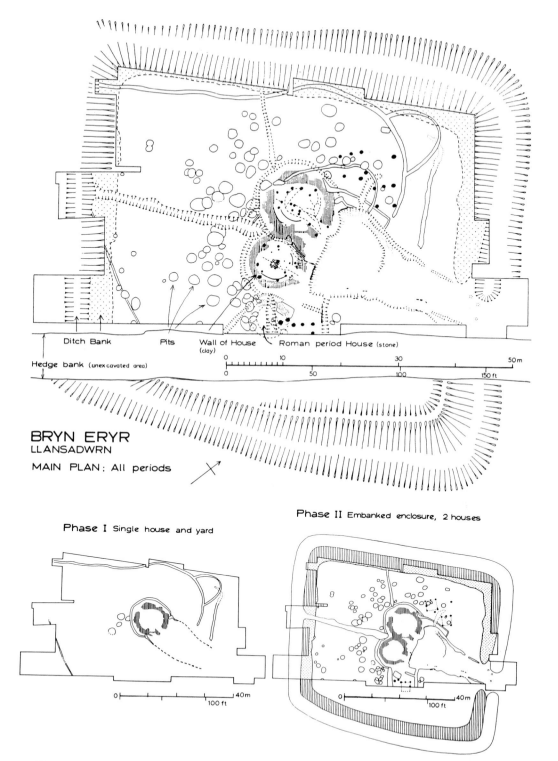

FIG. 20a. Bryn Eryr, Llansadwrn. General plan and pre-Roman phase plans kindly supplied by David Longley prior to his own publication of the excavations.

was no evidence for the metalworking so prominent at Tŷ Mawr and the establishment seems to have been purely agricultural; the most common finds were querns and mortars for processing crops. Plough marks under the bank suggest that crops were grown close to the earliest stockaded yard even though no cereal pollen or grains were found in deposits of that date. Botanical analysis of the ditch silts has shown the presence of glume wheat at a time when the ditch was well maintained — probably in Phase 2 during the later Iron Age. Bones reveal the presence of cattle and sheep, but no pigs.

The only pottery of Iron Age date was the very coarse gritty material known as stony VCP (Very Coarse Pottery) which, it is now generally agreed, represents packing material for salt loaves from the Cheshire mines[19]. This material, which has been the subject of a good deal of controversy (PA 277), is now recognised as very useful evidence for a trading network linking the more prosperous sites of the later Iron Age. At the beginning of the period it has a limited distribution within about 30 miles of Nantwich but by the third century bc it is found much more widely across North Wales and down the Marches, and the trade continues until disrupted by the Roman invasion.

It is possible that Stanley's coarse pottery might have been of this kind, for another Anglesey farmstead, Pant y Saer near Benllech (PA 278-9) has produced this material. An Iron Age origin can now be postulated for Pant y Saer with more confidence and a serious reconsideration of all the excavation records from this homestead would be highly desirable. Certain elements of the groundplan, it has been suggested, hint at the possibility of an early phase with wooden buildings and it is one of the very rare sites to produce artefactual evidence of Dark Age occupation — a fine tinned bronze brooch of fifth to sixth century AD date[20].

On the other hand the stoneless pottery from Dinas, Plas Cadnant, which has been mentioned in this same context (PA 277-8) has been examined microscopically and shown not to belong to this class of material[21]. Moreover the split-structure entrance may now be compared to the Roman-period 'threshing barn gateway' at Cefn Graeanog[22], rather than hillfort guard chambers.

The late Iron Age was the most prosperous time in the history of the farm at Bryn Eryr, but occupation is recorded there as late as the fourth century AD. Botanical evidence for scrub vegetation and the absence of cereal grains and pollen in the silted ditch might suggest that the farm had been abandoned, perhaps due to the Roman invasion. The excavator, however, believes that occupation was uninterrupted for the site was certainly occupied not long afterwards when the central house seems to have been still habitable since Romano-British pottery was found on its floor. The original, northern house had decayed and a new one

[19] Elaine Morris, 'Prehistoric Salt Distributions...' BBCS, 32, 1985, 326-35.
[20] Suggestion of early wooden phase in R.S. Kelly, *Proc. Prehist. Soc.*, 54, 1988, 148; N. Edwards and A. Lane, *Early Mediaeval Settlement in Wales: AD 400-1100*, Bangor and Cardiff, 1988, 99. The brooch was previously described as silver.
[21] NMW 38.643/1. Ms notes in NMW.
[22] Cefn Graeanog, GAT excavations, *forthcoming*.

with stone walls was built to the south where, earlier, granaries had stood. The occupants at this time favoured barley rather than wheat. New drains had to be cut across the yard as it became increasingly waterlogged, perhaps because of the neglect of the surrounding enclosure ditch which was almost completely silted up at this time. However, like moated sites of the present day, the defences might have been neglected but the standard of living (indicated by the presence of trade goods in this third phase) seems to have been reasonably high.

The excavations at Tŷ Mawr and Bryn Eryr have demonstrated the very long period of time during which the stone huts, which are some of the commonest antiquities of Anglesey, might have been occupied. Without excavation it would be unwise to claim that all these sites would show the same longevity and it remains true that most of the casual finds from them are undatable. In the course of cataloguing the collections in the Museum of Welsh Antiquities in Bangor a certain amount of material from Anglesey huts has come to light and attention should be drawn to the pair of fine Romano-British oxhead escutcheons found at Dinas near Holyhead, a site whose antiquity was previously only grudgingly admitted (PA 272)[23]. Excavations at Trefadog (PA 273) have not produced prehistoric material, but the earliest rampart, beneath the mediaeval bank is undated and might be early[24]. On the other hand the putative Iron Age phase at Castell Bryn Gwyn (PA 103) should perhaps be abandoned[25]. Another promontory (now an island) on the north coast, Ynys y Fydlyn (NGR SH 290 917) was cut off by a previously unnoticed bank which may have been defensive[26]. Aerial photography is continually augmenting the record of enclosures on the island but without excavation it would be unwise to claim that they are all prehistoric[27].

The only recent excavation within any major hillfort has been at Caer y Tŵr on Holyhead Mountain. No prehistoric material was found but the 'Roman lighthouse' (PA 266) was shown to be a fourth century AD signal station. This establishment was probably part of a series linking the fort at Chester to the naval outpost at Holyhead in much the same way and on many of the same sites as the Mersey Docks and Harbour Board system of the last century[28].

No new evidence for formal Iron Age burial has come to light, but the sixth century bc bone in a pit at Capel Eithin should not be forgotten (p 353), nor the renewed interest in the burial chamber at Trefignath, though this may have been no more than casual vandalism (p 334).

Difficulties of interpretation and dating always surround the carved stone

[23] FM Lynch, *Bangor Museum Catalogue of Archaeological Material*, nos.245-7, 255-8; 267, 273,77; J. Ellis Jones, TAAS, 1987, 19-26.

[24] Gwynedd Arch. Trust excavations directed by David Longley; publication forthcoming in *Mediaeval Archaeology*.

[25] See review by J.L. Davies, *Arch. Camb.*, CXXI, 1972, 114.

[26] I am grateful to Dr Jane Rees for drawing my attention to this site.

[27] Flying by Mrs Mary Aris (Gwynedd Archives Service) RCAM (Aberystwyth), and GAT. The Sites and Monuments Record in GAT is available for consultation. Two UCNW dissertations list much relevant information (Owenna Grey (1984) and Bob Becker (1990)). An undated enclosure is recorded at SH 498 779, near Talwrn by H.S. Chapman and R.H. Roberts (BBCS, XXIX, 1981-2, 845-6).

[28] P. Crew, *Arch. in Wales*, 21, 1981, no. 49, 35-6.

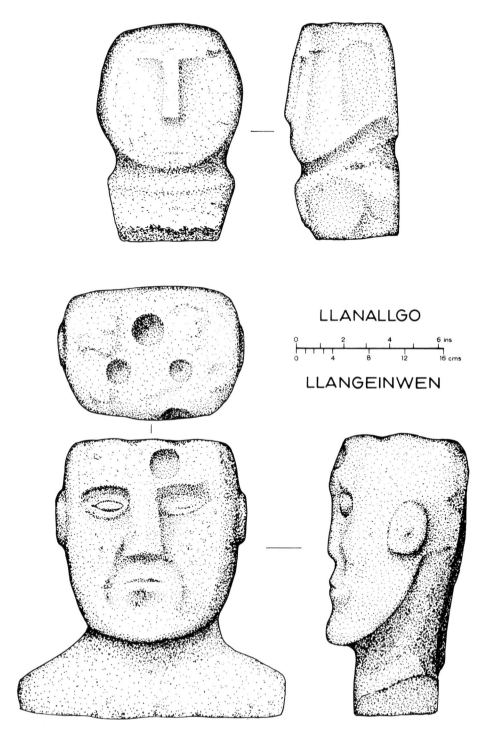

LLANALLGO

LLANGEINWEN

FIG. 21a. Stone heads from Llanallgo and Llangeinwen.

heads which are found from time to time on the island (PA 316). Of those found or recorded since 1970 only two are likely to be prehistoric. Both are illustrated in Fig. 21a. The upper one is a small head with very simple features; only the nose and the neck are clearly defined. It is made from a fine grained sandstone and was found in 1983 when a wall was demolished at Cae Marl, Llanallgo (NGR SH 501 849)[29]. Mary Vaughan Jones, in publishing the head in 1984, drew attention to the holy well, Ffynnon Allgo, not far away and made the very plausible suggestion that the head might originally have had some connection with the well since the Celtic association of heads with wells was common.

The second head, from the collection of Col. Lloyd Hughes of Plas Penrhyn is now in the National Museum of Wales, Cardiff[30]. It is said to have been found close to Llangeinwen Church (NGR SH 440 658) but no details about its discovery survive. The head and shoulders are much more elaborately carved than the previous one and it is possible to note some stylistic points which suggest that it is Iron Age or Romano-British rather than mediaeval. The left eye has been damaged but the right one retains a clear double outline, very similar to the treatment of the eyes on the Hendy Head, as is the straight profile and the flat top of the head (PA 316, Fig. 92). This flat top has three deep cups cut into it which may be a version of the 'offering cup' found on some early heads[31]. The stone is a coarse conglomerate, almost certainly from Anglesey.

Tacitus, in speaking of the political reasons for the Roman invasion of Anglesey, mentioned the number of refugees from the Belgic areas of south eastern England who had fled to the Island and were causing trouble for the Roman authorities[32]. In 1970 it was possible to point to the slave chains and some other Belgic pieces from the great deposit at Llyn Cerrig Bach[33], and to the sword from Gelliniog Wen as evidence for their presence (PA 284, 312). Two brooches from the Moelfre area may now be added to the list of finds which substantiate Tacitus's claim that southern refugees were here in some numbers.

The first of these brooches was found in 1983 while clearing a ditch in one of the fields of Glyn, Llanbedrgoch (NGR SH 520 810)[34]. It belongs to a well-known type, rare in the north west but extremely common in south east England where it is particularly characteristic of the first century AD levels in the Belgic town of Camulodunum (Colchester)[35].

The brooch is of copper alloy, probably bronze, of the *fibula* or safety pin type and, apart from a bent pin and catchplate, it is in very good condition. It

[29] *Arch. Camb.*, CXXXIII, 1984, 154-5. I am grateful to Mrs Owen for permission to study the head and to make a new drawing of the side view.
[30] *Arch. Camb.*, CXXVIII, 1979, 156-9. The head from Llandegfan listed here is unlikely to be ancient despite the hole in the mouth. It appears to be an architectural piece. It is in Bangor Museum, 77/23.
[31] A. Ross, *Pagan Celtic Britain*, 1967, Pl. 17.
[32] Tacitus, *Agricola*, XIV.
[33] Since 1970 another spearhead, almost identical to PA Fig. 82, 13 had been recorded (TAAS, 1969-70, 243-6). It was found shortly after the main group and has now been donated to Oriel Môn.
[34] TAAS, 1983, 121-4. The finder, Peter Corbett, and the landowner, Roger Tebbutt, have very generously given the brooch to Bangor Museum (2/83).
[35] C.F.C. Hawkes and M.R. Hull, *Camulodunum: First Report on the Excavations at Colchester 1930-1939*, Soc. Antiq. London Research Report XIV, 1947, 308-10.

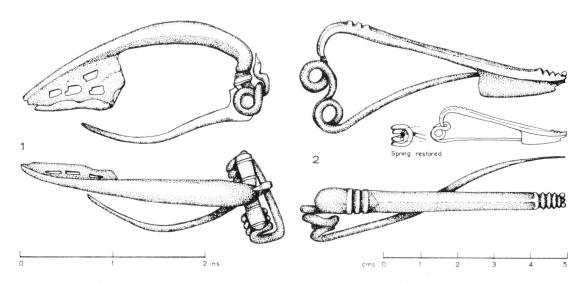

Fig. 22a. Late Iron Age copper alloy brooches from Glyn, Llanbedrgoch (1) and Moelfre (2)

has a facetted, curved bow, a pierced catchplate, an eight-coil spring covered by two side-wings with engraved lines and an external chord caught by a small hook. The pin is a separate piece held by a spindle inside the coils of the spring[36]. This use of what is in effect a false spring is unusual and suggests that this particular brooch is probably a late example of the type. None of the 'Colchester brooches' from Colchester itself use this arrangement but it was used as a repair system on some contemporary examples and such hinges become increasingly popular on later brooches[37].

The second brooch was found by Andrew Gillespie of Stockport in 1988 while he was examining the banks of a recently dredged stream near Din Lligwy, Moelfre (NGR SH 504 857)[38]. This brooch, too, is of copper alloy and is in good condition apart from a badly twisted spring. It seems probable that this damage occurred in antiquity because the pin has been bent back so that it would be possible to continue to use the brooch. Unlike the brooch from Glyn, this example does not belong to any well known group. In fact it has proved impossible to find any close parallels for it, though it may be broadly compared to the rare *knotenfibeln* and to the 'Nauheim Derivative' brooches which are known from southern England[39].

The brooch has a straight gently ridged bow decorated with three sharply moulded transverse grooves at the top and four transverse ridges at the tip ending with two little knobs like the eyes of a snail. The transition from the round-

[36] The description of the manufacture of the brooch in TAAS 1983 is defective because of the loss of some words in the printing. It is hoped that the structure of the brooch is clear from the expanded drawing in that publication.

[37] C.F.C. Hawkes, *Antiq. J.*, 20, 1940, 492-5 and C.F.C. Hawkes and M.R. Hull, *op. cit.*, 316.

[38] I am most grateful to Peter Corbett for drawing this brooch to my attention and arranging for its loan for study.

[39] R. Hattatt, *Ancient and Romano-British Brooches*, Oxford, 1982, 59, 36.

sectioned rod of the spring to the flattened bow is marked by a sharp shoulder and two engraved lines. The bold angle of the head is gently domed, but below the moulding the bow is ridged and tapers very gently towards the tip. The spring was of four coils with an internal chord, a significant difference from the Colchester type with its external chord and hook. The pin is a continuation of the end of the spring and, prior to the damage, would have engaged neatly with the solid catchplate.

No close parallel has been found for this brooch in Britain; the nearest comparison is an unprovenanced example in the Musée de Picardie, northern France[40]. This piece, described as a *fibula* with moulded rod bow, is of a type rare even in France but found occasionally on early Gallo-Roman sites and probably dating from the very beginning of the first century AD. Typologically it is thought to lie between the *knotenfibel*, a type which is rare in northern France and belongs to the period 40-20 bc, and the 'Nauheim' brooch which is much more common and was fashionable at the turn of the century. The *knotenfibel* has its roots in the La Tène II type of brooch in which the foot of the bow is extended and turns back on itself, the junction forming a small knob. Later only the knob survived on a smooth bow, but the back turn was reflected in a preference for an openwork catchplate. The 'Nauheim brooch' is characterised by a flat bow and normally a solid catchplate. Both types have a four coil spring usually with internal chord. The intermediate type has a moulding in place of the knob or button on a broader bow and may have either a pierced or solid catchplate.

About forty *knotenfibeln* (Hull's Type 19) have been found in Britain, all of them close to or south of the Thames[41]. The best known examples are a pair of silver brooches from a cremation burial found near the Belgic town of Great Chesterford in Essex dating from the end of the first century bc[42], but there is an example from Maiden Castle in Dorset which may belong to a later horizon, closer to the middle of the first century AD[43]. The 'Nauheim derivative' type is a great deal more common but is similarly restricted to the southern half of the country except for some outliers which, like the Anglesey examples, may have been lost when their owners fled before the Roman advance[44]. Without any British examples with which to compare the Moelfre brooch it would be unwise to be dogmatic about its date and context, but despite its link with earlier types, it is possible that the intermediate style might have remained in fashion up to the period of the Roman conquest to come north with its wearer.

The Welsh distribution of La Tène III brooches (like both Anglesey examples) echoes that of Belgic material in general. In the south there are examples from Sudbrook, Usk and — a very late instance — Caerwent, all in the south east where contact with Belgic-influenced tribes to the east was close[45]. Further west

[40] G. Dilly 'Les Fibules Gallo-Romaines du Musée de Picardie' *Cahiers Archeol. de Picardie*, 5, 1978, 157-75. I am grateful to Adrian Olivier for drawing my attention to this publication and to him and to Janet Webster and George Boon for help with the identification of this brooch.
[41] R. Hattatt, *Brooches of Antiquity*, Oxford, 1987, 26-9.
[42] C. Fox, *Pattern and Purpose*, Cardiff, 1958, Pl. 40b.
[43] R.E.M. Wheeler, *Maiden Castle*, London, 1943, 258.
[44] B. Raftery, *La Tène in Ireland*, Marburg, 1984, Map 13.
[45] H.N. Savory, *Guide Catalogue of the Iron Age Collections*, NMW, 1975, Fig. 35. I am grateful to Janet Webster for information on more recent finds.

there is one from Coygan Camp and from Solva, Pembrokeshire[46]. The discovery of a splendid gilt brooch from Carmarthen which, though made at a later date, has native decoration suggests that in south Wales some of these ornaments may have been locally made[47]. In the north there are only four examples, all chance finds[48], and material of Belgic origin in the region is all exceptional rather than domestic. The impression given is of wealth snatched up and carried into foreign lands to finance a refugee lifestyle. It is interesting that a Colchester brooch almost identical to the one from Glyn has been found still further west, in Ireland (sadly unprovenanced within that island) and similar brooches occur amongst the grave goods at Lambay[49] (PA 321).

As in 1970 the artefacts bring us face to face with the end of independence; but the new site evidence from Tŷ Mawr and Bryn Eryr has demonstrated, more clearly than could be hazarded twenty years ago, the continuity, through that period of political change, of so many aspects of everyday life.

[46] RCAM, *Pembrokeshire Inventory*, 1925, 339, Fig. 279.
[47] G.C. Boon and H.N. Savory, *Antiq. J.*, 55, 1975, 41-61.
[48] Rhuddlan: Webster in Manley 'Cledamutha: A Late Saxon Burh' *Mediaeval Archaeol.*, 31. 1987, 36-7; River Conwy near Caerhun: Bangor Museum 668, and the two Anglesey examples.
[49] Raftery, *A Catalogue of Irish Iron Age Antiquities*, Marburg, 1983, vol. 2, Fig. 128 no 388 and Fig. 158.

CHANCE FINDS OF STONE AXES

(R.O. = Roughout; pt = broken implement; ★ = post 1960 find or record; ns = not sectioned)

No.	Find spot	N.G.R.	Location	Petrology & CBA No.
1.	Kingsland, Holyhead	SH 250 815	Bangor 28.42	VII (AN 27)
2.	Kingsland, Holyhead, (found with 1)	SH 250 815	Bangor 2907	VII (ns AN 52)
3.	Tŷ Du, Holyhead	SH 241 815	BM 75.4-24.2	?
4.	Cwm. Holyhead (hoard of 4, 3 lost)	SH 21 82	BM 75.4-24.1	Flint
5.R.O.★	Caer Elen, Bodedern	SH 326 780	Private coll.	VII (AN 63)
6.R.O.	Llanfair yng Nghornwy	SH 31 91	Geol.Mus.S.Ken.	VII (ns)
7.	Pwllcoch, Rhos y bol	SH 425 871	NMW 49.452	VII (AN 9)
8.	Llaneilian	SH 47 91	Bangor 2841	VI (AN 35)
9.★	Near Llaneilian	SH 473 927	AAS 6/59	Flint
10.R.O.	Llwydiarth Esgob, Llandyfrydog	SH 435 845	Bangor 2775.1	XXI (AN 42)
11.R.O.★	Llwydiarth Esgob, Llandyfrydog	SH 443 852	Private coll.	VII (AN 55)
12.R.O.★	Rhostrehwfa, Llangefni	SH 445 755	AAS 9/60	VII (ns)
13.R.O.★	Rhostrehwfa, Llangefni, (found with 12)	SH 445 755	AAS 10/60	VII (ns)
14.★	Rhostrehwfa (found near 12 & 13)	SH 445 755	Private coll.	? chert
15.	County Hospital, Llangefni	SH 463 757	Private coll.	Quartz dolerite (AN 56)
16.	Cerrig Dewi, Llangwyllog	SH 440 780	BM 70.7-6.4	?
17.	Cerrig Dewi, Llangwyllog	SH 440 780	BM 70.7-6.5	?
18.	Glyn near Plas Penmynydd, Penmynydd	SH 491 749	NMW 56.74	I (AN 12)
19.	Plas Penmynydd, Penmynydd	SH 495 751	??	? (RCAM Suppl. 22)
20.★	Plas Penmynydd (in wall)	SH 495 751	Private coll.	VII (AN 62)
21.	Rectory, Penmynydd	SH 517 749	Warrington Ra.13	VII (AN18)
22.	Llanfihangel Esceifiog	SH 495 718	Bangor 2764	VII (AN 26)
23.R.O.★	Clegyrdy Mawr, Talwrn (in wall)	SH 473 764	Private coll.	VII (ns)
24.★	Ynys Uchaf, Brynteg (? re-used)	SH 497 815	Private coll.	?
25.★	Ynys Uchaf, Brynteg (in wall)	SH 497 815	Private coll.	?
26.	Cae Marl, Llanallgo	SH 503 849	Private coll.	VII (ns RCAM Suppl. 4)
27.★	Ysgubor Fawr, Llaneugrad	SH 508 843	Private coll.	VII (AN 19)
28.	Marianglas, Llaneugrad	SH 505 855	??	? (RCAM Suppl.9a)
29.	Bryn Caeau, Penmon	SH 62 80	AAS Evans 8	VII (ns)
30.	Pentraeth	SH 527 781	AAS Evans 5	VII (ns)
31.	Pentraeth (found with 30)	SH 527 781	AAS Evans 6	?
32.pt.	Pentraeth	SH 52 78	AAS Evans 20	?
33.	Pentraeth (? with 2 others in barrow)	SH 52 78	NMW 39.579.3	Dolerite (AN 8)
34.	Red Wharf Bay ? Pentraeth	SH 52 79	Manchester 0.1479	VII (AN 61)
35.★	Pentraeth (3 found together, 1920s)	SH 543 783	Lost	? (info. O.S)
36.	Ffynnon Tudur, Bwlch, Pentraeth	SH 525 774	Bangor 2775.5	VII (AN 39)
37.★	Gweithdy, Pentraeth	SH 537 769	Private coll.	VII (ns info. O.S)

38.	Near Trefor Wen, Llansadwrn	SH 543 779	AAS Evans 7	?
39.pt.	Hendrefor, Llansadwrn	SH 552 772	AAS Evans 17	VII (AN 22)
40.	Near Hendrefor, Llansadwrn	SH 551 773	AAS Evans 11	Rhyolite
41.pt	Rhos Owen, Llansadwrn	SH 537 762	AAS Evans 76	VII (AN 24)
42.	Between Cae Isaf & Bryn Eryr,	SH 541 754	AAS Evans 4	Rhyolite
43.pt.	Castellior, Llansadwrn	SH 544 742	AAS Evans 9	VII (AN 21)
44.pt.	Castellior, Llansadwrn	SH 544 742	AAS Evans 75	VII (AN 23)
45.pt.	Castellior, Llansadwrn	SH 544 742	NMW 54.273.1	VII (AN 49)
46.	Castellior, Llansadwrn	SH 544 742	AAS Evans 10	ns
47.*	Wern, Llandegfan	SH 551 748	Private coll.	VII (AN 14)
48.pt.*	Wern, Llandegfan	SH 550 748	Private coll.	VI (AN 17)
49.R.O.	Refail Newydd, Menai Bridge	SH 542 736	Bangor 2130	VII (AN 34 ns)
50.*	Hen Penclip, Menai Bridge	SH 557 726	Bangor 1984/177	Gabbro (AN 20)
51.	Menai Bridge	SH 55 72	NMW 25.155.672	VII (AN 1)
52.	Menai Bridge (not found with 51)	SH 55 72	NMW 25.155.672A	near VII (AN 2)
53.	Menai Bridge	SH 55 72	?	VII (ns RCAM Suppl.6)
54.*	Pwll Fanogl, Llanfairpwll	SH 530 709	Private coll.	VII
55.pt.*	Pwll Fanogl, Llanfairpwll	SH 530 709	Private coll.	VII
56.	Cae'r Carreg Wen, Llanddaniel	SH 505 702	Bangor 2039	VII (AN 33)
57.	Near Bryn Celli Ddu, Llanddaniel Fab	SH 507 702	Bangor 16/56	VII (AN 32)
58.pt.	Hologwyn, Llanddaniel Fab	SH 506 710	Bangor 1984/12 F4	VII (AN 36)
59.pt.	Hologwyn, Llanddaniel Fab	SH 506 710	Bangor 1984/12 F5	VII (AN 37)
60.*	Hologwyn, Llanddaniel Fab	SH 506 710	Bangor 1984/46	sandstone/tuff
61.*	Penrhyn Gwyn, Llanddaniel Fab	SH 480 697	Private coll.	near VIII (AN 60)
62.	Rhuddgaer, Llangeinwen	SH 445 642	Private coll.	? (RCAM Suppl.11a)
63.*	Trefarthen, Llangeinwen (+2 broken)	SH 490 662	Private coll.	?
64.pt.	Newborough Warren, Newborough	SH 39 64	Cambridge Univ. Mus.	VII (AN 48)
65.	Newborough Warren	SH 39 64	?	? (RCAM Suppl. 20)
66.pt.	Anglesey	—	Bangor 2129	XXI (AN 31)
67.	Anglesey	—	Bangor 2775.4	VI (AN 41)
68.pt.	Anglesey	—	AAS Evans 77	ns
69.	Dubious axe, Anglesey	—	Bangor 2775.2	Altered shale (AN 40)

AXES FROM EXCAVATED SITES

70.*	Tranchet axe, Trwyn Du, Aberffraw	SH 352 678	NMW (GAT Excav)	Crystal tuff (AN 57)
71.*	Flake (polished) Trwyn Du, Aberffraw	SH 352 678	NMW (CHH Excav)	near XXI (AN 29)
72.*	Flake, Trwyn Du, Aberffraw	SH 352 678	NMW (CHH Excav)	Chert (AN 30)
73.*	2 Flakes, Trwyn Du,	SH 352 678	Private coll.	VIII (AN 53 & 54)
74.	2 axes, Bryn yr Hen Bobl	SH 518 690	NMW 37.7.1 & 2	Dolerite (AN 3 & 4)
75.	2 broken axes Bryn yr Hen Bobl	SH 518 690	NMW 37.7.3 & 4	Dolerite (AN 5 & 6)
76.	Rough-out, Bryn yr Hen Bobl	SH 518 690	NMW 37.7.5	VII (ns AN 7)
77.	Numerous flakes, Bryn yr Hen Bobl	SH 518 690	NMW 37.7.6-21	VII (ns AN 7)

78.*	Broken axe (burnt) Din Dryfol	SH 395 724	NMW	Crystal tuff (AN 58)
79.	Chip from axe, Tŷ Newydd	SH 344 738	NMW	Flint
80.*	Broken axe, Tyn Lôn, Dothan, Llanbeulan	SH 373 744	Private coll.	Rhyolite (close VII)

APPENDIX 2
ANALYSIS OF BRONZE AGE METALWORK FROM ANGLESEY

by

Dr J.P. Northover, Dept. of Materials, University of Oxford

ALL analyses of bronze objects other than those in the collections of the British Museum were performed by Dr J.P. Northover at UCNW using JXA-3A electron microprobe, with detection limits of 0.02% for all elements except 0.04% for As, Zn; 0.06% for Au and 0.08% for Ag. Those marked * were performed by Dr P.T. Craddock, British Museum Research Laboratory, using atomic absorption spectrophotometry. A programme of standardisation was carried out between the two series and, apart from the lower limits of detection for atomic absorption spectrophotometry, the two sets of results can be regarded as equivalent. Exceptions are the razor, axe and chisel from the Llanddyfnan grave group analysed by D. Britton using optical emission spectroscopy[1]. The gold analyses are by A. Hartmann, Wurttembergisches Landesmuseum, Stuttgart, using optical emission spectroscopy.

The elements recorded in the analyses listed below are (in order) tin (Sn), arsenic (As), antimony (Sb), lead (Pb), cobalt (Co), nickel (Ni), iron (Fe), silver (Ag), gold (Au), zinc (Zn) and bismuth (Bi). The major element, copper (Cu), is not listed.

EARLY BRONZE AGE

		Sn	As	Sb	Pb	Co	Ni	Fe	Ag	Au	Zn	Bi
Castell Bryn Gwyn												
Awl	Fig.27.6	11.37	0.12	0.23	.	0.02	0.27	.	.	.	.	.
Talwrn												
Flat axe	Fig.58	10.63	0.37	0.23	1.8	.	0.05	.	.	.	.	.
GRAVE FINDS[2]												
Merddyn Gwyn												
Knife	Fig.34.6a	9.62	0.06	.	.	.	0.05	.	.	.	.	.
Llanddyfnan												
Gr.6.razor	Fig.47.6a	8.25	.	.	.	.	.	0.032	.	.	.	0.011
Gr.7.axe	Fig.48.7a	11.30	0.13	.	.	.	.	0.007	0.01	.	.	.
chisel	7c	13.20	0.15	.	.	.	0.01	0.021	0.009	.	.	0.0056
knife	7b	11.54	0.11	.	.	.	.	0.02	.	.	.	.
rivet	7b	11.59	.	.	.	.	.	.	.	.	.	.

[1] D. Britton *Proc. Prehist. Soc.*, *XXIX*, 1963, 258-325.
[2] Two metal identifications were carried out by Dr Francis James on the Bangor microprobe. The awl from Bedd Branwen (PA Fig.43.Lb) was a standard tin/bronze with a significant concentration of iron; the awl from Cae Mickney (PA Fig.55.1a) was shown to be a mixture of copper and lead without any tin (PA original edition p.291).

HOARD
Menai Bridge[3]

		Sn	As	Sb	Pb	Co	Ni	Fe	Ag	Au	Zn	Bi
*Flanged axe	Fig.60.1	12.10	0.25	0.19	0.12	.	0.07	0.03	0.075	.	.	0.003
Flanged axe	Fig.60.2	12.14	0.54	0.09	.	.	0.12	.	.	.	.	.
Flanged axe	Fig.60.3	12.83	0.57	0.16	.	.	0.07	0.03	.	.	.	.

MIDDLE BRONZE AGE PALSTAVES

		Sn	As	Sb	Pb	Co	Ni	Fe	Ag	Au	Zn	Bi
Holyhead												
Axe/palstave	Fig.63.1	11.03	0.75	.	1.5	0.08	0.34	0.35	.	.	.	.
Bodwryd												
Early pal.	Fig.63.4	10.44	0.66	.	.	0.02	0.20	0.02	.	.	.	.
Llangwyllog												
*Grp.II pal.	Fig.63.2	12.50	1.10	0.05	0.03	0.02	0.40	0.06	0.03	.	.	.
Cerrigceinwen												
Grp.III pal.	Fig.63.7	8.81	0.72	0.04	2.1	0.04	0.38	0.07	.	.	.	.
Llanddaniel Fab												
Grp.III pal.	Fig.63.5	5.61	0.55	.	7.5	0.03	0.35	0.02	.	.	.	.
? Anglesey												
Grp.III lp'd	Fig.63.6	7.52	0.70	.	4.2	0.19	0.56	1.04	.	.	.	.
Marianglas												
Transit.pal.	Fig.63.14	9.48	0.41	0.07	.	0.06	0.07	0.03	.	.	.	.

LATE BRONZE AGE

		Sn	As	Sb	Pb	Co	Ni	Fe	Ag	Au	Zn	Bi
Llangefni												
*Late palstave	Fig.63.13	8.30	0.15	0.23	5.2	.	0.10	0.01	0.14	.	.	.
Lligwy												
Late palstave	Fig.63.12	5.93	0.23	0.21	4.4	.	0.19	.	0.09	.	.	.
Llangristiolus (Parc)												
Socketed axe	Fig.66.2	7.70	0.15	0.18	7.6	.	0.11	.	.	.	.	.

HOARDS
Cors Bodwrog

		Sn	As	Sb	Pb	Co	Ni	Fe	Ag	Au	Zn	Bi
Late palstave	Fig.18a.1	8.04	0.26	0.22	4.8	.	0.10	.	.	.	.	.
Late palstave	2	9.44	0.17	0.17	8.2	.	0.12	.	.	.	.	.
Socketed axe	6	11.24	0.17	0.71	7.5	.	0.09	.	.	.	.	.
Socketed axe	5	10.57	0.05	0.19	3.36	.	0.08	0.01	0.14	.	.	0.02
Sword blade	3	5.50	0.21	0.17	5.0	.	0.16	.	.	.	.	.
Sword blade	4	6.10	0.21	0.17	2.0	.	0.16	.	.	.	.	.
Chape	7	12.54	0.05	0.20	0.73	.	0.10	0.28	0.12	.	.	0.03
Gouge	9	8.27	0.32	0.14	4.11	.	0.08	0.28	0.10	.	.	0.01
Razor	8	10.85	0.10	0.22	2.08	.	0.10	0.01	0.11	.	.	.

Tŷ Mawr, Holyhead

		Sn	As	Sb	Pb	Co	Ni	Fe	Ag	Au	Zn	Bi
*Socketed axe	Fig.69.1	12.10	0.60	0.50	2.2	.	0.05	0.01	0.11	.	0.01	0.006
*Spearhead	3	8.00	0.25	0.15	2.9	.	0.08	0.03	0.085	.	.	0.006
*Spearhead	4	7.70	0.20	0.17	10.7	.	0.19	0.015	0.014	.	.	.
*Ring	11	9.00	0.55	0.40	8.0	.	0.12	0.035	0.17	.	.	0.006
*Ring	13	10.00	0.07	0.10	3.0	0.015	0.05	0.04	0.08	.	.	.
*Bracelet	5	9.20	0.20	0.25	5.8	.	0.10	0.05	0.10	.	.	.

[3] The footnote (PA 219) which identifies the surviving axes in the Menai Bridge Hoard is incorrect. Fig.60.1 is in the British Museum; no.2 is in Bangor Museum and no. 3 is in the National Museum of Wales, Cardiff. The histories are correct.

		Sn	As	Sb	Pb	Co	Ni	Fe	Ag	Au	Zn	Bi
Llangwyllog												
*Razor	Fig.68.1	11.00	0.20	0.17	9.1	.	0.10	0.015	0.25	.	.	.
*Button	Fig.68	9.60	0.13	0.25	3.8	.	0.11	0.025	0.30	.	.	.
*Button	8-12	13.40	1.20	0.25	10.0	.	0.11	0.10	0.11	.	.	0.005
*Button		11.50	0.07	0.17	5.9	.	0.09	0.02	0.11	.	.	.
*Button		9.70	0.60	.	3.3	.	0.09	0.02	0.02	.	.	0.001
Button		9.70	0.10	0.20	3.5	.	0.08	0.008	0.17	.	.	0.001
Waste tin	Fig.68.4	99.00	.	0.045	0.7	.	0.01	0.03	.	.	0.003	.
*Pierced ring	13	11.80	0.15	0.13	5.0	.	0.06	0.01	0.13	.	.	0.005
*Harness ring	Fig.68.	10.80	0.35	0.20	5.4	.	0.13	0.06	0.18	.	.	0.002
*Harness ring	20	10.10	0.30	0.085	2.8	.	0.025	0.03	0.88	.	.	0.001
*Harness ring	(all)	11.20	0.60	0.30	5.5	.	0.08	0.02	0.13	.	.	0.001
*Harness ring		7.20	0.20	0.25	6.4	.	0.08	0.01	0.26	.	.	0.004
*Harness ring		7.70	0.02	0.30	17.0	.	.	0.10	0.03	0.20	.	0.001
*Harness ring		14.00	0.35	0.10	8.8	.	0.035	0.02	0.075	.	.	0.001
*Harness ring		9.10	0.10	0.20	6.5	.	0.075	0.03	0.10	.	.	0.002
*Harness ring		9.20	0.35	0.20	6.9	0.01	0.07	0.02	0.10	.	.	0.001
*Harness ring		16.80	0.35	0.025	1.4	.	0.11	0.055	0.03	0.01	.	0.002

BRONZE AGE GOLD FROM ANGLESEY

			Ag	Cu	Sn	
Beaumaris	Bracelet	Fig.67.6	14.0	5.91	0.18	
	Bracelet	5	14.0	5.99	0.20	In all cases the balance is gold.
Gaerwen	Bracelet	Fig.67.4	16.0	5.86	0.08	
	Bracelet	3	13.0	5.75	0.034	

Discussion

Fifteen years of research into the metallurgy of the Welsh Bronze Age have produced a detailed history and chronology of developments in technology and the exploitation of metal resources. The accumulated data provide a firm framework in which the varied Bronze age metalwork of Anglesey can be set in context. An outline of this basic structure can be found in the appendix on Bronze age metal analysis in the *Guide Catalogue to the Bronze Age Collections* of the National Museum of Wales (1980), while a discussion of wider, European aspects of Bronze Age trade in metals can be found in J.P. Northover 'The exploration of the long-distance movement of bronze in Bronze and Early Iron Age Europe' *Bulletin of the Institute of Archaeology, University of London,* 19, 1982, 45-72.

Despite its proximity to Ireland, no copper objects have survived from Anglesey (although one or two lost pieces might have been copper). The earliest surviving metalwork is already of bronze and the quantity is surprisingly small considering the metal resources of the island. It has not been possible to establish any direct connection between this metalwork and Parys mountain which we now know was being mined at this time.

Neither the flat axe from Talwrn nor the Castell Bryn Gwyn awl is likely to be made from Anglesey or even Welsh metal. Metal that can be said with some confidence to have been produced in Wales does not have the important antimony impurity seen in both these items. The Talwrn axe probably has an As/Sb/Ag impurity pattern typical of early Irish bronze, the silver content being obscured by the high detection limit of the microprobe used. On the other hand the As/Sb/Ni/Ag pattern of the Castell Bryn Gwyn awl is more indicative of an ultimate

European origin for the metal and is matched by the Arreton axes of the Menai Bridge hoard which are clearly imports to Anglesey. The Arreton axe is characteristic of the last stages of the Early Bronze Age in southern and south eastern England and is often made of metal imported from Europe.

The metal from the Anglesey grave groups is different in character having very low impurity levels, a small amount of arsenic up to 0.15% being the only one of any significance. Metal of this type could very easily derive from the chalcopyrites of Parys Mountain, but such compositions are very widespread in Early Bronze Age Britain. A situation where heavy products such as axes are imported to an area, while a small scale local industry produces lighter items such as knives, small tools and ornaments has been identified elsewhere in prehistoric Europe (Northover, *unpublished*) and would match the pattern in Anglesey. On this basis the knife from Merddyn Gwyn and the razor from Llanddyfnan, Grave 6 and perhaps the chisel and small axe from Llanddyfnan, Grave 7 could be local products. On the other hand typological considerations would suggest that the decorated knife from Grave 7 is an import. It is also technically different in that the cutting-edges of the blade have been finished to a much greater hardness than, say, the Merddyn Gwyn knife. Indeed the Llanddyfnan knife has the highest hardness recorded for any Bronze Age object in Britain at over 300HV, but it is the only example of its type to have been tested for hardness. The hardness permits an extremely sharp cutting-edge to be made, but it would have been very brittle.

With the palstaves of the Acton Park and Taunton/Cemmaes phases of the Middle Bronze Age we can say with some confidence that North Welsh metal is involved in their manufacture. The bronze industry in Early Bronze Age Wales was fragmented into a number of regional groups with a significant amount of imported metal being used. During the 15th century bc this pattern changed. Although regional metalworking groups can still be identified on a typological basis all were using the same metal, either primary close to the source, or re-cycled further away. The metal typically has 0.7-1.1% As, 0.25-0.45% Ni and a consistent cobalt trace. There is a range of iron contents with some primary metal having iron up to 1%. Frequently there is a significant lead content, usually 1-3%, but with instances up to 7%. It is presumed that this lead addition was made by co-smelting galena with chalcopyrite ore; the lead content is sufficient to noticeably improve casting properties and to improve the toughness of the finished product.

This metal (labelled 'M' in the scheme of metal groups given in the National Museum Catalogue) accounts for over 95% of surviving production from the Acton Park phase. A chain of circumstantial evidence points very strongly to Snowdonia being the source of the copper, alloyed with tin from Cornwall or, just possibly, Brittany. The alloy standard used in the Acton Park period was maintained with considerable consistency at 11-12% tin, with an equally consistent finish to the cutting edge with a hardness of 210-220HV. In the Acton Park phase the thin-bladed axe from Holyhead (PA Fig.63.1) and the Group II palstave from

Llangwyllog can both be assigned to this alloy and metal group. The primitive palstave from Plas Bodwryd belongs to a developmental stage of the classic Acton Park palstave and has a composition rather similar to the preceding Early Bronze Age metal.

In the Taunton/Cemmaes phase (Ornament Horizon in earlier terminology) the production of 'M' metal gradually declined and the centre of metal extraction seems to have shifted further south in Wales to the Aberystwyth/Cemmaes area. At the same time the alloy standard was no longer kept up, possibly because of economic or political difficulties affecting the supply of tin. Thus the three Group III palstaves can be assigned to metal group 'M' but all have reduced tin contents ranging from 5.6% to 8.8%.

During the crisis-ridden Penard phase there is a decline in surviving metalwork and it tends to be rather uniform in composition throughout Britain. The analysed Anglesey example, the palstave from Marianglas, fits with this group and experience suggests that the Valley basal-looped spearhead and Tre'r Dryw dirk (PA Fig.65) would have very similar analyses.

There is something of a break between the metalwork of the Penard phase and the Late Bronze Age metalwork of Anglesey as no material definitely attributable to the Wilburton or Wallington traditions survives, though the pair of spearheads from Valley may belong. Certainly the distinctive high impurity leaded bronze of the Wilburton hoards ('S' metal) has not been identified. The analysed metalwork is dominated by the Bodwrog, Tŷ Mawr and Llangwyllog hoards and the pattern set by these is maintained by the three single finds, the late palstaves from Llangefni and Lligwy and the socketed axe from Llangristiolus.

Almost all the objects analysed are of leaded bronze. The addition of lead metal to bronze was pioneered in Britain by the Wilburton industry, which developed the technique to assist in the casting of elaborate thin-walled products such as tongue chapes and hollow-bladed spearheads. The effect of the lead is to reduce the viscosity of the melt and to substantially lower the liquids temperature, i.e. that temperature at which the alloy is fully molten. It appears that only certain industries, notably those producing South Welsh and Yorkshire socketed axes (PA 238), made very heavy additions of lead, up to 20%. Other industries made smaller additions or even none at all; lead in their products being residual from the use of scrap. Although scrap had been a factor in metal trading throughout the Bronze age it achieved its greatest importance in this Ewart Park period. As a result impurity patterns are no longer sharply defined but from Wales there are now sufficient analyses to highlight the basic trends.

It is impossible at present to identify extraction of copper in Wales during the Late Bronze Age, but it is reasonable to assume that some mining was taking place and this mining activity might also include lead. The analytical record points to two major flows of metal into Wales. In the southern half of the Principality the metal is very similar to that in southern England and can ultimately be linked to imports from the Continent. In North Wales the impurity patterns are rather different and best matched in Ireland, the key future being moderate impurity levels, usually below 0.3% for all elements, with antimony higher than arsenic and nickel around 0.08-0.12% (some metal of European origin being similar but with higher impurity levels all round). There are several exceptions to this pattern indicating that metal from other sources was also reaching Anglesey, but the Irish connection (PA 232, 239) was the most important. The presence of a piece of tin in the Llangwyllog hoard also shows the long-distance movement of metal to Anglesey. Its significance is unfortunately limited to demonstrating this broad point since its presence in a hoard of ornaments does not tell us whether it had a basic metallurgical purpose in the making up of alloys, or was to be used for some decorative or ornamental item or technique.

The Irish connection is reinforced by the character and distribution of Late Bronze Age gold in Anglesey and North Wales generally. In the Middle Bronze Age gold objects concentrate in Mid Wales and some have a sufficiently idiosyncratic form to suggest local manufacture, perhaps from Welsh gold. In the Late Bronze Age the distribution is radically different, being concentrated in Anglesey and close to the North Welsh coast, with Irish types such as 'lock-rings' (PA 239) being common. Compositionally the objects are also identical to the Irish material.

The end of the Ewart Park period (the period of local workshops) sees an end to Bronze Age style metalwork in Anglesey, i.e. with bronze used for tools and weapons as well as ornaments. The final phase of Bronze Age metalworking, named after the Llyn Fawr deposit in South Wales, is not represented in Anglesey. The quantity of bronze in circulation clearly declined rapidly and the contemporary introduction of iron did nothing to increase the overall availability of metal.

ANALYSIS OF IRON AGE BRONZE METALWORK FROM LLYN CERRIG BACH

by

Dr J.P. Northover, Dept. of Materials, University of Oxford

		Sn	As	Sb	Pb	Co	Ni	Fe	Ag	Au	Zn	Bi
Horse-bit 49	Fig.87.49	9.62	0.07	.	0.40	0.48	0.02	0.52	0.01	.	.	.
Ring of bit 50	Fig.87.50	9.28	0.23	0.02	0.15	0.08	0.05	0.04	0.03	tr	.	.
Plated bit 47	Fig.87.47											
Bronze plate		7.96	0.86	0.05	0.25	0.05	0.13	1.19	0.05	.	0.40	0.03
Iron core		.	.	.	.	0.03	0.05	99.90	0.02	.	.	.
Horse-bit 53*	Unillus.	10.39	tr	0.45	0.05	0.01	.	0.01	0.10	0.04	tr	0.04
Horse-bit 54	Unillus.	10.51	0.59	0.02	0.04	0.06	0.09	0.02	0.06	.	0.03	0.01
Bronze strip 68 similar to Fig.84.67	Unillus.	9.97	0.29	0.01	tr	0.12	0.06	0.09	0.07	.	0.07	0.03
Cauldron (sheet)	Fig.89.76	18.81"	0.05	.	0.05	0.01	0.01	0.01	tr	.	.	.
Cauldron (sheet)	Fig.89.77	11.54	0.49	0.03	0.02	0.14	0.04	0.05	0.02	.	tr	0.03
Unnumbered sheet	Unillus.	9.06	0.35	tr	1.20	0.02	0.06	0.25	0.05	.	0.23	.

* Fig.85.53 is wrongly numbered; it should be 58.

" Value affected by corrosion.

All analyses performed by Dr J.P. Northover using the CAMEBAX automated electron microprobe in the Department of Materials, University of Oxford; detection limits 0.01-0.02% for all elements except Au at 0.04%.

Discussion

RECENT years have seen an extensive analysis of Iron Age non-ferrous metalwork in Britain. This has tended to be on a post-excavation basis and so the general framework established for the Bronze Age on the basis of museum collections does not yet exist. However, the accumulation of data is now sufficient for some features of chronology and distribution to become clear. As pointed out at the end of the discussion of the Bronze age metalwork, metal became very scarce in Britain during the Early Iron Age and from the 6th and 5th centuries bc very little survives anywhere. From the 3rd century bc, with the introduction of La Tene related styles and technology, especially the first extensive use of lost-wax casting in Britain, the amount of bronze and iron begins to increase, the expansion becoming rapid from the 2nd century bc onwards. It is during this phase of expansion that much of the bronze in the Llyn Cerrig Bach deposit was produced.

The re-establishment of flourishing bronze industries in Britain during the La Tene Iron Age can be associated with new impurity patterns not seen in the Bronze Age. Although the same general areas, such as North or Mid Wales or south west England are involved, it is clear that new deposits are being worked.

The first, seen in horse-bits 49 and 50 and sheet fragments 68 and 77, has the unusual pattern of having more cobalt than nickel (markedly so in 49); arsenic and iron are the other principal impurities. A precursor of this pattern is seen in the Middle Bronze Age in the area around Dartmoor but, pre-eminently, it is the bronze type used in southern and south western Britain during the La Tene Iron Age and there is very good reason to believe that the source was in the south west, possibly in the Tamar Valley/Dartmoor area. It first appears with La Tene I brooches and early La Tene style pieces such as the Standlake sword scabbard. At two Iron Age metalworking sites, Beckford in Hereford and Worcester and Maiden Castle in Dorset it is the sole metal type being worked. Despite this extensive use it disappears totally and rapidly in the mid-1st century bc.

Thus, without advancing any typological arguments, it is possible to say that the metal with this composition at Llyn Cerrig Bach used copper mined in south west England, was made into bronze and shaped somewhere in southern Britain and was certainly produced before the mid-1st century bc. Like virtually all Iron Age bronze analysed in Britain the alloy has around 10% tin with no added lead, leaded bronze having been abandoned in the 7th century bc[1].

The second distinctive type is seen in the bronze plate on the horse-bit 47 and the unnumbered sheet fragment. The important feature is the zinc content. In the past this zinc content might have been used to suggest that the bronze incorporated brass scrap and therefore was likely to date to the 1st century ad at the earliest. However, it is now clear that copper deposits in the Welsh Marches, possibly in the area of Llanymynech, were being exploited which were capable of producing raw copper with up to 3% zinc[2]. This metal was produced from at least the 3rd century bc onwards but for how long is not known. Thus, some of the metal at Llyn Cerrig Bach was produced in Wales. Horse-bit 53 is marked by a high antimony content (0.45%) and only a trace of arsenic. Such composition is reasonably common in later Iron Age metalwork; the source is as yet unknown but Ireland is one possibility. The other analyses presented have no distinctive characteristics and no particular comments can be made.

---

[1] J.P. Northover, *Forthcoming* 'Non-ferous metalwork and metalworking debris from Maiden Castle' in N. Sharples *(forthcoming) The excavations at Maiden Castle, Dorset, 1985-6* (London, English Heritage Monographs).

[2] C.R. Musson and J.P. Northover, 'Llanymynech Hillfort...' *Montgomeryshire Collections*, 77, 1989, 15-26 and C.R. Musson *et al.*, 'Excavations and metalworking at Llwyn Bryn Dinas Hillfort, Llangedwyn, Clwyd.' *forthcoming* in *Proc. Prehist. Soc.*

LIST OF RADIOCARBON
DATES FROM ANGLESEY

THE first figure in these lists is the laboratory number identifying where and when the date was calculated, then the sample number and context from which it came; then the result and its standard deviation to 1 sigma quoted as a date bp (ie before 1950), then the uncalibrated date bc and finally the range of calibrated years (to 2 sigma) within which there is a 95% chance of the real date falling. With a standard deviation of about 70 years, dates which are less than 200 years apart may not be deemed to be significantly different in statistical terms.

The calibration has been obtained from the University of Washington Quaternary Isotope Laboratory 1987 Radiocarbon Calibration program, Rev. 2.0. No laboratory error multiplier has been applied. I am grateful to Gwynedd Archaeological Trust for use of their computing facilities.

Trwyn Du, Aberffraw

Q. 1385	F13 hollow in occup. layer	8640 ±150 bp	6690 bc	c.7500 BC[1]
HAR 1194	F13 as before	8590± 90 bp	6640 bc	c.7500 BC[1]
HAR 1193	F16 stratig. pre-F13	7980±140 bp	6030 bc	7024-6825 BC

Trefignath

HAR 3932	S.8, beneath W. Chamber	5050± 70 bp	3100 bc	4000-3700 BC
HAR 3933	S.15, disturb. in E. Portal	2210± 70 bp	260 bc	400-100 BC

Tŷ Mawr (early dates)

HAR 4694	113, in yard, level uncert.	4170± 80 bp	2220 bc	2920-2502 BC
HAR 4695	99, beneath occup. in yard	3890± 80 bp	1940 bc	2580-2140 BC

Capel Eithin

CAR 619	F69, ? building PH.H	6330± 90 bp	4385 bc	5480-5069 BC
CAR 485	F69, Post Hole G	5890± 90 bp	3945 bc	5037-4546 BC
CAR 797	F78, lowest fill of PH	6510± 90 bp	4560 bc	5620-5241 BC
CAR 480	F78, ? building PH fill	5520± 80 bp	3570 bc	4520-4230 BC
CAR 618	F78	5350 ±100 bp	3400 bc	4451-3980 BC
CAR 481	F83, pit fill; Gr. Ware	4740± 80 bp	2790 bc	3700-3350 BC
CAR 446	F17, pit fill; Gr. Ware	3950± 80 bp	2005 bc	2859-2207 BC
CAR 488	Hearth near urns	4380± 80 bp	2430 bc	3340-2781 BC
CAR 447	Pit cut by Grave 35	3580± 70 bp	1625 bc	2140-1740 BC
CAR 453	Urn C6	3760± 60 bp	1810 bc	2454-2030 BC
CAR 452	Urn C12	3760± 70 bp	1810 bc	2460-1978 BC
CAR 451	Urn C11	3675± 70 bp	1725 bc	2290-1890 BC
CAR 448	Urn C2	3610± 70 bp	1660 bc	2192-1771 BC
CAR 450	Urn C1	3590± 70 bp	1645 bc	2178-1750 BC
CAR 482	Urn C16	3410± 70 bp	1455 bc	1890-1520 BC
CAR 449	Urn C10	3390± 70 bp	1440 bc	1890-1520 BC
CAR 456	Urn C8	3090± 70 bp	1135 bc	1520-1161 BC

[1] Date beyond the range of calibration.

CAR 487	Charcoal pit 38	3155 ± 70 bp	1205 bc	1604-1267 BC
CAR 486	Charcoal pit 42A	3040 ± 70 bp	1090 bc	1450-1069 BC
CAR 454	OGS[2] beneath 'Cairn'	3110 ± 70 bp	1145 bc	1520-1217 BC
CAR 455	Coarse pot C15	2530 ± 70 bp	580 bc	820-410 BC
CAR 483	Enclosed grave at N	1870 ± 60 bp	80 ad	10-316 AD
CAR 484	Enclosed grave at N	1120 ± 90 bp	830 ad	680-1040 AD

Bedd Branwen

BM-452	B, pre-barrow hollow	4923 ± 75 bp	2973 bc	3946-3530 BC
BM-456	Q, charcoal on OGS	3353 ± 60 bp	1403 bc	1871-1520 BC
BM-455	L, from close to Pot B	3257 ± 80 bp	1307 bc	1740-1400 BC
BM-453	D, contents of Pot La	3224 ± 81 bp	1274 bc	1690-1321 BC

Parys Mountain Mine tips

BM-2584	Mature oak: Site 3/20	3550 ± 50 bp	1600 bc	2040-1750 BC
BM-2585	Charcoal: Site 3/13	3490 ± 50 bp	1540 bc	1950-1690 BC
BM-2586	Charcoal: Site 3a	3500 ± 50 bp	1550 bc	1970-1695 BC

'Metalworking pit', Dwigyr

HAR 1920	Pit 1	4130 ± 70 bp	2180 bc	2910-2494 BC

Tŷ Mawr (later dates)

HAR 5403	164, shell midden Hut S	2560 ± 80 bp	610 bc (205 bc)	c. 390-0 BC
HAR 5404	164, same source	2440 ± 70 bp	490 bc (85 bc)	c.336 BC-AD 100

Brackets: correction for marine shell dates[3]

HAR 6684	269, inside Hut T4	1700 ± 80 bp	250 ad	130-540 AD
HAR 5730	90, inside Hut T3	1430 ± 80 bp	520 ad	430-758 AD
HAR 7081	17, burnt straw in Hut T1	1420 ±110 bp	530 ad	410-850 AD
HAR 5731	269, inside Hut T4	1410 ± 80 bp	540 ad	450-770 AD
HAR 6803	296, burnt plants, Hut T4	1370 ±130 bp	580 ad	420-950 AD

Bryn Eryr

CAR 1058	882, fence slot at W. end predating main ditch	2240 ± 80 bp	290 bc	478-90 BC
CAR 1060	446, gully beneath S. house Phase 2	2350 ± 80 bp	400 bc	766-210 BC
CAR 1000	643, pit cutting Ph.1 slot	2010 ± 60 bp	60 bc	97 BC-AD 126
CAR 944	999, wood from main ditch	1770 ± 70 bp	180 ad	25-230 AD
CAR 989	999, repeat	1780 ± 70 bp	170 ad	
CAR 990	999, repeat	2030 ± 60 bp	80 bc	
CAR 945	032a, wood from main ditch	1960 ± 60 bp	10 bc	110 BC-AD 209
CAR 946	032b, repeat	2110 ± 70 bp	160 bc	
CAR 1002	032c, repeat	2120 ± 70 bp	170 bc	198 BC-AD 23
CAR 947	029a, wood from main ditch	2070 ± 70 bp	120 bc	
CAR 1004a	653, turf in main ditch	2160 ± 70 bp	210 bc	349 BC-AD 20
CAR 1004b	653, repeat	2030 ± 60 bp	80 bc	
CAR 1063	325, floor: Central house	1960 ± 60 bp	10 bc	110 BC-AD 209
CAR 1064	329, same context	1990 ± 60 bp	40 bc	169 BC-AD 130
CAR 1065	305, drain: Central house	1940 ± 60 bp	10 ad	93 BC-AD 221
CAR 999	518, burning in S. house	1750 ± 60 bp	200 ad	129-382 AD
CAR 1043	518, repeat	1800 ± 60 bp	150 ad	
CAR 1003	210, eaves gully S. house	1850 ± 60 bp	100 ad	83-280 AD
CAR 1042	210, repeat	1720 ± 60 bp	230 ad	
CAR 1001	039, stones of 'farmyard'	1730 ± 70 bp	220 ad	130-527 AD

[2] OGS = Old ground surface.
[3] Harkness in Mook and Waterbolk (edd) *Proc. First Internat. Symposium Radiocarbon and Archaeology*, Groningen, 1983, Part 8, 351-64.

ENVIRONMENTAL STUDIES RELEVANT TO PREHISTORIC ANGLESEY

RANGE OF INFORMATION AVAILABLE

Site Name	Soils	Pollen	Plant Macro-fossils	Charcoal identific-ation	Animal bone identific-ation	Molluscs lists	Insects
Mesolithic							
Trwyn Du			x				
Neolithic							
Tŷ Newydd				x			
Din Dryfol	x			x	x		
Trefignath	x	x	x				x
Barclodiad y Gawres	x	x	x		x		x
Bryn Celli Ddu				x	x	x	
Bryn yr Hen Bobl				x	x	x	
Pant y Saer					x		
Lligwy				x	x		
Capel Eithin (setlmt)	x		x				
Bronze Age							
Bedd Branwen		x		x			
Treiorwerth				x			
Iron Age							
Bryn Eryr	x	x	x	x	x		
Tŷ Mawr (Iron Age)	x					x	
(post Roman)	x		x		x		
Pant y Saer hut group (Date uncertain)				x	x	x	

MESOLITHIC
Trwyn Du, Aberffraw. R.B. White *Arch. Camb.* CXXVIII, 1978, 16-39.
Hazel nut shells found in a pit.

NEOLITHIC TOMBS
Tŷ Newydd. C.W. Phillips, *Arch. Camb.* XCI, 1936, 998-9.
Charcoal from chamber floor, mainly (82%) hazel.

Din Dryfol. Smith & Lynch *Trefignath and Din Dryfol* CAA Monograph 3, 1987, 129-31.
Charcoal identifications by P.M. Denne, quantifiable. A large range of species came from post-Neolithic contexts with possible industrial activity.
Animal bone identification by T.P. O'Connor; very small quantities of human bone from chamber and amongst cairn stones.
Soil analysis by J.S. Conway for identification of later activity.

Trefignath. Monograph as above, 39-44.
Pollen analysis of monolith from nearby bog and from buried soils by J. Greig.
Results summarised in text, p.340

Barclodiad y Gawres. Powell and Daniel *Barclodiad y Gawres* Liverpool Univ.
Press, 1956, 23; also *Arch. Camb.* CVII, 1958, 125.
Report on pollen by Sir H. Godwin. There was no pollen surviving in the old
ground surface but the turves of the mound itself, assumed to have been derived
from the valley below, suggested a woodland environment with clearings. Birch,
pine, elm, hazel and alder were recorded, together with *plantago lanceolata*. The
animal bones are from a ceremonial context (PA 37) and are exceptional.

Bryn Celli Ddu. W.J. Hemp, *Archaeologia*, 80, 1930, 209, 213-4.
The charcoal from general contexts was mainly hazel; pine was found in two
postholes near the ox burial which constituted the only animal bone found. Cockle,
mussel, limpet and winkle shells were found in the chamber.

Bryn yr Hen Bobl. W.J. Hemp, *Archaeologia*, 85, 1935, 279-81.
Mixed animal bones came from the forecourt filling; ox was found at the end
of the 'terrace'. The charcoal was mainly oak (37%) with hazel (20%) and hawthorn
(16%) — its context is not precisely identified. Land snails from the old ground
surface suggested a 'damp scrub' environment as did the 15 species from other
contexts of variable date. Marine shells, cockle, limpet and mussel, were plentiful;
periwinkle, oyster and whelk were rare. The context is not indicated.

Pant y Saer Tomb. Lindsay Scott. *Arch. Camb.* LXXXVIII, 1933, 228.
All the animal bones (see chart below) were from the chamber deposit. There
were several cattle bones, at least one identifiable as *bos longifrons;* a few sheep/goat
and very few of the others. The fox was assumed to be intrusive.

Lligwy. E. Neil Baynes *Arch. Camb.* 1909, 224-5.
All the animal bones (presumably identified by Sir Arthur Keith) came from
the chamber deposit which was covered by a layer of limpet shells.

NEOLITHIC SETTLEMENT
Capel Eithin. Interim account only: S.I. White. TAAS, 1981, 19.
Carbonised grains of emmer wheat and barley were found in one of the large
Late Neolithic postholes. Identified by G.C. Hillman.

BRONZE AGE
Bedd Branwen. F.M. Lynch *Arch. Camb.* CXX, 1971, 73-4.
Pollen studied by Prof. G.W. Dimbleby. There was no pollen from the truncated
old ground surface, but turves from the mound produced pollen of grassland
and meadow plants, especially buttercups, with rather more hazel, alder, oak
and birch than was present in the modern surface. It suggested a Bronze age

landscape of cleared meadows with some woodland nearby; some cereals were growing in the vicinity. The same range of trees was identified amongst the charcoal.

Treiorwerth. F.M. Lynch, *Arch. Camb.* CXX, 1971, 38.
Charcoals from the old ground surface were identified by Dr G.K. Elliott. Oak and alder were common; there was some birch and hawthorn; the identification of Scots pine is less certain.

IRON AGE
Byn Eryr. *Publication forthcoming.* Environmental studies by A. Caseldine.
Glume wheat and barley have been identified from the later contexts. The results are summarised in the text, p.376.

Tŷ Mawr. C.A. Smith, *Arch. Camb.* CXXXV, 1986, 54-74.
Molluscs from general contexts were mainly limpets and periwinkles. The Iron Age midden was almost entirely limpets with a few *littorina* and six other species. Detailed study by J. and V. Evans.
The report on the charred plant remains by D. Williams was written before the late C14 dates for deposits in Huts T4 and T1 were available. Hut T4 produced oats, barley, bread/club wheat and spelt wheat; goosefoot and plantain were present as weeds. T1 contained emmer and spelt wheat as well as sedge, spike-rush and heather which might have been used for bedding.
The animal bones were not closely datable.
The soil study by Helen Keeley covers modern and buried soils and discusses their agricultural use.

Pant y Saer hut group. C.W. Phillips, *Arch. Camb.*, LXXXIX, 1934, 32-3.
The contexts of the animal bones, identified by J.W. Jackson, are not specified except that pig teeth and tusks were found in the make-up of the enclosure wall. The molluscs were identified by A.S. Kennard. The 13 land species from the occupation soil inside huts included the edible snail and probably belong the the post-Roman phase. They all occur in present day Anglesey. There were relatively few marine shells (winkle, mussel, limpet, cockle and whelk) which also came from hut floors.
Yew and gorse were identified by J.C. Maby in charcoal from the building in which the brooch was found; oak came from a small building on the north east side of the enclosure which produced VCP (Iron Age pottery).

MIRE POLLEN STUDIES
Cors Goch. B. Seddon *Geology and Vegetation of the Late Quaternary period in North Wales,* unpublished PhD thesis, University of Cambridge, 1958.
Llyn Hendref. R. Watkins *Flandrian vegetational history of lowland lake sites in Gwynedd,* unpublished PhD thesis, UCNW, Bangor 1991.

Trefignath. J. Greig in Smith and Lynch *Trefignath and Din Dryfol* CAA Monograph 3, 1987.
Tre'r Gof. E.M. Botterill *A Palaeoecological study of Gors Gyfelog and Tre'r Gof: lowland mires in north-west Wales,* unpublished PhD thesis, University of Keele, 1988.

Charcoal Identifications

Site Name	Oak	Hazel	Birch	Ash	Alder	Willow	Hawthorn	Pine	Cherry	Blackthorn	Gorse	Maple	Yew
Trwyn Du		x											
Tŷ Newydd	x	x		x		x							
Din Dryfol (Neol)	x	x				x							
(RB)	x	x	x	x	x	x			x			x	
Bryn Celli Ddu	x	x					x	x		x			
Bryn yr Hen Bobl	x	x	x	x	x	x	x					x	
Bedd Branwen	x	x	x		x								
Treiorwerth	x		x		x		x	x					
Bryn Eryr		x			x								
Pant y Saer hut	x										x		x

Animal Bone Identifications

Site Name	Cattle	Sheep	Sheep/Goat	Pig	Dog	Horse	Roe Deer	Red Deer	Fox	Otter
Din Dryfol	?	x	x	x		?				
Bryn Celli Ddu	x									
Bryn yr Hen Bobl	x		x	x						
Pant y Saer	x		x	x		x		x	x	
Lligwy	x	x		x	x		x	x	x	x
Bryn Eryr	x	x								
Tŷ Mawr	x	x				x				
Pant y Saer Hut	x	x		x	x	x				

Barclodiad y Gawres — exceptional context: not listed (see PA 37)

A summary of environmental history for the whole of Wales has recently been published: A Caseldine, *Environmental Archaeology in Wales,* Cadw and St. David's University College, Lampeter, 1990.

INDEX

An asterisk indicates an illustration (unless they are within the general discussion, in which case they are not shown separately).